D0386790

At Coney Island, New York, in the early 1900s

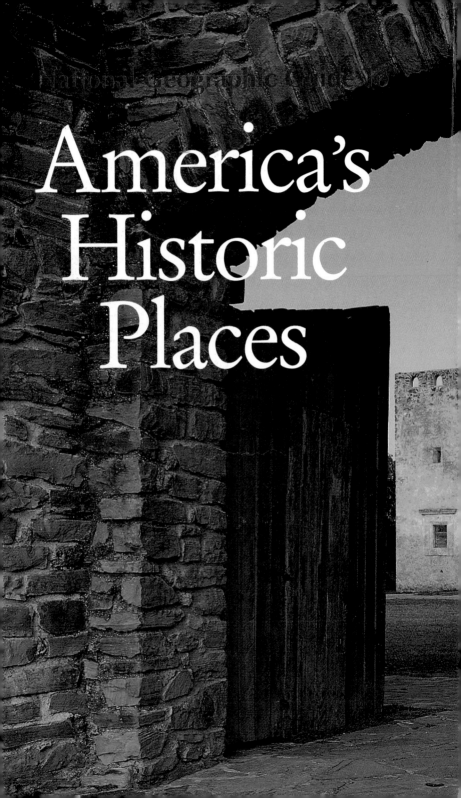

National Geographic Guide to

America's
Historic
Places

Prepared by
The Book Division
National Geographic Society
Washington, D.C.

Credits

Published by
THE NATIONAL GEOGRAPHIC SOCIETY

Reg Murphy
President and Chief Executive Officer
Gilbert M. Grosvenor
Chairman of the Board
Nina D. Hoffman
Senior Vice President

Prepared by The Book Division
William R. Gray
Vice President and Director
Charles Kogod
Assistant Director
Barbara A. Payne
Editorial Director

Staff for this book
Elizabeth L. Newhouse
Editor and Director of Travel Books
Cinda Rose
Art Director
Caroline Hickey, Barbara A. Noe
Research Editors
Mary Jenkins
Illustrations Editor
Carolinda E. Hill, K. M. Kostyal,
Barbara A. Noe
Text Editors
Carl Mehler
Map Editor and Designer

Gettysburg National Military Park, Pennsylvania

Donald A. Bluhm
Bob Devine
Jerry Camarillo Dunn, Jr.
Alison Kahn
K. M. Kostyal
Mark Miller
Barbara A. Noe
Geoffrey O'Gara
Kay and William G. Scheller
Thomas Schmidt
John M. Thompson

Mel White
Susan Young
Writers

Michael P. Donovan
Jennifer Emmet
Sean M. Groom
Michael H. Higgins
Mary Jennings, *Map Coordinator*
Keith R. Moore
Daniel M. Nonte
Tara Taghizadeh
Shana E. Vickers
Researchers

Lise S. Sajewski
Copy Editor

Christin A. Conaway, Thomas L. Gray,
Peter A. Jolicoeur, Joseph F. Ochlak,
Louis J. Spirito
Map Researchers

Michelle H. Picard, *Chief, Map Production*
Louis J. Spirito, Martin S. Walz, and
Mapping Specialists, Limited
Map Production
Tibor G. Tóth
Map Relief

Marianne R. Koszorus
Assistant Art Director
Meredith C. Wilcox
Illustrations Assistant

Richard S. Wain
Production Project Manager
Lewis R. Bassford, Lyle Rosbotham
Production

Rhonda J. Brown, Kevin G. Craig,
Dale M. Herring, Peggy J. Purdy
Staff Assistants

Diane L. Coleman, *Indexer*

Thomas B. Blabey, Martha C. Christian,
Banafsheh Ghassemi, Gwen Shaffer,
Elizabeth H. Wagley, Leslie Whedbee,
Robert J. Weatherly, Jayne Wise
Contributors

**Manufacturing
and Quality Management**

George V. White, *Director*
John T. Dunn, *Associate Director*
Vincent P. Ryan, *Manager*

Cover: Mount Rushmore, South Dakota
Previous pages: Church of San José y San
Miguel de Aguayo, San Antonio Mission
N.H.P., Texas

Contents

Living History Farms, Des Moines, Iowa

5

Library of Congress CIP data: page 384

The Measure of a People

The best way to understand a people—any people—is to look at, and think about, what they preserve and protect from their past, since the past controls the future. Whether one wants to learn about America, or France, or South Africa hardly matters: What does matter is that one must go over the ground of history, see the places that tell their stories, and not limit oneself to books. The American people are very fortunate, for despite how quickly they can remake themselves, they have many visible reminders from the invisible past. By visiting these reminders, the nation's treasure-house of historic parks, sites, monuments, and trails, that invisible past is made visible.

Many people, many organizations, have protected our historic heritage. No place survives simply because it is forgotten, no place is protected by simple neglect for long. The National Register of Historic Places lists over 50,000 structures with nationally significant historic value, though the criteria for listing these places are local and regional. The National Park Service has designated over 2,000 National Historic Landmarks, places neither owned nor administered by the Park Service but nonetheless deemed important to the nation and its sense of identity. Not all these places, to be honest, are interesting to visit (indeed, many if not most remain in private hands, and a goodly number are not open to the public). But all these places contribute to the fabric of the historical landscape, to the integrity of the nation's cities, and to the education of its citizens, and they do so simply by existing.

There are people who think they do not like history. Let them visit a handful of the places described and listed in this book and they will change their minds. History is about real places and real people, things that happened to create the time in which we live, a time we call the present, which becomes the past in the blink of an eye. This guidebook singles out the most accessible places where we can enjoy the past and learn what it can tell us about the present; it directs the traveler to places with historical integrity, from the 17th century (and, at the great ancient Native American sites, far, far deeper into the past) to yesterday's blink of an eye. History is about three things: what actually happened in the past, what people believe happened in the past, and what we are told, by historians, journalists, and people with an ax to grind, happened in the past. To separate out these three notions of history is not easy. The best way to start is to walk the very ground where history happened.

Robin W. Winks
Randolph W. Townsend Professor of History,
Yale University

About the Guide

*T*his guidebook brings together in a single volume the major historic and prehistoric sites in the United States and organizes them around central points of interest to help you in planning trips. Each site opens a window into America's past; taken together, they present a complete picture of our human history.

Lincoln Memorial, Washington, D.C.

The book divides the country into regions, the regions into states, and the states into categories of sites. Main Sites, usually cities or large towns or places of particular historical significance, are listed alphabetically. Immediately following them come Excursion Sites—towns, historic districts, museums, forts, battlefields, living history farms, prehistoric mounds, Indian dwellings—and many other places within relatively easy driving distance of the Main Sites. These are arranged geographically with mileages and general directions, but be sure to consult a road map before setting off to find them. Listed alphabetically at the end of each state chapter are Other Sites; usually they're a distance from the Main Sites but worth seeing if you're in the area.

We chose the sites with generous help from the staffs of the National Park Service and the National Register of Historic Places, as well as from state and local historians in all the states. A great many of the sites have been designated National Historic Landmarks by a federal program that helps preserve historic places not in the National Park System.

We make no claim to comprehensive coverage. Ours is a visitors' guide, so the included sites had to offer more than significance and diversity; they had to have something of interest for the visitor to see or experience. Our writers personally went to nearly every site to make their own assessments.

To further enhance your visits, we have put together numerous walking and driving tours of historic districts and areas and keyed them to maps to help you get around. Since space limitations kept us from including all historic districts, we strongly recommend you stop at the local Visitor Centers or Chambers of Commerce to gather information and touring maps.

The information about every site has been checked and, to the best of our knowledge, is correct as of the press date. However, it's advisable to phone ahead when possible, as visitor information changes frequently. Be warned that area codes also change often. Many sites close on national holidays; on other days the

Soo Locks, Sault Ste. Marie, Michigan

Lighthouse at Cabrillo National Monument, San Diego, California

sites in the book are open unless otherwise stated. All mileages are approximate, and the times suggested for walking and driving tours allow for less stopping than you are likely to want to do.

Many fascinating historical experiences await the reader of this guide —and, even more, the traveler who follows it to the sites.

MAP KEY and ABBREVIATIONS

		ABBREVIATIONS	
	Historic District		
	Historic Neighborhood	H.S.	Historic Site
	Cemetery, Forest,	I.R., Indian Res.	Indian Reservation
	Monument, Park	Intl.	International
		Mem.	Memorial
	Indian Reservation	N.B.	National Battlefield
	Tribal Park	N.B.P.	National Battlefield Park
	Featured Drive	N.B.S.	National Battlefield Site
		N.F.	National Forest
(94)	Interstate Highway	N.H.C.	National Heritage Corridor
		N.H.L.	National Historic Landmark
(12)	U.S. Federal Highway	N.H.P.	National Historical Park
		N.H.S.	National Historic Site
(29)	State or Local Road	N.M.P.	National Military Park
		N.P.	National Park
••••••ooooooo	Historic Walk/Trail	N. Pres.	National Preserve
		N.R.A.	National Recreation Area
––––––––	State or Nat. Border	Nat. Mem.	National Memorial
		Nat. Mon.	National Monument
••••••••••••••••	Ferry	S.A.A.	State Archaeological Area
		S.H.A.	State Historical Area or
⌐⌐⌐⌐⌐⌐	Canal		State Heritage Area
		S.H.P.	State Historic, -al Park
	POPULATION	S.H.S.	State Historic Site
● **Boston**	500,000 and over	S. Mem.	State Memorial
● Decatur	50,000 to under 500,000	■ ■	**Point of Interest**
● Thibodaux	under 50,000	) (	Tunnel or Bridge

New England

English settlement in North America, the struggle for independence, and the beginnings of American industry all have cornerstones in New England. Beginning with the Pilgrims' landing at Plymouth in 1620, Massachusetts set the pace for the region in colonization, shipbuilding, and trade. In 1775 the first battles of the Revolution were fought at Lexington, Concord, and Bunker Hill.

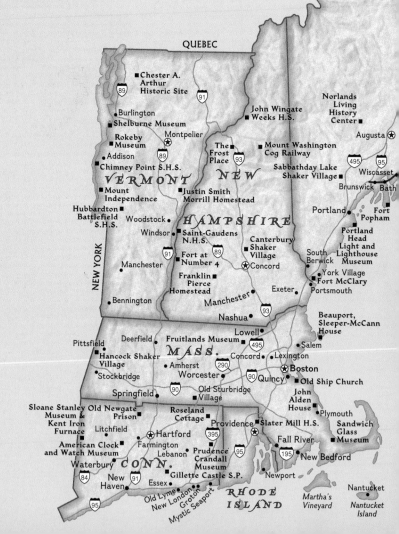

The small towns and agricultural economy that marked the area during the early decades of independence shifted quickly in the mid-19th century, as great industrial enterprises began to dominate the river valleys. By the 20th-century, however, the region was suffering as textile mills moved south. Turning its focus to high technology, finance, and tourism, New England has rebounded in recent decades.

Fort Kent Blockhouse

Acadian Village

NEW BRUNSWICK

95

M A I N E

Bangor

Lubec

Machias

Roosevelt Campobello International Park

Fort O'Brien

Mid-Coast Driving Tour

1

3

Bar Harbor

Camden

Bass Harbor

Mt. Desert Island

Rockland

1

Pemaquid Point

Old Ironsides—USS *Constitution*, Charlestown, Massachusetts

Maine

1879 Nubble Lighthouse, York Beach

After Samuel de Champlain's exploration of the rugged coastline of present-day Maine in 1604, the French attempted settlements in the area. Soon thereafter, beginning in 1607, the English made their own claims to parts of Maine, and for the next century and a half the two nations contested a boundary along the Penobscot River. Only in 1759 was British rule at last firmly established. By 1652 Maine was joined politically with Massachusetts, a link that continued until 1819. The following year Maine was granted statehood in the nation.

Since the colonial period—when tall pines were used as masts for British ships—logging has been an economic mainstay in the Maine interior. By the late 19th century Maine's forests were feeding the enormous appetites of lumber and paper mills. To this day, in the state's North Woods, pulpwood is king, while along the coast the long-held traditions of shipbuilding, fishing, and lobstering continue. In recent decades, the economy of southern Maine has become oriented to the high-technology and service industries.

Augusta

(Chamber of Commerce, 21 University Dr. 207-623-4559. Mon.-Fri.) Augusta is the creation of the Kennebec River. Native Americans once met in this place where "the tide runs no farther up the Kennebec." Later,

white traders and lumber barons found the spot equally inviting. The town was incorporated in 1797 and became the state capital in 1831. Buildings of the **Kennebec Arsenal Historic District** (*On the grounds of Kennebec Valley Medical Center, Arsenal St.*), a federal weapons-storage facility from 1828 to 1903, still stand along the banks of the Kennebec and are now used by the state.

Maine State Museum (*Statehouse Complex. 207-287-2301*) The state's natural environment and social history are presented here in creative and dramatic exhibits. The exhibit "12,000 Years in Maine" traces the natural and human history of the Pine Tree State from the last ice age forward. The "Made in Maine" exhibit details the state's diverse products and manufacturing methods. A highlight is one of the oldest surviving locomotive engines made in the U.S.

Old Fort Western (*16 Cony St. 207-626-2385. Daily Mem. Day–Labor Day, call for off-season hrs.; adm. fee*) Though most of this 1754 fort was dismantled, the garrison building—possibly the oldest surviving wooden fort in New England—is still standing, and outbuildings have been reconstructed. Costumed interpreters reenact a typical day's activities.

Excursion

NORLANDS LIVING HISTORY CENTER (*25 miles NW via US 202 and Maine 4, near Livermore. 207-897-4366. Tours July 4–Columbus Day, by appt. rest of year; adm. fee*) Former estate of the Washburn family, Norlands is now a 19th-century working farm and living history museum. You can observe activities for a few hours or experience 19th-century rural living during scheduled sessions that last several days. The Washburn house is itself a magnificent time capsule, and the restored walls and ceilings, frescoed with decorative trompe l'oeil designs, are particularly fine. Children get a dose of early education from a costumed teacher in the 1850s one-room schoolhouse.

Lumber Drives

As recently as the 1960s, Maine's rivers and streams were conduits that drained timber from the North Woods. After cutting all winter, lumbermen would pile logs into the tributaries of rivers like the Kennebec and the Penobscot. Spring's high water would carry the timber downriver. At intervals, makeshift dams were built to gather water behind the log drives. When the dams were opened, the surge drove the tangle of timber forward. The strong, skilled lumbermen muscled apart logjams using pike poles and occasionally dynamite. They took immense pride in their labor, knowing that they were working one of the most dangerous jobs America had to offer.

Bangor ··

(*Chamber of Commerce, 519 Main St. 207-947-0307. Mon.-Fri.*) Shipping and lumbering were major Bangor activities in the early 1800s. Later in the century the city was dubbed "lumber capital of the world," as timber floating down the Penobscot River from the northern wilderness was destined for mills here. Today Bangor offers little evidence of its heyday, save for its exuberant downtown architecture and the mansions of its timber barons. The **Bangor Historical Society Museum** (*159 Union St. 207-942-5766. April-Dec. Tues.-Fri., weekends by appt.; adm. fee*), housed in the 1836 Thomas A. Hill House, exhibits 19th-century furnishings and paintings by local artists.

Although a fire in 1911 devastated much of the downtown, some superb buildings were spared. Many present-day merchants have set up shop in the 1830s **West Market Square Historic District.** Wealthy entrepreneurs built their mansions in the **High Street Historic District,** and lumber merchants built theirs in what is now the **Broadway Historic District.** The **Isaac Farrar Mansion** (*Union and 2nd Sts. 207-941-2808. July–Sept. Thurs*) is one of the most magnificent.

Brunswick ···

(*Chamber of Commerce, 59 Pleasant St. 207-725-8797*) This site on Casco Bay was first settled in the early 1600s by English traders and fishermen, but hostilities with Indians hindered its development over the next hundred years. By the early 1800s, however, Brunswick was becoming an industrial and cultural center. Bowdoin—the state's first college—was founded here in 1794.

Brunswick's **Federal Street Historic District** is an early 19th-century example of zoning that called for large lots and limited buildings to only two stories. You can see another example of early urban planning in the **Lincoln Street Historic District,** a precisely laid-out subdivision.

Pejepscot Museum (*159 Park Row. 207-729-6606. Mon.-Fri., and Sat. in summer*) In one half of an 1858 Italianate double mansion, the historical society exhibits local memorabilia; the other half, the **Skolfield Whittier House** (*Late May–Labor Day Tues.-Sat.; adm. fee*), was sealed from 1925 to 1982 and now serves as a fascinating and moody Victorian time capsule. The **Joshua L. Chamberlain Museum** (*226 Maine St. Late May–Sept. Tues.-Sat.; adm. fee*) was the home of the Battle of Gettysburg hero who later became the governor of the state.

14

Peary-MacMillan Arctic Museum (*Hubbard Hall, Bowdoin College. 207-725-3416. Tues.-Sun.*) The museum imaginatively presents the polar explorations of two of Bowdoin's most famous alumni, Adm. Robert Peary and his associate Adm. Donald MacMillan. The exhibits include documents, navigational tools, artifacts, and even taxidermied wildlife brought back from the Arctic.

Penobscot Marine Museum, Searsport

Excursions

Bath (*10 miles E on US 1. Chamber of Commerce, 45 Front St. 207-443-9751. Mon.-Fri.*) For more than two centuries, Bath was one of the country's great shipping ports, and its prosperous merchants constructed fine houses and public buildings. All aspects of the state's rich maritime heritage are chronicled at the superb **Maine Maritime Museum** (*243 Washington St. 207-443-1316. Adm. fee*). On the banks of the Kennebec River, the museum encompasses a restored shipyard where wooden schooners were built from 1894 to 1920; you can also tour working fishing boats when they are in port.

Fort Popham *(15 miles S via US 1 and Maine 209. 207-389-1335. Late May–Sept.)* The granite, crescent-shaped fort at the mouth of the Kennebec River was begun in 1861 by Maine volunteers in the Union Army, to guard against a Confederate invasion. Circular staircases lead to the towers. At nearby **Popham Beach** *(End of Maine 209)* an English encampment in 1607 was the first European attempt to settle New England. After a severe winter, the colonists gave up and returned to England.

Mid-Coast Driving Tour •••••••••••• 200 miles, 3 days

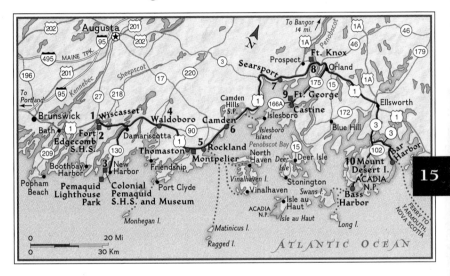

Maine's middle coast offers a rich amalgam of Revolutionary War-era forts, historic seaports, and tiny fishing villages.

1. Begin in **Wiscasset**, once the state's major port. In the early 19th century wealthy sea captains and merchants built stately houses and commercial buildings in what is now the **historic district**. The magnificent, federal **Nickels-Sortwell House** *(Main and Federal Sts. 207-882-6218. June–mid-Oct. Wed.-Sun.; adm. fee)* is an example.

2. Turn right just over the Wiscasset Bridge to **Fort Edgecomb State Historic Site** *(N. Edgecomb. 207-882-7777. Mem. Day–Labor Day; adm. fee).* Built in 1808 on the Sheepscot River to protect Wiscasset, the superbly preserved installation has its original octagonal blockhouse and earthworks and a reconstructed palisade.

3. Return to US 1, then follow Maine 129 and 130 to **Colonial Pemaquid State Historic Site and Museum** *(207-677-2423. Mem. Day–Labor Day; adm. fee includes Fort William Henry).* Archaeologists unearthed 14 foundations at this early 17th-century English settlement; the museum displays artifacts from prehistoric through colonial times. A replica of the 1692 **Fort William Henry** is adjacent. The much photographed lighthouse at **Pemaquid Lighthouse Park** *(Pemaquid Point. Parking fee)* was built in 1827.

4. Continue east on US 1 past **Waldoboro**, founded by German immigrants in 1748, to **Thomaston**, first settled in 1630 as a trading post.

Montpelier (*US 1. 207-354-8062. June–mid-Oct. Tues.-Sun.; adm. fee*) is a reproduction of the home of Gen. Henry Knox (1750-1806), the country's first secretary of war; it contains many of the furnishings from the original house.

5. Rockland, "schooner capital of Maine," is also one of its largest fishing ports. The Greek Revival **Farnsworth Homestead** (*352 Main St. 207-596-6457. Oct.-May Tues.-Sun.; adm. fee*) reflects the lifestyle of a wealthy Victorian family.

6. Camden (*Chamber of Commerce, on the Public Landing. 207-236-4404 or 800-223-5459. Daily June-Sept., Mon.-Sat. Oct.-May*) has been a summer resort since the mid-19th century; later in the century, well-to-do vacationers discovered the town and built extravagant cottages here. **Norumbega** (*61 High St. 207-236-4646*)—now a bed-and-breakfast—was one of the grandest.

7. From the late 1700s to the late 1800s, the shipyards of **Searsport** built approximately 250 sailing vessels, while the town supplied a quarter of the country's sea captains. This rich legacy is preserved in the artifacts, paintings, and antiques housed in eight historic buildings at the **Penobscot Marine Museum** (*Church St. off US 1. 207-548-2529. Mem. Day–mid-Oct.; adm. fee*).

8. Turn onto Maine 174 just west of the Waldo-Hancock Bridge to visit **Fort Knox** (*207-469-7719. May-Oct.; adm. fee*). Construction of the massive granite fort overlooking the Penobscot River began in 1844 and continued for 25 years, though it was never completed. The tour takes in the fort's spiral staircases, interior rooms, and cannon emplacements.

9. Follow Maine 175 and 166 to **Fort George** (*Wadsworth Cove Rd., in Castine*). Earthworks and fortifications are all that remain of the fort built by the British in 1779. They hoped to keep **Castine,** a strategic town on Penobscot Bay, from falling into the hands of the Colonials. Twenty-two days after construction began, British soldiers at the fort repelled a patriot force led by Col. Paul Revere.

10. Conclude the tour with a visit to **Mount Desert Island.** The island's main town, **Bar Harbor** (*Maine 3*), has been a fashionable summer resort since the late 19th century, when such East Coast elite as the Rockefellers, Astors, and Vanderbilts constructed Gilded Age cottages here, a few of which still stand. At the island's southern tip, the classic coastal village of **Bass Harbor** (*Maine 102*) is a cluster of clapboard houses belonging to families for whom groundfishing and lobstering have been a way of life for generations.

Portland ···

(*Convention & Visitors Bureau, 305 Commercial St. 207-772-5800. Closed Sun.*) This coastal site was sparsely settled and subject to Indian attack through much of the 17th century. In 1820 it became Maine's first capital, yielding to Augusta in 1831. The city is a veritable phoenix, since fire has destroyed it twice since 1623. Both times its citizens rebuilt, and today Portland is a lively seaport.

Victoria Mansion (*109 Danforth St. 207-772-4841. May-Oct. Tues.-Sun.; adm. fee*), in the **Spring Street Historic District,** is also known as the Morse-Libby Mansion (1858-1860). Its restrained Italianate facade, topped by a Tuscan tower, belies a riotously ornate interior with original furnishings.

Wadsworth-Longfellow House (*485 Congress St. 207-879-0427. June-Oct.*

Tues.-Sun.; adm. fee) Poet Henry Wadsworth Longfellow (1807-1882) spent his boyhood in the city's first brick house, built in 1785 by his grandfather. It is still filled with family furnishings and mementos. The adjacent **Maine History Gallery** offers changing exhibitions on Maine's past, based on the historical society's collections.

Waterfront Historic District *(Old Port Exchange)* The six-block neighborhood, built between 1850 and 1875, is one of the few intact historic waterfronts left on the East Coast. It has changed little over the years except for its occupants—now a conglomerate of restaurants, shops, and boutiques. The Italianate 1871 **U.S. Customshouse** *(312 Fore St. 207-780-3316. Mon.-Fri.)* is an elegant reminder of earlier prosperity.

Excursions

EAGLE ISLAND *(3 miles off coast, via boat from S. Harpswell, Freeport, and Portland. Boat information 207-624-6076. Maine Bureau of Parks and Recreation 207-287-3821. Mid-June–Labor Day; donations)* North Pole explorer Robert Peary and his family spent summers on the tiny island until Peary's death in 1920. Occupying a rocky bluff, the shingled **Peary house** features a hearth decorated with Arctic quartz. It was in this home that Mrs. Peary received her husband's telegram: "Have made good at last."

PORTLAND HEAD LIGHT AND LIGHTHOUSE MUSEUM *(15 miles SE via I-95 and Maine 77. 1000 Shore Rd., Cape Elizabeth. 207-799-2661. Museum daily June-Oct., weekends April-May and Nov.-Dec.; adm. fee)* George Washington ordered the completion of Maine's first lighthouse—and one of

Shaker Village and Museum, New Gloucester

its most scenic—in 1791. Ruins of **Fort Williams** (1898) are also here.

SHAKER VILLAGE AND MUSEUM *(18 miles N via Maine Tpk. and Maine 26. 707 Shaker Rd., New Gloucester. 207-926-4597. Mem. Day–Columbus Day Mon.-Sat.; adm. fee)* The Shaker village founded here at Sabbathday Lake in 1794 is the only active Shaker community left in the U.S., with fewer than a dozen followers. A guided tour takes in four of the buildings, including the original 1794 **meetinghouse.**

York Village ⋯⋯⋯

First settled in the early 1600s, the town was badly damaged by fire in the Candlemas Massacre of 1692, when Abenaki Indians launched a surprise attack. The nearby York Harbor area has been a popular resort since the Civil War.

Old York *(Old York Historical Society, 207 York St. 207-363-4974. Early June–Sept. Tues.-Sun.; adm. fee)* A guided tour of seven well-preserved

18th- and 19th-century period buildings begins at the 1750 **Jefferd's Tavern** and includes the 1719 **Old Gaol**, one of the country's oldest public buildings and in use until 1860; the 1745 **Old Schoolhouse**, one of the oldest one-room schoolhouses in the state; the **John Hancock Warehouse;** the colonial revival **Elizabeth Perkins House;** and the 1742 **Emerson-Wilcox House,** with period rooms and the country's most extensive collection of crewel bed hangings.

Excursions

FORT MCCLARY S.H.S. *(9 miles S via Maine 103, in Kittery. Kittery Point Rd. 207-439-2845. Mem. Day–Sept.; adm. fee)* Forts have occupied this site since 1690. The present structure—manned during five wars beginning with the Revolution—reflects several periods of construction. Maine's last blockhouse was erected here from 1844 to 1846.

SOUTH BERWICK *(15 miles via US 1 and Maine 91 and 236)* The **Sarah Orne Jewett House** *(5 Portland St. 603-436-3205. June–mid-Oct. Tues., Thurs., and Sat.-Sun.; adm. fee),* the Piscataqua Georgian family home of the late 18th-century writer, holds an eclectic collection of furnishings and antiques. Begun in 1774, the house was completed after the Revolution. The 1787 **Hamilton House** *(Vaughan's Ln. 603-436-3205. June–mid-Oct. Tues., Thurs., and Sat.-Sun.; adm. fee)* is interpreted as a colonial revival villa.

Other Sites in Maine

Acadian Village *(US 1, in Van Buren. 207-868-5042. Mid-June–mid-Sept.; adm. fee)* French Acadians expelled from Nova Scotia by the British settled Van Buren in the late 1700s. Their lives and times are re-created in 16 reconstructed buildings spanning the late 18th through the early 20th centuries.

Burnham Tavern *(Maine and Free Sts., in Machias. 207-255-4432. Mid-June–Oct. 1; adm. fee)* Patriots met in the 1770 gambrel-roofed tavern in 1775 and planned the first naval battle of the Revolution, sailing their small sloop out to capture the British warship *Margaretta.* The only building in eastern Maine with a direct link to the Revolutionary War, the tavern also serves as a local history museum.

Fort O'Brien *(Maine 92, Machiasport. 207-255-4402. Mem. Day–Labor Day).* The fort, also known as Fort Machias, was built overlooking Machias Bay in 1775 and maintained by the British until 1777. The well-preserved earthworks were erected in 1863.

Fort Kent Blockhouse *(Fort Kent. 207-834-3866. Mem. Day–Labor Day)* The fort was built in 1839, right after the bloodless Aroostook War with Canada, to protect Maine's claim to the northern forests. The blockhouse contains a pictorial display and a collection of lumbering equipment.

Roosevelt Campobello International Park *(Via Maine 189 from Lubec, across Franklin D. Roosevelt Memorial Bridge to Campobello Island, in Canada. 506-752-2922. Mem. Day–early Oct.)* Franklin D. Roosevelt first visited Canada's Campobello Island in 1883, when he was a year old. He spent his boyhood summers here, and in 1909 his mother gave him and his wife, Eleanor, a 34-room "cottage" on the island as a belated wedding present. In 1921, while at Campobello, FDR discovered he had polio; he returned to the island three times as President. The house, now part of a 2,800-acre memorial park occupying much of the island's southern tip, is filled with Roosevelt furnishings and memorabilia.

18

New Hampshire

Candlelight tour through Portsmouth's Strawbery Banke Museum

Originally part of a 1620s royal grant, New Hampshire was, at various times during the next hundred years, a fiefdom of Massachusetts and a separate colony. In 1741 it spun off on its own permanently and endorsed independence from Britain a full six months before July 4, 1776. Later, it cast the deciding vote that ratified the federal Constitution.

By 1800 the state's focus was turning inland, away from Portsmouth and the coast. In 1808 Concord became the new capital, and soon thereafter Manchester's Amoskeag Mill Yard grew to be the world's largest textile manufacturer. With the arrival of the railroad, New Hampshire's White Mountains were transformed from forbidding wasteland to America's first alpine playground. The textile days are long gone, but a prosperous industrial and post-industrial southern New Hampshire clings to the Massachusetts border like an outer suburb of Boston, while far to the north wilderness still holds sway.

Concord ··

(Chamber of Commerce, 244 N. Main St., 603-224-2508. Mon.-Fri.) The Abenaki people who lived along the winding Merrimack River called it

Penacook—"crooked place." The Europeans who arrived in the mid-1600s dubbed the area Pennycook. Later renamed Concord, it has been the state capital since 1808.

Museum of New Hampshire History *(Hamel Center, 6 Eagle Square. 603-226-3189. Closed Mon.; adm. fee)* The history of the people who helped build the Granite State is brought to life in diaries, photographs, and documents that also provide an excellent overview of New Hampshire's relations with the rest of New England.

State House *(Main St. 603-271-2154. Mon.-Fri.)* Dedicated in 1819, this ranks as the oldest state capitol in

"The Mill Girl," Amoskeag Mill Yard

the nation in which a legislature still meets in its original chambers. The federal structure has been modified over the years, but the magnificently preserved legislative chambers retain their simple elegance.

Pierce Manse *(14 Penacook St. 603-224-5954. Mid-June–Labor Day Mon.-Fri.; adm. fee)* Before becoming the country's 14th President, Franklin Pierce lived in this house, then located in the city center, for four years. Moved here in 1971, the manse is filled with family furnishings and memorabilia.

Excursions

CANTERBURY SHAKER VILLAGE *(15 miles N via I-93. 288 Shaker Rd., Canterbury Center. 603-783-9511. Daily May-Oct., Fri.-Sun. Nov.-Dec. and April; adm. fee)* In the 1850s, during the peak of the Shaker movement, 300 of the religion's followers lived here in a hundred buildings. The grounds and 24 buildings have been restored to depict the community's simple lifestyle and many practical achievements.

FRANKLIN PIERCE HOMESTEAD *(25 miles W via N.H. 9/US 202, near jct. of N.H. 9 and 31, in Hillsboro. 603-478-3165. Call for hours; adm. fee)* President Pierce's father, a hero of the Revolutionary War and governor of the state, completed this federal house in 1804, just a few weeks after Franklin was born. The handsome structure has been restored to its early 1800s appearance.

Manchester ·······································

New Hampshire's oldest and most populous city began as Derryfield, a poor farming community. In 1810 it was renamed Manchester, and by 1840 it had become a thriving milltown, its factories benefiting from the immense waterpower generated by Amoskeag Falls. The town's Amoskeag Manufacturing Company grew to be the largest textile producer in the world.

Amoskeag Mill Yard *(Off Commercial St. Tours offered by Manchester Historic Association, 129 Amherst St. 603-622-7531. Tues.-Sat.; adm. fee)* At its height, the enormous redbrick complex covered more than 8 million square feet of floor space along the Merrimack River. Its 17,000 employees worked in more than 30 mills. Though the mills declared bankruptcy in 1936, when you walk past them now, it isn't hard to conjure the sound of 23,000 clanking looms turning out 4 million yards of cloth a week.

John Stark House (*2000 Elm St. 603-622-5719. By appt.; adm. fee*) Revolutionary War hero Gen. John Stark (who declared "Live free or die") grew up in what is now Manchester's oldest house (1736); it is decorated with authentic 18th-century furnishings.

Excursions

NASHUA (*18 miles S via F.E. Everett Tpk.*) At the confluence of the Merrimack and Nashua Rivers, this area was the first inland region in New Hampshire to be settled. In the 1800s it was a major industrial center. The Nashua Historical Society (*5 Abbott St. 603-883-0015. Call for hours*) offers tours of the federal **Abbott-Spalding House.** Along the Nashua River, the **Nashua Manufacturing Company,** a massive brick-and-stone complex now housing condominiums, was a major textile plant from 1823 to 1948. A portion of the statewide **Heritage Trail** provides a view of the complex. The Gothic Revival **Hunt Memorial Building** (*6 Main St.*) served as city library from 1903 to 1971.

LOWELL, MASS. (*25 miles SE via F. E. Everett Tpk. and US 3*) See page 35.

Portsmouth •••••••••••••••••••••

(*Seacoast Council on Tourism, 235 West Rd. 603-436-7678 or 800-221-5623*) Europeans first sailed up the Piscataqua River to present-day Portsmouth in 1603. Twenty years later, the first colonists settled at Odiborne Point. An English trading company established bases along the Piscataqua a few years later, but dissolved after a short time. One settlement—Strawbery Banke—held on and grew into Portsmouth.

Market Square The city's central square, lined with redbrick buildings, is home to the elegantly pilastered federal **Athenaeum** (*9 Market Square. 603-431-2538. Research library open Tues., Thurs., Sat.*). Its collections include documents, ship models, paintings, and artifacts pertaining to local history.

> **Workers at the Amoskeag**
> For nearly a century, beginning in the 1830s, the Amoskeag Mill Yard dominated the city of Manchester. Like other New England factories, the textile giant first relied for labor on Yankee "mill girls," young women from New England farms. The Irish migrations of the mid-19th century added a foreign element to Manchester's labor force, and skilled German and Scandinavian workers soon followed, along with "Scotch girls" from Glasgow mills. But the greatest influx came from Canadian farmers who answered advertisements in Quebec newspapers. By 1910, over a third of Manchester's residents were sons and daughters of these Quebecois.

21

Portsmouth Trail In the 1700s, the town's shipyards built ships, and its wealthy citizens built mansions. This trail leads past six historic houses from the colonial and federal periods: the 1784 **Gov. John Langdon House** (*143 Pleasant St. 603-436-3205. June–mid-Oct. Wed.-Sun.; adm. fee*), described by George Washington as one of the town's finest; the 1758 **John Paul Jones House** (*Middle and State Sts. 603-436-8420. Mem. Day–mid-Oct.; adm. fee*), where the captain lived while outfitting his ships; the 1763 **Moffatt-Ladd House** (*154 Market St. 603-436-8221. Mid-June–mid-Oct.; adm. fee*); the 1716 Georgian **Warner House** (*Daniel and Chapel Sts. 603-436-5909. June-Oct.; adm. fee*); and the Georgian 1710 **Wentworth-Gardner House** (*140 Mechanic St. 603-436-4406. Mid-June–mid-Oct.; adm. fee*).

Strawbery Banke Museum (*Marcy St. 603-433-1100. Late April–early Nov.; adm. fee*) Established in the early 1600s, Portsmouth's first settlement mushroomed into a thriving community. In the oldest quarter, 42 houses have been restored, with furnishings that reflect virtually every era of Portsmouth's history, from the 17th to the mid-20th century.

Excursion

EXETER (*20 miles SW via N.H. 108 and 101. Chamber of Commerce, 120 Water St. 603-772-2411*) Founded in 1638, the town was a hotbed of pre-Revolutionary sedition and became the state capital during the war. The **American Independence Museum** (*1 Governor's La. 603-772-2622. May–Oct. Wed.-Sun.; adm. fee*), built in 1721, served as the state treasury from 1775 to 1789 and as the home of the state governor in the late 1790s and early 1800s. Using museum documents and artifacts, docents recount stories of the Revolution and Exeter's part in it. The **Gilman Garrison House** (*12 Water St. 603-436-3205. June–mid-Oct. Tues., Thurs., Sat.- Sun.; adm. fee*), one of the state's oldest houses (circa 1690), was fortified to withstand Indian attacks; later additions trace colonial tastes and styles.

Founded in 1781 by town merchant John Phillips, **Phillips Exeter Academy** (*Front St. 603-772-4311, ext. 3437. Mon.-Fri.*), a college preparatory school, boasts more than one hundred buildings from the late 1800s and early 1900s.

Other Sites in New Hampshire

Fort at No. 4 (*Off N.H. 11, near Charlestown. 603-826-5700. Late May–mid-Oct. Wed.-Mon., closed first 2 weeks in Sept.; adm. fee*) In 1744 Charlestown was New England's northwesternmost outpost. Villagers, fearing attack from French and Indians during King George's War with France, turned their settlement into a fort. Number 4 is an authentic reconstruction, the only living history museum in New England focusing on that era.

John Wingate Weeks Historic Site (*Off US 3, in Lancaster. 603-788-4004. June–early Sept. Wed.-Sun., early Sept.–early Oct. Sat.-Sun.; adm. fee*) On top of Mount Prospect, this was once the estate of the Massachusetts senator who helped establish national forests in the eastern U.S. His house is one of the best preserved of New Hampshire's grand, turn-of-the-century summer homes. Climb to the top of the adjacent tower for spectacular views.

Mount Washington Cog Railway (*Off US 302, E of Fabyan. 603-846-5404 or 800-922-8825. Late May–late Oct.; fare*) Since 1869 coal-fired engines have been wheezing and belching their way up one of the steepest railway grades in the world, the 3.5-mile track leading to the summit of 6,288-foot Mount Washington. The world's first mountain-climbing locomotive, Old Peppersass, is on exhibit in the small **museum** (*Base of Mount Washington. Late May–late Oct.*).

The Frost Place (*Off N.H. 116, in Franconia. 603-823-5510. Mem. Day–June Sat.-Sun., July–mid-Oct. Wed.-Mon.; adm. fee*) Poet Robert Frost purchased this simple farmhouse overlooking the White Mountains in 1915. It's filled with memorabilia, including several first editions of his works. The half-mile poetry-nature trail is delightful.

Saint-Gaudens National Historic Site (*N.H. 12A, in Cornish. 603-675-2175. Late May–Oct., grounds open year-round; adm. fee*) Irish-born sculptor Augustus Saint-Gaudens converted an 1805 inn on the Connecticut River into a home and studio he called Aspet. He lived and worked here from 1885 until his death in 1907; many of his pieces are exhibited.

Vermont

· ·

President Calvin Coolidge State Historic Site, Plymouth Notch

One of only two New England states not to have been among the 13 original Colonies, Vermont began to be settled in the 18th century, through land grants made by New Hampshire governors. These Hampshire Grants were disputed by New York, whose surveyors were harassed by the legendary Ethan Allen and his Green Mountain Boys. Allen and other independent-minded Vermonters fought the British during the Revolution. But instead of joining with the other rebellious colonies, Vermont declared itself a sovereign republic in 1777. Finally, in 1791, Vermont capitulated and became the 14th state in the Union.

In the 19th century Vermont remained a region of small, self-sufficient farming communities, with few major population centers. During the post-Civil War era, agriculture began a long decline in the state. Today, dairying is the main farming activity, but Vermont bases its economy on high-tech industry and on the tourists who come to enjoy winter skiing and the appealing rural character of the state.

Bennington ·

(Chamber of Commerce, Veterans Mem. Dr. 802-447-3311) Named for colonial governor Benning Wentworth, grantor of the township, Bennington

Ethan Allen

Ethan Allen straddles the border between fact and legend. Born in Connecticut in 1738, he migrated in 1769 to the Hampshire Grants—townships carved out of the Vermont wilderness by New Hampshire's governors. Within a year Allen was caught up in the struggle against New York grant holders who recognized only those titles issued by their own government. To harass them, Allen and like-minded firebrands organized the vigilante Green Mountain Boys. Celebrated for seizing Fort Ticonderoga from the British, Allen lost standing later for his controversial negotiations with the British and for his enthusiasm for land speculation.

was the pre-Revolutionary headquarters of the Green Mountain Boys.

Bennington Battle Monument (*15 Monument Circle. 802-447-0550. Mid-April–Oct.; adm. fee*) The 306-foot obelisk commemorates the 1777 battle in which Gen. John Stark's Continental troops and Green Mountain Boys under Seth Warner halted a British advance in nearby Walloomsac, New York.

Old Bennington Historic District (*Monument Ave. area, W of downtown*) The district encompasses the original Bennington settlement, along with 200-year-old homes and the exquisite 1805 **Old First Church** The adjacent **Old Burying Ground** holds the graves of Battle of Bennington casualties and of poet laureate Robert Frost.

Bennington Downtown Historic District (*Main St. at North and South Sts.*) The brick Victorian architecture here recalls the town's busy 19th-century manufacturing era. Note the **Putnam Block** (*Main and South Sts.*) and the **Pennysaver Building** (*107 South St.*).

Bennington Museum (*W. Main St. 802-447-1571. Adm. fee*) In 1938, 78-year-old Anna Mary Robertson "Grandma" Moses began painting scenes of rural life that would make her famous. The museum, just a few miles from her former farmhouse, preserves the largest public collection of her work.

Burlington ························

Vermont's largest city was settled at the end of the 18th century and became a leader in commercial navigation on Lake Champlain. The 1798 **Gideon King House** (*35 King St. Closed to public*) was built by an early steamship magnate. At the crest of the hill above the lake spreads the campus of the **University of Vermont** (*802-656-3480*), founded in 1791. Oldest of the handsome buildings that face the university green (*between Pearl and College Sts.*) is the redbrick **Old Mill** (1825).

Ethan Allen Homestead Historic Site (*Vt. 127. 802-865-4556. Early May–mid-Oct.; call for hours in spring and fall; adm. fee*) The reconstructed farmhouse was believed to be the home of Ethan Allen, controversial leader of the Green Mountain Boys. A Visitor Center offers exhibits and a multimedia presentation on Allen.

Excursions

SHELBURNE MUSEUM (*7 miles S on US 7, in Shelburne. 802-985-3346. Late May–late Oct., limited daily tours rest of year; adm. fee*) New York heiress Electra Havemeyer Webb created this renowned 45-acre museum village in 1947. Dedicated to American folk art and artifacts, it preserves handcrafted and utilitarian items, historic structures, and a turn-of-the-century Lake Champlain steamboat.

SHELBURNE FARMS (*9 miles S via US 7, in Shelburne. 102 Harbor Rd. 802-985-8686. Grounds open daily, guided tours mid-May–mid-Oct.; adm. fee*) Tycoon William Seward Webb's turn-of-the-century country retreat has survived largely intact. Shelburne House, his Queen Anne mansion, operates seasonally as an elegant inn; the site also features a model dairy and enormous shingled barns.

ROKEBY MUSEUM (*18 miles S via US 7, in Ferrisburg. 802-877-3406. Mid-May–Columbus Day Thurs.-Sun.; adm. fee*) This 1780s farmhouse was home to Rowland Evans Robinson, popular 19th-century author of Yankee and French-Canadian stories. His abolitionist father used the house as a stop on the Underground Railroad.

Manchester ············

(*Chamber of Commerce, 2 Main St. 802-362-2100. Daily Mem. Day– Columbus Day, Mon.-Fri. Columbus Day–Mem. Day*) Long a popular resort area, tree-shaded **Manchester Village** (*Vt. 7A*) is still graced by marble sidewalks and anchored by the white-colonnaded **Equinox Hotel** (*802-362-4700 or 800-362-4747*), a handsomely restored survivor of Manchester's 19th-century heyday.

First Congregational Church, Bennington

25

Hildene (*Vt. 7A. 802-362-1788. Mid-May–late Oct.; adm. fee*) Robert Todd Lincoln, Abraham Lincoln's son, built this Georgian Revival retreat in 1903-05. The house retains many Lincoln furnishings and several Abraham Lincoln mementos. Highlights include a thousand-pipe organ and formal gardens.

Windsor ·····················

American Precision Museum (*196 Main St. 802-674-5781. Late May– Oct.; adm. fee*) Built in 1846, this onetime factory houses a vast collection of machine tools, with demonstrations on working equipment and displays explaining the principles of mechanics.

Old Constitution House (*Main St. 802-828-3051. Mid-May–mid-Oct.*) In this tavern, representatives adopted a constitution for the Republic of Vermont in 1777. Period rooms recall early life in Vermont.

The 450-foot **Windsor-Cornish Bridge** (1866) ranks as New England's longest covered wooden span.

Excursions

SAINT-GAUDENS NATIONAL HISTORIC SITE, NEW HAMPSHIRE (*5 miles E via Vt. 44 and N.H. 12A, in Cornish*) See page 22.

WOODSTOCK (*17 miles NW via US 5, Vt. 12, and US 4*) A resort town for over 60 years (the state's first ski tow was installed nearby), the town boasts a manicured green surrounded by a **historic district** of Georgian brick and stone houses. Nearby, the **Billings Farm and Museum** (*Vt. 12 and River Rd. 802-457-2355. Daily May-Oct., Sat.-Sun. Nov.-Dec.; adm. fee*) is a working model of a turn-of-the-century New England farm, with period equipment and farm animals such as horses, oxen, and sheep. It is the former property of Frederick Billings, a 19th-century railroad magnate and advocate of scientific agriculture.

FORT AT NO. 4, NEW HAMPSHIRE (*20 miles SE via US 5 and N.H. 11, near Charlestown*) See page 22.

PRESIDENT CALVIN COOLIDGE S.H.S. (*30 miles NW via US 5, Vt. 12, US 4, and Vt. 100A. 802-828-3226. Mem. Day–Columbus Day, small exhibit open weekdays rest of year; adm. fee*) The hilltop hamlet where President Calvin Coolidge (1872-1933) was born looks as it did during Coolidge's boyhood. A tour includes his family store and the parlor where Vice President Coolidge was sworn in as 30th President by his father, when President Harding died. Also at the site are Coolidge's summer White House, an operating cheese factory run by Coolidge's son, and 17 other buildings.

Other Sites in Vermont

Chester A. Arthur Historic Site (*Off Vt. 36, in Fairfield. 802-933-8362. Mem. Day–Columbus Day Wed.-Sun.*) The little clapboard house on this remote site is a 1953 replica of the boyhood home of Chester Alan Arthur, 21st President. Inside the present structure are exhibits on Arthur's family and on his Presidency.

Chimney Point State Historic Site (*Vt. 125 at Champlain Bridge, near Addison. 802-759-2412. Mem. Day–Columbus Day Wed.-Sun.; adm. fee*) A museum housed in an 18th-century tavern focuses on the Indian and French heritage of the Lake Champlain basin. Native Americans had long encamped near this narrow spot in the lake which Samuel de Champlain explored in 1609; later, a French fort stood here.

Hubbardton Battlefield State Historic Site (*Off Vt. 30, in E. Hubbardton. 802-273-2282. Mem. Day–Columbus Day Wed.-Sun.*) On July 7, 1777, Lt. Col. Seth Warner's forces slowed a British advance here and made possible an orderly Colonial retreat south. A small museum explains the action; the site itself is a lovely, lofty meadow with fine views.

Justin Smith Morrill Homestead (*Off Vt. 132, in S. Strafford. 802-828-3051. Mid-May–mid-Oct. Wed.-Sun.; adm. fee*) Vermont congressman and senator Justin Morrill built this pink Gothic Revival home during a brief retirement before he entered politics in 1854. Morrill later authored the law that created the land-grant college system. Family furnishings fill the home's 17 rooms; outdoors, many of the senator's plantings survive, and a carriage house now serves as an interpretive center with exhibits outlining Morrill's achievements.

Mount Independence (*Off Vt. 73, near Orwell. 802-948-2000. Grounds open year-round, Visitor Center Memorial Day–Columbus Day Wed.-Sun.; adm. fee*) During the Revolution, a fort at this spot guarded southern Lake Champlain. Trails threading through the site reveal foundation remnants; a new interpretive center features exhibits pertaining to the fort's role in the Revolution. In summer you can take a tour boat from Mount Independence across the lake to **Fort Ticonderoga, New York** (*see page 57*).

Vermont Historical Society Museum (*109 State St., Montpelier. 802-828-2291. Tues.-Sun.; adm. fee*) The museum celebrates the Vermont experience from the days of the Abenaki Indians through the early 19th-century agricultural era to the coming of industrialization and tourism.

Massachusetts

Reenactment of Patriots' Day Battle, Lexington

The history of the New England colonies began in Massachusetts, with the 1620 landing of the Pilgrims at Plymouth. Ten years later a group of Puritans founded Boston, which grew to be the colony's commercial center and one of the largest cities in the British Colonies. By 1700 Massachusetts had developed a more secular, less theocratic character and a strong spirit of independence that would eventually lead to the American Revolution. Defiance toward the crown centered in Boston during the years immediately preceding hostilities, and the first battles of the war were fought at Lexington, Concord, and Bunker Hill. In the early years of independence, ports such as Boston and Salem grew rich, and the capital that accrued from the sea trade later financed vast manufacturing enterprises in Lowell, Lawrence, Brockton, and other burgeoning cities. Still the most populous state in New England, Massachusetts continues to be a leader in finance, electronics, and higher education.

Boston ···

(Convention & Visitors Bureau, 147 Tremont St. 617-536-4100 or 800-888-5515) When John Winthrop and the Puritan settlers arrived here aboard

the *Arbella* in 1630, they found an irregular peninsula inhabited only by English hermit William Blackstone. The colonial era saw Boston rise to prominence as a major seaport and New England's de facto political capital, as well as a lightning rod for the frustrations that culminated in the American Revolution.

Nineteenth-century Bostonians nurtured their city's reputation as the "Athens of America," but with the 20th century came a long commercial decline in Boston's fortunes. Today, Bostonians cling to their traditions and proudly preserve the downtown area where the city's colonial life was centered.

Beacon Hill Historic District

Beacon Hill is the gaslit, redbrick haunt of real Boston Brahmins and such fictional stereotypes as John P. Marquand's George Apley. Bounded by Boston Common on the south, the statehouse complex on the northeast, Cambridge Street on the north, and the Charles River on the west, the "Hill" was once three steep summits, named after a colonial beacon. Just before 1800 the burgeoning city engulfed Beacon Hill, the tops of the three summits were leveled, and Charles Bulfinch erected his magnificent statehouse on the northeast slope. New streets were lined with elegant brick row houses, designed by Bulfinch and other adherents of his federal-style architecture.

For a primer on that period, visit the Society for the Preservation of New England Antiquities, quartered in the superbly furnished **Harrison Gray Otis House** (*141 Cambridge St. 617-227-3956. Tues.-Sat.; adm. fee*). It is the first of three Beacon Hill mansions designed by Bulfinch for Otis, an influential Boston lawyer. Elsewhere on Beacon Hill, stroll through **Louisburg Square,** between Mount Vernon and Pinckney Streets; its bow-fronted 1840s Greek Revival row houses face each other across a

Acorn Street, Beacon Hill Historic District

small private park. Along Beacon Street, look for the purple windowpanes that were part of an early 19th-century glass shipment and are now a sign of Beacon Hill distinction.

Back Bay Historic District

Long before it was a desirable residential quarter, the Back Bay was in fact a baylike backwater of the Charles River. Beginning in 1857 and continuing for 30 years, landfill reclaimed the marshes, transforming them into a 450-acre tract laid out with broad, straight avenues quite unlike those in the older parts of town.

The Back Bay neighborhood is a rectangle tucked between the Charles River and Boylston Street on the north and south, and the Public Garden and Massachusetts Avenue on the east and west. With the exception of Boylston and Newbury Streets, which are now given over to upscale shops, the Back Bay remains residential, with Victorian homes, mostly brownstones, that look much as they did in the 19th century. For a glimpse of a virtual time capsule of domestic Victoriana, visit the 1859 **Gibson House Museum** *(137 Beacon St. 617-267-6338. May-Oct. Wed.-Sun., Nov.-April Sat.-Sun.; adm. fee).*

Freedom Trail Walking Tour ·········· Half to full day

(Information on sites available at the Boston National Historical Park Visitor Center, 15 State St. 617-242-5642, or at the Visitor Information Center on Boston Common at Tremont and Park Sts.) Most of Boston's most important Revolutionary sites lie along the Freedom Trail, a walking route through the city indicated by a red line on the sidewalk.

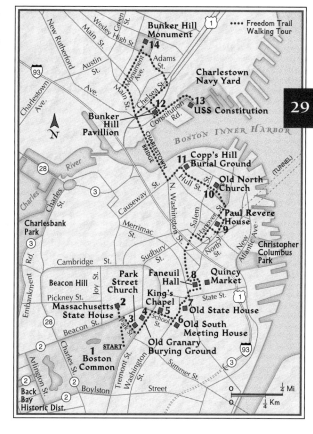

29

1. The nation's oldest public park, the 44-acre **Boston Common** has belonged "in common" to the city's residents since Boston's founding in 1630.

2. The **Massachusetts State House** *(Beacon St. 617-727-3676)* was designed in the late 1700s by Charles Bulfinch. It houses the handsomely appointed Senate and House Chambers, a Hall of Flags of Massachusetts regiments, and portraits of governors dating from early colonial times.

Directly across Beacon Street stands Augustus Saint-Gaudens's famous

Robert Gould Shaw and the 54th Regiment Memorial, honoring the first Union regiment of free black volunteers. Shaw, a Bostonian, and his men distinguished themselves at the Civil War Battle of Fort Wagner, in South Carolina.

3. Park Street Church *(Park and Tremont Sts. 617-523-3383),* designed by Peter Banner and built in 1809, echoes the influence of English architect Christopher Wren in its graceful steeple. Here in 1829 abolitionist William Lloyd Garrison made his first antislavery address in Boston.

4. Next to the church the **Old Granary Burying Ground** *(Tremont St.)* is the resting place of such luminaries as Paul Revere, John Hancock, and Samuel Adams, as well as other patriots.

5. Built in 1754, **King's Chapel** *(Tremont and School Sts. 617-227-2155)* housed

Statue of Paul Revere near Old North Church

Boston's first Anglican congregation; the burial ground alongside the church is the oldest in the city.

6. The **Old South Meeting House** *(310 Washington St. 617-482-6439. Under restoration until August 1997)* was a popular pre-Revolutionary gathering place. It was from here that Samuel Adams launched the pivotal Boston Tea Party protest.

7. Now functioning as a museum of city history, the **Old State House** *(State and Washington Sts. 617-720-1713)* was built in 1713 as the seat of colonial government. In March 1770 an altercation between British soldiers and an angry mob began outside its doors and escalated into the Boston Massacre, resulting in the deaths of five Bostonians.

8. Faneuil Hall *(Merchants Row. 617-242-5642)* was built in 1742 and enlarged in 1806. Built as a combination market and meeting place, it became known as the "cradle of liberty" because the colonists frequently held protest gatherings here. Directly opposite the hall, the restored, early 19th-century **Quincy Market** now houses restaurants and shops.

9. The **Paul Revere House** *(19 North Square. 617-523-2338)* is notable not only as the home of the patriot but also as the oldest building in Boston (circa 1680). The interior features rooms decorated in 17th- and 18th-century styles.

10. Old North Church *(193 Salem St. 617-523-*

30

Passion for Education

In the beginning was the word—and nothing except faith itself mattered more to the Puritan founders of the Massachusetts Bay Colony. The Puritans held that each congregation have an educated minister and that believers be able to read the Bible. By 1647 all Massachusetts townships of 50 families were required to have a primary school, "that learning may not be buried in the graves of our forefathers." In 1636 the colony opened its own college. Two years later, the institution received a substantial bequest from a deceased young minister whose name was John Harvard.

Excursion

WALDEN POND *(2 miles S via Mass. 126 at Walden Pond State Reservation. 508-369-3254. Parking fee in summer)* On the shores of this half-mile-long pond Henry David Thoreau conducted the two-year experiment in solitude and self-sufficiency that he described in his classic, *Walden*. Thoreau's cabin site is marked by a cairn, accessible by trail from the parking area.

Lowell

Lowell was the first successful large-scale industrial city in North America. Its core is now a shrine to the industrial revolution.

Lowell N.H.P. *(Visitor Center, 246 Market St. 508-970-5000)* At the Visitor Center, you can learn how capital, labor, machinery, and waterpower came together to produce cotton cloth—by 1848, 50,000 miles of cloth a year. From the Visitor Center, foot, trolley, and canalboat tours *(summer only)* lead to other park sites in former mills. These include the **Working People Exhibit** *(40 French St. 508-970-5000. Call for hours)*, which honors Lowell's native and immigrant workers; and the **Boott Cotton Mills Museum** *(End of John St. 508-970-5000. Adm. fee)*, where the experience of answering the morning work bell and the cacophony of the power looms is re-created. An entire floor is filled with them, their racket so loud that visitors are given earplugs (the workers were not). An upstairs floor contains an engaging exhibit on how Lowell's textile enterprises were organized and run.

Whistler House Museum of Art *(243 Worthen St. 508-452-7641. March–late Dec. Wed.-Sun.; adm. fee)* The birthplace of 19th-century artist James Abbott McNeill Whistler is a gallery featuring a permanent collection of American paintings and contemporary art shows.

35

Martha's Vineyard

(Chamber of Commerce, Beach St., Vineyard Haven. 508-693-0085. For ferry info call 508-477-8600) Seven miles off Cape Cod, this ruggedly picturesque island is a mix of small villages and exclusive private retreats. The Vineyard's oldest settlement, **Edgartown** was founded in 1642 and served as the island's whaling port during the early 19th century. The whaling era is recalled at the **Dr. Daniel Fisher House** *(99 Main St. 508-627-4440. Mem. Day–Columbus Day)*, an 1840 mansion built by a whale-oil manufacturer and dealer and local physician. Captains and shipowners worshiped at the **Old Whaling Church** *(89 Main St., included in tours of Vincent and Fisher Houses)*, an 1843 Greek Revival masterpiece. The **Vincent House Museum** *(Rear of Fisher House. 508-627-8619. Mem. Day–Columbus Day)*, built in 1672, is the oldest house on the island. Some of the interior trim, glass, and hardware are original.

Nantucket

(Chamber of Commerce, 48 Main St. 508-228-1700. Ferry schedules available) Whaling capital of the early 1800s, Nantucket is the only real town on the island of the same name. The **Nantucket Historical Association** *(2 Whalers Ln. 508-228-1894)* maintains all the sites listed below, except for the Maria Mitchell Birthplace and Observatory.

Whaling Museum *(15 Broad St. Daily in summer, weekends late April–late May; adm. fee)* Originally a whale-oil candle factory, the museum features

1849 Sankaty Lighthouse, Nantucket

a fine exhibit of scrimshaw (whalebone carving and engraving), harpoons and other whaling equipment, and a 40-foot finback whale skeleton; lectures on whaling daily.

Hadwen House *(96 Main St. Daily late June–Labor Day, weekends late spring and early fall; adm. fee)* Whale-oil merchant William Hadwen built this stately Greek Revival home in 1845 and its furnishings and gardens represent the peak of Nantucket's prosperity.

Peter Foulger Museum *(17 Broad St. June–Labor Day; adm. fee)* Dedicated to life on Nantucket from the time of the Indians and first English settlers, the museum features changing exhibits.

Oldest House–Jethro Coffin House *(16 Sunset Hill. Daily in summer; adm. fee)* This austere frame dwelling was built for Jethro and Mary Coffin in 1686. Exhibits interpret the hardships and adaptations of the earliest period of Nantucket settlement.

Maria Mitchell Birthplace and Observatory *(1 Vestal St. 508-228-2896. June-Aug. Tues.-Sat.; adm. fee)* The 1790 Nantucket Quaker-style house was the birthplace of Maria Mitchell, a pioneer astronomer who discovered the comet named after her in 1847. The Maria Mitchell Association sponsors lectures, classes, and observation nights at the observatory.

New Bedford

(Visitor Centers at 33 Williams St. 508-991-6200 or 800-508-5353, and at Pier 3, 508-979-1745) The former hub of America's 19th-century whaling industry celebrates its heritage at the **New Bedford Whaling Museum** *(18 Johnny Cake Hill. 508-997-0046. Adm. fee)*. Harpoons, a whaleboat, scrimshaw, a humpback whale skeleton, marine paintings and documents, and an 89-foot-long model of the 1826 whaling ship *Lagoda* are exhibited in the nation's most comprehensive whaling museum.

Seamen's Bethel *(15 Johnny Cake Hill. 508-992-3295. Check at Mariner's Home next door for adm.)* Opened in 1832, this chapel was made famous by Herman Melville in *Moby-Dick*.

Rotch-Jones-Duff House and Garden Museum *(396 County St. 508-997-1401. Closed Mon. Jan.-May; adm. fee)* The 1830s Greek Revival mansion belonged to three prominent New Bedford families and reflects the wealth gained from the whaling industry. Period gardens have been preserved.

Excursion

FALL RIVER *(19 miles W via I-195)* Although Fall River's historic attractions are principally maritime, the somber brick mills that line the highway approaches to the city are a legacy of its past as a textile town. At **Battleship Cove** *(508-678-1100. Adm. fee)* the World War II battleship USS *Massachusetts* is permanently berthed; several decks are accessible to visitors. Also on site are the destroyer ***Joseph P. Kennedy, Jr.,*** the submarine ***Lionfish,*** and two PT boats.

Old Sturbridge Village ·····························

(1 Old Sturbridge Village Rd. 508-347-3362. Daily April-Oct., call for off-season hours; adm. fee) Carefully designed to represent a New England village as it would have appeared in the 1830s, this superb living history museum is made up of some 40 authentically furnished period buildings, collected from across New England. Each retains its original character and is appropriately staffed with knowledgeable, costumed interpreters and tradespeople. Printers, blacksmiths, bookbinders, coopers, cobblers, storekeepers, schoolteachers, and even a minister go about their business as they welcome visitors. Authenticity extends to farming practices as well—the livestock at Sturbridge are, as closely as possible, bred to resemble old New England varieties, as are the crops planted and harvested on site. Such activities as a choir practice or a black-powder musket drill re-create life in a typical rural community of 175 years ago.

Plymouth ··

(Information Center, 130 Water St. 508-747-7525 or 800-USA-1620) It was at this site on the Atlantic coast that the Pilgrims made their historic landing in 1620.

Plymouth Rock *(Water St.)* is where tradition marks the Pilgrims' first footsteps in New England. Still washed by the tide, it lies beneath a neoclassical canopy along the waterfront.

Cole's Hill *(Water St., opposite Plymouth Rock)* The Pilgrims' numbers were halved by the hardships of the first winter. The dead were buried on this hill by night, so that the Indians could not gauge the numbers of the living. A monument marks their remains; another honors Chief Massasoit, who helped the survivors.

Plimoth Plantation

Mayflower II *(Water St. 508-746-1622. April-Nov.; adm. fee. Combination ticket also covers admission to Plimoth Plantation, below).* This full-size reproduction of the *Mayflower* sailed from England to Plymouth in 1957. On board, sailors and passengers in period dress discuss the events of 1620 as they tend ship.

Pilgrim Hall Museum *(75 Court St. 508-746-1620. Closed Jan.; adm. fee)* The museum's exhibits include a number of articles believed to have been carried across the Atlantic on the *Mayflower.* On display are John Alden's Bible, Miles Standish's sword, furniture, armor, and even the primitive cradle of Peregrine White, the first European child born in New England.

Plymouth also opens three 17th-century houses to the public: the circa 1667 **Howland House** *(33 Sandwich St. 508-746-9590. Mem. Day–Columbus Day and last weekend in Nov.; adm. fee);* the pre-1640 **Richard Sparrow House** *(42 Summer St. 508-747-1240. Mem. Day–Thanksgiving Thurs.-Tues. or by appt.; adm. fee);* and the 1677 **Harlow Old Fort House** *(119 Sandwich St. 508-746-0012. June–mid-Oct. Fri.-Sat.; adm. fee).*

Plimoth Plantation *(137 Warren Ave. 508-746-1622. April-Nov.; adm. fee)* On a seaside hilltop just outside town, this painstakingly researched reproduction of Plymouth as it appeared around 1627 is the home of costumed interpreters so thoroughly versed in the Pilgrims' lives—and even in their dialects—that either they or you seem like time travelers to another century. Also on the site is the **Hobbamock's Homesite,** a reconstruction of Wampanoag Indian dwellings where Native American crafts are demonstrated.

Excursion

JOHN ALDEN HOUSE *(12 miles N via Mass. 3 and 3A. 105 Alden St., Duxbury. 617-934-9092. Late June–Labor Day Tues.-Sun., mid-May–late June and Labor Day–mid-Oct. Sat.-Sun.; adm. fee)* Pilgrims John and Priscilla Alden, made famous in Longfellow's poem, "The Courtship of Miles Standish," lived in this snug little house, built by Alden in 1653.

Pittsfield

(Visitors Bureau, Berkshire Common at South St. 413-443-9186 or 800-237-5747. Mon.-Fri.) A popular 19th-century resort and the seat of Berkshire County, Pittsfield enjoyed ample waterpower, which made it an industrial center, particularly for the manufacture of paper and textiles. Paper for U.S. currency is still made nearby.

Arrowhead *(780 Holmes Rd. 413-442-1793. Daily Mem. Day–Labor Day, Fri.-Mon. Labor Day–Oct. or by appt.; adm. fee)* As a young man, Herman Melville lived in this 1780s farmhouse off and on between 1850 and 1863 and wrote his masterpiece, *Moby-Dick,* in an upstairs room. During his early sojourns in the Berkshires he became friends with another local resident, Nathaniel Hawthorne, to whom he dedicated *Moby-Dick.*

Berkshire Athenaeum *(1 Wendell Ave. 413-499-9486. Mon.-Sat.)* Pittsfield's public library, the Athenaeum houses the Herman Melville Memorial Room, with the world's largest collection of Melville's personal belongings; it includes a number of first editions of his works.

Excursion

HANCOCK SHAKER VILLAGE *(5 miles W via US 20 at Mass. 41. 413-443-0188. April-Nov. or by appt.; adm. fee).* The community, founded in 1790, was the third established in the U.S. by the Shakers, followers of English visionary Mother Ann Lee. Now fully preserved, its 20 restored buildings—including a beautifully crafted 1826 round stone barn—feature collections of elegantly simple Shaker furniture and implements.

Quincy ···········

Called the "city of Presidents" for its connections to the Adams family, Quincy was part of the farming community of Braintree when John Adams (1735-1826) and his son John Quincy Adams (1767-1848) were born. The town was also famous for its granite quarries, which supplied stone for the Bunker Hill Monument and for the vast local naval shipyard.

Adams National Historic Site *(Visitor Center, 1250 Hancock St. 617-770-1175. Mid-April–mid-Nov.; adm. fee for house tours)* From the Visitor Center, take shuttle buses to tour the **John Adams Birthplace,** a 1681 farmhouse where the second President was born; and the **John Quincy Adams Birthplace,**

Stone Library, Adams National Historic Site

another clapboard structure, where the sixth President was born. The **Old House** *(3 miles away)* was the home of four generations of Adamses, from 1787, when it was purchased by John Adams, to 1946, when it was given by the family to the nation. All of the furnishings and paintings in the big, rambling clapboard house belonged to John Adams or to his descendants, who included diplomat Charles Francis Adams and historian Henry Adams. On the grounds is the **Stone Library,** built in 1870 to house the family's collection of some 14,000 books and manuscripts.

Excursion

OLD SHIP CHURCH *(10 miles E via Mass. 3A. 90 Main St., Hingham. 617-749-1679. July-Aug., by appt. rest of year; donations)* The nation's oldest continuously used wooden church was built in 1681. It may have been named for the shiplike construction of its massive roof timbers. Adjacent is a burial ground with many stones from the colonial era.

Salem ···

(Office of Tourism and Cultural Affairs, City Hall, 93 Washington St. 508-745-9595) First settled in 1626, Salem is famed for its 17th-century witch trials and its maritime heyday following the Revolution. The most vivid relic of the latter period is superbly preserved **Chestnut Street,** a 60-foot-wide thoroughfare laid out in 1796 and lined with federal and Greek Revival homes.

Peabody Essex Museum *(East India Square. 508-745-9500. Daily Mem. Day–Oct., Tues.-Sun. rest of year, call for daily house tour schedules; adm. fee)*

In 1799 Salem's traders and captains founded a museum to house the artworks, natural specimens, and cultural artifacts they were bringing back from across the seas. In recent years it has merged with the Essex Institute, and the joint collections include superb Asian export art, marine paintings, and American decorative arts, as well as several restored 17th, 18th-, and early 19th-century houses, many designed and ornamented by the brilliant Salem architect Samuel McIntire.

Salem Maritime National Historic Site (*174 Derby St. 508-740-1660. Fee for tours*) This collection of buildings, all on or near the waterfront, celebrates the golden age of the China trade, from roughly 1790 to 1812. The site encompasses the 1819 **Custom House,** where onetime employee Nathaniel Hawthorne wrote that he had found an ancient tattered cloth letter *A*; the 1762 **Elias Hasket Derby House,** home of the wealthiest Salem shipowner of his day; and a number of other homes, wharves, and historic warehouses.

Witch House (*310 1/2 Essex St. 508-744-0180. Mid-March–Nov.; adm. fee*) This steep-gabled 1642 house was the home of Judge Jonathan Corwin, a judge during the infamous Salem witch trials that were held in the early 1690s.

Salem Witch Museum (*Washington Square. 508-744-1692. Adm. fee*) Housed in an appropriately spooky-looking old church, the museum gives a sensational but accurate sound-and-light presentation on the witch hysteria and its resultant trials and executions of 20 men and women.

House of the Seven Gables (*54 Turner St. 508-744-0991. Closed two weeks in Jan.; adm. fee*) This is the 1668 house immortalized by Salem native Nathaniel Hawthorne, descendant of a witch-trial judge. Rooms are furnished in a variety of period styles, from the 17th to the early 19th century. A secret staircase winds between two floors.

Stockbridge ·······································

Stockbridge, a market and mill town serving the colonial farmers of the southern Berkshires, became the center of a region of sumptuous summer estates in the late 19th century.

Chesterwood (*4 Williamsville Rd. in Glendale neighborhood. 413-298-3579. May-Oct.; adm. fee*) Sculptor Daniel Chester French (1850-1931), whose works include the seated statue of Lincoln in the U.S. capital's Lincoln Memorial, spent his summers at this gracious home from 1897 until his death. His studio stands amid the serenely elegant gardens that he designed.

Mission House (*Main St. 413-298-3239. Mem. Day–Columbus Day; adm. fee*) Originally located outside Stockbridge on Eden Hill, this 1739 house was built by Rev. John Sergeant as both his home and an Indian mission. It now houses a fine collection of furniture and decorative arts from the 17th through the 19th centuries.

Norman Rockwell Museum at Stockbridge (*Mass. 183. 413-298-4100. Museum open daily; studio open May-Oct.; adm. fee*) Rockwell (1894-1978), the most beloved American illustrator of his day, lived in Stockbridge for the last 25 years of his life. The museum preserves and exhibits the world's largest collection of original Rockwell art, including many paintings done for magazine covers and such masterworks as "The Four Freedoms"; his studio, originally located downtown, has been moved to the grounds.

Excursion

THE MOUNT *(6 miles N via US 7, at southern junction with Mass. 7A in Lenox. 2 Plunkett St. 413-637-1899. May-Oct.; adm. fee)* Edith Wharton, who wrote so perceptively of turn-of-the-century mores in such novels as *Ethan Frome* and *The House of Mirth*, designed and built this setting for her own gracious lifestyle in 1902. Both the American classical-style mansion and the formal gardens reflect Wharton's love of symmetry and balance.

Other Sites in Massachusetts

Beauport: The Sleeper-McCann House *(75 Eastern Point Blvd., Gloucester. 508-283-0800. Mid-May–mid-Sept. Mon.-Fri., daily mid-Sept.–mid-Oct.; call for tour schedules; adm. fee)* Pioneer interior decorator Henry Davis Sleeper made his own oceanfront home the crowning achievement of his career. Rambling—almost labyrinthine—the 40-room Beauport is a monument to sheer eclecticism, from colonial-era rooms to the grandeur of New England's China trade years.

Emily Dickinson Homestead *(280 Main St., Amherst. Reservations recommended. 413-542-8161. May-Oct. Wed.-Sat., March-April and Nov.–mid-Dec. Wed. and Sat.; adm. fee)* Reclusive poet Emily Dickinson (1830-1886) spent most of her life in the brick house her grandfather built. Period furnishings (not Dickinson's) re-create her surroundings; knowledgeable guides explain her physically confined but intellectually spacious world.

Fruitlands Museums *(102 Prospect Hill Rd., Harvard. 508-456-3924. Mid-May–mid-Oct. Tues.-Sun.; adm. fee)* Transcendentalist Bronson Alcott and his followers set up an experiment in communal living here in 1843-44. Though it failed after seven months, the transcendentalists' ideas have resonated into our own time. The farmhouse is a museum of the transcendentalist movement; other buildings house Shaker and Native American exhibits and a 19th-century American art exhibit.

Sandwich Glass Museum *(129 Main St., Sandwich. 508-888-0251. Daily April-Oct., Wed.-Sun. rest of year. Closed Jan.; adm. fee)* Cape Cod's oldest town was a 19th-century glassmaking capital. Located in the village center, this museum traces the changing demands of taste and the developments in technology that affected the local glass industry. A wealth of fine glass is displayed.

Springfield Armory National Historic Site *(State and Federal Sts., Springfield. 413-734-8551. Wed.-Sun.)* Many of America's battles were won at Springfield, where weapons ranging from muzzle-loading muskets to M14s were mass-produced for over 170 years. One armory

Sandwich Glass Museum

building now houses a comprehensive firearms collection. An organlike array of rifles inspired Longfellow's "Arsenal at Springfield".

41

The Breakers, Newport

Rhode Island was permanently settled by the English in 1636, when religious maverick Roger Williams arrived following his expulsion from the Massachusetts Bay Colony. Other dissidents soon followed, but problems with the Indians during King Philip's War in 1675-76 slowed the colony's growth. After 1700 the population expanded rapidly in conjunction with a lucrative maritime trade that made Newport one of the wealthiest towns in the American Colonies.

During the 19th century, as the industrial revolution inaugurated at Pawtucket took hold, the tide of prosperity turned toward Providence and the communities at the head of Narragansett Bay. Newport's second era of prominence came later in the century, when it became a millionaires' summer colony, famous for its lavish mansions. As in the past, the population of this diminutive state—smallest geographically in the nation—remains centered in and around the heavily industrialized Providence area.

Newport

(Convention & Visitors Bureau, 23 America's Cup Ave. 401-849-8098 or 800-326-6030) Now famed as a yachting mecca, Newport was at first a working seaport. The most vivid reminders of colonial Newport, including the cobblestoned, 18th-century **Bowen's** and **Bannister's Wharves,** are

clustered in the **historic district** that comprises the Easton's Point and Midtown neighborhoods, close by the Newport Harbor.

Trinity Church (*Queen Anne Square, Spring and Church Sts. 401-846-0660*) The traditional lines of Christopher Wren's London churches are echoed in this 1726 structure, which houses a splendid collection of Communion silver and parts of the second organ ever installed in America.

Touro Synagogue (*85 Touro St. 401-847-4794. Mid-May–mid-Sept. Sun.-Fri., call for off-season hours*) Founded as a place of worship by Sephardic Jews from Spain and Portugal, this is the oldest synagogue (1763) in North America. George Washington proclaimed America's commitment to religious freedom here in 1790.

Wanton-Lyman-Hazard House (*17 Broadway. 401-846-0813. Call for hours; adm. fee*) Built circa 1675, this ranks as the oldest restored house in Newport. Once the home of a Tory lawyer, it was the focus of a Stamp Act riot in 1765.

Colony House (*Washington Square. Private*) Once the headquarters of Rhode Island's colonial and state governments, this 1739 structure was one of the colony's first brick buildings. Representatives gathered here and rejected King George's rule on May 4, 1776. Later that year, the Declaration of Independence was first read to Rhode Islanders from the Colony House balcony.

Hunter House National Historic Landmark (*54 Washington St. 401-847-1000. Daily in summer, weekends April and Oct.; adm. fee*) The 1748 house is a textbook study in high Georgian style. It was the home of two Rhode

43

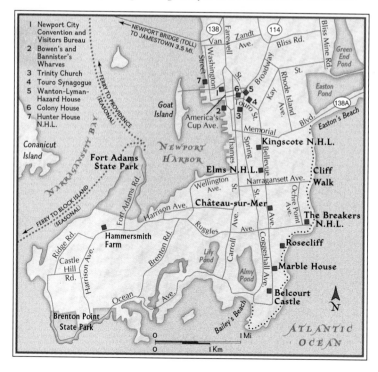

Touro Synagogue, Newport

44

Island governors and is today a showcase for work by master 18th-century Newport cabinetmakers Job Townsend and John Goddard.

Newport "Cottages" *(Preservation Society of Newport County. 424 Bellevue Ave. 401-847-1000. Call for individual house schedules; different adm. fees apply to different combination house tours, including Hunter House, above)* The preservation society maintains the finest of the summer cottages built by 19th-century financial titans and captains of industry. Standing along Bellevue Avenue and surrounding streets, these include the oldest of the mansions, **Kingscote,** designed by the Gothic Revival architect Richard Upjohn in 1839 and now a national historic landmark; the French-inspired **Elms National Historic Landmark;** William S. Wetmore's **Château-sur-Mer,** built in 1852 and enlarged in a later Victorian style in 1872; **The Breakers N.H.L.,** built by Cornelius Vanderbilt II and the largest of the Newport mansions; **Rosecliff,** designed by Stanford White in imitation of the Grand Trianon at Versailles; and William K. Vanderbilt's **Marble House,** which incorporates rare marbles from around the world.

Belcourt Castle *(Bellevue Ave. 401-846-0669. Closed Jan.; call for winter hours; adm. fee)* This reproduction of the hunting lodge at Versailles showcases 13th-century glass and an extensive art collection.

Cliff Walk For magnificent ocean vistas and a backdoor view of many of the Newport mansions, follow this oceanfront pedestrian pathway that runs from Easton's Beach to Bailey's Beach.

Fort Adams State Park *(Harrison Ave. 401-847-2400. Adm. fee in summer)* Between 1824 and 1857, military engineers created this formidable granite-walled defense at the approach to Narragansett Bay. With the decline of its military usefulness during the 1960s, the fort became a state park. President Dwight Eisenhower summered in a Victorian house on the grounds *(By appointment).*

Providence

(Visitor Center, 2 American Express Plaza. 401-274-1636) Rhode Island's capital was founded by Roger Williams, whose disagreement with Massachusetts

Triangle Trade

Colonial Rhode Island's greatest resource was its access to the sea. The ports of Providence and Newport soon became leaders in the era's lucrative "Triangle Trade," which profited from several of the 18th century's harsher realities: The sugar planters of the Caribbean depended upon slaves for labor. They also depended upon New England distillers to turn their molasses into rum, and rum was a negotiable commodity along the slave coasts of West Africa. Rhode Islanders and other Yankee traders kept the Triangule Trade in motion, bartering rum for Africans taken as slaves and transporting the slaves back to the West Indies.

Puritans was the result not only of his liberal theology but also of his sympathetic attitude toward the Indians. He proclaimed that his new settlement would be a refuge for the oppressed, and he named it after God's providence. Not far from where Williams once lived, along a hillside between downtown and Brown University, **Benefit Street** is lined with Georgian and federal mansions, including the 1810 **Sullivan-Dorr House** *(109 Benefit St. Private).* The **Providence Athenaeum** *(251 Benefit St. 401-421-6970. Mon.-Fri., call about weekend hours)* is an 1836 members-association library housed in handsome Greek Revival quarters. Edgar Allan Poe courted a sweetheart here.

John Brown House *(52 Power St. 401-331-8575. Closed Mon. year-round and weekdays Jan.-Feb.; adm. fee)* Built in 1786 for John Brown, wealthiest of Providence's merchant-prince Brown brothers, this 3-story, 14-room brick mansion is a crowning achievement of the Georgian style. John Quincy Adams pronounced it the "most magnificent and elegant private mansion" in North America. The Rhode Island Historical Society maintains it very much in that style, with fine 18th-century furniture, silver, and Chinese export porcelain.

Excursion

SLATER MILL HISTORIC SITE *(5 miles N via I-95. Roosevelt Ave., Pawtucket, 401-725-8638. Closed Mon., call for tour information; adm. fee)* In 1790 near this site on the Blackstone River, Samuel Slater introduced the water-powered spinning frame to this country; three years later he built the wooden mill that still stands. It now features an extensive collection of vintage textile machinery and demonstrations of their uses. The site also includes a machine shop and working waterwheel, at nearby Wilkinson Mill. Pawtucket and the Slater Mill lie at the southern end of the **Blackstone River National Heritage Corridor** *(Visitor Center 401-762-0440),* which extends north along the river into Massachusetts. In the mid-19th century, the Blackstone was the nation's most heavily industrialized river valley, and the corridor focuses on that history.

45

Slater Mill Historic Site, Pawtucket

Connecticut

State Capitol, Hartford

In 1633 Dutch settlers built the first European outpost at what is now Hartford, in a region that a few years before had been thickly populated by Algonquin Indians. English migrants from Massachusetts dispossessed the Dutch, organized a General Court in 1636, and three years later wrote the "Fundamental Orders," the world's first written constitution. A strong supporter of the independence movement of 1776, Connecticut became known as the "provision state" because of its liberal supply of food to the Continental forces. A postwar economic decline was reversed by the rise of manufacturing, the result of the ingenuity of such "Connecticut Yankee" inventors as revolver-creator Samuel Colt and clockmaker Seth Thomas. Manufacturing supported the state from the 1840s until the 1970s and attracted Irish, German, Italian, and Polish immigrants. Connecticut remains today one of the most culturally heterogeneous states in the nation. Service industries, recreation, and tourism now dominate the economy.

Essex

The houses of former sea captains line the winding streets of this trim little town, which functioned as a major port and shipbuilding center for a hundred years beginning in the mid-1700s.

Connecticut River Museum (*67 Main St. 860-767-8269. Tues.-Sun.; adm. fee*) has exhibits on shipbuilding, archaeology, and local history, and a reproduction of the 1775 submarine, *American Turtle*, in the boathouse.

Valley Railroad Company *(Railroad Ave. 860-767-0103. Call for schedule; adm. fee)* Hop aboard one of the restored vintage passenger cars and let a snorting, puffing steam locomotive carry you through the Connecticut valley. A further bit of history: the 1930s bar car was once a Pullman on which a young porter later known as Malcolm X allegedly worked.

Excursions

GILLETTE CASTLE STATE PARK *(8 miles N via Conn. 9 and Conn. 82, in E. Haddam. 860-526-2336. Daily Mem. Day–Columbus Day, weekends Columbus Day–late Dec.; adm. fee to castle)* The park centerpiece is the hilltop fieldstone mansion of early 20th-century actor William Gillette, who designed the house himself, with, as one wag put it, an "uncanny inventive ability, a precocious and daring initiative and a total disregard for accepted standards and ways."

OLD LYME *(6 miles SE via Conn. 9, I-95, and Conn. 156)* The stately 18th- and 19th-century houses that line Lyme Street are a reminder that this resort town was once a shipping and shipbuilding hub. The **Florence Griswold Museum** *(96 Lyme St. 860-434-5542. June-Nov. Tues.-Sun., Jan.-May Wed.-Sun., Dec. daily; adm. fee)* Two major U.S. art movements—the American Barbizon school and American impressionism—were brought to life by painters staying at "Miss Florence's" boardinghouse, which now displays a superb art collection, including works by Childe Hassam.

Hartford ···························

(Visitors Bureau, 1 Civic Center Plaza. 860-728-6789 or 800-446-7811) The English colonial history of Connecticut's capital began with the arrival of Rev. Thomas Hooker and an estimated one hundred followers from Massachusetts in 1636. In 1687, in defense of their political liberties, colonists refused to relinquish a charter from King Charles II and hid the document in a tree later called the Charter Oak. Hartford's rise to its present-day prominence as America's insurance capital began in the 18th century, when underwriters met here to insure merchant vessels.

Old State House *(800 Main St. 860-522-6766. Mon.-Sat.)* Prominent federal architect Charles Bulfinch designed one of the country's oldest statehouses in 1796. It now boasts a restored Senate Chamber and a Gilbert Stuart portrait of George Washington.

Museum of Connecticut History *(231 Capitol Ave. 860-566-3056. Mon.-Fri.)* The 1687 charter defended by the Colonists and hidden in the Charter Oak is displayed here, along with locally manufactured Colt firearms and an exhibit on the state's government and politics and its industrial and military history.

Connecticut State Capitol *(210 Capitol Ave. 860-240-0222. April-Oct. Mon.-Sat., Nov.-March Mon.-Fri.)* Topped by a gold-leafed dome, the mar-

Yankee Ingenuity

Connecticut might properly be described as the fountainhead of American industry. Short on fertile farmland but favored with ample waterpower and a crossroads location, the state cultivated its tinkerers from the earliest days of the Republic. In the 1790s Eli Terry began producing clocks in Watertown, and Eli Whitney perfected his cotton gin in New Haven. The new century saw Seth Thomas found a clockmaking dynasty in Thomaston, while Whitney's system of interchangeable parts revolutionized all industries—particularly the one founded by Hartford revolver-maker Samuel Colt, of whom it was said, "God made all men...and Samuel Colt made them equal."

47

ble and granite building houses an eclectic assortment of Connecticut artifacts, including an inscribed Civil War wagon wheel and banners from past wars.

Connecticut Historical Society *(1 Elizabeth St. 860-236-5621. Closed Mon. year-round, and Sat. Mem. Day–Labor Day; adm. fee)* Changing exhibits highlight various aspects of the state's history, and a permanent exhibit covers decorative arts in Connecticut from the 17th through the 19th centuries.

Harriet Beecher Stowe House *(71 Forest St. 860-525-9317. Daily June–Columbus Day and Dec., closed Mon. rest of year; adm. fee)* Beecher, the author of the seminal abolitionist novel, *Uncle Tom's Cabin,* lived here from 1873 until her death in 1896. The house is still filled with the writer's personal and professional memorabilia.

Mark Twain summering in New Hampshire

Mark Twain House *(351 Farmington Ave. 860-493-6411. Daily Mem. Day–Columbus Day and Dec., closed Tues. rest of year; adm. fee)* Samuel Langhorne Clemens commissioned this whimsically elegant, 19-room Picturesque Gothic mansion and lived here from 1874 to 1891. During that time, he wrote such classics as *The Adventures of Tom Sawyer* and *Adventures of Huckleberry Finn.* The house contains the only remaining domestic interiors by the design firm of Louis Comfort Tiffany.

Excursions

WETHERSFIELD *(5 miles S via I-91. Visitor information at the Keeney Memorial, 200 Main St. 860-529-7161. Tues.-Sun.)* One of the state's first permanent English settlements now boasts Connecticut's largest historic district. The **Buttolph-Williams House** *(249 Broad St. 860-529-0612. May-Oct. Wed.-Mon.; adm. fee)* features "Ye Great Kitchin," an 18th-century kitchen showcasing 17th-century appliances. At the **Webb-Deane-Stevens Museum** *(211 Main St. 860-529-0612. May-Oct. Wed.-Mon., Nov.-May Sat.-Sun.; adm. fee),* three 18th-century homes are furnished to reflect distinctive American architectural styles, beginning with the Revolutionary War era, then into the industrial revolution and on to the colonial revivalism of the early 20th century. In 1781 George Washington visited the Webb House.

NOAH WEBSTER HOUSE *(4 miles W via I-84. 227 S. Main St., West Hartford. 860-521-5362. Thurs.-Tues.; adm. fee)* The books, papers, and personal possessions of the man who compiled the first American dictionary, published in 1828, are displayed at his restored 18th-century farmhouse.

FARMINGTON *(9 miles W via I-84 and Conn. 4 and 10)* Once an industrial center, this town is now a wealthy bedroom community of Hartford. The lives of colonial families are depicted at the **Stanley-Whitman House** *(37 High St. 860-677-9222. May-Oct. Wed.-Sun., Nov.-April Sun. and by appt.; adm. fee),* a 1720 post-and-beam structure. Housed in industrialist Alfred Atmore Pope's turn-of-the-century country home, the **Hill-Stead Museum** *(35 Mountain Rd. 860-677-9064. Tues.-Sun.; adm. fee)* holds a magnificent mélange of

French Impressionist paintings, decorative arts, and antique furnishings.

AMERICAN CLOCK & WATCH MUSEUM *(20 miles W via I-84 and US 6. 100 Maple St., Bristol. 860-583-6070. Daily April-Nov.; adm. fee)* Focusing on the Bristol area as the "cradle of the American clock industry," the museum exhibits more than 3,000 timepieces. A special exhibit chronicles clockmaking history in this region.

MASSACOH PLANTATION *(15 miles N via US 44 and US 202. 800 Hopmeadow St., Simsbury. 860-658-2500. May-Oct.; adm. fee)* This settlement was established early in the 1600s and burned to the ground in King Philip's War. Nine historic structures have been rebuilt and are used to recount the plantation's past.

OLD NEW-GATE PRISON AND COPPER MINE *(15 miles N via I-91, Conn. 20. Newgate Rd., E. Granby. 860-653-3563. Mid-May–Oct. Wed.-Sun.; adm. fee)* During the Revolution, the country's first chartered copper mine was used to house Loyalist prisoners; later it was the state's first prison. Ruins of the prison remain, and a museum holds historic photographs and memorabilia.

OLIVER ELLSWORTH HOMESTEAD *(6 miles N via I-91 and Conn. 305. 778 Palisado Ave., Windsor. 860-688-8717. Mid-May–Oct. Tues.-Wed. and Sat.; adm. fee)* Built in 1780, the birthplace of the third Chief Justice of the United States has many of its original furnishings.

Litchfield ·· 49

(Historical Society, 7 South St. 860-567-4501) Settled in 1721, the center, with its magnificent village green, was the first in Connecticut to be designated a **historic district.** The town is regarded by many as New England's quintessential village.

Tapping Reeve House and Law School *(82 South St. 860-567-4501. Closed 1997 for renovation; adm. fee)* A number of prominent national figures, including Aaron Burr and John C. Calhoun (both later Vice Presidents), attended this law school, founded in 1773 as the country's first school of legal instruction. The museum presents exhibits and programs that explore daily life in early 19th-century Litchfield, the significance and impact of its law school, and the accomplishments of its graduates.

New Haven ··

(Visitors Bureau, 1 Long Wharf Dr. 203-777-8550 or 800-332-STAY) English Puritans from Massachusetts came to this area in 1638 and set about establishing a Puritan theocracy on land they purchased from local Indians, laying it out in a grid pattern of nine squares, with a public green at the center. The colony of Connecticut absorbed the New Haven colony in 1665, but the town still preserves its original grid pattern.

Yale University *(Guided tours offered at the Information Center, 149 Elm St. 203-432-2300. Call for hours)* Founded in 1701 as the Collegiate School, the Ivy League university borders one side of the town green. While a student here, Revolutionary War hero Nathan Hale ("I only regret that I have but one life to lose for my country") lived in what is now the school's oldest building—the 1752 Connecticut Hall. The several superb museums on campus include the **Beinecke Rare Book and Manuscript Library** *(121 Wall St. 203-432-2977. Closed Sun. year-round and Sat. in Aug.),* which displays an original copy of the circa 1455 Gutenberg Bible.

Excursion

HENRY WHITFIELD STATE MUSEUM (*15 miles N via I-95 and Conn. 77. Stone House Ln., Guilford. 203-453-2457. Wed.-Sun.; adm. fee*) New England's oldest stone house, built by one of the founders of Guilford in 1639, is now a repository for the state's collection of 17th- through 19th-century furniture and household items. Greatly modified over the years, it has been restored to recall the days of Connecticut's first settlers.

New London ···

(*Visitor information at Downtown New London Association, Eugene O'Neill Dr. at Golden St. 860-444-7264*) Puritan John Winthrop, Jr., and his followers founded New London in 1646. Two hundred years later it was the second largest whaling port in the world. During the Revolution, Benedict Arnold's forces burned much of the city to the ground. The **historic district** preserves several structures that predate the fire.

Joshua Hempsted House (*11 Hempstead St. 860-443-7949. Mid-May–mid-Oct. Thurs.-Sun.; adm. fee*) New London's oldest surviving house, built in 1678, is also one of the oldest frame buildings in New England. Lived in by members of the Hempsted family until 1937, it was restored according to a diary kept by Joshua from 1711 to 1758.

Nathan Hale School (*The Parade. 860-443-7949. Under restoration*) The Revolutionary War hero was schoolmaster here before enlisting in George Washington's army.

Shaw-Perkins Mansion (*11 Blinman St. 860-443-1209. May-Oct. Wed.-Sat.; adm. fee*) Used as the state's naval office during the Revolutionary War, this shipowner's home, built in 1756, has been restored and is decorated with original 18th- and 19th-century furnishings and holds a treasure trove of local artifacts.

The *Joseph Conrad*, Mystic Seaport

Monte Cristo Cottage (*325 Pequot Ave. 860-443-0051. Mem. Day–Labor Day Tues.-Sun.; adm. fee*) The boyhood home of Nobel Prize-winning playwright Eugene O'Neill (1888-1953), who wrote such ground-breaking works as the autobiographical *Long Day's Journey into Night* and *The Iceman Cometh,* is filled with family furnishings and mementos.

Excursions

GROTON (*4 miles E via I-95*) Long known as a major shipbuilding town and port, Groton is home of a U.S. Naval Submarine Base. **Fort Griswold Battlefield State Park** (*Monument St. and Park Ave. 860-445-1729. Park open year-round; monument and Monument House open Daily Mem. Day–Labor Day, weekends Labor Day–Columbus Day*) preserves the site of the 1781 Revolutionary War battle in which British troops under the command of Benedict Arnold massacred more than 80 patriots after they surrendered. The **Historic Ship *Nautilus* and Submarine Force Museum** (*Crystal Lake Rd., U.S. Naval Submarine Base. 860-449-3174 or 800-343-0079. Nov.-May Wed.-Mon., closed first week of May and last week of Oct.*) showcases the first nuclear-powered vessel in the world; *Nautilus* has also shattered every submerged speed and distance record. The museum features comprehensive exhibits on the history of underwater navigation, including three working periscopes.

MYSTIC SEAPORT (*9 miles NE via I-95 and Conn. 27. 75 Greenmanville Ave. 860-572-5315. Adm. fee*) The rich maritime history of Mystic—and America—are brought to life in this re-created 19th-century village on the Mystic River. Historic ships, period buildings, a working shipyard, and maritime paraphernalia all help tell the story. America's last surviving wooden whaleship, the *Charles W. Morgan,* now a national historic landmark, is docked here.

Other Sites in Connecticut

Governor Jonathan Trumbull House (*on the Green, W. Town St., Lebanon. 860-642-7558. Mid-May–mid-Oct. Tues.-Sat.; adm. fee*) Revolutionary governor Trumbull and his advisors helped plot military strategy in this mid-1700s house on the green and in the nearby war office. Washington and Lafayette were among the officers who met here.

Prudence Crandall Museum (*Canterbury Green, jct. Conn. 14 and 169, Canterbury. 860-546-9916. Closed mid-Dec.–Jan., Wed.-Sun. rest of year; adm. fee*) Prudence Crandall operated the first private school in New England to accept a black girl, in 1832. Two years later, irate townspeople forced the school's closing. In 1995 Crandall was designated a State Female Hero. The school now features exhibits on local and African-American history.

Roseland Cottage (*556 Conn. 169, Woodstock. 860-928-4074. Mem. Day–Labor Day Wed.-Sun., Labor Day–mid-Oct. Fri.-Sun.; adm. fee*) Nineteenth-century publisher Henry Bowen entertained four Presidents at his pink, Gothic Revival summer retreat, built in 1846. One of the country's oldest surviving bowling alleys occupies the barn.

Sloane-Stanley Museum and Kent Iron Furnace (*US 7, Kent. 860-927-3849 or 860-566-3005. Mid-May–Oct. Wed.-Sun.; adm. fee*) Artist and author Eric Sloane donated and arranged early American tools to tell the story of America's heritage of craftsmanship. The ruins of a 19th-century iron furnace are a reminder that the area was once a leading producer of pig iron.

51

Middle Atlantic

Long a leader in the affairs of the nation, the Middle Atlantic region is a compelling mix of historic cities and bucolic countryside. In the 17th century, the Dutch, Swedes, and English all claimed pieces of the Atlantic coastline, for centuries the home of native peoples. The mingling of—and conflicts among—these different cultures left marks that still linger on the land.

The American Revolution ripped mercilessly through the region, but it was followed by a period of great hopes and dreams. A new capital city was laid out and industrialization burgeoned, bringing prosperity—and a growing rift with the slave-holding, agrarian South. After the horrors of the Civil War, the area resumed its growth, with an influx of African Americans and whites from the South, and a massive wave of European immigrants at the turn of the century. Their traditions continue to give the Middle Atlantic a rich cultural diversity.

Old Fc
Niaga
Buf
Milla
Fillm
Muse

Chautauqua
Institution

Erie

Titusville

Drake Well
Museum

OHIO

Horseshoe   Altoor
Curve
Old Economy
Village
Bushy   Johnstown
Run   Flood
Pittsburgh   Battlefield   Nat.
Mon.
Fort
Searights Ligonier Johnstown
Tollhouse
N.H.L.   Uniontown
Fallingwater
Fort Necessity
Nat. Battlefield
Friendship
Hill N.H.S. La Vale
Toll Gate House
Cumberland

WEST
VIRGINIA

Valley Forge National Historical Park, Pennsylvania

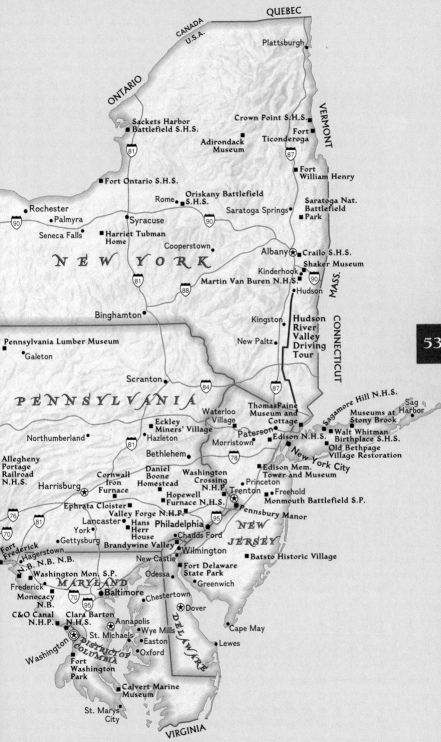

QUEBEC

Plattsburgh

CANADA
U.S.A.

ONTARIO

VERMONT

Sackets Harbor
Battlefield S.H.S.

Crown Point S.H.S.

Adirondack
Museum

Fort
Ticonderoga

Fort Ontario S.H.S.

Fort
William Henry

Rochester
Palmyra

Rome

Oriskany Battlefield
S.H.S.

Saratoga Nat.
Battlefield
Park

Syracuse

Saratoga Springs

Seneca Falls

Harriet Tubman
Home

N E W   Y O R K

Cooperstown

Albany

Crailo S.H.S.

Shaker Museum

Kinderhook

Binghamton

Martin Van Buren N.H.S.

Hudson

MASS.

CONNECTICUT

Kingston

New Paltz

Hudson
River
Valley
Driving
Tour

53

Pennsylvania Lumber Museum

Galeton

Scranton

P E N N S Y L V A N I A

Waterloo
Village

Thomas Paine
Museum and
Cottage

Sagamore Hill N.H.S.

Sag
Harbor

Eckley
Miners' Village

Paterson

Museums at
Stony Brook

Northumberland

Hazleton

Morristown

Edison N.H.S.

Walt Whitman
Birthplace S.H.S.

Bethlehem

Old Bethpage
Village Restoration

New York City

Allegheny
Portage
Railroad
N.H.S.

Cornwall
Iron
Furnace

Daniel
Boone
Homestead

Washington
Crossing
N.H.P.

Edison Mem.
Tower and Museum

Harrisburg

Princeton

Hopewell
Furnace N.H.S.

Trenton

Freehold

Monmouth Battlefield S.P.

Ephrata Cloister

Valley Forge N.H.P.

Pennsbury Manor

Lancaster

Hans
Herr
House

Philadelphia

N E W

York

J E R S E Y

Gettysburg

Brandywine Valley

Chadds Ford

Fort
Frederick

Hagerstown

N.B. N.B. N.B.

Wilmington

Batsto Historic Village

Washington Mon. S.P.

New Castle

Odessa

Fort Delaware
State Park

M A R Y L A N D

Frederick

Greenwich

Monocacy
N.B.

Baltimore

Chestertown

C&O Canal
N.H.P.

Clara Barton
N.H.S.

Dover

Annapolis

DELAWARE

Cape May

Washington

St. Michaels

Wye Mills

DISTRICT OF
COLUMBIA

Easton

Lewes

Fort
Washington
Park

Oxford

Calvert Marine
Museum

St. Marys
City

VIRGINIA

54

Fort Ticonderoga

Henry Hudson sailed up the river that now bears his name in 1609, giving the Dutch an early claim to New York. They prospered in the fur trade until 1664, when the English took the colony. A century later, during the French and Indian War, the English expanded their territory by winning France's lands to the north. One-third of all Revolutionary War battles were fought on New York soil, and the British defeat at Saratoga turned the course of the war. In 1825 the Erie Canal opened a link to the Midwest, spurring the state's growth. Although New York supplied more soldiers to the Civil War than any other state, its prosperity continued throughout the 1860s and into the "Boss Tweed" era of political corruption. By the late 19th century, John D. Rockefeller, J. P. Morgan, and Cornelius Vanderbilt were generating new growth with their industrial empires, beginning the process that has made New York City the world's leading financial center.

Albany

Dutch fur traders built Fort Orange in 1624 on the banks of the Hudson. When the English gained control in 1664, they changed the settlement's name to Albany, after the Duke of Albany. Chartered in 1686, Albany remains the oldest city operating under its original constitution. Begin a city tour at the **Albany Urban Cultural Park Visitor Center** (*25 Quackenbush Square. 518-434-6311*), where exhibits detail Albany's history. The pamphlet "Capital! Capital! A City Walk Tour" outlines a walk that includes such landmarks as the ornate **State Capitol** *(Upper State St. 518-474-2418).*

New York State Museum *(Empire State Plaza. 518-474-5877. Donations)* Highlights include sophisticated displays on the Adirondack wilderness, New York metropolis, and the area's native peoples.

Albany Institute of History and Art *(125 Washington Ave. 518-463-4478. Wed.-Sun.; adm. fee)* Four centuries of regional history and culture are traced with Albany-made silver, 18th- and 19th-century furniture, and Hudson River school landscape paintings.

Schuyler Mansion State Historic Site *(32 Catherine St. 518-434-0834. Mid-April–Oct. Wed.-Sun.; donations)* Revolutionary War general Philip Schuyler (1733-1804) built this Georgian house in the 1760s and lavishly decorated it. You'll see the house (now in a less-than-fashionable neighborhood) as it looked in Schuyler's day, complete with family items.

Historic Cherry Hill *(523½ S. Pearl St. 518-434-4791. Closed Mon.; adm. fee)* The 1787 Georgian house, originally part of a 900-acre Dutch farm, stayed in the van Rensselaer family until 1963 and overflows with the furnishings of five generations.

Shaker Heritage Society *(Albany-Shaker Rd. 518-456-7890. Closed Sun.-Mon.; adm. fee)* Just north of Albany, Mother Ann Lee established America's first Shaker community in 1776. Eight remaining buildings (private), an apple orchard, and cemetery where Lee is buried can be visited on a self-guided walking tour. Pick up maps at the 1848 meetinghouse, which houses a small Shaker museum.

Excursions

CRAILO STATE HISTORIC SITE *(1 mile E on I-90 in Rensselaer. 9½ Riverside Ave. 518-463-8738. April-Nov. Wed.-Sun.; adm. fee)* Built about 1705 by Hendrick van Rensselaer, the fortified Dutch Colonial house now holds a museum on the region's early Dutch settlers.

SHAKER MUSEUM *(19 miles SE via I-90 in Old Chatham. 518-794-9100. April-Oct.; adm. fee)* Housed in a picturesque farmstead, this premier museum describes 200 years of Shaker life in America and displays finely crafted furnishings, clothing, and tools. Difficult to find but well worth it.

KINDERHOOK *(22 miles S via I-90 and N.Y. 9H)* This village holds a prize collection of 18th- and 19th-century houses. Tours of the circa 1820 **James Vanderpoel House** *(16 Broad St. 518-758-9265. Mem. Day–Labor Day Thurs.-Sun.; adm. fee)* highlight fine New York furniture. Á mile away, the 1737 **Luykas Van Alen House** *(N.Y. 9H. 518-758-9265. Mem. Day–Labor Day Thurs.-Sun.; adm. fee)* typifies 18th-century Dutch domestic architecture with its open fireplace, delft tiles, and hewn beams.

MARTIN VAN BUREN NATIONAL HISTORIC SITE *(2 miles S of Kinderhook on N.Y. 9H. 518-758-9689. Daily May-Oct., March-April and Nov.–early Dec. Wed.-Sun.; adm. fee)* The eighth U.S. President retired in 1841 to this lavish Italianate estate, built in 1797. The upstairs bedrooms boast magnificent sleigh beds.

Buffalo ···

(Visitor Center, 617 Main St. 716-852-2356 or 888-228-3369) Laid out by Joseph Ellicott in 1799, Buffalo fell victim to British torches in 1813. The arrival of the Erie Canal in 1825 brought prosperity in the manufacturing trade. The city made international headlines in 1901 when an assassin

shot President McKinley after he spoke at the Pan-American Exposition. Today, Buffalo is noted for fine architecture that includes a few houses by Frank Lloyd Wright. His 1904 **Darwin Martin House** (*125 Jewett Pkwy. 716-829-2648. Under restoration*) and the nearby 1903 **George Barton House** (*118 Summit Ave. Same phone as above. By appt.*) are worth a look.

Buffalo and Erie County Historical Society (*25 Nottingham Court. 716-873-9644. Closed Mon.; adm. fee*) Housed in the only surviving structure from the 1901 Pan-American Exposition, the regional museum offers well-done exhibits and a re-created 1870s Main Street.

Theodore Roosevelt Inaugural National Historic Site (*641 Delaware Ave. 716-884-0095. Closed Sat. Jan.-March; adm. fee*) After McKinley died on Sept. 14, 1901, Vice President Theodore Roosevelt took the presidential oath in this stately mansion. Guided tours include the library where he became 26th President and an exhibit room that details the McKinley assassination. Guided and self-guided walking tours of the nearby **Delaware Avenue Historic District**—a neighborhood of Gilded Age mansions—depart from here.

Excursions

OLD FORT NIAGARA (*35 miles N via I-190, in Old Fort Niagara State Park. 716-745-7611. Adm. fee*) In 1726 the French built this château-style fort to strengthen their foothold in the Niagara area. The restored fortress includes pre-Revolutionary War buildings, mounted cannon, and a museum of uniforms and weapons.

MILLARD FILLMORE MUSEUM (*15 miles SE via N.Y. 400, in E. Aurora. 24 Shearer Ave. 716-652-8875. Wed., Sat., and Sun. in summer; adm. fee*) As a young country lawyer in 1825, Fillmore built this small cottage. Restored to the period, it contains original furnishings.

Cooperstown ·····················

(*Chamber of Commerce, 31 Chestnut St. 607-547-9983*) On glimmering Lake Otsego, Cooperstown was founded in 1785 by Judge William Cooper. The frontier setting inspired his son, James Fenimore Cooper, to write such works as *The Leatherstocking Tales.*

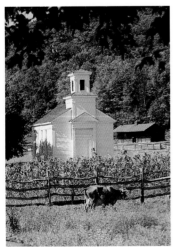

Farmers' Museum (*1 mile N of town on N.Y. 80. 607-547-1400. Closed Mon. April, Nov., and Dec.; adm. fee*) You enter this country village re-creation through the great barn, where exhibits and craftspeople portray rural life in this region a century ago. A dozen other antique-filled historical buildings are centered around a village green.

Fenimore House Museum (*1 mile N of town on N.Y. 80. 607-547-2533. Closed Mon. April, Nov., and Dec.; adm. fee*) Featuring Indian artifacts, American folk art, and Cooper memorabilia, this modern complex stands on the former site of young Cooper's cabin.

National Baseball Hall of Fame and Museum (*Main St. 607-547-7200. Adm. fee*) Whether or not Cooperstown resident Abner Doubleday invented the American game of

Cooperstown Farmers' Museum

baseball in 1839, this museum celebrates the national pastime with all kinds of compelling memorabilia, including Doubleday's own threadbare baseball and exhibits on revered Hall of Famers.

Fort Ticonderoga ·································

(1 mile E of Ticonderoga on N.Y. 74. 518-585-2821. Closed late Oct.–mid-May; adm. fee) Standing sentry over Lake Champlain—strategic gateway to both Canada and the Hudson River—the 1755 star-shaped fort has at times flown French, British, and American flags. Fort Ticonderoga gained its greatest fame on May 10, 1775, when Benedict Arnold, Ethan Allen, and the Green Mountain Boys stormed the British-held fortress and scored the first Colonial victory in the fight for independence. The reconstructed barracks hold Revolutionary War relics.

Excursions

CROWN POINT STATE HISTORIC SITE *(16 miles N via N.Y. 9N, near Crown Point. 518-597-3666. Late May–Oct. Wed.-Sun.)* A fort built on this strategic site in 1734 gave the French control of the Champlain Valley. The British ousted them in 1759 and built another fort, opening the way for attack on Montreal. Ruins of the forts have been preserved, along with French and British relics found at the site.

FORT WILLIAM HENRY *(39 miles SW on N.Y. 9N. Canada St., Lake George. 518-668-5471. May–mid-Oct.; adm. fee)* This replica recalls the colonial days of Fort William Henry, the site of the 1757 massacre of British Colonial forces by French and Indian soldiers. Musket balls, surgical instruments, and other excavated artifacts are displayed. Costumed interpreters demonstrate how to mold bullets, musket and cannon firing, and troop drilling.

New York City ·································

(Convention & Visitors Bureau, 2 Columbus Circle at W. 59th St. 212-397-8222 or 800-NYC-VISI) Peter Minuit, Director General of New Netherland, purchased Manhattan from the Indians in 1626 for $24 worth of baubles, and the Dutch proceeded to settle on the island's southern tip. Prized for its location on the Hudson River, Manhattan was the object of fierce fighting during the Revolutionary War. First capital of the new nation from 1789 to 1790, New York City blossomed, and by 1844 it was the country's most populous city. By the mid-1800s, Wall Street—home to the world's preeminent financiers—had become first in world trade and finance. Such promise of the good life lured millions of immigrants, who helped shape New York's ever changing, multiethnic culture. By the turn of the century, a frantic race to build the world's tallest structure began to fashion the city's legendary skyline.

Lower Manhattan Walking Tour ············· Half day

1. Castle Clinton National Monument *(Battery Park. 212-344-7220)* Built between 1807 and 1811 to protect the harbor from British attack, the brownstone structure never saw a single shot fired. Roofed over in the 1840s, the "castle" served over the next century as a concert hall, an immigrant-processing center, then an aquarium. Now restored as the original fort, its small museum has dioramas that depict the building's various incarnations.

Lower Manhattan Walking Tour

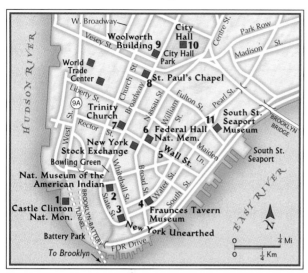

2. In 1994 the **National Museum of the American Indian** (*Alexander Hamilton Custom House, 1 Bowling Green. 212-668-6624*), part of the Smithsonian Institution, moved into this customshouse, a 1907 beaux arts palace. The collection of Indian artifacts spans over 10,000 years of the native cultures of North, Central, and South America.

3. Tucked behind 17 State Street, **New York Unearthed** (*212-748-8628. Closed Sun. year-round and Sat. Jan.-March*) features a fascinating archaeological gallery with a reconstructed cross section of the layers beneath the pavement, speckled with long forgotten bones and sherds of pottery.

4. Fraunces Tavern Museum (*54 Pearl St. 212-425-1778. Adm. fee*) Gen. George Washington bade farewell to his triumphant officers after the Revolutionary War in this 1719 Georgian tavern. Fully reconstructed, the tavern features changing exhibits and period rooms with mementos of Washington's farewell dinner, and American decorative arts.

5. In 1653 the Dutch built a wall for protection against hostile Indians. By the mid-19th century, **Wall Street** had become the nation's financial center. Among the district's regal-looking facades is the 1903 **New York Stock Exchange** (*20 Broad St. 212-656-3000. Closed weekends*), where tours showcase the frenetic trading room.

6. Federal Hall National Memorial (*26 Wall St. 212-825-6888. Closed weekends*) George Washington stood on the balcony of City Hall in 1789 and, before a cheering crowd, became the first U.S. President. The City Hall no longer stands, but a bronze statue of Washington marks the inauguration spot. Federal Hall, a Greek Revival structure built in 1842 as the U.S. customshouse, serves as a mini-museum with exhibits on the U.S. Bill of Rights and Constitution.

7. At the foot of Wall Street, the 1846 **Trinity Church** (*Broadway and Wall St. 212-602-0872. Guided tours 2 p.m. daily*) is the third church on the site. Until 1860 the needle-shaped steeple of the Gothic Revival church was the tallest structure in town (280 feet). A small museum contains relics relating to the history of the church. Statesman Alexander Hamilton and steamboat inventor Robert Fulton lie buried in the church's moss-softened cemetery.

8. St. Paul's Chapel (*Broadway at Fulton St. 212-602-0874. Closed Sat.*) After his swearing-in as the country's first President, George Washington prayed in this 1766 Georgian gem. The chapel is now Manhattan's oldest public building in continuous use.

9. Built in 1913 as headquarters of the chain of five-and-dime stores, the **Woolworth Building** (*233 Broadway*) set the standard for skyscrapers. The graceful 792-foot-high, 60-story structure reigned as the world's tallest building until the completion of the Chrysler Building in 1930.

10. The stately federal-style **City Hall** (*City Hall Park. 212-788-7100. By appointment*) has been the seat of New York government since 1812. The magnificent rotunda, with its twin-spiral marble staircase beneath a soaring dome, has welcomed kings, astronauts, and heads of state. The governor's room now exhibits art objects.

11. An 11-block historic district, the **South Street Seaport Museum** (*Fulton St. at East River. Visitor Center, 12 Fulton St. 212-669-9400. Adm. fee*) preserves the heart of New York's busy 19th-century waterfront. Six full-rigged sailing vessels are moored at Piers 15 and 16. Other sites include a printing shop and a children's museum.

1913 Woolworth Building flanked by the twin towers of the World Trade Center

Other Sites in Manhattan

Museum of the City of New York (*5th Ave. at 103rd St. 212-534-1672. Closed Mon.; adm. fee*) Period rooms from the 17th to the 20th century, including the 1860s bedroom of John D. Rockefeller (removed from his town house), and a toy gallery are some of the items splendidly displayed here.

New-York Historical Society (*2 W. 77th St. 212-873-3400. Closed Mon.-Tues.; donations*) Among the treasures of this repository of New York history (founded in 1804) are original watercolors by John Jay Audubon, an exceptional collection of colonial silver, federal furniture, and Tiffany lamps.

Abigail Adams Smith Museum (*421 E. 61st St. 212-838-6878. Sept.-July Tues.-Sun.; adm. fee*) The daughter of President John Adams never lived in this elaborate 1799 carriage house, though she and her husband owned the property before going bankrupt. Restored as a federal-era museum, the house currently offers a glimpse into its days as a country inn, when much of Manhattan was countryside.

Central Park (*Between 5th Ave., Central Park West, 59th St., and 110th St. 212-360-3444*) In 1857 landscape architects Frederick Law Olmsted and Calvert Vaux began to transform an area of pig farms and swamps into a "place where city dwellers could go and forget all about the city." Today, Central Park covers a lush 843 acres, and its old Gothic Revival **Dairy** (*65th St., near carousel. 212-794-6564. Closed Mon.*) serves as a Visitor Center. The **Arsenal** (*5th Ave. at 105th St.*) contains a museum with an original copy of the Olmsted and Vaux park plan.

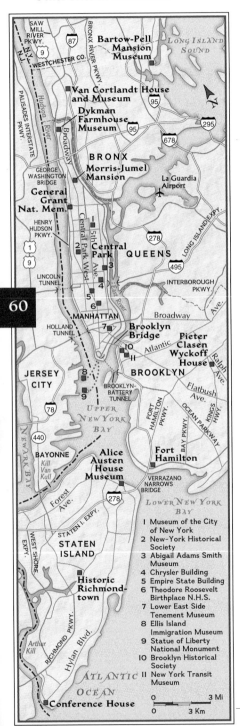

1 Museum of the City of New York
2 New-York Historical Society
3 Abigail Adams Smith Museum
4 Chrysler Building
5 Empire State Building
6 Theodore Roosevelt Birthplace N.H.S.
7 Lower East Side Tenement Museum
8 Ellis Island Immigration Museum
9 Statue of Liberty National Monument
10 Brooklyn Historical Society
11 New York Transit Museum

Chrysler Building (*405 Lexington Ave. at 42nd St.*) The art deco masterpiece, commissioned by auto magnate Walter Chrysler in 1930, ruled briefly as the world's tallest building (1,046 feet).

Empire State Building (*5th Ave. at 34th St. 212-736-3100. Adm. fee*) At 1,250 feet, the 1931 national icon reigned longer as the world's tallest building than any other—42 years. Today, only the twin towers of the city's World Trade Center and Chicago's Sears Tower are closer to the sky. Observation platforms on the 86th and 102nd floors afford city views.

Theodore Roosevelt Birthplace National Historic Site (*28 E. 20th St. 212-260-1616. Wed.-Sun.; adm. fee*) This re-creation of the 26th President's birthplace displays an extensive collection of memorabilia, including childhood toys and a Rough Rider uniform. The tour of five rooms includes the library, which Roosevelt called a room of "gloomy respectability."

Lower East Side Tenement Museum (*90 Orchard St. 212-431-0233. Closed Mon.; fee for tours and films*) The appalling conditions endured by immigrants in the Lower East Side slums come alive at 97 Orchard Street, a tenement that housed more than 10,000 people from the 1860s to 1935. The guided tour wanders through a dark hallway to two cramped apartments—the 1870s home of a Jewish family and the 1935 home of a Sicilian Christian family—both meticulously re-created. Tours of the surrounding ethnic neighborhoods, a museum with objects recovered from the tenement house, and films are also offered.

Ellis Island Immigration Museum (*Ellis Island, New Harbor. Via ferry from Battery Park. 212-363-7260. Fare for ferry*) More than 12 million men, women, and children came through Ellis Island between 1892 and 1954, during North America's greatest immigration wave. The island's refurbished main building houses a museum that tells the stories of individual immigrants and the processing procedures they endured.

Statue of Liberty

Statue of Liberty National Monument *(Liberty Island, New York Harbor. Via ferry from Battery Park. 212-363-3200. Fare for ferry)* An 1886 gift of France, Lady Liberty has greeted millions of immigrants from her New York Harbor perch. Frédéric-Auguste Bartholdi sculptured her, perhaps in his mother's likeness, and Gustave Eiffel of Eiffel Tower fame devised an iron frame for the enormous copper sheets. A museum explores the statue's history. Views are breaktaking from the observation deck at the top of the pedestal, accessible by elevator. Even better are the views from the top of her crown, a 354-step climb.

Harlem and Washington Heights

Dykman Farmhouse Museum *(4881 Broadway at 204th St. 212-304-9422. Closed Mon.; donations)* Manhattan's only surviving 18th-century Dutch farmhouse (circa 1783) is filled with original furnishings and period pieces.

General Grant National Memorial *(122nd St. at Riverside Dr. 212-666-1640. Wed.-Sun.)* Both Ulysses S. Grant and his wife, Julia, are buried in Grant's tomb, a grandiose open crypt similar to Napoleon Bonaparte's in Paris. The main hall has exhibits on Grant's careers as Civil War general and 18th President. Visit by daylight only.

Morris-Jumel Mansion *(160th St. at Edgecombe Ave. 212-923-8008. Wed.-Sun.; adm. fee)* Reminiscent of Harlem's era of magnificent estates, the 1765 Georgian mansion served as headquarters for George Washington in 1776. Georgian, federal, and French furnishings now fill the elegant house.

The Bronx

Bartow-Pell Mansion Museum *(895 Shore Rd. N., in Pelham Bay Park. 718-885-1461. Wed. and Sat.-Sun.; adm. fee)* Completed in 1842, the federal mansion has a Greek Revival interior with period furnishings; lovely sunken gardens surround it.

Van Cortlandt House and Museum *(Broadway at W. 246th St. in Van Cortlandt Park. 718-543-3344. Closed Mon.; adm. fee)* Frederick Van Cortlandt, a wealthy New

Brooklyn Bridge, completed in 1883

Yorker of Dutch heritage, built this Georgian fieldstone house about 1748, and George Washington headquartered here during part of the war. The restored house showcases period antiques and delftware.

Brooklyn

Brooklyn Bridge The world's longest suspension bridge (1,595 feet) when opened in 1883, the Brooklyn Bridge was the inspiration of engineer John A. Roebling. It took 14 years to build and cost some 20 lives, including Roebling's own. Walk across for excellent views of Lower Manhattan.

Brooklyn Historical Society *(128 Pierrepont St. 718-624-0890. Closed Sun.-Mon.; adm. fee)* The society offers exhibits on the Dodgers, the Brooklyn Bridge, Coney Island, the Navy yard, and the borough's famous residents over the years. The surrounding **Brooklyn Heights Historic District** is filled with 19th-century brownstones. Note the 1849 **Plymouth Church of the Pilgrims** *(75 Hicks St.)*, where abolitionist Henry Ward Beecher (the brother of *Uncle Tom's Cabin* author Harriet Beecher Stowe) preached.

New York Transit Museum *(Boerum Pl. and Schermerhorn St. 718-243-3060. Closed Mon.; adm. fee)* Vintage cars, signal equipment, and photographs trace the development of the city's subway and bus systems.

Pieter Clasen Wyckoff House *(Clarendon Rd. and Ralph Ave., in Flatlands. 718-629-5400. Thurs.-Fri.; adm. fee)* The state's oldest building, circa 1652, holds 17th- and 18th-century furnishings.

Harbor Defense Museum at Fort Hamilton *(101st St. and Fort Hamilton Pkwy. 718-630-4349. Call for weekend hrs.)* Housed in the original 19th-century fort, the museum explains how the harbor has been defended over the years.

Staten Island

Alice Austen House Museum *(2 Hylan Blvd. 718-816-4506. Thurs.-Sun.; donations)* Overlooking the harbor, the Victorian cottage known as Clear Comfort was the lifetime home of pioneer photographer Alice Austen (1866-1952). One of America's finest social documentarians, she captured images of turn-of-the-century life in New York.

Conference House *(7455 Hylan Blvd. 718-984-6046. April-Nov. Thurs.-Sun.; adm. fee)* The only conference called to prevent the Revolutionary War took

Philipsburg Manor, North Tarrytown

place in this 1675 house on Sept. 11, 1776, when British Vice-Admiral Lord Richard Howe invited three American delegates—Benjamin Franklin, John Adams, and Edward Rutledge—to discuss possible terms. Today, period furnishings and costumed interpreters help the visitor contemplate the consequences of that failed peace attempt.

Historic Richmondtown *(441 Clarke Ave. 718-351-1611. Wed.-Sun.; adm. fee)* Richmondtown's early days are preserved at the 103-acre museum village, which includes the Dutch-era Voorlezer House (ca 1696), the oldest elementary school in the country; an 1837 courthouse; houses; and shops.

Excursions

PATERSON, NEW JERSEY (*25 miles NW via N.J. 495, N.J. 3, Garden State Pkwy., and N.J. 19*) See page 85.

EDISON NATIONAL HISTORIC SITE, NEW JERSEY (*30 miles W via N.J. Turnpike and I-280*) See page 85.

MORRISTOWN NATIONAL HISTORICAL PARK, NEW JERSEY (*35 miles W via I-287, N.J. Turnpike, and I-280*) See page 83.

Hudson River Valley Driving Tour ···· 100 miles, 2-3 days

Winding along the wooded banks of New York's legendary waterway, this tour takes in the history of the Hudson River Valley, from early Dutch settlers to Revolutionary War soldiers to Gilded Age industrialists.

1. Begin in Tarrytown at **Sunnyside** (*US 9. 914-631-8200. Closed Tues. and Jan.-Feb.; adm. fee*), the retirement home of internationally successful author Washington Irving (1783-1859). The romantic country villa on the banks of the Hudson is particularly notable for Irving's book-lined study and mahogany desk. Be sure to stroll the lovely grounds.

Also in Tarrytown, **Lyndhurst** (*US 9. 914-631-4481. May-Oct. Tues.-Sun., Nov.-April Sat.-Sun.; adm. fee*) is a superior example of Gothic Revival architecture. Built in 1838, the fairy tale palace of towers and spires was home to three prominent New York families for a period of 100 years; railroad magnate Jay Gould was its most famous resident. The interior is graced with vaulted ceilings, gilding, and elaborate plasterwork.

2. In **North Tarrytown,** kids love to chase chickens at **Philipsburg Manor** (*US 9. 914-631-8200. Closed Tues.; adm. fee*), an early 18th-century working farm. A video at the Visitor Center and brief guided tours of the original house reveal that the Philipses—a long line of Dutch entrepreneurs—lost all of their holdings after the Revolution, due to their Tory sympathies.

3. Kykuit (*Via shuttle from Philipsburg Manor. 914-631-9491. April-Oct. Wed.-Mon. Reservations necessary; adm. fee*) Modest by Gilded Age standards, Kykuit (KY-cut) was home to four generations of Rockefellers. Built in the early years of this century for John D. Rockefeller, Sr., founder of Standard Oil, the 40-room beaux arts mansion contains superb antiquities and modern art. The guided tour—expensive for what you actually see—takes in the first floor, preserved as it was when Gov. Nelson Rockefeller lived here in the 1960s and 1970s; a below-ground gallery displays Rockefeller's extensive collection of modern art.

4. In **Croton-on-Hudson** elegant **Van Cortlandt Manor** (*Off US 9. 914-631-8200. Closed Tues. and Jan.-Feb.; adm. fee*), built in the late 1600s, remained home to members of the eminent Van Cortlandt family until 1945. While it's not lavish—planks in the parlor have been painted to resemble marble—European furnishings and high ceilings attest to the family's wealth. Costumed guides weave and cook in the 18th-century style.

Vanderbilt Mansion National Historic Site, near Hyde Park

5. U.S. Military Academy *(Off US 9W in West Point. 914-938-2638)* George Washington chose the beautiful promontory on the Hudson River known as West Point as a strategic military vantage. The resulting English Tudor fortification (1788) still stands on the magnificent grounds of the U. S. Military Academy. The best place to start a tour is at the **West Point Museum** *(Behind Visitor Center. Adm. fee),* which features a comprehensive collection of 16th- to 20th-century arms, uniforms, and flags. Down the hill, you'll find the **Plain** (parade ground) and **Trophy Point,** which affords a breathtaking view of the Hudson River Palisades.

6. New Windsor Cantonment State Historic Site *(N.Y. 300 in Vails Gate. 914-561-1765. Mid-April–Oct. Wed.-Sun.; adm. fee)* A year after the 1781 Battle of Yorktown, 7,000 soldiers made their final winter encampment here. A living history area re-creates life in Washington's army. Nearby, the **Last Encampment of the Continental Army** *(914-562-6397. Mid-April–Oct. Tues.-Sun.)* preserves some campsites.

7. While the Colonial Army encamped at New Windsor, **Washington's Headquarters** *(Liberty and Washington Sts., Newburgh. 914-562-1195. Mid-April–Oct. Wed.-Sun., weekends rest of year; adm. fee)* were situated in this austere, eight-room house in **Newburgh,** overlooking the Hudson River. The guided tour shows the house furnished in military fashion. The adjacent museum offers a slide show and displays of Revolutionary War memorabilia.

8. In **Hyde Park,** the **Franklin D. Roosevelt National Historic Site** *(US 9. 914-229-9115. Closed Mon.-Tues; adm. fee)* encompasses part of the family estate known as Springwood. Members of the Roosevelt clan settled in this region long before Franklin's father, James, enlarged the orginal Roosevelt farmhouse, turning it into a colonial revival mansion in 1867. Franklin was born here in 1882 and raised on the estate, in turn raising his own family here. Among the well-worn rooms on the self-guided tour are his boyhood bedroom and the living room where he gave his first fireside chat. Personal touches such as his wheelchair and a collection of mounted birds add to the intimacy. The President and his wife, Eleanor, are buried in the rose garden. The grounds also contain his presidential library and a museum.

Two miles away, Mrs. Roosevelt's weekend retreat, Val-Kill, is now the **Eleanor Roosevelt National Historic Site** *(Daily April-Oct., Nov.-Dec. and March Sat.-Sun.),* where you can see a short film about her life.

Continue 2 miles north of Hyde Park on US 9 to **Vanderbilt Mansion National Historic Site** *(914-229-9115. Closed Nov.-March Tues.-Wed.; adm. fee).* At the sumptuous, 54-room Italian Renaissance palace, built in 1898, guides lead you in but let you tour at your leisure. Almost everything looks as it did in the days of Frederick Vanderbilt, grandson of railroad magnate Cornelius Vanderbilt.

9. Farther north in **Staatsburg** you'll find the 65-room French Renaissance **Mills Mansion S.H.S.** *(Off US 9 on Old Post Rd. 914-889-8851. April–Labor Day Wed.-Sun.; adm. fee),* designed in 1896 by New York architect Stanford White around an earlier Greek Revival building. The elaborate interior is full of exquisite oak paneling, marble, and gilded wood.

10. Built in 1805, **Montgomery Place** *(Off US 9. 914-758-5461. April-Oct. Wed.-Mon., Nov.-Dec. and March Sat.-Sun.; adm. fee),* a stately 23-room mansion in **Annandale-on-Hudson,** remained in the Livingston family until 1986. Filled with family belongings, the house boasts fine portraits by Gilbert Stuart and Rembrandt Peale.

11. Clermont State Historic Site *(Off N.Y. 9G in Germantown. 518-537-4240. Mid.-April–Oct. Tues.-Sun., Nov. weekends; adm. fee)* Negotiator of the Louisiana Purchase, drafter of the Declaration of Independence, and a partner in the development of the first steamboat, Robert R. Livingston (1746-1813) rebuilt this late Georgian mansion after the British burned the first in 1777. The furnishings reflect seven generations of Livingstons.

12. Olana *(N.Y. 9G, S of Hudson. 518-828-0135. Mid-April–Oct. Wed.-Sun.; adm. fee)* Sitting high on a hill above the Hudson, the 1870s Persian Gothic castle resembles an exotic work of art. Designed by renowned Hudson River school artist Frederick Edwin Church as his own home, the mansion features jewel-colored rooms with stenciled doorways and enormous windows that overlook the magnificent valley. The 250-acre grounds laid out by Church are a romantic mix of open countryside bordered by woodland.

65

Rochester ·······························

(Visitor information at Center at High Falls, 74-78 Brown's Race. 716-325-2030) Just north of the Genessee River's High Falls, Ebenezer "Indian" Allan built the region's first gristmill in 1789. When the Erie Canal came through town in 1825, so many flour mills lined the riverbanks that the city was called "flour city." Restored buildings in the small **High Falls and Brown's Race Historic District** recall the early days.

George Eastman House *(900 East Ave. 716-271-3361. Closed Mon.; adm. fee)* The fortune that George Eastman (1854-1932) acquired by inventing a camera for the masses is reflected in the lavishness of his 50-room colonial revival mansion, built at the turn of the century. Guided tours wander through the well-appointed rooms, including the two-story conservatory draped with lush vegetation. In an adjoining wing, the **International Museum of Photography** showcases a vast collection of photographs and camera equipment.

Surrounding the museum, the fashionable **East Avenue Historic District** boasts such luxurious mansions as 1838 **Woodside** *(485 East Ave. 716-271-2705. Closed weekends; adm. fee),* where the Rochester Historical Society preserves a fine collection of paintings, costumes, and furnishings.

Susan B. Anthony House National Historic Landmark *(17 Madison St. 716-235-6124. Thurs.-Sat.; adm. fee)* Champion fighter for women's suffrage,

Susan B. Anthony (1820-1906) lived in this modest house during her last 40 years. Tours showcase original furnishings and personal photographs.

Excursions

PALMYRA *(24 miles E on N.Y. 31)* Mormons believe an angel appeared to young Joseph Smith in 1823 and told him of a recorded history of the Americas, inscribed on golden plates. According to Mormon doctrine, Smith found these plates at **Hill Cumorah** *(4 miles S of Palmyra on N.Y. 21. 315-597-5851)*. You can either drive or walk to the hilltop monument that now marks the spot. The nearby white-frame **Smith Family Home** *(Off N.Y. 21. 315-597-5851)*, where Joseph Smith lived between the ages of 19 and 22, is furnished with period pieces. Across the road is the **Sacred Grove** where the 14-year-old boy experienced the vision that would lead to the founding of the Church of Jesus Christ of Latter-day Saints.

Rome

Erie Canal Village *(3 miles W on N.Y. 49. 315-337-3999. May–Labor Day; adm. fee)* Located near the spot where ground was broken for the Erie Canal, this 1800s living history village relives the canal's early days with a tavern, schoolhouse, and mule-drawn packet rides along the canal.

Fort Stanwix National Monument *(112 E. Park St. 315-336-2090. Closed Jan.-March; adm. fee)* During the French and Indian War, the British colonists used Fort Stanwix to protect a valuable portage—the Oneida Carry—between the Great Lakes and the Atlantic. The fort's strength wasn't tested until the Revolution, when a desperate, three-week battle resulted in an American victory and indirectly influenced the strategic Colonial victory at Saratoga.

Excursion

ORISKANY BATTLEFIELD STATE HISTORIC SITE *(6 miles E on N.Y. 69. 315-768-7224. Mem. Day–Labor Day Wed.-Sun.)* Marching to relieve Fort Stanwix on August 6, 1777, Gen. Nicholas Herkimer's Colonials were ambushed by Tories and Indians. The Americans finally warded off the enemy in a bloody battle but not before Herkimer was mortally wounded.

Saratoga Springs

(Visitor information at Urban Cultural Park, 297 Broadway. 518-587-3241) Native Americans long knew of the life-giving properties of the local springwaters here. By the late 19th century, their secret was out. As people began coming to "take the cure," a summer culture of casinos, hotels, and horse racing grew up, still obvious in the town's several elegant **historic districts**.

Congress Park *(Congress St. and Broadway. 518-584-6920. Closed Jan.; adm. fee)* The exquisite 1870 Italianate Canfield Casino now contains gambling paraphernalia and Victorian furniture. On the lovely park grounds, you can still sample the town's famous springwaters.

66

Erie Canal

For a century, people had talked of a waterway that would join the Great Lakes with the Atlantic Ocean. Former New York mayor DeWitt Clinton finally made the dream a reality. Construction on "Clinton's Big Ditch," as it was called, began in 1817. Thousands signed on to work, drawn by the 80-cents-a-day pay, a whiskey ration, and all-they-could-eat pork, squirrel, venison, and corn bread. Hundreds died in accidents or from malaria, but in 1825 the 40-foot-wide trench—by then called the Grand Canal —opened, allowing easier access to lands and goods west of the Appalachians.

"Lockport on the Erie Canal," 1832, by Mary Keys

Saratoga Spa State Park (*S. Broadway. 518-584-2535. Seasonal; appts. necessary in summer. Fee*) The grand Lincoln and Roosevelt Bathhouses are part of the reservation created in 1909 to exploit the town's most precious resource. Baths and spa amenities are available.

National Museum of Racing (*191 Union Ave. 518-584-0400. Adm. fee*) This glamorous museum guides you through the history of Thoroughbred racing with such memorabilia as trophies and the gavel that closed the sale of the legendary racehorse, Man O' War. Across the street, the 1864 **Saratoga Race Track**—the oldest still operating in the country— has its original gabled bandstand and a turreted clubhouse.

Excursions

SARATOGA NATIONAL BATTLEFIELD PARK (*17 miles SE via N.Y. 29 and US 4. 518-664-9821. Adm. fee*) Hoping to take control of the Hudson River, the British clashed with American troops here in 1777. Outnumbered and surrounded, British general John Burgoyne finally surrendered to American general Horatio Gates. The victory is considered a turning point of the Revolutionary War. Begin at the Visitor Center and museum, where a small collection of battle artifacts and a film provide background. Then take the 9-mile auto loop through the park.

In nearby Schuylerville, the 155-foot-high **Saratoga Battle Monument** commemorates the surrender. Also part of the park is the 2-story **Gen. Philip Schuyler House** (*S of Schuylerville on US 4. 518-664-9821. Summer only; adm. fee*).

Seneca Falls ·······································

Elizabeth Cady Stanton, Lucretia Mott, and others called the first convention for women's rights on July 19 and 20, 1848. At that historic meeting in Seneca Falls, the assembly drafted the Declaration of Sentiments that outlined women's grievances and gave birth to the modern women's rights movement.

Women's Rights National Historical Park (*136 Fall St. 315-568-2991. Tours Mem. Day–Labor Day*) Interactive exhibits and a film describe the evolution of the women's movement. Next door at Declaration Park, brick walls are all that remain of the 1848 convention venue; the **Elizabeth Cady Stanton House** and **M'Clintock House** still stand in the park.

Seneca Falls Historical Society (*55 Cayuga St. 315-568-8412. Closed weekends Sept.-June; adm. fee*) Exhibits in the 1880 Queen Anne mansion explore Victorian lifestyles and the women's rights movement.

Syracuse ···

(Visitor information at Urban Cultural Park, 318 Erie Canal Blvd. 315-471-0593) Salt from Onondaga Lake attracted settlers to the Syracuse area as early as 1788. With the arrival of the Erie Canal in the 1820s, Syracuse soon became the country's largest salt producer.

Erie Canal Museum *(318 Erie Blvd. E. 315-471-0593)* Housed in the only surviving canal weigh station, the museum describes the grueling lives of "canallers" with exhibits and displays. You can climb aboard a 65-foot-long passenger boat. The adjoining Urban Cultural Park has walking tour maps of nearby **Hanover Square Historic District,** once a bustling neighborhood along the Erie Canal.

Salt Museum *(Onondaga Lake Pkwy. in Liverpool. 315-453-6767. May-Sept. Tues.-Sun.; adm. fee)* This rustic structure and its equipment tell the story of the area's 140-year-old salt industry.

Sainte Marie Among the Iroquois *(Onondaga Lake Pkwy., Liverpool. 315-453-6767. Closed Mon. year-round and Tues. Jan.-April; adm. fee)* In 1657 French Jesuit missionaries came to the remote shores of Onondaga Lake to teach the local Iroquois about Christianity. At this re-created mission, costumed interpreters portray life on the frontier, and the Visitor Center has extensive exhibits on the Iroquois.

Excursion

HARRIET TUBMAN HOME *(26 miles SW via N.Y. 5, Auburn. 180 South St. 315-252-2081. April-Nov. Tues.-Fri.; donations)* During the Civil War, Harriet Tubman, an escaped slave born in Maryland, helped some 300 fugitive slaves flee to safety in the northern states and Canada. Tubman's work earned her the affectionate epithet, "Moses." At war's end she moved into this white clapboard house, a former Underground Railroad station. Here she worked with indigent blacks until her death in 1913. The house contains some Tubman possessions.

Adirondack Museum, Blue Mountain Lake

Other Sites in New York

Adirondack Museum *(N.Y. 30, Blue Mountain Lake. 518-352-7311. Mem. Day–mid-Oct.; adm. fee)* Adirondack history—farming, logging, furniture-making—is described in 22 exhibit areas.

Chautauqua Institution *(N.Y. 394. 716-357-6200 or 800-836-ARTS. Late June–late Aug; adm fee)* Founded in 1874 on the shores of Chautauqua Lake, this arts and education center still presents lectures, concerts, and drama.

Portrait of Harriet Tubman

Fort Ontario State Historic Site *(1 E. 4th St., Oswego. 315-343-4711. Mid-May–Oct. Wed.-Sun.; adm. fee)* Built in 1755, the fort played important roles in both the French and Indian and Revolutionary Wars. It is now being restored to its 1867-1872 appearance.

Huguenot Street *(New Paltz. Tours given by Huguenot Historical Society 914-255-2660)* From 1692 to 1712, French Huguenots built six stone houses on this street, now one of the nation's oldest.

Museums at Stony Brook (*1208 N.Y. 25A, Stony Brook. 516-751-0066. Daily July-Aug. and Dec.; Jan.-June and Sept.-Nov. Wed.-Sun.; adm. fee)* A museum and period buildings portray regional 19th- and 20th-century life.

Old Bethpage Village Restoration *(Round Swamp Rd., Old Bethpage. 516-572-8400. Closed Jan.-Feb.; adm. fee)* A hundred acres of pre-Civil War Long Island preserve farms, houses, shops, and gardens.

Plattsburgh Bay The American victory at the 1814 Battle of Plattsburgh thwarted a British takeover of New York. The British headquartered at the **Kent-Delord House** *(17 Cumberland Ave. 518-561-1035. Tues.-Sat.; adm. fee)*, now restored with period furnishings.

69

Sackets Harbor Battlefield State Historic Site *(Sackets Harbor. 315-646-3634. Mid-May–mid-Oct. Wed.-Sun.; adm. fee)* The 1800s commandant's house and Navy yard interpret the two War of 1812 battles that occurred here.

Sag Harbor An important seaport for whalers in the late 1700s and early 1800s, the town preserves its federal-style **Customs House** *(Main and Garden Sts. 516-941-9444. Mid-May–Sept. Tues.-Sun.; adm. fee),* furnished with original and period pieces. At the **Sag Harbor Whaling and Historical Museum** *(Main St. 516-725-0770. Mid-May–Sept.; adm. fee)*, whaling days are remembered with scrimshaw, ship models, and gear.

Sagamore Hill National Historic Site *(20 Sagamore Hill Rd., Oyster Bay. 516-922-4447. Adm. fee)* As a young Harvard graduate in 1885, Theodore Roosevelt helped design this 23-room house and subsequently used it as his main residence (and as the summer White House). Hunting trophies and original furnishings decorate the rooms, which have been kept as in Roosevelt's day. Next door, the **Old Orchard Museum** contains exhibits and a documentary film on the 26th President's life.

Kingston *(Information at Urban Cultural Park, 20 Broadway. 914-331-7517 or 800-331-1518)* Dating from the Dutch West India Company days, this town preserves its early history in the **Stockade Historic District.** In 1777 New York's first Senate met to form a new state government at the simple stone **Senate House** *(312 Fair St. 914-338-2786. Mid-April–Oct. Wed.-Sun.).* Exhibits detail life and government in 18th-century New York.

Thomas Paine Museum and Cottage *(20 Sicard Ave., New Rochelle. 914-632-5376. Fri.-Sun.)* The master pamphleteer resided in this cottage during the Revolutionary War. Exhibits trace Huguenot history and Paine's life.

Walt Whitman Birthplace State Historic Site *(246 Old Walt Whitman Rd., Huntington Station. 516-427-5240. Wed.-Sun.; adm. fee)* The esteemed poet (1819-1892) spent his first four years at this early 1800s farmhouse. Rustic furnishings and a museum detail his life.

Civil War reenactment, Gettysburg National Military Park

Claimed first by the Swedes then the Dutch in the early 17th century, Pennsylvania became an English colony in 1664. The British proprietor, Quaker William Penn, promptly granted religious freedom to all citizens. Roughly a century later, George Washington and his troops, on behalf of the English Crown, skirmished with the French over control of western Pennsylvania, sparking the French and Indian War. By the 1770s, Philadelphia stirred with Revolutionary fervor. In 1774-75 patriots gathered in the city to protest English rule; on July 4, 1776, representatives of the 13 Colonies met to sign the Declaration of Independence; and in 1787 the Constitutional Convention met here. Though Pennsylvania played a lesser role in the Civil War, it was the scene of the bloody 1863 Battle of Gettysburg that turned the war to the North's advantage. The state's rich coal, iron, and steel industries brought prosperity after the war and into this century.

Altoona

Thousands of cars and locomotives were built and maintained in Altoona, the 19th-century heart of the Pennsylvania Railroad. The legacy comes to life at the **Railroaders Memorial Museum** (*1300 9th Ave. 814-946-0834. Closed Mon. Nov.-April; adm. fee*), where a large yard is filled with vintage rolling stock.

Excursions

HORSESHOE CURVE (*5 miles W on Pa. 4008. 814-941-7960. Closed Mon. Nov.-March*) Carved by hand from a mountainside in 1854, the amazing horseshoe curve enabled steam engines to conquer the Alleghenies. The Visitor Center has fine exhibits detailing the engineering marvel. Take the funicular (*fee*) or climb 194 steps to the observation platform at the center of the curve, where dozens of loaded trains on the main line of Conrail and Amtrak rumble by daily.

ALLEGHENY PORTAGE RAILROAD NATIONAL HISTORIC SITE (*10 miles SW via US 220 and US 22. 814-886-6150*) Built in 1831 to pull sectional canalboats over the formidable Allegheny Mountains, the portage railroad cut travel time between Philadelphia and Pittsburgh from 23 days to 4. From the Visitor Center, a short boardwalk zigzags to the portage route, the remains of the engine, and an 1832 tavern.

Chadds Ford ···

As early as 1736 John Chads ferried travelers across Brandywine Creek. (No one knows where the extra "d" in the current spelling came from.) The 1725 two-story **John Chads House** (*Pa. 100 just N of US 1. 610-388-7376. Weekends May-Sept.; adm. fee*) is shown by costumed interpreters. The 1714 **Barns-Brinton House** (*US 1. 610-388-7376. Weekends May-Sept.; adm. fee*), built by an English Quaker, is noted for its Flemish bond brickwork.

Brandywine Battlefield (*US 1. 610-459-3342. Visitor Center and buildings closed Mon.; grounds closed Mon. except in summer. Adm. fee for buildings*) At the 1777 Battle of Brandywine, British troops outmaneuvered George Washington's forces, enabling them to move unopposed into the patriot capital of Philadelphia. The 50-acre park features Washington's rebuilt headquarters and the farmhouse where the Marquis de Lafayette stayed.

Gettysburg ···

Founded in the 1780s, Gettysburg sits at the strategic crossroads of four major roads. Here Union and Confederate soldiers clashed on July 1, 1863, fighting the bloodiest battle of the Civil War. Three days later, 51,000 men were dead, wounded, or missing, and the South had suffered a defeat from which it would not recover.

Gettysburg National Military Park (*Main Visitor Center on Pa. 134. 717-334-1124*) Only cannon, stone walls, and countless monuments recall the horrors that unfolded in this placid country setting. The Visitor Center houses the excellent Gettysburg Museum of the Civil War and a 750-square-foot electric map (*fee*), depicting troop movements. Next door, the Cyclorama Center's 360-degree painting (*fee*) portrays Pickett's Charge. An 18-mile self-guided battlefield driving tour includes McPherson Ridge, where the battle began, and the open field where Pickett led his famous charge. On Nov. 19, 1863, Abraham Lincoln gave his 272-word Gettysburg Address at the Evergreen Cemetery that lies adjacent to the Gettysburg National Cemetery.

Eisenhower National Historic Site (*Via shuttle bus from national military park Visitor Center. 717-334-1124. Adm. fee*) The 34th President, Dwight D. Eisenhower, and his wife, Mamie, relaxed and entertained on this 189-acre estate. The pleasant Georgian house appears much as it did during Ike's tenure here.

Harrisburg ·····················

(Walking-tour maps available at the Office of the Mayor, 10 N. 2nd St. 717-255-3040) The town derives its name from Indian trader John Harris, who settled here about 1712. It was his son who actually platted the town and built the **John Harris Mansion** *(219 S. Front St. 717-233-3462. Closed weekends; adm. fee).* Harrisburg became the state capital in 1812. The **State Museum of Pennsylvania** *(3rd and North Sts. 717-787-4978. Closed Mon.; adm. fee)* recounts Pennsylvania's history.

Excursion

CORNWALL IRON FURNACE *(23 miles E via US 322 in Cornwall. 717-272-9711. Closed Mon.; adm. fee)* The stately red-sandstone exterior of this building belies the once inferno-like interior that produced cannon for the Revolution. Visitor Center exhibits explain the process of ironmaking, and an open-pit mine and an ironmaster's mansion are nearby.

Johnstown ·····················

When an earthen dam owned (and allegedly maintained) by coal and steel tycoons burst on May 31, 1889, it unleashed 20 million tons of water from an exclusive resort lake. The 35-foot wave tore down a narrow valley, collecting uprooted trees, railroad cars, and buildings on its way to Johnstown, 14 miles away. Of 30,000 citizens, some 2,200 were presumed killed, and thousands were left homeless.

Johnstown Flood Museum *(304 Washington St. 814-539-1889. Adm. fee)* The horrors of that day, as well as the story of the town's rebuilding, are recounted in exhibits, including a wall of flood debris and an Academy Award-winning film.

Johnstown Inclined Plane *(711 Edgehill Dr. 814-536-1816. Adm. fee)* Fearful of future floods, the town built this incline in 1891 as an escape route. From the Visitor Center, you can see the path taken by the flood.

Aftermath of 1889 Johnstown flood

Excursion

JOHNSTOWN FLOOD NATIONAL MONUMENT *(10 miles NE via US 219. 814-495-4643)* A compelling movie and exhibits at the Visitor Center relive the tragedy, and old dam abutments stand above the empty lake basin.

Lancaster ···

(Historic Lancaster Information Center, 100 S. Queen St. 717-397-3531. Closed Jan.-March) According to legend, the first settler here opened a tavern in 1721, near what is now Penn Square. By mid-century, the frontier village—famed for producing the Kentucky rifle—was one of the colony's largest inland towns. Fleeing the British in Philadelphia, the Continental Congress paused here on Sept. 27, 1777, making Lancaster the nation's capital for a day. Some 70 historic buildings have been restored, among them **Trinity Church** (1761) and the 1852 **Fulton Opera House.**

Heritage Center Museum of Lancaster County *(Penn Square. 717-299-6440. April–mid-Nov. Tues.-Sat., Sat.-Sun. only in Dec.; donations)* The small but splendid museum showcases 18th- and 19th-century decorative arts, including painted furniture typical of the Pennsylvania Dutch, who first settled in the region in the mid-1700s.

Wheatland *(1120 Marietta Ave. 717-392-8721. April-Nov.; adm. fee)* The nation's only bachelor President, James Buchanan bought this elegant federal mansion in 1848, while secretary of state. Tours feature the study where he conducted his election campaign and the upstairs bedroom of his niece, who acted as surrogate First Lady.

Excursions

LANDIS VALLEY MUSEUM *(2.5 miles N on Pa. 272. 717-569-0401. Closed Mon.; adm. fee)* Pennsylvania German culture and history come to life at this village and farm complex. Some 75,000 regional artifacts dating from before 1900 fill 15 historic structures, and costumed interpreters—quilters, weavers, blacksmiths—demonstrate traditional crafts.

EPHRATA CLOISTER *(10 miles N via US 272, in Ephrata. 632 W. Main St. 717-733-6600. Adm. fee)* This tree-shaded site was the 18th-century home of a self-sufficient German religious community famed for its printing and publishing. Guided tours of the German-style structures include the gabled-roofed *Saal* (meetinghouse) and the log cabin that belonged to the community's founder.

HANS HERR HOUSE *(5 miles S via US 222. 717-464-4438. Closed Sun. and Dec.-March; adm. fee)* A German Mennonite minister and his family, among the first settlers in what is now Lancaster County, built this German-style house in 1719.

Philadelphia ·····································

(Visitor Center, 16th St. and JFK Blvd. 215-636-1666 or 800-537-7676) William Penn's "greene Countrie towne" gained fame early on, for it was here that the Colonists decided to break their ties with England and create a new nation based on freedom and equality. The momentous events—proclamation of war against the English, signing of the Declaration of Independence in 1776, inauguration of two Presidents, drafting of the U.S. Constitution—unfolded in the few square miles now preserved as Independence National Historical Park. After independence, the prosperous city served as the nation's capital from 1790 to 1800, when the government moved to Washington.

Independence Walking Tour ·············· 4 to 6 hours

1. Begin at **Independence National Historical Park Visitor Center** *(3rd*

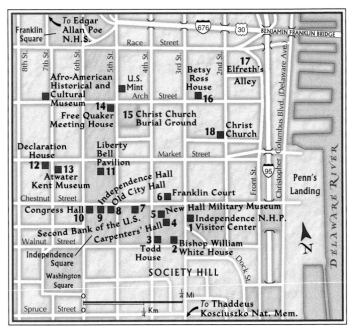

and Chestnut Sts. 215-597-8974. Free, same-day tickets required for tours of Bishop White and Todd houses; arrive early). In this modern building, you can pick up maps and tour tickets, learn about daily park activities, watch an introductory film by John Huston, and see interactive exhibits.

2. Bishop William White House (*309 Walnut St. 215-597-8974*) The revered rector of both Christ Church and St. Peter's Church, Bishop William White built and lived in this elegant federal town house between 1786 and 1836.

3. A simple Georgian structure, **Todd House** (*4th and Walnut Sts. 215-597-8974*) typifies the middle-class Quaker lifestyle of colonial Philadelphia. Dolley Todd (who later married James Madison) resided here with her first husband, John Todd.

4. Carpenters' Hall (*320 Chestnut St. 215-925-0167. Closed Mon. year-round and Tues. Jan.-Feb.*) The Carpenters' Company of Philadelphia—the country's oldest crafts guild (founded 1724)—built this Georgian structure in 1770 and uses it to this day. The First Continental Congress convened here in September 1774 to air grievances against England. A small display includes Windsor chairs used by the delegates and early carpentry tools.

5. Nearby, the **New Hall Military Museum** (*Chestnut St. between 3rd and 4th Sts. 215-597-8974*) recounts the histories of the Army, Navy, and Marine Corps between 1775 and 1800 with weapons, scale models, and a slide show.

6. Franklin Court (*Between 3rd, 4th, Chestnut, and Market Sts. 215-597-8974*) Don't miss this celebration of Benjamin Franklin, tucked unexpectedly behind Chestnut Street's commercial buildings. In the courtyard, a house-shaped steel frame hovers over the remains of the residence that the inventor and statesman owned from 1763 to 1790; glass portals let you peer into the original foundations. The state-of-the-art **Franklin Museum** has samples of Franklin's inventions, plus interactive exhibits and a film on his life. Several row houses, once rented out by Franklin, contain exhibits on architecture and 18th-century printmaking.

7. The Greek Revival **Second Bank of the United States** (*420 Chestnut St. 215-597-8974*) ranked as one of the world's most important financial institutions when it was chartered in 1816. The beautifully restored interior houses the **National Portrait Gallery,** featuring more than 185 works of art (many by Charles Willson Peale).

8. Old City Hall (*5th and Chestnut Sts. 215-597-8974. Under restoration*) John Jay presided over the U.S. Supreme Court in a stately chamber here between 1791 and 1800. The restored building contains exhibits on early courts and late 18th-century Philadelphia.

9. Independence Hall (*Chestnut St. between 5th and 6th Sts. 215-597-8974. Tour lines can be long in summer.*) The United States of America was born in this beautiful marble-trimmed Georgian, originally constructed between 1732 and 1756 as the State House of the Province of Pennsylvania. The centerpiece is the stately Assembly Room, where delegates from the 13 Colonies adopted the Declaration of Independence on July 4, 1776. The guided tour also includes the Pennsylvania Supreme Court chamber, the governor's council chamber, the long room, and the committee room.

10. Congress Hall (*6th and Chestnut Sts. 215-597-8974*) The Congress met in the federal-style Philadelphia Court House from 1790 to 1800, and both George Washington (second term) and John Adams took their presidential oaths of office here.

75

11. Philadelphia's most visited site, the **Liberty Bell Pavilion** (*Market St. bet. 5th and 6th Sts. 215-597-8974*) enshrines America's most cherished emblem of liberty. Cast in 1753, the bell's ringing called the town's citizens for the first public reading of the Declaration of Independence on July 8, 1776. The venerable bell, cracked from decades of use, rang for the last time on George Washington's birthday in 1846. It was moved from Independence Hall to this brick-and-glass pavilion in 1976, where it can be viewed 24 hours a day.

12. Declaration House (Graff House) (*7th and Market Sts. 215-597-8974*) In 1776, 33-year-old Thomas Jefferson rented rooms in this reconstructed Georgian house and penned the Declaration of Independence. The first floor con-

Independence Hall

tains exhibits and a short film on the drafting of the document. The parlor and bedroom have been re-created with period furnishings.

13. Atwater Kent Museum *(15 S. 7th St. 215-922-3031. Closed Sun.-Mon.)* Toys and other everyday objects recall Philadelphia's history from its 1682 founding to the nation's 1876 centennial celebration.

Liberty Bell

14. Free Quaker Meeting House *(5th and Arch Sts. 215-597-8974. Mem. Day–Labor Day Tues.-Sun.)* Declaring their support for the Revolutionary cause, the Free Quakers splintered from the pacifist Quakers and built their own meetinghouse in 1783. The brick structure has been restored to its appearance in 1784.

15. Five signers of the Declaration of Independence, including Benjamin Franklin, are buried in moss-covered **Christ Church Burial Ground** *(5th and Arch Sts. 215-922-1695).* You can see Franklin's penny-covered grave through the fence on Arch Street.

16. Betsy Ross House *(239 Arch St. 215-627-5343. Closed Mon.; donations)* Whether Betsy Ross designed the first American flag or simply sewed an early one is widely disputed. But this dimly lit brick house (which may or may not be hers) portrays the 1740s lifestyle of a seamstress, Quaker, and patriot. Rooms seen on the short, self-guided tour include a restored upholstery shop.

17. Thirty colonial and federal houses line charming **Elfreth's Alley** *(2nd between Arch and Race Sts. 215-574-0560)*, considered the country's oldest, continuously inhabited residential street. **Elfreth's Alley Museum** *(No. 126. Adm. fee)*, housed in a 1750s brick row house, belonged to a mantuamaker and now contains period furnishings.

18. Christ Church *(2nd between Arch and Market Sts. 215-922-1695. Closed Mon.-Tues. Jan.–mid-March)* One of North America's largest buildings when completed in 1754, this lovely Georgian church, with its wine-glass pulpit, served a venerable congregation of patriots.

Other Sites in Philadelphia

Historical Society of Pennsylvania *(1300 Locust St. 215-732-6201. Closed Sun.-Mon.; adm. fee)* The first draft of the Constitution and William Penn's wampum belt are among a plethora of artifacts.

Afro-American Historical and Cultural Museum *(70 Arch St. 215-574-0380. Closed Mon.; adm. fee)* The history of black culture both in the region and in the Americas is traced in this modest collection of artifacts, photographs, and video presentations.

Edgar Allan Poe National Historic Site *(532 N. 7th St. 215-597-8780)* The itinerant author of "The Raven" and other poems lived in this small brick house in 1843-44. Because no record exists of Poe's furnishings, the house has been left vacant, but a seven-minute film and a self-guided tour fuel the imagination.

Penn's Landing *(Between Market and Lombard Sts. along Delaware River. 215-629-3200. Adm. fee to ships)* Moored near the site where William Penn landed in 1682 are several historic ships that may be toured, including the 1883 *Gazela of Philadelphia* and the USS *Becuna,* a guppy-class World War II-era submarine.

Thaddeus Kosciuszko National Memorial *(301 Pine St. 215-597-9618)* When patriot and engineer Kosciuszko was exiled from Poland, he stayed in this 1775 row house in 1797-98. The rooms are virtually empty, but a slide show tells his life story. The site is surrounded by the colonial houses of **Society Hill,** the town's original residential district.

Gloria Dei (Old Swedes') Church *(Christian St. at Christopher Columbus Blvd. 215-389-1513. Weekends)* The oldest church in Philadelphia—built by Swedish Lutherans in 1700—is still active and contains some original furnishings. A small museum displays the Bible presented by William Penn.

Germantown Philadelphia's first borough was settled in 1683 by Germans. Over time, the neighborhood lured the moneyed class, who built refined houses. Today, poverty marks Germantown but several architectural gems remain, including **Stenton** *(18th and Windrim Sts. 215-329-7312. Tues.-Sat.; adm. fee),* the unaltered home of James Logan, secretary to William

77

Old Ferry Inn, Washington Crossing N.H.P.

Penn; **Cliveden** *(6401 Germantown Ave. 215-848-1777. April-Dec. Thurs.-Sun.; adm. fee),* the scene of a pivotal Revolutionary War battle; and the **Deshler-Morris House** *(5442 Germantown Ave. 215-596-1748. Closed Mon. and mid-Dec.–March; adm. fee),* where George Washington came to escape the 1793 yellow fever epidemic.

Excursions

PENNSBURY MANOR *(25 miles NE via I-95 and US 13, S of Morrisville. 215-946-0400. Closed Mon.; adm. fee)* The only home William Penn ever built for himself, this gracious place memorializes the Quaker founder of Pennsylvania. The 43-acre estate has only a few of Penn's personal objects, but its collection of 17th-century furnishings is Pennsylvania's largest.

TRENTON, NEW JERSEY *(25 miles NE via I-95)* See page 83.

WASHINGTON CROSSING NATIONAL HISTORIC PARK *(25 miles NE via US 1 and Pa. 532, in Washington Crossing. 215-493-4076. Adm. fee to buildings)* On Christmas night in 1776, Gen. George Washington and 2,400 soldiers stole across the ice-choked Delaware River with hopes of taking British and Hessian troops in Trenton, New Jersey, by surprise. The picturesque, 500-acre park, commemorating the daring maneuver, is divided into two sections. A Visitor Center in the **Washington Crossing** section offers tours of several restored buildings; one building contains replicas of the troops' flat-bottomed Durham boats. In the **Bowman's Hill** section you'll find restored officers quarters.

VALLEY FORGE NATIONAL HISTORICAL PARK *(22 miles NW via US 1, I-76, US 422, Pa. 23. 610-783-1077. Adm. fee)* During the frigid winter of 1777-

French and Indian War

Three times from 1689 to 1748, European wars between France and Britain spilled over into the New World, sparked by local conflicts over territory and the fur trade. Each side had its Indian allies. In 1753 the French built a chain of forts along the Allegheny River to strengthen their claim on the Ohio fur trade. British Virginia also claimed the river valley, and in 1754 young Maj. George Washington was sent to chase the French. At Fort Necessity, he was routed in the first battle of the war. After early losses, British luck turned. The Treaty of Paris in 1763 ended the war, leaving Britain to dominate eastern North America.

78, George Washington's ragged troops, encamped at Valley Forge, shivered, starved, and died. Despite their condition, drillmaster Friedrich von Steuben mercilessly trained the men, shaping them into a formidable army. A film, reconstructed huts, Washington's headquarters, and well-preserved fortifications recall that winter. The Valley Forge Historical Society Museum exhibits Washington memorabilia.

BRANDYWINE VALLEY, DEL. *(25 miles SW via US 1 or I-95)* See page 86.

Pittsburgh ···························

(Convention & Visitor Bureau, 4 Gateway Center. 412-281-7711 or 800-366-0093) The British chose the spot where the Allegheny and Monongahela Rivers join to form the Ohio for Fort Pitt. A protection for their wilderness claims at the close of the French and Indian War, the fledgling settlement grew steadily through independence. When Andrew Carnegie modernized the steel industry after the Civil War, Pittsburgh—with its hills full of coal for fuel—became the nation's steel capital. That era's wealth is represented by **Clayton** *(7227 Reynolds St., Pt. Breeze. 412-371-0606. Closed Mon.; adm. fee)*, the French château-style estate of Carnegie associate Henry Clay Frick.

Of the 15 cable railways built on the sides of Mount Washington, two remain. The **Monongahela Incline** *(E. Carson St. 412-442-2000. Fare)* was the city's first, built in 1870. A mile downriver, cars on the **Duquesne Incline** *(412-381-1665. Fare)* still have their original hand-carved wood interiors. Both inclines offer superb city views.

Point State Park *(Off Commonwealth Place. 412-471-0235)* All that remains of Fort Pitt (1759) is the redoubt, but the fort's history is recounted at the **Fort Pitt Museum** *(412-281-9285. Closed Mon.-Tues.; adm. fee)* with dioramas, artifacts, and a re-created barracks room.

Sen. John Heinz Pittsburgh Regional History Center *(1212 Smallman St. 412-681-5533)* Four floors

Duquesne Incline (lower left) and the Pittsburgh skyline

78

of exhibits pertain to western Pennsylvania's history, from the Native American cultures through the steel era.

Excursions

BUSHY RUN BATTLEFIELD (*25 miles E via I-376, I-76, Pa. 130, and Pa. 993, near Greensburg. 412-527-5584. Closed Mon.-Tues.; adm. fee for museum*) The British victory here in 1763 broke the series of Indian uprisings called Pontiac's Rebellion. A small museum displays artifacts belonging to both sides.

FORT LIGONIER (*50 miles E via US 30, in Ligonier. 216 S. Market St. 412-238-9701. Closed Nov.-April; adm. fee*) Constructed in 1758, the wilderness fort served as a British stronghold during the French and Indian War. A large Visitor Center includes a film, two elegant period rooms, and artifacts from the site. A reconstructed stockade portrays military life here.

OLD ECONOMY VILLAGE (*15 miles NW on Pa. 65. 14th and Church Sts., Ambridge. 412-266-4500. Closed Mon.; adm. fee*) Seventeen trim structures and a formal garden are all that remain of the 19th-century utopian community that thrived here. The structures now contain the shops of artisans and the former Feast Hall, now the **Harmonist Museum,** which exhibits thousands of handicrafts.

Scranton

The four vast fields of anthracite—considered the world's largest concentration—that lie beneath Scranton's tree-covered hills transformed the once remote town into a booming city in the early 19th century.

Steamtown National Historic Site (*150 S. Washington St. 717-340-5204. Adm. fee*) At the restored 1902 roundhouse—laced with boardwalks for close-up views—mechanics tinker at shining black engines now used for sight-seeing excursions. A history museum, a technology museum, and a yard full of locomotives and railcars are some of the other exhibits that describe the importance of the steam railroad to the nation's development.

Pennsylvania Anthracite Heritage Museum (*McDade Park. 717-963-4804. Adm. fee*) The story of the immigrant coal miners who flocked to the region in the last century is told through personal belongings and other regional artifacts. At the nearby **Lackawanna Coal Mine Tour** (*717-963-MINE. Closed Nov.-April; adm. fee*), railcars carry you 300 feet beneath the earth, for a guided walking tour through a coal mine.

Excursion

ECKLEY MINERS' VILLAGE (*45 miles S via I-81 on Pa. 940, near Hazleton. 717-636-2070. Adm. fee*) This anthracite mining village of 51 buildings, settled in 1853, portrays the hard lives of miners and their families.

Pennsylvania coal car

Uniontown Vicinity

Fort Necessity National Battlefield (*10 miles E of Uniontown on US 40. 412-329-5512. Adm. fee*) Sent to western Pennsylvania to build a military road in 1754, 22-year-old George Washington launched a surprise attack on a French force at remote **Jumonville Glen** (*5 miles NW of Fort Necessity* *via US 40 and Collspring Rd. Closed Nov.-April).* Fearing a counterattack, Washington hastily put up a stockade. As expected, the French soldiers besieged his Fort Necessity, and by nightfall, he and his troops were forced to surrender. The events marked the beginning of the French and Indian War. A Visitor Center now recounts the story, and a short trail leads to the reconstructed fort. The nearby 1828 **Mount Washington Tavern,** once a popular stagecoach stop, recounts the early years of the National Pike—constructed in the early 1800s as the first federally funded road.

Fallingwater *(15 miles E of Uniontown via US 40. 412-329-8501. April-Dec. Tues.-Sun., Jan.-March weekends only; adm. fee)* Cantilevered over a waterfall, Frank Lloyd Wright's architectural masterwork—built in 1936 of reinforced steel, concrete, and stone—blends smoothly into the surrounding woodlands. Numerous windows and wide terraces draw the eye to the natural setting; Wright also decorated the interior.

Friendship Hill National Historic Site *(15 miles S of Uniontown on Pa. 166, near Point Marion. 412-725-9190)* Though devoid of furniture, the rambling house features an audiovisual tour that recalls the days when this was the wilderness estate of Albert Gallatin, secretary of the treasury under Jefferson and Madison. At the Visitor Center, a holographic Gallatin chats about his lifetime of achievement.

Searights Tollhouse National Historic Landmark *(5 miles W of Uniontown on US 40. 412-245-2477. Summer only; adm. fee)* The 1835 brick tower—one of several tollhouses on the National Pike—is now a tiny museum.

York ·

When the British invaded Philadelphia in 1777, the Continental Congress fled to York, making this provincial town the nation's capital for nine months. During their stay, the esteemed group, which included George Washington and Thomas Jefferson, adopted the Articles of Confederation. Combination tickets for the sites listed below are available at the **Historical Society Museum of York County** *(250 E. Market St. 717-848-1587. Adm. fee),* which houses permanent exhibitions on York's early automobile history, an 1830 Conestoga wagon (such wagons originated in Lancaster County), and a reconstructed street of shops.

Horatio Gates House *(157 W. Market St. 717-848-1587. Adm. fee)* While the Continental Congress was in York, several members moved to replace Gen. George Washington, commander of the Continental forces, with Gen. Horatio Gates, hero of Saratoga. The conspiracy was thwarted at Gates's elegant Georgian home where, it is said, the Marquis de Lafayette pledged his loyalty to Washington. Period furnishings decorate the house. The adjacent, half-timbered **Golden Plough Tavern** (1740s) recalls York's days as a tiny frontier village, and the **Barrett Bobb Log House** (1812) was the residence of early German settlers.

York County Colonial Court House *(205 W. Market St. 717-846-1977. Adm. fee)* This 1976 replica of the courthouse where the Continental Congress met—with its 13 tables, quill pens, and original case clock—gives a feel for the nation's days of infancy. A three-screen slide show provides historical background.

Other Sites in Pennsylvania

Bethlehem *(Visitor Center, 52 W. Broad St. 610-868-1513)* The large stone buildings of this picturesque Moravian village—known for its music and art—are prime examples of pre-Revolutionary War German architecture. Several of the many houses in the historic district have been turned into museums, including the 1741 Gemein Haus, now the **Moravian Museum** (*66 W. Church St. 610-867-0173. Feb.-Dec. Tues.-Sat.*), a five-story log building whose exhibits showcase Moravian skill in the decorative arts.

Daniel Boone Homestead (*10 miles E of Reading off US 422. 610-582-4900. Closed Mon.; adm. fee*) The peripatetic frontiersman was born in 1734 in this two-story stone house, which contains mid-18th-century furnishings.

Drake Well Museum (*1 mile SE of Titusville off Pa. 8. 814-827-2797. Adm. fee*) Col. Edwin Drake drilled the world's first commercial oil well here in 1859, ushering in the modern age of oil. This 218-acre park at the edge of beautiful Oil Creek contains a museum and outdoor exhibits, including an oil well and a working replica of Drake's derrick. The **Oil Creek & Titusville Railroad** (*814-676-1733. Fare*) takes you on a 2.5-hour trip past some of the early boomtowns.

Hopewell Furnace National Historic Site (*5 miles S of Birdsboro on Pa. 345. 215-582-8773. Adm. fee*) This restored 18th- and 19th-century company town—one of hundreds of Pennsylvania "iron plantations" that supplied iron to the Colonies—housed many of the employees of the nearby Hopewell Furnace. The office store, tenant houses, furnace stack, and other buildings are now open to the public.

81

Joseph Priestley House (*472 Priestley Ave. in Northumberland. 717-473-9474. Closed Mon.; adm. fee*) Exiled from England, Joseph Priestley built this elegant Georgian house—filled with period furnishings—in 1794. The lab wings (*under construction*) will feature equipment similar to the kind the scientist and freethinker used in his experiments, including a model of the "burning glass" in which he first identified oxygen.

Pennsylvania Lumber Museum (*10 miles W of Galeton via US 6. 814-435-2652. April-Nov.; adm. fee*) The state's lucrative 19th-century lumber industry is recalled with a reconstructed logging village and an 1890 steam-powered circular sawmill, plus more than 3,000 artifacts.

Hopewell Furnace National Historic Site

U.S. Brig Niagara (*164 E. Front St. in Erie. 814-452-2744. Open daily Mem. Day–Labor Day, Sat.-Sun. spring and fall; closed Nov.-March; adm. fee*) The reconstructed brig—with a full rig and cannon—gained fame in the 1813 Battle of Lake Erie, in which Commodore Oliver Perry's fleet defeated the British. The flagship, with its cramped captains and officers quarters, its storerooms and its galley, now displays early nautical equipment.

Ford Mansion, George Washington's 1779-80 headquarters, Morristown National Historical Park

The Swedes and Dutch who settled New Jersey's wooded shores in the 1600s shared dreams of riches to be made in trade with the Indians. They fared well enough until 1664, when control of the area passed peacefully to England. Under the British crown, the colonists tamed and tilled the wilderness lands until the Revolution, when the small colony—wedged strategically between New York and Pennsylvania—endured a hundred battles on its soil. Fiercely independent, New Jersey adopted the nation's first state constitution on July 2, 1776. In the Civil War, 88,000 New Jerseyites joined the Union cause. By the end of the 19th century, industrialization was deeply entrenched in the north, and steel, cable-wire, and ceramic factories assured the state's prosperity well into this century.

Morristown

(Visitor Center, 14 Elm St. 201-993-1194) Iron ore in the surrounding Watchung Mountains first lured settlers to the region in the early 1700s. And it was iron for munitions, combined with mountain defenses, that drew George Washington and his troops to Morristown for winter

encampments in 1777 and 1779. In the 19th century, industrial tycoons passed leisurely summers here, leaving behind a showcase of Victorian mansions along broad avenues. Several venerable houses are open to the public, including **Macculloch Hall** (*45 Macculloch Ave. 201-538-2404. Sun. and Thurs.; adm. fee*). Begun in 1810 by the founder of the Morris Canal, it is now a national historic landmark. **Acorn Hall** (*68 Morris Ave. 201-267-3465*), an 1850s Italianate Victorian, now houses the Morris County Historical Society. At the **Schuyler-Hamilton House** (*5 Olyphant Pl. 201-267-4039. Tues. and Sun.; adm. fee*), Alexander Hamilton (then Washington's aide-de-camp and later secretary of the treasury) courted Elizabeth Schuyler in 1780.

Historic Speedwell (*333 Speedwell Ave. 201-540-0211. Thurs.-Sun.; adm. fee*) Owned by the self-made Stephen Vail, the Speedwell Iron Works manufactured the first engine to power a steamship across the Atlantic and was responsible for making improvements on the first telegraph. Factory buildings filled with antique tools have been preserved, as has the Vail house and its furnishings.

Morristown National Historical Park (*Washington Pl. 201-539-2085. Adm. fee for headquarters*) Washington's troops shivered and starved as much during their winter encampments at Morristown as they did during the 1777-78 Valley Forge winter. In fact, the winter of 1779 proved to be the century's cruelest. Unable to take the hardships, many of the 10,000 soldiers who had encamped at Morristown deserted Washington. A film at the Visitor Center elucidates the adversities suffered here.

Washington set up his military headquarters in the Georgian **Ford Mansion** (*Next to Visitor Center*), still furnished with various Chippendale pieces. Off Chestnut Street are the remains of **Fort Nonsense**, built in 1777. Legend says Washington had his troops build the fort to keep them busy, hence the name. Five miles south of town, in another section of the historical park, densely wooded **Jockey Hollow** recalls the campsites of Washington's troops with reconstructed log huts.

Trenton ···

(*Visitor Center, corner of Lafayette and Barrack Sts. 609-777-1770*) Originally settled by English Quakers, Trent's Town was laid out by William Trent in 1714. The Georgian **William Trent House** (*15 Market St. 609-989-3027. Adm. fee*), one of the state's oldest dwellings completed in 1719, includes fine examples of William and Mary furniture. Trenton became the state capital in 1790; today it is known for its manufacturers of fine china—such as the Lenox Company—and for its steel-cable industries.

Old Barracks Museum (*Barrack St. 609-396-1776. Adm. fee*) After their daring crossing of the ice-clogged Delaware on Christmas night, 1776, George Washington and his ragged troops surprised sleeping Hessian soldiers at this barracks. The two ensuing battles (December 26, 1776, and January 2, 1777) were patriot victories. The barracks now offer a look at 18th-century military life.

New Jersey State Museum (*205 W. State St. 609-292-6464. Closed Mon.*) Opened in 1895, the four-story museum houses an eclectic collection that includes historic New Jersey-made furnishings and ceramics. The surrounding **State House Historic District** is full of dwellings once belonging to Trenton's prominent 19th-century families.

Excursions

PRINCETON *(10 miles NE of Trenton via US 206. Visitor information at Historical Society of Princeton, 158 Nassau St. 609-921-6748. Tues.-Sun.)* Founded by Quakers in the 1690s, Princeton maintains a genteel charm despite the high-tech research institutions and corporate headquarters that surround it. Its tree-canopied streets are edged by houses dating from the 18th-century.

Fourth oldest university in the country, **Princeton University** *(Campus tours offered by Orange Key Guide Service; reserve 3 days in advance. 73 Nassau St. 609-258-3603)* is centered around Nassau Hall, the original school structure (1756). Both British and American troops used it as a barracks during the Revolutionary War, and for several months in 1783, the Continental Congress met in the hall, making it a temporary Capitol of the nation. Capt. William Bainbridge, commander of the USS *Constitution* and a hero of the War of 1812, was born in **Bainbridge House** *(158 Nassau St. 609-921-6748. Tues.-Sun.),* now repository of the Historical Society of Princeton.

The **Princeton Battlefield State Park** *(500 Mercer St. 609-921-0074)* commemorates the short but decisive battle won by Washington's forces in early January 1777, just a week after the famous crossing of the Delaware. Coupled with the recent victory at Trenton, the Princeton battle marked an important turning point in the Revolutionary War. The **Thomas Clarke House** *(Wed.-Sun.)* is furnished in period style.

WASHINGTON CROSSING STATE PARK *(10 miles NW of Trenton, off N.J. 29. 609-737-0623. Visitor Center and ferry house open Wed.-Sun.)* After the 1776 crossing of the Delaware, George Washington and his troops landed along this stretch of New Jersey shoreline. A small museum at the Visitor Center, along with the restored ferry house where Washington rested, recount the historic crossing. Markers along **Continental Lane** show the route the patriots took on their way to attack Trenton.

PENNSBURY MANOR STATE SITE, PA. *(5 miles S via US 1)* See page 77.

Other Sites in New Jersey

Batsto Historic Village *(Rte. 542, Wharton State Forest. 609-561-3262. Daily summer, Labor Day–Memorial Day Wed.-Sun.; adm. fee)* Deep in the state's Pine Barrens, this 18th-century village was once the center of New Jersey's bog-iron industry. Though the original furnace that produced munitions for the Revolutionary War no longer stands, a gristmill, sawmill, general store, cabins, and the 36-room ironmaster's house have all been restored.

Cape May *(Chamber of Commerce, 609 Lafayette St. 609-884-5508)* More than 600 pastel Victorian buildings grace the streets of Cape May, one of the nation's oldest seaside resorts. For most of the 19th century, droves of sunseekers (including several Presidents) flocked to the town. Rediscovered in the 1960s, the buildings—adorned with cupolas, wraparound porches, wrought-iron fences, and gingerbread—have been meticulously restored, and many now operate as bed-and-breakfasts. The 1879 **Emlen Physick Estate** *(1048 Washington St. 609-884-5404. Adm. fee)* showcases Victorian furniture, toys, and clothing.

Edison Memorial Tower and Museum *(Christie St. in Edison State Park, Menlo Park. 908-549-3299. Wed.-Sun.)* A lightbulb-shaped tower marks the site of Thomas Edison's Menlo Park laboratory, where he invented the

Victorian Cape May

incandescent light bulb. The lab itself was moved to Greenfield Village in Dearborn, Michigan (*see p. 229*), by Henry Ford, but the small museum here has worthwhile exhibits that include early light bulbs.

Edison National Historic Site (*Main St. and Lakeside Ave.,W. Orange. 201-736-0550. Adm. fee*) While working at his ivy-covered "invention factory" between 1887 and 1931, Thomas Alva Edison conceived of many new devices, including the phonograph and the motion picture camera. The extensive guided tour takes in Edison's chemistry lab, his library, and a replica of the world's first motion picture studio. A tinfoil recording captures Edison reciting "Mary Had A Little Lamb." A half mile away stands **Glenmont** (*201-736-0550. Wed.-Sun.; tickets at historic site Visitor Center*), Edison's opulent Victorian mansion.

Greenwich (*Off N.J. 49*) The 1774 site of a tea-burning party, Greenwich is a charming village whose large historic district brims with colonial, federal, and Victorian houses. The **Cumberland County Historical Society** (*Ye Greate St. 609-455-4055*) is located in the 1730 Gibbon House.

Monmouth Battlefield State Park (*N.J. 33, 2 miles W of Freehold. 908-462-9616*) After rigorous drilling at Valley Forge, George Washington's troops clashed head-on here with the British Army on June 28, 1778. During the battle—the longest of the Revolutionary War—Molly Pitcher earned her nickname by carrying water to fallen soldiers.

Paterson (*Great Falls Visitor Center, 65 McBride Ave. 201-279-9587. Sun.-Fri.*) Diverting water from the Passaic River to power textile mills, Alexander Hamilton planned the nation's first industrial community here in 1791. The **Great Falls Historic District** (*Between Grand St. and Ryle Ave.*) preserves early factories, including the Old Gun Mill, where Samuel Colt manufactured the first successful revolver. The **Paterson Museum** (*2 Market St. 201-881-3874. Closed Mon.; donations*) offers exhibits that explore the city's urban and industrial past.

Waterloo Village (*Off US 206 in Stanhope. 201-347-0900. Mid-April–Dec. Wed.-Sun.; adm. fee*) During the Revolution, Waterloo was an ironmaking village; in the 1830s it became an important way station on the Morris Canal. Both eras are represented at this living history museum.

Winterthur Museum in the Brandywine Valley

Though geographically the second smallest state in the nation, Delaware justifiably claims status as the "First State," since it was first to ratify the U.S. Constitution. But Delaware had struggled hard to establish itself as a colony prior to that event. The Dutch arrived here first, attempting several tentative footholds along the coastline, but it was the Swedes who managed to create the first permanent settlement in the area. In the mid-1600s the English entered the landscape, laying claim to all territory between the Delaware and Connecticut Rivers and granting much of what is now Delaware to Quaker leader William Penn. The conservative Quaker standards met with opposition from the non-Quakers, and in 1704, Delaware became a separate colony. The du Ponts led the way in industrializing the northern tip of the state, beginning in the early 19th century. In this century, the Atlantic beaches have seen increasing development, but much of the rest of the state has kept its rural character.

Brandywine Valley

(Convention & Visitors Bureau, 1300 Market St., Suite 504, Wilmington. 302-652-4088) The historic Brandywine Valley that threads through Wilmington's lush northern outskirts is replete with the stupendous estates of the du Pont barons. Their forebear, E.I. du Pont, made this area an industrial powerhouse when he founded black-powder mills on the Brandywine River

in the early 19th century. In downtown Wilmington the **Delaware History Museum** (*504 Market St. 302-655-7161. Tues.-Sat.; donations*) offers changing exhibits on state history. Next door the **Old Town Hall** (*Under restoration*), built in 1798, is Wilmington's oldest public building.

Hagley Museum and Library (*Del. 141. 302-658-2400. Daily mid-March–Dec., call for off-season hours; adm. fee*) This picturesque spot on the banks of the Brandywine River preserves a remarkable collection of buildings related to America's early industrialization. In the early 1800s, French entrepreneur Éleuthère Irénée du Pont established a black-powder mill here that heralded the birth of the du Pont empire. The world's largest manufacturer of black powder, Hagley Mills stretched for 2 miles along the Brandywine and was in constant use until 1921. Ruins and restorations of the granite buildings still stand on the 230-acre museum site, with exhibits and demonstrations on the early industrial age. A small workers village climbs a hillside, and the original du Pont estate, **Eleutherian Mills,** offers a look at period rooms and furnishings from the Crown-inshield era, depicting the life of the last du Pont heiress to live here.

Nemours Mansion and Gardens (*1600 Rockland Rd. off Del. 141N. 302-651-6912. May-Nov. Tues.-Sun.; adm. fee*) Another du Pont heir, Alfred I. du Pont, built this lavish 102-room mansion in 1909-10. Modeled on a Louis XVI-style French château and designed by Carrere and Hastings of New York, the house is furnished in elegant antiques, paintings, rugs, and tapestries; extravagant formal gardens surround it.

87

Rockwood Museum (*610 Shipley Rd. 302-761-4340. March-Dec. Tues.-Sun., Jan.-Feb. Tues.-Sat.; adm. fee*) The rural Gothic mansion (1851) of Joseph Shipley—great-grandson of Wilmington's founder, William Shipley—was modeled on a British country house and features Edwardian and Irish manor house furnishings. The high, rounded shrubs and evergreens of the grounds typify mid-19th-century "gardenesque" landscaping.

Winterthur Museum, Garden, and Library (*Del. 52, 6 miles N of Wilmington. 302-888-4600 or 800-448-3883. Adm. fee*) The country's premier collection of American decorative arts owes its existence largely to one man—industrial scion Henry Francis du Pont (1880-1969), who turned his family home in the lush Brandywine Valley suburbs of Wilmington into a vast museum and garden. Originally interested in European decorative arts, du Pont shifted his focus to American items early in this century and became an avid collector. In the coming decades he expanded his home enormously to hold his collections and in 1951 opened it as a museum. Today, Winterthur compasses 175 period rooms with more than 89,000 artifacts that reflect the best in American decorative arts. Du Pont limited his collection to pieces from the 1640s to the 1860s, when industrialization brought an end to handcrafting. A new gallery building exhibits highlights of the collection, and the grounds are justifiably famous for du Pont's extensive naturalized gardens.

Excursion

CHADDS FORD, PA. (*8 miles N via Del./Pa. 100*) See page 71.

See page 71.

Dover ···

(*Delaware State Visitor Center, North and Federal Sts. 302-739-4266*) Since 1781 this small town has served as the state capital. On December 7,

1787, Delaware's legislators, meeting in a tavern on the green, became the first to ratify the Constitution. The 1792 **State House** (*Tours begin at State Visitor Center. 302-739-4266. Tues.-Sun.*) still faces the green. Seat of government for 140 years, the gracefully proportioned Georgian brick, with its double interior staircases, contains the restored federal-era courtroom, legislative chambers, and offices. Nearby, the **Sewell C. Biggs Museum of American Art** (*Located above State Visitor Center. 302-674-2111. Wed.-Sun.*) boasts a distinguished collection of American decorative arts from the 18th and 19th centuries, as well as paintings and sculpture by prominent American artists.

Christ Church (*S. State and Water Sts. 302-734-5731. Donations*) was constructed in 1734 and has undergone many additions and changes since then; the lovely

Zwaanendael Museum, Lewes

neo-Gothic stained-glass windows were added in the late 19th century. Dover's old 1790s Presbyterian Church and its 1880s Sunday school are now the **Meeting House Galleries** (*316 S. Governors Ave. 302-739-4266. Tues.-Sat.*), where a "Main Street, Delaware" exhibit features the shops found in turn-of-the-century southern Delaware. The galleries also display archaeological finds, particularly relating to Native Americans.

Delaware Agricultural Museum and Village (*US 13N. 302-734-1618. April-Dec. Tues.-Sun., Jan.-March Mon.-Fri.; adm. fee*) Buildings moved here from the countryside re-create a small farming town of the late 19th century. In the barnlike museum, antique farm implements and machinery are displayed, including Delawarean Cecile Steele's original broiler house, developed in 1923 for raising chickens. Her innovation lead to the development of the commercial broiler industry that is still thriving on the Eastern Shore.

John Dickinson Plantation (*340 Kitts Hummock Rd. off US 113S. 302-739-3277. March-Dec. Tues.-Sun., Jan.-Feb. Tues.-Sat.*) This was the boyhood home of the "penman of the American Revolution," as Dickinson, a major formulator of the U.S. Constitution, was known. The original 1740 brick mansion burned in 1804, and Dickinson rebuilt it.

Lewes

(*Visitor information at the 18th-century Fisher Martin House, 120 Kings Hwy. 302-645-8073. Daily Mem. Day–Labor Day, Mon.-Fri. rest of year*) The Dutch first settled this site on Delaware Bay in 1631, calling it Zwaanendael, or "valley of the swans."

Zwaanendael Museum (*102 Kings Hwy. 302-645-1148. Tues.-Sun.*) The distinctive redbrick facade of the museum was modeled on a Dutch town hall. Exhibits center on local history and on artifacts salvaged from the HMS *De Braak*, which went down off Cape Henlopen in 1798.

Lewes Historical Society Complex (*110 Shipcarpenter St. 302-645-7670.*

Mid-June–Labor Day Tues.-Sat.; adm. fee) Occupying a spacious greensward, the cluster of 18th- and 19th-century houses and shops spans two centuries of life in this part of the Eastern Shore.

New Castle

(Visitors Bureau 302-322-8411 or 800-758-1550) This pristinely preserved village on the upper Delaware River has enjoyed a rich past. The Dutch arrived here first, establishing Fort Casimir in 1651 to solidify their control over the area. In the ensuing decades, the area passed between the Dutch, the Swedes, and finally the British. In 1682 they granted it to Quaker leader William Penn, who first set foot on American soil here. In 1704, when Delaware separated from Pennsylvania, New Castle became the colonial capital and remained such until 1777.

The town's 18th- and 19th-century houses center around a village green, anchored on one end by **Immanuel on the Green Episcopal Church** *(302-328-2413)*—completed in 1703 and restored after a 1980 fire—and on the other by the 1732 **Courthouse** *(302-323-4453. Tues.-Sun.),* which served as the colonial capitol and now houses exhibits on state history; adjacent to it is the old **town hall.** The diminutive 1700 **Dutch House** *(32 E. 3rd St. 302-322-2794. March-Dec. Tues.-Sun., Jan.-Feb. Sat.-Sun.; adm. fee)* recalls the town's Dutch heritage in its furnishings. The Georgian 1738 **Amstel House** *(2 E. 4th St. 302-322-2794. March-Dec. Tues.-Sun., Jan.-Feb. Sat.-Sun.; adm. fee)* re-creates the life of a prominent 18th-century family.

Read House *(42 The Strand. 302-322-8411. March-Dec. Tues.-Sun., Jan.-Feb. Sat.-Sun. or by appt.; adm. fee)* Fronting the Delaware River, the elegant house boasts elaborate punch-and-gouge woodwork. The builder, George Read II, was son of a prominent Revolutionary statesman and signer of the Declaration of Independence. The house now features both federal rooms and colonial revival rooms from a 1920s restoration.

Excursions

FORT DELAWARE STATE PARK *(Via ferry from the end of Clinton St. in Delaware City. 302-834-7941. Mid-June–Labor Day Wed.-Sun., call for hours in April and Sept.; adm. fee)* Living history actors reenact life here on Pea Patch Island in the summer of 1864, when the moated, pentagonal brick fortress served as a Civil War fortification and hub of the prisoner-of-war camp that took in the rest of the island. The island's wartime population reached 14,000, making it the state's largest city.

CHADDS FORD, PA. *(15 miles N via Del. 141 to Del./Pa. 100)* See p. 71.

Odessa

(Historic Houses of Odessa, Main St. 302-378-4069. March-Dec. Tues.-Sun.; adm. fee) Time passed by this thriving 18th-century river port, leaving many of its old houses intact. Winterthur Museum now owns four Main Street buildings. The imposing Georgian **Corbit-Sharp House** (1774) contains original woodwork and some original furnishings. The **Wilson-Warner House** (1769), another Georgian, is portrayed as it was at the time of an 1829 bankruptcy sale. The 19th-century **Brick Hotel Gallery** displays the ornate Victorian furniture made by mastercraftsman John Henry Belter. The **Collins-Sharp House,** one of the town's earliest structures, dates from the early 1700s.

89

Maryland

The Irish Lord Baltimore launched Maryland, sending the earliest settlers forth under his younger brother Leonard Calvert in 1634. The Catholic Calverts hoped to establish a colony that would be lucrative in the fur and tobacco trade and would offer religious freedom. The dream of religious tolerance faded when the Protestant population staged a rebellion against Calvert's Catholic governor in 1689. Still, Maryland has through the centuries retained a more liberal atmosphere than its neighbor states to the south, staying with the Union in the Civil War. Much of the state has the rural, agricultural flavor it had in the past century, though Baltimore and its growing environs are characterized by a vibrant urbanism.

Annapolis

(Visitors Bureau, 26 West St. 410-280-0445) In 1694 Royal Governor Francis Nicholson established a new colonial capital here on the banks of the Severn, moving it from its former Catholic stronghold in St. Marys City and naming it after Queen Anne. The city quickly became one of the most cosmopolitan centers in the Colonies. Surviving 18th-century structures and the colonial layout of narrow, radiating streets give it a charming quaintness.

Historic Annapolis Walking Tour · · · · · · · · · · · · 5 hours

1. Begin at the **State House** (*State Circle. 410-974-3400*). The oldest capitol in continuous use in the country, the columned and cupolaed redbrick structure has been the seat of the state legislature since 1780. It also briefly served as the national Capitol, when the newborn U.S. Congress met here in the early 1780s. During that time George Washington appeared to resign his commission as commander-in-chief. Among its historic paintings is

Annapolis, on the Severn River

Charles Willson Peale's "Washington, Lafayette, and Tilman at the Battle of Yorktown."

2. Housed in a former church and dedicated to the state's African-American history, the **Banneker-Douglass Museum** (*84 Franklin St. 410-974-2893. Tues.-Sat.*) is named for abolitionist Frederick Douglass and for Benjamin Banneker, an African-American surveyor who helped lay out Washington, D.C.

3. A colonial town house in the grand style, the **Chase-Lloyd House** (*22 Maryland Ave. 410-263-2723. Tues.-Sat.; adm. fee*), is ornamented with woodwork by William Buckland, who executed the woodwork at George Mason's Gunston Hall, in Virginia.

4. Mathias Hammond built the gracious Georgian **Hammond-Harwood House** (*19 Maryland Ave. 410-269-1714. Adm. fee*) in the 1770s; it also highlights the craftsmanship of William Buckland. One of Buckland's descendants, William Harwood, became a proprietor of the house, and many Harwood family pieces now decorate it.

5. Described by an 18th-century observer as the most elegant house in

Annapolis, the **William Paca House** (*186 Prince George St. 410-263-5553. Daily March-Dec., Sat.-Sun. Jan.-Feb.; adm. fee*) was the home of a prominent colonial statesman and signer of the Declaration of Independence. Two acres of gardens add to its manorial appearance.

6. U.S. Naval Academy (*Visitor Center, Randall and King George Sts. 410-263-6933. Guided tours available*) Since 1845, the "Yard" has dominated the northern side of town. Its green-roofed beaux arts buildings were designed by turn-of-the-century architect Ernest Flagg, and the

91

domed **chapel** streams with light reflected through Tiffany windows. The chapel's crypt is a shrine to Revolutionary War hero John Paul Jones. The academy **museum** (*Preble Hall*) exhibits naval memorabilia.

7. Once a colonial inn, the **Shiplap House Museum** (*18 Pinkney St. 410-267-7619. Mon.-Fri.*) has been restored to its early 18th-century appearance.

Baltimore ···

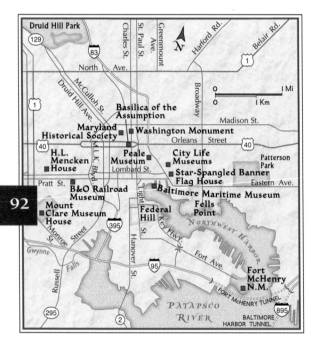

(*Visitor Center, 301 E. Pratt St. 410-837-4636 or 800-282-6632*) Named for the Lords Baltimore, Maryland's largest town traces its beginnings to 1729. The area's potential as a deepwater port was recognized in 1750, and from that time forward, the town thrived on maritime commerce and shipbuilding. In the War of 1812, the city's reputation as a haven of privateers led the British to target it, but with little success. A major industrial center in this century, Baltimore drew the European immigrants whose traditions give the town its distinctive flavor.

Baltimore Maritime Museum (*Piers 3 and 4 at Pratt St., Inner Harbor. 410-396-3854. Adm. fee*) Three pierside vessels constitute this museum: the Lightship *Chesapeake;* the USS *Torsk,* a World War II-era submarine; and the U.S. Coast Guard cutter *Roger B. Taney,* now the only ship afloat that survived the Japanese raid on Pearl Harbor.

Fells Point (*Foot of Broadway*) This historic neighborhood jutting into the Patapsco below the Inner Harbor was the focus of the colonial port town and still retains row houses from the 18th and 19th centuries.

Star-Spangled Banner Flag House (*844 E. Pratt St. 410-837-1793. Tues.-Sat.; adm. fee*) Vexologist—flagmaker—Mary Pickersgill was living in this house during the War of 1812, when she produced the 30-by-42-foot version of the Stars and Stripes that later inspired Francis Scott Key to write the national anthem.

City Life Museums (*33 S. Front St. 410-396-3523. Adm. fee*) The museum complex comprises several structures centered around the old **Carroll Mansion.** Respected statesman and signer of the Declaration of Independence, Charles Carroll spent his last winters amid the refined Empire furnishings of his federal town house. Adjacent to it, the **1840 House** depicts the moderate lifestyle of a middle-class wheelwright's family. The new **Morton K. Blaustein City Life Exhibition Center** includes lively exhibits on the Baltimore area, from the prehistoric to the modern period. The landmark redbrick **Shot Tower** (*801 E. Fayette. 410-396-3523*) rears up within sight. Built in 1828, the 215-foot tower, like other such towers of the time, was constructed to produce lead shot.

Peale Museum (*225 N. Holliday St. 410-396-1149. Sat.-Sun.; adm. fee*) One of the oldest museum buildings in the country, the federal brick structure was built in 1814 by artist Rembrandt Peale, son of famous Maryland portraitist Charles Willson Peale. It now contains works by Peale family members and scientific curiosities such as would have been in the original museum.

Basilica of the National Shrine of the Assumption of the Blessed Virgin Mary (*Cathedral and Mulberry Sts. 410-727-3564*) The massive Greek Revival structure ranks as the nation's first Roman Catholic cathedral and mother church of U.S. Catholicism. Washington architect Benjamin Latrobe designed the original part of the structure, completed in 1821.

Washington Monument (*N. Charles St. at Mount Vernon Pl.*) Respected Washington, D.C., architect Robert Mills designed this Doric shaft topped by an image of the first President. Completed in 1829, the monument predates the one in the U.S. capital.

Maryland Historical Society (*201 W. Monument St. 410-685-3750. Sept.-June. Tues.-Sun., July-Aug. Mon.-Sat.; adm. fee*) The history of the state is traced here in exhibits, decorative arts, and artifacts. The museum complex includes the 1840s mansion of philanthropist Enoch Pratt.

H. L. Mencken House (*1524 Hollins St. 410-396-7997. Sat.-Sun., or by appt.; adm. fee*) A perspicacious editorialist whose writings earned him the sobriquet "sage of Baltimore," Mencken (1880-1956) lived and worked in the comfortable row house on Union Square. The house is still furnished with his effects.

B&O Railroad Museum (*901 W. Pratt St. 410-752-2490. Adm. fee*) This impressive complex encompasses 5 historic buildings and 37 acres. The well-preserved 1884 roundhouse now shelters vintage steam, diesel, and electric locomotives. An exhibit area displays railroadiana, and the museum entrance occupies the 1830 Mount Clare Station, the nation's first railroad station. The railyards are filled with one of the most extensive collections of rolling stock on the continent.

Mount Clare Museum House (*1500 Washington Blvd., Carroll Park. 410-837-3262. Closed Mon.; adm. fee*) The stately 1760s brick house that was the home of Charles Carroll, a barrister, and his wife is the only pre-Revolution house still standing in the city. Period furnishings,

Fells Point, Baltimore

including Carroll family pieces and portraits by Charles Willson Peale, decorate it.

Federal Hill This historic district overlooking the Patapsco River is filled with brick 19th-century row houses, and the park holds a statue of the 1812 hero Samuel Smith.

Fort McHenry National Monument

Fort McHenry National Monument and Historic Shrine *(E. Fort Ave. 410-962-4290. Adm. fee)* Built in the 1790s, the fortress became critical to the defense of Baltimore when the British attacked the city in September 1814. In a night battle that raged along the waterfront, the Colonials repulsed the British. Washington lawyer Francis Scott Key watched the battle from a ship downriver and was so taken with the site of Old Glory flying above the fort that he was inspired to pen "The Star-Spangled Banner."

Cumberland ······································

(Visitor Center, Western Maryland Station Center, 13 Canal St. 301-777-5905) Situated at a gap in the Alleghenies, this spot was chosen by the British in the 1750s for the site of a fort to counter threats from the French and Indians to the west. All that is now left of Fort Cumberland is **George Washington's Headquarters** *(Riverside Park at Greene St.)*, a small log cabin the young commander of the Virginia militia occupied while posted here. In 1785 the town was laid out around the fort and grew to be a major transportation center. The **Washington Street Historic District** harbors gracious Queen Anne and classical revival houses that testify to the town's 19th-century prosperity as a railroad shipping center.

History House *(218 Washington St. 301-777-8678. Closed Mon.; adm. fee)* Built in 1867 as the home of Chesapeake & Ohio Canal president Josiah Gordon, the house reflects the lavish style of the period.

Western Maryland Station Center *(13 Canal St. 301-777-5905)* The town's cavernous 1913 railroad terminal houses a small museum with exhibits on local glassmaking and railroad memorabilia, and a Visitor Center for the **Chesapeake & Ohio Canal National Historical Park** *(301-722-8226. Closed Mon.)*. The 184.5-mile canal, begun in 1828, terminates here.

Excursion

LA VALE TOLL GATE HOUSE *(5 miles W via US 40A. 301-729-3047. Late May–Oct. Sat.-Sun.)* The octagonal brick structure is the first tollhouse (1833) built on the old National Road and the last one surviving in Maryland.

Easton ···

(Visitor Center, 210 Marlboro Ave., Suite 3. 410-822-4606. Mon.-Fri.) The

seat of Talbot County, Easton offers a glimpse into the area's past at the **Historical Society of Talbot County** *(25 S. Washington St. 410-822-0773. Closed Mon.; adm. fee)*. The society maintains two adjacent historic houses: the 1810 **James Neall House**, built for a well-to-do Quaker cabinetmaker; and his brother Joseph's modest cottage. The town's Quaker heritage is also preserved at the **Third Haven Friends Meeting House** *(405 S. Washington St. 410-822-0293)*, a simple frame building erected in the 1680s. The adjacent brick meetinghouse was built in 1880.

Excursions

ST. MICHAELS *(10 miles W via Md. 33)* A respected shipbuilding center in the 18th century, this small town continues its association with the sea at the renowned **Chesapeake Bay Maritime Museum** *(Mill St. 410-745-2916. Daily March-Jan., Sat.-Sun. in Feb.; adm. fee)*. One of the country's finest maritime museums, the 18-acre complex offers eight exhibition buildings, including the 1870 Hooper Strait Lighthouse. The **St. Mary's Square Museum** *(410-745-9561. Weekends May-Oct.; donations)*, housed in an 1800s mill, also details local history.

OXFORD *(10 miles SW via Md. 333. Also by Oxford-Bellevue Ferry; landing outside St. Michaels on Md. 329. 410-745-9023. Fare)* Wide, gracious streets and fine houses bespeak this town's former importance as the first colonial port-of-entry established on the Eastern Shore. The **Oxford Museum** *(Morris and Market Sts. 410-226-0191. Weekends Mid-April–mid-Oct.)* showcases local memorabilia and offers walking-tour maps. Fronting the Tred Avon River, the **Robert Morris Inn** *(314 N. Morris St. 410-226-5111)* incorporates the home of the famous Revolutionary financier.

WYE MILLS *(13 miles N via US 50 and Md. 662)* The restored 17th-century **gristmill** *(410-827-6909. April-Nov.)* still grinds grains, as it did for George Washington's troops. Near it sprawls the famous 400-year-old **Wye Oak**, said to be the nation's largest white oak.

Frederick ··

(Visitor Center, 19 E. Church St. 301-663-8687 or 800-999-3613) Laid out in 1745, the historic core of this small, picturesque town centers around **Courthouse Square.** Distinguished federal row houses front the square, as does **All Saints Episcopal Church** *(106 W. Church St.)*, whose elegant Gothic Revival interior boasts Tiffany-style stained-glass windows. Francis Scott Key was an active member here, and the small brick **law offices of Roger Brooke Taney and Francis Scott Key** *(104 N. Court St. Not open to public)* lie across the square. Brothers-in-law, the two later became famous—Key as author of the "Star-Spangled Banner" and Taney as the U.S. chief justice who handed down the controversial Dred Scott decision that added to the mounting tensions between pro- and antislavery factions.

Barbara Fritchie House and Museum *(154 W. Patrick St. 301-698-0630. April-Nov. Thurs.-Mon.; adm. fee)* Standing at the edge of Carroll Creek, this small brick house is a reconstruction of the one occupied by Frederick's famous old lady, Barbara Fritchie. The 95-year-old Fritchie became a legend in the Civil War when she waved a Union flag at a passing column of Confederate troops. Her original cabin was damaged beyond repair by flooding in 1868, but original furnishings and building materials are incorporated in the current structure.

95

National Museum of Civil War Medicine *(48 E. Patrick St. 301-695-1864. Tues.-Sun.; adm. fee)* This ambitious new museum houses an extensive collection of medical memorabilia depicting the primitive state of medicine during the Civil War and the dreadful suffering endured by victims of battle and disease.

Roger Brooke Taney House/Francis Scott Key Museum *(121 S. Bentz St. 301-663-8687. Weekends May-Oct.; adm. fee)* Taney lived in this stately federal home from 1815 to 1823, and Key was a frequent visitor. Decorated in period furnishings with pieces of family memorabilia, the house preserves a desk used by Key and law books of the brothers-in-law.

Rose Hill Manor Park *(1611 N. Market St. 301-694-1648. Daily April-Oct., weekends only in Nov.; adm. fee)* The stately white Georgian house and its surrounding dependencies re-create 19th-century life.

Schifferstadt Architectural Museum *(1110 Rosemont Ave. 301-663-3885. April–mid-Dec. Tues.-Sun.; donations)* Typifying the architectural style used by mid-18th-century German settlers, the large stone house (1750s) is unfurnished but notable for its hand-hewn oak beams and other details.

Excursions

MONOCACY NATIONAL BATTLEFIELD *(5 miles S via Md. 355. 301-662-3515. Visitor Center open daily Mem. Day–Labor Day, Wed.-Sun. rest of year)* In July 1864 Confederate general Jubal Early attempted to attack the Federal capital by approaching it along this route. On July 9 opposing Union forces engaged Early's forces here along the Monocacy River, slowing the Southern advance on Washington.

WASHINGTON MONUMENT STATE PARK *(10 miles W via US 40A. 301-791-4767)* A short wooded path leads to the top of South Mountain, where George Washington is honored by a stone monument (1827), the first ever erected to him. During the Civil War this high summit was used as a Union signal station.

HARPERS FERRY, W.VA. *(20 miles W on US 340)* See page 201.

LEESBURG, VIRGINIA *(25 miles S via US 340 and 15)* See page 112.

Hagerstown ··

(Visitor Center, 16 Public Square. 301-791-3246 or 800-228-STAY) The heritage of the early German pioneers who came from Pennsylvania to

settle Maryland's western frontier is preserved at the restored stone **Jonathan Hager House and Museum** *(110 Key St., City Park. 301-739-8393. April-Nov. Tues.-Sun.; adm. fee)*. Hager, the town's namesake, was the first to settle the area, arriving in 1739. An adjacent stone building displays archaeological artifacts found on the site. The 1818 **Miller House** *(135 W. Washington St. 301-797-8782. April-*

Sunken Road, Antietam National Battlefield

Dec. Wed.-Sat.; adm. fee) now houses the collection of the Washington County Historical Society.

Excursions

ANTIETAM NATIONAL BATTLEFIELD *(15 miles S on Md. 65. 301-432-5124. Adm. fee)* On September 17, 1862, these farm fields witnessed the bloodiest one-day battle of the Civil War, when Lee's army clashed with McClellan's and 23,000 men fell in battle. A driving tour leads past the Sunken Road, Dunker Church, and other sites associated with the ferocious fighting, and an observation tower allows a sweeping overview of the battlefield. Many of the Union dead are buried in the **Antietam National Cemetery.**

FORT FREDERICK *(20 miles SW via I-70 and Md. 56. 301-842-2155. Visitor Center open daily May-Oct.; grounds open year-round)* Built in the 1750s to protect against encroachment from the French and Indians, the massive stone fortress was restored in the 1930s by the Civilian Conservation Corps.

MARTINSBURG, W.VA. *(16 miles SW via US 11)* See page 201.

SHEPHERDSTOWN, W.VA. *(17 miles SW via Md. 65 and 34)* See page 201.

HARPERS FERRY, W.VA. *(27 miles S via Md. 65, Md. 34, W. Va. 230, and US 340)* See page 201.

Other Sites in Maryland

Calvert Marine Museum *(Md. 2 in Solomons. 410-326-2042. Adm. fee)* Centered around the old Drum Point Lighthouse, the museum's several buildings celebrate the human and natural history of the Chesapeake Bay.

Chesapeake & Ohio Canal National Historical Park The 184.5-mile canal was begun in 1828 as a trade route between Washington and the western frontier. It now serves as a recreation corridor. **Great Falls Tavern Visitor Center** *(MacArthur Blvd. and Falls Rd., Potomac. 301-299-3613. Adm. fee)* offers historical exhibits and short cruises on a canalboat *(fee).*

Chestertown *(Chamber of Commerce, 400 S. Cross St. 410-778-0416)* Graced with fine houses from the 1700s, the old port on the Chester River celebrates its past at the **Geddes-Piper House** *(101 Church Alley. 410-778-3499. Wed.-Mon.; adm. fee),* a museum operated by the historical society. You can take tea at the **White Swan Tavern B&B** *(410-778-2300)* on High Street.

Clara Barton National Historic Site *(5801 Oxford Rd., Glen Echo. 301-492-6246)* Barton, a former Pension Office clerk and famed Civil War nurse who founded the American Red Cross, lived in this house in the late 19th and early 20th centuries; the house served briefly as Red Cross headquarters.

Fort Washington Park *(Fort Washington Rd. off Indian Head Hwy., Prince Georges County. 301-763-4600. Adm. fee)* Begun in 1815, the fort was completed in 1824 and became a strategic Union defense during the Civil War.

Historic St. Marys City *(Off Md. 5. 301-862-0990 or 800-SMC-1634. Mid-March–Nov. Wed.-Sun.; adm. fee)* In 1634 a group of colonists led by Leonard Calvert landed here on the banks of what they called the St. Marys River and established a settlement that would serve as Maryland's colonial capital until 1694. The 800-acre living history complex now on the site features reconstructions of colonial buildings, the Archaeology Exhibit Hall, and a replica of the 17th-century pinnace, the *Maryland Dove,* that accompanied the first group of settlers across the Atlantic.

Washington, D.C.

West front of the U.S. Capitol

In 1790 the fledgling Congress of the newly founded United States empowered President Washington to find a suitable site for the new seat of government. Washington chose a plot of land on the Potomac River, about 16 miles upriver from his own plantation at Mount Vernon, and engaged young French architect Pierre L'Enfant to design a capital worthy of the new ideals of democracy. L'Enfant's grand baroque plan envisioned a city of broad avenues, greenswards, and memorials. But lack of finances, skilled labor, and building materials thwarted such dreams. And wars perpetually interceded. In the War of 1812, the British set fire to the few official buildings; the Civil War turned the town into a vast garrison; and the World Wars saw makeshift offices and barracks sprawled across the city. Only in recent decades has Washington become the "city beautiful" that the founding fathers envisioned.

The Mall and West Potomac Park

Lincoln Memorial *(202-426-6841)* Standing to the west of the Reflecting Pool, the colonnaded marble monument (1922) houses a brooding, 19-foot-high statue of the Great Emancipator by sculptor Daniel Chester French. Thirty-six Doric columns represent the states in the Union at the time of Lincoln's death. In 1963 Martin Luther King, Jr., delivered his "I have a dream…" speech from the monument steps.

Vietnam Veterans Memorial *(Constitution Gardens at 21st St. and Constitution Ave. 202-426-6841)* The polished granite "Wall," two joined triangles set into a hillside, is inscribed with the names of the 58,000 casualties of Vietnam. Three more conventional war monuments stand nearby—one to women (1994) and another (1984) to men who served in Vietnam, and a third (1995) to Korean War soldiers.

Washington Monument *(15th St. and Constitution Ave. NW. 202-426-6841)* This 555.5-foot obelisk, the tallest masonry tower in the world, has become a symbol of the nation. Begun in 1848 with private funding, the monument remained an uncompleted shaft throughout the Civil War. When construction resumed in 1876, marble was quarried from a different source, resulting in a subtle color differentiation. An elevator whisks the perpetual line of visitors to an observation room with panoramic views.

Jefferson Memorial *(Off Ohio Dr. 202-426-6841)* Modeled on the Roman Pantheon, the domed Ionic colonnade was designed in the 1930s by John Russell Pope. At its center stands a bronze statue of the third President, with his writings on individual freedoms inscribed on the surrounding walls. Situated on the south bank of the Tidal Basin, the monument is showcased in early April by hundreds of blooming cherry trees.

U.S. Holocaust Memorial Museum *(100 Raoul Wallenberg Pl. SW. 202-488-0400. Passes necessary for Permanent Exhibit: advance passes through Protix 800-400-9373, same-day passes available from 10 a.m. at museum; arrive early.)* The highly acclaimed new addition to the Mall area is dedicated to the stories of victims of the Holocaust. Inside the massive limestone exterior, redbrick walls evoke the architecture of such death camps as Auschwitz. The Permanent Exhibit dominates the museum, tracing the rise of Hitler and his persecution of Jews and other groups.

Smithsonian Institution *(For all museums call 202-357-2700 or visit the Castle, mid-Mall on Jefferson Dr.)* Perhaps the world's most extensive collection of museums (now numbering 16), the Smithsonian owes its existence to a British man of letters, James Smithson, who bequeathed funds "to found at Washington…an Establishment for the increase and diffusion of knowledge…." Of the ten Smithsonian buildings on the Mall, three are specifically devoted to history. The **Arts and Industries Building** *(Mid-Mall on Jefferson Dr.)* reflects the Victorian decor it had when it opened in 1881 as the first National Museum. It still displays artifacts from the 1876 Philadelphia International Exhibition, as well as exhibits on the histories of African Americans and Native Americans.

Vietnam Veterans Memorial

The **National Air and Space Museum** *(Jefferson Dr. at 6th St. SW. Adm. fee for theater and planetarium shows)* celebrates aviation with such vintage aircraft as the Wright brothers' 1903 *Flyer*, Charles Lindbergh's *Spirit of St. Louis*, and the Apollo 11 capsule.

The Mall

The **National Museum of American History** (*Madison Dr. on the Mall bet. 12th and 14th Sts. NW*) displays the country's most cherished memorabilia, including many First Ladies' inaugural gowns and the original Star-Spangled Banner that inspired Francis Scott Key to write the national anthem.

Downtown Washington

National Archives (*Constitution Ave. bet. 7th and 9th Sts. NW. 202-501-5000*) The imposing neoclassical structure, another work by John Russell Pope, enshrines the country's most prized documents. Encased on a marble altar in the Rotunda are the original **Declaration of Independence,** two pages of the **Constitution,** and the **Bill of Rights.** A 1297 copy of England's **Magna Carta,** on loan from Texas financier Ross Perot, is displayed nearby.

Ford's Theatre (*10th St. between E and F Sts. 202-426-6924. Closed for tours during performances*) On April 14, 1865, President Lincoln was mortally wounded in this ornate Victorian theater by actor and Southern sympathizer John Wilkes Booth. Rebuilt to look as it did then, Ford's Theatre now functions both as a performing arts hall and a memorial to the loss of Lincoln. After the shooting, Lincoln was carried across 10th Street to **Petersen House** (*516 10th St. 202-426-6830*), where he died of his injuries.

White House Area

White House (*1600 Pennsylvania Ave. NW. 202-456-7041. Visitor Center at 15th St. near E St. NW has exhibits on the White House and issues free, same-day tickets on a first-come, first-served basis, Tues.-Sat. Contact your congressional office*

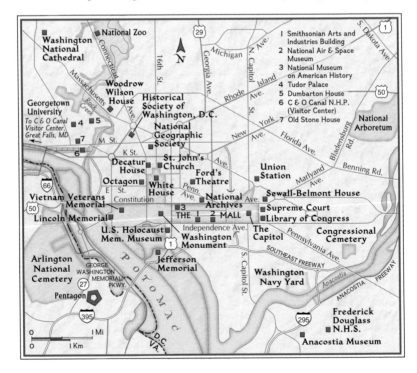

8-10 weeks in advance for guided tour tickets.) Home of the nation's First Family for almost 200 years, the White House has evolved over time, its architecture and decor frequently changing with the changing fashions and tastes of its occupants. To preserve the historical character of the house, First Lady Jacqueline Kennedy launched a campaign in the 1960s to furnish it with objects of artistic and historical note.

Great Hall of the Library of Congress

Tours include the ground-floor federal-style library and Vermeil Room, and the more elaborate first-floor reception rooms. The East Room, scene of White House parties and concerts, houses a piano played by such notables as Vladimir Horowitz and Richard Nixon. A 1797 portrait of Washington, saved by Dolley Madison in the War of 1812, also hangs here. The remains of five Presidents, including Abraham Lincoln, have lain in state in the East Room. Three small reception rooms—the Green, Red, and Blue Rooms—are decorated in early 19th-century American, British, and French Empire pieces. After a look at the ornate State Dining Room, you exit through hallways hung with presidential portraits.

St. John's Church at Lafayette Square *(16th and H Sts. N.W. 202-347-8766)* The small, beautifully proportioned church designed by Benjamin Latrobe is called the "church of the Presidents," as every Chief Executive has worshiped here since the church opened in 1815.

Decatur House *(748 Jackson Pl. N.W. 202-842-0920. Tues.-Sun.; adm. fee)* The first house (1819) to be erected on Lafayette Square was built for naval hero Stephen Decatur and designed by Latrobe. The house and its various owners played a prominent role in capital life.

Octagon *(1799 New York Ave. NW. 202-638-3105. Tues.-Sun.; adm. fee)* This federal-style house, designed by Capitol architect William Thornton, was home to President and Mrs. Madison after the "President's House" burned in the War of 1812. Here, Madison signed the Treaty of Ghent, ending the war.

Capitol Hill

The Capitol *(1st St. bet. Independence and Constitution Aves. 202-225-6827. Special pass to congressional sessions available through your congressman's office. Congress recesses in Aug. and at other times during the year.)* Dominating the high ground at the east end of the Mall, the richly embellished Capitol embodies representative government in action. Begun in 1793, the building has undergone many alterations. The cast-iron dome was completed during the Lincoln Administration and soars 180 feet above the floor of the Rotunda with its paintings, murals, and statuary. The semicircular Statuary Hall, originally the House Chamber, is edged by statues of famous Americans. The Old Senate Chamber

101

Capital Architects

A handful of early architects gave Washington many of its most compelling buildings. William Thornton, educated as a medical doctor, submitted the original Capitol drawings and designed several well-known houses. Professional architect Benjamin Latrobe had a hand in both the White House and Capitol and was responsible for St. John's Church and Decatur House. Robert Mills, who trained under Latrobe, designed the first version of the Washington Monument, as well as several government buildings. Much later, in the 1930s, John Russell Pope left a legacy of classical revival buildings.

Frederick Douglass National Historic Site

contains original furnishings. Below the Rotunda, the crypt is notable for an enormous head of Abraham Lincoln, sculptured by Gutzon Borglum. The nearby Old Supreme Court Chamber contains its original, early 19th-century furnishings. The current House and Senate Chambers are located on the second floor.

Supreme Court *(1st and E. Capitol Sts. NE. 202-479-3211. Mon.-Fri. Court terms run Oct.-April; call for hours. Public access to court sessions is on a first-come, first-served basis.)* The austere white-marble building, designed by Cass Gilbert in 1928, houses the historic courtroom where the nine highest justices of the land sit. "We are very quiet here," Justice Oliver Wendell Holmes, Jr., once said, "but it is the quiet at the storm center." On the ground floor, changing exhibits and a film recount the history of the court; a massive statue of John Marshall honors the "great chief justice."

Library of Congress *(1st St. and Independence Ave. SE. 202-707-8000. Mon.-Sat.)* The extravagant Italian Renaissance Thomas Jefferson Building is the oldest and most ornate of the three Library of Congress buildings on Capitol Hill. Opened in 1897, it is ornamented with an exuberance of murals, mosaics, statuary, and staircases in its Great Hall and Main Reading Room. In addition to serving Congress, it acts as the national library.

Sewall-Belmont House *(144 Constitution Ave. NE. 202-546-3989. Tues.-Sat.)* The federal house (1798) survives as one of the oldest structures on the Hill; exhibits tell the history of the house and of the national suffragist movement.

Union Station *(50 Massachusetts Ave. NE. 202-371-9441)* When it opened in 1907, the beaux arts edifice ranked as the largest train station in the world. A 1980s renovation returned the main lobby to its former glory.

Southeast

Anacostia Museum *(1901 Fort Pl. SE. 202-287-3369)* This Smithsonian Institution museum is dedicated to African-American history and culture.

Frederick Douglass National Historic Site *(1411 W St. SE. 202-426-5961)* The eloquent African-American orator, abolitionist, and leader lived in this pleasant Victorian clapboard from 1877 to his death in 1895.

Congressional Cemetery *(1801 E St. SE. 202-543-0539)* Created in 1807, the cemetery contains the remains of such prominent figures as Civil War photographer Mathew Brady, composer John Philip Sousa, and capital architects William Thornton and Robert Mills.

Washington Navy Yard *(9th and M Sts. SE)* Dating from 1799, the Navy's oldest shore facility celebrates naval history in its **Navy Museum** *(202-433-4882)*. The **Marine Corps Museum** *(202-433-3534. Closed Tues.)* houses memorabilia and exhibits on the history of the Corps.

Northwest

National Geographic Society's Explorers Hall *(17th and M Sts. NW. 202-*

857-7588) Interactive exhibits in the Society's headquarters museum highlight geography, Society-sponsored exploration, and stories of human adventure. Temporary exhibits focus on world culture, science, and wildlife.

Historical Society of Washington, D.C. *(1307 New Hampshire Ave. NW 202-785-2068. Wed.-Sat.; adm. fee)* The society and its archives are housed in the richly embellished 1890s mansion built by brewer Christian Heurich.

Woodrow Wilson House *(2340 S St. NW. 202-387-4062. Tues.-Sun.; adm. fee)* The dignified brick house, in the city's embassy district, was the final home of the 28th President and contains many Wilson furnishings. Wilson died here in 1924, and his body lay in state in the drawing room.

Washington National Cathedral *(Mass. and Wis. Aves. NW. 202-364-6616)* The second largest cathedral in the country, the immense Gothic edifice was begun in 1907 and completed in 1990. Three 26-foot-high rose windows dominate the Episcopal cathedral's nave. Other stained glass and sculpture throughout the nave and side chapels bear patriotic motifs.

Georgetown

Established in the mid-18th century, Georgetown predates Washington, not becoming part of the federal district until 1871. Many of its well-preserved 19th-century houses now belong to Washington's elite.

Tudor Place *(31st and Q Sts. NW. 202-965-0400. Tues.-Sat; donations)* Designed by Capitol architect William Thornton for the granddaughter of

103

Martha Washington, the federal house was occupied by family descendants until 1983; its decor and furnishings span six generations.

Dumbarton House *(2715 Q St. NW. 202-337-2288. Donations)* The late 18th-century house typifies Georgetown's federal architecture and now features furnishings and decorative period costumes.

Chesapeake and Ohio Canal National Historical Park

Chesapeake and Ohio (C&O) Canal National Historical Park *(Below M St. NW. Visitor Center, 1057 Thomas Jefferson St. NW. 202-653-5844)* Built as an early 19th-century shipping route, the 184.5-mile canal has become a major recreation corridor, though flooding in 1996 damaged portions of it.

Old Stone House *(3051 M St. NW. 202-426-6851. Wed.-Sun.)* Oldest house still standing in the city, the simple stone structure dates from 1765.

Excursions

ARLINGTON NATIONAL CEMETERY, VA. *(1 mile E across Memorial Bridge)* See page 122.

ALEXANDRIA, VA. *(5 miles S via George Wash. Mem. Pkwy.)* See p. 106.

CLARA BARTON N.H.S., MD. *(7 miles W via MacArthur Blvd.)* See p. 97.

C&O CANAL N.H.P., MD. *(10 miles W via MacArthur Blvd.)* See p. 97.

The South

No part of the country boasts a greater consciousness of itself as a region nor a greater obsession with its history than the South. With the Spanish establishment of St. Augustine in 1565 and the English settlement of Jamestown in 1607, the South began its long, varied story. In 1619 the first African slaves landed in Virginia, presaging a system that would define the region for generations to come. After a difficult start, the colonists struck on tobacco, rice, indigo, sugar, and cotton as cash crops that would ensure success for both the large planters and the more numerous small farmers.

Virginia and the Carolinas played strong roles in the American Revolution, contributing many of the country's early leaders and heroes. Yet by 1861 a majority of white Southerners—led by South Carolinians and Mississippians—opted

to secede from the Union.

After the dual traumas of the Civil War and Reconstruction, it took decades for much of the region to recover its economic health and sense of direction. Not until the mid-20th century did the South at last stand on the brink of industrial development and improved race relations.

Thomas Jefferson's University of Virginia

MD.

Leesburg

Manassas N.B.P.

Winchester

Arlington Nat. Cemetery

Alexandria

WEST VIRGINIA

Shenandoah Valley Driving Tour

Front Royal

Montpelier

Gunston Hall Plantation

Fredericksburg

George Washington Birthplace Nat. Mon.

Museum of American Frontier Culture

Charlottesville

Appomattox Court House N.H.P.

Richmond

Williamsburg

Lexington

Lynchburg

Roanoke

Poplar Forest

Red Hill

Petersburg

VA.

James River Plantations

Norfolk

Virginia Beach

KY.

Booker T. Washington Nat. Mon.

Historic Crab Orchard Museum

Blue Ridge Institute

Halifax

Wright Brothers Nat. Mem.

Edenton

Roanoke Island

TENN.

Winston-Salem

Greensboro

Durham

Raleigh

Cherokee Indian Reservation

Fort Dobbs S.H.S.

Asheville

Salisbury

NORTH CAROLINA

Dallas

Reed Gold Mine S.H.S.

New Bern

Russell Cave Nat. Mon.

Carl Sandburg Home N.H.S.

Charlotte

Beaufort

Huntsville

Chickamauga and Chattanooga N.M.P.

Spartanburg

Kings Mt. N.M.P.

Moores Creek N.B.

Rome

New Echota S.H.S.

Clemson

McConnells

Wilmington

Gadsden

Kennesaw

Abbeville

Ninety Six N.H.S.

Camden

Brunswick Town S.H.P.

Fort Fisher S.H.S.

Anniston

Atlanta

Athens

Columbia

SOUTH CAROLINA

Childersburg

Washington

Brookgreen Gardens

Dadeville

Little White House

Augusta

Milledgeville

Georgetown

Hampton Plantation S.P.

Columbus

Macon

Middleton Place

Charleston

Tuskegee Institute N.H.S.

Montgomery

Westville

GEORGIA

Americus

Beaufort

Hunting Island Lighthouse

Eufaula

Savannah

Fort McAllister S.H.P.

Kolomoki Indian Mounds S.H.P.

Tifton

Fort King George S.H.S.

Thomasville

Brunswick

Tallahassee

Stephen Foster State Folk Culture Center

Kingsley Plantation

San Marcos de Apalache S.H.S.

Jacksonville

St. Augustine

Fort Matanzas Nat. Mon.

Marjorie Kinnan Rawlings S.H.S.

Bulow Plantation S.H.S.

Ormond Beach

Daytona Beach

Ponce de Léon Inlet Lighthouse

Dade Battlefield S.H.S.

Orlando

FLORIDA

Tampa

Gamble Plantation S.H.S.

Gilbert's Bar House of Refuge

Bradenton

Sarasota

Fort Myers

Palm Beach

Fort Lauderdale

Miami

Dry Tortugas National Park

Key West

Duke of Gloucester Street, Colonial Williamsburg

In 1607 a band of English adventurers arrived on Virginia's shores and established a tentative toehold on the continent, calling it Jamestown. Though the settlement seemed destined to fail, its fortunes reversed dramatically when a young man named John Rolfe managed to hybridize a mellow, smokable tobacco. In the next century, the great Georgian houses of tobacco barons sprouted along riverfronts, as did the invidious institution of slavery. As the Colonies grew, war with Britain became imminent. By the 1770s Virginia's patriots—Washington, Jefferson, Madison, and others—were at the forefront of revolution. Afterward, as the new country began its experiment with representative government, Virginia contributed four of the first five Presidents. But in less than a century, the state had ceded its place in the Union to join the Confederacy. For four bloody years, much of Virginia became a battleground, and the memories of that lost cause still haunt the Old Dominion. More recent wars brought Virginia—with its strong federal, military, and industrial areas—a prosperity that has lasted to the present.

Alexandria

Just across the Potomac River from the U.S. capital, Alexandria actually predates Washington. Established in 1749, it has played its own role in the nation's history, serving as a meeting place for Revolutionary patriots and early Federalists. Rows of well-tended Georgian and federal houses still line its 30-block historic area.

Historic District Walking Tour ·············· 1 day

1. Begin at **Ramsay House Visitor Center** (*King and N. Fairfax Sts. 703-838-4200*), a small clapboard moved here from an outlying area and now the town's oldest building (1724).

2. The **Stabler-Leadbeater Apothecary Shop** (*105-107 S. Fairfax St. 703-836-3713. Adm. fee*) is lodged in two historic town houses; one of them is a museum that retains the appearance and pharmaceutical accoutrements of the mid-19th century, including prescriptions once filled here for illustrious Virginians.

3. The dignified 18th-century town houses in the 200 block of **Prince Street** have earned it the sobriquet **Gentry Row,** while the quaint houses of the cobbled 100 block are called **Captain's Row.**

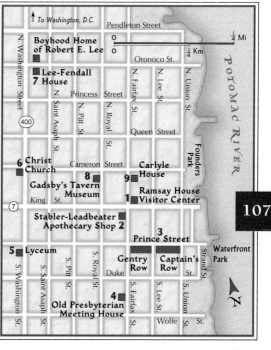

To Washington, D.C.

4. At George Washington's death in 1799, a public memorial service was held at the **Old Presbyterian Meeting House** (*321 S. Fairfax St. 703-549-6670*). The original 1772 church was destroyed by lightning in 1835 but rebuilt in 1837. The tomb of the Unknown Soldier of the Revolutionary War lies in the cemetery.

5. Constructed as a cultural center and lecture hall in the 1830s, the Greek Revival **Lyceum,** Alexandria's History Museum (*201 S. Washington St. 703-838-4994. Donations*), traces the town's history from colonial seaport to the present.

6. In the simple but elegant interior of 1773 **Christ Church** (*118 N. Washington St. 703-549-1450. Donations*), the pews where George Washington and Robert E. Lee worshiped are marked by plaques. Much of the original woodwork remains.

7. The **Lee-Fendall House** (*614 Oronoco St. 703-548-1789. Tues.-Sun.; adm. fee*) was built by Robert E. Lee's uncle in 1785 and occupied by family members for over a century, later becoming home to labor leader John L.

Stabler-Leadbeater Apothecary Shop

107

Lewis. It is filled with Lee possessions. The more modest 1795 brick town house across Oronoco Street was the **Boyhood Home of Robert E. Lee** (*607 Oronoco St. 804-548-8454. Feb.–mid-Dec.; adm. fee*). Fatherless at a young age, Lee shouldered much of the responsibility for his arthritic mother.

8. Gadsby's Tavern Museum (*134 N. Royal St. 703-838-4242. Tues.-Sun.; adm. fee*), an 18th-century tavern and hotel frequented by such notables as Washington and Jefferson, offers tours of its dining rooms, bedchambers, and two ballrooms.

9. The most imposing dwelling in town, the Georgian Palladian **Carlyle House** (*121 N. Fairfax St. 703-549-2997. Tues.-Sun.; adm. fee*) was built by John Carlyle, one of the prominent Scottish entrepreneurs who helped develop Alexandria in its early decades. In 1755 British general Edward Braddock held a Governors Council here, attended by five royal governors.

Other Sites in Alexandria

George Washington Masonic National Memorial (*King St. and Callahan Dr. 703-683-2007*) The imposing monument, built in 1932, boasts a collection of Washington's personal effects and dioramas on his life.

Fort Ward Museum and Historic Site (*4301 W. Braddock Rd. 703-838-4848. Tues.-Sun.*) The 45-acre site preserves earthworks from one of the series of Civil War forts constructed to protect Washington, D.C. The museum features Civil War artifacts.

Excursions

ARLINGTON NATIONAL CEMETERY (*7 miles N via George Washington Mem. Pkwy.*) See page 122.

WASHINGTON, D.C. (*5 miles N via George Washington Mem. Pkwy.*) See page 98.

GEORGE WASHINGTON'S MOUNT VERNON ESTATE AND GARDENS (*10 miles S via George Washington Mem. Pkwy. 703-780-2000. Adm. fee*) Now a national icon, George Washington's plantation occupies the bluffs above the Potomac, its well-known, red-roofed mansion meticulously restored to its appearance when George and Martha lived here in the mid- to late 18th century. The plantation life that Washington loved is re-created in scattered dependencies. He and Martha are entombed in a vault near the river, and a museum holds family memorabilia.

WOODLAWN PLANTATION (*13 miles S via George Washington Mem. Pkwy. to Mount Vernon, then Va. 235W to US 1. 703-780-4000. March-Dec., weekends Jan.-Feb.; adm. fee*) Designed by Capitol architect William Thornton, the stately 1805 Georgian was the home of Nelly and Lawrence Lewis. (Nelly was the granddaughter of Martha Washington, and Lewis was Washington's nephew.) The house now contains pieces from Mount Vernon and Lewis family furnishings. Moved to the grounds, the **Pope-Leighey House,**

Virginia's Presidents

Virginia has given the country eight Presidents, more than any other state. Four of the first five Chief Executives were Virginians: George Washington, Thomas Jefferson, James Madison, and James Monroe. The ninth President, 68-year-old William Henry Harrison, was also a Virginian. He survived only a month in office and was succeeded by his Vice President and fellow Virginian, John Tyler. Both men were born within miles of one another on James River estates. The 12th President, military hero Zachary Taylor, was born in the Virginia Piedmont, not far from James Madison's Montpelier. Woodrow Wilson, the state's final contribution to date, served as 28th President during World War I. His efforts in establishing the League of Nations earned him the 1919 Nobel Peace Prize.

a modest low-slung structure, was designed by Frank Lloyd Wright in 1940 as one of his Usonian residences—affordable homes for the middle class.

GUNSTON HALL PLANTATION *(20 miles S via US 1. 703-550-9220. Adm. fee)* Completed in 1758-59, the Georgian house of influential colonial statesman George Mason is justifiably renowned for its extravagant wood carving, the work of indentured servant William Buckland. The estate grounds contain outbuildings and impressive boxwood gardens.

George Washington's Mount Vernon, near Alexandria

Appomattox Court House N.H.P. ....

(Va. 24. 804-352-8987. Adm. fee) Set amid the rural Virginia Piedmont, this cluster of buildings was the scene of Robert E. Lee's surrender to Ulysses S. Grant on April 9, 1865. The 1,700-acre site includes a score of restored or reconstructed buildings, including the courthouse and the Clover Hill Tavern, where Southern paroles were printed. Lee and Grant signed the surrender in the parlor of the two-story Wilmer McLean house, since reconstructed.

Excursions

THOMAS JEFFERSON'S POPLAR FOREST *(25 miles W via US 460. Va. 662 and 661, outside Lynchburg. 804-525-1806. Late April–Nov. Wed.-Sun.; adm. fee)* Thomas Jefferson began building this lovely octagonal villa-style retreat in 1806. Now under restoration, the house allows visitors a firsthand look at the historic restoration process.

RED HILL PATRICK HENRY NATIONAL MEMORIAL *(25 miles S via US 460, Va. 47, and 40. Off Rte. 619, near Brookneal. 804-376-2044. Adm. fee)* The fiery orator of the Revolution, Patrick Henry, spent the last five years of his life here. His simple, five-room house has been reconstructed, along with several dependencies, his law office, and a modern museum.

Charlottesville ....

(Monticello Visitor Center, Va. 20 S. 804-977-1783) Charlottesville and surrounding Albemarle County are frequently called Jefferson Country because of Thomas Jefferson's abiding influence on this part of the Piedmont.

University of Virginia *(Visitor information in Rotunda, on University Ave. at Rugby Rd. 804-924-1019)* Jefferson founded and designed this university between 1817 and 1826, basing its architectural plan "on the illimitable freedom of the human mind to explore…." Now a UNESCO world heritage site, the historic core of the university centers on the domed Rotunda, modeled on Rome's Pantheon, its interior restored to its original Jeffersonian appearance. Flanking the central green space, called the

Lawn, Jefferson's "academical village" stretches in Tuscan colonnades fronting student rooms and pavilions. **Edgar Allan Poe's room,** where the poet spent a year as a student before lack of funds forced him to leave, is preserved on the west range.

Jefferson's bedroom, Monticello

Monticello (Va. 53. 804-984-9822. Adm. fee) Architectural critics consider Jefferson's domed home one of America's most distinctive houses. An inveterate architect himself, Jefferson modified Monticello frequently throughout his lifetime. Its rooms and their innovative furnishings reflect his restless intellect and love of the classical. A meticulous restoration of his gardens has put Monticello at the forefront of historical horticulture. Jefferson died here on Independence Day 1826. The obelisk on the grounds above his grave bears the epitaph he wrote.

Ash Lawn-Highland (James Monroe Pkwy. 804-293-9539. Adm. fee) Thomas Jefferson enticed his compatriot James Monroe to this spot. Monroe and his family lived in the simple farmhouse he called Highland from 1799 to 1823; it still contains Monroe furnishings.

Excursion

MONTPELIER (20 miles NE via Va. 20, near Orange. 540-672-2728. March-Dec., weekends only Jan.-Feb.; adm. fee) The "Great Little Madison" retired here to the family estate after serving as the country's fourth President, and he and his wife, Dolley, are buried on the grounds. At the turn of the century, the du Pont family purchased the estate and doubled the size of the house. Now very sparsely furnished and undergoing architectural and archaeological research, the glowing salmon-colored house reflects both families' tenures.

Fredericksburg ······································

(Visitor Center, 706 Caroline St. 540-373-1776 or 800-678-4748) This strategic site just below the fall line of the Rappahanock River was laid out as a tobacco port in 1728 and has many associations with George Washington's family. During the Civil War, Fredericksburg's location midway between Washington and Richmond resulted in four major battles in the area. Today the town remembers its past at the **Fredericksburg Area Museum and Cultural Center** (907 Princess Anne St. 540-371-3037. Adm. fee). The historic core of town, centered around Caroline Street, boasts a number of restored 18th- and 19th-century buildings.

James Monroe Museum and Memorial Library (908 Charles St. 540-654-1043. Adm. fee) Located on land owned by Monroe in the 1780s, the museum holds a large number of family pieces, including two Rembrandt Peale portraits of Monroe and the directoire desk on which the fifth President wrote his 1823 annual message to Congress, a part of which is now called the Monroe Doctrine.

Hugh Mercer Apothecary Shop (1020 Caroline St. 540-373-3362. Adm. fee) George Washington's friend and Scottish patriot Hugh Mercer established an apothecary in the mid-1700s. This re-creation features period items.

Rising Sun Tavern (1304 Caroline St. 540-371-1494. Adm. fee) Built as a private home about 1760 by George Washington's brother Charles, the clapboard building was converted to a tavern in 1792 and is now interpreted as such with exceptional authenticity.

Mary Washington House *(1200 Charles St. 540-373-1569. Adm. fee)* George Washington bought this pleasant clapboard house for his mother in 1772 and often visited here. It still contains some of her effects.

Kenmore Plantation and Gardens *(1201 Washington Ave. 540-373-3381. March-Dec., weekends Jan.-Feb.; adm. fee)* The elegant Georgian residence, renowned for its plasterwork, once stood at the heart of a 1,300-acre plantation that was home to George Washington's sister, Betty, and her husband, Fielding Lewis.

Fredericksburg and Spotsylvania National Military Park *(Visitor Center, 1013 Lafayette Blvd. 540-371-0802)* This park preserves several historic structures and four major battlefields associated with the Civil War. The **Fredericksburg Battlefield** centers on Marye's Heights, where the Union suffered horrific losses while attempting to storm the Confederate-held hill in December 1862. The **Battle of Chancellorsville** (May 1863) is recalled in a Visitor Center and self-guided drive through woodlands in the countryside west of town. During this engagement, Stonewall Jackson was mistakenly shot by southern riflemen. He died ten days later. The farm office in which he succumbed is now the park's **Stonewall Jackson Shrine.** In May 1864 the forces of Lee and Grant squared off in the tangled brushland known as the **Wilderness,** and a day later they met again at **Spotsylvania Court House,** where they fought for two weeks. The park also offers exhibits at **Chatham** *(120 Chatham La., Stafford),* an 18th-century house used as headquarters by the Union Army.

111

Excursions

GEORGE WASHINGTON BIRTHPLACE NATIONAL MONUMENT *(40 miles SE via Va. 3 to Va. 204. 804-224-1732. Adm. fee)* In 1732 Washington was born here in a modest plantation house on the banks of Popes Creek. Destroyed by fire in 1779, the original house was replaced by a colonial revival "memorial house" in the 1930s. The National Park Service now operates the grounds as a working colonial-era farm.

STRATFORD HALL PLANTATION *(40 miles SE on Va. 3 to Va. 214. 804-493-8038. Adm. fee)* The grand, H-shaped mansion, now sparsely furnished, was the ancestral home of the Lees, one

Marye's Heights, Fredericksburg Battlefield

of the state's—and the early nation's—most respected families. Thomas Lee, who built the brick house in the 1730s, fathered two signers of the Declaration of Independence—Richard Henry and Francis Lightfoot Lee. Their cousin "Light Horse" Harry Lee, a famous Revolutionary cavalry commander, was living here when his son Robert was born.

James River Plantations ....

Upriver from Williamsburg, along the banks of the James, Virginia's colonial gentry established large plantations crowned by baronial 18th-century houses, a number of which still stand. *(Combination tickets available at plantations.)*

Shirley Plantation *(Shirley Plantation Rd. off Va. 5 and Rte. 608. 804-829-5121 or 800-232-1613. Adm. fee)* Shirley Plantation was established in 1613, and the impressive hipped-roof Queen Anne house, built by the Carters in the 1720s is still occupied by Hill-Carter family members. (Robert E. Lee's mother, Anne Hill Carter Lee, was born here.) Furnished with impressive 18th- and 19th-century family pieces, the house is justifiably famous for the square-rigged, or flying, staircase.

112

Shirley Plantation on the James

Berkeley Plantation *(12602 Harrison Landing Rd. off Va. 5. 804-829-6018. Adm. fee)* The redbrick Georgian plantation house (1726) witnessed the birth of Benjamin Harrison, signer of the Declaration of Independence, and William Henry Harrison, the 9th President; the 23rd President, Benjamin Harrison, considered it his ancestral home. During the 1862 Union campaign to take Richmond, the Northern commander, Maj. Gen. George McClellan, headquartered on the grounds.

Westover *(7000 Westover Rd. off Va. 5. 804-829-2882. Grounds open year-round, house open Garden Week in April; adm. fee)* The aristocratic Col. William Byrd constructed Westover, perhaps the most elegant Georgian house in America, in 1730. A line of century-old tulip poplars now adorns its riverfront facade.

Sherwood Forest *(Va. 5. 804-829-5377. Adm. fee)* John Tyler retired to this long, graceful frame house after serving as tenth President (1841-45). Built about 1730, the house was "modernized" by Tyler's young wife. Still occupied by Tyler descendants, it is furnished with family antiques.

Leesburg ·······················

(Visitor Center, Market Station. 703-777-0519 or 800-752-6118) Established in 1758, the small town has long served as the seat of Loudoun County. The **Loudoun Museum** *(16 Loudoun St. SW. 703-777-7427. Closed Jan.; donations)* features artifacts and a video on area history. Walking tours originating here take in the federal buildings in the town's historic core.

Morven Park *(1.5 miles W on Va. 7 and Morven Park Rd. 703-777-2414. April-Oct. Tues.-Sun., Nov. weekends; adm. fee)* The dignified 19th-century Greek Revival mansion was home of Maryland governor Thomas Swann early in the 19th century and of Virginia governor Westmoreland Davis from 1903 to 1942. Davis's wife collected the European tapestries and furnishings now ornamenting it. The estate's 1,200 acres include a boxwood garden, the **Museum of Hounds and Hunting,** and a carriage collection.

Excursions

OATLANDS *(8 miles S on US 15. 703-777-3174. April-Dec. Tues.-Sun. Adm. fee)* Reflecting more than a century of tastes and styles, the white stucco Greek Revival mansion was built in 1810 by George Carter, a great-grandson of Robert "King" Carter, colonial Virginia's major landholder. The current furnishings belonged to the house's early 20th-century owners, the Eustices. The estate is renowned for its restored gardens.

MANASSAS NATIONAL BATTLEFIELD PARK *(21 miles S via US 15 to Va. 234E. 703-361-1339. Adm. fee)* In July 1861 these rolling hills cut by a stream called Bull Run witnessed the first major land battle in the Civil War—an unexpected Union defeat that shocked the Northern public. During the fighting, the heroics of Confederate commander Thomas Jonathan Jackson earned him his legendary sobriquet, "Stonewall." A year later the Second Battle of Manassas also ended in a victory for the South. A Visitor Center and self-guided drive interprets the battles and their effects on the morale of both sides. In the nearby city of Manassas, the **Manassas Museum** *(9101 Prince William St. 703-368-1873. Tues.-Sun.; adm. fee)* covers the history of Virginia's Piedmont region.

WATERFORD *(10 miles NW via Va. 7W, Va. 9N, and Rte. 662)* This well-preserved Quaker mill town, with its 250-year history and old stone buildings, now enjoys the status of a national historic landmark and a reputation as one of the state's most charming spots.

FREDERICK, MARYLAND *(20 miles N via US 15)* See page 95.

HARPERS FERRY, W.VA. *(17 miles NW via Va. 9)* See page 201.

Shenandoah Valley Civil War Driving Tour ············
2 days, 150 miles

"Breadbasket of the Confederacy," the Shenandoah Valley became one of the most hotly contested areas of the Civil War. A strategic route linking western Virginia with the Federal capital of Washington, the valley witnessed one battle after another, its peaceful fields becoming a killing ground. This route leads past some of the major battlefields and other sites that were associated with the war. The state publishes a brochure entitled "Civil War Campaigns of Virginia's Shenandoah Valley."

1. Begin in **Winchester,** founded in 1754 and the northern gateway to the valley. Due to its strategic location, it changed hands often throughout the Civil War. The **Shenandoah Valley Civil War Center** *(Old Town Welcome Center, 2 N. Cameron St. 540-722-6367)* provides an

Civil War reenactment, New Market Battlefield State Historical Park

overview of the military engagements that took place in the valley over the course of the war. Two cemeteries, the **National Cemetery** (*National Ave.*) and the nearby **Stonewall Cemetery** (*Mount Hebron Cemetery, Boscawen St.*) honor soldiers who fell in the Winchester battles. **Stonewall Jackson's Headquarters** (*415 N. Braddock St. 540-667-3242. April-Oct.; adm. fee*) were set up in this pleasant Gothic Revival house during the winter of 1861-62, prior to the general's legendary Valley Campaign through the Shenandoah. In early March, he evacuated Winchester as Union forces overran the town.

2. A few miles out of town, a marker off US 11 commemorates the first **Battle of Kernstown,** where on March 23, 1862, Jackson's forces fired the first salvo in the Valley Campaign, considered one of the most brilliant campaigns in military history. For two months, Jackson's vastly outnumbered forces outmanuevered and outfought several Union contingents, keeping them occupied in the Shenandoah and unable to participate in the Northern Army's march on Richmond.

3. About 5 miles farther south, a sign marks the **Battle of Cedar Creek,** where later in the war the Union enjoyed a resounding victory under Phil Sheridan. In 1864 General Grant sent Sheridan into the valley to "make of it a wasteland, so that even crows flying overhead would have to bring their own provender." Some of Sheridan's officers headquartered at adjacent **Belle Grove Plantation** (*540-869-2028. Mid-March–Oct.; adm. fee*), an imposing stone mansion built in the late 1700s by Isaac Hite, Jr., brother-in-law of James Madison. Thomas Jefferson is believed to have had a hand in its design.

4. In **Strasburg,** Union commanders Nathaniel Banks and James Shields headquartered at what is now the **Hupp's Hill Battlefield Park and Study Center** (*US 11. 703-465-5884*) during the Valley Campaign.

5. The flamboyant Confederate spy Belle Boyd frequently visited this modest home of her aunt and uncle in **Front Royal** during the Civil War. Since moved from its original location, the **Belle Boyd Cottage** (*101 Chester St. 540-636-1446. Daily May-Oct., Nov.-April Mon.-Fri.; adm. fee*) now details area events during the war. The adjacent **Ivy Lodge** (*Mon.-Fri.*) offers more local history exhibits. Also in Front Royal the **Warren Rifles Confederate Museum** (*95 Chester St. 540-636-6982. Mid-April–mid-Nov.; adm. fee*) celebrates the exploits of Stonewall Jackson, Belle Boyd, and others.

6. Placid green fields now mark the **New Market Battlefield State Historical Park** (*8895 Collins Dr. 540-740-3101. Adm. fee*), where in May 1864 cadets of the Virginia Military Institute distinguished themselves in a battle

Flag Ceremony, Virginia Military Institute, Lexington

that ended in Confederate victory. The **Hall of Valor** recounts their role in the battle. The 19th-century **Bushong Farm** still stands on the battlefield. The nearby **New Market Battlefield Military Museum** *(9500 Collins Dr. 540-740-8065. Mid-March–Nov.; adm. fee)* displays a collection of Civil War and other military memorabilia.

7. In March 1865, in the town of **Waynesboro**, Jubal Early's war-weary troops made their final attempt to hold off Federal forces in the Shenandoah. Bested by Union troops under Custer (later of the Little Bighorn), Early managed to escape capture. A pillar commemorates Confederate heroism.

8. The home of two Confederate greats, the lovely college town of **Lexington** *(Visitor Center, 106 E. Washington St. 540-463-3777)* preserves the simple brick **Stonewall Jackson House** *(8 E. Washington St. 703-463-2552. Adm. fee)*, where the then obscure Jackson lived while a professor at VMI. The **Stonewall Jackson Memorial Cemetery** contains the Confederate hero's remains and a statue of him by Edward Valentine.

After the war, Robert E. Lee became president of Washington College, since renamed **Washington and Lee University** *(Letcher Ave. 540-463-8400)*. The school honors its former president in the Victorian **Lee Chapel.** Built under Lee's supervision, the chapel shelters the famous recumbent statue of Lee by Edward Valentine and a Charles Willson Peale portrait of George Washington, who helped fund an early academy that was a precursor of the university. In the lower-level crypt, Lee is buried with his family.

The nearby **Virginia Military Institute** *(Letcher Ave. 540-464-7000)* encompasses the **VMI Jackson Memorial Hall** *(Letcher Ave.)*, where a mural depicts the charge of VMI cadets at the 1864 Battle of New Market. Downstairs, the **Virginia Military Institute Museum** *(540-464-7232. Donations)* traces the institute's history and the contributions of its faculty and graduates.

Norfolk ···

(Visitor Center, End of Fort View St. 757-441-1852) This pivotal naval town, founded in the 1680s, has played a role in every American war since the Revolution. In 1776 royal governor Lord Dunmore ordered the town shelled, and one of his cannonballs still lodges in the wall of **St. Paul's Episcopal Church** *(201 St. Paul's Blvd. 757-627-4353. Tues.-Fri.; donations)*, the only building to survive the subsequent burning of the town.

MacArthur Memorial *(MacArthur Square. 757-441-2965)* The 1850s city hall designed by Thomas U. Walter (a U.S. Capitol architect) has been transformed into a mausoleum and museum to the controversial 20th-century general.

Moses Myers House *(331 Bank St. 757-664-6283. Tues.-Sun.; adm. fee)* The elegant 15-room town house (1792) was the home of Norfolk's first Jewish family, the Myers, and remained in family hands until 1931. Still furnished with family pieces, it includes portraits by Stuart and Sully.

115

Nauticus: The National Maritime Center *(1 Waterside Dr. 757-664-1000. Daily Mem. Day–Labor Day, Tues.-Sun. rest of year; adm. fee)* Inside this cavernous new hands-on, high-tech museum, the Navy maintains the **Hampton Roads Naval Museum** *(757-444-8971)*, dedicated to the naval history of the area from the Revolutionary War to the present.

Excursions

FORT MONROE *(5 miles N via I-64 and US 258 in Hampton)* Begun as a link in the chain of coastal defenses designed by Simon Bernard after the War of 1812, the hexagonal, moated fortress, with its sod roof, now holds the **Casemate Museum** *(757-727-3391)*. Tracing the area's long military history, it also showcases the cell where Jefferson Davis was held prisoner after the Civil War. The early 19th-century **Old Point Comfort Lighthouse** rises nearby.

FORT WOOL *(Via commercial tour boat or private boat. April-Sept. Inquire at Hampton Visitor Center 757-727-1102)* Originally designed by Simon Bernard and modified by subsequent engineers, such as Robert E. Lee, the fortress provided artillery backup to the USS *Monitor* during the famous 1862 Battle of the Ironclads in Hampton Roads. Lincoln observed the first, unsuccessful Union invasion of Norfolk from the fort.

ADAM THOROUGHGOOD HOUSE *(17 miles E via I-264, Va. 44, and Va. 225, in Virginia Beach. 1636 Parish Rd. 757-664-6283. April-Dec. Tues.-Sun., Jan.-March Tues.-Sat.; adm. fee)* The simple English-style cottage, offset by gardens, dates from the 1600s.

LYNNHAVEN HOUSE *(15 miles E via I-264, Va. 44, and Va. 225, in Virginia Beach. 4405 Wishart Rd. 757-460-1688. June-Sept. Tues.-Sun., May and Oct. Sat.-Sun.; adm. fee)* The exceptionally well-preserved English medieval-style house dates from 1725 and recalls the lives of colonists during that period.

CAPE HENRY *(10 miles E via US 60. Through the Fort Story gate on US 60)* At the juncture of the Chesapeake Bay and the Atlantic, the cape is anchored by two lighthouses—**Old Cape Henry Lighthouse** *(757-422-9421. Mid-March–Oct.; adm. fee)*, ordered built by George Washington in 1791, and the more recent 1880s light. Nearby a cross commemorates the landing of English colonists on Virginia soil in 1607, and a statue celebrates the heroics of the Comte de Grasse, whose victory over the British in the 1781 Battle of the Capes eventually lead to Cornwallis's defeat at Yorktown.

BACON'S CASTLE *(35 miles NW via US 17 and Va. 10. 757-357-5976. April-Oct. Tues.-Sun., March and Nov. Sat.-Sun.; adm. fee)* This impressive 1665 house was commandeered in 1676 by followers of Nathaniel Bacon, who staged an early, portentous rebellion against royal power in the Colonies.

Petersburg ....

Incorporated in 1748 and a major transportation center on the Appomattox, Petersburg endured a ten-month siege by Grant's bluecoats near the end of the Civil War. That ordeal is commemorated at the **Siege Museum** *(15 W. Bank St. 804-733-2402. Adm. fee)*.

Centre Hill Mansion *(1 Centre Hill Court. 804-733-*

2401. Adm. fee) This stately residence reflects Petersburg's elegant past. The original federal house was built by a businessman in 1823. Later embellished with Greek and colonial revival details, the rooms contain impressive Victorian furnishings, a few from the original Bolling family.

Blanford Church *(319 S. Crater Rd. 804-733-2396. Adm. fee)* The 1735 church became a Confederate memorial in 1901. Louis Comfort Tiffany designed its 15 stained-glass windows, each commemorating the men of a different southern state. The church's vast cemetery dates from the early 1700s and contains the graves of some 30,000 Southern soldiers.

Petersburg National Battlefield *(Va. 36. 804-732-3531. Adm. fee)* A self-guided, 37-mile driving tour loops past earthworks erected by Union and Confederate troops during the 1864-65 siege, you can still see the infamous 30-foot-deep crater that Northern troops blasted out. In April 1865 Lee withdrew his army from Petersburg, hoping to join with Confederate forces in North Carolina. He made it as far as Appomattox. The route of **Lee's final retreat** can be traced via a narrated driving tour *(800-6RETREAT)*.

Excursion

HOPEWELL *(4 miles NE on Va. 36. Visitor Center, 201D Randolph Sq. 804-541-2206)* Formerly called City Point, this small town on the James became a massive Federal supply depot during Grant's Siege of Petersburg. Grant headquartered on the grounds of **Appomattox Manor** *(Pecan Ave. and Cedar La. 804-458-9504)*, an 18th-century house at the confluence of the Appomattox and James Rivers. The National Park Service now uses the house as an interpretive center for events at City Point; Grant's restored cabin stands on the grounds. Nearby on the Appomattox River, white frame **Weston Manor** *(Weston La. and 21st Ave. 804-458-4682. April-Oct.; adm. fee)* still contains much of its mid-18th-century woodwork.

117

Richmond ·······································

(Visitor Center, off I-64/95. 804-358-5511 or 800-444-2777) From its 1737

Union encampment near Richmond during McClellan's 1862 Peninsula Campaign

origins as a colonial port at the fall line of the James, Richmond grew steadily, becoming the state capital in the 1780s, a major industrial center, and eventually capital of the Confederacy. Though devastated by the Civil War, it has largely recovered, still serving as state capital and a corporate center, particularly for tobacco interests.

Downtown Area

State Capitol (Between 9th and 11th Sts. 804-786-4344) The domed neoclassical capitol that Thomas Jefferson designed has been in use since 1788, making it the second oldest working capitol in the U.S. Beneath its rotunda stands a statue of George Washington by French sculptor Jean-Antoine Houdon, the only statue of Washington done from life. Busts of Virginia's seven other Presidents and one of Revolutionary war hero, the Marquis de Lafayette, surround Washington. In the capitol's Hall of the House of Delegates the dashing Aaron Burr was tried for treason in 1807, with Chief Justice John Marshall presiding.

Also located on Capitol Square is the **Executive Mansion** (804-371-2642. Mon.-Fri. by appt.). Completed in 1813, it ranks as the oldest continuously occupied governor's mansion in the nation. At the northwest corner of the square, the **Washington Monument** depicts Washington on horseback, surrounded by other notable Virginians.

John Marshall House (818 E. Marshall St. 804-648-7998. April-Dec. Tues.-Sat., Jan.-March by appt.; adm. fee) The "great chief justice," John Marshall, lived in this large but unpretentious brick house for much of his adult life, and the restored rooms now contain many family furnishings reflecting Marshall's simple tastes. The country's fourth chief justice, Marshall served through the early 1800s, establishing the judicial branch of government as a major force in the federal balance of power.

Museum and White House of the Confederacy (1201 E. Clay St. 804-649-1861. Adm. fee) The stuccoed brick mansion (1818) that was home to Confederate president Jefferson Davis and his family during the Civil War has been restored to the ornate Victorian appearance it had during his tenure. The adjacent museum displays an extensive collection of battle flags, weaponry, paintings, and other exhibits relating to the war.

Valentine Museum (1015 E. Clay St. 804-649-0711. Adm. fee) From its comprehensive archival repository, the museum mounts superb exhibits on "the life and history of Richmond." Its 1812 **Wickham House** preserves fine regency-style architectural details, such as a cantilevered spiral staircase and rare neoclassical wall paintings. The house interprets the life of both master and slave in early 19th-century Richmond.

Edgar Allan Poe Museum (1914-16 E. Main St. 804-648-5523. Adm. fee) Occupying the Old Stone House (circa 1740)—the city's oldest residential dwelling—the museum honors the tragic life of Richmond's greatest literary genius. Poe was raised in Richmond by foster parents, later returning to work on the Southern Literary Messenger.

St. John's Church (2401 E. Broad St. 804-648-5015. Donations) In the large frame church Revolutionary patriot Patrick Henry gave his immortal 1775 "liberty...or death" speech. Poe's mother is buried in the churchyard.

Richmond National Battlefield Park (Visitor Center, 3215 E. Broad St. 804-226-1981) In 1861 this hilltop became the site of Chimborazo, a sprawling Confederate hospital complex that, during the course of the war, housed some 76,000 patients. Today, the hill serves as headquarters for a National Park Service complex that comprises ten different Civil War battle sites in and around the Richmond area; a self-guided, 80-mile tour takes in the entire complex.

Maggie L. Walker National Historic Site (*110½ E. Leight St. 804-780-1380. Wed.-Sun.*) Maggie Walker, a pioneering African-American entrepreneur, was also the first American woman to found a bank and serve as president. The brick row house where she lived from 1905 to 1934 is furnished with turn-of-the-century pieces.

West End

Monument Avenue This wide, gracious thoroughfare, lined with stately 19th-century houses, derives its name from the monuments that punctuate it. Robert E. Lee, Stonewall Jackson, Jefferson Davis, Jeb Stuart, and pioneering oceanographer Matthew Fontaine Maury are honored here. A new monument to native Richmonder and tennis great, Arthur Ashe, now stands at the avenue's west end.

Virginia Historical Society (*428 N. Boulevard. 804-358-4901. Adm. fee*) A major repository and innovator in historical research, the society and its museum mount insightful exhibits into various aspects of Virginia's past. Its historic Cheek Gallery features epic murals honoring Southern heroism in the Civil War.

Maymont (*1700 Hampton St. 804-358-7166. Tues.-Sun.; donations*) This stone Romanesque Revival house, built by Maj. James and Sallie May Dooley in the 1890s, still contains its extravagant Gilded Age furnishings, including an elaborate swan-shaped bed and a Tiffany-designed table of silver and carved narwhal tusks. The estate's extensive grounds include elaborate Italian, Japanese, and English gardens.

Hollywood Cemetery (*412 S. Cherry St. 804-648-8501*) The serenely wooded hills of the historic cemetery, established in 1847, shelter the remains of Presidents James Monroe and John Tyler, Confeder-

Jefferson Davis memorial on Richmond's Monument Avenue

ate heroes Jefferson Davis and Jeb Stuart, and more than 18,000 Confederate soldiers.

Wilton (*215 S. Wilton Rd. 804-282-5936. Closed Mon.; Feb. by appt.; adm. fee*) A memorable example of Georgian architecture, the colonial mansion originally stood on the James River near Shirley Plantation and was home to members of the prestigious Randolph family. Moved to its present location upriver on the James in the 1930s, it is renowned for its extensive wood paneling and a superb collection of 18th- and early 19th-century furnishings.

Williamsburg ·····································

(Visitor Center, Va. 132Y. 757-220-7645 or 800-246-2099. General adm. fee to most Colonial Williamsburg buildings and museums listed below. Overall site and some re-created buildings are free.) Colonial Williamsburg, the celebrated 173-acre restoration of Virginia's 18th-century capital, re-creates the atmosphere here on the eve of the Revolution. Duke of Gloucester Street and its side streets are lined with 88 original and hundreds of replicated colonial structures. Well-versed costumed interpreters offer insights into life in Williamsburg during the colonial era.

Capitol *(E end of Duke of Gloucester St.)* The original 1701 capitol, destroyed by fire in 1747, has been reconstructed on its original site. The H-shaped brick edifice houses the re-created Hall of the House of Burgesses (where Patrick Henry intoned his "Caesar...had his Brutus" warning to George III), the general court, and the elegant room in which the Governor's Council met.

Governor's Palace, Colonial Williamsburg

Public Gaol *(Beside Capitol)* The small building contrasts the jail keeper's pleasant upper-level living quarters with the abysmal lower-level jail cells.

Raleigh Tavern *(E end of Duke of Gloucester St.)* The reconstructed tavern, with its gaming rooms, reception halls, and bedchambers, interprets the lively social life of the colonial capital. In 1774 patriot burgesses, disbanded by the royal governor for "treasonous" words, reconvened in the tavern's Apollo Room.

Governor's Palace *(End of Palace St.)* This elaborate reconstruction of the 1722 royal governor's palace is replete with elegant woodwork, furnishings, and an unforgettable ornamental display of firearms. Home to seven royal governors and Virginia's first two independent governors, the original palace burned in 1781. Extensive formal gardens and a boxwood maze have been resurrected behind the current reconstruction.

Peyton Randolph House *(Nicholson and N. England Sts.)* Patriot Peyton Randolph, who presided over the First and Second Continental Congresses in Philadelphia, entertained many of the colony's most notable lawmakers and revolutionaries in his spacious clapboard home.

George Wythe House *(West side of Palace St.)* The unadorned Georgian brick home of jurist and William and Mary law professor George Wythe typifies the lifestyle and architectural preferences of early 18th-century Virginia gentry. A mentor to such founding fathers as Thomas Jefferson and John Marshall, Wythe exerted an influence beyond his own lifetime.

Bruton Parish Church *(Palace and Duke of Gloucester Sts.)* Completed about 1712, the elegant cruciform brick church has held services continuously ever since. Weathered gravestones spanning centuries still punctuate the churchyard.

College of William and Mary *(West end of Duke of Gloucester St.)* King

William and Queen Mary chartered this college in 1693, and in 1695 foundations for the **Wren Building** were laid. Now the oldest academic building in use in America, the Wren contains spare, colonial-style classrooms, an ornate chapel, and a Great Hall that served as a dining room. Two Georgian structures flank the Wren: the **President's House** (1732) and the **Brafferton** (1723), the latter funded by English scientist Robert Boyle as a school for Native Americans.

Public Hospital (*S. Henry and Francis Sts.*) The stolid brick hospital that housed the mentally ill from 1773 to 1885 has been reconstructed with hospital rooms that trace the evolution of treatment for mental illness. Acclaimed architect Kevin Roche has used the hospital as an entryway to the below-ground **DeWitt Wallace Decorative Arts Gallery.** Its premier collection of decorative arts from the colonial period includes Charles Willson Peale's military portrait of a young George Washington.

Abby Aldrich Rockefeller Folk Art Center (*Off Francis St. on S. England St.*) One of the world's finest collections of American folk art boasts such masterpieces as "Baby in Red Chair" and one rendition of Edward Hick's classic "Peaceable Kingdoms."

Excursions

COLONIAL NATIONAL HISTORICAL PARK AT JAMESTOWN (*10 miles SW via Colonial Pkwy. 757-229-1733. Adm. fee*) The first colonists to Virginia founded a settlement on this small marshy island in the James. A Visitor Center now details their ordeal, and foundations from the early town that served as the colonial capital until 1699 have been excavated. A driving tour loops through the pine woods of the now virtually deserted island; across the causeway on the mainland, the park's popular **Glasshouse** features costumed artisans demonstrating colonial glassmaking.

JAMESTOWN SETTLEMENT PARK (*10 miles SW via Colonial Pkwy. 757-253-4838. Adm. fee*) The state-run facility offers a museum; re-creations of the palisaded fort of America's first permanent English colonists and an Indian village; and reproductions of the three ships that crossed the Atlantic in 1607.

COLONIAL NATIONAL HISTORICAL PARK AT YORKTOWN (*15 miles E via Colonial Pkwy. 804-898-3400*) Earthworks on these bluffs above the York River mark the site of the last major battle of the Revolution. The Visitor Center features exhibits and a docudrama on Washington's crucial victory here over Cornwallis in the autumn of 1781. A self-guided driving tour leads through the battlefields to **Moore House**—where terms of surrender were discussed—and on to **Surrender Field**—where the British capitulated on October 19.

Statue of John Smith, Jamestown

Yorktown's **Main Street** is dotted with colonial buildings, including the oldest **customshouse** in the country and the 1729 **Nelson House** (*Consult park Visitor Center for hours*), home to Revolutionary hero Thomas Nelson, Jr. Nelson is buried a block away at **Grace Church** (1697).

YORKTOWN VICTORY CENTER (*15 miles E via Colonial Pkwy., on Old Va. 238. 757-253-4838. Adm. fee*) Exhibits extensively chronicle the Revolution, from the start of colonial unrest through the Revolution and into the formation of a new nation.

CARTER'S GROVE *(8 miles SE on US 60. March-Dec. Tues.-Sun. 757-229-7453; adm. fee)* Built in the 1750s, this stately Georgian house was extensively renovated in the colonial revival style of the 1930s. Off the richly paneled entrance hall lie rooms of antiques collected by the McCrea family, the owners at the time of renovation. Fronting the James, the estate grounds encompass the remains of **Wolstenholme Towne,** a palisaded settlement built by the early colonists. An **archaeology museum** displays artifacts recovered from the town. A cluster of re-created **slave quarters** detail conditions faced by blacks on an 18th-century Virginia plantation.

Other Sites in Virginia

Arlington National Cemetery *(US 50 and Va. 110. 703-607-8052)* The simple white headstones of this compelling national cemetery sprawl across some 600 acres. Reserved for veterans of America's armed services and their families, the cemetery is punctuated by memorials to distinguished groups and persons. The **Tomb of the Unknowns** is honored by a perpetual ceremonial guard, and an eternal flame burns at the **gravesite of President John F. Kennedy;** his brother Robert lies close by. These hillsides above the Potomac River became a national cemetery in 1864, when, as an act of vengeance, Quartermaster Gen. Montgomery Meigs began burying Union dead here on the former estate of Robert E. Lee and his wife, Mary. The imposing columned portico of **Arlington House,** the Robert E. Lee Memorial, still dominates the high point in the cemetery. George Washington Parke Custis, Lee's father-in-law and George Washington's step-grandson, completed the Greek Revival mansion in 1818. Below the veranda a small monument marks the grave of **Pierre L'Enfant,** designer of the nation's capital.

Blue Ridge Institute *(Va. 40, in Ferrum. 540-365-4416. Museum galleries open Mon.-Sat. year-round; farm museum open mid-May–mid-Aug. Sat.-Sun. or by appt.; adm. fee)* Operated by Ferrum College, the institute features museum galleries and an early 19th-century farm museum dedicated to the traditional crafts and folkways of the Appalachian culture.

Booker T. Washington National Monument *(20 miles SE of Roanoke via Va. 116S and 122N. 540-721-2094)* In 1856 the African-American educator was born into slavery on this small tobacco farm. When Washington was nine, the Emancipation Proclamation set him and his family free. A re-creation of the mud-and-log slave cabin the boy lived in now stands amid the working fields and barns of the national monument.

Historic Crab Orchard Museum *(US 19/460, near Tazewell. 540-988-6755. Adm. fee)* On the site of an archaeological dig, this park displays fossilized bones and Native American artifacts. Its 13 log-and-stone buildings trace the region's pioneering and mining heritage.

Museum of American Frontier Culture *(1250 Richmond Rd., Staunton. 540-332-7850. Adm. fee)* The major groups that settled the Shenandoah Valley are superbly represented by the painstakingly reconstructed farmsteads featured here. The Ulster, German, and English farmhouses were moved to the site from Europe; the American farm is native to the valley. Costumed interpreters work the farmsteads and explain what life was like on them, both in this country and in Europe.

North Carolina

Wright brothers' historic 1903 flight, Kitty Hawk

123

The English established their first American footholds on what is now the North Carolina coast in 1585 and 1587. The tiny settlements were short lived, and the second vanished completely, becoming known as the Lost Colony. Not until the early 18th century had enough settlers moved into the Carolina region for towns to appear. The early North Carolinians, a fiercely independent lot, deposed a number of English governors and were the first colonists to vote for independence. Yet, showing a stubborn resistance to being led, the state was the second to last to ratify the Constitution, and in 1861 it was second to last to join the Confederacy. Once committed to civil war, however, North Carolina fought hard, suffering more than a fourth of the South's total casualties. Humbled and impoverished by the war, the state slowly revived in the 20th century, becoming a standard-bearer for higher education and industrial research.

Asheville

(Visitor Center, 151 Haywood St. 704-258-6101 or 800-257-1300) Soon after the completion of the grandiose Biltmore House in 1895, Asheville became one of the leading mountain resorts in the East. The resulting building boom lasted through the 1920s and left Asheville with some of the South's most impressive early 1900s architecture.

Thomas Wolfe Memorial State Historic Site *(48 Spruce St. 704-253-8304. Closed Mon. Nov.-March; adm. fee)* Stepping onto the wide front porch of this rambling late 19th-century boardinghouse is like stepping into the

Biltmore Estate, outside Asheville

pages of *Look Homeward, Angel* (1929). Family furnishings occupy the home where the novelist spent most of his childhood.

Biltmore Estate (*Off US 25. 704-255-1700 or 800-543-2961. Adm. fee*) George Vanderbilt, grandson of railroad baron Cornelius, built his French Renaissance-style château between 1889 and 1895. The nation's largest private residence, Biltmore rises in overwhelming splendor amid 8,000 hilly acres. Typifying the excesses of the Gilded Age, it boasts a medieval banquet hall with a 70-foot-high vaulted ceiling, a 10,000-volume library, a bowling alley, and an indoor swimming pool. Frederick Law Olmsted, designer of New York's Central Park, planned the 75 acres of gardens and grounds, which gradually merge into fields and woods. Plan to spend at least a half day here.

Excursions

ZEBULON B. VANCE BIRTHPLACE STATE HISTORIC SITE (*12 miles N via US 19/23, near Weaverville. 704-645-6706. Closed Mon. Nov.-March*) This site honors the state's Civil War governor. An oak-shingle cabin reconstructed around the homestead's original chimney holds furnishings typical of 1790 to 1840.

CHEROKEE INDIAN RESERVATION (*50 miles W via I-40 and US 19, in Cherokee. 704-497-9195 or 800-438-1601*) More than 7,000 Cherokee live on this 56,000-acre reservation. Historical attractions include the **Museum of the Cherokee Indian** (*704-497-3481*) and the **Oconaluftee Indian Village** (*704-497-2315. Mid-May–Oct.*), a living history complex with demonstrations of basketmaking, beadworking, and other crafts.

CARL SANDBURG HOME NATIONAL HISTORIC SITE (*30 miles SE via I-26, in Flatrock. 704-693-4178. Adm. fee to house*) The first national historic site to honor an American poet contrasts with the opulence of Biltmore. The 264-acre farm comprises ponds, pastures, a goat barn, and a book-filled house with intact Sandburg family furnishings.

Charlotte ··

(*Visitor Center, 330 S. Tryon St. 704-331-2700*) British general Charles Cornwallis briefly occupied the colonial town of Charlotte in 1780, but patriot harassment drove him from this "hornet's nest"—a moniker still used in the city seal and by local concerns.

Charlotte Museum of History (*3500 Shamrock Dr. 704-568-1774. Tues.-Sun.*) Exhibits trace area history from the late 1700s to the early 1900s; the **Hezekiah Alexander Homesite** (*Adm. fee*) features a 1774 stone house, a restored springhouse, and a reconstructed log kitchen.

Mint Museum of Art (*2730 Randolph Rd. 704-337-2000. Closed Mon.; adm.*

fee) Housed in a reconstructed Greek Revival structure that served as the country's first branch of the U.S. Mint (1837-1861 and 1867-1913), the museum's collection includes European and American paintings, locally minted gold coins, and regional crafts.

Excursions

JAMES K. POLK MEMORIAL STATE HISTORIC SITE *(10 miles S via US 521, in Pineville. 704-889-7145. Closed Mon. Nov.-March)* This unimposing site preserves 21 acres of the Polk farm, 1795 birthplace of the 11th President.

HISTORIC LATTA PLACE *(12 miles NW via Beatties Ford Rd., near Huntersville. 704-875-2312. March-Dec. Tues.-Sun.; adm. fee)* A restored plantation house (circa 1800), a replica kitchen and well house, and other buildings give insight into the life and times of a wealthy planter.

GASTON COUNTY MUSEUM OF ART AND HISTORY *(25 miles W via I-85, in Dallas. 131 W. Main St. 704-922-7681. Tues.-Sun.)* The museum is housed in the 1852 Hoffman Hotel. The former county seat preserves a handful of 19th- and early 20th-century buildings in the **Dallas Historic District.**

REED GOLD MINE STATE HISTORIC SITE *(27 miles E via N.C. 24, near Locust. 704-786-8337. Closed Mon. Nov.-March)* The first discovery of gold on U.S. soil was made here in 1799, and the area's 100 mines produced more gold than any other place in the country until the California rush of 1848-49. Exhibits explain gold formation and mining; you may try your luck at panning *(April-Nov.).*

Edenton ···

(Visitor Center, 108 N. Broad St. 919-482-2637. Guided walking tours of historic area offered) This small waterfront town, incorporated in 1722 as a colonial capital, became a hub of 18th- and early 19th-century politics, culture, and commerce. Its early citizens included two state governors, as well as signers of the Declaration of Independence and the Constitution.

The historic area along Edenton Bay is lined with old oaks and private homes with two-story porches. Buildings open to the public include **St. Paul's Episcopal Church** *(W. Gale and Church Sts. 919-482-3522),* built in the mid-1700s; the **James Iredell House State Historic Site** *(108 N. Broad St. 919-482-2637. Daily April-Oct., Tues.-Sun. Nov.-March; adm. fee),* home of a justice of the first U.S. Supreme Court; the 1767 Georgian **Chowan County Courthouse;** and the 1750s Jacobean **Cupola House.**

Edenton waterfront

Greensboro ·······································

(Visitor Center, 317 S. Greene St. 910-274-2282 or 800-344-2282) Founded in 1808, Greensboro was named for patriot general Nathanael Greene, who stood against British general Cornwallis at Guilford Courthouse. On

April 11, 1865, Jefferson Davis met here with Gen. Joseph Johnston to discuss surrender. Almost a century later, four black students made history by remaining seated at a Woolworth lunch counter after they were refused service. Their action sparked civil rights protests throughout the South, which led to passage of the 1964 federal law banning the segregation of public facilities.

Greensboro Historical Museum (*130 Summit Ave. 910-373-2043. Closed Mon.*) Two floors of exhibits highlight locals Dolley Madison and short-story writer O. Henry, the 1960 lunch counter sit-ins, transportation, and 19th-century Piedmont lifestyles. Well worth a visit.

Guilford Courthouse National Military Park (*6 miles NW, off US 220. 910-288-1776*) Though technically a defeat, the fierce battle Nathanael Greene's army waged here on March 15, 1781, against Cornwallis's Redcoats set the British up for final defeat seven months later at Yorktown. A 2.3-mile auto tour loops the battlefield.

Excursion

CHARLOTTE HAWKINS BROWN MEMORIAL STATE HISTORIC SITE (*10 miles E via I-85, in Sedalia. 6136 US 70. 910-449-4846. Closed Mon. Nov.-March*) The Palmer Memorial Institute, a respected black prep school founded by Dr. Brown, operated here from 1902 to 1971. Exhibits and a video vividly portray Brown's successful experiment in education.

New Bern ···························

(*Convention & Visitor Bureau, 219 Pollock St. 919-637-9400*) Swiss and German settlers established this picturesque town in 1710, naming it for Bern, Switzerland. Considered the state's second oldest community, New Bern (NEW-bern) served as a colonial capital from 1766 to 1776 and, later in the century, as the first state capital of North Carolina. Situated at the confluence of the Neuse and Trent Rivers, the historic district harbors 18th- and 19th-century churches, houses, and other landmarks of federal and Greek Revival design; several historic houses have been converted to fine inns.

Christ Episcopal Church (*320 Pollock St. 919-320-2109*), an 1875 Gothic Revival edifice, was built around an earlier church; on display is a Bible, prayer book, and silver Communion service given by King George II in 1752. The federal **First Presbyterian Church** (*418 New St.*) was completed in 1822. The 1808 **New Bern Academy** (*509 New St.*) operated as a Union hospital during the Civil War and now houses a history museum.

Tryon Palace Restoration Complex (*610 Pollock St. 919-638-1560 or 800-767-1560. Adm. fee*) An accidental fire in 1798 destroyed the original Georgian mansion 28 years after royal governor William Tryon took up residence here. The current 1950s reconstruction, from original plans,

---

Eastern Cherokee

North Carolina boasts a larger population of Indians than any state east of the Mississippi, thanks largely to the bravery of the few hundred Cherokee who eluded the infamous Trail of Tears march by disappearing into the Blue Ridge mountains. In 1830 an official Indian Removal Act called for the forced displacement of all eastern natives, even though the Cherokee had accommodated to the presence of white settlers. But the newcomers pressed for more and more land, and, under Army supervision, some 18,000 Cherokee were forced to walk to Oklahoma in the icy winter of 1838-39. Sick and despondent, nearly a fourth perished along the way. Those who escaped formed the core of the Eastern Band of the Cherokee, which today numbers about 9,000.

features period furnishing and artwork and is offset by 12 acres of surrounding gardens. Be sure to stop at the nearby 1780s **John Wright Stanley House** and 1830s **Dixon-Stevenson House** (*Tickets available at Tryon Palace Visitor Center*).

Raleigh

(Visitor Center, 301 N. Blount St. 919-733-3456. March-Nov. Tours of capitol and executive mansion offered) Named for Sir Walter Raleigh, North Car-

State Capitol, Raleigh

olina's capital city was planned in 1792 and laid out in the mile-square grid that still serves as the heart of the city.

Mordecai Historic Park (*1 Mimosa St. 919-834-4844. March–mid-Dec.; adm. fee*) The park encompasses the Greek Revival Mordecai House (circa 1785), once the manor of a large plantation; the relocated 1795 birthplace of President Andrew Johnson; and other structures from early Raleigh.

North Carolina Museum of History (*5 E. Edenton St. 919-715-0200. Closed Mon.*) Opened in 1994, the monolithic edifice covers almost an entire city block. Exhibits trace the state's history from precolonial days to the present, while special areas highlight folklife, women, and sports.

State Capitol (*Capitol Sq. 919-733-4994*) This neoclassical building was constructed from 1833 to 1840. In 1889 the former President of the Confederate States of America, Jefferson Davis, lay in state here.

Excursions

DURHAM (*25 miles NW via US 70*) Prestigious Duke University, which flavors the town's atmosphere, was endowed by the Duke family, whose simple beginnings are recalled at the **Duke Homestead State Historic Site and Tobacco Museum** (*2828 Duke Homestead Rd. 919-477-5498. Closed Mon. Nov.-March*). The site features the 1852 home of tobacco pioneer Washington Duke, a reconstruction of his first tobacco factory, a curing barn, and other outbuildings. A first-class museum displays packing machines, cigarette advertisements, and other cigarette paraphernalia.

The **Bennett Place State Historic Site** (*4409 Bennett Memorial Rd. 919-383-4345. Closed Mon. Nov.-March*) preserves the site where Gen. Johnston surrendered to General Sherman on April 26, 1865, 17 days after Lee surrendered to Grant. Johnston's action ended the war in the Carolinas, Georgia, and Florida. A reconstructed farmhouse, a film, and artifacts recreate the scene.

Roanoke Island

Fort Raleigh National Historic Site (*US 64. 919-473-5772*) A few months after establishing a fledgling colony here in 1587, John White returned to England for supplies, leaving more than a hundred colonists behind. Delayed for three years, he came back to Roanoke in 1590 and found no one left. Scholars have never solved the mystery of the Lost Colony, but

127

a film, a reconstructed earthen fort, and a 400-year-old Elizabethan room from England re-create their saga. *The Lost Colony* symphonic drama is performed outdoors during the summer months *(fee)*.

Elizabeth II State Historic Site *(Manteo waterfront. 919-473-1144. Nov.-March Closed Mon.; adm. fee)* This full-scale replica of a 16th-century sailing ship recalls the rugged realities of the early transatlantic voyages.

Excursion

WRIGHT BROTHERS NATIONAL MEMORIAL *(14 miles N via US 64 and US 158 in Kill Devil Hills. 919-441-7430. Adm. fee)* Aviation pioneers, brothers Orville and Wilbur Wright made the world's first powered airplane flight here on December 17, 1903. On display are model gliders, a reconstructed hangar, and the brothers' living quarters. The locally famous site historian presents a spellbinding program on early flight.

Wilmington ·····························

(Convention & Visitor Bureau, 24 N. 3rd St. 910-341-4030) North Carolina's main seaport, Wilmington was incorporated in 1739 and had become the state's largest town by 1780. An early hotbed of resistance, the town defied the Stamp Act in 1765 and later was the Confederacy's principal entry for blockade-runners and its last port to fall.

Wilmington has lovingly preserved its history in an extensive downtown waterfront teeming with antebellum houses and churches, as well as charming restaurants and shops. The 1770 Georgian **Burgwin-Wright House** *(224 Market St. 910-762-6570. Tues.-Sat.; adm. fee)* briefly served as headquarters to General Cornwallis in 1781, and the elegant Italianate **Zebulon Latimer House** *(126 S. 3rd St. 910-762-0492),* dating from 1852, is now headquarters of the Lower Cape Fear Historical Society.

Cape Fear Museum *(814 Market St. 910-341-7413. Closed Mon.; adm. fee)* The museum holds thousands of artifacts and photographs that recount southeastern North Carolina's history from the Indian era to modern times.

USS *North Carolina* Battleship Memorial *(US 421 on Eagle Island. 910-251-5797. Adm. fee)* A colossal feat of engineering, the 1941 warship fought in every major naval battle in the Pacific during World War II. Self-guided tours twist through labyrinthine passageways to the galley, officers quarters, pilothouse, and gun turret, providing an intimate look at life aboard a 2,300-man war vessel.

Excursions

BRUNSWICK TOWN STATE HISTORIC PARK *(20 miles S via N.C. 133. 910-371-6613. Closed Mon. Nov.-March)* Settled in 1726, this port town quickly became a leading center for the export of naval stores and lumber. Hurricanes, malaria, and the rise of Wilmington spelled decline for Brunswick. Few citizens remained in the town when the English burned it in 1776. A trail leads under moss-strewn trees, through the ruins of buildings, and around the 15-foot-high earthworks of a Confederate fort.

FORT FISHER STATE HISTORIC SITE *(20 miles S via US 421 at Kure Beach. 910-458-5538. Closed Mon. Nov.-March)* The South's last major link to the outside world, the earth-and-sand stronghold allowed passage of Confederate blockade-runners into Wilmington until a Union assault in early 1865. Roughly ten percent of the fort's earthworks remain; the

Visitor Center displays items recovered from sunken blockade-runners.

MOORES CREEK NATIONAL BATTLEFIELD *(23 miles NW via US 421 and N.C. 210. 910-283-5591)* The 86-acre park and its interpretive trail memorialize the Revolutionary War battle fought in February 1776. The colonists' victory over a band of loyalist Highland Scots put an end to royal rule in North Carolina.

Winston-Salem ··································

(Visitor Center, 601 N. Cherry St. 910-777-3796) A coupling of the 1766 Moravian settlement of Salem with the 1849 county seat of Winston, this Piedmont city owes its growth to the latter's success in tobacco and textiles.

Old Salem *(Old Salem Rd. 910-721-7300 or 800-441-5305. Adm. fee to buildings)* Time and busy highways have bypassed the impressive collection of some 90 restored 18th- and early 19th-century buildings. Visitors may stroll pleasant streets and brick sidewalks lined by frame houses and tidy gardens. Twelve buildings are open to the public and costumed workers demonstrate period cooking and crafts.

Other Sites in North Carolina

Beaufort *(Visitor Center, Turner St. 919-728-5225)* Dating from the early 18th century, the pretty waterfront town of Beaufort (BO-fort) began as a fishing village and port of safety. Guided tours of the **Beaufort Historic Site** *(Check at Visitor Center; fee)* take in three restored houses that were built between 1767 and 1825. The **North Carolina Maritime Museum** *(315 Front St. 919-728-7317)* does a fine job of interpreting the cultural and natural history of the coast.

129

Fort Dobbs State Historic Site *(438 Ft. Dobbs Rd., Statesville. 704-873-5866. Closed Mon. Nov.-March)* On this ground in 1756, colonial soldiers constructed a fort to defend against attacks by the Indians. The fort saw action in 1760 and was then abandoned. Artifacts and plaques now recall the colonial era.

Historic Halifax State Historic Site *(Visitor Center, St. David and Dobb Sts. 919-583-7191. Closed Mon. Nov.-March)* A river port established in 1760, Halifax later blossomed into a center of commerce and culture. Several buildings are open to visitors.

Salisbury Historic District *(Visitor Center, 215 Depot St. 704-638-3100 or 800-332-2343)* Started in 1755 by Scotch-Irish and German settlers, this trading village served as Revolutionary headquarters for both

Old Salem, Winston-Salem

Cornwallis and Nathanael Greene. One of the Confederacy's largest prison camps was also located here. You can visit preserved historic structures and the prison site.

Dr. Joseph Johnson House, built in 1850, Beaufort

South Carolina dates its history from 1670, when the first European settlement took root near present-day Charleston. Though a land-owning gentry in the Low Country controlled the political scene, they were eventually outnumbered by upcountry pioneer farmers. Despite differences, citizens united in opposition to British rule: Nearly 200 Revolutionary War battles were fought here, believed to be more than in any other state. Meanwhile, another class of South Carolinians was laboring in the fields. Leaving an indelible mark on state history and culture, blacks accounted for the majority of early South Carolina's population. By the mid-19th century, the state's slave-based agrarian economy was so entrenched that the ruling class was willing to go to war to preserve it. In April 1861 Confederate troops fired on Fort Sumter in Charleston Harbor, heralding the Civil War. Crushed as much by Reconstruction as by the war, South Carolina did not pull out of its economic slump until after World War II.

Beaufort

(Chamber of Commerce, 1006 Bay St. 803-524-3163) The Spanish and French attempted settlements here in the 16th century, but Beaufort (BEW-furt) was not officially chartered until 1711, only to be burned a few years later by the Yemassee Indians. South Carolina's second oldest town was occupied by the British during the Revolutionary War and by the Union throughout the Civil War, resulting in the survival of the hundred pre-

Revolutionary and antebellum houses that still edge quiet lanes arched by live oaks. Some have served as locations for such movies as *The Big Chill*, *The Great Santini*, and *The Prince of Tides*. Among the town's many fine private houses, the circa 1717 **Thomas Hepworth House** (*214 New St.*) ranks as the oldest in town. With money he earned from helping capture a Confederate gunboat, Robert Smalls, the state's first black U.S. congressman, bought the 1834 **Henry McKee House** (*511 Prince St.*), where he had worked as a slave. The federal **Thomas Fuller House** (*1211 Bay St.*), built by a prominent planter in 1786, commands a wonderful view of Beaufort River.

Beaufort County Museum (*713 Craven St. 803-525-7077. Closed Wed. and Sun.*) Exhibits include Indian artifacts, cannon, and Revolutionary and Civil War relics, housed in a 1798 arsenal.

John Mark Verdier House (*801 Bay St. 803-524-6334. Mon.-Sat.; adm. fee*) Built about 1790 by a wealthy merchant, this elegant federal structure was rescued and preserved by the local historical foundation in the 1940s. Early 19th-century furnishings grace the two floors.

St. Helena's Episcopal Church (*501 Church St. 803-522-1712*) dates, in its present form, from 1724. Both British officers from the Revolution and Confederate officers from the Civil War are buried in the churchyard; Union surgeons reputedly used grave slabs as operating tables.

Excursions

PENN CENTER HISTORIC DISTRICT (*10 miles SE via US 21, on St. Helena Island. 803-838-2235. Tues.-Fri.*) In a sandy grove under moss-hung oaks, Quakers from Philadelphia established a school for freed blacks in 1862. A museum contains weavings, sweetgrass baskets, photographs, and recordings of Gullah (a Sea Islands dialect).

HUNTING ISLAND LIGHTHOUSE (*16 miles SE on US 21, in Hunting Island State Park. 803-838-2011*) Built in 1875, the lighthouse operated as a beacon until 1933. It now affords excellent views of the ocean, salt marsh, and surrounding islands.

PARRIS ISLAND MUSEUM (*6 miles S via S.C. 281, on Parris Island. 803-525-2951*) Museum displays trace the history of warrior training, and a driving tour (*brochure available at nearby Visitor Center*) takes you around the Marine Corps recruit training station, past the late 19th-century naval base to the sites of early Spanish and French settlements and on to fields where battalions of young men drill incessantly.

Charleston ·····································

(*Visitor Center, 375 Meeting St. 803-853-8000*) The history of the state—and of the entire South—is exemplified by the stately houses and the postcard-perfect streets of Charleston. The first English settlement in South Carolina, Charles Towne was named for King Charles II and first located in 1670 across the Ashley River. Moving to the peninsula ten years later, the young city quickly became a thriving port, where wealthy rice planters built fine town houses. During the Revolutionary War, the British lay siege to Charleston, finally overcoming it in 1780. In April 1861 Southern troops fired the first shots of the Civil War, when they shelled Fort Sumter in Charleston Harbor. First in the nation to zone for a historic district (1931), the city encompasses more than a thousand buildings that predate the Civil War.

Charleston Historic District Walking Tour ····· 6 hours

1. Start at the **Charleston Visitor Center** (*375 Meeting St. 803-853-8000*), which has maps, brochures, a multimedia show, and information on carriage and guided walking tours. Most of the historic sites lie several blocks south—you can either walk, take DASH (Downtown Area Shuttle), or drive and park in a lot.

2. The **Charleston Museum** (*360 Meeting St. 803-722-2996. Adm. fee*) displays Low Country memorabilia that includes dueling pistols, a signed

Charleston historic district's East Battery, on the Cooper River

dueling contract, copper slave badges, and rice-farming exhibits.

3. The **Joseph Manigault House** (*350 Meeting St. 803-723-2926. Adm. fee*), a federal mansion built in 1803 for a rice planter, is furnished with many Charleston-made pieces.

4. The monumental Greek Revival **Kahal Kadosh Beth Elohim Synagogue** (*90 Hasell St. 803-723-1090*), constructed in 1840, replaced an 18th-century structure that served one of the country's largest Jewish communities.

5. Across the street, the 1839 **St. Mary's Catholic Church** (*89 Hasell St. 803-722-7696*) stands as the mother church for the Carolinas and Georgia.

6. The busy open-air **City Market** (*Market St. from Meeting St. to E. Bay St.*) dates back to the late 18th century, though the present buildings were constructed in the 1840s. At the head of the row of stalls, Market Hall housed the **Confederate Museum** until damaged by Hurricane Hugo in 1989. The museum's collection (*currently at 34 Pitt St. Sat.-Sun.; adm. fee*) contains the first and last flags to wave over Fort Sumter, hair of Robert E. Lee and Jefferson Davis, and other Confederate relics.

7. The 1835 **St. Philip's Episcopal Church** (*142 Church St. 803-722-7734*) boasts a 200-foot steeple that was an easy target for Union batteries. John C. Calhoun and other notable South Carolinians are buried in the cemetery.

8. The oldest public building in town, the 1713 **Old Powder Magazine** (*79 Cumberland St. 803-722-3767. Under restoration*) squats at the northwest corner of the original walled city and was used as an ammunition depot during the Revolution.

9. The grand old **Dock Street Theatre** (*135 Church St. 803-720-3968. Mon.-Fri.*) boasts ornate ironwork and a plush interior. The original the-

South Carolina

ater, opened in 1736, probably burned in the fire of 1740, along with 300 other buildings.

10. The Gothic Revival **Huguenot Church** *(136 Church St. 803-722-4385. Feb.-Dec. Mon.-Fri.),* built in 1845, is one of the last surviving French Protestant churches in the country.

11. A small plaque at 6 Chalmers Street serves as a reminder of the once active **Old Slave Mart,** the main site of the city's antebellum slave trade.

12. The South Carolina Historical Society now occupies the Palladian-style **Fireproof Building** *(48 Meeting St. 803-723-3225),* completed in 1827 as the first such building in the United States.

13. Yet another prominent city spire, the brilliant white steeple of **St. Michael's Episcopal Church** *(Meeting and Broad Sts. 803-723-0603)* contains bells that have made at least four Atlantic crossings. George Washington and Robert E. Lee both worshiped in pew 43.

14. At the east end of Broad Street stands the Palladian **Old Exchange and Provost Dungeon** *(122 E. Bay St. 803-727-2165. Adm. fee),* built by the British in 1771 as an exchange and customshouse. One of the most significant and popular historical sites in the city, the building was used to imprison pirates and patriots, including three signers of the Declaration of Independence. The two upper floors contain colonial artifacts; the dank dungeon, dating from the early 18th century, exhibits chained pirate mannequins and a portion of the city's original brick seawall, discovered in a 1965 excavation. Just to the south, the pastel-colored attached houses called **Rainbow Row** *(79-107 E. Bay St.)* date from the mid-18th century and typify the style favored by merchants who lived above their ground-floor shops.

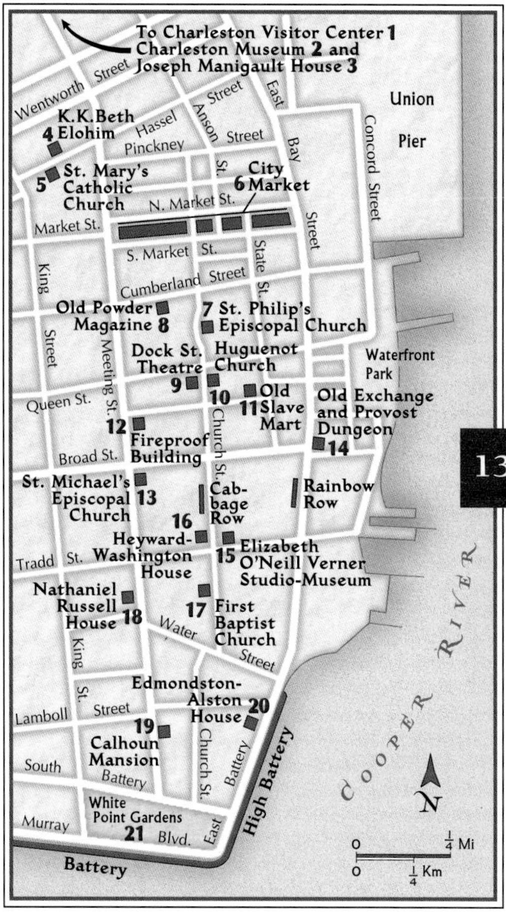

15. For an artist's-eye view of Charleston, stop by the **Elizabeth O'Neill Verner Studio-Museum** *(38 Tradd St. 803-722-4246. Mon.-Sat.),* which exhibits street scenes and portraits dating from the early 20th century.

133

Along Tradd Street are examples of Charleston's ubiquitous single and double houses—dwellings one or two rooms wide, many with front doors that open onto a long breeze-catching porch, or piazza. Also note the earthquake bolts, with decorative ends, that date from just after the 1886 earthquake, when residents repaired structural damage by inserting long iron rods through their walls and tightening them with turnbuckles.

16. The **Heyward-Washington House** (*87 Church St. 803-722-0354. Adm. fee*) was built in 1772 by wealthy rice planter Daniel Heyward and occupied by George Washington during a visit to the city in 1791; 18th-century furnishings made in Charleston exemplify fashionable tastes of that period. Just to the north a colorful line of row houses, **Cabbage Row** (*89-91 Church St.*), shows a West Indian architectural influence and was the model for "Catfish Row" in DuBose Heyward's 1925 novel *Porgy.*

17. Founded in 1682, the **First Baptist Church** (*48 Meeting St. 803-722-3896*) is the oldest Baptist church in the South; the present building is among the state's first Greek Revival structures.

18. A triumph of federal architecture, the 1808 **Nathaniel Russell House** (*51 Meeting St. 803-724-8481. Adm. fee*) was built by a Rhode Island merchant for his family and slaves. A three-story, freestanding spiral staircase is the highlight of the house, which also features period antiques and artwork and a formal garden with year-round flowers.

19. The 1876 **Calhoun Mansion** (*16 Meeting St. 803-722-8205. Thurs.-Sun. Adm. fee*), with its massive walnut front doors, gilt mirrors, and 45-foot-high ballroom ceiling, offers a look at the high Victorian style.

20. The Greek Revival **Edmondston-Alston House** (*21 E. Battery St. 803-722-7171. Adm. fee*) ranks among the grandest of the many magnificent homes shouldering the tip of the Charleston peninsula. Still owned and partly occupied by descendants of the Alston rice-planting dynasty, this 1825 house harbors rooms of priceless family furniture, books, and silver. The second-floor piazza claims a breathtaking view of Charleston Harbor; from here, family members watched the bombardment of Fort Sumter.

21. Occupying the end of the peninsula, the **Battery** (or White Point Gardens) provides pleasant waterfront strolling under canopies of live oaks and palmettos. Cannon symbolize fortifications placed here to defend the city against British and Union Armies.

Also in Charleston

The Citadel Museum (*The Citadel, 171 Moultrie St. 803-953-6846*) Exhibits shed light on the history of South Carolina's military college, from the 1822 slave revolt that led to the founding of The Citadel, to the code of discipline and the plebe system still enforced there today.

Excursions

FORT SUMTER (*Charleston Harbor via 2.5-hour boat tours that leave from City Marina. 803-883-3123. Fee*) Built between 1829 and 1860 on a man-made island, Fort Sumter became the target of the opening salvos in the Civil War, on April 12, 1861. Two days later, Union commander Robert Anderson surrendered the fort to his former West Point student, Gen. Pierre Beauregard. Tours traverse the impressive brick bastion; a small museum houses relics.

CHARLES TOWNE LANDING (*5 miles NW via S.C. 61 and 171, W side* *of Ashley River. 803-852-4200. Adm. fee)* A park with 80 acres of gardens, a full-scale replica of a 17th-century trading ship, a native animal enclosure, and a living history area re-create the 1670 English settlement.

DRAYTON HALL *(9 miles NW via S.C. 61. 3380 Ashley River Rd. 803-766-0188. Adm. fee)* Built between 1738 and 1742 by planter John Drayton (whose father owned nearby Magnolia Plantation), this splendid Georgian Palladian plantation house remained in the family until the 1970s. Still grand on the outside but unfurnished inside, the house boasts elaborate handcrafted woodwork.

MAGNOLIA PLANTATION AND GARDENS *(10 miles NW via S.C. 61. 803-571-1266. Adm. fee)* Held by the Drayton family for more than 300 years, this estate prides itself on its 50 acres of meticulously landscaped gardens. The cottage, which displays family heirlooms, was built on the ruins of an earlier plantation house burned by Sherman's troops.

MIDDLETON PLACE *(14 miles NW via S.C. 61. 803-556-6020. Adm. fee)* One hundred slaves labored from 1741 to 1751 to complete the exquisite gardens and estate of rice planter Henry Middleton, whose son Arthur signed the Declaration of Independence. Among the oldest formal gardens in the country, they include a terraced lawn, lakes, and surrounding parks. The 1755 house, originally a guest wing, contains family treasures; charred foundation stones are all that remain of the central house, torched by Union troops in 1865.

135

Drayton Hall, outside Charleston

PATRIOTS POINT NAVAL AND MARITIME MUSEUM *(2 miles E via US 17. 803-884-2727. Adm. fee)* A floating armada of World War II vessels provides hours of self-guided touring. Flagship of the fleet, the 888-foot *Yorktown* aircraft carrier engaged in numerous battles in the Pacific; its flight deck exhibits more than 20 World War II aircraft. A submarine, destroyer, and Coast Guard cutter round out the fleet. Also of interest, a re-created, full-size Vietnam-era naval support base brings to life the realities of modern warfare.

FORT MOULTRIE *(10 miles SE via US 17 and S.C. 703 on Sullivans Island. 803-883-3123)* Active through World War II, the strategically placed fortification helped successfully defend Charleston Harbor in both the Revolution and Civil War. Visitors may explore the extensive passageways and ramparts, with fine views of Fort Sumter, the harbor, and the city.

Clemson ··

(Chamber of Commerce, 103 Clinton St. Mon.-Fri. 864-654-1208) The city of Clemson grew up around **Clemson University,** founded as an agricultural and scientific college by Thomas Green Clemson, the son-in-law of fiery states' rights advocate and U.S. Vice President John C. Calhoun.

Fort Hill *(Clemson University. 864-656-4789. Donations)* Anchor of a 1,100-acre plantation, the 1803 federal house was owned by John C. Calhoun from 1825 until his death in 1850. The restored house contains a mahogany sideboard made from the 1797 frigate *Constitution* and a Windsor chair owned by George Washington.

Hanover House *(Botanical Gardens, E side of Clemson University campus. 864-656-4789. Sat.-Sun.; donations)* The 1716 clapboard offers an interpretation of the lifestyles of the state's indigo, rice, and cotton planters.

Excursion

PENDLETON *(5 miles SE off US 76)* In the late 18th century, Pendleton was a successful center of commerce and government. The **historic district** encompasses scores of public and private buildings, including **Ashtabula Plantation** *(Hwy. 88. 864-646-3782. April-Oct. Sun. or by appt.; adm. fee)* and the 1850s **Hunter's Store** *(125 E. Queen St. 864-646-3782. Mon.-Fri.).*

Columbia ··

(Visitor Center, 1012 Gervais St. Mon.-Sat. 803-254-0479 or 800-264-4884) In 1786, to ease tension between South Carolina's up country farmers and its aristocratic Low Country planters, the state legislature called for the creation of Columbia, a capital city in the middle of the state. In 1865 Union troops invaded the city and set fire to it. Bronze stars on the **Capitol** *(Main and Gervais Sts. Closed for renovation)* mark hits from Union artillery.

First Baptist Church *(1306 Hampton St. 803-256-4251. Mon.-Fri.)* In 1860 the first Secession Convention was held in the church's original Greek Revival core.

Hampton-Preston Mansion *(1615 Blanding St. 803-252-1770. Tues.-Sun.; adm. fee)* Built in 1818, the elegant classical revival showplace belonged to three generations of the prominent Wade Hampton family. A Union headquarters during the Civil War, the house later served as a governor's residence, convent, women's college, and boardinghouse. Most of the furniture on display belonged to the Hamptons.

Mann-Simons Cottage *(1403 Richland St. 803-252-1770. Tues.-Sun.; adm. fee)* With money earned as a midwife, Charleston slave Celia Mann bought her freedom and walked to Columbia, where she purchased this white clapboard cottage about 1850.

Robert Mills House *(1616 Blanding St. 803-252-1770. Tues.-Sun.; adm. fee)* Original designer of the Washington Monument, Mills designed this graceful house in 1823 for a wealthy merchant. Never used as a private residence, it served instead as a theological seminary for nearly a century. Tours cover the many fine architectural details and period furnishings that reflect upper-class styles of the 1800s.

South Carolina State Museum *(301 Gervais St. 803-737-4921. Adm. fee)* In the old warehouse district on the riverfront, the former Columbia textile mill (1894) houses excellent exhibits on art, natural history, science, prehistoric Indians, slave life, and sharecroppers.

Woodrow Wilson Boyhood Home (*1705 Hampton St. 803-252-1770. Tues.-Sun.; adm. fee*) Built by Reverend Wilson in 1872, the Tuscan-style dwelling was the home of young Woodrow from age 14 to 17. A well appointed interior includes the birth bed of the 28th President.

Excursions

CAYCE HISTORICAL MUSEUM (*3 miles S via State St. 803-796-9020. Tues.-Sun.; adm. fee*) A complex centering around a reconstructed 1765 trading post presents local memorabilia.

FORT JACKSON MUSEUM (*6 miles E via Jackson Blvd. 803-751-7419. Tues.-Sun.*) Dating from 1917, Fort Jackson became a World War II training facility for 500,000 people. Displays focus on area contributions to wars from the Revolution to the present.

HISTORIC CAMDEN (*32 miles NE via I-20, in Camden. 803-432-9841. Guided tours available except Mon.*) The state's oldest inland settlement, Camden was platted in 1733 and witnessed a disastrous American defeat in a 1780 Revolutionary War battle. A 98-acre historical area comprises numerous restored buildings, as well as reconstructed fortifications. Scores of antebellum houses still stand in the **Camden Historic District.**

Georgetown

(*Chamber of Commerce, Front and Broad Sts. 803-546-8436*) In 1526 the Spanish had a settlement here on Winyah Bay but abandoned it because of disease. English settlers began arriving in the early 18th century and established a town named for George II. Held by the British during the Revolution, Georgetown was a favorite target of guerrilla raider Francis Marion, the "swamp fox."

Harold Kaminski House (*1003 Front St. 803-546-7706. Adm. fee*) Located in the historic district, this 1760s town house, home of a wealthy merchant, contains an outstanding collection of antiques.

Prince George Winyah Episcopal Church (*301 Broad St. 803-546-4358*) The cemetery of the early 18th-century church holds the graves of Revolutionary and Civil War soldiers.

Rice Museum (*Front and Screven Sts. 803-546-7423. Mon.-Sat.; adm. fee*) Exhibits in the Old Market Building (1842) explain the story of area rice production from 1700 to 1900, during

Middleton Place, near Charleston

which time Georgetown became the world leader in rice exports.

Excursions

HOPSEWEE PLANTATION (*12 miles S on US 17. 803-546-7891. March-Oct. Tues.-Fri.; adm. fee*) The restored 1740 home of Continental Congressman Thomas Lynch houses period furnishings. Thomas, Jr., born here, was a signer of the Declaration of Independence.

HAMPTON PLANTATION STATE PARK (*16 miles S via US 17.*

803-546-9361. Thurs.-Mon.; adm. fee) Built in the mid-18th century as an enlargement of a modest farmhouse, this fine, unfurnished plantation house is notable for its two-story ballroom and an eight-column portico added in 1791 before a visit by George Washington.

BROOKGREEN GARDENS *(18 miles N via US 17. 864-237-4218. Adm. fee)* One of the preeminent collections of American sculpture finds an Edenesque setting amid the ancient oaks and bare remains of a mid-1700s rice and indigo plantation. Sculptor Anna Hyatt Huntington and her railroad-heir husband, Archer Huntington, created the gardens in 1931.

Spartanburg

This upcountry county seat prospered before the Civil War with ironworks and cotton, and afterward as a railway hub. The **Regional Museum of Spartanburg County** *(501 Otis Blvd., adjoining library. 864-596-3501. Tues.-Sun.; adm. fee)* has cotton mill displays and a 1567 etched stone trail marker used by the Spanish and said to be the oldest European artifact in the state.

Excursions

WALNUT GROVE PLANTATION *(12 miles SW via US 221. 1200 Otts' Shoals Rd. 864-576-6546. Sun. year-round, April-Oct. Tues.-Sun.; adm. fee)* This rustic, two-story log house (built circa 1765), once the headquarters of a 3,000-acre estate, offers a good introduction to backcountry plantation life in the late 1700s. Hunting rifles and powder horns hang ready by the front and back doors, while bloodstains on the plank floor upstairs mark where a patriot soldier was supposedly stabbed to death by Tories.

COWPENS NATIONAL BATTLEFIELD *(16 miles NE via I-85 and S.C. 110, near Chesnee. 864-461-2828)* On these rolling pasturelands in 1781, Daniel Morgan led a small army of Continental soldiers and untutored militia to a stunning victory against Banastre Tarleton's larger, better trained British troops. A walking trail, auto tour, and slide show highlight the battle.

KINGS MOUNTAIN NATIONAL MILITARY PARK *(35 miles NE off I-85, near Blacksburg. 864-936-7921)* In 1780 a band of colonial mountainmen advanced uphill against Maj. Patrick Ferguson's Loyalists, taking both the mountain and Ferguson's life in a pivotal battle. The Visitor Center contains life-size dioramas and a film; a 1.5-mile trail leads through the thick woods and hilly terrain traversed by the patriots.

Other Sites in South Carolina

Abbeville *(Chamber of Commerce, 104 Pickens St. 803-459-4600)* A charming small town centers around a downtown square with 19th-century storefronts and a 1908 Opera House. The 1830 **Burt-Stark Mansion** *(N. Main St. 803-459-4297. Adm. fee)* witnessed the last meeting of the Confederate Council of War; the **Abbeville County Museum** *(Poplar St. 803-459-2740. Wed. and Sat.; adm. fee)* displays items of regional history in an 1850s county jail.

Brattonsville Historic District *(McConnells. 864-684-2327. March-Nov. Tues.-Sun.; adm. fee)* A restored village offers 24 buildings interpreting 18th- and 19th-century rural life.

Ninety Six National Historic Site *(11036 S.C. 248, in Ninety Six. 864-543-4068)* Site of two major Revolutionary War battles, this field has earthworks, a reconstructed fort, a foot trail, and a Visitor Center.

Georgia

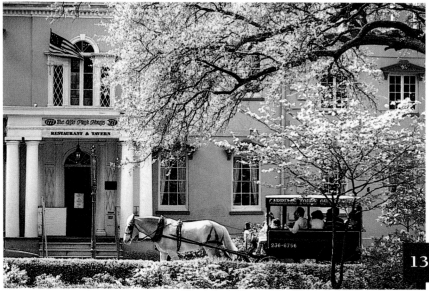

Historic Savannah

Brainchild of English general and philanthropist James Oglethorpe, the colony of Georgia began in Savannah in 1733 as an opportunity for debtors to gain a fresh start. King George II granted the charter for the new colony, trusting that Georgia would serve as a buffer between his Carolinas and the Spanish territory to the south. After the Revolution, inland settlement boomed, and by the 19th century cotton had become the economic linchpin. But in pushing west settlers encroached on Indian lands. With the Dahlonega, Georgia, gold rush of the 1820s and 1830s came the forced removal of Cherokee and Creek in the infamous Trail of Tears march. In 1864 the Union Army set out on a different sort of march—this one to the sea. Their purpose, declared leader William Tecumseh Sherman, was to "make Georgia howl." At war's end many of the state's proud plantations lay in ashes, much of its wealth gone up in smoke. Recovery, however, proceeded relatively smoothly, with Atlanta leading the way into a new era of prosperity.

Americus

(Chamber of Commerce, 400 W. Lamar St. 912-924-2646. Mon.-Fri.) Dating from 1832, this former cotton-growing center boasts a wealth of handsome Victorian homes and buildings. The castle-like 1891 **Windsor Hotel** *(125 W. Lamar St. 912-924-1555)* blends Victorian Gothic and neo-classical details into a magnificent creation of towers, arches, and balconies.

Excursions

ANDERSONVILLE NATIONAL HISTORIC SITE *(10 miles NE on Ga. 49. 912-924-0343)* More than a fourth of the 45,000 Union soldiers held in this infamous Civil War prison camp perished, most from disease caused by overcrowding and poor water. The driving tour passes earthworks, the remains of escape tunnels, and row upon row of white headstones.

JIMMY CARTER NATIONAL HISTORIC SITE *(10 miles W on US 280, in Plains. Plains High School, 300 N. Bond St. 912-824-3413)* Exhibits of photographs, campaign posters, and a film follow the career and 1976 campaign of the 39th President. Carter's boyhood home and the 1888 railroad depot that served as his campaign headquarters are slated for restoration before being opened to the public.

WESTVILLE *(36 miles W via US 280 and Ga. 27, in Lumpkin. 912-838-6310. Tues.-Sun.; adm. fee)* A living history village of 32 restored and relocated buildings illustrates rural Georgia in 1850.

Atlanta ···

(Convention & Visitors Bureau, 233 Peachtree St. N.E. 404-521-6600) Founded in 1837 as a railroad terminus, Atlanta soon became a transportation center, a distinction that marked it for destruction when Gen. William T. Sherman invaded the area in 1864. With most of the city gone up in flames, a bold new Atlanta arose to become the financial and commercial magnet of the Southeast. Though a giant of the New South, Atlanta faithfully preserves its history in several worthwhile attractions. The striking 1889 **State Capitol** *(Capitol Sq. 404-656-2844. Mon.-Fri.)* boasts a dome gilded with Georgia gold.

Martin Luther King, Jr., National Historic Site *(501 Auburn Ave. 404-331-3919)* The Nobel laureate and civil rights leader was born and raised in this Queen Anne house. The surrounding Sweet Auburn neighborhood—once the heart of black Atlanta—includes the **Ebenezer Baptist Church** and **King's gravesite.**

Atlanta Cyclorama *(Grant Park. 404-658-7625. Adm. fee)* A gigantic circular painting (358 by 42 feet) of the Battle of Atlanta brings the 1864 event to life. A Civil War museum is also housed in the building.

Atlanta History Center *(130 W. Paces Ferry Rd. N.W. 404-814-4000. Adm. fee)* A banquet of area history, this site shows off two houses and a museum, surrounded by 32 acres of lovely gardens. The grand **Swan House** (1928) holds a wealth of furnishings and embellishments; the relocated 1840s **Tullie Smith Farm** includes a wooden plantation house and outbuildings and exhibits on Georgia history.

Excursions

STONE MOUNTAIN PARK *(16 miles E on US 78. 770-498-5690. Adm. fee)* Situated around an 800-foot granite outcropping, the popular 3,200-acre park features a Civil War museum and an antebellum

Martin Luther King, Jr., N.H.S.

plantation (moved here from elsewhere). A colossal relief carving of Confederate heroes Lee, Jackson, and Davis dominates the mountain face.

KENNESAW MOUNTAIN NATIONAL BATTLEFIELD PARK *(23 miles NW via I-75. 770-427-4686)* Here in June 1864 Gen. Joseph Johnston's outnumbered Confederate forces stalled Sherman's march to Atlanta for about two weeks. An auto trail winds past interpretive markers to the top of a summit with a panoramic view.

KENNESAW CIVIL WAR MUSEUM *(25 miles NW via I-75, Kennesaw. 2829 Cherokee St. 770-427-2117. Adm. fee)* A renovated cotton gin houses "the general," the locomotive stolen by Union soldiers in April 1862 and recaptured in a chase to Chattanooga. Exhibits and a video detail the episode.

Stone Mountain Park

Augusta ··························

(Welcome Center, 8th and Reynolds Sts. 706-724-4067) Located on the Savannah River fall line, Georgia's second oldest city was established as a fur-trading post in 1736 by James Oglethorpe, who had founded Savannah three years earlier. Until the mid-1900s, Augusta was the country's second leading inland cotton market (after Memphis). The town's life support, the river was also its worst enemy, prone to heavy flooding. Today tourists congregate along a new **riverwalk,** with shops and eateries. The **Historic Cotton Exchange Welcome Center** (1886) features high ceilings with coffers of pressed tin and exhibits on the early cotton market.

Augusta-Richmond County Museum *(560 Reynolds St. 706-722-8454. Tues.-Sun.)* This massive repository spotlights regional and natural history in 48,000 square feet of space and 23 permanent exhibit areas.

Ezekiel Harris House *(1822 Broad St. 706-724-0436. Tues.-Sat.; adm. fee)* Built in 1797 by a tobacco merchant, the meticulously restored frame house features a gambrel roof, double piazza, and period antiques.

Meadow Garden *(1320 Independence Dr. 706-724-4174. Mon.-Fri.; adm. fee)* This white two-story house was the home of George Walton (1749-1804), a signer of the Declaration of Independence, Georgia governor and U.S. senator. He is buried at the **Signers Monument** *(500 Greene St.).*

Sacred Heart Cultural Center *(1301 Greene St. 706-826-4700. Mon.-Fri.)* The magnificent Romanesque Revival building served as a Catholic church from 1900 to 1971. Now headquarters for an area arts organization, it retains its soaring spires, stained glass, and carved Italian marble.

Brunswick ··

(Chamber of Commerce, 4 Glynn Ave. 912-265-0620) A commercial fishing port, this gateway to the Golden Isles dates back to 1771 and preserves many buildings from the Victorian period.

Excursions

ST. SIMONS ISLAND *(5 miles E via F. J. Torras Causeway)* Scene of Spanish explorations in the 16th century and bloody conflicts between Native Americans and missionaries, lovely St. Simons was finally brought to heel in 1736 by James Oglethorpe. His **Fort Frederica** *(912-638-3639. Adm. fee)*

141

stood until 1758. Now a national monument, the site holds ruins and a Visitor Center. At the south tip of the resort island, the 1872 **St. Simons Lighthouse** (*912-638-4666. Tues.-Sat.; adm. fee*) offers views of island and ocean.

JEKYLL ISLAND HISTORIC DISTRICT (*10 miles S via US 17 and Ga. 520. Visitor Center, Stable Rd. 912-635-2762. Adm. fee for island*) In 1886 a group of millionaires bought this island and formed the Jekyll Island Club, an exclusive retreat for hunting, fishing, and general indulgence. The club's members, among the world's wealthiest men, included William Rockefeller, the Gould Brothers, J. P. Morgan, and Joseph Pulitzer. The 240-acre historic area includes 33 structures in a lush setting along Jekyll Creek; tram tours stop at several cottages. At the island's north end stand the ruins of **Horton House,** built of oyster shells, lime, and sand around 1740 by William Horton, Oglethorpe's successor as the colony's leader.

HOFWYL-BROADFIELD PLANTATION STATE HISTORIC SITE (*10 miles N on US 17. 912-264-7333. Tues.-Sun.; adm. fee*) William Brailsford built his rice plantation at the edge of a cypress swamp in 1807. The buildings and land survived through five generations until bequeathed to the state in 1973. Cows still graze in pastures, and magnolias, camellias, and gnarled live oaks adorn the property. The Visitor Center offers exhibits on planters and slaves.

FORT KING GEORGE STATE HISTORIC SITE (*15 miles N via US 17, in Darien. Fort King George Dr. 912-437-4770. Tues.-Sun.; adm. fee*) England's southernmost outpost in America from 1721 to 1727, the fort protected British soldiers from the French, Spanish, and Indians. A reconstructed three-story blockhouse stands at the edge of a vast marsh of spartina grass.

Columbus

Founded in 1828, this industrial city was a leading cotton port and textile center, fueled by hydraulic power from the Chattahoochee River. The downtown **historic district,** covering almost 30 blocks, includes a variety of architectural styles. The **Historic Columbus Foundation** (*700 Broadway.*

706-322-0756) offers tours of five houses, including the foundation headquarters, an 1870 Italianate town house; the 1840 Pemberton House, once owned by the inventor of Coca-Cola; an 1828 federal cottage; and an 1820s log cabin and farmhouse. The 1871 **Springer Opera House** (*103 10th St. 706-324-5714*) has been a venue for such celebrities as Edwin Booth, Oscar Wilde, and Will Rogers.

Confederate Naval Museum (*202 4th St. 706-327-9798. Tues.-Sun.*) In addition to models, 1860s weapons, and relics,

1886 Christ Church, St. Simons Island

the museum contains the salvaged remains of two Southern warships—the gunboat *Chattahoochee* and the Civil War ironclad ram *Jackson*.

Excursions

NATIONAL INFANTRY MUSEUM (*5 miles S via I-185. Bldg. 396, Baltzell Ave., Fort Benning. 706-545-2958*) No ordinary military museum, this sprawling collection fills three floors and more than 30 exhibit areas with weapons, uniforms, and equipment from the 16th century to the present.

LITTLE WHITE HOUSE *(40 miles NE via Ga. 85, near Warm Springs. 706-655-5870. Adm. fee)* Built by Franklin Roosevelt in 1932, this modest but comfortable retreat is furnished the way it was when the 32nd President died here in 1945. A self-guided tour takes in the main house, guesthouse, servants quarters, and garage with FDR's hand-operated 1938 Ford convertible.

Macon ······························

(Convention & Visitors Bureau, Terminal Station, 200 Cherry St. 912-743-3401 or 800-768-3401. Mon.-Sat.) On the banks of the Ocmulgee River, Macon's broad streets were laid out in 1822. The pleasant hilly town soon became a rail and river transport center. During the Civil War, it served as a supply depot and gold depository, making it a prime target for Federal forces. The city surrendered in 1865, and its many antebellum buildings were thus spared destruction.

Hay House *(934 Georgia Ave. 912-742-8155. Adm. fee)* The splendid Italianate mansion was built between 1855 and 1859 by entrepreneur William Johnston, who became treasurer of the Confederacy. Among its riches the house counts stained-glass windows, arched ceilings with elaborate plasterwork and woodwork and fabulous trompe l'oeil effects.

Old Cannonball House *(856 Mulberry St. 912-745-5982. Adm. fee)* A Union cannonball hit this sturdy Greek Revival house in 1864 and rolled into the hallway, where it remains on display today. Built in 1853 by Judge Asa Holt, who reputedly survived three hangings by Union soldiers, the house contains period furnishings; a separate servants' quarter holds a museum of Confederate artifacts.

Ocmulgee National Monument *(207 Emory Hwy. 912-752-8257)* In addition to stone tools and pottery, the site claims several awe-inspiring ceremonial mounds built by Mississippian Indians more than a thousand years ago.

Sidney Lanier Cottage *(935 High St. 912-743-3851. Mon.-Sat.; adm. fee)* The birthplace of southern poet Sidney Lanier (1842-1881), who wrote "The Marshes of Glynn," holds mementos from his life and work.

Sherman's March

After three long years of civil war, with the hard-pressed South still not ready to give up the fight, Union general William T. Sherman set off on his infamous March to the Sea—his mission to destroy Confederate morale and bring the war to an end. Starting from Atlanta in November 1864, the army of 62,000 blazed a path of destruction through Georgia, pillaging and burning as they went. They twisted rail ties into "Sherman neckties" and used heirloom silver for target practice; they stole food from rich and poor alike; and they successfully spread fear throughout the South, trailing in their wake bands of freed slaves. "The devil himself," Sherman reputedly said, "couldn't restrain my men." By Christmas he had captured Savannah. Leaving a devastated Georgia behind, he and his army turned their attention next to the Carolinas.

143

Excursion

MILLIDGEVILLE *(30 miles NE via Ga. 49. Welcome Center, 200 W. Hancock St. 912-452-4687)* State capital from 1803 to 1868, this charming Old South town boasts shady streets shouldered by wonderful houses. Among the many significant structures scattered through the town are the Greek Revival **Old Governor's Mansion** (1838), the Gothic **Old State Capitol** (1807), and the federal **Stetson-Sanford House** (1825).

Rome ··

(Visitor information at railway depot, 402 Civic Center Dr. 706-295-5576)

Nestled in hills, Rome was captured and put out of service by Union forces in 1863 during the Civil War but has since regained its prominence as a manufacturing capital.

Chieftains Museum *(501 Riverside Pkwy. 706-291-9494. Tues.-Sat.; adm. fee)* Exhibits on Indian history, including Cherokee scholar Sequoyah's alphabet, are displayed here in the 1790s home of a Cherokee leader. Assimilated to the ways of the white man, he signed the Treaty of New Echota, which led to the ouster of his own people from Georgia.

Excursions

Sequoyah, inventor of the Cherokee alphabet

ETOWAH INDIAN MOUNDS STATE HISTORIC SITE *(27 miles E via US 411, near Cartersville. 770-387-3747. Tues.-Sun.; adm. fee)* Large temple and burial mounds built by Native Americans between A.D. 900 and 1500 are preserved here. A museum has effigies and other ceremonial and ornamental objects.

NEW ECHOTA STATE HISTORIC SITE *(30 miles NE via Ga. 53 and Ga. 225. 706-629-8151. Tues.-Sun.; adm. fee)* Capital of the Cherokee Nation from 1825 until the Indians' expulsion to Oklahoma in 1838, the site enshrines Cherokee efforts to copy the white system of government. A restored tavern, a courthouse, newspaper office, and missionary house are authentically furnished as they were in the early 19th century.

Savannah ··

(Visitor Center, 301 Martin Luther King, Jr., Blvd. 912-944-0455) Gen. James Oglethorpe sailed up the Savannah River with 144 settlers and chartered the Georgia Crown Colony here in 1733. The town flipped back and forth between British and Colonial control throughout the Revolution, and suffered again in the Civil War. On December 22, 1864, Union general William T. Sherman claimed but did not destroy this gracious seaport town, writing with understated bravado to Lincoln: "I beg to present you as a Christmas gift the city of Savannah." Downtown Savannah still bears the imprint of Oglethorpe's original colonial grid of wide streets punctuated by public squares—now lush parks of semitropical shade trees and heroic statuary. Along the busy waterfront, tourists stroll past converted warehouses where antebellum merchants once made fortunes in the cotton trade.

Etowah Indian Mounds State Historic Site, near Cartersville

Historic Savannah
Walking Tour ···································· **5 hours**

1. Begin at the **Visitor Center** *(301 Martin Luther King, Jr., Blvd. 912-*

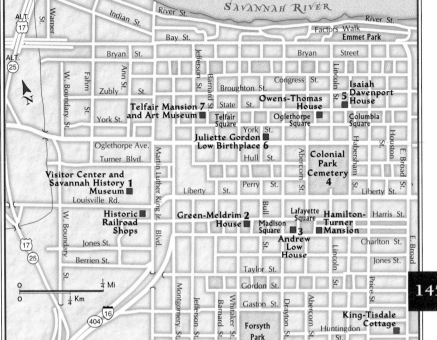

944-0455), housed in a restored 19th-century railroad station. The attached **Savannah History Museum** (*912-238-1779. Adm. fee*) displays a cotton gin, a Central of Georgia steam locomotive, and a standard sampling of war items. Just to the south, the **Historic Railroad Shops** (*601 W. Harris St. 912-651-6823. Adm. fee*) preserve an extensive complex of 1850s repair shops—considered the most significant antebellum railroad buildings in the country; the site also includes a roundhouse, turntable, and 125-foot brick smokestack.

   2. Constructed in the early 1850s by a cotton broker, the **Green-Meldrim House** (*Madison Sq. 912-233-3845. Tues. and Thurs.-Sat.; adm. fee*), ranks as one of the outstanding examples of Gothic Revival architecture in the South. Its nine massive rooms, bright with natural light, are decorated with elegant ironwork, marble, and carved walnut.

   3. Another wealthy cotton broker built the 1848 **Andrew Low House** (*329 Abercorn St. 912-233-6854. Fri.-Wed.; adm. fee*), a model of classical restraint. Notable guests were Robert E. Lee and British writer William Thackeray. Across the square stands the imposing French Empire **Hamilton-Turner Mansion** (*330 Abercorn St. 912-233-4800. Adm. fee*), erected in 1873 for banker-mayor Samuel Hamilton.

   4. Colonial Park Cemetery (*E. Oglethorpe Ave. and Abercorn St.*) was the city's burial ground from 1750 to 1853; interred here are a royal governor, soldiers and officers, and Button Gwinnett, a signer of the Declaration of Independence who died in a duel.

5. Exemplifying a middle-class dwelling of the 1820s, the federal-style **Isaiah Davenport House** *(324 E. State St. 912-236-8097. Adm. fee)* boasts original plaster and horsehair molding and decorative columns. By the 1930s the house had become a tenement for up to 13 families. Its rescue from demolition in 1955 by

Andrew Low House, Savannah

a handful of local women was the city's first preservation effort and the beginning of the Historic Savannah Foundation. Far up the social ladder, the grand 1819 **Owens-Thomas House** *(124 Abercorn St. 912-233-9743. Adm. fee)* is a landmark of English Regency architecture.

6. The **Juliette Gordon Low Birthplace** *(142 Bull St. 912-233-4501. Thurs.-Tues.; adm. fee)*, a regency-style house completed in 1821, is furnished with Victorian pieces belonging to Low's family. Low founded the Girl Scouts of America in 1912.

7. Another fine regency building, the 1818 **Telfair Mansion and Art Museum** *(Telfair Sq. 912-232-1177. Tues.-Sun.; adm. fee)* features fine and decorative arts, as well as furnished period rooms.

Also in Savannah

King-Tisdale Cottage *(514 E. Huntingdon St. 912-236-5161. Tues.-Sun.; adm. fee)* The cottage houses furniture, art, and documents related to the history of blacks in Savannah and on the Sea Islands.

Excursions

WORMSLOE STATE HISTORIC SITE *(10 miles SE via Skidaway Rd. 7601 Skidaway Rd. 912-353-3023. Tues.-Sun.; adm. fee)* An awesome 1.5-mile avenue lined with more than 400 live oaks vanishes into a dense wilderness where original Savannah colonist Noble Jones carved out a plantation in the 1730s. Sparse ruins of his fortified tabby house remain. A Visitor Center has a film and excavated artifacts.

FORT JACKSON *(3 miles E via President St. 912-232-3945. Adm. fee)* Completed in 1812, Georgia's oldest surviving brick fortification protected Savannah from attack by water during the Civil War. A self-guided tour offers riverside views of barges and tugboats and their factory ports-of-call upriver in the city.

FORT PULASKI NATIONAL MONUMENT *(15 miles E via US 80. 912-786-5787. Adm. fee)* The state's most impressive fort, this tremendous 1847 brick structure was captured by the Union in 1862. Visitors cross a drawbridge over a moat to explore battlements, furnished quarters, and dark tunnels. Audio stations heighten the tour: one recounts the harrowing tale of a Confederate prisoner's escape attempt.

TYBEE ISLAND LIGHTHOUSE AND MUSEUM *(18 miles E via US 80, on*

146

Tybee Island. 912-786-5801. Wed.-Mon.; adm. fee) Completed in 1867, the 154-foot beacon replaced three earlier structures dating as far back as 1736. If you climb the 178 steps, you'll be rewarded with sweeping views of land and sea. Housed in a crumbling 1897 gun battery, the museum interprets coastal history.

FORT MCALLISTER STATE HISTORIC PARK *(30 miles S via US 17 and Ga. 144. 912-727-2339. Tues.-Sun.; adm. fee)* A well-preserved example of a Confederate earthwork fortification, the fort survived Union naval bombardments in 1862 and 1863 but fell to Sherman's ground forces in 1864.

Washington

Laid out in 1780, this off-the-beaten-track town boasts a large number of elegant antebellum houses in Greek Revival and other styles. A marker on the downtown square indicates the site where Jefferson Davis performed his last duties as President of the Confederacy on May 4, 1865. Legend maintains that some $400,000 in Confederate gold is buried nearby.

Robert Toombs House State Historic Site *(216 E. Robert Toombs Ave. 706-678-2226. Tues.-Sun.; adm. fee)* Outfitted with a two-story columned portico, the dignified mansion was the home of the brash U.S. senator and frustrated Confederate presidential hopeful who urged Georgia into secession and war. Family furnishings and a film document his life.

Washington Historical Museum *(308 E. Robert Toombs Ave. 706-678-2105. Tues.-Sun.; adm. fee)* Among the holdings in this wonderfully creaky 1830s house are Jefferson Davis's campaign chest, Civil War-era Texas Ranger jackets, Reconstruction-era Ku Klux Klan robes, and a Rosewood piano plundered by Sherman's troops and later recovered.

147

Excursion

CALLAWAY PLANTATION *(5 miles W on US 78. 706-678-7060. Tues.-Sun.; adm. fee)* An 1869 brick Greek Revival house, log cabin (circa 1785), log barn (1790), and other buildings portray early farm life in the area.

Other Sites in Georgia

Agrirama *(I-75 and 8th St., in Tifton. 912-386-3344. Tues.-Sun.; adm. fee)* A living history museum of 35 structures depicts late 19th-century farm, industrial, and rural life-styles.

Athens *(Visitor Center, 280 E. Dougherty St. 706-353-1820)* Home of the University of Georgia (chartered 1785), Athens has a wealth of fine Italianate and Greek Revival houses, including the 1840s **Taylor-Grady House** *(634 Prince Ave. 706-549-8688. Tues.-Fri.; adm. fee).*

Chickamauga and Chattanooga N.M.P. *(Fort Oglethorpe)* See page 185.

Kolomoki Indian Mounds State Historic Park *(Blakely. 912-723-5296)* Creek and Weeden Island Indians built the mounds still standing here more than a thousand years ago. A museum *(Tues.-Sun.; adm. fee)* explains the prehistoric Indian culture.

Thomasville *(Visitor Center, 109 S. Broad St. 912-225-3919)* After the Civil War, this town became a highly popular winter resort for northerners. Among historic sites are the fanciful 1884 Victorian **Lapham-Patterson House** *(912-225-4004. Tues.-Sun.; adm. fee)* and **Pebble Hill Plantation** *(US 319 S. 912-226-2344. Closed Mon. and Sept.; adm. fee)*, a grandiloquent 1820s house rebuilt after a 1934 fire.

Florida

Fort Jefferson, Dry Tortugas National Park

The first European to claim Florida soil was Juan Ponce de Léon. Searching for the fountain of youth, he landed in 1513 near present-day St. Augustine. Just over 50 years later, the Spanish put up a permanent settlement in the same area and managed to fend off other colonizers for two centuries. In 1763 Britain took Florida from Spain in exchange for Havana. But only 20 years later, drained by the Revolutionary War, the British gave it back. The Spanish held on until 1819, when they turned over the region to the U.S. The ensuing Seminole Wars with the Indians lasted nearly until the Civil War and were among the bloodiest and costliest fought in this country. In the late 1800s financial giants Henry Flagler and Henry Plant laid train tracks through the wilderness along both coasts, encouraging a tide of tourists that continues today.

Daytona and Ormond Beaches ················

In 1871 Ohio developer Mathias Day laid out Daytona on an old plantation along the Halifax River. The new railroad soon brought prosperous vacationers who enjoyed racing their automobiles on the firm beaches. Motorists may still drive the 23-mile stretch of coast, while professional racers congregate at the Daytona International Speedway.

The Casements (*25 Riverside Dr., Ormond Beach. 904-676-3216. Mon.-Sat.; donations*) Named for its windows, the 1912 mansion served as the winter residence of John D. Rockefeller, from 1918 to 1937.

Excursions

BULOW PLANTATION STATE HISTORIC SITE *(12 miles N off Fla. A1A. 904-517-2084. Adm. fee)* Slaves erected a sugar mill and plantation house here in 1821, but the Seminole burned them down 15 years later; ruins remain.

PONCE DE LÉON INLET LIGHTHOUSE *(11 miles S via Fla. A1A. 4931 S. Peninsula Dr. 904-761-1821. Adm. fee)* Dating from the late 1880s, the 175-foot sentinel offers visitors an inspiring view of inland waterway and ocean. Keepers' cottages display maps, photos, and nautical items.

Fort Myers

After the Second Seminole War (1835-1842) an Army post here protected settlers, then served as a Union fortification in the Civil War. Incorporated in 1886, Fort Myers became a center for the area's large cattle ranches, pineapple plantations, and substantial fishing industry.

Edison and Ford Winter Estates *(2350 McGregor Blvd. 941-334-3614. Adm. fee)* Vacationing in Florida for his health in 1885, inventor Thomas Edison bought this lovely riverside property and built two adjoining houses and a laboratory. In 1916 his friend Henry Ford bought a cottage next door, and here they vacationed together until Edison's death in 1931. Tours wind through lush botanical gardens and into the roomy house, with family furnishings. Don't miss the laboratory and museum.

Fort Myers Historical Museum *(2300 Peck Ave. 941-332-5955. Tues.-Sat.; adm. fee)* The 1923 railroad depot houses exhibits on area history from Indian to modern times, including an elegant private railcar (1930s).

Jacksonville

Laid out in 1822, Jacksonville became a popular winter resort in the late 19th century, before the development of South Florida.

Museum of Science and History *(1025 Museum Circle. 904-396-7061. Adm. fee)* A summary of local history includes exhibits on the *Maple Leaf* steamship, sunk by a Confederate mine in the St. Johns River.

Excursions

FORT CAROLINE NATIONAL MEMORIAL *(13 miles E via Fort Caroline Rd. 904-641-7155)* French Huguenots established an outpost here in 1564 but were massacred the next year by the Spanish, who set up operations just to the south, in what became St. Augustine. A short nature trail leads to a reconstructed fort, and a small museum displays 16th-century weapons and a 9-foot owl effigy (circa 1500) carved by the Timucuan.

KINGSLEY PLANTATION *(25 miles E via Fla. 105 to Fla. A1A. 1676 Palmetto Ave., Mayport. 904-251-3537)* A 1798 main house, outbuildings, and ruins of 23 tabby slave cottages remain on this once vast plantation. Exhibits highlight the slave trade and slave life.

Key West

(Chamber of Commerce, 402 Wall St. 305-294-2587 or 800-527-8539) Purchased from Spain in 1821, the country's southernmost port of call became a naval base and a center for fish, shrimp, and sponges. Salvaging of sunken ships gave Key West the country's highest per capita income by mid-century. Though a hurricane blew away a portion of Henry Flagler's railroad to Key West in 1935, the Overseas Highway linked the island to the

mainland three years later and continues to bring a stream of visitors. The

Ernest Hemingway Home

historic district harbors a mix of Bahamian- and New England-style architecture.

Audubon House *(Whitehead and Greene Sts. 305-294-2116. Adm. fee)* Built by a sea captain in the 1840s and named for the naturalist who visited Key West in 1832, this restored neoclassical dwelling features elegant 1840s furnishings and original Audubon engravings.

Mel Fisher Maritime Heritage Society *(Front and Greene Sts. 305-294-2633. Adm. fee)* In the 1980s treasure hunter Fisher located the wreckage of Spanish galleons that went down off the Keys in a 1622 hurricane. The museum showcases some of the remarkable gold, silver, and artifacts recovered from them and explains the hardships and thrills of treasure hunting.

Harry S Truman Little White House Museum *(111 Front St. 305-294-9911. Adm. fee)* A short video and a tour explore Harry S Truman's Key West retreat. Furnishings include the President's mahogany poker table.

Fort Zachary Taylor State Historic Park *(Southard St. and Truman Annex. 305-292-6713. Adm. fee)* Constructed from 1845 to 1866, this stronghold seized so many Confederate blockade-runners that it claims the nation's largest collections of Civil War armaments, most still lodged within the fort's walls. The crumbling battlements afford fine ocean views.

Ernest Hemingway Home *(907 Whitehead St. 305-294-1575. Adm. fee)* The Nobel laureate owned the Spanish Colonial house from 1931 to 1961 and wrote much of his oeuvre here. Tours cover the house—furnished with antiques the author collected on his travels—the gardens, and his writing studio.

Miami ·······································

(Visitor Center, 401 Biscayne Blvd. 305-539-8070) When Henry Flagler's Florida East Coast Railroad made it to Miami in 1896, the area held little more than orange groves and a handful of military deserters and Bahamian settlers. But by the 1920s, the city was a bustling resort. Slowed like the rest of Florida during the 1930s land bust, greater Miami has, since the 1950s, burst its seams with a growing population of Haitian, Cuban, and Latin American immigrants.

South Florida's oldest settlement, **Coconut Grove** was started in the 1880s by black Bahamians and New England intellectuals and retains a sophisticated bohemian flavor. Another old neighborhood, **Coral Gables** was laid out in the 1920s; a drive along **Miracle Mile** *(24th St. S.W.)* offers a good sampling of the community's elaborate Mediterranean Revival architecture. For a dazzling array of art deco hotels from the 1930s, cruise Miami Beach's recently renovated **Ocean Drive** *(5th to 15th Sts.)*.

Church of St. Bernard de Clairvaux *(16711 W. Dixie Hwy. 305-945-1461. Adm. fee)* The 12th-century Spanish monastery was purchased in 1925 by newspaper tycoon William Randolph Hearst, shipped here, and reassembled. Piped-in chants whisper down stone cloisters and into chapels and gardens.

Historical Museum of Southern Florida *(Metro-Dade Cultural Center,*

101 W. Flagler St. 305-375-1492. Adm. fee) Early Indian artifacts, an exhibit on Everglades dredging, and photographs of Cuban immigrants are among the offerings in this cornucopia of history.

Vizcaya *(3251 S. Miami Ave. 305-250-9133. Adm. fee)* A must-see for Miami visitors, industrialist John Deering's Italian Renaissance villa (1914-16) holds a dizzying quantity of European decorative art treasures from the 16th to 19th centuries. In addition, the property boasts absolutely splendid formal gardens and views of Biscayne Bay.

Barnacle State Historic Site *(3485 Main Hwy., in Coconut Grove. 305-448-9445. Fri.-Sun.; adm. fee)* Five acres of hardwood hammock on Biscayne Bay surround the 1891 house of Coconut Grove pioneer Ralph Monroe.

Gold Coast Railroad Museum *(12450 S.W. 152 St. 305-253-0063. Adm. fee includes 20-minute train ride)* Among historic rail cars here is the *Ferdinand Magellan,* the private car-

South Beach art deco district, on Miami Beach

rier for Presidents Roosevelt, Truman, Eisenhower, and Reagan.

Excursions

FORT LAUDERDALE *(30 miles N via I-95)* This oceanside community recalls South Florida's early past at the **Stranahan House** *(335 S.E.6th Ave. 954-524-4736. Sept.-June Wed.-Sun.; adm. fee),* the 1901 store-turned-home of businessman Frank Stranahan. Spacious verandahs wrap around the house, built of Dade County pine and furnished with Victorian pieces. A 35-acre oceanfront estate, **Bonnet House** *(900 N. Bird Rd. 954-563-5393. May-Nov. Tues.-Fri. and Sun.; adm. fee)* features the winter home and gardens of artist Frederic Clay Bartlett. Built in the 1920s, the house contains a hand-painted ceiling, carved carousel animals, and other works by the artist and his wife.

Pensacola ···

(Convention & Visitors Bureau, 1401 E. Gregory St. 904-434-1234) From its founding in 1698 until the end of the Civil War, the City of Five Flags has passed back and forth between nations: Spain, France, England, the Confederate States of America, and the U.S. have all claimed possession of this natural port in the Florida Panhandle. Its contiguous historic districts (easily managed on foot) rank second in the state only to St. Augustine's in significance. The **Pensacola Historical Museum** *(Currently relocating; phone for new address. 904-433-1559. Adm. fee)* details local history.

Historic Pensacola Village *(Tickets to houses and museums available at Tivoli House, 205 E. Zaragoza St. 904-444-8905; and at T.T. Wentworth, Jr., Florida State Museum)* The village offers a number of fine buildings open to the public: The 1871 Greek Revival **Dorr House** *(Church and Adams Sts.)* exemplifies refined 19th-century living; the modest **Julee Cottage** *(210 E. Zaragoza St.)* was owned in the early 1800s by a free black woman; one of Pensacola's oldest

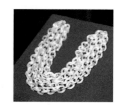

Treasure from Mel Fisher Maritime Heritage Society

houses, the **Lavalle House** (*205 E. Church St.*) was built in 1805 in the French Creole style; the **Museum of Commerce** (*Tarragona and Zaragoza Sts.*) features a replica turn-of-the-century street; the **Museum of Industry** (*200 E. Zaragoza St.*) highlights forestry, shipping, and fishing; and the eclectic **T.T. Wentworth, Jr., Florida State Museum** (*330 S. Jefferson St. 904-444-8586*) inhabits a huge Renaissance Revival edifice.

Palafox Historic District (*Palafox St. between Garden and Pine Sts.*) The commercial backbone of Pensacola boasts many late 19th- and early 20th-century buildings. In the verdant **Plaza Ferdinand VII,** Spain ceded west Florida to Andrew Jackson in 1821.

Excursions

NATIONAL MUSEUM OF NAVAL AVIATION (*8 miles W via US 98 at Pensacola U.S. Naval Air Station. 904-452-3604*) One of the world's top air museums showcases a hundred aircraft, including a squadron of Blue Angels suspended in a seven-story glass atrium. The massive brick **Fort Barrancas,** occupying a point on the air station grounds, was built between 1839 and 1844 to protect Pensacola Bay.

FORT PICKENS (*18 miles SE via US 98 E and Fla. 399, on Santa Rosa Island. 904-934-2600. Adm. fee*) Slaves labored from 1829 to 1834 to build this formidable bastion, soon an anachronism thanks to rifled cannon and other new technology. Used briefly in the Civil War, the fort also held Apache prisoner Geronimo.

St. Augustine

The nation's oldest permanent European city, St. Augustine was the 1513 landing site of Ponce de Léon in his search for the fountain of youth. The permanent settlement dates from 1565 when the Spanish, after a few failed attempts at settling, found a new incentive to stay—to drive away the recently arrived French.

Castillo de San Marcos National Monument (*1 Castillo Dr. S. 904-829-6506. Adm. fee*) The country's oldest surviving fortress dates to 1672 and served as an important coastal defense until 1900. You will find the coquina fort impressive, ancient, and weighted with historical anecdotes.

Lightner Museum (*75 King St. 904-824-2874. Adm. fee*) The former Alcazar Hotel, built by Henry Flagler in 1888, maintains a stunning collection of Asian antiquities, Tiffany art glass, scrimshaw, and musical instruments. Across the street the opulent rotunda and lobby of the castle-like **Flagler College** (formerly Hotel Ponce de Léon) is adorned with mosaic-tile floors, marble arches, and carved wood pillars.

Memorial Presbyterian Church (*Valencia and Sevilla Sts. 904-829-6451*) Developer Henry Flagler built this Venetian Renaissance-style church in 1889 in memory of his daughter; Flagler, his first wife, and daughter are buried in the mausoleum.

152

Florida and Flagler

The Sunshine State's reputation as America's playground owes much to Henry Morrison Flagler, railroad magnate and visionary developer. In 1844 the 14-year-old Flagler left New York with nine cents in his pocket and headed west to seek his fortune. Twenty years later, broke again but full of business sense, he teamed up with John D. Rockefeller to found the Standard Oil Company. In the 1870s Flagler came to St. Augustine for his wife's health and stayed on to build two elegant hotels. In subsequent years, he studded Florida's Atlantic coast with luxury resorts, linking them with a railway that by 1912 stretched all the way to Key West.

Oldest House *(14 St. Francis St. 904-824-2872. Adm. fee)* Occupying the site of an early 17th-century dwelling, the tabby and coquina house dates from 1727 and is furnished to reflect Spanish, English, and American occupations.

Spanish Quarter Museum *(33 St. George St. 904-825-6830. Adm. fee)* Costumed guides interpret this restored and re-created clutch of 18th-century Spanish colonial buildings.

Ximenez-Fatio House *(20 Aviles St. 904-829-3575. Thurs.-Mon. Closed Sept.)* This late 18th-century structure has been restored to the appearance it had in the 1830s, when it operated as a boardinghouse.

Zorayda Castle *(83 King St. 904-824-3097. Adm. fee)* Impressive and bizarre, this 1883 replica of the Moorish

Castillo de San Marcos National Monument, St. Augustine

Alhambra—complete with harem and central courtyard—owes its existence to the imagination of Boston millionaire Franklin Smith.

153

Excursions

ST. AUGUSTINE LIGHTHOUSE AND MUSEUM *(1 mile E via Fla. A1A. 904-829-0745. Adm. fee)* Since 1874, the 165-foot tower has guided mariners; a climb up the 219 steps offers unparalleled vistas of St. Augustine, the Intracoastal Waterway, and beaches.

FORT MATANZAS NATIONAL MONUMENT *(14 miles S via Fla. A1A. 904-471-0116)* The small coquina fortress on an island in the Matanzas River was built by the Spanish in 1740 to replace an earlier outpost on the site.

Sarasota ···

In 1885 Scottish immigrants landed here and established a town. By the early 20th century, Sarasota was a resort. John Ringling's decision to begin wintering his famous circus here in 1927 gave the town a welcome boost during the land-bust years in Florida.

John and Mable Ringling Museum of Art *(5401 Bayshore Rd. 941-359-5700. Adm. fee)* The circus owner's treasury of high art contains thousands of art objects, including one of the finest baroque collections in the country. Ringling's winter home, **Ca' d'Zan** (1926), a magnificent Venetian-style villa on beautiful Sarasota Bay, is decorated with European antiques.

Bellm's Cars and Music of Yesterday *(5500 N. Tamiami Trail. 941-355-6228. Adm. fee)* For 40 years this museum has delighted visitors with some 150 vintage automobiles, 1000 antique musical instruments, and scores of old-fashioned penny arcade games that still work.

Excursions

BRADENTON *(10 miles N via US 41)* Named after mid-19th-century settler Dr. Joseph Bradenton, this town on the Manatee River celebrates its past at the **Manatee Village Historical Park** *(604 15th St. E. 941-749-7165.*

Mon.-Fri.), a complex of late 19th- and early 20th-century buildings that includes a 1912 pioneer house and the first county courthouse (1860). The **De Soto National Memorial** (*75th St. NW. 941-792-0458*) preserves the site where Hernando de Soto and his 610 men started on the 4,000-mile inland expedition that would cost him his life. A 22-minute film, an interpretive trail, and exhibits recount the perils faced by the 16th-century Europeans, as well as their impact on the Indians of the area. Among the many offerings at the **South Florida Museum** (*201 10th St. W. 941-746-7827. Tues.-Sun; adm. fee*) are dioramas of prehistoric Indian life, replicas of de Soto's home and a Spanish chapel, a maritime history exhibit, and a doctor's and dentist's office.

GAMBLE PLANTATION STATE HISTORIC SITE (*18 miles N via I-75. 941-723-4536. Thurs.-Mon.; adm. fee*) South Florida's only extant antebellum plantation house, this handsome 1844 mansion once was at the hub of a 3,500-acre sugar plantation. Period furnishings grace the interior of the house.

HISTORIC SPANISH POINT (*10 miles S via US 41 in Osprey. 941-966-5214. Adm. fee*) The tranquil 30-acre site holds a glassed-off cross section of a prehistoric shell midden, restored gardens of cattle baron Bertha Palmer, early 1900s cottages, and a reconstructed 1894 chapel.

Tallahassee

(*Visitors Bureau, New Capitol Bldg., Duvall and Jefferson Sts. 904-413-9200*) This area was winter camp for conquistador de Soto in 1539. Almost 300 years later, in 1824, Tallahassee (Creek for "old town") was chosen as the new state capital because it lay halfway between the state's leading cities of St. Augustine and Pensacola. During the Civil War, Tallahassee was the only Southern capital east of the Mississippi not captured.

Old Capitol (*Monroe St. and Apalachee Pkwy. 904-487-1902*) The 1845 American Renaissance structure, restored to its 1902 appearance, features exhibits and former house, senate, and supreme court chambers, and a governor's suite.

Museum of Florida History (*500 S. Bronough St. 904-488-1484*) This well-conceived museum features a 12,000-year-old mastodon skeleton found in the area, naval stores equipment, and replicas of a steamship and early camper truck.

Cigarmaker, Ybor City, Tampa

Knott House Museum (*301 E. Park Ave. 904-922-2459. Wed.-Sat.; adm. fee*) Set in the historic district, the 1840s house has been restored to its 1930s look, when it was owned by state politician William V. Knott. Victorian furnishings predominate.

San Luis Archaeological and Historic Site (*2020 W. Mission Rd. 904-487-3711*) The site of an Indian village and 17th-century Spanish mission features a council house and an archaeology research lab.

Tallahassee Museum of History and Natural Science (*3945 Museum Dr. 904-576-1636. Adm. fee*) Children particularly enjoy this outdoor attraction that re-creates a late 19th-century farm.

Lake Jackson Indian Mounds State Archaeological Site (*US 27 to 3600 Indian Mounds Rd. 904-922-6007*) A small park with a nature trail embraces three Indian mounds dating from A.D. 1200.

Excursion

SAN MARCOS DE APALACHE STATE HISTORIC SITE *(20 miles S via Fla. 363, in St. Marks. 904-925-6216. Thurs.-Mon.; adm. fee)* Over the centuries, this much contested spit of land at the confluence of the Wakulla and St. Marks Rivers has claimed the attention of Spanish explorer Hernando de Soto, a band of pirates, the English army, Gen. Andrew Jackson, and Confederate forces. A museum displays artifacts from the various periods of occupation, and ruins of old Fort Ward can be seen.

Tampa ···

(Convention & Visitors Bureau, 111 E. Madison St. 813-223-1111. Mon.-Sat.) Though Spanish explorers came through in their searches for gold, the Tampa Bay area was left mostly to the Indians until a few fishermen and homesteaders found their way here in the early 1800s. Fort Brooke was set up in 1824 to displace the newly arrived Seminole, and Tampa was officially launched in 1855. By the turn of the century, Tampa had become the world's leading cigarmaking center, supported by thousands of Cuban, Spanish, and Italian immigrants. The renewed **Ybor City,** one of Florida's three national historic landmark districts, preserves a strongly Latin flavor in the shops and restaurants along 7th Street.

Ybor City State Museum *(1818 9th Ave. 813-247-6323. Tues.-Sat.; adm. fee)* Exhibits detail Tampa's cigarmaking industry and its ethnic heritage. Also included is an 1885 shotgun-style cigarworker's cottage, furnished with period pieces.

Henry B. Plant Museum *(U. of Tampa, 401 W. Kennedy Blvd. 813-254-1891. Tues.-Sun.; adm. fee)* Housed in the former Tampa Bay Hotel (1891), this fine museum is known for its landmark Moorish minarets. Exhibits trace the state's early tourism and Tampa's contribution to the Spanish-American War.

Other Sites in Florida

Dade Battlefield State Historic Site *(Bushnell. 904-793-4781. Adm. fee)* A Visitor Center and trail recount the beginning of the Second Seminole War in 1835, when Seminole ambushed 108 U.S. soldiers here.

Dry Tortugas National Park *(Via excursion boat or floatplane from Key West. 305-242-7700)* Initiated in 1846 to protect shipping interests in the Gulf, massive, moated Fort Jefferson, occupying most of Garden Key in the Dry Tortugas, was never completed. Dr. Samuel Mudd, implicated in Lincoln's assassination, was imprisoned in the fort before it was abandoned in 1873.

Gilbert's Bar House of Refuge *(Hutchinson Island. 407-225-1875. Tues.-Sun.; adm. fee)* This is the only survivor of the nine aid stations built on the Florida coast in 1875 to save stranded mariners.

Henry Morrison Flagler Museum *(1 Whitehall Way, Palm Beach. 407-655-2833. Tues.-Sun.; adm. fee)* Railroad tycoon Flagler built the 1902 Gilded Age mansion known as Whitehall; sumptuous furnishings and artwork fill it.

Marjorie Kinnan Rawlings State Historic Site *(Rte. 325, Cross Creek. 352-466-3672. Oct.-July Thurs.-Sun.; adm. fee)* The Pulitzer Prize-winning author of *The Yearling* (1939) lived here from 1928 to 1953.

Stephen Foster State Folk Culture Center *(US 41, White Springs. 904-397-2733. Adm. fee)* On the Suwannee River, the museum has dioramas that honor the composer of Florida's official state song, "Old Folks At Home."

Alabama

Russell Cave National Monument, outside Bridgeport

In 1540 near present-day Montgomery, Spanish explorer Hernando de Soto and his 500 men killed about 2,500 Indians in an all-day frenzy that ranked as one of the bloodiest battles ever fought on this continent between Indians and Europeans. For the next 275 years, the various tribes formed shifting allegiances with the foreign powers struggling for dominance of the region. By 1820 Andrew Jackson had driven out the Indians, and the new state of Alabama had entered the golden era of cotton. To prolong its plantation system, Alabama sent roughly 100,000 men to war; some 35,000 did not return. After the war, white politicians, embittered by Reconstruction, forced African Americans from power. In the mid-20th century, the civil rights movement exploded in the state, and disenfranchised blacks in Montgomery, Birmingham, and Selma led the way in national social reform.

Birmingham

(Visitor Bureau, 2200 9th Ave. N. 205-458-8000 or 800-458-8085. Mon.-Fri.) A post-Civil War town, Birmingham was founded in 1871 at the junction of two railroads and named for the industrial city in England. Blessed with the necessary raw materials—limestone, coal, and iron ore—the city

soon led the South in production of iron and steel. In the early 1960s Birmingham became a flash point of racial conflict, but by the late 1970s race relations had improved, and an integrated city council and African-American mayor had been elected.

Birmingham Civil Rights Institute (*520 16th St. N. 205-328-9696. Tues.-Sun.; donations*) A dramatic new facility with a marble rotunda and polished wood floors, the institute presents a walk-through of civil rights history. After an introductory film, the screen rises and you enter a series of realistic sets peopled with life-size figures and enhanced with audio and video programs. The institute is adjacent to **Sixteenth Street Baptist Church** (*1530 6th Ave. N. 205-251-9402. Tues.-Sat.*), where a bomb in 1963 killed four African-American children.

Arlington (*331 Cotton Ave. SW. 205-780-5656. Tues.-Sun.; adm. fee*) Built by Judge William Mudd in the 1840s, the Greek Revival mansion was used by the Union as a base of operations for destroying Alabama's factories, furnaces, and railroads. Period antiques adorn the house.

Sloss Furnaces (*20 32nd St. N. 205-324-1911. Tues.-Sun.*) From 1882 to 1971 Sloss produced a prodigious amount of pig iron—400 tons a year—for the city's foundries and mills. The blast furnaces that once bubbled with molten iron are preserved.

Southern Museum of Flight (*4343 73rd St. N. 205-833-8226. Tues.-Sun.; adm. fee*) An F-4 jet fighter mounted outside greets visitors to this fine overview of aviation history. Exhibits include a Delta Air Lines crop duster; a display on Germany's famous World War I hero, the Red Baron; and the Alabama Aviation Hall of Fame.

Vulcan Park (*20th St. S and Valley Ave. 205-328-2863. Adm. fee*) Honoring Birmingham's industrial heritage, the 55-foot-high cast-iron figure of the Roman god of fire and metalworking was built in 1904 for the St. Louis World's Fair. An observation deck provides excellent views of the city.

Excursions

BESSEMER HALL OF HISTORY (*15 miles SW via I-20/59, in Bessemer. 1905 Alabama Ave. 205-426-1633. Tues.-Sat.*) Housed in the renovated Southern Railway Depot (1916), this museum offers a potpourri of area history from fossils and Indian artifacts to Civil War items and exhibits on Bessemer's early years as a steel- and iron-producing town.

TANNEHILL IRONWORKS HISTORICAL STATE PARK (*30 miles SW via I-20/59, near Bucksville. 205-477-5711. Adm. fee*) From 1829 to their destruction by Union forces in 1865, Tannehill's huge stone furnaces turned out iron for plows, kitchenware, guns, and cannons. Predating Birmingham by more than 40 years, Tannehill and a few smaller area furnaces produced about 70 percent of the Confederacy's iron. In addition to the furnaces, the 1,500-acre wooded park holds the **Iron and Steel Museum of Alabama** and numerous 19th-century log cabins used as artisan studios.

Demopolis ·······································

(*Chamber of Commerce, 102 E. Washington St. 334-289-0272. Mon.-Fri.*) A group of exiles from defeated Napoleonic France settled Demopolis ("city of the people") in 1817. Congress granted them land for the cultivation of wines and olive oil. Unable to produce either, the French by the mid-1820s had scattered to New Orleans and other areas. Not long thereafter, cotton planters moved in and made far better use of the rich, black Alabama soil.

Bluff Hall *(405 Commissioners Ave. 334-289-1666. Tues.-Sun.; adm. fee)* Overlooking the Tombigbee River, this imposing white brick structure started as a federal town house (1832), then was modified around 1850 to the more popular Greek Revival style, with a columned portico and other additions. Period furniture and clothing are on display.

Gaineswood *(805 S. Cedar St. 334-289-4846. Adm. fee)* One of the state's finest house museums, Gaineswood (1842-1860) is the result of nearly 20 years of building and tinkering by owner-architect Gen. Nathan Bryan Whitfield. Originally a clapboard cabin anchoring a plantation, the dwelling evolved into a 20-room mansion with graceful porticos, glass domes, detailed friezes, and landscaped grounds. Family furnishings are still found throughout the house.

Gaineswood, in Demopolis

Excursion

GREENSBORO *(22 miles NE via US 80 and Ala. 69)* Scores of 19th-century commercial buildings and residences survive in this agricultural town, including **Magnolia Grove** *(1002 Hobson St. 334-624-8618. Wed.-Sun.; adm. fee)*, birthplace of Spanish-American War hero Richmond Hobson.

Florence ·······························

(Tourism Office, 1 High Tower Pl. 205-740-4140 or 888-356-8687. Mon.-Fri.) Named by the Italian surveyor who laid out its wide streets in 1818, the town benefited from its proximity to the Natchez Trace and the Tennessee River. In 1855 Florence became the home of the University of North Alabama, and in 1918 construction began on the massive Wilson Dam.

Indian Mound and Museum *(S. Court St. 205-760-6427. Tues.-Sat.; adm. fee)* At 42 feet high, the pre-Columbian ceremonial mound ranks as the biggest on the Tennessee River. A museum displays tools as old as 10,000 years and a case containing artifacts buried with an 18th-century chief.

Pope's Tavern Museum *(203 Hermitage Dr. 205-760-6439. Tues.-Sat.; adm. fee)* Built in the 1830s of handmade brick, the stage stop and tavern was used as a hospital for wounded Civil War soldiers throughout the war. Period furnishings depict conditions as they would have been at an outpost drinking establishment.

W.C. Handy Home and Museum *(620 W. College St. 205-760-6434. Tues.-Sat.; adm. fee)* The father of the blues was born in 1873 in this primitive log cabin, originally located six blocks north. An attached museum houses his personal belongings.

Excursion

IVY GREEN *(6 miles S via US 43/72, in Tuscumbia. 300 W. North Commons Rd.. 205-383-4066. Adm. fee)* A moving experience awaits visitors to the birthplace of Helen Keller (1880-1968). Rendered blind and deaf by an early childhood illness, Keller went on to graduate cum laude from Radcliffe College and to symbolize courage and hope for millions. One room contains personal effects, writings, and photos. The 1820 clapboard cottage, built by Keller's grandparents, has mostly family furnishings. Out back is the water pump where a seven-year-old Helen, with the help of her teacher, Anne Sullivan, suddenly unlocked the mystery of language.

Huntsville ···

(Visitor Center, Clinton and Monroe Sts. 205-533-5723) Popular with squatters in the early 1800s, the town was officially established in 1809 as Twickenham, but the name was changed two years later to honor John Hunt, one of the squatters. In 1819 the state's first constitutional convention was held in Huntsville. A cotton mill town in the mid-20th century, Huntsville received a boost in its fortunes in 1960, when NASA's Marshall Space Flight Center opened here. The **Twickenham Historic District** preserves more than 65 antebellum structures, and the adjacent **Old Town Historic District** has a concentration of ornate Victorian houses.

Constitution Hall Village *(109 Gates Ave. 205-535-6565. March-Dec. 23 Mon.-Sat.; adm. fee)* The living history complex comprises several early 1800s buildings reconstructed on their original sites, including the cabinetmaker's shop where Alabama's first constitutional meeting was held in 1819. Costumed guides illustrate pioneer life.

Huntsville Depot Museum *(320 Church St. 205-539-1860. March-Dec. Mon.-Sat.; adm. fee)* The 1860 railroad station holds three floors of entertaining exhibits, including train cars, Civil War graffiti, and robots that tell how the old trains operated.

U.S. Space and Rocket Center *(1 Tranquility Base. 205-837-3400. Adm. fee)* A highly popular hands-on showcase of space history includes original Apollo spacecraft, spacesuits, full-scale models of the space shuttle and Skylab, a 363-foot Saturn V rocket, spectacular Omnimax movies, and training simulators. Tours include the Marshall Space Flight Center, where scientists continue to develop the technology for further space exploration.

Weeden House Museum *(300 Gates Ave. 205-536-7718. Tues.-Sun.; adm. fee)* The 1819 federal house is the birthplace of 19th-century artist Maria Howard Weeden and features Weeden's paintings of slaves.

Burritt Museum and Park *(3101 Burritt Dr. 205-536-2882. Tues.-Sun. Closed late Dec.-Feb.; adm. fee)* Built in 1938 by a prominent physician, the 14-room house sits on 167 wooded acres atop Monte Sano. An eclectic collection includes Indian artifacts, early medical instruments, and pioneer outbuildings. The quiet setting offers fine views of the city.

U.S. Space and Rocket Center

Excursions

DECATUR *(20 miles SW via I-565)* This Tennessee River town was burned during the Civil War and decimated by a yellow fever epidemic in 1888 but held on to become an industrial and agricultural center. The **Old Decatur District** encompasses a number of Victorian buildings; the 1833 **Old State**

Bank (*925 Bank St. 205-350-5060. Call for hours*) served as a Civil War hospital and now houses a museum and visitor center.

MOORESVILLE (*10 miles W via I-565*) An all-but-forgotten village of a few dozen residents preserves the charm of the early 19th century with its tall trees and picket fences. Its handful of buildings includes a stagecoach tavern and a Greek Revival church where James Garfield once preached.

Mobile ·····································

German stained glass in Mobile's cathedral

(*Visitor information at Fort Conde, 150 S. Royal St. 334-434-7304*) Alabama's oldest town originated in 1711 as a French fort. Ceded to the English in 1763, it was grabbed by Spain during the American Revolution and then taken by the U.S. during the War of 1812. One of the Confederacy's most vital ports, Mobile was home base for blockade-runners, and their activity precipitated the Battle of Mobile Bay in August 1864. The town itself fell to the Union April 12, 1865, three days after Lee's surrender to Grant. After the war, Mobile recovered quickly, becoming a major shipping hub during the World Wars. The city's Mardi Gras celebrations started in the early 1700s, predating those in New Orleans. The downtown and surrounding neighborhoods preserve a large number of homes and buildings from the colonial through the Victorian periods.

Battleship *Alabama* (*2703 Battleship Pkwy. 334-433-2703. Adm. fee*) Mobile's most popular attraction, the enormous World War II ship protected convoys in the North Sea, destroyed enemy fortifications, and shot down numerous Japanese planes. Self-guided tours explore decks, mess rooms, sick bays, the captain's cabin, and more.

Bragg-Mitchell Mansion (*1906 Springhill Ave. 334-471-6364. Sun.-Fri.; adm. fee*) Framed by towering live oaks, the 1855 mansion is Mobile's largest house museum. Fluted columns support a wide portico; inside, original pier mirrors hang in a cavernous double parlor and fine period furniture fills the rooms.

Carlen House Museum (*54 S. Carlen St. 334-470-7768. Tues.-Sat.*) An unpretentious Creole cottage illustrates 19th-century rural life with a kitchen, dining room, parlor, bedroom, and upstairs nursery.

Cathedral of the Immaculate Conception (*Dauphin and Claiborne Sts. 334-434-1565*) The imposing antebellum house of worship boasts twin belfries; stained-glass windows made in Munich, Germany, that depict the life of Jesus; a barrel-roofed nave; and candles flickering in an immense silence.

Conde-Charlotte Museum House (*104 Theatre St. 334-432-4722. Tues.-Sat.; adm. fee*) Built between 1822 and 1824 as the city's first jail, the structure was converted into a residence in 1849. Each room is furnished to reflect a different period in Mobile history.

Museum of the City of Mobile (*355 Government St. 334-434-7569. Tues.-Sun.*) More than 100,000 items pack this elegant 1872 town house, including a large collection of historic armaments, a glittering display of Mardi Gras costumes, the ceremonial sword of Confederate naval hero Raphael Semmes, and a chair belonging to Union admiral David Farragut, hero of the Battle of Mobile Bay.

Oakleigh (*350 Oakleigh Pl. 334-432-1281. Adm. fee*) Constructed from 1833 to 1838 by a cotton broker who died a pauper, the Greek Revival house features bricks made on-site, high ceilings, and period furnishings. Informative tours illustrate mid-19th-century life in upper-class Mobile.

Richards—D.A.R. House *(256 N. Joachim St. 334-434-7320. Tues.-Sun.; adm. fee)* The Italianate townhouse, built in 1860 by a cotton-boat captain, stands out for its highly ornate wrought-iron facade. Interior delights include a fancy Carrara marble fireplace and brass and pewter gasoliers.

Excursions

BELLINGRATH GARDENS AND HOME *(10 miles S via Rte. 59, in Theodore. 334-973-2217. Adm. fee)* In the 1930s Coca-Cola-bottling pioneer Walter Bellingrath turned 65 acres of subtropical jungle into a paradise of year-round blooms. Though the gardens are the star attraction, the house contains an outstanding collection of 19th-century furnishings. A small museum exhibits Boehm porcelains.

FORT GAINES *(40 miles S via Ala. 193 on Dauphin Island. 334-861-6992. Adm. fee)* The pentagonal brick fort was completed just in time for the Civil War. The Battle of Mobile Bay occurred between here and Fort Morgan, directly east, and resulted in a Union victory. During the intense conflict federal admiral David Farragut became a naval legend when he declared, "Damn the torpedoes. Full speed ahead!"

HISTORIC BLAKELEY STATE PARK *(12 miles E via I-10 and Ala. 225, near Spanish Fort. 334-626-0798. Adm. fee)* This 3,800-acre site honors a major battle fought at the end of the Civil War.

161

Montgomery ··

(Visitor Center, 401 Madison Ave. 334-262-0013) Founded in 1819 near a former Indian village and French fort, the town soon became a prosperous cotton market. In 1861 it was made the first capital of the Confederacy and was captured by Union forces in 1865. In 1955 the arrest of Rosa Parks, an African-American woman who refused to give up her seat on a city bus, precipitated a year-long bus boycott and turned Montgomery into the focus of much civil rights activity. The boycott helped lead to the 1956 U.S. Supreme Court ruling that made segregated public transportation illegal.

Alabama Department of Archives and History *(624 Washington Ave. Mon.-Sat.)* A worthwhile compendium of state history, this museum offers memorabilia from various wars, Indian artifacts, and a display on country singer and native Alabaman Hank Williams (1923-1953).

Bellingrath Gardens and Home

Alabama State Capitol *(E. end of Dexter Ave. 334-242-3935)* The handsome Greek Revival structure (1851) has served as the backdrop to momentous occasions. In 1861 Jefferson Davis was sworn in as President of the Confederacy in front of the capitol, and just over a hundred years later, the Selma-to-Montgomery civil rights march ended here. The interior boasts twin two-story spiral staircases and an embellished rotunda that rises 90 feet to a skylight. The house and senate chambers, used by the legislature until the mid-1980s, have been

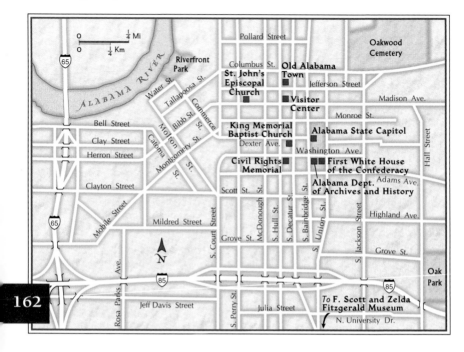

restored to their late 19th-century appearance, with trompe l'oeil effects on the walls and ceilings. The first Confederate Constitution was drafted in the senate chambers in February 1861.

Civil Rights Memorial (*400 Washington Ave.*) Water flows across a black granite wall inscribed with the names of people killed in the struggle for equal rights. The 1989 memorial was designed by Maya Lin, creator of the Vietnam Veterans Memorial in Washington, D.C.

Dexter Avenue King Memorial Baptist Church (*454 Dexter Ave. 334-263-3970. Mon.-Fri.*) Martin Luther King, Jr., was pastor in this 1880s red-brick church from 1954 to 1960.

First White House of the Confederacy (*664 Washington Ave. 334-242-1861. Mon.-Fri.*) Jefferson Davis and his wife lived in the 1835 two-story house for the few months that Montgomery was the Confederate capital. Some of Davis's belongings are on display.

Old Alabama Town (*310 N. Hull St. 334-240-4500. Adm. fee*) A clutch of 19th-century buildings, moved from locations around the state, illustrates urban and rural life. An audio tour describes the old days at such institutions as the corner grocery, one-room school, and doctor's office. Another assemblage of buildings across the street includes a cotton gin and active crafts shops.

St. John's Episcopal Church (*113 Madison Ave. 334-262-1937. Mon.-Fri.*) Jefferson Davis worshiped in an earlier version of this church. Dating from 1869, the present structure features Tiffany stained glass and a vaulted ceiling of colorful panels.

F. Scott and Zelda Fitzgerald Museum (*919 Felder Ave. 334-264-4222.*

Wed.-Sun.; donations) The novelist and his wife leased this modest house in Zelda's hometown briefly in 1931-32, while Fitzgerald worked on *Tender Is the Night* and Zelda continued the long descent into mental illness that would plague her the rest of her life.

Excursions

CONFEDERATE MEMORIAL PARK *(30 miles N via I-65 in Mountain Creek. 205-755-1990)* The former site of a home for Confederate veterans and their wives now makes a peaceful spot for a picnic under tall trees. The grounds encompass two cemeteries and a small museum.

FORT TOULOUSE-JACKSON PARK *(12 miles NE via US 231 near Wetumpka. 334-567-3002. Adm. fee)* An archaeological dig site features living history exhibits at two reconstructed forts. The first was a French trading post occupied during the 18th century; the second was built by Andrew Jackson in 1814. A treaty signed with the Indians here opened 20 million acres to white settlement.

LOWNDESBORO *(15 miles SW via US 80)* Planters from Virginia and South Carolina settled here at a bend in the Alabama River around 1820. The quiet wayside town now holds a handful of antebellum mansions and churches.

TUSKEGEE INSTITUTE NATIONAL HISTORIC SITE *(40 miles E via I-85. 334-727-6390)* Founded in 1881 by former slave Booker T. Washington, the prestigious college started in a run-down church and now boasts more than 150 buildings and an enrollment of nearly 5,000. One building houses the **George Washington Carver Museum** *(334-727-3200)*, honoring the institute's well-known professor and inventor, who lived from 1864 to 1943. Carver's laboratory equipment, his paintings, and films about him and the school are featured. Another highlight, **The Oaks,** was the home of Booker T. Washington. The attractive Queen Anne house (1899) contains family furniture.

Selma ···

(Visitor Center, 2207 Broad St. 334-875-7485) A lovely river bluff town of antebellum houses and old trees, Selma served as a major manufacturing center and supply depot during the Civil War. In April 1865 Gen. James Wilson's Raiders blazed through, destroying the munitions plant, foundry, and about a hundred houses. A century later, in March 1965, the town received national attention when a showdown between several hundred African-American marchers and Gov. George Wallace's state troopers resulted in violence on the **Edmund Pettus Bridge.** Two weeks later the Alabama National Guard protected civil rights activists on their 54-mile march to Montgomery to protest for voting rights.

George Washington Carver and students, Tuskegee Institute

Anchoring the north end of the Edmund Pettus Bridge, the five-block **Water Avenue** business district contains many antebellum structures. A few blocks north stands the **Brown**

Chapel A.M.E. Church (*410 Martin Luther King St. Mon., Wed., Fri.*), used as headquarters by organizers of the 1965 civil rights march.

Old Depot Museum (*4 Martin Luther King St. 334-874-2197. Mon.-Sat.; adm. fee*) A compendium of area history housed in an 1891 railway station includes pioneer tools, antique medical equipment, Civil War crutches, and an extraordinary collection of plantation-era photographs.

Smitherman Historic Building (*109 Union St. 334-874-2174. Mon.-Fri.; adm. fee*) Built by members of the local Masonic lodge as a school for orphans and indigents, the 1847 Greek Revival structure became a Confederate hospital and then a county office building. A museum room displays handbills for slave sales, runaway reward posters, and other interesting documents and artifacts.

Sturdivant Hall (*713 Mabry St. 334-872-5626. Tues.-Sun.; adm. fee*) Selma's finest house (1852) at first appears to be a standard grand Greek Revival box. But closer inspection reveals an immaculately restored home of extreme elegance, with tasteful marble and plasterwork and an L-shaped floor plan that lends an airy feel. Period furnishings include a coin silver service and a rare 18th-century ormolu clock. A spiral stairway winds to a third-floor cupola; the kitchen building now houses a gift shop.

National Voting Rights Museum (*1012 Water Ave. 334-418-0800. Mon.-Sat.; adm. fee*) Just west of the Edmund Pettus Bridge, this small museum pays tribute to the 1965 protest movement in Selma, where, as President Lyndon Johnson said, history and fate met "to shape a turning point in man's unending search for freedom." Featured are photographs and the PBS documentary "Eyes on the Prize."

Excursion

CAHAWBA (*14 miles SW via Ala. 22. 334-872-8058*) Only vine-wrapped ruins remain of Alabama's former capital city (1820-1826), victim of repeated floods. Interpretive markers along dirt roads show the location of the courthouse, capitol, and other buildings.

Tuscaloosa

(*Visitor information at the Jemison-Van de Graaff House, 1305 Greensboro Ave. 205-391-9200 or 800-538-8696. Mon.-Fri.*) Named for the Choctaw chief Black Warrior, who was defeated in 1540 by Hernando de Soto, Tuscaloosa was founded in 1816 on the Black Warrior River. It served as state capital from 1825 to 1847 and in 1831 became the home of the University of Alabama.

More than a hundred antebellum houses remain, including the 1835 Greek Revival **Battle-Friedman House** (*1010 Greensboro Ave. Tues.-Sun.; adm. fee*) and the 1820 **Mildred Warner House** (*1925 8th St. 205-345-4062. Sat.-Sun.*), with a fine collection of American art.

University of Alabama (*University Blvd.*) Though destroyed by Union

---

Reconstruction and After
The end of the Civil War began a period of both frustration and hope for thousands of freed slaves. With the Southern states determined to restrict freedmen's rights, Congress ordered the Army to occupy and reconstruct the South in 1867. African Americans held political office and voted for the first time, courts were restructured, and public education was made available. But these changes were overshadowed by continued racial conflict: The Ku Klux Klan and other outlaw groups rose up to intimidate blacks and their white sympathizers. By the time the Army withdrew in 1877, Southern white democrats were back in power. The old caste system held firm until the civil rights movement of the 1950s and '60s eventually led to more parity between the races.

forces in 1865, the school was quickly rebuilt. Its Gothic Revival and neoclassical buildings center around a quadrangle. Across the boulevard stands the stately 1841 **President's Mansion** *(Not open to public)*, one of four buildings not burned; another was the 1829 **Gorgas House** *(205-348-5906. Tues.-Fri. and Sun.)*.

Excursion

MOUNDVILLE ARCHAEOLOGICAL PARK *(16 miles S via Ala. 69. 205-371-2572. Adm. fee)* The 317-acre site preserves more than 20 mounds from one of the Southeast's largest pre-Columbian Mississippian villages. Concentrating on the period A.D. 900 to 1500, the museum displays stone and bone tools, shell ornaments, and a mysterious stone disk possibly used for war or religious ceremonies.

Other Sites in Alabama

Anniston *(Chamber of Commerce, 1330 Quintard Ave. 205-237-3536 or 800-489-1087. Mon.-Fri.)* Buildings of interest in this late 19th-century industrial town include the 1888 Richardson Romanesque **Church of St. Michael and All Angels** *(1000 W. 18th St. 205-237-4011)*, with its alabaster reredos and 95-foot bell tower.

Clarkson Covered Bridge *(9 miles W of Cullman. 205-739-3530)* Built in 1904, one of Alabama's largest covered bridges measures 270 feet long. Nearby are a reproduction pioneer cabin and gristmill.

Cullman County Museum *(211 2nd Ave. N.E., in Cullman. 205-739-1258. Sun.-Fri.; adm. fee)* A reconstruction of the house of the German refugee who founded the town in 1873, the museum contains early farm implements, 1800s household items, and a replica Main Street with shops and offices.

DeSoto Caverns Park *(Childersburg. 205-378-7252. Adm. fee)* Occupied about 1000 B.C. by Woodland Indians, the marble-onyx caves were used as a speakeasy during Prohibition.

Eufaula *(Off US 431. Chamber of Commerce, 102 N. Orange Ave. 334-687-6664)* The

Moundville Archaeological Park, near Tuscaloosa

small town boasts more than 700 buildings of architectural or historical significance, including the 1884 **Shorter Mansion** *(340 N. Eufala Ave. 334-687-3793. Adm. fee)*, a prosperous cotton planter's vision of grandeur.

Horseshoe Bend National Military Park *(12 miles N of Dadeville. 205-234-7111)* After the Creek massacred 250 settlers near Mobile, Andrew Jackson and his 3,000 men crushed 1,000 warriors here in March 1814. The park has a 3-mile interpretive road, hiking trails, and a museum.

Noccalula Falls Park *(Gadsden. 205-549-4663. Adm. fee)* A legendary Cherokee princess leapt to her death from these picturesque 90-foot falls. Close by are a covered bridge and reassembled pioneer farm and homestead.

Russell Cave National Monument *(8 miles NW of Bridgeport. 205-495-2672)* Occupied from about 7000 B.C. to A.D. 1000, the vast limestone cavern was home to a long procession of cultures. The site comprises 310 acres donated in 1961 by the National Geographic Society and includes a Visitor Center, nature trails, and a viewing area at the cave's mouth.

Frontier camp at Biloxi, sketched in 1720

Conquistador Hernando de Soto and his army dashed through here in 1540 during their search for gold and fame. They reached the Mississippi River in 1541, encountering the Chickasaw Indians along the way. More than two centuries would pass before farmers from Georgia and the Carolinas began settling the area. In 1817 the western part of the Mississippi Territory became the state of Mississippi, with the eastern part becoming Alabama two years later. The next 50 years witnessed the rapid rise and fall of the plantation system, with its paradoxical legacy of beauty and pain. Landowners tamed the wilderness with vast cotton fields, then erected palatial houses to symbolize their wealth. Slaves and imported artisans made a genteel life-style possible for the very few, but the Civil War put an end to the Southern aristocracy's idyllic life. The second state to secede from the Union, Mississippi had much to lose by defeat. Left in economic ruin by the war, the state began to pick up momentum in the mid-20th century, as it gradually industrialized.

Biloxi

(Visitor Center, 710 Beach Blvd. 601-374-3105) The French settlement got its start in 1699 as the seat of government for the vast Louisiana Territory. Named for the Biloxi ("first people") Indians, the Gulf Coast town volleyed between nations for 150 years or so. In the early 1900s, Biloxi was the world's leading seafood producer; today casinos dominate the waterfront.

Beauvoir *(2244 Beach Blvd. 601-388-1313. Adm. fee)* Confederate President Jefferson Davis lived and wrote at this serene estate from 1877 until his death in 1889; from 1903 to 1957 it served as a Confederate veterans home. Now a national historic landmark, the site features a museum of Confederate relics, a breezy high-ceilinged house furnished mostly with Davis family pieces, and some 50 acres of lovingly maintained grounds.

Pedestrians-only side streets hold such points of interest as the 1847 **Magnolia Hotel** (119 Magnolia Ave. 601-435-6245), which contains a Mardi Gras museum, and the 1835 classical revival **Brunet-Fourchy House** (116 Magnolia Ave.), now a restaurant.

Maritime and Seafood Industry Museum (115 1st St. 601-435-6320. Mon.-Sat.; adm. fee) The small informative museum highlights Biloxi's leading industry with exhibits on boatbuilding, oystering, and related topics.

Tullis-Toledano Manor (360 Beach Blvd. 601-435-6293. Mon.-Fri.; adm. fee) Built by New Orleans cotton broker Christoval Toledano in 1854 and damaged by flooding from Hurricane Camille in 1969, the spacious two-story brick house has been restored to its former elegance.

Excursions

FORT MASSACHUSETTS (12 miles S via excursion boat from Gulfport Yacht Harbor to West Ship Island. 601-864-1014. March-Oct.; fare for boat) As U.S. Secretary of War, Jefferson Davis advised constructing a masonry fortification here in 1855. Ironically, the island outpost (built 1859-1866) became a Union blockade and staging platform during the Civil War.

OLD SPANISH FORT MUSEUM (20 miles E via US 90, in Pascagoula. 601-769-1505. Adm. fee) Constructed in 1718 with thick tabby walls, the Mississippi Valley's oldest building was actually a settler's home, not a fort. A museum has Indian and 18th-century artifacts.

Columbus ···

(Convention & Visitors Bureau, 321 7th St. N. 601-329-1191) Established as a trading center in the late 1700s, Columbus began attracting planters from Georgia and the Carolinas. They raised cotton in the rich soil along the Tombigbee River and built elegant Greek Revival houses. Spared the flames that ravaged many southern cities during the Civil War, Columbus boasts more than a hundred noteworthy antebellum houses. The first home of playwright Tennessee Williams (1911-1983) now holds the city's **Welcome Center** (300 E. Main St. 601-328-0222 or 800-689-3983. Mon.-Sat.).

Waverley, near Columbus

Excursions

ABERDEEN (28 miles N via US 45 and Miss. 25) A pre-Civil War social and commercial hub, this gracious county seat prides itself on its well-preserved antebellum and Victorian houses. **The Magnolias** (732 W. Commerce St. 601-369-9440 or 800-634-3538. Mon.-Fri.), a magnificent 1850 Greek Revival mansion with twin curved staircases, is now site of the Visitor Center.

WAVERLEY (11 miles NW via US 45 and Miss. 50. 601-494-1399. Adm. fee) One of the most splendid houses in the South, Waverly (1852) once presided over a 50,000-acre plantation. A breathtaking ballroom lifts the eye up to octagonal second- and third-floor balconies and a 65-foot-high dome. The building was painstakingly restored by a Mississippi family.

Corinth

(*Chamber of Commerce, 1810 Pate St. 601-287-5269. Mon.-Fri.*) Located at the junction of two major railroads, Corinth became a mobilization center for Confederate troops and much contested strategic ground, resulting in 1862 in the bloody battle of Shiloh, 20 miles north, and the Battle of Corinth later that year. Federal victories opened the way to control of the Mississippi Valley. Scene of intense fighting, **Battery Robinette** (*W. Linden St.*) is now a quiet park with interpretive markers.

Corinth Museum (*4th and Washington Sts. 601-287-3120*) Three rooms display a collection of historical artifacts, with emphasis on the Civil War, including photographs and a violin reputedly owned by Jefferson Davis.

Curlee House (*301 Childs St. 601-287-9501. Adm. fee*) During the Civil War this dignified Greek Revival house (1857) served as headquarters for both Confederate and Union generals. The house features 16-foot ceilings, plaster molding, and period furnishings. The former guesthouse now serves as the **Civil War Center**, interpreting Corinth's role in the war.

Excursion

SHILOH NATIONAL MILITARY PARK, TENN. (*23 miles NW via US 45 and Tenn. 22*) See page 190.

Jackson

(*Convention & Visitors Bureau, 921 N. President St. 601-960-1891 or 800-354-7695. Mon.-Fri.*) French-Canadian Louis Le Fleur established a trading post here on a bluff over the Pearl River in the 1790s, and in 1821 state legislators selected the site for a new capital city. General Sherman's troops burned the town so thoroughly in July 1863 that it became known as "Chimneyville."

Governor's Mansion (*300 E. Capitol St. 601-359-3175. Tues.-Fri.*) One of the few buildings not destroyed by Sherman, the well-proportioned Greek Revival house, completed in 1842, is furnished with 19th-century antiques.

Manship House (*420 E. Fortification St. 601-961-4724. Tues.-Sat.; donations*) Charles Henry Manship, ornamental painter and Civil War mayor of Jackson, built his Gothic Revival home in 1857 and decorated it with faux wood-graining and marbling.

Jim Buck Ross Mississippi Agricultural and Forestry/National Agricultural Aviation Museum (*1150 Lakeland Dr. 601-354-6113. Adm. fee*) A slick complex of buildings details state history from the Indians to the 20th century. The vast Heritage Center presents early farm machinery, sawmill exhibits, and crop dusters, while the outdoor Small Town comprises numerous relocated structures from the 1920s.

The Oaks House Museum (*823 N. Jefferson St. 601-353-9339. Tues.-Sat. Adm. fee*) Considered the oldest private house extant in Jackson, the one-story cottage was built in 1846 by Mayor James Boyd and occupied by Sherman during the siege of Jackson.

Old Capitol (*100 S. State St. 601-359-6920*) Dating from 1833, the Greek Revival edifice, now housing the state historical museum, served as the seat of state government until the completion of a grander capitol in 1903.

Natchez

(*Convention & Visitors Bureau, 422 Main St. 601-446-6345. Mon.-Fri.*) A city-size museum of the antebellum South, Natchez started in 1716 as Fort Rosalie, built by the French on the site of an old Natchez Indian village. The sun-worshipping Natchez attempted to retake their land, and were destroyed in the process. After English and Spanish occupations, the town in the early 1800s settled down to its golden age of building. Profiting from the Mississippi's rich earth, cotton planters put up great neoclassical showplaces. Situated at the southern end of the Natchez Trace, which extends to Nashville, the port town became a lively center of culture and

169

Stanton Hall, Natchez

business. Reserves of timber and oil buoyed Natchez through the first half of the 20th century, but tourism fuels the current economy.

The town encompasses an astounding 300 antebellum houses and other buildings, more than 30 of which are open during the annual spring and fall pilgrimages; several offer year-round tours and bed-and-breakfast stays. Since the finest residences were not built side by side, but scattered and set off by parklike estates, driving is the best way to take in the large quantity and variety of Natchez architecture.

Natchez Driving Tour ················· 35 miles, 6 hours

1. In the southeast part of town, the oldest settlement, the **Grand Village of the Natchez Indians** (*400 Jefferson Davis Blvd. 601-446-6502*) preserves mounds from a Natchez ceremonial center occupied from 1200 to 1730.

2. Longwood (*140 Lower Woodville Rd. 601-442-5193. Adm. fee*), one of the two or three most memorable Natchez houses, features an octagonal design surmounted by a six-story-high minaret. Interior construction on

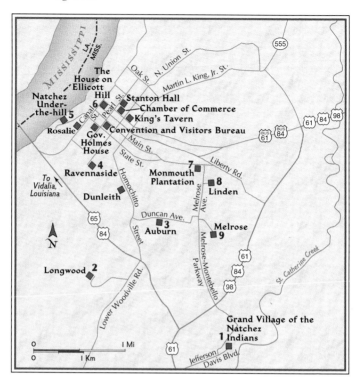

the house was interrupted by the Civil War and was never completed.

3. An early Greek Revival, **Auburn** (*400 Duncan Ave. 601-442-5981. Adm. fee*) boasts an elegant freestanding spiral staircase and some original furnishings. The nearby 1856 Greek Revival **Dunleith** (*84 Homochitto St. 601-446-8500. Adm. fee*), now an inn, shows off its many white columns. Tours cover only the first floor—the upstairs is reserved for overnight guests.

4. Ravennaside (*601 S. Union St. 601-442-8015. Adm. fee*) was built just after the Civil War to entertain visiting dignitaries and local elite. The Gold Room has an ornate marble fireplace and gleaming parquet floor.

5. Rosalie (*100 Orleans Sts. 601-445-4555. Adm. fee*), an 1823 Georgian mansion, commands fine views of the river from its wide galleries, perhaps enjoyed by Ulysses S. Grant, who occupied the house in 1863. Exquisite furnishings, original to 1858, abound.

Just down the street, refurbished **Natchez Under-the-Hill** (*Silver St.*) attracts tourists to bars, shops, and a riverboat casino docked at the infamous landing where gamblers, thieves, and prostitutes once thrived. One of the oldest domiciles in town, **Governor Holmes House** (*207 S. Wall St. 601-442-2366*) dates from the 1790s and offers bed-and-breakfast accommodations. It was owned by the last governor of the Mississippi Territory and the first governor of the new state.

6. The **House on Ellicott Hill** (*211 N. Canal St. 601-442-2011. Adm. fee*), though it pales in comparison with later houses, illustrates graceful French

Monmouth Plantation, Natchez

Caribbean living in 1798. Period furnishings match with inventories kept for tax purposes.

White-stuccoed **Stanton Hall** (*401 High St. 601-442-6282. Adm. fee*), a true gem of antebellum splendor, occupies an entire city block and boasts 17-foot-high ceilings, navelike central hallways, 10-foot-high cypress doors, and intricate rococo woodwork and plasterwork.

The oldest known building in Natchez, **King's Tavern** (*619 Jefferson St. 601-446-8845*) dates from 1789 and served as a stage stop and mill station; it now houses a restaurant.

7. The 1818 home of Gen. John Quitman, **Monmouth Plantation** (*John Quitman Pkwy. and Melrose Ave. 601-442-5852. Adm. fee*) is surrounded by lovely formal gardens. The house operates as an inn.

8. Another inn of note, **Linden** (*1 Linden Pl. 601-445-5472. Adm. fee*) dates from circa 1790, with family furnishings from six generations.

9. Anchoring Natchez National Historical Park, the majestic 1840s **Melrose** (*1 Melrose Montabello Pkwy. 601-446-5790. Adm. fee*) is a textbook Greek Revival edifice of perfect symmetry. Informative tours discuss the Natchez nabobs and their slave-driven economy.

Excursions

EMERALD MOUND (*12 miles NE, off Natchez Trace Pkwy.*) Constructed between 1250 and 1600 by ancestors of the Natchez Indians, the second largest earthen mound in the U.S. measures 8 acres and towers 35 feet.

SPRINGFIELD PLANTATION (*22 miles NE via US 61 and Natchez Trace Pkwy. 601-786-3802. Adm. fee*) This operating plantation features a colonnaded home built by planter Thomas Green, Jr. In 1791 Andrew Jackson is said to have married Rachel Robards at the newly completed house.

ROSSWOOD PLANTATION (*35 miles NE via US 61, in Lorman. 601-437-4215. March-Dec.; adm. fee*) Functioning now as a bed-and-breakfast, the 1857 mansion was designed by David Shroder, whose **Windsor** stands in ghostly ruins nearby. Rosswood served briefly as a hospital during the Civil War.

ROSEMONT PLANTATION (*35 miles S via US 61, Woodville. Miss. 24E. 601-888-6809. March-Dec. Mon.-Fri.; adm. fee*) This modest two-story house (1810), graced by family furnishings, was the boyhood home of Jefferson Davis.

Tupelo ....

(*Visitor Center, 399 E. Main St. 601-841-6521 or 800-533-0611*) Tupelo was built on the Chickasaw trade route that became known as the Natchez Trace. A later link to the outside—the railroad—was targeted in two fierce Civil War battles. Tupelo's most famous son, Elvis Presley (1935-1977) was born in a modest house on the east side of town.

City Museum (*Miss. 6 W, in Ballard Park. 601-841-6438. Adm. fee*) A real curio shop of area history, this museum contains room after room of assorted artifacts and curios—from an iron lung and other medical equipment to an Apollo 15 spacesuit and pieces of old aircraft. Pioneer life is depicted in an 1870 farmhouse and other buildings.

171

Tupelo National Battlefield Site (*Natchez Trace Pkwy. 601-680-4025 or 800-305-7417*) After the Union defeat at Brices Cross Roads, Gen. Sherman ordered his Memphis commander to "follow Forrest to the death." A small park with markers recalls the July 1864 battle here, which ended in a draw.

Excursion

BRICES CROSS ROADS NATIONAL BATTLEFIELD SITE (*20 miles N via US 45 and Miss. 370W. 601-680-4025*) To learn battle tactics, cadets visit this country crossroads where wily Gen. Nathan Bedford Forrest and his men outfoxed a Federal force more than twice their number in June 1864. Cannon and a cemetery mark the hallowed ground.

Vicksburg ···

(*Visitors Bureau, Clay St./US 80. 601-636-9421*) Methodist minister Newit Vick established a mission here in 1817 on the site of 18th-century French and Spanish forts. Developing into a major port, the town became the Confederacy's key bastion on the Mississippi River. It succumbed on July 4, 1863, after a 47-day siege engineered by Gen. Ulysses S. Grant. Several historic antebellum houses open their doors for tours as well as overnight stays. They include **Anchuca** (*1010 First East St. 601-631-6800 or 800-469-2597. Adm. fee*), **Balfour House** (*1002 Crawford St. 601-638-7113 or 800-294-7113. Mon.-Sat.; adm. fee*), and **Cedar Grove** (*2200 Oak St. 601-636-1000 or 800-862-1300. Adm. fee*).

Vicksburg National Military Park (*3201 Clay St. 601-636-0583. Adm. fee*) Knowing the war could not be won without the capture of Vicksburg, Lincoln repeatedly urged his commanders to attempt to take the city. Finally, in the late spring of 1863, General Grant and his 50,000 men began their siege of the blufftop town. Residents took shelter in caves and suffered hunger and other privations. The 1,700-acre park offers a 16-mile auto tour past monuments, markers, and re-created earthworks. A corner of the park contains the wreckage of the Union ironclad *Cairo,* a time capsule of naval history. The adjacent national cemetery contains the graves of nearly 17,000 Union men.

Wisconsin State Memorial, Vicksburg National Military Park

Martha Vick House (*1300 Grove St. 601-638-7036. Adm. fee*) Built in 1830 for a daughter of Vicksburg's founder, the house has 18th- and 19th-century furnishings, Impressionist paintings, and Haviland china.

McRaven (*1445 Harrison St. 601-636-1663. Adm. fee*) Distinguished by the three periods in which it was built, this house dates from before the found-

ing of Vicksburg and contains a wealth of local artifacts. The 1797 wing has a frontier feel; the 1836 section is decorated in federal empire style; and the 1849 addition exemplifies Greek Revival luxury, with Belter and Mallard furniture, Rose Medallion porcelain, and ornate plasterwork.

Old Court House Museum (*1008 Cherry St. 601-636-0741. Adm. fee*) A harmonious building with Ionic columns and a cupola dating from 1858, the museum houses nine rooms filled with items ranging from Ku Klux Klan and Confederate artifacts to a chair used by Grant during the siege. In the upstairs courtroom Jefferson Davis attempted to regain his nearby plantation seized during the war and sold to his former slaves; he lost the case but won on appeal to the state supreme court.

Excursions

GRAND GULF MILITARY MONUMENT (*33 miles S via US 61 and Miss. 462, near Port Gibson. 601-437-5911. Adm. fee*) Here in April 1863 Confederates prevented Grant's forces from crossing the river, thus staving off the fall of Vicksburg. The defeated Union troops simply pulled out and crossed farther south. The 450-acre park includes two forts, several restored buildings, a small museum, and a 30-foot observation tower.

PORT GIBSON (*30 miles S via US 61. Chamber of Commerce, US 61. 601-437-4351. Mon.-Sat.*) This small town resonant of the Old South boasts fine homes, churches, and other buildings. General Grant purportedly spared the town because he thought it too beautiful to burn. Landmarks include **Oak Square,** an 1850 mansion (*1207 Church St. 601-437-4350. Adm. fee*), and the **First Presbyterian Church** (*Walnut and Church Sts. 601-437-5428*), with its signature steeple crowned by a tremendous hand.

Other Sites in Mississippi

Delta Blues Museum (*114 Delta Ave., in Clarksdale. 601-624-4461*) Housed in the 1914 Carnegie Public Library, exhibits and recordings trace the origins of the blues through the work of such regional musicians as W.C. Handy, John Lee Hooker, and Muddy Waters.

Holly Springs (*Chamber of Commerce, 154 S. Memphis St. 601-252-2943. Mon.-Fri.*) Established by a Virginian in the 1830s, this cotton-era rail town experienced 59 Civil War skirmishes and raids, including the December 1862 attack on Grant's stockpiled supplies. Confederate general Earl Van Dorn took 1,500 prisoners and delayed Grant's advance toward Vicksburg. Privately owned antebellum houses grace the town.

Greenville (*Welcome Center, US 82 and Reed Rd. 601-378-3141*) The river port and agricultural town was burned by Federal forces, rebuilt during Reconstruction, then partially destroyed by flood in 1927. In the 1930s a levee system pushed the Mississippi west. **Winterville Mounds State Park** (*3 miles N on Miss. 1. 601-334-4684. Wed.-Sun.; adm. fee*) displays jewelry and pottery of the Choctaw who lived in the area nearly 1,000 years ago.

Nanih Waiya State Historic Site (*Miss. 397, Louisville. 601-773-7988*) The traditional cradle of the Choctaw nation, the site was first occupied about A.D. 400 and contains large mounds.

Rowan Oak (*Old Taylor Rd., in Oxford. 601-234-3284. Tues.-Sun.*) Tucked into a grove of oak and cedar trees is the 1848 house where Nobel laureate novelist William Faulkner lived and worked. His home looks the way he left it at his death in 1962.

Louisiana

Oak Alley, near Vacherie

In 1682 French explorer La Salle claimed the entire Mississippi Valley for France, naming it in King Louis XIV's honor. A fort built near a village of Natchitoches Indians in 1714 became the Louisiana Territory's first permanent settlement. Four years later, Nouvelle Orleans was founded on the steamy, mosquito-infested banks of the Mississippi; in 1722 it became the territorial capital. Over the next several decades, the royal colony's population grew with the arrival of French and Spanish settlers (whose descendants became Creoles), exiled Acadians (or Cajuns), and African-born slaves. From 1762 to 1803, the Louisiana Territory alternated between Spanish and French rule. In 1803 the Americans purchased it for 15 million dollars, and in 1812 Louisiana became the 18th state to join the Union. The slave-run plantation economy boomed along fertile rivers and bayous until the Civil War. Ravaged by the war, the state faltered economically until the turn of the century, when the discovery of black gold brought a much needed boost.

Baton Rouge

(Convention & Visitors Commission, 730 North Blvd. 504-383-1825 or 800-LA-ROUGE) In 1699 French explorers noticed a red tree marking the boundary between two Indian nations and called the place Baton Rouge—"red stick." Seven flags have flown over the city since. Chosen state capital in 1849, Baton Rouge was occupied by Union forces during the Civil War.

Old State Capitol (*North Blvd. at River Rd. 504-342-0500. Tues.-Sun.; adm. fee*) Built on a perch above the Mississippi in the 1840s, the turreted, Gothic Revival castle oversaw the state's secession from the Union in 1861 and the impeachment proceedings against controversial Gov. Huey P. Long in 1929. Replaced by a new state house in 1932, the restored edifice now contains a museum on the history of state government.

Pentagon Barracks (*Capitol Complex. 504-342-1866*) A portion of the 1820s barracks now holds an interpretive center on city history.

Spanish Town (*Bounded by Spanish Town Rd., North St., N. 8th St., and N. 5th St.*) The city's oldest neighborhood was laid out in 1805 for Spanish families who wished to remain under their own flag after the Louisiana Purchase.

Magnolia Mound (*2161 Nicholson Dr. 504-343-4955. Tues.-Sun.; adm. fee*) The leisurely world of a cotton and sugar planter comes to life in this 1791 French Creole house, furnished with federal pieces.

LSU Rural Life Museum (*Off I-10, Essen Lane exit. 504-765-2437. Adm. fee*) While most of the area's 19th-century house museums focus on the wealth and prestige of the plantation owners, this outdoor complex showcases the lifestyle of the laboring folk. The site includes a barn with hundreds of artifacts and an orientation film; an overseer's house; a small Baptist church; several slave quarters; and other buildings.

Excursions

PORT HUDSON STATE COMMEMORATIVE AREA (*14 miles N via US 61. 504-654-3775*) The last Confederate stronghold on the Mississippi, Port Hudson withstood 48 days of fierce fighting in 1863 before Southern troops surrendered. The defeat helped turn the tide of war. Begin a tour at the interpretive center, where a video and a small museum describe the battle. The park's 6 miles of wooded trails include a boardwalk above the breastworks of Fort Desperate, where vicious fighting took place.

AUDUBON STATE COMMEMORATIVE AREA (*3 miles E off US 61 on La. 965. 504-635-3739. Adm. fee*) John J. Audubon painted many of his "Birds of America" here at **Oakley** plantation in 1821.

ST. FRANCISVILLE (*25 miles N via US 61. Visitor information at the W. Feliciana Historical Society, 11757 Ferdinand St. 504-635-6330*) Built around a French fort in the early 1700s and later ruled by Spain, St. Francisville took on a decidedly English flavor in the late 18th century when Anglo-Americans with Spanish land grants settled here. The attractive **historic district,** centered on Ferdinand and Royal Streets, boasts 146 notable buildings, including the 1850s Gothic Revival **Grace Episcopal Church** (*494 Ferdinand St.*). Grand plantation houses from the cotton era dot the region's rolling hills. Of particular note is **Rosedown** (*La. 10 and US 61. 504-635-3332. Adm. fee*), famed for its 19th-century French-inspired gardens and original family furnishings.

PARLANGE PLANTATION HOUSE (*35 miles NW via US 190 and La. 1, near New Roads. 504-638-8410. Adm. fee*) At the heart of a working sugar plantation, the brick and cypress manor has been in the same family for 225 years.

PLAQUEMINE LOCK (*10 miles S via La. 1. Main St., in Plaquemine. 504-687-7158. Tues.-Sun.*) Plaquemine Lock was built in 1909 to shortcut the journey between the Mississippi River and Louisiana's interior. The white-brick lockhouse has exhibits on the lock's history. Nearby, Plaquemine's historic downtown is worth a visit.

Lafayette ··

(Visitor Center, 1400 N.W. Evangeline Thruway. 318-232-3808 or 800-346-1958) Chased by the English from their Nova Scotian homeland more than 200 years ago, the Acadians (or Cajuns) fled to the swampy, remote landscape surrounding Vermilionville, Lafayette's original name. These hardy, industrious people created a particularly colorful culture, still evi-

dent in their French dialect, spicy cuisine, and distinctive traditions.

Alexandre Mouton House *(1122 Lafayette St. 318-234-2208. Tues.-Sun.; adm. fee)* Town founder Jean Mouton built the oldest part of this frame house in 1800. His belongings and Mardi Gras costumes are on display.

Acadian Cultural Center *(501 Fischer Rd. 318-232-0789)* Part of the Jean Lafitte National Historical Park, the center offers a broad overview of the Cajun story with a 40-minute film, cultural artifacts, and pictorial exhibits.

Acadian Village

Vermilionville *(1600 Surrey St. 318-233-4077 or 800-992-2968. Adm. fee)* Though commercialized, the 23-acre folk museum does a good job of interpreting early Acadian and Creole life in southern Louisiana. Twenty-three reconstructed or relocated historic structures create a typical 18th-century Cajun settlement, peopled with costumed weavers, quilters, storytellers, and fiddlers. Cajun guides lead the tours.

Acadian Village *(Ridge Rd. 318-981-2364. Adm. fee)* Clustered around a pretty bayou is a collection of authentic 19th-century Cajun structures—including a general store, a blacksmith shop, and a chapel—all filled with period pieces. The **Mississippi Valley Museum** showcases artifacts relating to missionary efforts among the tribes.

Excursions

ST. MARTINVILLE *(18 miles SE via US 90 and La. 96)* Acadian refugees who flocked to St. Martinville in the 1760s were joined by French aristocrats fleeing the guillotine during the 1789 French Revolution. For a glimpse into the past, visit the 1844 **St. Martin de Tours Catholic Church** *(Main St. 318-394-7334)*, the Mother Church of Acadiana; and the adjoining **Petit Paris Museum** *(318-394-7334. Adm. fee)*, which displays a Mardi Gras rendition of a fabled 18th-century plantation wedding. In the nearby **Longfellow-Evangeline State Commemorative Area** *(Off La. 31. 318-394-3754. Adm. fee)*, a raised Creole cottage built by a sugar planter in the mid-1800s is now furnished with period pieces.

SHADOWS-ON-THE-TECHE *(25 miles SE via US 90 and La. 182. 317 E. Main St., New Iberia. 318-369-6446. Adm. fee)* Surrounded by shady oaks on the Bayou Teche, this coral-colored, colonnaded villa was built in 1834 for rich sugar planter David Weeks and still has most of its original furnishings.

FRANKLIN *(49 miles SE via US 90. Tourist Commission, 1600 Northwest Blvd. 318-828-2555)* Largely settled by colonists from the Northeast, the gracious village was kept safe during the Civil War by its strong Union sympathies. On **Main Street** stately Greek Revival houses hide behind moss-bearded oaks. Open to the public are the 1837 **Oaklawn Manor** (*Irish Bend Rd. 318-828-0434. Adm. fee*), once the center of a large sugar plantation; and the 1851 **Grevemberg House** (*Sterling Rd. 318-828-2092. Adm. fee*), which features 19th-century furnishings and memorabilia from the Civil War.

PRAIRIE ACADIAN CULTURAL CENTER (*42 miles NW via I-49 and US 190. 250 W. Park Ave., Eunice. 318-457-8499*) Fiddles and rag dolls are among the artifacts that expertly tell the story of the Cajun "cowboys" who left the swamps for the prairies west of Lafayette.

Natchitoches ···

(*Natchitoches Parish Tourist Commission, 781 Front Street. 318-352-8072 or 800-259-1714*) In 1714 French traders built a small fort near a village of Natchitoches Indians. That wooden outpost became Natchitoches (NAK-i-tush), the oldest permanent European settlement in the Louisiana Territory. **Fort St. Jean Baptiste** (*130 Morrow St. 318-357-3101. Adm. fee*) was reconstructed using 18th-century technology and offers a glimpse into early frontier life. In the town's 33-block **historic district**, French Creole cottages and pillared mansions line tree-shaded streets.

Excursions

CANE RIVER PLANTATIONS (*Driving-tour map available from Natchitoches Parish Tourist Commission; see above*) In the early 1800s, the narrow valley along the Red River south of Natchitoches supported a huge cotton kingdom. French Creole plantation houses still dot the scenic valley. Best preserved is **Melrose** (*20 miles via La. 1 and Rte. 493. 318-379-0055. Adm. fee*), a complex of 18th- and 19th-century structures that once belonged to freed slave Marie Thérése Coin-coin.

FORT JESUP STATE COMMEMORATIVE AREA (*25 miles W via La. 6. 318-256-4117. Adm. fee*) Only stone pillars and a kitchen remain of the once sprawling frontier military complex, built by Col. Zachary Taylor in 1822.

177

New Orleans ···

(*Convention & Visitors Bureau, 1520 Sugar Bowl Dr. 504-566-5011 or 800-672-6124*) Hurricanes, fires, yellow fever, constant flooding—18th-century French settlers faced all these in the fledgling, thatched-hut settlement called Nouvelle Orleans. The hardy people persevered, and a sophisticated city emerged out of the wilderness. In the late 1700s, it was shuffled with the rest of the Louisiana Territory between French and Spanish rule, then became American (at least on paper) under the Louisiana Purchase of 1803. Prospering on the tobacco, cotton, and sugarcane trades, New Orleans became one of the nation's largest cities by 1840—and one of its liveliest. Indeed, the first Mardi Gras parade sashayed down city streets in the 1840s. For a good historical overview of the French Quarter and Garden District, take the guided walking tour offered by the **Jean Lafitte National Historical Park and Preserve** (*Visitor Center, 916 N. Peters St. 504-589-2636*).

French Quarter Walking Tour ·················· 2 hours

Under Spanish rule between 1762 and 1800, New Orleans burned twice. Out of the ashes rose the magnificent, Spanish-style French Quarter, graced by wrought-iron galleries, shuttered doors, and bountiful flowers.

1. Begin at **Jackson Square,** whose long history has encompassed a cast of characters. Originally called Place d'Armes, it was renamed in the mid-1800s to honor the hero of the Battle of New Orleans. Still surrounded by government, religious, and commercial buildings, the iron-fenced square—with its French-style gardens—remains the heart of the French Quarter.

2. The crown jewel of Jackson Square, **St. Louis Cathedral Basilica** *(504-525-9585)* is a quiet reminder of the city's religious ties. The nation's oldest active cathedral, with soaring ceilings and a painted altar, was the gift of a Spanish benefactor in 1794.

3. The Spanish Council ruled New Orleans and the rest of Louisiana from the Spanish Colonial **Cabildo** *(504-568-6968. Tues.-Sun.; adm. fee)*. In an upstairs chamber, the transfer papers for the Louisiana Purchase were signed in 1803. Part of the Louisiana State Museum, it now contains historical exhibits, including Napoleon Bonaparte's death mask. Flanking the other side of the cathedral is the nearly identical **Presbytere** *(504-568-6968. Tues.-Sun.; adm. fee)*, built in 1795 to house priests (though it never served that purpose). It now houses changing exhibits.

4. Facing one another across Jackson Square, the redbrick **Pontalba Buildings** were constructed as apartments between 1849 and 1851 by Baroness de Pontalba, daughter of the cathedral's wealthy benefactor. You can glimpse the Creole life-style of the first residents at the **1850 House** *(523 St. Ann St. 504-568-6968. Tues.-Sun.; adm. fee)*, re-created with plush, locally made furniture.

5. Under orders from King Louis XV, France's Ursuline Sisters came to the outpost city in 1727 to found a convent and girls school. Built in

178

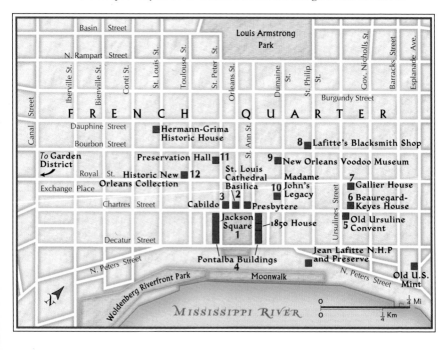

Royal Café, French Quarter

1734, the beautifully restored **Old Ursuline Convent** (*Chartres and Ursulines Sts. 504-866-1472. Tues.-Sun.; adm. fee*) is the original colony's only remaining building, and may well be the Mississippi Valley's oldest structure built by Europeans.

6. The late federal-Greek Revival **Beauregard-Keyes House** (*1113 Chartres St. 504-523-7257. Tues.-Sun.; adm. fee*) was the home of Confederate general P.G.T. Beauregard and novelist Frances Keyes: he from 1866 to 1868 and she in the 1940s. Decorated as it appeared in the mid-1800s, the house holds personal belongings of both former residents, plus an 1830s walled garden.

7. Noted local architect James Gallier, Jr., designed his 1857 Victorian **Gallier House** (*1118-1132 Royal St. 504-523-6722. Mon.-Sat.; adm. fee*) with such fabulous, then modern features as bedroom ventilators and a flush toilet.

8. Lafitte's Blacksmith Shop (*941 Bourbon St.*) The notorious 18th-century freebooter Jean Lafitte is said to have used this weathered, colonial cottage—now a rustic, smoke-filled bar—as a blacksmith shop to front his illicit contraband trade.

9. Voodoo queens and doctors once reigned in this niche of the French Quarter, practicing the religion of their African ancestors. Packed with old and new *gris-gris,* altars, voodoo dolls, and other objects, the somewhat spooky **New Orleans Voodoo Museum** (*724 Dumaine St. 504-523-7685. Adm. fee*) loosely traces the religion's history in the city.

10. Though the West Indian cottage known as **Madame John's Legacy** (*632 Dumaine St. Private*) doesn't look like much, it's one of the oldest buildings in the Mississippi Valley. The present structure is an exact replica, built in 1788, of the circa 1726 original.

11. Preservation Hall (*726 St. Peter St. 504-522-2841. Nightly at 8:00; adm. fee*) In this city where jazz made some of its most significant advances, no place recalls the old-time, no-frills music as well as this bare bones venue for native singers and musicians. Lines are long to enter the no-food, no-drink establishment, so show up early.

12. Historic New Orleans Collection (*533 Royal St. 504-523-4662. Tues.-Sat.; fee for tour*) Part of a well-endowed private research facility, the 1792 **Merieult House**—a rare survivor of the 1794 fire—showcases a collection of documents pertaining to New Orleans history. Visitors may also view the changing exhibits in the **Williams Gallery.**

Other Sites in the French Quarter

Hermann-Grima Historic House (*820 St. Louis St. 504-525-5661. Mon.-*

179

Preservation Hall in New Orleans

Sat.; adm. fee) With its formal doorways, central hallway, and tall sash windows, this 1831 federal house stands out in the otherwise Spanish quarter. Boasting the city's only functioning Creole kitchen, it features cooking demonstrations *(Thurs. May-Oct.).*

Built in 1835, the thick-walled **Old U.S. Mint** *(400 Esplanade Ave. 504-568-6968. Tues.-Sun.; adm. fee)* operated as a federal mint from 1838 to 1861, and then produced Confederate money. Now part of the Louisiana State Museum, it houses glittering Mardi Gras costumes and artifacts and such jazz icons as Louis Armstrong's trumpets.

Uptown New Orleans

St. Charles Street Car *(504-248-3900)* Clanging up and down St. Charles Street since 1835, the shining red streetcar is still the best way to travel uptown.

Confederate Museum *(929 Camp Street. 504-523-4522. Adm. fee)* Battle flags, uniforms, rare guns, and portraits of war heroes are some of the treasures to be found at the nation's second largest collection of Confederate memorabilia.

Garden District *(Bounded by St. Charles Ave. and Magazine St., and Jackson and Louisiana Aves.)* Following the 1803 Louisiana Purchase, Yankees poured into New Orleans. Ostracized by the French Creoles, they settled 2 miles upriver and built flashy mansions in lush garden settings. Among the many houses, best seen by walking, are **Toby's Corner** *(2340 Prytania St.),* believed to be the district's oldest house (circa 1838); and the 1849 **Payne-Strachan House** *(1134 1st St.),* where Jefferson Davis died.

In the heart of the district, **Lafayette Cemetery Number 1** *(1428 Washington Ave.)* is a prime example of the "cities of dead" that evolved above ground, due to the region's marshy terrain. The best (and safest) way to visit is by tour *(inquire at the New Orleans Convention & Visitors Bureau).*

Excursions

CHALMETTE NATIONAL HISTORICAL PARK *(6 miles E via La. 46. 504-589-4430)* On Jan. 8, 1815, in the last major land battle in the War of 1812, Gen. Andrew Jackson's makeshift command defeated British regulars at Chalmette Plantation, on the banks of the Mississippi River. The two-hour battle clinched America's claim to the Louisiana Purchase, thus facilitating westward expansion. Begin at the Visitor Center, which has a film and exhibits. The winding road through the 141-acre battlefield park is dotted with interpretive plaques.

FORT PIKE STATE COMMEMORATIVE AREA *(23 miles E via US 90. 504-662-5703. Adm. fee)* Built after the War of 1812 to command the narrows, Fort Pike figured in the 1830s Seminole Wars, the Mexican War, and the Civil War. Its 3-foot-thick walls are crumbling, but much of the citadel, casement, and exterior walls remain.

RIVER ROAD PLANTATIONS *(For listings and information contact the New*

Orleans Convention & Visitors Bureau) Legacies of the southern aristocracy, oak-shaded plantation houses still line the languid banks of the Mississippi River and its sleepy bayous. Lavishly restored, their flower-graced rooms are open to visitors; some offer dining and overnight accommodations. You'll find them on and off the **Great River Road** that runs between New Orleans and Baton Rouge. The 1856 Steamboat Gothic **San Francisco Plantation** (*3 miles W of Reserve on La. 44. 504-535-2341. Adm. fee*) was originally named Sans Fruscins ("without a penny in my pocket"), owing to its exorbitant cost. The restored house, with its peach-and-blue shutters, faux marble fireplaces, and painted cypress ceilings, reflects the antebellum Creole style.

An unknown French settler planted 28 live oak trees in two rows in the mid-1700s, about 150 years before sugar planter Jacques Telesphore Roman built his classic Greek Revival mansion. The impeccable, gleaming rooms of **Oak Alley Plantation** (*3 miles W of Vacherie on La. 18. 504-265-2151. Adm. fee*) portray the elegant lifestyles of southern aristocrats. But nothing gives a feeling of the antebellum South more than a slow walk down to the Mississippi River beneath the magnificent alley of oaks, now grown enormous and gnarled. Nearby stands the **Laura Plantation** (*2247 La. 18, Vacherie. 504-265-7690),* an 1805 Creole house.

Set in a verdant garden, the imposing Greek Revival **Houmas House Plantation** (*La. 942, just N of Burnside. 504-473-7841. Adm. fee for guided tours*) suffered little during the Civil War, thanks to its Irish owner, John Burnside, who threatened international complications should Union soldiers set foot inside. Filled with early Louisiana pieces, it is actually two houses—an 1840s mansion linked to an 18th-century Spanish-French-style building by a carriageway.

As imposing as a Greek temple, the magnificent Palladian **Madewood Plantation** (*La. 308, near Napoleonville. 504-369-7151. Adm. fee*) was built in 1846 by renowned New Orleans architect Henry Howard for the Pugh family. Period antiques now decorate its lovingly restored rooms.

Other Sites in Louisiana

Mansfield State Commemorative Area (*La. 175, 4 miles S of Mansfield. 318-872-1474. Adm. fee*) Monuments, a museum, and an interpretive trail commemorate the bloodiest Civil War battle fought on Louisiana soil.

Marksville State Commemorative Area (*700 Martin Luther King, Jr., Dr., Marksville. 318-253-8954; adm. fee*) Earthen mounds built by the Marksville people who flourished from A.D. 100 to 400 dot the 39-acre park; a museum houses archaeological finds.

Poverty Point State Commemorative Area (*4 miles E of Epps via Rte. 134 and Rte. 577N. 318-926-5492. Adm. fee*) A complex of earthen mounds built by the highly advanced Poverty Point culture date from 1700-1100 B.C. A museum, observation tower, and walking trails provide interpretation.

Shreveport Historic District (*Visitor Center, 629 Spring St. 318-222-9391 or 800-551-8682*) Established in 1839 on the banks of the Red River, Shreveport grew rich as a transportation hub for cotton. Never occupied during the Civil War, the prosperous town was spared destruction.

Thibodaux Boasting 1840s structures, the **Laurel Valley Village Museum** (*La. 308. 504-447-7352*) depicts a 19th-century sugar plantation. The **Acadian Cultural Center** (*314 St. Mary St. 504-448-1375*)—part of Jean Lafitte National Historical Park—tells the Acadian story.

Pricketts Fort State Park, Fairmont, West Virginia

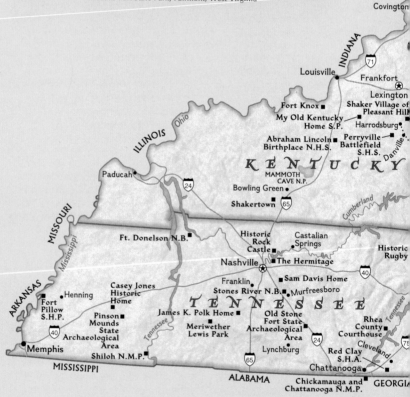

Covington

INDIANA

71

Louisville

Frankfort

Lexington

Fort Knox ■

Shaker Village of
Pleasant Hill

My Old Kentucky
Home S.P.

Harrodsburg ●

Abraham Lincoln
Birthplace N.H.S. ■

Perryville
Battlefield
S.H.S.

Danville

K E N T U C K Y

Ohio

ILLINOIS

Paducah ●

24

MAMMOTH
CAVE N.P.

Bowling Green ●

Shakertown

65

Cumberland

MISSOURI

Ft. Donelson N.B. ■

Historic
Rock
Castle ■

Castalian
Springs

Historic
Rugby

Mississippi

Nashville ■ The Hermitage

40

ARKANSAS

Henning ●

Casey Jones
Historic
Home ■

Franklin ●

Sam Davis Home ■

Stones River N.B. ■

Murfreesboro

T E N N E S S E E

Fort
Pillow
S.H.P. ■

Pinson
Mounds
State
Archaeological
Area

James K. Polk Home ■

Meriwether
Lewis Park ■

Old Stone
Fort State
Archaeological
Area ■

24

Rhea
County
Courthouse ■

Cleveland

75

40

Memphis ●

Shiloh N.M.P. ■

Tennessee

Lynchburg ●

65

Red Clay
S.H.A. ●

Chattanooga ●

Tennessee

MISSISSIPPI

ALABAMA

Chickamauga and
Chattanooga N.M.P.

GEORGIA

Appalachians

The Appalachian region takes its name from the mountains that once defined the western frontier of the newly founded nation. By the close of the 18th century, Daniel Boone's Wilderness Road was leading a stream of settlers through the Cumberland Gap into Kentucky and Tennessee. Nearly a century later the residents of western Virginia, Kentucky, and Tennessee found themselves bitterly divided in their sentiments

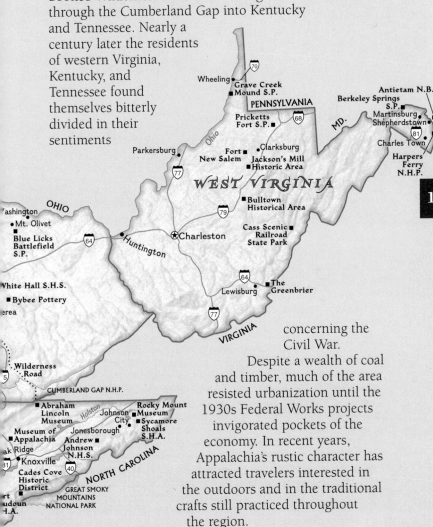

concerning the Civil War.

Despite a wealth of coal and timber, much of the area resisted urbanization until the 1930s Federal Works projects invigorated pockets of the economy. In recent years, Appalachia's rustic character has attracted travelers interested in the outdoors and in the traditional crafts still practiced throughout the region.

Cades Cove Historic District, Great Smoky Mountains National Park

The region known as Tennessee—from the Cherokee name, Tanasi, for the long dissecting river that runs through it—was claimed by France, Spain, and Great Britain before being subsumed by the British colony of North Carolina. In 1790 it became part of the U.S. Territory South of the River Ohio. The first backcountry settlers, known as overmountain men, trickled in during the late 1700s, and on June 1, 1796, Tennessee became the nation's 16th state. Three future Presidents—Andrew Jackson, James K. Polk, and Andrew Johnson—played integral roles in the state's development.

Officially Confederate, Tennessee's loyalties were split during the Civil War, with East Tennessee strongly Unionist leaning. After the war, it took some 40 years for farms to recover, and during that time industries developed. By the mid-1930s, Tennessee's economy was shifting from agriculture to industry, thanks to the power supplied by two New Deal projects—the Tennessee Valley Authority and Norris Dam. World War II further boosted the state's economy.

Chattanooga

(Visitor Center, 2 Broad St. 423-266-7070 or 800-322-3344) Situated in the Tennessee River Valley where Tennessee, Georgia, and Alabama meet, Chattanooga is thought to have derived its name from the Creek term for "rock that comes to a point"—a likely reference to looming Lookout Mountain. A crossroads since prehistoric times, Chattanooga was a gate-

way to the Confederacy during the Civil War—and a prize sought and at last won by the Union in a protracted campaign waged during the autumn of 1863. The **Chattanooga National Cemetery** (*1200 Bailey Ave. 423-855-6590*) contains the graves of more than 12,000 Union soldiers.

Chattanooga African-American History Museum (*200 E. Martin Luther King, Jr., Blvd. 423-267-1076. Closed Sun.; adm. fee*) The museum is dedicated to the contributions and achievements of African Americans.

Chattanooga Regional History Museum (*400 Chestnut St. 423-265-3247. Adm. fee*) Exhibits trace the city's history from the prehistoric period through the present.

Lookout Mountain Incline Railway (*827 E. Brow Rd. 423-821-4224. Adm. fee*) Built in 1895 to link the city with the summit of Lookout Mountain, the mile-long trolley system reaches a grade of 72.7 percent, making it the world's steepest passenger railway. From the summit, walk down the road to spectacularly situated **Point Park** (*Visitor Center, 1112 E. Brow Rd. 423-821-7786*), a unit of the Chickamauga and Chattanooga National Military Park (below). The site of one of the key engagements in the 1863 Chattanooga Campaign, it contains batteries, monuments, the historic 1865 **Cravens House** (*Adm. fee*), and exhibits.

Tennessee Valley Railroad (*Grand Junction Station, 4119 Cromwell Rd. or E. Chattanooga Depot, 2200 N. Chamberlain Ave. 423-894-8028. Daily April-Oct., Sat.-Sun. Nov.; adm. fee*) The South's largest operating historic railroad preserves the legacy of steam locomotion. At either depot, each a turn-of-the-century reproduction, you can board an authentic 1930s passenger train for a 6-mile round-trip ride. A shop tour offers a glimpse of train maintenance, and the **museum** preserves six vintage engines.

Excursions

CHICKAMAUGA AND CHATTANOOGA NATIONAL MILITARY PARK (*10 miles S via US 27 to Main Visitor Center, in Fort Oglethorpe, Ga. 706-866-9241*) America's first and largest national military park, the 8,000-acre park contains 17 units in Georgia and Tennessee, all related to the bloody series of Civil War battles fought in and around Chattanooga in the fall of 1863. On September 20, Confederate general James Longstreet's troops forced Union forces under Gen. George H. Thomas to retreat from Chicamauga Creek to Chattanooga. Two months later, with the Siege of Chattanooga over, Union troops were in control of the city—and most of the state. In the spring, using Chattanooga as a base, Gen. William Tecumseh Sherman launched his march to Atlanta and the sea. This part of the park offers a 7-mile auto tour, monuments, and a Visitor Center with exhibits and a film (*fee*) on the Battle of Chickamauga.

RED CLAY STATE HISTORICAL AREA (*20 miles E via I-75 and Tenn. 317E, near Cleveland. 1140 Red Clay Rd. Follow signs carefully. 423-478-0339*) The 260-acre park commemorates the Cherokee capital-in-exile from 1832 to 1838. Here, Cherokee leaders learned they would have to surrender their homeland. Red Clay marks the start of the Trail of Tears—the route the tribe followed on its forced removal to Oklahoma. Grounds feature a Visitor Center, a sacred spring, and several Cherokee structures.

Johnson City ·······························
(*Convention & Visitors Bureau, 603 E. Market St. 423-461-8000*) Tennessee's

northeast corner was settled in the late 1700s by pioneers of mostly Scotch-Irish descent. The railroad opened the mountainous region in the mid-1800s.

Tipton-Haynes Historic Site *(2620 S. Roan St. 423-926-3631. Daily April-Oct., Mon.-Fri. Nov.-March; adm. fee)* Landon Carter Haynes designed his home around the log house built circa 1784 by Col. John Tipton. The grounds contain ten original and reconstructed buildings from the pioneer period.

Excursions

ROCKY MOUNT MUSEUM *(4 miles NE via US 11E. 423-538-7396. Closed weekends Jan.-Feb.; adm. fee)* The oldest U.S. territorial capital was built by William Cobb in 1770. This living history farmstead re-creates the year 1791 through first person interpretation and demonstrations of seasonal chores and tasks. The **Massengill Museum of Overmountain History** on the grounds details the area's frontier history.

JONESBOROUGH *(5 miles SW on US 11E. Visitor Center, 117 Boone St. 423-753-5961)* The first township in what is now Tennessee was founded in 1779. When North Carolina ceded its western claims in 1784, settlers formed their own government, called the State of Franklin, with Jonesborough as the capital. You can get the whole story at the Visitor Center's **Jonesborough-Washington County History Museum.** The restored downtown **historic district** contains more than 150 vintage buildings.

SYCAMORE SHOALS STATE HISTORIC AREA *(12 miles E via US 321, Elizabethton. 1651 W. Elk Ave. 423-543-5808)* In 1772 the first permanent settlement outside the original 13 Colonies was established here, along with the Watauga Association—the first majority-rule system of government in America. The park includes a Visitor Center and a reconstructed fort (the original fort site was a mile south). The park also maintains the unfurnished but well-preserved 1780 **Carter Mansion** *(Broad St. Ext. May-Aug.)*, built by a Watauga founder, John Carter, and his son Landon.

FDR and the TVA
Hard luck has been no stranger to the Tennessee Valley, long one of the nation's poorest regions. Its fortunes turned in 1933 when President Franklin D. Roosevelt, spurred by the momentum of his first hundred days in office, signed into being the Tennessee Valley Authority. A monumental experiment, it established a network of dams to harness the Tennessee River and generate cheap electric power for the valley.

Knoxville

Gen. James White came here from North Carolina in 1786 and built a stockade and cabins overlooking the Tennessee River. In 1791 territorial governor William Blount chose White's Fort as the site for the capital of the U.S. Territory South of the River Ohio. Renamed Knoxville—after George Washington's Secretary of War, Henry Knox—it became Tennessee's first state capital in 1796. White, Blount, and other early settlers are buried in the cemetery of the **First Presbyterian Church** *(620 State St.)*.

James White Fort *(205 E. Hill Ave. 423-525-6514. Mon.-Sat. March–mid-Dec.; adm. fee)* Reconstructed near the original fort location, this site contains White's 1786 log home, reconstructed buildings, and a museum.

Blount Mansion *(200 W. Hill Ave. 423-525-2375. March-Oct. Tues.-Sun., Nov.-Feb. Tues.-Fri.; adm. fee)* The simple house built by territorial governor William Blount in 1792 was referred to locally as a mansion. The restored house contains period and original furnishings. The **Governor's**

Office here served as territorial capital from 1792 to 1796, during which time the state constitution was drafted.

Marble Springs *(1220 W. Gov. Sevier Hwy. 423-573-5508. Tues.-Sun.; adm. fee)* Tennessee's first governor, John Sevier, resided here from around 1790 until his death in 1815. The plantation site, now covering 37 acres, contains Sevier's original two-story log house, with some family furnishings.

C o n f e d e r a t e Memorial Hall *(3148 Kingston Pike. 423-522-2371. Closed Sat.-Mon. March-Oct.; adm. fee)*

Blount Mansion, Knoxville

The 15-room, Italianate house (1858) served as Confederate general James Longstreet's headquarters during his 1863 siege of Knoxville. Along with Civil War graffiti, bloodstains, and bullet holes, the restored home contains period furnishings, war memorabilia, and historical photographs.

187

Excursions

MUSEUM OF APPALACHIA *(16 miles NW via I-75 and Tenn. 61, outside Norris. 423-494-7680. Adm. fee)* The culture and pioneer past of southern Appalachia come to life at this 65-acre outdoor museum, where 35 relocated and restored structures display some 200,000 artifacts.

OAK RIDGE *(22 miles W via I-40 and Tenn. 162)* During World War II, the federal government chose this rural area to locate part of the top secret Manhattan Project, which produced the first atomic bomb. The story is well told at the **American Museum of Science and Energy** *(300 S. Tulane Ave. 615-576-3200)*. The **Graphite Reactor** *(Bethel Valley Rd. 615-574-4163)* is the world's first, continuously operated nuclear reactor.

Memphis ···

(Visitor Center, 340 Beale St. 800-873-6282 or 901-543-5333) Tennessee's largest city, Memphis was platted on a Mississippi River bluff by entrepreneurs Andrew Jackson, John Overton, and James Winchester in 1819. By mid-century, it claimed the world's largest inland cotton market, thanks to the area's prodigious, slave-driven plantations and to riverboats and railroads. The city's wealthy cotton brokers, bankers, and other tycoons built great mansions in the preserved **Victorian Village Historic District,** where you may visit the circa 1836 **Magevney House** *(198 Adams Ave. 901-526-4464. Tues.-Sat.; donations)*; the circa 1852 **Mallory-Neely House** *(652 Adams Ave. 901-523-1484. Tues.-Sun.; adm. fee)*; and the 1870 **Woodruff-Fontaine House** *(680 Adams Ave. 901-526-1469. Adm. fee)*. Elsewhere, the newly restored **Hunt-Phelan Home** *(533 Beale St. 901-525-8225)*, built from 1828 to 1832 and enlarged in the 1850s, was a hub of

antebellum society. During the Civil War, it served as headquarters for Gen. Ulysses S. Grant.

Beale Street Historic District (*Between 2nd and 4th Sts.*) Early in the century, a new musical genre called the blues, introduced by black composer W. C. Handy, took hold in this quarter's honky-tonks. A short trail provides a history of the refurbished corridor. Highlights include **W. C. Handy's Museum and Gallery** (*352 Beale St. 901-522-1556. Tues.-Sun.; adm. fee*); the **Center for Southern Folklore** (*130 Beale St. 901-525-3655. Tues.-Sun.*), with exhibits on the heritage of southern music; and the **Memphis Music and Blues Museum** (*97 S. 2nd St. 901-525-4007. Adm. fee*).

Sun Studio (*706 Union Ave. 901-521-0664*) Famed as the birthplace of rock and roll, the still operating studio made musical history in the 1950s by launching the careers of Elvis Presley, Jerry Lee Lewis, B. B. King, Johnny Cash, and Roy Orbison.

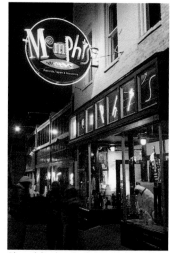

Blues clubs along Beale Street in Memphis

Mississippi River Museum (*Mud Island. 901-576-7241. Daily Mem. Day–Labor Day, Tues.-Sun. April-May and Sept.-Nov.; adm. fee*) On 52-acre Mud Island Park, this museum chronicles 10,000 years of river history; exhibits include the reconstructed prow of an 1870s packet boat. The park also features the **river walk,** a topographically correct, scale model of the river terrain from Cairo, Illinois, to New Orleans, Louisiana.

National Civil Rights Museum (*Lorraine Motel, 450 Mulberry St. 901-521-9699. Wed.-Mon.; adm. fee*) The preserved site of Dr. Martin Luther King, Jr.'s, assassination on April 4, 1968, forms the core of this must-see museum. Focusing on the seminal events of the civil rights movement, audiovisual and graphic displays re-create scenes that make for a powerful, often chilling journey through this chapter in American history.

Memphis Pink Palace Museum (*3050 Central Ave. 901-320-6320. Adm. fee*) The original, pink Georgia-marble mansion was built in 1922 by Clarence Saunders, the founder of Piggly Wiggly—the country's first self-service food market. Much expanded, the museum's new wing covers the natural and cultural history of Memphis and the mid-South.

Nashville ·····························

(*Convention & Visitors Bureau, 161 4th Ave. N. 615-259-4700*) In 1779 two pioneer parties from the Carolinas pushed into the western frontier, guided by frontiersman James Robertson and Col. John Donelson. They settled along the Cumberland River, where their Fort Nashborough became the center of the Middle Tennessee settlements. With the advent of the steamboat, the settlement developed as a major river port. In 1843 Nashville became Tennessee's permanent state capital.

Nashville's downtown **historic district** contains the 1859 Greek Revival **Tennessee State Capitol** (*Charlotte Ave. bet. 6th and 7th Aves. 615-741-2692. Mon.-Fri.*), designed by William Strickland and still the government seat.

President James K. Polk and his wife, Sarah, are buried on the grounds.

Tennessee State Museum (*5th and Deaderick Sts. 615-741-2692. Tues.-Sun.*) Exhibits colorfully chronicle and preserve the state's history and culture.

Belmont Mansion (*1900 Belmont Ave. 615-386-4459. Daily June-Aug., Tues.-Sat. Sept.-May; adm. fee*) The 36-room, Italianate villa—built in the 1850s by Adelicia Acklen, one of America's wealthiest women—contains original and period furnishings and art.

Belle Meade Plantation (*5025 Harding Rd. 615-356-0501. Adm. fee*) Famed in the 1800s as a Thoroughbred nursery and stud farm, the property includes a 1790 log cabin; an 1853 Greek Revival mansion, built by Gen. William G. Harding; and an 1890 carriage house.

Travellers' Rest Historic House Museum (*636 Farrell Pkwy. 615-832-2962. Tues.-Sun.; adm. fee*) Built by John Overton in 1799, the house reflects Middle Tennessee's transition from a frontier to a plantation economy. Overton ran Andrew Jackson's presidential campaign from here.

Country Music Hall of Fame and Museum (*4 Music Square E. 615-255-5333. Adm. fee*) The history of the "Nashville Sound" is presented through multimedia exhibits, displays of instruments and celebrity memorabilia, and a tour of RCA's Studio B—famous for its recordings of country music in the 1950s.

The Hermitage (*4580 Rachel's Ln. 615-889-2941. Adm. fee*) In 1804 Andrew Jackson, who would become the seventh President, bought farmland here and built a complex of log structures. The family's original 1821 home, ravaged by fire in 1834, was rebuilt as a Greek Revival mansion. Authentically restored, it holds the most complete collection of furnishings and personal effects of any early presidential home. **Jackson's tomb** is on the grounds. Nearby stands the **Old Hermitage Church** and the 1836 **Tulip Grove,** the home of Jackson's nephew and presidential secretary, Andrew Donelson.

189

Excursions

HISTORIC ROCK CASTLE (*15 miles NE via US 31E, in Hendersonville. 139 Rock Castle Ln. 615-824-0502. Closed Mon.-Tues. Feb.-Dec.; adm. fee*) Daniel Smith—Revolutionary War officer and senator—built the territory's first stone masonry house about 1790; it is furnished with period pieces.

CASTALIAN SPRINGS (*35 miles NE via US 31E and Tenn. 25*) Site of a wilderness post and a popular mineral spring, the town harbors **Wynnewood** (*210 Old Tenn. 25. 615-452-5463. Closed Sun. Nov.-March; adm. fee*), a well-preserved, two-story log stagecoach inn built in 1828 as a stop between Knoxville and Nashville. From 1830 to 1940 it served as a spa. Inside are a doctor's office with period furnishings, sleeping rooms, a kitchen, and the 1780s log cabin of pioneer Isaac Bledsoe. Nearby stands the Georgian **Cragfont** (*300 Cragfont Rd. 615-452-7070. Daily mid-April-Nov., Tues.-Sat. rest of year; adm. fee*).

The Hermitage, Nashville

Built circa 1800 by Gen. James Winchester, it was the first mansion in the Tennessee region.

FRANKLIN (*15 miles S via I-65 and Tenn. 96. Williamson County Chamber* *of Commerce, 209 E. Main St. 615-794-1225)* Founded in 1799 and the seat of wealthy Williamson County, Franklin preserves a downtown **historic district** boasting many 19th-century buildings. The area was a Civil War hot spot and the site of the Battle of Franklin, which took place on November 30, 1864. Nearby landmarks include the 1830 **Carter House** *(1140 Columbia Ave. 615-791-1861. Adm. fee),* a Federal command post and center of the battle. Bloodstained floors at the 1826 **Historic Carnton Plantation** *(1345 Carnton Ln. 615-794-0903. Adm. fee)* recall the home's service as a Civil War field hospital. The adjacent **McGavock Confederate Cemetery** holds the graves of 1,480 soldiers.

SAM DAVIS HOME *(18 miles S via US 41, in Smyrna. 1399 Sam Davis Rd.*

615-459-2341. Adm. fee) The boyhood plantation of the young Confederate scout, hanged as a spy in 1863, dates from 1820 and features family items, original outbuildings, and slave cabins.

MURFREESBORO *(32 miles SE via I-24)* The former state capital (1819 to 1826) is the location of **Oaklands Historic House Museum** *(900 N. Maney Ave. 615-893-0022. Tues.-Sun.; adm. fee),* an architecturally significant planter's home (1815) that was occupied by Northern and Southern troops during the Civil War. **Stones River National Battlefield** *(3501 Old Nashville Hwy. 615-893-9501)* preserves the site of the pivotal battle that took place from December 31, 1862, to January 2, 1863. While both sides claimed victory, the Confederacy lost the valuable agricultural region of Middle Tennessee. The site features a Visitor Center museum and driving tour.

Shiloh National Military Park

Shiloh National Military Park ················

(Tenn. 22 E of US 64. 901-689-5275. Adm. fee) One of the Civil War's bloodiest battles took place around a small church here. The largest engagement of the 1862 campaign waged in this region began on April 6, when Gen. A. S. Johnston's Confederate forces surprised and forced back Union troops under Gen. Ulysses S. Grant. Federal reinforcements enabled Grant to counterattack the next day, routing the Confederates. A 9.5-mile tour loops through the park's nearly 4,000 acres of fields and woods, scattered with 151 monuments, 600 troop position markers, and

more than 200 cannon. The Visitor Center exhibits battle artifacts and traces events in a 25-minute film. The site also contains **Shiloh National Cemetery** and **Shiloh Indian Mounds National Historic Landmark.**

Excursion
CORINTH, MISSISSIPPI *(23 miles S via Tenn. 22 and US 45)* See p. 168.

Other Sites in Tennessee
Abraham Lincoln Museum and Lincoln Memorial University *(Cumberland Gap Pkwy., in Harrogate. 423-869-6235. Adm. fee.)* The museum contains one of the nation's largest collections of Lincolniana—rare personal items, books, manuscripts, photographs, paintings, sculptures, and Civil War artifacts. Union general O. O. Howard founded the university in 1897 to fulfill Lincoln's wish to "do something" for the people of East Tennessee, who had stayed loyal to the Union during the Civil War.

Andrew Johnson National Historic Site *(Greeneville. Visitor Center, College and Depot Sts. 423-638-3551)* The 17th President assumed office upon Lincoln's death in 1865; three years later he was impeached but acquitted. The site includes a Visitor Center; the **family home** from the 1830s to 1851; the **Andrew Johnson National Cemetery** *(Monument Ave.)*; and the **Homestead** *(S. Main St. Adm. fee),* where Johnson lived from 1851 until his death in 1875.

Cades Cove Historic District *(7 miles S of Townsend off Tenn. 73, in Great Smoky Mountains National Park. 423-448-2472)* In 1818 the cove's first settler arrived. The isolated community, which had reached some 700 people by 1900, hung on to its land and its folk traditions until the 1930s. Several buildings have been preserved. Visitor Center exhibits offer a glimpse of life in the cove.

Casey Jones Historic Home and Railroad Museum and Casey Jones Village *(56 Casey Jones Lane, in Jackson. 901-668-1222. Adm. fee)* Fast-rolling engineer for the Illinois Central Railroad, Jonathan Luther "Casey" Jones was immortalized for his fateful ride of April 30, 1900. Unable to avoid a collision, he remained with the engine, thereby sacrificing his own life but saving others aboard the train. The deed moved Wallace Saunders, a black engine wiper, to compose the ballad that would make Casey Jones an American legend.

James K. Polk Home *(301 W. 7th St., in Columbia. 615-388-2354. Adm. fee)* Polk's father, Samuel, built the house in 1816, and James began his legal and political career here, eventually leading to his election in 1844 as the 11th President. The only existing Polk residence, it contains family and White House furnishings and memorabilia. Polk's sisters lived next door in the 1818 federal **Sisters' House.**

Fort Donelson National Battlefield *(US 79, in Dover. 615-232-5706)* The Union won its first major Civil War victory with the capture of this fort, part of the Confederate western defense line. The 1862 battle made a hero of Gen. U. S. Grant, who became known after the battle as "Unconditional Surrender" Grant.

Fort Loudoun State Historic Area *(Near Vonore. Tenn. 360. 423-884-6217)* Built in 1756, the first British fort and trading post in Cherokee territory was besieged in 1760 by Indians who forced the garrison to surrender. The site features a reconstructed fort and Visitor Center exhibits. Nearby stand the remains of the 1794 **Tellico Blockhouse,** which the federal government built to protect the Cherokee from the settlers. The Cherokee-owned **Sequoyah Birthplace Museum** (*Tenn. 360. 423-884-6246. Adm. fee*) honors the creator of the tribe's writing system and features cultural and archaeological exhibits.

Jack Daniel's Distillery, Lynchburg

Fort Pillow State Historic Park (*18 miles W of Henning via Rtes. 87 and 207. 901-738-5581*) The fort witnessed one of the Civil War's most controversial battles, when, on April 12, 1864, Confederate troops under Gen. Nathan Bedford Forrest brutally attacked garrisoned Union troops—many of them black—under Maj. Lionel F. Booth.

Henning (*6 miles S of Ripley via Tenn. 209*) This tiny town claims the **Alex Haley House Museum** (*200 S. Church St. 901-738-2240. Tues.-Sun.; adm. fee*). Haley (1921-1992), the author of *Roots,* spent much of his youth here at his grandparents' home. Restored to its 1919 appearance, the house displays some family pieces and memorabilia. Haley's boyhood friend, Fred Montgomery, personalizes his site interpretation with firsthand memories.

Historic Rugby (*Visitor Center, Tenn. 52, in Rugby. 423-628-2441. Adm. fee*) In 1880 English author and social reformer Thomas Hughes founded a cooperative, class-free, agricultural society here, in part for the younger sons of British gentry, who were customarily excluded from inheritances. The restored utopian village consists of 20 restored or reconstructed buildings, including a Visitor Center, a library whose original 7,000 volumes constitute a superlative collection of Victoriana, and Hughes's home.

Lynchburg (*Welcome Center, Town Square. 615-759-4111*) Settled around 1800, the town counts Davy Crockett among its early homesteaders. You can tour **Jack Daniel's Distillery** (*Tenn. 55. 615-759-6180*), established in 1866 and the country's oldest registered distillery. Northeast of town, **Old Stone Fort State Archaeological Area** (*Off US 41. 615-728-0751*) preserves an ancient ceremonial site, built before A.D. 430. Visitor Center exhibits and an interpretive trail orient you to the site's mysteries.

Meriwether Lewis Park (*Natchez Trace Pkwy. Milepost 385.9. 601-680-4025*) A reconstruction of the old log **Grinder's Inn** marks the place where the explorer died in 1809·of a mysterious gunshot wound—believed to have been a suicide. The grounds contain a pioneer cemetery with **Lewis's grave** and a monument.

Pinson Mounds State Archaeological Area (*10 miles S of Jackson via US 45. 460 Ozier Rd. 901-988-5614. Closed weekends Dec.-Feb.*) An ancient ceremonial site dating from A.D. 1 to 300 preserves the country's largest surviving Middle Woodland mound group, featuring 12 flat-topped mounds and a great circular enclosure, a museum, and interpretive trails.

Rhea County Courthouse and Museum (*Courthouse Square, in Dayton. 423-775-7801. Closed Sat.-Sun.*) In 1925 the courtroom was the site of the famed "monkey trial" of John T. Scopes. The trial tested a state law banning the teaching of evolutionary theory and pitted defense lawyer Clarence Darrow against prosecuting attorney William Jennings Bryan. The courtroom appears as it did at the time of the trial; trial-related memorabilia are exhibited at the museum.

Kentucky

My Old Kentucky Home State Park, Bardstown

Virginia's interest in the land west of the Alleghenies spurred a series of explorations, beginning in 1750. With the establishment of Kentucky County as an extension of Virginia in 1776, Virginians began pouring in. Isolated by the mountains and beyond the protection of the established East, the new settlers were prey to repeated Indian attacks. In 1778 George Rogers Clark launched a campaign that forced the Indians north beyond the Ohio River. His attacks on British outposts also succeeded in extending the western frontier to the Mississippi. In 1792 Kentucky became the 15th state in the U.S. Its farmers thrived on the cultivation of hemp, tobacco, and grains used to manufacture whiskey. Though it stayed with the Union during the Civil War, Kentucky was split in its loyalties. After the war, Thoroughbred horse farms began to burgeon in the central Bluegrass region, and coal mining took hold in eastern Appalachia. Hit hard by the depression of the 1930s, Kentucky's coal capital, Harlan County, erupted in the now famous clashes between workers and management that resulted in the recognition of the United Mine Workers of America.

Danville

(Chamber of Commerce, 304 S. 4th St. 606-236-2361) Located along the Wilderness Road, Danville was founded in 1775. In 1785 it was made

the capital of Virginia's expansive new county west of the Alleghenies. Between 1784 and 1792 Danville was the site of ten conventions to discuss separation from Virginia, resulting at last in the drafting of a state constitution and statehood for Kentucky. The **Central Constitution Square State Historic Site** *(105 E. Walnut St. 606-239-7089)* memorializes the original spot with replicas of the old log courthouse, meetinghouse, jail, and other structures.

McDowell House and Apothecary Shop *(125 S. 2nd St. 606-236-2804. Closed Mon. Nov.-Feb.; adm. fee)* On Christmas Day in 1809, Dr. Ephraim McDowell made medical history when he successfully removed, without anesthesia—and without precedent—a 22.5-pound tumor from 46-year-old Jane Todd Crawford. Henceforth, McDowell was known as the "father of abdominal surgery." His house, built between the late 18th and early 19th centuries, contains some original furnishings. The adjoining shop displays a collection of vintage medical instruments.

Wilderness Road

By 1795 some 300,000 migrants had pushed over the Appalachian Mountains in search of "a New Sky & Strange Earth"—the legendary Bluegrass lowlands of central Kentucky. Their journey was greatly eased by the Wilderness Road, blazed 20 years earlier by Daniel Boone. Dispatched by North Carolina speculator and judge, Richard Henderson, Boone was to break trail across the Appalachians into Kentucky, where Henderson was haggling, illegally, with the Indians for land. Boone and his entourage of 30 woodsmen cut the Wilderness Road during the summer of 1775.

Excursions

PERRYVILLE BATTLEFIELD STATE HISTORIC SITE *(10 miles W via US 150 and US 68. 606-332-8631. Park open daily, museum open April-Oct.; adm. fee)* Kentucky's bloodiest Civil War battle occurred here on October 8, 1862, when Confederate troops under Gen. Braxton Bragg met Union general Don Carlos Buell's soldiers. Outnumbered, Bragg retreated, marking the end of the Confederate campaign to take Kentucky. The 250-acre park features self-guided interpretive walking and driving tours; a burial ground and monuments; and a small museum.

HARRODSBURG *(9 miles NW via US 127)* In 1774 Pennsylvania captain James Harrod led a company of 32 frontiersmen to lay out a settlement near the Wilderness Road. Kentucky's first permanent settlement, Harrodsburg was also the site of its first law court, school, and religious service. At **Old Fort Harrod State Park** *(Junction of US 68 and 127. 606-734-3314. Adm. fee)*, you'll find a replica of the fort, with period cabins and blockhouses; frontier craft demonstrations; the oldest pioneer cemetery west of the Alleghenies; and the **Lincoln Marriage Temple,** housing the relocated cabin in which Abraham Lincoln's parents were married in 1806. The 1830 **Mansion Museum** *(125 S. College St. 606-734-2927. Mid-March–Nov.)* features exhibits on Kentucky history from pre-statehood through the Civil War.

Frankfort

(Visitor Center, 100 Capital Ave. 502-875-8687) Tucked among the hills of the Kentucky River Valley, Kentucky's capital was founded in 1786 by Revolutionary War general James Wilkinson and named after pioneer Stephen Frank. Despite two major fires and lobbying by Louisville and Lexington to move the capital, Frankfort continues to hold its place as

the headquarters of state government. **Old State Capitol** (*Broadway and Lewis Sts.*) Built around 1830 and in use until 1910, the Greek Revival edifice contains a self-supporting, stone spiral staircase. Next door, the 1798 **Old Governor's Mansion,** home to 33 governors, is now the lieutenant governor's residence. Just east of here, the **Frankfort Cemetery** (*215 E. Main St.*) may hold the grave of Daniel Boone.

Spiral staircase and dome of the Old State Capitol, Frankfort

The city's oldest district, known as the **Corner of Celebrities,** has claimed over time more nationally prominent residents than perhaps any other four acres in the country. The luminaries who lived here included cabinet officers, Supreme Court justices, U.S. senators, congressmen, governors, and ambassadors. The focal points of the district are two historic homes: The Georgian **Liberty Hall** (*218 Wilkinson St. 502-227-2560. Closed Mon. March-Dec.; adm. fee*) was built in the 1790s by Kentucky's first senator, John Brown, and remained in his family for four generations, until 1934. Sharing the property is the 1835 **Orlando Brown House** (*202 Wilkinson St. 502-875-4952. Closed Mon. March-Dec.; adm. fee*) The only residence designed by Kentucky's famous Greek Revivalist architect, Gideon Schryock (he also created the Old State Capitol), the home was built by the senator's second son.

Kentucky State Capitol (*Capital Ave. 502-564-3449*) In 1904 legislators planned to build a new capitol—the fourth—on Frankfort's public square. Too large for the lot, the domed beaux arts masterpiece went up in south Frankfort instead. Begun in 1905 and dedicated in 1910, the limestone and granite edifice weds Greek and French design elements. The inside is embellished with a rotunda modeled after Napoleon's tomb, a 403-foot columned nave, marble floors, and a riot of murals, sculptures, and stained glass. The showpiece State Reception Room was inspired by the palace at Versailles.

Governor's Mansion (*Capitol Grounds. 502-564-3449. Tours Tues. and Thurs.*) This beaux arts mansion, the governor's residence since 1914, was modeled after the Petit Trianon, Marie Antoinette's villa at Versailles.

Lexington

(*Convention & Visitors Bureau, 301 E. Vine St. 606-233-7299 or 800-845-3959*) The heart of Bluegrass country, Kentucky's second largest city began as a campsite that frontiersmen named after Lexington, Massachusetts.

The town was established by the General Assembly of Virginia in 1782, two years after the founding of **Transylvania University** *(300 N. Broadway. 606-233-8120)*—the first college west of the Alleghenies and the alma mater of Confederate President Jefferson Davis.

The city has several historic districts, the oldest being **Gratz Park Historic District** *(Between 2nd and 3rd and Limestone and N. Broadway Sts.)*, named for hemp manufacturer and town leader, Benjamin Gratz. Lexington's most prominent antebellum families once lived in this neighborhood.

Hunt-Morgan House *(201 N. Mill St. 606-253-0362. Closed mid-Dec.–mid-March; adm. fee)* Kentucky's first millionaire, John Wesley Hunt, built the 1814 federal mansion, which features family furnishings and portraits, an unusual cantilevered staircase, and a fanlit doorway.

Mary Todd Lincoln House *(578 W. Main St. 606-233-9999. Closed Dec.–mid-March; adm. fee)* As a young woman, Abraham Lincoln's wife lived in this homey 14-room house between 1832 and 1839. Originally built as a tavern and inn in 1803, it now contains few original furnishings but a nice collection of portraits and personal effects. The Todd family and other notable locals, including John Hunt Morgan and Henry Clay, are buried in **Lexington Cemetery** *(833 W. Main St. 606-255-5522)*.

Ashland, The Henry Clay Estate *(120 Sycamore Rd. 606-266-8581. Closed Mon. and Jan.; adm. fee)* The mansion is a reconstruction of the original home built by statesman Henry Clay, who lived here from 1806 to 1852. His son James rebuilt the house, using its federal floor plan but adding Italianate elements. In the 1880s, a granddaughter redecorated it in Victorian style. Nearly all of the furnishings are original. Once 600 acres, now 20, the estate includes gardens and original outbuildings.

Centre Family Dwelling, Shaker Village of Pleasant Hill

Red Mile *(1200 Red Mile Rd. 606-255-0752. Grounds open daily. Racing late April–June and late Sept.–early Oct.; adm. fee for races)* Kentucky's oldest harness track, established in 1875, preserves Lexington's heritage as a center of horse sales and racing.

Keeneland Association *(4201 Versailles Rd. 606-254-3412. Grounds open daily. Racing April and Oct.; adm. fee for races)* Reminiscent of Britain's Ascot, the manicured course opened in 1936 on Keene family land bought from Virginia patriot Patrick Henry.

Waveland State Historic Site *(225 Higbee Mill Rd. 606-272-3611. Closed mid-Dec.–Feb.; adm. fee)* Legend claims that Daniel Boone surveyed this site for his nephew, Daniel Boone Bryan, who established the original plantation here. Bryan's son built the Greek Revival Waveland mansion, named for the breezy acres of grain and hemp that once surrounded it.

Excursions

SHAKER VILLAGE OF PLEASANT HILL *(25 miles SW via US 68. 3501 Lexington Rd. 606-734-5411. Adm. fee)* Shaker missionaries from New Lebanon, New York, came here in 1805, and they and their converts established a farm community on this plateau above the Kentucky River. It boasted about 270 structures on some 4,500 acres before closing in 1910. Today, the nation's largest restored Shaker village is an outdoor museum consisting of 33 restored structures, with Shaker furnishings and tools and other artifacts.

WHITE HALL STATE HISTORIC SITE *(15 miles S via I-75. 500 White Hall Shrine Rd. 606-623-9178. Daily April-Oct., Wed.-Sun. Sept.-Oct.; adm. fee)* The distinctive brick mansion was reconstructed in the mid-1860s by Cassius Marcellus Clay—abolitionist, publisher, politician, ambassador to Russia under Abraham Lincoln, and a promoter of Berea College. Built around his father's simpler 1798 home, the house combines Georgian, Gothic Revival, and Italianate elements.

BYBEE POTTERY *(30 miles SE via I-75 and Ky. 52. 606-369-5350. Mon.-Fri.)* The oldest existing pottery producer west of the Alleghenies, Bybee is said to date from 1845, although its records go back as far as 1809. Based in the original log building and run by the same family for six generations, Bybee uses the pit-mined clay that early settlers at Fort Boonesborough used.

BEREA *(40 miles S via I-75)* Set in the Appalachian foothills, the area became the center of abolitionist mission activity in 1855. Called Berea,

after the biblical town where people "received the Word with all readiness of mind," tuition-free **Berea College** *(Visitor information at Boone Tavern, Main St. 606-986-9358)* was founded as one of the South's first interracial colleges. A center for traditional Appalachian crafts, the college became a leader in the American Crafts Revival movement during the first half of this century; the town continues to be a haven for craftspeople. The **Berea College Appalachian Museum** *(Jackson St. 606-986-9341. Adm. fee)* offers exhibits on the culture and history of Appalachia.

197

Finish line at the Kentucky Derby, Churchill Downs

Louisville ···········

(Visitor Center, 400 S. 1st St. 502-582-3732 or 800-792-5595) Founded in the 1770s by George Rogers Clark, the town was named in honor of French king Louis XVI and prospered as an Ohio River port. The steamboat era is recalled by the 1914 ***Belle of Louisville*** *(4th and River Rd. 502-574-2355. Cruises Mem. Day–Labor Day; fare),* one of the last stern-wheelers in use.

Churchill Downs *(700 Central Ave. 502-636-4400)* The nation's oldest continuously operated racetrack played host to the first Kentucky Derby in May 1875. At the adjacent **Kentucky Derby Museum** *(704 Central Ave. 502-637-7097. Adm. fee),* you can experience the thrill of the race through a 360-degree, multi-image show and learn about the history and culture of Thoroughbred racing.

Farmington *(3033 Bardstown Rd. 502-452-9920. Adm. fee)* The 1810 federal house, modeled on a plan by Thomas Jefferson and built largely by slaves, belonged to John and Lucy Speed, owners of a 554-acre hemp plantation. Abraham Lincoln was a guest here in 1841.

Locust Grove *(561 Blankenbaker Lane. 502-897-9845. Adm. fee)* Built in 1790 by Maj. William Croghan, the Georgian mansion was the retirement home of his brother-in-law, Gen. George Rogers Clark. Among the estate's famous visitors were three Presidents and Clark's youngest brother, William, who returned here with Meriwether Lewis in 1806, after their expedition to the Pacific.

Excursions

FORT KNOX *(16 miles SW via US 31W)* Opened in 1918, this U.S. military reserve stores much of the nation's gold in the **U.S. Gold Depository.** Also on site, the **Patton Museum of Cavalry and Armor** *(Fayette Ave. 502-624-3812)* exhibits personal items that belonged to World War II Gen. George S. Patton, Jr., and an array of historic military equipment.

MY OLD KENTUCKY HOME STATE PARK *(25 miles SE via US 31E/150 in Bardstown. 502-348-3502. Adm. fee to house)* Focal point of the 280-acre park is the federal mansion built in 1818 by Judge John Rowan. After a

Mammoth Cave National Park

visit to his cousins here in 1852, Stephen Foster was inspired to write his famous ballad. The **"Stephen Foster Story,"** an outdoor musical, is performed annually at the amphitheater *(June–Labor Day Tues.-Sun. Adm. fee).*

HODGENVILLE *(55 miles S via I-65 and Ky. 61)* Epicenter of Kentucky's Lincoln heritage, the area preserves the **Abraham Lincoln Birthplace N.H.S.** *(3 miles S of town on US 31E and Ky. 61. 502-358-3874),* where Lincoln was born on February 12, 1809. A symbolic cabin is enshrined in the Memorial Building, designed by John Russell Pope. A Visitor Center offers exhibits and a film. In 1811 the Lincoln family moved to **Knob Creek Farm** *(8 miles E of town on US 31E. 502-549-3741. April-Oct.; adm. fee).* On the site today stands a replica of the cabin Lincoln lived in until the age of seven, when the family moved to Indiana.

Other Sites in Kentucky

Blue Licks Battlefield State Park *(US 68, near Mount Olivet. 606-289-*

5507. *Grounds open year-round, museum open April-Oct.; adm. fee)* The park memorializes the site of the Battle of Blue Licks, the last Revolutionary War battle in Kentucky. In 1782 Shawnee Indians and British troops routed a Kentucky militia here along the Licking River. Among the many casualties was Daniel Boone's son, Israel. The site includes a history museum, a soldiers' burial ground, and portions of a buffalo trail.

Covington *(Visitor Center, 605 Philadelphia St. 606-655-4159 or 800-STAY-NKY)* Cincinnati's charming neighbor across the Ohio River grew from a 150-acre farm into an industrial center by the mid-1830s. Several designated **historic districts**—the oldest being the **Riverside Historic District**—preserve the city's impressive collection of 19th-century Italianate, Second Empire, Queen Anne, Romanesque, and Greek Revival row houses and mansions. The old German quarter, settled in the 1800s, has been nicely restored as **MainStrasse Village,** a five-block commercial area of cobbled lanes and renovated structures. You'll also want to visit **Cincinnati, Ohio,** just across the Ohio River (see page 208).

Cumberland Gap National Historical Park *(Park straddles Kentucky, Virginia, and Tennessee. Visitor Center, Cumberland Gap Pkwy., in Middlesboro, Ky. 606-248-2817)* Focal point of the nation's largest historical park, covering more than 20,000 acres, is the 800-foot-deep gap that provided a natural pass through the Appalachian Mountains. Bison originally pounded out the trail, followed by Indian hunters and warriors and white trappers. Part of the Wilderness Road marked by Daniel Boone, it was a main commercial and transportation route for west-bound settlers and east-bound livestock and produce, and was later used by Civil War troops. The park has restored three of twelve farmsteads at the **Hensley Settlement** *(Via 4-mile hike on Chadwell Gap Trail, off US 58 in Va.),* an Appalachian community that was established in 1904 and thrived for half a century.

Mammoth Cave National Park *(Off I-65, in Mammoth Cave. 502-758-2251. Adm. fee for cave tours; reservations recommended)* The world's longest known cave system, rediscovered in the 1790s, saw its first human presence as long ago as 4,000 years. Well-preserved prehistoric artifacts and other evidence date from 2500 B.C. During the War of 1812, the cave supported a saltpeter mine. It also served briefly as the site of an experimental tuberculosis hospital during the winter of 1842-43. All of this and more is covered on the **Historic Cave Tour.**

Shakertown *(US 68, in South Union. 502-542-4167. March–mid-Dec.; adm. fee)* Among 19 Shaker villages in the country, Shakertown was Kentucky's last, founded in 1807. The community grew to 6,000 acres and more than 200 buildings, sustained through the sale of packaged garden seeds and fruit preserves; it disbanded in 1922. Three of the six remaining buildings are open to the public, including the 1869 Shaker Tavern *(Ky.73),* now a bed-and-breakfast; the **Shaker Museum** *(US 68),* located in the 40-room, 1824 Centre Family Dwelling House and displaying Shaker furniture, textiles, and tools; and an 1835 smoke and milk house.

Washington *(Visitor Center in the Cane Brake, Old Main St. 606-759-7411. Mid-March–Dec.)* Settled as an outpost for travelers along the Buffalo Trace frontier trail and incorporated in 1786, Washington boasts a wealth of houses dating from 1785 to 1812. Guides in period costume offer tours of **Old Washington** that take you along its flagstone paths and through historic house museums, cemeteries, and churches.

West Virginia

Cass Scenic Railroad State Park

The 35th state to join the Union, West Virginia actually carved itself out of Virginia during the Civil War. Never dependent on slave labor, the pro-Union counties in the northern part of western Virginia broke away from secessionist eastern Virginia and applied to the federal government to accept them as a new state. President Lincoln signed the West Virginia Statehood Proclamation on June 20, 1863. The newly created state prospered in its early years, with industry thriving along the Ohio River Valley and coal mining spreading across much of the state. But labor unrest and poor working conditions among miners plagued West Virginia throughout much of this century. Now the state's rugged, largely rural character has become the backbone of a growing tourist industry.

Charleston

(Convention & Visitors Bureau, 200 Civic Center Dr. 304-344-5075 or 800-733-5469) After the formation of West Virginia, the new state's capital fluctuated between several places before this central city on the Kanawha River was finally chosen in 1885.

State Capitol *(1900 Kanawha Blvd. E. 304-558-3809)* Charleston's mighty American Renaissance landmark was designed in the 1920s by Cass Gilbert and is topped by a 292-foot-high, gold-leafed dome. The nearby **Cultural Center** *(Capitol Complex. 304-558-0220. Donations)* houses a historical museum featuring exhibits on West Virginia's past.

Craik-Patton House *(2809 Kanawha Blvd. E, Daniel Boone Park. 304-925-5341. Mid-April–Sept.; adm. fee)* Built in 1834, the elegantly proportioned

Greek Revival house is furnished with 18th- and early 19th-century antiques.

Harpers Ferry National Historical Park .....

(Visitor Center, US 340, in Harpers Ferry. 304-535-6298) The picturesque town occupies a deep, rock-riven gorge at the strategic confluence of the Potomac and Shenandoah Rivers. In the late 1790s, its waterpower potential lead to the development of a major federal armory and arsenal here. In October 1859, abolitionist John Brown and his 21-man "army of liberation" seized control of the armory but were quickly put down by a contingent of Marines under Lt. Col. Robert E. Lee. During the Civil War the town changed hands eight times. Today, Harpers Ferry's historic buildings house Park Service museums detailing the town's role in the war and in the early civil rights movement. (The second meeting of black activist W.E.B. Du Bois's Niagara movement was held here in 1906.) The town summit is crowned by **St. Peter's Catholic Church** (1830s). On **Virginius Island,** a trail leads past 19th-century industrial ruins.

Excursions

CHARLES TOWN *(5 miles SW via US 340)* George Washington surveyed this area in the 1740s, and his brother Charles laid out the town in 1786. The 1837 **Jefferson County Courthouse** *(Washington and George Sts.)* was the scene of John Brown's trial.

SHEPHERDSTOWN *(12 miles N via US 340 and W.Va. 230 N. Visitor Center, 102 N. King St. 304-876-2786)* The state's oldest town was laid out in the 1730s by Thomas Shepherd, and many 18th- and 19th-century buildings still stand. The museum in the 1786 **Entler Hotel** *(Princess and German Sts. 304-876-0910. Museum open April-Oct. Sat.-Sun.; donations)* chronicles local history and displays a replica of an early steamboat.

ANTIETAM NAT. BATTLEFIELD, MD. *(12 miles N via US 340, W. Va. 230, and Md. 34 and 65)* See p. 96.

MARTINSBURG *(20 miles via US 340 and W. Va. 230 and 45)* Laid out in 1773, the town served as a cultural and commercial center until the Civil War. The **Belle Boyd House** *(126 E. Race St. 304-267-4713. Wed.-Sat.; donations)* recounts the childhood and later exploits of the town's native daughter and features memorabilia of the Berkeley County Historical Society. The large stone **Gen. Adam Stephen House** *(309 E. John St. 304-267-4434. May-Oct.)*, built by the town founder in the 1770s and 1780s, is decorated with federal antiques. The adjacent 1874 **Triple Brick House** displays local memorabilia.

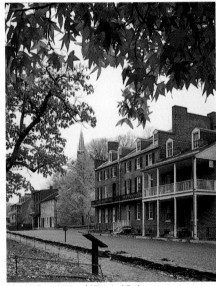

Harpers Ferry National Historical Park; above, portrait of John Brown

FREDERICK, MD. *(20 miles NE via US 340)* See page 95.
LEESBURG, VA. *(25 miles SE via US 340 and Va. 671 and 9)* See p. 112.

Lewisburg ·····························

(Visitor Center, 105 Church St. 304-645-1000 or 800-833-2068) In the 1750s Andrew Lewis surveyed this area of the Greenbrier Valley and in 1782 the town of Lewisburg was chartered, becoming the administrative and cultural center of the region. A number of late 18th- and early 19th-century buildings remain, including the **General Lewis Inn** *(310 E. Washington St. 304-645-2600)*, whose east wing dates from the early 1800s and is filled with antiques. The **Old Stone Presbyterian Church** *(200 Church St.)* and the adjacent **Lewisburg Cemetery** have withstood 200 years.

North House Museum *(301 W. Washington St. 304-645-3398. Tues.-Sat.; adm. fee)* Reflecting the prosperity of Greenbrier County, the 1820s house features 18th- and 19th-century rooms, local history exhibits, and the nation's first RFD (Rural Free Delivery) mail buggy (1896).

Excursion

THE GREENBRIER *(10 miles E via US 60, in White Sulphur Springs. 300 W. Main St. 800-624-6070)* A fashionable spa since antebellum days, the renowned resort preserves its neoclassical 1830s springhouse and white frame cottages. The two-story **President's Cottage Museum** *(April-Thanksgiving)* was used as a retreat for five Presidents in the early 19th century. Murals depict the Greenbrier's early years and Civil War scenes.

Parkersburg ·····························

(Visitor Bureau, 350 7th St. 304-420-4800 or 800-752-4982) Established at the confluence of the Little Kanawha and Ohio Rivers in the 1790s, the town gained notoriety when traitor Aaron Burr gathered his followers here in preparation for establishing a separate domain in the Southwest.

Blennerhassett Island Historical State Park and Museum *(137 Juliana Sts. 304-420-4800 or 800-CALL-WVA. Museum open April–early Dec. Tues.-Sun., mid-Dec.–March Sat.-Sun.; island via sternwheeler at Point Park and 2nd St. May-Oct.; adm. fee)* The late 18th-century Italian Palladian home of Irish aristocrats Harman and Margaret Blennerhassett has been reconstructed on Blennerhassett Island and decorated with original and period pieces. The downtown Blennerhassett Museum houses exhibits on regional history and prehistory and includes a film on the Blennerhassetts and their involvement with Aaron Burr, which led to their ruin.

Excursion

MARIETTA, OHIO *(15 miles N via I-77 and Ohio 7)* See page 212.

Wheeling ·····························

(Visitor Bureau, 1310 Market St. 304-233-7709 or 800-828-3097) This historic town began as a colonial river crossing and grew to be an important 19th-century commercial center and industrial town and the terminus of the National Road. In 1849 the **Wheeling Suspension Bridge** became the first bridge across the Ohio and the world's longest, spanning 1,010 feet. A well-preserved **Victorian district** edges downtown.

West Virginia Independence Hall *(1528 Market St. 304-238-1300. Closed*

Greenbrier Resort, White Sulphur Springs

Sun. Jan.-Feb.) Originally a mid-1800s customshouse, the Italianate brick building witnessed the birthplace of West Virginia when Northern loyalists convened here during the Civil War and formed a new state. From 1861 to 1863, the building served as capitol.

Oglebay *(W. Va. 88. 304-243-4010 or 800-624-6988. Adm. fee to attractions)* Wheeling's proud jewel, the park was a gift to the city by industrialist Earl Oglebay, who had a farm here. His Greek Revival mansion holds period rooms that span the frontier era to the Gilded Age. The **Carriage House Glass Museum** traces the region's glassmaking history.

Excursion

GRAVE CREEK MOUND STATE PARK *(12 miles S via W. Va. 2, in Moundsville. 801 Jefferson Ave. 304-843-1410. Adm. fee)* At 70 feet high and about 295 feet around, this mound is the largest surviving structure from the mound builder culture that dominated the Ohio River Valley from about 2000 B.C. to A.D. 700. The park's **Delf Norona Museum** houses dioramas and exhibits detailing the culture.

Other Sites in West Virginia

Berkeley Springs State Park *(US 522, in Berkeley Springs. 304-258-2711. Fee for baths)* George Washington took the mineral waters that made this town famous. The 4.5-acre park offers an 1815 **Roman Bath House,** with museum and working baths, and a 1928 **Main Bath House.**

Bulltown Historical Area *(10 miles N of Flatwoods, off US 19. 304-452-8170. Mid-May–early Oct.)* Cabins moved to this location re-create life in central West Virginia (then Virginia) in the 1800s.

Cass Scenic Railroad State Park *(W. Va. 66, near Snowshoe Resort. 304-456-4300 or 800-CALL-WVA. Daily Mem. Day–Labor Day, Thurs.-Sun. Sept.-Oct.; fare for train)* Narrated coal- and steam-powered rides take in the remains of the lumber town of Cass and breathtaking mountain scenery.

Fort New Salem *(W. Va. 23. 304-782-5245 April–Mem. Day Mon.-Fri., Mem. Day–late Dec. Wed.-Sun.; adm. fee)* Log buildings moved here and such regional traditions as weaving and open-hearth cooking preserve a passing culture. The original fort was settled in the 1790s by Seventh Day Baptists.

Jackson's Mill Historic Area *(15 miles S of Clarksburg, off US 19. 304-269-5100. Mem. Day–Labor Day Tues.-Sun.; adm. fee)* Confederate hero Stonewall Jackson was raised on this farm, and the 1841 family gristmill now functions as a museum of frontier life; several other period buildings have been reconstructed on the site.

Pricketts Fort State Park *(Off I-79 on W. Va. 3, near Fairmont. 304-363-3030. Mid-April–Oct.; adm. fee)* At the reconstructed stockaded refuge fort, costumed interpreters relive the hardships that settlers faced when they would gather here at the threat of Indian attack.

MANITOBA

CANADA
U.S.A.

ONTARIO

NORTH DAKOTA

Grand Mound

Soudan
Underground
Mine State Park

Hull Rust Mahoning
Open Pit Iron Mine
Chisholm

Forest History
Center

Grand Portage
Nat. Mon.

LAKE SUPERIOR

Split Rock
Lighthouse and
History Center

Coppertown
U.S.A.
Hancock
Copper Harbor
Keweenaw
Peninsula
Houghton

MINNESOTA

Duluth

Bayfield

Apostle
Islands

Old Victoria

Michigan Iron
Industry Museum

MICH.

Charles A.
Lindbergh
House

Mille Lacs
Indian Museum

North West
Company Fur Post

WISCONSIN

Iron Mountain
Iron Mountain
Iron Mine

Fayette
Historic
S.P.

Oliver H. Kelley Farm

SOUTH DAKOTA

Upper
Sioux
Agency

Minneapolis
St. Paul

Lower Sioux Agency

Fort Ridgely

Oneida
Nation
Museum

Green
Bay

Mississippi

Pipestone
Nat. Mon.

Jeffers
Petroglyphs

Wisconsin
Maritime Museum

LAKE MICHIGAN

IOWA

Circus
World
Museum

Old Wade
House

Taliesin

Villa Louis
Pendarvis H.S.
Stonefield H.S.
First Capitol H.S.

Galena

Little Norway

Madison

Aztalan S.P.

Milwaukee

Old World
Wisconsin

Lincoln-
Tallman
Restorations

John
Deere
H.S.

Oak Park
Chicago

Gary

Rock
Island
Arsenal

ILLINOIS AND
MICHIGAN
CANAL N.H.C.

Amish Acre
Historic Far.

Carl Sandburg
S.H.S.

Bishop Hill S.H.S.

ILLINOIS

Tippecanoe
Battlefiel

Dickson Mounds
State
Museum

Nauvoo
Carthage

Lincoln's New
Salem S.H.S.

Quincy

Bloomington

Lincoln

Decatur

Lafayette

Conn
Pra

MISSOURI

Springfield

Lincoln
Heritage
Trail Driving
Tour

Lincoln
Log Cabin
S.H.S.

Indianap

IND

Center for
American
Archaeology
Visitor Center

Vandalia

Cahokia
Courthouse
S.H.S.

Cahokia
Mounds

Vincennes

Fort de
Chartres
S.H.S.

New Harmony

Angel
Mounds
S.H.S.

Linco
Boyh
Nat.
Mem.

Cairo

Split Rock Lighthouse, Lake Superior, Minnesota

Great Lakes

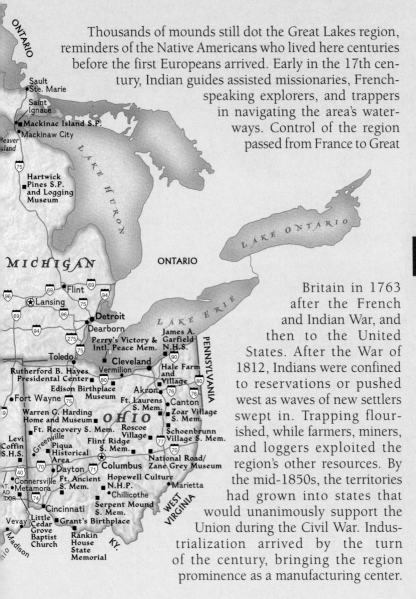

Thousands of mounds still dot the Great Lakes region, reminders of the Native Americans who lived here centuries before the first Europeans arrived. Early in the 17th century, Indian guides assisted missionaries, French-speaking explorers, and trappers in navigating the area's waterways. Control of the region passed from France to Great

Britain in 1763 after the French and Indian War, and then to the United States. After the War of 1812, Indians were confined to reservations or pushed west as waves of new settlers swept in. Trapping flourished, while farmers, miners, and loggers exploited the region's other resources. By the mid-1850s, the territories had grown into states that would unanimously support the Union during the Civil War. Industrialization arrived by the turn of the century, bringing the region prominence as a manufacturing center.

Hopewell Culture National Historical Park

As far back as 2,000 years, Ohio formed the heart of ancient Indian cultures, whose earthworks still imprint the landscape. Centuries later, when the Europeans arrived, it was the Delaware, Miami, Shawnee, Wyandot, among others, who inhabited the region. The British, victors of the French and Indian War, sought peace with the Indians by granting them, in the 1768 Treaty of Fort Stanwix, the lands northwest of the Ohio River. After the Revolutionary War, however, the Americans demanded the return of these lands and more. The Indians, of course, resisted. In 1790 President George Washington called for their forced removal. They fought a good fight for four years—the Ohio Indian Wars—before relinquishing most of their claims. In 1803 Ohio won statehood—the first state to be carved out of the Northwest Territory. In the years between 1830 and the Civil War, the building of canals, and the development of steamboats resulted in the growth in Ohio of cities, industry, and agriculture, drawing waves of European immigrants. After the Civil War, with the rise of the railroad and with coal and iron ore finds nearby, Ohio continued to grow industrially.

Canton

Incorporated in 1854, Canton is the largest of Stark County's industrial and manufacturing centers, and the county seat. The town boomed with the railroad. By century's turn, Canton had become a leading steel producer.

Pro Football Hall of Fame (*2121 George Halas Dr. N.W., off I-77. 330-456-8207. Adm. fee*) Home of the Bulldogs, Canton fought to host this entertaining shrine to America's most popular sport. The city was, after all, the birthplace of pro-football in 1920. Don't miss the NFL action film.

McKinley National Memorial (*800 McKinley Monument Dr. N.W. 330-455-7043. April-Nov.*) The neoclassical mausoleum of favorite son and assassinated 25th President, William McKinley, also holds the remains of his wife and two daughters. An impressive array of McKinleyana awaits at the adjacent **McKinley Museum** (*330-455-7043. Adm. fee*).

Excursions

FORT LAURENS STATE MEMORIAL (*10 miles S via I-77 just outside Bolivar, on Fort Laurens Rd. 330-874-2059 or 800-283-8914. Mem. Day–Labor Day Wed.-Sun., Labor Day–Oct. weekends; adm. fee for museum*) A shallow trench is all that remains of Ohio's only Revolutionary War outpost, built in 1778. The fort, abandoned in 1779, is recalled in a small museum and park.

ZOAR VILLAGE STATE MEMORIAL (*12 miles S via I-77, on Ohio 212. 330-874-3011 or 800-262-6195. Mem. Day–Labor Day Wed.-Sun., weekends April–Mem. Day and Labor Day–Oct.; adm. fee*) In 1817 German Separatists seeking religious freedom formed one of the country's most significant experiments in communal living. Zoar grew into a self-supporting farm community before the society was dissolved in 1898. Its legacy lives on in this quaint village's many restored structures. A ticket buys a tour (some self-guided) of nine building museums; start at the Visitor Center.

SCHOENBRUNN VILLAGE STATE MEMORIAL (*25 miles S via I-77 and US 250, on Ohio 259 in New Philadelphia. 330-339-3636. Daily Mem. Day–Labor Day, weekends Labor Day–Oct.; adm. fee*) In 1772 the Moravians—a pacifist German Protestant sect—founded a mission here for the Delaware Indians, Ohio's first Christian settlement. The reconstructed village contains log structures, the old cemetery, and a Visitor Center. A dramatization of the Schoenbrunn story, *Trumpet in the Land,* is performed in the nearby amphitheater (*330-339-1132. Mid-June–Aug. Mon.-Sat.; adm. fee*).

Chillicothe Region ······························

Thousands of years before Europeans came, prehistoric peoples—including the Adena, the Hopewell, and the Fort Ancient—centered their civilizations in this part of the Ohio River Valley. The southern Ohio landscape still bears their mark in the few remaining mounds and earthworks, the most important of which are located near Chillicothe. Founded in 1796 by Kentuckians and Virginians, who named it after the Shawnee word for "town," Chillicothe served as territorial, and later state, capital. A premier attraction is **Adena State Memorial** (*848 Adena Rd. 614-772-1500 or 800-319-7248. Mem. Day–Labor Day Wed.-Sun., Labor Day–Oct. weekends; adm. fee*), the 1807 estate of Thomas Worthington, Ohio's sixth governor and first U.S. senator.

Hopewell Culture N.H.P. (*3 miles N of Chillicothe on Ohio 104. 614-774-1125. Adm. fee*) Two thousand years ago, the Hopewell Indians established a village and burial site on the west bank of the Scioto River, where they interred the cremated remains of their elite. Dubbed the Mound City Group, this restored site preserves one of the largest known concentrations of

Hopewell burial mounds. The archaeological site is self-guided, with a peripheral interpretive trail.

Serpent Mound State Memorial (*45 miles SW via US 50 and Ohio 41 and 73. 513-587-2796. April-Oct.; adm. fee*) One of the nation's largest effigy mounds—*the* largest and finest serpent mound in North America—this 1,348-foot-long serpentine embankment, jaws gaping and tail coiled, slithers across the bluff top. Likely created by the Fort Ancient Indians around A.D. 1070, its purpose—probably religious, possibly astronomical—is a mystery. Climb the observation platform for the best view. You'll appreciate it more if you visit the museum first.

John A. Roebling Suspension Bridge, Cincinnati

Cincinnati

(*Convention & Visitors Bureau, 300 W. 6th St. 513-621-6994 or 800-246-2987*) The "Queen City" took root on the Ohio River flats, spreading north into the hills after the completion of the Miami and Erie Canal in 1845. Ohio's main port during the river's heyday as a major commercial and transportation route, the frontier's largest city was, by 1850, a center of art and culture. It was also a commercial and manufacturing hub, supplied with a large pool of migrant and immigrant labor. After the Civil War, with the expansion of the railroad, Cincinnati lost its preeminence to Chicago. Unique among the city's numerous landmarks is the **John A. Roebling Suspension Bridge,** the longest span of its kind when built in 1867, and a model for the engineer's famous Brooklyn Bridge.

Cincinnati Historical Society Museum (*Cincinnati Museum Center at Union Terminal. 513-287-7000. Adm. fee*) Part of the museum complex within Cincinnati's refurbished art deco terminal, this fine museum features detailed re-creations of historical settings through which visitors experience the city's story.

William Howard Taft N.H.S. (*2038 Auburn Ave. 513-684-3262*) In 1857 America's 27th President was born in this house—the only national Taft memorial—in the hilltop neighborhood of Mount Auburn. The tour focuses on his public and private life. (Don't confuse the birthplace with the Taft Museum, formerly the home of William's half-brother, Charles.)

Harriet Beecher Stowe House (*10 miles NE of downtown via 7th St. 2950 Gilbert Ave, Walnut Hills. 513-632-5120. Tues.-Thurs.*) As a young woman, Stowe moved from Connecticut in 1832 to her father's simple, newly built home here. Minister and abolitionist Lyman Beecher helped organize the city's Underground Railroad network, a fact that no doubt inspired Stowe to write her famed antislavery novel, *Uncle Tom's Cabin*. Self-guided tours showcase several rooms containing period furnishings.

Excursions

COVINGTON, KENTUCKY *(1 mile S via I-75)* See p. 199.

FORT ANCIENT STATE MEMORIAL *(35 miles NE via I-71 on Ohio 350, near Lebanon. 513-932-4421. Wed.-Sun. Mem. Day–Labor Day, weekends only April–Mem. Day and Labor Day–Oct.)* These outstanding bluff-top earthworks—including ceremonial mounds and more than 3.5 miles of walls forming a 100-acre enclosure—were built by the Hopewell Indians between 100 B.C. and A.D. 500. Fort Ancient Indians lived here between A.D. 1000 and 1200.

ULYSSES S. GRANT HISTORIC SITES Grant's Birthplace *(20 miles SE via US 52 at junction with Ohio 232, in Point Pleasant. 513-553-4911. April-Oct. Wed.-Sun.; adm. fee)* On April 27, 1822, America's 18th President and famous Civil War general was born along the Ohio River in this small frame house, now containing Grant memorabilia and period furnishings. **Grant's Boyhood Home** *(30 miles farther E via US 52 and Ohio 221 in Georgetown. E. Grant Ave. and N. Water St. 513-378-4222. Mon.-Sat.; Sun. by appt.; adm. fee)* preserves the more gracious house, where the family moved in 1823.

RANKIN HOUSE STATE MEMORIAL *(45 miles SE via US 52 in Ripley. Rankin Hill Rd. 513-392-1627. Wed.-Sun. Mem. Day–Labor Day, weekends late April–Mem. Day and Labor Day–Oct.; adm. fee)* The preserved 1828 home of abolitionist Rev. John Rankin was a major station on the Underground Railroad. The house is immortalized in Harriet Beecher Stowe's *Uncle Tom's Cabin.*

Cleveland

(Information Booth in the Terminal Tower, 50 Public Square. 216-621-4110 or 800-321-1004) In 1796 Moses Cleaveland led a survey team from Connecticut to the east bank of the Cuyahoga River at Lake Erie. Their mission? To plan a central town site in the Western Reserve—the last of the lands granted Connecticut by King Charles II in 1662. Cleaveland bought the land from the Iroquois for 500 pounds, two beef cattle, and 100 gallons of whiskey. His namesake town became the main terminus of the Ohio and Erie Canal and, later, an industrial center that drew thousands of immigrants.

Rock and Roll Hall of Fame and Museum *(E. 9th St. and Erieside Ave. 216-781-7625. Adm. fee)* In 1951 Cleveland's WJW disc jockey Alan Freed popularized the term "rock and roll." More than four decades later, rock and roll came home to Cleveland. Housed in a geometric glass-fronted structure designed by I.M. Pei, the museum is a loud, fast-paced, and high-tech trip through rock history.

Western Reserve Historical Society *(10825 East Blvd. 216-721-5722. Adm. fee)* Cleveland's oldest cultural institution, the complex includes a history museum, where unfolds the story of the Western Reserve and the city's cultural and economic development; the Frederick C. Crawford Auto-Aviation Museum, which represents the city's role in these industries; and the Italianate Hay-McKinney Mansion, designed by President James Garfield's son.

Excursions

HALE FARM AND VILLAGE *(25 miles SE via I-77 in Bath. 2686 Oak Hill Rd. 330-666-3711. Mid-May–Oct. Tues.-Sun.; adm. fee)* In 1810 Jonathan Hale brought his family here from Connecticut to carve out a farm in the Cuyahoga Valley. Their land now holds a re-created, mid-1800s Western Reserve village consisting of the original homestead and restored period buildings from around the region.

JAMES A. GARFIELD NATIONAL HISTORIC SITE *(25 miles NE via I-90 and Ohio 306 in Mentor. 8095 Mentor Ave. 216-255-8722. Tues.-Sun.; adm. fee)* America's 20th President campaigned from his front porch here at Lawnfield, his 30-room Victorian home, which now holds family furnishings and memorabilia, and a presidential library.

STAN HYWET HALL AND GARDENS *(40 miles SE via I-77 in Akron. 714 N. Portage Path. 330-836-5533. Call for hours; adm. fee)* Thought to be Ohio's largest private residence, and considered America's premier example of Tudor Revival architecture, the 65-room mansion was built between 1911 and 1915 by Goodyear cofounder Franklin A. Seiberling. Its lavish interior brims with art and antiques; equally magnificent are the 70 acres of gardens. The history of the rubber industry itself is presented at the **Goodyear World of Rubber** *(1144 E. Market St. 330-796-6546. Closed weekends)*.

VERMILION *(35 miles W via I-90 and Ohio 2 and 60)* This picturesque port town—named by the local Erie Indians after the Vermilion River's red-clay banks—was settled by New Englanders in 1808-1811 and became a shipbuilding and shipping center. The **Harbour Town historic district** *(Self-guided tour brochure available at museum)* preserves the character of the original village, while artwork and artifacts at the **Inland Seas Maritime Museum** *(480 Main St. 216-967-3467. Adm. fee)* offer Great Lakes lore and history.

Columbus

(Visitor Center, City Center Mall, 2nd floor. 614-222-6262) When Ohio won statehood in 1803, it had no permanent capital. In 1812 residents of the prosperous town of Franklinton convinced state officials to locate the capital across the river from them, on the Scioto's boggy east banks. The town took off, boosted by subsequent linkups with the Ohio and Erie Canal, the National Road, and five railroads.

German Village *(German Village Society Meeting Haus, 588 S. 3rd St. 614-221-8888)* Columbus's original German neighborhood thrived between 1840 and 1914, then fell into decline before its restoration as a 233-acre historic district. Quaint cottages now house restaurants and shops.

Ohio Historical Center and Ohio Village *(I-71 and 17th Ave. 614-297-2300. April-Dec. Wed.-Sun., Jan.-March weekends only; adm. fee)* The museum showcases thousands of years of Ohio's human and natural history, with galleries dedicated to Ohio's story. Behind the museum, a re-created Civil War-era Ohio village features costumed interpreters and artisans who demonstrate typical period activities.

Excursion

FLINT RIDGE STATE MEMORIAL *(35 miles E via I-70 and Ohio 668, near Brownsville. 614-787-2476 or 614-344-1919. Park open April-Oct.; museum*

Western Reserve
In 1662 King Charles II gave Connecticut a great swath of land stretching to the Pacific. (Never mind that King James had previously promised part of it to Virginia.) Charles also offered parts of the same area to the Duke of York and to Admiral William Penn. Predictably, the unequal parceling of lands later caused strife. To appease the smaller states, Congress proposed that landed states turn over all or part of their western turf. Connecticut, thanks to its persistent efforts, kept a 3.3 million-acre chunk (modern-day northeastern Ohio) called the Western Reserve. Settlement proved difficult, though, and in 1800 the last piece of "New Connecticut" became part of the Northwest Territory.

open Wed.-Sun. Mem. Day–Labor Day, weekends only Labor Day–Oct. Adm. fee) As many as 9,000 years ago, prehistoric Indians from around the Midwest made tracks to this mother lode of flint, which they quarried to make weapons and tools. Museum exhibits present the geological and cultural history of the stone. Nature trails

Ohio Village, Columbus

wend past some of the many ancient flint pits pockmarking the ridge.

Dayton ···

(Convention & Visitors Bureau, 1 Chamber Plaza, Suite A. 513-226-8211 or 800-221-8235) The first settlement in the fertile Miami Valley, Dayton Township was founded on April Fool's Day in 1796, and later divided into present-day Montgomery and Greene Counties. Despite Dayton's battle with floods, the city became a center of trade, industry—and invention: It's home to the airplane, the cash register, and the ignition starter.

Dayton Aviation Heritage National Historical Park Comprised of four separate locations, this park is dedicated to Dayton's significant legacy of flight: The **Wright Cycle Company Shop** *(22 S. Williams St. 513-225-7705. Daily Mem. Day–Labor Day, weekends or by appt. rest of year)* preserves the city's last Wright brothers shop where, from 1895 to 1897, Wilbur and Orville made bicycles, operated a printshop, and considered researching their flying machine. The nearby Hoover Block marks the site of an earlier printshop, where they printed a newspaper for acclaimed African-American poet Paul Laurence Dunbar. His restored home, the **Dunbar House State Memorial** *(219 N. Paul Laurence Dunbar St. 513-224-7061. Mem. Day–Labor Day Wed.-Sun., Sept.-Oct. weekends only; adm. fee),* is the first publicly owned African-American historic site. **Carillon Historical Park** *(2001 S. Patterson Blvd. 513-293-3638. May-Oct. Tues.-Sun.; adm. fee)* counts among its varied exhibits the 1905 Wright Flyer III, the world's first practical airplane. The Wrights tested the plane and established the first permanent flying school at **Huffman Prairie Flying Field** *(Wright-Patterson Air Force Base. 513-257-5535. Historic walking trail guide available.).*

SunWatch Archaeological Park *(Just S of downtown via I-75 and Nicholas Rd., at 2301 W. River Rd. 513-268-8199. Closed Mon. Nov.-March; adm. fee)* In the late 12th century, Fort Ancient Indians—part of a larger Mississippian culture—built a significant farm village and a kind of sun calendar here along the Great Miami River. The archaeological site consists of a reconstructed village and Visitor Center, with detailed cultural and archaeological exhibits.

Excursions

CARRIAGE HILL METROPARK FARM *(8 miles NE of downtown via Brandt Pike/Ohio 201 in Huber Heights. 7800 E. Shull Rd. 513-879-0461)* Settled in 1830, Carriage Hill is a working historical farm, restored to demonstrate

life on a late 19th-century farmstead. The self-guided tour takes in original buildings, representative animals and crops, and craft demonstrations.
PIQUA HISTORICAL AREA (30 miles N via I-75 in Piqua. 9845 N. Hardin Rd.

513-773-2522. Mem. Day–Labor Day Wed.-Sun., Labor Day–Oct. weekends; adm. fee) The 174-acre farm of 19th-century federal Indian agent John Johnston has a range of sites covering the history of the Great Miami River Valley, including a prehistoric Indian mound, restored Johnston farm buildings, and a restored section of the Miami and Erie Canal, with an operating canalboat.

GREENVILLE (35 miles NW via Ohio 49) Gen. Anthony Wayne built his headquarters here in 1793 to establish an American presence

Canalboat on Miami and Erie Canal, Piqua Historical Area

on the wild frontier. Two years later he negotiated the Treaty of Greenville, which ceded two-thirds of present-day Ohio from Indian to federal control, and opened the Northwest Territory for settlement. The story is told at the landmark **Garst Museum** (205 N. Broadway. 513-548-5250. Closed Mon. and Jan.), which also displays memorabilia of sharpshooter Annie Oakley, who was born and buried in surrounding Darke County.

212

Marietta ···

(Convention & Visitors Bureau, 316 3rd St. 614-373-5178 or 800-288-2577)
Rich in Ohio River Valley history, the town originated with the late 18th-century Campus Martius fort, the first significant American settlement in the Northwest Territory. Exhibits and artifacts at the **Campus Martius Museum** (601 2nd St. 614-373-3750. Daily May-Sept., Wed.-Sun. March-April and Oct.-Nov.; adm. fee) trace the history of that era and the subsequent expansion into the Northwest Territory. The Putnam House, part of the original fort, has been incorporated into the modern museum building. The nearby **Ohio River Museum** (601 Front St. 614-373-3750. Daily May-Sept., Wed.-Sun. March-April and Oct.-Nov.; adm. fee) contains steamboat memorabilia; docked on the river nearby is the **W.P. Snyder, Jr.,** a steam-powered stern-wheeler towboat.

Excursion
PARKERSBURG, WEST VIRGINIA (15 miles S via I-77) See page 202.

Toledo ···

Among the world's busiest freshwater ports, Toledo sits on Lake Erie at the mouth of the Maumee River. Ohio came by this prime Great Lakes port after winning a boundary skirmish, known as the Toledo War, with Michigan. It was incorporated in 1837. With the arrival of two major canals, followed by a rail network, Toledo became a major industrial center (famed as a glass manufacturer), its output fueled by local natural gas fields.

Excursions
RUTHERFORD B. HAYES PRESIDENTIAL CENTER (35 miles SE via

·I-80/90 and Ohio 53 in Fremont. 1337 Hayes Ave. 419-332-2081. Adm. fee) From 1863 to his death in 1893, 19th President Rutherford B. Hayes made his home at Spiegel Grove, the lovely wooded, 25-acre estate he inherited from his uncle. The property includes the Hayes's 33-room Victorian mansion, a history museum, a presidential library, and the graves of Hayes and his wife.

PERRY'S VICTORY AND INTL. PEACE MEMORIAL (*55 miles E via Ohio 2 and ferry from Port Clinton or Catawba Point, to Put-in-Bay; ferry fee. 419-285-2184. Mid-May–Sept.; adm. fee*) During the War of 1812, on Sept. 10, 1813, Comm. Oliver Hazard Perry defeated British naval forces here in the Battle of Lake Erie. "We have met the enemy and they are ours," he reported to Gen. William Henry Harrison. The 352-foot-tall monument, ribboned by an observation deck, is said to be the world's largest Greek Doric column.

JOHNSON'S ISLAND (*70 miles E off Marblehead Peninsula, via Ohio 2 and Ohio 163, turn right at Gaydos Dr. and cross causeway to island. Information at Ottawa County Visitors Bureau, 109 Madison St., Port Clinton. 419-734-4FUN or 800-441-1271. Toll*) From 1862 to 1865, the U.S. Army maintained a prisoner-of-war camp, mostly for thousands of captured Confederate officers, on this wooded, then remote island. The island's Civil War legacy is preserved in two earthen forts and the bayside **Confederate Cemetery,** containing at least 206 graves and a monument to the Confederate dead.

Other Sites in Ohio

213

Edison Birthplace Museum (*9 Edison Dr., Milan. 419-499-2135. Closed Mon. Feb.-Nov.; adm. fee*) On Feb. 11, 1847, pioneer son and inventor Thomas Alva Edison was born in this three-story brick house, where he lived until age seven. The house has been restored to 1847 vintage and exhibits examples of many early Edison inventions.

Fort Recovery State Memorial (*Jct. of Ohio 49 and Ohio 119, Fort Recovery. 419-375-4649. Museum open daily June-Aug., weekends May and Sept.; park open year-round. Adm. fee*) Here in 1791, Miami chief Little Turtle's coalition crushed Gen. Arthur St. Clair's troops in perhaps America's worst military defeat by Indians. On the same spot 3 years later, Gen. "Mad Anthony" Wayne, garrisoned at his new fort, Recovery, routed the Indians. The 9-acre site includes two reconstructed blockhouses, a museum, and a cemetery.

National Road/Zane Grey Museum (*US 40 near Norwich. 614-872-3143. Daily May-Sept., Wed.-Sun. March-April and Oct.-Nov.; adm. fee*) The museum colorfully interweaves the story of America's first federally funded interstate highway (now US 40) with that of Zanesvillian Zane Grey, father of the Western adventure novel. There's also an exhibit of the region's famous art pottery from the early 1900s.

Roscoe Village (*Ohio 16/36 in Coshocton. 614-622-9310 or 800-877-1830. Adm. fee to building museums*) The arrival of the Ohio and Erie Canal in 1830 saw Roscoe prosper as a canal port and milling center. Now restored as a mid-19th-century living museum community, it offers nine building museums, costumed interpreters, and craft demonstrations.

Warren G. Harding Home and Museum (*380 Mt. Vernon Ave., Marion. 614-387-9630. Mem. Day–Labor Day Wed.-Sun., Labor Day–Oct. weekends; adm. fee*) From this house in 1920, the future 29th President ran his successful "front porch campaign." The restoration is authentic, down to the gaslights and wallpaper. A museum outlines Harding's career. Also in town, the **Harding Memorial** (*Ohio 423*) holds the tombs of Harding and his wife.

Indiana

First State Capitol, Corydon

In the mid-1700s the great Maumee-Wabash river system, joining Indiana with Lake Erie, formed the backdrop for territorial struggles among the French, British, Americans, and Indians. The French ceded their claims to Britain in 1763. Britain lost its stronghold to the Americans 16 years later at Vincennes. Subsequently, Indiana was swallowed by the Northwest Territory until Congress established the Indiana Territory in 1800, sweeping present-day Indiana, Illinois, Wisconsin, and parts of Michigan and Minnesota. The young governor William Henry Harrison negotiated for millions of acres of Indian lands in southern Indiana, over which he fought, and defeated, Tecumseh's Confederation in the 1811 Battle of Tippecanoe. After Harrison's victory over the British in the 1813 Battle of the Thames in Canada, the territory was free for settlement. In 1816 Indiana became the 19th state. The young state went bankrupt in 1841, after overspending on and mismanaging its canal systems. The railroads, however, soon put the canalboats out of business, and Indiana's economic and cultural center shifted northward, away from the Ohio and its port towns, toward Indianapolis and later the industrial shores of Lake Michigan, now bustling with giant corporations such as Standard Oil and U.S. Steel.

Corydon

(Chamber of Commerce, 310 N. Elm St. 812-738-2137) In 1808 town father

William Henry Harrison established Corydon. The village replaced Vincennes as Indiana's territorial capital in 1813, becoming the first capital of the new state three years later. Corydon's original core has been well preserved in the town's **historic district.** Laid out in a grid around the public square, the district boasts numerous 19th-century buildings—noteworthy among them, the 1817 **Posey House Museum** *(225 Oak St. Tues.-Sun.)*, where the unmarried son of the territorial governor raised 14 orphans.

Corydon Capitol State Historic Site *(202 E. Walnut St. 812-738-4890. Mid-March–mid-Dec. Tues.-Sun., call for winter hours)* On these grounds in 1816-25, the square-shaped **First State Capitol** held the state senate, house, and supreme court. The restored landmark contains period furnishings and fixtures. The 1817 federal-style **Governor's Headquarters** preserves the home and headquarters of Indiana's second elected governor, William Hendricks, while the massive **Constitution Elm Monument** *(High St.)*, located nearby, marks where delegates drafted the state's first constitution in 1816.

Battle of Corydon Memorial Park *(Just S of town on Old Ind. 135. 812-738-8236)* Indiana's only Civil War fighting occurred here on July 9, 1863, when Gen. John Hunt Morgan's Confederate Raiders defeated the Home Guard troops. Markers interpret the site.

Excursion

LOUISVILLE, KENTUCKY *(22 miles E via I-64)* See page 197.

Indianapolis ························

(City Center, Pan Am Plaza Bldg., 201 S. Capitol Ave. 317-237-5206 or 800-468-INDY) In 1820 state officials dispatched a commission to find a new, and third, locale for the capital. It chose a boggy settlement on an impossible stretch of the White River in central Indiana. Undeterred by its lack of navigable waterways, Indianapolis became an overland transportation hub, thanks to the arrival of the Michigan and National Roads in the 1830s, followed by the railroads in the 1850s. It subsequently boomed as an agricultural, commercial, and manufacturing center. Factories, notably automakers, came in the early 20th century, spawning a significant labor movement. The **Indiana State Museum** *(202 N. Alabama St. 317-232-1637)* showcases the state's cultural and natural history.

Eiteljorg Museum of American Indian and Western Art *(500 W. Washington St. 317-636-9378. Daily June-Aug., closed Mon. rest of year; adm. fee)* Complementing its exhibits of Western art and sculpture is the museum's acclaimed collection of Native American art and artifacts.

Riley Museum Home *(528 Lockerbie St. 317-631-5885. Tues.-Sun.; adm. fee)* James Whitcomb Riley, the "Hoosier poet" and author of *Little Orphan Annie, The Raggedy Man,* and other classics, spent his last 23 years in this home of friends. He died here in 1916. Pride of the Victorian **Lockerbie**

Underground Railroad

One would be hard put to invent the tales linked with the Underground Railroad, a system of secret routes by which untold thousands of slaves escaped to the North in the years leading up to the Civil War. It was risky business, both for the fugitives, ever in danger of recapture, and for the operators—both black and white—who helped them, facing criminal charges if caught. Runaways moved by night and hid by day. Some disguised themselves as whites in mourning. Railroad workers used code "agents," "conductors," "stations"—and secret signs and signals, such as handshakes and passwords, lanterns and flags. By 1860, as many as 50,000 escapees had found refuge in Canada, beyond reach of the harsh Fugitive Slave Law of 1850.

Indianapolis

Indianapolis Motor Speedway

Square Historic District, the house museum contains original furnishings and personal articles.

President Benjamin Harrison Home *(1230 N. Delaware St. 317-631-1898. Feb.-Dec., call for Jan. hours; adm. fee)* In 1875, 23rd President Harrison moved his family into the 16-room, Italianate mansion, where in 1888 he campaigned from the porch. Original furnishings and political memorabilia fill the home.

Indianapolis Motor Speedway and Hall of Fame Museum *(4790 W. 16th St. 317-484-6747. Adm. fee for museum and track tours)* Since 1911 the home of the Indianapolis 500—one of the world's largest sporting events—the speedway's 2.5-mile oval track is the world's oldest continually operated race course. It was built in 1909 as a testing ground for autos. Museum exhibits include race car winners.

Excursions

CONNER PRAIRIE *(20 miles NE via I-495 near Fishers. 13400 Allisonville Rd. 317-776-6000. May-Oct. Tues.-Sun., April and Nov. Wed.-Sun.; adm. fee)* A re-created pioneer settlement brings to life the year 1836. Guides in period costume use first-person interpretation. You'll also find the 1823 brick home of settler William Conner, a hands-on area, and a museum center.

NATIONAL ROAD CORRIDOR *(Extending 50 miles E on US 40. Call Historic Landmarks Foundation of Indiana 317-639-4646, or contact local Visitor Centers)* America's first federally funded interstate, the National Road—stretching between Cumberland, Maryland, and Vandalia, Illinois—was the Midwest's main overland route in the early 1800s. It was re-engineered as US 40 in the 1920s and superseded by I-70 in the 1960s. Eastern Indiana's portion, built between 1829 and 1834 and now a designated historic corridor—is strung with typical "pike towns"—notably **Greenfield, Knightstown, Lewisville, Dublin, Mount Auburn, Cambridge City, East Germantown, Centerville,** and **Richmond.** Each has a historic district with an array of 19th-century architecture. You'll also see classic 20th-century gas stations, diners, and early motor and cabin courts. Significant landmarks include the circa 1853 **James Whitcomb Riley Boyhood Home** *(250 W. Main St., Greenfield. 317-462-8539. April-Dec. Tues.-Sun.)* and the 1841 **Huddleston Farmhouse Inn Museum** *(US 40, near Cambridge City. 317-478-3172. Tues.-Sun. May-Aug., Tues.-Sat. Feb.-April and Sept.-Dec.),* the state's only intact "movers' house"—a way station for westward-bound emigrants.

LEVI COFFIN S.H.S. *(75 miles E via I-70 and US 27 in Fountain City. 113 N. Main St. 317-847-2432. June-Aug. Tues.-Sat.; Sept.-Oct. Sat. only; adm. fee)* For 20 years, Levi and Catharine Coffin, Quakers and antislavery leaders from North Carolina, provided haven for some 2,000 fugitive slaves en route to freedom in the North. Their eight-room federal house, known as the "Grand Central Station of the Underground Railroad," contains period furnishings.

Lafayette ···

(Convention & Visitors Bureau, 301 Frontage Rd. 317-447-9999 or 800-872-6648) Founded in 1825, the old river town honors the French general who served under George Washington during the Revolutionary War. Its location above the Wabash enabled it to become a prosperous trade center, served in the 1840s by the Wabash and Erie Canal, and later by the railroads. The 40-square-block **downtown historic district** exemplifies 19th-century, midwestern-style, urban development.One sure stop is the restored, eclectic-style **Tippecanoe County Courthouse** *(Public Square between 3rd and 4th Sts.),* completed in 1884 and still in use.

Moses Fowler House *(909 South St. 317-742-8411. Closed Mon. and Jan.)* A self-aggrandizing merchant and cattleman, Fowler designed his grand Gothic Revival mansion in the early 1850s after a British country manor. Now home of the Tippecanoe County Historical Museum, it displays pioneer and Indian artifacts, as well as relics from the Battle of Tippecanoe and Fort Ouiatenon.

Excursion

TIPPECANOE BATTLEFIELD *(7 miles N via I-65 and Ind. 43 in Battle Ground. Railroad St. 317-567-2147. Adm. fee)* After several years of arguing over land ownership in the Indiana Territory, William Henry Harrison's infantry clashed here in 1811 with the intertribal Indian alliance under Chief Tecumseh and his brother Tenskwatawa (known as the Prophet). The Indian defeat at the Battle of Tippecanoe was one of the main events leading to the War of 1812 with Britain—and to Harrison's Presidency. A memorial obelisk marks the campsite and battlefield, centerpiece of the 108-acre park. The Visitor Center presents a broad and equitable historical picture.

217

Madison ··

(Convention & Visitors Bureau, 301 E. Main St. 812-265-2956) Laid out in 1809, the Ohio River town boomed as a trade and commercial center. By the mid-1800s it had become Indiana's largest city, with pork packing leading the early industries. Madison also served as a gateway to the Northwest Territory along the Michigan Road. With the arrival of the first railroad in 1847, Madison's status began to change as its business, like that of other Ohio River ports, was diverted. The legacy of its boom years lives in the potpourri of 19th-century architecture found here, including federal, Queen Anne, Greek Revival, and Italianate styles. The **downtown historic district**—133 square blocks—is best explored on foot.

Among the finest houses in the valley, the **J.F.D. Lanier State Historic Site** *(511 W. 1st St.*

Levi Coffin State Historic Site, in Fountain City

812-265-3526. Tues.-Sun.) and the **Shrewsbury-Windle House Museum** *(301 W. 1st St. 812-265-4481. Adm. fee),* both 1840s Greek Revivals, were built by Indiana's premier 19th-century architect, Francis Costigan. Madison's first mansion, the 1818 **Jeremiah Sullivan House** *(304 W. 2nd St. 812-265-2967. Adm. fee)* features the only known federal-era serving kitchen.

Excursion

VEVAY *(20 miles E via Ind. 56. Switzerland County Welcome Center, 209 Ferry St. 812-427-3237 or 800-HELLO VV)* Pronounced "VEE VEE," this river town was settled by Swiss winemakers around the turn of the 19th century—which accounts for the county's name. The hometown of Edward Eggleston, writer and editor of *The Hoosier Schoolboy* and *The Hoosier Schoolmaster*, contains some impressive 19th-century architecture.

Metamora ·····················

J.F.D. Lanier S.H.S., Madison

Looking every bit a storybook hamlet, this restored 19th-century canal village was founded in 1812 on the Whitewater River. First called Duck Creek Crossing, Metamora prospered during the mid-1800s, while the Whitewater Canal was active, and the gristmills and woolen mills were rolling. But railbed replaced towpath, the canal and mills fell into ruin, the population declined, and a main road came through, later rerouted to bypass the town altogether. Today, Metamora lives on as a commercial and tourist hub and artists' community. Along Main Street you can see the symbols of America's transportation eras and of westward settlement.

Whitewater Canal S.H.S. *(Just S of town on US 52. 317-647-6512. Closed Mon. and Jan.–mid-March)* The restored 14-mile stretch of the old canal includes an original lock, a feeder dam, an operating aqueduct, and an 1845 gristmill, plus a horse-drawn canalboat *(May-Oct. Tues.-Sun.; fee)*.

Excursions

CONNERSVILLE *(18 miles N via US 52 and Ind. 121)* This sister canal town is the main terminus for the **Whitewater Valley Railroad** *(317-825-2054)*, a vintage train that shuttles passengers 16 miles to and from Metamora along the old canal towpath. The 1842 **Canal House** *(E. 4th St. and Central Ave.)* served as the canal company's clearinghouse.

LITTLE CEDAR GROVE BAPTIST CHURCH *(10 miles SE via US 52, just S of Brookville)* The Franklin County seat has a gem in this rustic brick church, dedicated by Baptist pioneers in 1812 and said to be the oldest church in Indiana standing on its original foundation.

Vincennes ··

(Information at George Rogers Clark N.H.P., 401 S. 2nd St. 812-882-1776) Set on the banks of the Wabash, Indiana's oldest community began as a French fur-trading post and fort, built in 1732 by François Marie Bissot, Sieur de Vincennes. French missionaries followed, founding the first church here in 1749. The church's last incarnation, built in the 1820s on the original spot, is the brick **Basilica of St. Francis** *(205 Church St.)*. Behind

the basilica lies the **old French cemetery,** burial ground for hundreds of French settlers and Indians. In 1800, when the Indiana Territory was carved out of the Old Northwest, Vincennes became the territorial capital, and William Henry Harrison its first governor. It was from here that Harrison mounted his campaign against Tecumseh in the Battle of Tippecanoe. Most sites are concentrated in Vincenne's historic old town. The **Vincennes State Historic Sites** *(1st and Harrison Sts.)* includes the 1805 territorial capitol building and a replica of the territory's first printshop.

George Rogers Clark National Historical Park *(401 S. 2nd St. 812-882-1776. Adm. fee)* Here on Feb. 25, 1779, George Rogers Clark and his small band of French and American frontiersmen took Fort Sackville from the British. Their victory facilitated America's westward expansion. Centerpiece of the park is a monumental, Greek Revival memorial. Don't miss the excellent orientation film at the Visitor Center.

Grouseland *(3 W. Scott St. 812-882-2096. Adm. fee)* The abundance of birds here inspired William Henry Harrison's name for his 17-room, 300-acre, federal-style estate, completed in 1804 for his term in Vincennes as territorial governor. The home of the future ninth President contains period furnishings and political memorabilia.

Other Sites in Indiana

Amish Acres Historic Farm *(1 mile W of Nappanee via US 6, 1600 W. Market St. 219-773-4188. March-Dec.; fee for guided tour)* In an agricultural region characterized by a substantial Amish population, this 80-acre outdoor museum was the site of a 19th-century Amish farm. Today it offers 18 restored buildings and crafts demonstrations.

Angel Mounds S.H.S. *(8215 Pollack Ave., Evansville. 812-853-3956. Mid-March–Dec. Tues.-Sun.)* The 103-acre site marks the location of an ancient village of Mississippian Moundbuilders, who lived along the Ohio River around A.D. 1000-1300. The park features a reconstructed village.

Fort Wayne *(Convention & Visitors Bureau, 1021 S. Calhoun. 219-424-3700 or 800-767-7752)* The manufacturing hub of Fort Wayne began as a French trading post. After Gen. Anthony Wayne defeated the Miami in 1794, he built the area's first American fort here. The **Old City Hall Historical Museum** *(302 E. Berry St. 219-426-2882. Closed Mon. and Jan.; adm. fee),* housed in an 1893 Romanesque landmark, presents regional history. Nearby, the **Lincoln Museum** *(200 E. Berry St. 219-455-3864)* houses possibly the world's largest privately owned collection of Lincolniana.

Lincoln Boyhood National Memorial *(Ind. 162 in Lincoln City. 812-937-4541. Adm. fee)* Heart of the 200-acre memorial is the farm where Abraham Lincoln lived in 1816-1830. The grounds include the **Lincoln Living Historical Farm** *(Mid-April–Sept.),* a re-created Indiana farm of that period. The Visitor Center contains historic and interpretive exhibits and halls dedicated to Lincoln and his mother, Nancy Hanks Lincoln, who is buried on the grounds.

New Harmony *(Visitor Center, North and Arthur Sts. 812-682-4474)* Among the country's most famous utopian experiments, New Harmony was settled in 1814 by a German religious separatist group. They never fully created their model utopian community, but their contributions to education, science, and women's suffrage were significant. Your first stop should be the Atheneum Visitor Center, offering museum exhibits and a film. Guided walking tours of restored properties are arranged through Historic New Harmony *(fee).*

Illinois

Fort de Chartres State Historic Site

Jacques Marquette and Louis Joliet were the first known Europeans to visit Illinois, when they ventured up the Illinois River during their 1675 exploration of the Mississippi River. The French took possession of the region soon after and ruled it until 1763, when it was ceded to the British. The American Revolution challenged British ownership, and in 1778 a group of Virginians captured British forts at Cahokia, Prairie du Rocher, and Kaskaskia. After Illinois gained statehood in 1818, Kaskaskia became the state capital, though two years later the capital was moved to Vandalia. Springfield became the third, and final, capital in 1839. Illinois' fertile prairies lured settlers, who thrived with the help of such innovations as barbed wire and John Deere's steel plow. The state's perch on Lake Michigan and its many waterways—crucial trade links—made its largest city, Chicago, a busy 19th-century center for trade, transportation, and communications. The city's immigrant labor force served the iron and steel industries, which headed U.S. production into the 1950s.

Cahokia Mounds

(2 miles SW of Collinsville, off I-55/70. 618-346-5160. Adm. fee) At 6 square miles the largest prehistoric Indian city north of Mexico, Cahokia Mounds

flourished between A.D. 700 and 1400. Its peak population in 1100 numbered some 20,000 people of the Mississippian culture. The complex encompasses 68 of the original 120 mounds, most of which served as a base for ceremonial buildings or residences of the elite. Monks Mound—measuring 100 feet tall and covering 14 acres—is said to be the largest prehistoric earthen structure in the Americas. It's not known exactly why Cahokia was abandoned, though it's generally accepted that resource depletion and possibly a crop failure following a climate change played a role. The interpretive center displays artifacts, a model reproduction of the original city, and dioramas depicting the way of life during Cahokia's thriving years.

Excursions

CAHOKIA COURTHOUSE STATE HISTORIC SITE (*10 miles SW from Collinsville via I-55 and I-255, in Cahokia. 107 Elm St. 618-332-1782. Tues.-Sat.; donations*) Built in 1737 as a French residence, the French colonial courthouse became a center for political and judicial activity in the Northwest Territory. The building was dismantled and displayed at the 1904 St. Louis World's Fair, then reassembled on its original site in 1939.

ST. LOUIS, MISSOURI (*7 miles SW via I-55/70*) See page 267.

Chicago ···

(*Office of Tourism, 78 E. Washington St. 312-744-2400 or 800-2CONNECT*) Jean Baptiste Point Du Sable, a fur trader of French-African descent, built a cabin on the Chicago River's north bank around 1779. To protect the area's growing trade routes from the British and Indians, Fort Dearborn was constructed on the south bank in 1803. Early in the War of 1812, Indians massacred 52 of the fort's occupants. The arrival of the Illinois and Michigan Canal in the 1830s and of the railroad in 1848 made it a bustling port city. In 1871 the Great Chicago Fire razed one-third of the city, leaving more than 250 people dead and 100,000 homeless. At the hands of the nation's best architects and engineers, a thicket of structures rose from the ashes, heralding the era of the skyscraper. The world was forever changed again in 1942, when University of Chicago physicists achieved the first nuclear chain reaction.

Architectural Walking Tour ·············· 1 mile, 2 hours

Reinforced with iron and steel frames and equipped with new-fangled mechanical elevators, Chicago "skyscrapers" towered higher than buildings had ever before. This walking tour takes in a celebrated cluster of these early-day skyscrapers, centered around Chicago's Loop area (bounded by the "El" subway system).

1. Housed in the old Railway Exchange Building, the **Chicago Architecture Foundation Shop and Tour Center** (*224 S. Michigan Ave. 312-922-8687. Fee for tours*) stocks a plethora of architecture-related literature and offers more than 50 guided tours. The building itself, built in 1904 by D.H. Burnham & Co., boasts a delicate glass facade decorated with white terra-cotta.

2. Combining office space with a hotel and acoustic theater and using forced-air ventilation, the 1889 **Auditorium Building** (*430 S. Michigan Ave.*) made its architects, Dankmar Adler and Louis H. Sullivan, world famous.

Roosevelt University occupies much of the structure today; it's worthwhile attending a theatrical performance if only to see the lavish interior design.

3. The first tall office building to use skeleton construction throughout, Jenney's 1891 **Manhattan Building** (*431 S. Dearborn St.*) was also the first building ever to employ a sophisticated wind-bracing system.

4. When the 16 stories of the landmark **Monadnock Building** (*53 W. Jackson Blvd.*)—designed by Burnham & Root—first rose above Chicago in 1891, they constituted the world's tallest office building. But architectural scholars are more interested in the engineering of it all: Load-bearing masonry walls, 6 feet thick at ground level, support unadorned brick bays. The terra-cotta-walled southern addition (by Holabird & Roche) relies on one of the first steel frames.

5. A rusticated masonry base, Romanesque arches, and terra-cotta ornamentation highlight the 1888 **Rookery Building** (*209 S. La Salle St.*), an important precursor to the skyscraper. Frank Lloyd Wright designed the stunning gold and ivory atrium.

6. Elegant columns and fragile-looking windows combine with a solid steel-frame design to make the 1894 **Marquette Building** (*140 S. Dearborn St.*) an exemplar of Chicago School architecture. The aesthetics established here were used in skyscrapers over the next 30 years. Note the Chicago windows—a large central plane flanked by double-hung windows that open for air.

7. With its slender piers, narrow spandrels, and delicate Gothic ornamentation, Burnham & Root's 1895 **Reliance Building** (*32 N. State St.*) is

one of the most elegant early skyscrapers. Its open glass walls make it an obvious predecessor to the glass-sheathed monoliths built in the 1950s and 1960s.

8. As graceful as its cast-iron grillwork may be, the **Carson Pirie Scott building** (*S. State and E. Madison Sts.*) was designed in 1899 by Louis H. Sullivan with functionality in mind. The shopper's eye is drawn to the richly ornamented display windows below, ignoring the unadorned office floors above.

Other Sites in Chicago

Chicago Historical Society (*1601 N. Clark St. 312-642-4600. Walking and bus tours offered. Adm. fee except Mon.*) Exhibits explore such topics as Fort Dearborn, pioneer life

Carson Pirie Scott building, designed in 1899

in Illinois, the Civil War, and the city's growth into an important midwestern trade center.

Jane Addams' Hull House Museum (*800 S. Halsted St., Univ. of Ill.-Chicago campus. 312-413-5353. Sun.-Fri.*) Built as a country home in 1856, the Hull mansion became the center of Jane Addams's pioneer work with immigrants in the late 1800s. Next door stands the former residents' dining hall.

Prairie Avenue House Museums (*1800 S. Prairie Ave. 312-326-1480. Wed.-Sun.; fee for house tours*) Prairie Avenue embraced Chicago's most fashionable neighborhood in the years following the 1871 fire. Two houses are open for tours: the circa 1836 Greek Revival **Henry B. Clarke House**, Chicago's oldest building; and the 1887 **Glessner House**, designed by H. H. Richardson.

Pullman Historic District (*Headquarters at the Hotel Florence, 11111 S. Forestville Ave. 312-785-8181. Self-guided tours year-round; guided walking tours first Sun. in May-Oct.; fee for tours*) In 1880 George M. Pullman began building his "model industrial town" for the employees of his Pullman Palace Car Company. The centerpiece of the four-block Victorian historic district is the grand 1881 **Hotel Florence**, which still serves lunch; it also has historical exhibits, including the George Pullman suite. Artists and other professionals now occupy the brick row houses.

Excursions

OAK PARK (*10 miles W via I-290. Visitor Center, 158 N. Forest Ave. 312-848-1500*) In this shady

Detail of 1891 Manhattan Building

Chicago suburb, Frank Lloyd Wright developed many aspects of the Prairie School of architecture, which emphasized large, open, free-flowing spaces. Here you'll find the biggest concentration of houses (25) designed by Wright, including what's now the **Frank Lloyd Wright Home and Studio** (*951 Chicago Ave. 708-848-1976. Adm. fee*), his first residence.

Thirteen other Wright-designed structures line **Forest Avenue.**

The Nobel Prize-winning author of *The Sun Also Rises, For Whom the Bell Tolls,* and other classics was born in Oak Park on July 21, 1899. The **Hemingway Home** *(339 N. Oak Park Ave. 708-848-2222. Fri.-Sun. and Wed. p.m.; adm. fee)* showcases memorabilia from his first 20 years. On the second floor of the Pleasant Home Mansion, the small **Historical Society of Oak Park and River Forest Museum** *(217 Home Ave. 708-848-6755. Thurs.-Sun.; adm. fee)* offers exhibits on local history and notable residents, including Wright and Hemingway.

Italianate-style Belvedere Mansion, Galena

ILLINOIS AND MICHIGAN CANAL NATIONAL HERITAGE CORRIDOR *(Extending 100 miles SW, accessed by various roads. National Heritage Corridor office 815-740-2047. Mon.-Fri.)* This long, skinny corridor encompasses the 96.4-mile-long Illinois and Michigan Canal, excavated by hand in 1836-1848 to link Lake Michigan and the Illinois River and, ultimately, open a trade route between New York and the Gulf of Mexico. Numerous towns grew up along the canal's banks, many of which still contain historic districts and other canal-related sites. In the town of **Lockport** *(35 miles SW of Chicago via I-55 and Ill. 53)*, the **Gaylord Building** *(200 W. 8th St. 815-838-4830. Wed.-Sun.)*, in the 1838 canal warehouse, contains a Visitor Center and a gallery of the Illinois State Museum.

Galena

(Visitor Information Center, 101 Bouthillier St. 815-777-9050 or 800-747-9377) Named after the Latin word for "lead ore," which turned this river town into a booming mining center in the mid-19th century, Galena still has a well-preserved commercial district and a fine collection of historic houses in many styles including Queen Anne, Italianate, federal, and Greek Revival. In fact, 85 percent of the town's buildings are listed on the National Register of Historic Places. Among them, the Italianate **Ulysses S. Grant Home State Historic Site** *(500 Bouthillier St. 815-777-0248. Donations)* was presented by town citizens to the general, who lived in Galena before and after the Civil War. The 1845 **Old Market House** *(Market Sq. on Commerce St. 815-777-2570. Thurs.-Mon.; donations)* served as a market center; it now houses an old general store display. For a glimpse into the early mining history, stop by the **Vinegar Hill Historic Lead Mine and Museum** *(6 miles N of town, 8885 N. Three Pines Rd. 815-777-0855. Daily June-Aug., weekends only May and Sept.-Oct.; adm. fee)*, which offers underground tours; its museum contains samples of ore and mining tools.

Excursion
DUBUQUE, IOWA *(16 miles NW via US 20)* See p. 255.

Nauvoo

In 1839 a group of Mormons led by Joseph Smith settled on a bend in the Mississippi River and named their settlement for the Hebrew word meaning "beautiful place." As more Mormons flocked to the area and gained political power, non-Mormons saw them as a threat. In 1844 an angry mob killed Smith and his brother Hyrum in the nearby town of Carthage, where they had been jailed for treason. Mormons soon deserted Nauvoo, fleeing for safer territory in Utah. More than 20 of their structures—including a printshop, bakery, log cabin, school, shoe shop, and post office, as well as an archaeological temple site—have been preserved in the **Nauvoo Historic District** *(Latter-day Saints Visitor Center, Main and Young Sts. 217-453-2237)*. Nearby, the **Joseph Smith Historic Center** *(149 Water St. 217-453-2246)* offers guided tours of the **Joseph Smith Homestead** and the **Mansion House.** You can also visit the **Red Brick Store** (once operated by Smith) and the **Smith Family Gravesite.**

Excursion

CARTHAGE *(20 miles SE via Ill. 96 and US 136)* The town jail where Smith and his brother were killed has been preserved as the **Historic Carthage Jail and Visitor's Center** *(US 136. 217-357-2989)*. Tours of the seven-room jail include the bedroom where the shooting took place.

Springfield ···

(Lincoln Home Visitor Center, 426 S. 7th St. 217-492-4150) For the 24 years before becoming the 16th President, Abraham Lincoln lived and worked in the Illinois capital, which now promotes itself as the "city Lincoln loved." Of the many monuments and historic buildings devoted to the statesman, the most important cluster near the Old State Capitol building, in the historic downtown area. Among them are his law offices, preserved as the **Lincoln-Herndon Law Offices State Historic Site** *(1 S. Adams St. 217-785-7289. Donations)* and filled with period furniture. The first and only house he owned, purchased for $1,500 in 1844, is now the **Lincoln Home National Historic Site** *(8th and Jackson Sts. 217-492-4150 ext.*

221). It's been restored with some original furnishings. In accepting the Republican nomination to the U.S. Senate in 1858, Lincoln gave his famous "House Divided" speech at the nearby **Old State Capitol** *(Old Capitol Mall. 217-785-7960. Donations)*, completed in 1853, which houses an original copy of the Gettysburg Address. Leaving for Washington, D.C., the President-elect bade farewell to Springfield at the **Great Western Depot** *(Monroe and 10th Sts. 217-544-8695. April-Aug.)*; restored waiting rooms and exhibits show

Lincoln Home National Historic Site, Springfield

how it may have looked. Finally, on the north side of the city, the **Lincoln Tomb State Historic Site** *(Oak Ridge Cemetery, 1441 Monument Ave. 217-782-2717)* was built with public donations and contains the Lincoln family burial vaults.

Other Sites in Springfield

Dana-Thomas House (*301 E. Lawrence Ave. 217-782-6776. Wed.-Sun.; adm. fee*) Frank Lloyd Wright designed this early 1900s prairie-style house and much of its contents for socialite and women's activist Susan Lawrence Dana.

Illinois State Museum (*Spring and Edwards Sts. 217-782-7386*) History exhibits explore decorative arts and the lives of early Native Americans.

Lincoln Heritage Trail Driving Tour ················
266 miles, 1 to 2 days

(*Springfield Convention &Visitors Bureau, 109 N. 7th St. 217-789-2360 or 800-545-7300. Mon.-Fri.*) The official Lincoln Heritage Trail wanders about west-central and southern Illinois for some 1,100 miles, visiting many of the major sites in Abraham Lincoln's life. This tour begins in Springfield and takes in 266 miles of the trail, focusing on his early years as attorney and state legislator.

1. Lincoln's New Salem State Historic Site (*20 miles N of Springfield via Ill. 97, near Petersburg. 217-632-4000. Donations*) In 1831-1837, young Abe Lincoln lived in this now re-created pioneer village, where he worked as a postmaster, clerk, store owner, and surveyor; during this time he also ran for state office. On the grounds, 22 timber buildings (including one original) are furnished in period style.

2. When the town of **Lincoln** named itself after Lincoln even before he became famous, he christened it with watermelon juice, saying "nothing named Lincoln ever amounted to much." The **Postville Courthouse S.H.S.**

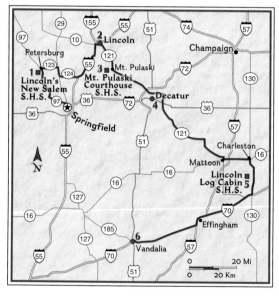

(*914 5th St. 217-732-8930. Fri.-Sat. p.m.; donations*) is a reproduction of the courthouse where Lincoln tried many cases.

3. In 1848-1855 Lincoln practiced law at the **Mount Pulaski Courthouse S.H.S.** (*City Square, Mount Pulaski. 217-732-8930*).

4. On **Decatur**'s square in 1830, 21-year-old Lincoln is thought to have made his first political speech. The **Richard J. Oglesby Mansion** (*421 W. William St. Last Sun. of month March-Oct., or by appt.*) belonged to the Illinois governor who first promoted Lincoln for the White House. Lincoln argued some of his first cases at the courthouse now located at the **Macon County Historical Museum and Prairie Village** (*5580 N. Fork Rd. 217-422-4919. Tues.-Sun.; donations*).

5. At the **Lincoln Log Cabin S.H.S.** (*8 miles S of Charleston via S.4th Rd. 217-345-6489*), the two-room Lincoln family cabin has been reconstructed from old photographs. Lincoln's father and stepmother are buried at nearby **Shiloh Cemetery.**

6. The Greek Revival **Vandalia Statehouse** *(315 W. Gallatin St. 618-283-1161. Donations)*, dating from the days when Vandalia was the state capital (1820-1839), contains many original furnishings, along with a copy of a Lincoln life mask. The **Evans Public Library** *(215 S. 5th St. 618-283-2824. Mon.-Sat.)* has a collection of Lincolniana.

Other Sites in Illinois

Lincoln's New Salem S.H.S.

Bishop Hill S.H.S. *(10 miles SW of Kewanee, via US 34. 309-927-3345. April-Dec.)* Founded in 1846 as an agrarian communal society by Swedish religious dissenters, the site has 18 original buildings.

Cairo The small town served as a major Union supply depot during the Civil War. The 1872 **Custom House** *(14th St. and Washington Ave. 618-734-1019 or 618-776-5407. Mon.-Fri.; donations)* contains relics, including the desk Gen. Ulysses S. Grant used while stationed here. Grant stayed at the 14-room, fully restored **Magnolia Manor** *(2700 Washington St. 618-734-0201. Adm. fee).*

Carl Sandburg State Historic Site *(313 E. 3rd St., Galesburg. 309-342-2361. Donations)* The Pulitzer Prize-winning poet was born in this three-room wood-frame cottage in 1878. The site includes Sandburg memorabilia.

Center for American Archaeology Visitor Center *(Ill. 100 at Oak St., Kampsville. 618-653-4316. Mid-April–mid.-Nov. Wed.-Mon.; dig sites open May–mid-Aug.; donations)* The Visitor Center and digs are located in the "Nile of North America," where humans have lived for nearly 10,000 years. The center offers excavation projects at active sites and displays artifacts.

Dickson Mounds State Museum *(10956 N. Dickson Mounds Rd., Lewiston. 309-547-3721)* The museum traces the 12,000 years of Native American history in the Illinois River Valley. A discovery center has hands-on activities.

Fort de Chartres State Historic Site *(1350 Ill. 155, Prairie du Rocher. 618-284-7230)* Begun in 1753, the fort was the French colonial seat of government in the New World. The storehouse holds a small museum.

John Deere Historic Site *(8393 S. Main St., Grand Detour. 815-652-4551. April-Oct.; adm. fee)* Young John Deere designed a superior plow blade here in 1836, paving the way for the cultivation of the vast midwestern prairie. The site includes a Visitor Center and several reconstructed buildings.

Quincy *(Convention & Visitors Bureau, 300 Civic Center Plaza, Ste. 237. 217-223-1000 or 800-978-4748)* Named for John Quincy Adams, this town was a stop on the Underground Railroad. The Greek Revival **Gov. John Wood Mansion** *(425 S. 12th St. 217-222-1835. Daily June-Aug.; weekends April-May, Sept.; adm. fee)*, built in 1835-38, belonged to Quincy's founder.

Rock Island Arsenal *(Off 14th St., Rock Island. 309-782-5021 and -5182)* In the middle of the Mississippi River, Rock Island was used as a Confederate prisoner of war camp during the Civil War; an arsenal, begun in 1862, continues as a U.S. Army factory. Exhibits at the **Arsenal Museum** *(Bldg. 60. 309-782-5021 and -5182)* trace area history. The oldest civilian dwelling in the area is the 1835 **Colonel Davenport House** *(W end of island. 309-786-7336. Call for tour information).*

227

Fort Michilimackinac, Mackinaw City

The story of Michigan is etched in the millions of tons of copper and iron ore taken from the state's precambrian heart and in the steel that was forged into automobiles in the assembly plants of Detroit, Flint, and Dearborn. The written history of Michigan, in 1837 the 26th state to enter the Union, began when Father Jacques Marquette founded a Jesuit mission in 1668 at Sault Ste. Marie, an area inhabited principally by Ojibwe people. John Jacob Astor's American Fur Company ran its operations from Mackinac Island. Commercial copper mining began in the 1840s; and, in 1855, the opening of the Soo Locks connecting Lake Superior and Lake Huron increased iron ore production in the north. Before the Civil War, Michigan was a principal northern terminus for southern slaves escaping to Canada via the Underground Railroad. From 1900 to 1930 the auto industry dominated the state's economy, but it badly faltered during the Depression. World War II brought relief as the entire industry turned to making war materials. Michigan has since continued to lead the nation in automobile production, while working to attract new industries.

Detroit

(Convention & Visitors Bureau, 100 Renaissance Center. 313-259-4333 or 800-DETROIT) In 1701 a French explorer, Antoine de la Mothe Cadillac, founded a trading post on the banks of the Detroit River. The early blossoming of Detroit—spurred by shipbuilding and maritime commerce in the 19th cen-

tury—pales in comparison to the revolution that occurred around the turn of the century, when Henry Ford introduced his Model T. Today Detroit is world headquarters for two of the globe's largest automakers, General Motors and Chrysler, with Ford located in nearby Dearborn.

Dossin Great Lakes Museum *(100 Strand Dr., Belle Isle. 313-267-6440. Wed.-Sun.; adm. fee)* Devoted to Great Lakes history, the museum's exhibits include one of the world's largest collections of Great Lakes ship scale models.

Detroit Historical Museums *(5401 Woodward Ave. 313-833-1805. Wed.-Sun.; adm. fee)* Exhibits include a reconstruction of the city's 19th-century main street, antique toys, and a display on the Underground Railroad.

Motown Historical Museum *(2648 W. Grand Blvd. 313-875-2264. Adm. fee)* A young businessman, Barry Gordy, started Motown Corporation in Detroit in 1957, producing popular music that became known as the "Motown Sound." The museum includes photos, records, and artifacts.

Museum of African-American History *(301 Frederick Douglass St. 313-833-9800. Wed.-Sun.; adm. fee)* Exhibits celebrating the culture of black Americans include one on the Underground Railroad in Michigan.

Excursion

DEARBORN *(Just SW of metropolitan Detroit via I-94)* Auto pioneer Henry Ford founded the **Henry Ford Museum and Greenfield Village** *(20900 Oakwood Blvd. 313-271-1620. Village buildings closed Jan.-March; adm. fee)*, the country's largest indoor-outdoor museum, to portray America's industrial development since the 19th century. The 12-acre indoor portion includes a multimedia extravaganza on U.S. auto culture. The adjacent 81-acre village contains more than 80 historical buildings—including the actual laboratories and workplaces of Thomas Edison, the Wright brothers, and other famous inventors—that Ford purchased and had moved here. Also in town you'll find the **Henry Ford Estate–Fair Lane** *(Univ. of Michigan-Dearborn campus. 313-593-5590. Adm. fee)*. Built in 1914, the 56-room home of Ford and his wife was inspired by Frank Lloyd Wright's prairie style. It includes original furnishings and a self-sufficient powerhouse.

Motor City

On March 6, 1896, Charles Brady King, a Detroit inventor, drove the first horseless carriage down the streets of the Motor City. But many people contributed to the industry that would secure Detroit's place in history. Sir Isaac Newton developed a steam-propelled engine in 1680. The first successful "self-propelled road vehicle" is credited to French engineer Nicholas J. Cugnot, in 1769. Henry Ford brought Detroit to automotive prominence when he designed the first assembly line in 1913. The big auto plants followed: William C. Durant established General Motors in 1908, and Walter Chrysler joined the Maxwell Motor Co. in 1921, changing its name to his own in 1925.

Flint ···

Once a summer Indian encampment, Flint was the nation's largest producer of carriages in the early 1900s. Here in 1916, William C. Durant, owner of the Buick Motor Company, incorporated General Motors.

Alfred P. Sloan Museum *(1221 E. Kearsley St. 810-760-1169. Adm. fee)* At this museum named for the former president of General Motors, antique cars, including an early Flint roadster, and more than 600 artifacts—old neon signs, period clothing, and household furnishings, to name a few—offer a unique glimpse into U.S. car culture.

Labor Museum and Learning Center of Michigan *(711 N. Saginaw St. 810-*

762-0251. Tues.-Fri.; adm. fee) Exhibits trace the state's and America's labor movement from pre-statehood to the present, including the "Sit-Down Strike" of 1936-37, mining camps, and Saginaw Valley lumber camps.

Iron Mountain ·····································

In the central Upper Peninsula, an iron mine prospector reported in 1845 that he had found a "mountain of iron." The discovery led to the establishment of the Menominee Iron Range, one of three mining areas that contributed large amounts of iron ore to U.S. industry. In the town of Iron Mountain, exhibits and artifacts at the **Menominee Range Historical Foundation Museum** *(300 E. Ludington St. 906-774-4276. Mid-May–mid-Oct. Mon.-Sat.; adm. fee)* depict life on the Michigan Iron Ranges, including the histories of Native Americans, fur trading, mining, and lumbering. The nearby **Chapin Mine Historic District** preserves an assortment of mine-related buildings, including the **Cornish Pumping Engine and Mining Museum** *(Kent St. 906-774-1086. Mid-May–mid-Oct. Mon.-Sat.; adm. fee),* which shows mining equipment and geological specimens. Don't miss the 1890 water pump, the largest ever built. Because much of the land in the area was swampy, causing frequent cave-ins, miners used such pumps to drain water.

Excursions

IRON MOUNTAIN IRON MINE *(5 miles E on US 2 in Vulcan. June–mid-Oct.; adm. fee)* A train tour takes visitors 400 feet beneath the surface, through the underground drifts and tunnels of a mine that was active from 1877 to 1945. Former miners explain mine operations and demonstrate equipment.

MICHIGAN IRON INDUSTRY MUSEUM *(70 miles N via Mich. 95 and US 41 in Negaunee. 73 Forge Rd. 906-475-7857. May-Oct.)* Overlooking the site of the region's first iron forge, the museum displays mining artifacts.

Keweenaw Peninsula ····························

(Keweenaw Tourism Council 906-482-2388 or 800-338-7982) In the northernmost reaches of the Upper Peninsula, the nation's first mineral boom exploded in 1842, when copper was discovered in the Houghton-Hancock region of the Keweenaw Peninsula.

Quincy Mine Hoist Association *(1 mile N of Hancock. 201 Royce Rd. 906-482-3101. Mem. Day–Oct.; adm. fee)* The 60-foot-tall steam-driven mine hoist, dating from 1920, is the world's largest; it hauled ten-ton loads of ore from 9,200-foot depths. You can tour the Civil War-era mine workings.

Houghton County Historical Museum Society *(5500 Mich. 26, Lake Linden. 906-296-4121. June-Sept. Mon.-Sat.; adm. fee)* An extensive collection of area mining artifacts are showcased in a former mill office.

Coppertown U.S.A. *(1197 Calumet Ave., Calumet. 906-337-4354. Mem. Day–Oct.; adm. fee)* Exhibits and artifacts trace area copper mining from methods used by Native Americans to modern extraction.

Copper Harbor The region's deepest port, Copper Harbor played an important transportation role in the copper boom. Begun in 1844 to protect miners from the local Ojibwe, **Fort Wilkins Historic Complex S.P.** *(US 41. 906-289-4215. Mid-May–mid-Oct.; adm. fee)* encompasses 19 buildings, 12 of them original and most with furnishings representing Army outpost life. Costumed guides are on duty seasonally. The park includes the restored 1845 **Copper Harbor Lighthouse** *(Mem. Day–Labor Day. 906-289-4966. Adm. fee).*

Lansing ···

(Chamber of Commerce, 117 E. Allegan St. 517-487-6340) In 1847 legislators chose the wilderness setting of Lansing for the state capital. After local resident R.E. Olds began making his "merry buggies"—gasoline-powered horseless carriages—in the late 1800s, Lansing became one of the nation's leading carmakers. The **R. E. Olds Transportation Museum** *(240 Museum Dr. 517-372-0422. Closed Sun. Nov.-April; adm. fee)* displays the first (1897) Oldsmobile, as well as early carriages, an Indy 500 race car, and more.

Michigan Historical Museum *(717 W. Allegan St. 517-373-3559)* Exhibits document state history, including the arrival of Paleo-Indians, the Civil War, lumbering and mining, and the growth of modern manufacturing. Don't miss the walk-through copper mine.

Quincy Mine shaft house, near Hancock

State Capitol *(Capitol and Michigan Aves. 517-373-2353. Mon.-Sat.)* One of the first state capitols to be modeled after the nation's Capitol, the Second Renaissance Revival structure was completed in 1879. Tours highlight building history and the legislative process.

231

Mackinaw City ·······································

(Chamber of Commerce, 706 S. Huron Ave. 616-436-5574 or 800-666-0164) In 1715 the French built a fortified palisade on the strategic Straits of Mackinac, which protected their fur-trading interests for more than half a century. **Fort Michilimackinac** (mish-ili-MACK-in-naw) *(I-75, S end of Mackinac Bridge. 616-436-5563. Mid-May–mid-Oct.; adm. fee)* has been reconstructed, including traders' houses, officers' quarters, and a chapel. Costumed interpreters act as guides. The 1892 **Old Mackinac Point Lighthouse** stands on the grounds.

Historic Mill Creek State Historic Park *(4 miles SE of Mackinaw City on US 23. 616-436-5563. Mid-May–mid-Oct.; adm. fee)* The site of one of the first industrial complexes on the Great Lakes, the 625-acre park encompasses reconstructions of the circa 1790 water-powered sawmill and other historic structures. Colonial-garbed artisans demonstrate log sawing.

Excursions

MACKINAC ISLAND S. P. *(Via passenger ferry from Mackinaw City or St. Ignace. For ferry info call 616-436-5542 or 616-436-5023. Fee for ferry. No cars allowed on island. Park info 616-436-5563. Mid-May–mid-Oct.)* Strategically located in the Straits of Mackinaw, this limestone outcrop—named after an Indian word for "great turtle"—has successively served as an Indian burial ground, a fort and fur-trading center for French and Americans, a 19th-century lumbering supply center, and a 20th-century resort. The state park encompasses **Fort Mackinac** *(Adm. fee)*, built in 1780-81 by the British, who had ousted the French from Fort Michilimackinac. When the island was passed to the U.S. after the Revolutionary War, the Americans garrisoned it until 1875. Fourteen original buildings remain, including officers' quarters and soldiers' barracks. Costumed interpreters perform rifle and cannon demonstrations on the parade ground. Nearby sites include an 1838 **Indian dormitory;** an 1820s **mission church;** and the **McGulpin House,** a restored French-Canadian log residence.

ST. IGNACE *(5 miles N via I-75)* In 1671 Father Jacques Marquette began a mission here and named it for St. Ignatius Loyola, founder of the Jesuit order. Two years later he left on his epic journey with Louis Joliet down the Mississippi. Marquette is believed to be buried beneath the chapel at the **Marquette Mission Park and Museum of Ojibway Culture** *(500 N. State St. 906-643-9161. Late May–Oct.; adm. fee for museum).* Housed in a 19th-century church building, the museum is devoted to the Ojibwe—the area's original inhabitants—and displays relics dating back as far as 6000 B.C. Typical Huron Indian village structures stand nearby. To learn about the meeting of French and Native American cultures, stop by the **Father Marquette National Memorial and Museum** *(2 miles W of St. Ignace off US 2. 906-643-9394. Mid-June–Aug.; phone for off-season schedule).* Finally, the **Fort de Baude Museum** *(334 N. State St. Mem. Day–Sept.; adm. fee),* built in 1681 to protect the French fur trade, displays artifacts from that era.

Sault Ste. Marie

(Chamber of Commerce, 2581 I-75 Bus. Spur. 906-632-3301 or 800-647-2858) The oldest permanent settlement in Michigan, Sault Ste. Marie dates back to the mission founded here by Father Jacques Marquette in 1668. Its strategic location on the St. Marys River, which connects Lake Superior with Lake Huron, made it highly desirable to Indians, French, British, and American settlers alike. Because of the river's tremendous rapids, however, the water route wasn't open to ship traffic until 1855, when a canal and the **Soo Locks** *(515 E. Portage Ave. 906-632-6301 or 800-432-6301. Mid-May–early Oct.)* were built. Once open, the locks enabled the transfer of iron ore from the northern iron territory to southern manufacturers. Narrated boat tours *(fare)* take visitors through the locks. The **St. Marys Falls Canal Visitor Center** *(W. Portage Ave. 906-632-3311)* has pictorial displays and three observation platforms.

Museum Ship Valley Camp *(Johnston and Water Sts. 906-632-3658. Mid-May–mid-Oct; adm. fee)* A 550-foot freighter houses the world's largest Great Lakes maritime museum.

Other Sites in Michigan

Beaver Island *(Via ferry from Charlevoix. 616-547-2311. Mid-April–mid-Dec.; adm. fee)* Mormon James Strang declared himself king of the island in 1850. He died six years later from wounds inflicted by residents whose wives objected to his strict dress code. A small museum tells the story.

Fayette Historic State Park *(7 miles S of Garden on Mich. 183. 906-644-2603. Mid-June–Aug.; adm. fee)* The remains of a Civil War iron-smelting center, including 19 original structures, are open to visitors.

Hartwick Pines State Park and Logging Museum *(3 miles N of Grayling on Mich. 93. 517-348-7068. Visitor Center open year-round; museum June–Labor Day. Adm. fee)* Building exhibits tell about the loggers, rivermen, mill hands, and entrepreneurs who developed Michigan's white pine industry.

Old Victoria *(Just N of Victoria. 906-884-4735. Mem. Day–Oct.; donations)* A group of circa 1899 log mining buildings, furnished in period style, depict the hardships of mining life.

Early settler's home, Madeline Island Historical Museum, La Pointe

Native Americans hunted and gathered in Wisconsin for more than 8,000 years before the first reported European, French explorer Étienne Brûlé, traversed a portion of Lake Superior in 1621. It was not until after the War of 1812, however, that the U.S. government built forts, at Prairie du Chien on the Mississippi River and at Green Bay on Lake Michigan, to establish a presence and protect settlers. The state's first permanent white settlers, in southwestern Wisconsin in the 1820s, were said to have been lead miners from Kentucky and Missouri. After Wisconsin attained statehood on May 29, 1848, a flood of immigrants brought skills in dairying, brewing, tanning, and iron-working. Heavy industry in the 1900s expanded rapidly in southeastern Wisconsin.

Apostle Islands

Prehistoric Indians once inhabited this 22-isle archipelago, named by missionaries who, along with fur traders, were the first European visitors. The 19th century brought loggers and fishermen; you can visit an old fishing camp on **Manitou Island**. In the late 1800s quarriers cut the brownstone that built elegant town houses as far away as New York City. Abandoned pits still exist on **Stockton, Hermit,** and **Basswood Islands.** Also of historical interest, four of six 19th-century **lighthouses** are open in summer. The islands' jumping-off point is the picturesque Victorian town of **Bayfield.** For ferry information, as well as exhibits, stop by the **Visitor Information Center** (*Washington and 4th Sts. 715-779-3397. Closed* *weekends mid-Sept.–mid-May),* in the Old Bayfield County Courthouse.

Madeline Island The largest of the Apostles and a popular summer resort, Madeline is the only island not included in the federally protected Apostle Islands National Lakeshore. Housed in four historic log buildings, the **Madeline Island Historical Museum** *(Ferry Landing, La Pointe. 715-747-2415. Mid-May–1st weekend in Oct.; adm. fee)* displays artifacts from the area's early Native American, missionary, and fur-trading days.

Green Bay

(Convention & Visitors Bureau, 1901 S. Oneida St. 414-494-9507 or 888-867-3342) In 1669 Father Allouez established a mission near the green waters of a long, narrow bay. By 1816, when the area was ceded to the U.S., the settlement—now flourishing as a fur-trading and military post—had been under both French and British rule.

Heritage Hill State Historical Park *(2460 S. Webster Ave. 414-448-5150. Mid-May–mid-Sept.; adm. fee)* The 48-acre park's 22 historic buildings represent pioneer, small-town, military, and agricultural settlements. Costumed interpreters act as guides.

National Railroad Museum *(2285 S. Broadway St. 414-435-7245. Daily May-Oct., weekdays rest of year; adm. fee)* One of the country's largest rail museums, its exhibits, including some 80 railroad cars and locomotives, span the history of U.S. railroading.

Excursions

ONEIDA NATION MUSEUM *(7 miles S via Wis. 57 and Rte. EE in De Pere. 886 Rte. EE. 414-869-2768. Tues.-Sun.; adm. fee)* A re-created longhouse and full-size dioramas tell the story of the "People of the Standing Stone," who migrated here in 1822 from upper New York State. The name "Oneida" is a corruption of an Indian word that refers to a sacred boulder near the site of an ancient tribal village on New York's Lake Oneida.

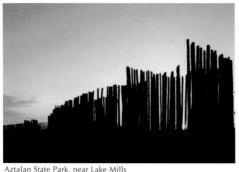

Aztalan State Park, near Lake Mills

WISCONSIN MARITIME MUSEUM *(40 miles S via I-43 in Manitowoc. 75 Maritime Dr. 414-684-0218. Adm. fee)* In the town known during the 19th century as "Clipper City" for its prolific schooner production, this large maritime museum spans a hundred years of Great Lakes history. Exhibits include a re-created facade of Manitowoc's 19th-century waterfront. Close by, you can tour the World War II-era submarine **USS Cobia.**

Madison

(Convention & Visitors Bureau, 615 E. Washington Ave. 608-255-2537 or 800-373-6376) Despite its remote wilderness setting, Madison was selected territorial capital in 1836; the capital prospered with the coming of statehood in 1848. The **State Historical Museum** *(30 N. Carroll St. 608-264-6555. Closed Mon.)* fleshes out the history.

Excursions

AZTALAN STATE PARK *(30 miles E via I-94 and Rte. B on Rte. Q, near Lake Mills. 414-648-8774. May-Oct.)* From A.D. 900 to 1200, some 500 Aztalan Indians occupied a stockaded village on this site. It's believed to have been the northernmost city of the Middle Mississippian culture, which was influenced by the Aztec in Mexico. Markers identify ancient mounds and parts of the stockade. Sitting on the site of a former pioneer village, the nearby **Aztalan Museum** *(Jct. of Rtes. Q and B. 414-648-8845. Mid-May–Sept.; adm. fee)* displays a log cabin, Baptist church, and school with period artifacts.

Norwegian church in Little Norway

LINCOLN-TALLMAN RESTORATIONS *(40 miles S via I-90 in Janesville. 440 N. Jackson St. 608-752-4519 or 608-756-4509. Daily June-Sept., weekends rest of year; adm. fee)* The complex includes the 26-room Italianate William Tallman House, a rest stop for Abraham Lincoln in 1859.

LITTLE NORWAY *(20 miles W via US 18/151 on Rte. JG, near Blue Mounds. 608-437-8211. May-Oct.; adm. fee)* Norwegian settlers built this farmstead in 1856. Four authentically furnished log buildings include a wood church built in Norway for Chicago's World's Fair of 1893.

PENDARVIS HISTORIC SITE *(50 miles W via US 151, in Mineral Point. 114 Shake Rag St. 608-987-2122. May-Oct.; adm. fee)* The local lead boom in the 1830s lured Cornish hard-rock miners to the settlement of Mineral Point. Their English heritage is preserved at Pendarvis, a collection of six limestone and log cottages filled with period furniture and mining tools.

TALIESIN *(35 miles W via US 14 and Rte. C, just S of Spring Green. 608-588-7900. May-Oct.; adm. fee)* Famed architect Frank Lloyd Wright was born in 1867 in the Spring Green vicinity, and in 1911 he built his house, Taliesin, overlooking the Wisconsin River. He retreated here often, though didn't live here permanently until the 1930s. Begin your tour of his famous workplace at the Visitor Center, originally designed by Wright as the Spring Green Restaurant. Tour options include Taliesin, as well as the Hillside Home School; originally designed as a boarding school, the school now headquarters the Frank Lloyd Wright School of Archictecture. At nearby **Unity Chapel** is the Lloyd-Jones family cemetery, where Wright's mother is buried. (Wright's ashes are buried at Taliesin West in Arizona.)

CIRCUS WORLD MUSEUM *(50 miles N via I-94 and Wis. 33 in Baraboo. 426 Water St. 608-356-0800. Adm. fee)* From 1884 to 1918, the Ringling Brothers Circus—the brainchild of a German juggler and his four brothers—wintered in Baraboo. This museum showcases the history of the American circus. From May through mid-August you can see live performances beneath the Big Top, and tours are available of the world's largest collection of circus wagons. The eldest Ringling brother built the nearby ornate **Al Ringling Theater** *(136 4th Ave. 608-356-8864. Fee for tours)*, which opened in 1915. The tour showcases the theater's architecture and history, and includes a demonstration of the 1928 Barton organ.

Milwaukee ....

(Convention & Visitors Bureau, 510 W. Kilbourn Ave. 414-273-7222 or

800-554-1448) Incorporated in 1846, the city was first settled in 1818 by fur traders led by French-Canadian Solomon Juneau. The Welsh brewed Milwaukee's first beer, though it was the Germans who introduced in the 1840s the first lager, and who went on to found Schlitz, Miller, and the other giant breweries that made Milwaukee famous.

Annunciation Greek Orthodox Church *(9400 W. Congress St. 414-461-9400. Tues. and Fri.; donations)* This widely praised example of Byzantine architecture, completed in 1961, is one of Frank Lloyd Wright's last major works.

Capt. Frederick Pabst Mansion *(2000 W. Wisconsin Ave. 414-931-0808. Adm. fee)* Finished in 1893 for beer baron Frederick Pabst, the 37-room manse is considered an exemplar of Flemish Renaissance Revival style.

Grain Exchange Room *(Mackie Bldg., 225 E. Michigan St., 2nd fl. 414-272-6230. Mon.-Fri.)* A reminder of Milwaukee's heyday as a grain-trading center, the elegant 1879 room's vibrant colors, large wall murals, and gold leaf have been brilliantly restored.

Milwaukee County Historical Center *(910 N. Old World 3rd St. 414-273-8288)* Two floors of exhibits on Milwaukee County history fill this neoclassical landmark, completed in 1913.

Milwaukee Public Museum *(800 W. Wells St. 414-278-2700. Adm. fee)* Among the museum's exhibits on natural and human history is a replica neighborhood portraying the city's many ethnic neighborhoods between the 1870s and 1917.

Pabst Theater *(144 E. Wells St. 414-286-3665. By appt.; fee for tours)* The restored 1895 building is one of the most ornate and beautiful Victorian theaters still in operation.

Excursion

OLD WORLD WISCONSIN *(35 miles SW via I-43 on Wis. 67, near Eagle. 414-594-6300. May-Oct.; adm. fee)* At this 576-acre outdoor museum, more than 60 authentic farmhouses, barns, and village shops portray 19th-century immigrant life around the state.

Other Sites in Wisconsin

First Capitol Historic Site *(3 miles NW of Belmont, on Rte. G. 608-264-6586. Mid-May–mid-Sept.)* In 1836 the territorial legislative council convened in Belmont, but the town declined when Madison was selected state capital that same year. The original **Council House** now contains exhibits, and the **courthouse** is furnished in period style.

Old Wade House and Wesley Jung Carriage Museum S.H.S. *(Jct. of Kettle Moraine Scenic Dr. and Plank Rd., in Greenbush. 414-526-3271. May-Oct.; adm. fee)* A stagecoach stop built in 1850, the Old Wade House has three floors of authentic furnishings. More than 100 horse-powered vehicles, dating from the late 1800s, are displayed at the nearby carriage museum.

Stonefield Historic Site *(1 mile NW of Cassville, on Rte. VV. 608-725-5210. May-Oct.; adm. fee)* Composed of three different sections, this historical park includes a replica 1890s rural Wisconsin village, an agricultural museum, and the reconstructed homestead of the state's first governor.

Villa Louis *(521 Villa Louis Rd., Prairie du Chien. 608-326-2721. May-Oct.; adm. fee)* Built on a prehistoric Indian site, the Victorian 1870 mansion belonged to millionaire fur trader Hercules Dousman and showcases a fine collection of Victorian decorative arts.

Minnesota

Canoe and Great Hall Grand Portage National Monument

   The legend's popularity notwithstanding, no reliable history proves that Paul Bunyan and his blue ox created Minnesota's 10,000-plus lakes. But the 32nd state to enter the Union, on May 11, 1858, owes much of its early story to the Dakota, who freely roamed the area until the Ojibwe began arriving in the early 18th century. This migration precipitated years of war between the tribes. The French were the first Europeans to come, in the 1600s. The British held sway from the 1760s until after the Revolutionary War. In the early 19th century, Americans built a series of forts to guard the Northwest frontier, including Fort Snelling—near the site that would become Minneapolis. One of the first large settlements in the territory was Mendota, established about 1822 as the main trading post for John Jacob Astor's American Fur Company. Later in the 19th century, jobs in lumbering, milling, and railroading, as well as farming, lured many European immigrants, especially Germans and Scandinavians.

Chisholm

   Less than a hundred miles from the ore-shipping port of Duluth, Chisholm lies in the heart of Minnesota's Iron Range. This area—comprised of three ranges, the Mesabi, the Vermilion, and the Cuyuna—has produced about four billion tons of iron ore since mining operations began in the late 1800s.

Minnesota Museum of Mining (*Top of Main St. in Memorial Park. 218-254-5543. May-Sept.; adm. fee*) Indoor and outdoor mining exhibits include an underground drift replica and giant trucks that once hauled iron ore.

Iron Range Interpretive Center (*Ironworld USA, just W of town on Minn. 169. 218-254-3321 or 800-372-6437. Mem. Day–Labor Day; adm. fee to park*) Located in the middle of the Mesabi Iron Range, which still produces about 75 percent of the nation's iron ore, the center features hands-on exhibits explaining the area's mining history.

Excursions

HULL RUST MAHONING OPEN PIT IRON MINE (*7 miles S via US 169, near Hibbing. 3rd Ave. E. 218-262-4900. Mid-May–Sept.*) Known as the world's largest open-pit iron-ore mine, this hole in the earth measures about 3 miles by 2 miles by 600 feet. At its peak in the 1940s, the mine provided up to one-fourth of all iron ore mined in the United States. You can observe the yawning canyon from an observation platform, or see it by bus tour in summer.

FOREST HISTORY CENTER (*45 miles SW via US 169 and US 2 in Grand Rapids. 2609 County Rd. 76. 218-327-4482. Daily Mem. Day–mid-Oct., Mon.-Fri. rest of year; adm. fee Mem. Day–mid-Oct. only*) Museum exhibits and an outdoor living history logging camp portray the history of Minnesota's timber industry, which began in the 1840s with the clear-cut harvest of immense white pine forests.

SOUDAN UNDERGROUND MINE STATE PARK (*40 miles N on US 169, Minn. 169, and Minn. 1, near Tower. 218-753-2245. Mem. Day–Sept. or by appt.; adm. fee*) An elevator takes visitors some 2,500 feet down into Minnesota's last operating underground iron mine, which closed in 1962.

Duluth ···

(*Convention & Visitors Bureau, 100 Lake Place Dr. 218-722-4011 or 800-4DULUTH*) First explored in 1679 by Frenchman Daniel de Greysolon, Sieur du Luth, Duluth grew with the discovery of copper and gold in the mid-1800s, followed by a lumber boom. With the opening of the Iron Range near Chisholm later in the century, the port city became the major shipper of iron ore that it remains today.

Canal Park Marine Museum (*End of Canal Park Dr. in Canal Park. 218-727-2497. Closed Mon.-Thurs. mid-Dec.–March*) Model ships and illustrations recount the history of commercial traffic on Lake Superior. The museum is located next to the 386-foot-long **Aerial Lift Bridge,** a unique elevator bridge built in 1905 to permit ships into Duluth Harbor.

The Depot (*506 W. Michigan St. 218-727-8025. Adm. fee*) Built in 1892 as a railroad station, the brownstone building now houses various museums and art galleries. Among them, the **Lake Superior Museum of Transportation** features the state's largest collection of antique railroad equipment; the **St. Louis County Historical Society Museum** displays exhibits on Native Americans, early logging, and fur trading; and old-fashioned shops at **Depot Square** depict 1910 commercial Duluth.

Glensheen (*3300 London Rd. 218-724-8864. Mem. Day–Labor Day; adm. fee*) Overlooking Lake Superior, the 22-acre estate—encompassing a 39-room Jacobean mansion, carriage house, bowling green, boathouse, and gardens—was built in 1908 for state legislator Chester A. Congdon.

Excursions

SPLIT ROCK LIGHTHOUSE AND HISTORY CENTER (*60 miles NE via Minn. 61. 218-226-6372. Mid-May–mid-Oct., history center also open Fri.-Sun. mid-Oct.–mid-May except Dec.; adm. fee*) Sitting atop a 130-foot headland, the light was completed in 1910 to guide ore carriers along Lake Superior's rocky shoreline. The history center features exhibits on lake navigation, shipwrecks, and the U.S. Lighthouse Service. You may also tour the fog-signal building and restored keeper's house.

GRAND PORTAGE NATIONAL MONUMENT (*150 miles NE via Minn. 61, near Grand Portage. 218-387-2788. Mid-May–mid-Oct.; adm. fee*) In the late 18th century, this remote outpost was a fur-trading hub for the North West Company. The partially reconstructed palisaded depot, which includes the warehouse, kitchen, and Great Hall, commemorates the French-Canadian voyageurs, or "travelers," who devoted their lives paddling canoes to transport furs and trade goods between the Canadian Northwest and Montreal. Every summer they flocked to Grand Portage to receive their wages and to feast. A midsummer rendezvous is reenacted every year. At the nearby Grand Portage, the "great carrying place," they carried their canoes along a 8.5-mile trail that bypassed unnavigable waters. Today the portage trail is popular among skiers and hikers.

Twin Cities

Quarters at Fort Snelling, Minneapolis

239

The boundaries of Minneapolis and St. Paul blur on a modern map, but their histories are quite distinct. Minneapolis dates back to the days of Fort Snelling, a military post established in 1819 at the confluence of the Mississippi and Minnesota Rivers. Soldiers built a gristmill and sawmill at the nearby Falls of St. Anthony; the milling and lumbering settlement that grew from there became Minneapolis. A separate settlement just below the falls—called Pig's Eye for an infamous settler—became known as St. Paul after a priest constructed the Chapel of St. Paul on the Mississippi's banks. St. Paul became a prosperous river port. In 1849 it was named territorial capital, and in 1858 state capital.

Minneapolis

(*Convention & Visitors Bureau, City Center Bldg., bet. 6th and 7th Sts. 612-661-4700 or 800-445-7412*)

St. Anthony Falls Historic District (*Visitor Center, 125 Main St. S.E. 612-627-5433. Self-guided tours year-round, guided tours Wed.-Sun. May-Oct; adm. fee for guided tours*) The industrial heart of Minneapolis until 1930, the Falls of St. Anthony provided waterpower for the town's lumber and flour mills. One of the first millwrights lived in what's now called the **Ard Godfrey House** (*Central and University Aves. 612-870-8001. Mem. Day–Sept. Fri.-Mon.; adm. fee*), built in 1849.

American Swedish Institute (*2600 Park Ave. 612-871-4907. Tues.-Sun.;*

adm. fee) The city's Swedish heritage is reflected in this 33-room Romanesque mansion, the 1929 gift of a self-made millionaire to further Swedish culture. The house museum includes hand-carved oak woodwork, glass and textiles, and immigrant artifacts.

Fort Snelling *(Minn. 5 and 55. 612-726-1171. May-Oct.; adm. fee.)* Minneapolis's first settlement encompasses 18 restored or reconstructed buildings, including a school, hospital, officers' quarters, and powder magazine. Costumed interpreters play the roles of early fort residents.

St. Paul ············
(Visitors Bureau, 55 E. 5th St., Suite 102. 612-297-6985 or 800-627-6101)

Summit Avenue Historic District *(W of Cathedral of St. Paul. Guided tours offered June-Sept. by James Hill House. Reservations required; fee)* Among the impressive 19th- and early 20th-

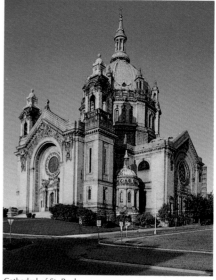
Cathedral of St. Paul

century mansions along Summit Avenue is the red sandstone 1891 **James J. Hill House** *(240 Summit Ave. 612-297-2555. Wed.-Sat.; adm. fee)*, which belonged to the Great Northern Railway founder. Across the way towers the 1915 Roman Catholic **Cathedral of St. Paul** *(239 Selby Ave. 612-228-1766)*, topped with a 306-foot copper dome. Modeled after St. Peter's in Rome, the classical renaissance structure seats 3,000 people.

Irvine Park Historic District *(Intersected by Ryan Ave. and Walnut St. Contact Ramsey House for walking tour information)* In 1849 John Irvine operated a ferry across the Mississippi River. A parcel of land he donated to the village was named in his honor. Of the district's many elegant Victorian houses, the most lavish is the 15-room **Alexander Ramsey House** *(265 S. Exchange St. 612-296-8760. May-Dec.; adm. fee)*, which belonged to the first territorial governor.

Sibley Historic Site *(1357 Sibley Memorial Hwy. 612-452-1596. May-Oct. Tues.-Sun.; adm. fee)* Built in 1836, the stone residence of the state's first governor contains period furnishings. The site also includes the **Jean Baptiste Faribault House,** which explores the history of Native Americans and the fur trade.

Gibbs Farm Museum *(2097 Larpenteur Ave., near Cleveland Ave., Falcon Heights. 612-646-8629. May-Oct. Tues.-Sun.; adm. fee)* Owned by the the same family for nearly a century, the 7-acre farmstead—including a 1900s farmhouse and one-room schoolhouse—depicts farm life in the late 1800s.

Excursions
OLIVER H. KELLEY FARM *(25 miles NW of Minneapolis via US 10. 612-*

240

441-6896. May-Oct.; Visitor Center exhibits open weekends Nov.-April; adm. fee) Oliver H. Kelley, who first farmed these 189 acres in 1850, is best remembered for founding the Order of the Patrons of Husbandry, better known as the Grange. At its peak in 1874, this national farmer's union was estimated to have more than 10,000 chapters across the nation. Kelley's land is now a living history farm, where work animals and costumed interpreters portray the rural life of mid-19th-century families.

NORTH WEST COMPANY FUR POST *(65 miles N of St. Paul via I-35, near Pine City. 320-629-6356. May–Labor Day Tues.-Sun.)* The reconstructed 1804-05 winter encampment of fur traders, Ojibwe trappers, and voyageurs depicts life in early Minnesota.

Others Sites in Minnesota

Charles A. Lindbergh House *(1200 Lindbergh Dr. S., Little Falls. 320-632-3154. Daily May–Labor Day, weekends Labor Day–Oct.; adm. fee)* The famed aviator spent many boyhood summers in this cottage on the Mississippi River. A history center tells the family story.

Fort Ridgely *(7 miles S of Fairfax, off Minn. 4. 507-426-7888. May–Labor Day; adm. fee)* The fort was constructed in 1853 without any protective walls to oversee the area's newly settled lands. Plaques mark a restored commissary building and several foundations, and the Visitor Center offers a scale model and video program.

Grand Mound *(17 miles W of International Falls via Minn. 11. 218-285-3332. May–Labor Day, weekends in Oct.; adm. fee)* Woodland people built the Grand Mound, one of five mounds at the site, as early as 200 B.C. Measuring 136 by 98 by 25 feet, it is one of the largest prehistoric mounds in the upper Midwest.

Jeffers Petroglyphs *(13 miles N of Bingham Lake. 507-877-3647 or 507-697-6321. Call for hours)* Some 2,000 rock carvings, dating from as early as 3000 B.C., decorate a red-quartzite outcrop. A self-guided trail has interpretive markers that explain some of the figures.

Mille Lacs Indian Museum *(10 miles N of Onamia on US 169. 320-532-3632. May-Oct.; adm. fee)* Life-size dioramas, contemporary powwow outfits, and a changing display of some 1,500 artifacts present the history and culture of this band of Ojibwe.

Pipestone National Monument *(US 75 in Pipestone. 507-825-5464. Adm. fee)* Native Americans still quarry pipestone (a special type of clay stone) here to carve peace pipes and other ceremonial objects. Exhibits at the Visitor Center examine the area's history, and a self-guided walking trail loops past the rocks.

Upper and Lower Sioux Agencies Displaced from their lands in the mid-19th century, the Dakota were moved to the Upper and Lower Sioux Agencies to learn how to farm. A subsequent treaty cut their reservation in half, fueling anger that erupted in a series of battles between infantry and Indians, known as the U.S.-Dakota Conflict of 1862. Only a warehouse building remains on the 240-acre **Lower Sioux Agency** *(10 miles E of Redwood Falls, off Minn. 19. 507-697-6321. May-Oct.; adm. fee)*, but Visitor Center exhibits and a slide program explain the history. A trail leads to Redwood Ferry Crossing, one of the skirmish sites. At the **Upper Sioux Agency** *(9 miles S of Granite Falls, on Minn. 67. 507-697-6321. Adm. fee)*, interpretive signs mark exposed foundations of agency buildings.

241

SASK. CANADA **MAN.**

U.S.A.

Fort Buford
S.H.S.

NORTH DAKOTA

Pembina
State Museum

Knife River
Indian Village
N.H.S.

Theodore
Roosevelt
N.P.

Fort Totten S.H.S.

Fort Mandan
Fort Clark S.H.S.

Medora

Bismarck

Bonanzaville U.S.A

Fort Abraham
Lincoln S.P.

Fort Abercrombie
S.H.S.

Mooreton

Whitestone Hill
Battlefield S.H.S.

Sisseton

SOUTH DAKOTA

MONT.

Deadwood

Pierre

Mt. Rushmore
Nat. Mem.

Rapid City

Chamberlain

Mitchell

MINN.

Custer S.P.

Badlands N.P.

Hot
Springs

Sioux Falls

Fort Atkinson
State Preserve

Effigy
Mounds
Nat. Mon.

Decorah

WYO.

Crawford

Chadron

Missouri

Abbie
Gardner
Cabin

Cedar
Rock

Dubuque

WIS.

Scotts Bluff
Nat. Mon.

Nel100

Bancroft

Fort Dodge

IOWA

Cedar Rapids

Chimney Rock
N.H.S.

Ash Hollow
S.H.P.

NEBRASKA

Des Moines

Amana

Herbert Hoover
N.H.S.

Iowa City

ILLINOIS

North
Platte

Grand
Island

Ft. Atkinson S.H.P.

Omaha

Council
Bluffs

Kalona

Lincoln

COLORADO

Fort Kearney S.H.P.

Nebraska City

Beatrice

Brownville

Hannibal

Red Cloud

Pawnee Indian
Village S.H.S.

St. Joseph

Atchison

Independence

Arrow
Rock S.H.S.

St. Charles

Fort
Riley

Topeka

Kansas
City

Fulton

St.
Louis

Fort Larned
N.H.S.

Abilene

Council Grove

Jefferson City

Hermann

Ste. Genevieve

Fort
Davidson
S.H.S.

Kauffman
Museum

MISSOURI

New
Madrid

Garden
City

Dodge
City

KANSAS

Wichita

Fort Scott
N.H.P.

Wilson's
Creek N.B.

George Washington
Carver Nat. Mon.

TENN.

Bartlesville

Eureka Springs

Black Kettle
Museum

Guthrie

Tulsa

Claremore

Fayetteville

Mountain
View

Kingfisher

Okmulgee

Muskogee

ARKANSAS

Amarillo

Indian City,
U.S.A.

Oklahoma
City

Sallisaw

Fort Smith

Little
Rock

Helena

Canyon

OKLAHOMA

Hot Springs
N.P.

Toltec
Mounds

Mississippi

Tishomingo

Durant

Arkansas Post
Nat. Mem.

MISS.

Lubbock

Wichita Falls

Old
Washington
Historic S.P.

Hueco
Tanks S.P.

Fort Worth

Dallas

LOUISIANA

El Paso

Midland

Pecos

Waco

Sam
Houston
Mem. Museum

Nacogdoches

TEXAS

Fort
Concho

Alabama-
Coushatta
I.R.

Fort Davis
N.H.S.

Washington-
on-the-Brazos
S.H.P.

Beaumont

Fredericksburg

Austin

Houston

LBJ State and
National Historical
Parks

New
Braunfels

San Jacinto
Battleground S.H.P.

San Antonio

Galveston

Goliad

George
Ranch
Historical Park

Rio Grande

Corpus Christi

Laredo

U.S.A.
MEXICO

Central Plains

Once frontier, now heartland, the central states saw more than their share of adversity and challenge as a young nation moved toward maturity in the 19th century. The trauma of the Civil War was followed by years of bloody conflict between federal troops and Native Americans, whose homeland shrank with each new wave of immigrants. Early routes such as the Santa Fe and Oregon Trails began populating the lonely plains. An expanding network of railroads brought more people into the region and shipped farm products back to eastern markets. Cattle, wheat, corn, cotton, and soybeans have all played their parts in the growth of the central states—rivaled only by natural gas and oil, the "black gold" that helped build cities such as Houston, Dallas, and Tulsa.

Mitchell Pass, Scotts Bluff National Monument

North Dakota

Maltese Cross Cabin, Theodore Roosevelt National Park

On February 22, 1889, President Benjamin Harrison signed the bill making North Dakota, South Dakota, Montana, and Washington states. The quill for the pen he used had been plucked from a North Dakota eagle, and it provided a rare moment of recognition for a place often viewed as last in line with the least to offer. But along this frontier lived seminal figures in American history. Lt. Col. George A. Custer embarked from his Fort Abraham Lincoln home on his journey to the Little Bighorn in 1876. Theodore Roosevelt, a New Yorker, transformed himself into a Rough Rider in the 1880s on a ranch near Medora. In the 1860s the Homestead Act opened the plains to settlers, and the Northern Pacific Railroad lured would-be landowners from as far away as Finland. Like the Hidatsa, Sioux, and other tribes, North Dakota's new residents endured and prospered despite harsh weather and isolation. Tough-minded farmers and ranchers sometimes tilted toward radicalism. Their independence is shaped by thinly populated geography: the spare beauty of glacier-carved plains, productive farms, and grassy wildlands.

Bismarck

(Convention & Visitors Bureau, 523 N. 4th St. 701-222-4308 or 800-767-3555)
In 1873, when the capital of Dakota Territory was moved from Yankton to Bismarck, political shenanigans were suspected. The move assured that the territory would split into two states. But Bismarck had its virtues: It was central to the northern territory, accessible by river, and seated prettily on

seven hills, a site that Indian communities had also found to their liking.

North Dakota Heritage Center *(State Capitol, 612 E. Blvd. Ave. 701-328-2666)* Exhibits ranging from the skeleton of a mastodon to the radio of a Depression-era living room give an overview of North Dakota's history and prehistory. Displays are selected from the state historical society's collections.

Capitol Building *(State Capitol, 600 E. Blvd. Ave. 701-328-2000)* Given the low-rise style of Bismarck, the 19-story Capitol is an art deco eye-catcher. The 1930s exterior seems dated, but the interior's soaring entry atrium, marble floors, and fine wood paneling lend grandeur to governance.

Former Governors' Mansion *(320 E. Ave. B. 701-328-2666. Mid-May–mid-Sept. Wed.-Sun.)* The quiet neighborhood and compact living rooms of the house where 23 North Dakota governors resided from 1893 to 1960 open a window on the private life of public figures. The mansion is decorated with modest Victorian furnishings, and the third floor is relinquished to a large play area for gubernatorial offspring.

Ward Earthlodge Village Historic Site *(N on Tyler Parkway, W on Burnt Boat Dr.)* Before 19th-century pioneers founded Bismarck, Mandan Indians chose these hills above the Missouri to build a community of dome-shaped earth lodges. Tucked behind a modern subdivision, this earlier housing tract—now a grassy walking tour of 43 lodge depressions—commands an impressive river view.

Excursions

FORT ABRAHAM LINCOLN STATE PARK *(10 miles SW via I-94, on N. Dak. 1806. Custer House 701-663-4758. Adm. fee)* The compact but luxurious home of Lt. Col. George A. Custer and wife, Libbie, faces Cavalry Square, flanked by the former commissary (now a store) and barracks. From here Custer left for his fateful 1876 meeting with Sitting Bull at Little Bighorn. Guides in period dress show visitors the room where George and his brother played billiards. During Frontier Days *(June)* there are cavalry drills and cannon firings.

ON-A-SLANT INDIAN VILLAGE *(Adj. to Fort Abraham Lincoln)* The spacious, softly lit earth lodges of the Mandan were in some ways cozier than Custer's quarters. Reconstructed during the 1930s, this secure agricultural village, surrounded by a moat, thrived during the 17th century.

FORT MANDAN *(45 miles NW via US 83 and Rte. 17. 701-462-8129. Tues.-Sun.)* The Missouri River site where historians think Lewis and Clark wintered in 1804-05 is underwater now, but this downstream copy of a triangular, shed-roofed fort illustrates the rough circumstance of their expedition. At a nearby Mandan village, the explorers met Toussaint Charbonneau and his Shoshone wife, Sacagawea, their interpreters for the journey.

FORT CLARK STATE HISTORIC SITE *(55 miles NW via US 83 and N. Dak. 200A. 701-794-8832. Mid-May–mid-Sept. Thurs.-Mon.)* Traders built two forts adjacent to settlements of Mandan and Arikara. Fort and earth-lodge foundations and a burial ground are still visible on a grassy hillside.

KNIFE RIVER INDIAN VILLAGE N.H.S. *(60 miles N via US 83 and N. Dak. 200A. 701-745-3309)* At the juncture of the Knife and Missouri Rivers, Hidatsa Indians built earth lodges alongside their allies, the Mandan and Arikara. Skiing and walking trails pass mounds of the original villages.

Theodore Roosevelt National Park ···········

(Visitor Center, I-94, South Unit. 701-623-4466) Theodore Roosevelt came

to North Dakota from New York to hunt bison in the badlands and stayed to raise cattle in the 1880s. Artifacts from these years are displayed at the Visitor Center near his ranch house. His Elkhorn Ranch, sans buildings, can be visited 25 miles north via a dirt road.

Excursion

CHATEAU DE MORES S.H.S. (*1 mile S of Medora via N. Dak. 10. 701-623-4355. Mid-May–mid-Sept. or by appt.; adm. fee*) Arriving about the same time as Roosevelt, the Marquis de Mores invested millions in ranches, a slaughterhouse, and railroad refrigerator cars. The Frenchman "roughed it" in a 26-room château, which remains standing and sumptuously furnished.

Other Sites in North Dakota

Bagg Bonanza Farm (*I-29, Mooreton. 701-274-8989. Mem. Day–Labor Day Fri.-Sun.*) A restored "Bonanza" farm, the site is the last surviving example of the large corporate or privately owned farms that successfully cultivated the verdant Red River Valley in the late 19th century.

Bonanzaville, USA (*I-94 at US 10, West Fargo. 701-282-2822. Adm. fee*) The eclectic "village" holds nearly 40 buildings built from the 1860s to the 1930s. Interesting items range from a dog-driven butter churn to the hand-carved pews of an 1898 Lutheran church.

Fort Abercrombie State Historic Site (*Rte. 81, SE of Abercrombie. 701-553-8513. Mid-May–mid-Sept.; adm. fee*) In 1862 this military post was besieged by Sioux. Still standing is a palisade wall and one building; blockhouses have been reconstructed.

Fort Buford State Historic Site (*N. Dak. 1804, 22 miles SW of Williston. 701-572-9034. Mid-May–mid-Sept.; adm. fee*) Sioux chief Sitting Bull surrendered at this fort near the confluence of the Missouri and Yellowstone Rivers. Nez Perce chief Joseph was brought here after capture. The site has 3 of 100 original buildings, a cemetery, and a museum.

Fort Union Trading Post N.H.S. (*N. Dak. 1804, 25 miles SW of Willis-

ton. 701-572-9083*) The fort was the region's biggest trading post in the early 19th century. Tools, clothing, and weapons were swapped for bison robes and furs; visitors can buy replica wares at the 1851 Indian Trade House. **Bourgeois House** has fur-trade exhibits.

Fort Totten State Historic Site (*N. Dak. 57, SW of Devils Lake. Interpretive Center 701-766-4441. Mid-May–mid-Sept.; adm. fee*) Seventeen buildings from 1868 to 1871 still remain. Exhibits cover the military era and the fort's later incarnation as a government-run boarding school for Indians.

Pembina State Museum (*N. Dak. 59, Pembina. 701-825-6840. Adm. fee*) The Ox Cart Trail, which brought supplies to settlers, is featured in exhibits.

Bourgeois House, Fort Union Trading Post

Whitestone Hill Battlefield S.H.S. (*12 miles NW of Ellendale, on country roads off US 281*) Seeking to "punish" the Sioux for their uprising in Minnesota in 1862, U.S. troops attacked and killed 150 Sioux at this site. The remote location is unadorned except for a monument to the soldiers and a plaque honoring the Indians.

South Dakota

Mount Rushmore National Memorial

Explorers Lewis and Clark stopped briefly along South Dakota's stretch of the Missouri River in 1804; emigrants on the Oregon Trail 40 years later looked at the treeless grasslands and continued West. The earliest non-Indian visitors to Dakota country found few reasons to stop, and soon the Indians of the Dakotas were unsettled too: Horses and rifles brought by Europeans quickened the lives of the Plains tribes, and disease turned Mandan earth lodges into ghostly smallpox hospices. In the 1870s, when settlers finally became interested in the Dakotas, the fate of the tribes was sealed. The final chapter was written in 1890 at Wounded Knee, where the U.S. Army attacked defenseless Lakota. While Indians were pushed aside, new residents pushed for statehood—"twin" states, north and south, because distances were great and territorial rivalries prickly. In 1889 South Dakota became a state. Descendants of homesteaders have held on through drought and depression, and passersby now look longingly at the small towns and open horizons.

Badlands National Park

"Les mauvaises terres à traverser" (bad lands to cross), said 19th-century French fur trappers trekking among the dry, colorful buttes, spires, and canyons of what is now Badlands National Park. The park is a 380-square-mile remnant of the great grasslands that once made up the Great Plains, grazed again today by herds of bison, pronghorn, and bighorn sheep.

Displays, a video, and helpful attendants at the **Ben Reifel Visitor Center** (*S. Dak. 240, NE Entrance. 605-433-5361. Adm. fee*) provide an excellent introduction to the geological and human history of the badlands. A drive west along the unpaved **Sage Creek Rim Road** provides access to short boardwalk hikes and overviews of the grasslands and sandstone.

The water in the badlands may have been "too thick to drink, too thin to plow," but that didn't stop homesteaders from trying. Just outside the Northeast Entrance, the **Prairie Homestead** (*I-90. 605-433-5400. Mid-April–mid-Oct.; adm. fee*), first settled in 1909, shows how cramped life was in cabins dug into hillsides. Descendants donated furnishings and farm equipment, including carriages, a rendering pot, and a small pump organ.

The southern portion of Badlands National Park is part of the Lakota Pine Ridge Reservation. The small **White River Visitor Center** (*Rte. 27. June-July*), housed in a trailer, tells the Lakota story. Farther south, outside the park, is the site of the 1890 **Wounded Knee Massacre** (*Rte. 28*), where U.S. Army troops opened fire and killed more than 200 Lakota men, women, and children. A simple sign marks the site, and a rutted dirt road leads up a hill to the cemetery where many of the Lakota, including the leader Big Foot, are buried.

Black Hills

248

The Lakota's sacred Paha Sapa, or "hills of black," were to be part of the Great Sioux Reservation under an 1868 treaty, but no treaty could cool gold fever among settlers. An 1874 expedition led by Lt. Col. George A. Custer sent word of gold in the hills, and the rush was on. Remnants of that brief, intense Wild West of the late 19th century survive today.

Historic Deadwood (*Main, Pine, and Sherman Sts. 605-578-1102 or 800-345-1876*) Many late 19th-century buildings have been restored to how they looked not long after Wild Bill Hickok was dealt the "Dead Man's Hand" (aces over eights) at **Saloon #10** (*657 Main St. 605-578-3346*). Today's cardsharps can pick up hands of their own in #10, which is noisy with drinkers, dancers, and gamblers; a small-stakes gambling industry has largely paid for Deadwood's restoration. The Victorian decor of the **Bullock Hotel** (*633 Main St. 605-578-1745 or 800-336-1876*) is a respite from smoky gambling halls. Barred cashiers' windows and mahogany pilasters inside the **First Western Bank** (*696 Main St.*) let customers transact business in turn-of-the-century style. The three-story **Adams Museum** (*54 Sherman St. 605-578-1714. May-Sept.; adm. fee*) houses Western guns and garb and a plesiosaur fossil. Follow Sherman Street up the south side of Deadwood Gulch to Boot Hill—windy **Mount Moriah Cemetery** (*Lincoln St. dead end*), the final resting place of Wild Bill, Calamity Jane, Potato Creek Johnny, and Vinegar Bill.

Black Hills Mining Museum (*Main St., in Lead. 605-584-1605. Mid-May–Sept. or by appt; adm. fee*) Photos, participatory panning, and displays of equipment show the ways that gold has been extracted, but visitors get the most authentic sense of what it was like by walking through timbered passages of a simulated underground mine. Lead is home to one of the oldest operating underground mines in the U.S., the **Homestake Gold Mine.** Black Hills gold-mining history is depicted at the **Visitor Center** (*Main St. 605-584-3110. Closed weekends Sept.-May*), and bus tours show off the mine's modern mining process.

Mount Rushmore National Memorial *(W of Keystone, on S. Dak. 244. 605-574-2523)* Sculptor Gutzon Borglum carved for 7 years, and more than 300 workers toiled 14 years to transform a Black Hills mountain into the 60-foot-tall granite faces of four American Presidents. The inspiring monument was finished on the eve of America's entry into World War II.

Just 17 miles west, at the **Crazy Horse Memorial** *(Between Hill City and Custer, on US 385. 605-673-4681)*, a large figure of the famed Lakota warrior on horseback has been blasted from mountain granite over the past 50 years.

Custer State Park *(US 16A. 605-255-4515. Adm. fee)* Pine forests, granite spires, prairie grass, and bison dot this preserve. The **Gordon Stockade** *(US 16, West Entrance)* re-creates frontier quarters and a way of life from 1874, when Lt. Col. George Armstrong Custer first came here. Spend the night and lounge on the stone porches of the **State Game Lodge,** President Calvin Coolidge's summer White House *(US 16A, near the East Entrance).*

Corn Palace, in Mitchell

Hot Springs *(US 18 and 385. 605-745-4140 or 800-325-6991)* On the southern end of the Black Hills, this site has an otherworldly quality because of its many 1890s sandstone buildings, some with turrets and minarets. A self-guided walking tour can be topped off by a sip of mineral water at the Kidney Springs Gazebo or a dip at Evans Plunge. You can also tour the huge **Mammoth Site** *(US 18. 605-745-6017)*, where archaeologists are unearthing Ice Age tusks and bones.

249

Sisseton Area ······························

In the 1830s Frenchman Joseph Nicollet mapped the glacial hill country of northeast South Dakota. The open-air **Nicollet Tower** *(3.5 miles W via S. Dak. 10)* offers a three-state view of lake-dotted prairie, and the **Interpretive Center** *(605-698-7672. May-Sept. Tues.-Sun., or by appt.)* has exhibits on Nicollet and Yankton Sioux.

Fort Sisseton State Park *(31 miles W off S. Dak. 10. Visitor Center open Mem. Day–Labor Day, grounds year-round)* Built in 1864 to protect settlers, Sisseton turned out to be a peaceful stopping place for travelers. A museum describes area history; barracks, guardhouse, and officers quarters are open.

Other Sites in South Dakota

Akta-Lakota Museum *(St. Joseph's Indian School, Chamberlain. 605-734-3452. Closed weekends Oct.-April)* Displays include traditional beadwork, ceremonial clothing, a tepee, and contemporary art.

Mitchell A monument to midwestern promotional kitsch, the vaguely Moorish **Corn Palace** *(604 N. Main. 605-996-7311. Closed weekends Sept.-May)* has been redecorated every year since 1892 with multihued corncobs, husks, grains, and grasses arranged in murals depicting Great Plains history. Archaeologists at the **Prehistoric Indian Village** *(Indian Village Rd. 605-996-5473. May-Sept. or by appt.; adm. fee)* near Lake Mitchell are digging up lodges from a 900-year-old hunting and farming village.

Fort Kearney State Historical Park

On bluffs overlooking the Missouri River, just north of where Omaha high-rises stand today, explorer Meriwether Lewis in 1804 met members of the Oto and Missouri tribes and told them of an oncoming civilization with "cities...as numerous as the stars." Forty years later, great streams of westward-bound immigrants would merge on trails along the Platte River, which some of them called "the coast of Nebraska," and follow them past Scotts Bluff and Chimney Rock, which tower above the landscape in the state's northwest corner. Rails replaced wagon ruts in the 1860s when the Union Pacific Railroad began laying track from Omaha, the company's western headquarters. Homesteaders in the 1860s liked the fertile valleys of eastern Nebraska; the buffalo-grass prairies of the west filled more slowly. Grasshoppers in the 1870s and drought in the 1890s tested the mettle of farmers and ranchers. Today, huge irrigation systems use deep aquifers to water western fields, and in the east Omaha is a thriving commercial center, one of Meriwether Lewis's "stars."

Beatrice

Homestead National Monument of America (*4 miles W of Beatrice on Nebr. 4. 402-223-3514*) Daniel Freeman joined the wave of 19th-century settlers who staked out 160-acre plots. His log cabin and a school give a glimpse of conditions in the 1860s; visitors can walk through a field reminiscent of the days when prairie tallgrass grew "taller than a man's head."

Excursion

ROCK CREEK STATION STATE HISTORICAL PARK (*26 miles SW via US 136 and S on 573 Ave. Visitor Center 402-729-5777. Daily mid-May–mid-Sept., weekends through Oct.; grounds open year-round*) In 1861 a stable hand at this Pony Express station ambushed and killed David McCanles, and was thereafter transformed by the press into glamorous Wild Bill Hickok. Buildings and corrals have been reconstructed and artifacts from the Pony Express are exhibited. Visitors can ride in ox-drawn wagons.

Lincoln ··

(*Convention & Visitor Bureau, 201 N. 7th St. 800-423-8212*) The village of Lancaster was renamed Lincoln when it was designated Nebraska's capital in 1867. The state legislature established the University of Nebraska here in 1869, and the first railroad arrived the following year.

Fairview (*49th and Sumner Sts. 402-483-8303. Tues.-Fri.*) William Jennings Bryan ran three times for President and never won, but the "silver-tongued orator" made a decent fortune on the lecture circuit and built this comfortable three-story house. The family entertained on the main floor and dined downstairs. Though once in the country, today it is surrounded by Lincoln and houses a bioethics institute.

Kennard House (*1627 H St. 402-471-4764. Closed Mon.; adm. fee*) Nebraska's first secretary of state campaigned to locate the state capital on the empty prairie near Salt Creek. He bolstered the controversial choice by building his own home here.

Museum of Nebraska History (*15th and P Sts. 402-471-4754*) On three floors, visitors travel from prehistory to the present. Among the displays are exhibits on various Indian tribes and a walk-through rural store.

Nebraska City ·····································

(*Tourism and Events, 806 1st Ave. 800-514-9113*) Once a trading post near the Oregon Trail, Nebraska City grew into a town of handsome 19th-century houses and commercial buildings. Publisher Julius Sterling Morton, who began Arbor Day to encourage tree planting, omitted few leafy species on his hilltop estate, now known as **Arbor Lodge State Historical Park and Mansion** (*Centennial Ave. 402-873-7222. Mansion March-Dec., grounds year-round; adm. fee*). The 52-room, colonial-style mansion displays newspaper wares upstairs and horse-drawn vehicles in the carriage barn. The grounds are now an arboretum.

Abolitionist Allen Mayhew hand-dug a cave beneath his cabin in the 1850s to provide a hiding place and escape route for fugitive slaves heading north. Moved from its original site, the cabin sits today with other 19th- and early 20th-century buildings in **John Brown's Cave and Historical Village** (*20th St. and 4th Corso. 402-873-3115. April-Nov.; adm. fee*).

Excursion

BROWNVILLE (*32 miles SE via US 75 and US 136. 402-825-6001*) Life along the Missouri River, 19th-century style, can be experienced in this town, with its restored Main Street and historic houses. The **Meriwether Lewis and Missouri River History Museum** (*402-825-3341. May–mid-Oct.; adm. fee*) is housed in an old side-wheeler dredge, where displays trace the river's role in opening the West. The *Spirit of Brownville* (*402-825-6441.*

Mid-June–mid-Aug. Thurs.-Sun.; adm. fee), a re-created paddle wheeler, takes passengers on cruises.

Omaha ·····························

(Visitor Center, 1212 Deer Park Blvd. 402-595-3990) Nebraska's largest city is named for "those who go against the current"—Indians who traveled up the Missouri River to the Great Plains. A fort, several trading posts, and a ferry crossing were in the area before Omaha was laid out in 1854.

Western Heritage Museum *(801 S. 10th St. 402-444-5071. Closed Mon.; adm. fee)* From art deco designs on the soaring walls to the old-fashioned soda fountain, this magnificently restored 1930s Union Pacific train station has become a museum to Omaha's past. An enclosure on the south side of the building houses restored train cars, and a glass elevator transports visitors to lower level exhibits.

Old Market District *(W from 10th and Howard Sts. 402-341-7151)* Where wagons rolled and produce merchants hawked their wares, tony shoppers and diners now walk cobblestone streets. Old brick warehouses hold artists' lofts and antique stores.

Great Plains Black History Museum and Archive Center *(2213 Lake St. 402-345-2212. Closed weekends)* Located in the original Webster Telephone Exchange Building, exhibits tell the story of African slaves, "buffalo soldiers," and black homesteaders.

General Crook House Museum *(Metropolitan Community College. 402-455-9990. Closed Sat. and Mon.; donations)* Living on the "edge of the frontier" in 1878 at Fort Omaha, Gen. George Crook commanded military campaigns and entertained visiting dignitaries, including Presidents Ulysses S. Grant and Rutherford B. Hayes. Perched atop a tree-shaded hill and looking across the parade grounds, Crook's Italianate brick house has been refurnished with ornate wallpaper and period furniture.

Mormon Trail Center at Historic Winter Quarters *(3215 State St. 402-453-9372)* In 1846, 12,000 Mormons headed west from Nauvoo, Illinois, and more than 4,000 stopped here to recover from the first part of their journey. The temporary community suffered many deaths—600 Mormons are buried in the cemetery. Outdoor displays include a handcart, replicated cabin, and wagon.

Excursions

FORT ATKINSON STATE HISTORICAL PARK *(8 miles N via US 75. 7th and Madison Sts. 402-468-5611. Visitor Center mid-May–mid-Sept., grounds open year-round; adm. fee)* The first military post west of the Missouri was built on bluffs overlooking the river. The spacious reconstructed fort has several bunkhouse rooms, stocked with rough furniture of the era, and meadow walks among the outbuildings. Lewis and Clark held their first parleys with Indians who lived near here.

GENERAL DODGE HOUSE, COUNCIL BLUFFS, IOWA *(8 miles E via I-80)* See page 258.

Other Sites in Nebraska

Ash Hollow State Historical Park *(3 miles S of Lewellen on US 26. 308-778-5651. Visitor Center Mem. Day–Labor Day or by appt.; grounds open year-round; adm. fee)* Oregon Trail pioneers got a break from the open road in this shady grove of ash trees. They were not the first campers at this site—diggings around Ash Hollow Cave unearthed artifacts 8,000 years old. Two miles south on US 26, visitors can visit ruts made by covered wagons when they were lowered by rope down steep Windlass Hill.

Buffalo Bill Ranch State Historical Park (*1 mile NW of North Platte on US 30. 308-535-8035. June-Aug., weekdays April-May and Sept.-Oct.; adm. fee*) William F. "Buffalo Bill" Cody unwound here after tours of his Wild West Show. The barn holds 19th-century farm equipment and a screening room for Thomas Edison's film of Cody's show.

Fort Kearney State Historical Park (*2 miles S of Kearney on Nebr. 44, 4 miles E on Rte. L-50A. 308-865-5305. Mid-May–mid-Sept.*) Built in 1848 along the Platte River to keep Indians away from pioneers, this "gateway to the Great Plains" was where westbound trails merged. Re-created buildings include a blacksmith shop and powder magazine. The fort was closed in 1871, after the transcontinental railroad opened.

Fort Robinson State Park (*3 miles W of Crawford on US 20. 308-665-2900. Mid-May–mid-Sept.; museum adm. fee*) Lakota warrior Crazy Horse was killed while trying to escape from this military outpost. Restored buildings include officers quarters with overnight accommodations for visitors. A museum in the 1905 Post Headquarters recounts the era of the Indian wars, and a smaller trailside museum exhibits fossils.

John G. Neihardt State Historic Site (*Elm and Washington Sts., Bancroft. 402-648-3388. Donations*) Nebraska's late poet laureate began his monumental *Cycle of the West* here, but he is best known for his book *Black Elk Speaks*. Visitors can wander in a Sioux prayer garden.

Museum of the Fur Trade (*3 miles E of Chadron on US 20. 308-432-3843. June–mid-Sept.; adm. fee*) Before homesteaders or soldiers arrived, traders swapped guns for furs at the now restored 1833 Trading Post. Museum exhibits describe the early fur trade.

Neligh Mill Historic Site (*N St. at Wylie Dr., Neligh. 402-887-4303. Mid-May–mid-Sept.; adm. fee*) In the 1880s a waterwheel drove the mill, which ground wheat grown in the Elkhorn Valley. The mill office is restored and the flume still brings water to the mill.

Scotts Bluff National Monument (*3 miles W of Gering on Nebr. 92. 308-436-4340. Adm. fee*) When Oregon Trail migrants saw this landmark, they knew they had made it a third of the way west.

Arbor Lodge State Historical Park, in Nebraska City

Twenty miles to the east stands another trail marker—a stone arrow pointing skyward at **Chimney Rock National Historic Site** (*US 26. 308-586-2581*).

Stuhr Museum of the Prairie Pioneer (*Jct. of US 34 and 281, 4 miles N of I-80, in Grand Island. 308-385-5316. Museum year-round, outdoor exhibits May–mid-Oct.; adm. fee*) The museum holds a 7-acre steam locomotive railyard and presents living history activities in summer.

Willa Cather Historical Center (*326 N. Webster, Red Cloud. 402-746-2653. Adm. fee*) A small display introduces Willa Cather and her subjects; the bookstore next door provides driving maps to the primitive farmstead where the real-life model for *My Antonia* lived.

Iowa

Walnut Hill, 1875 town at Living History Farms, Des Moines

Blessed with a bounty of rich soil, Iowa attracted serious agrarian people—many of them religious—whose concerns were for farming and right living rather than turf wars. This might explain, in part, the state's reasonably calm history, concentrated largely along its border rivers, the Missouri and the Mississippi. Centuries before French explorers Father Jacques Marquette and Louis Joliet arrived in 1673, Iowa's river valleys and bluffs supported mound-building Indian cultures. Europeans later encountered Woodland and Plains tribes, including the Ioway, for whom the state was named. After some 150 years of being passed among France, Spain, and five territories, and going unclaimed by any power from 1821 to 1834, the Iowa Territory was formed in 1838. It encompassed contemporary Iowa, most of the Dakotas, and a chunk of Minnesota. After much wrangling, Iowa became the 29th state in 1846. Congress, in an effort to promote the building of railroad facilities here, added four million acres in 1856. The first line was completed after the Civil War, and by 1880 four more sliced the prairie lands, ensuring markets for Iowa's farmers and leading to regulation of freight rates.

Des Moines

(Convention & Visitors Bureau, Two Ruan Center, 601 Locust St., Suite 222. 515-286-4960 or 800-451-2625) Iowa's capital and largest city stands at the confluence of the Raccoon and Des Moines Rivers, a strategic spot for Fort Des Moines, established in 1843 by the U.S. Army. Later, the fort

served as the core of a civilian enclave. The city's name may be traced to "les Moines," the French nickname for a local Indian tribe.

Crown jewel of Des Moines is the **Iowa State Capitol** (E. 9th St. and Grand Ave. 515-281-5591). Completed in 1886, the building boasts a gold-leaf dome, Venetian-glass mosaics, marbled corridors, carved wood, and a doll collection representing Iowa's first ladies in inaugural gowns. Exhibits at the nearby **Iowa Historical Building** (600 E. Locust St. 515-281-5111. Closed Mon.) showcase the state's frontier, cultural, and natural heritage.

Historic estates open to the public include **Hoyt Sherman Place** (1501 Woodland Ave. 515-243-0913. Mon.-Fri.; adm. fee), including the 1877 Italianate home of pioneer insurance entrepreneur Hoyt Sherman, a 1907 art gallery, and a 1922 theater. **Terrace Hill** (2300 Grand Ave. 515-281-3604. Mar.-Dec. Tues.-Sat.; adm. fee), an exemplary 1869 mansion in Second Empire-style, was donated in 1971 as the governor's residence, where visitors may view art, artifacts, and antiques. Hidden on 9 wooded acres, the 42-room, Tudor-style **Salisbury House** (4025 Tonawanda Dr. 515-279-9711. Mon.-Fri.; adm. fee) was modeled after the King's House in Salisbury, England, and built in the 1920s with architectural elements from centuries-old English buildings.

Excursions

LIVING HISTORY FARMS (10 miles NW of downtown, off I-35/80, in Urbandale. 2600 N.W. 111th St. 515-278-5286. May–mid-Oct.; adm. fee) The 600-acre open-air museum chronicles the development of Iowa agriculture through five historical sites, including three working farms. The sites represent different eras and span 300 years of history. Interpreters in period dress authentically raise crops and animals and perform domestic activities. Sites include the **1700 Ioway Indian Village, 1850 Pioneer Farm, 1875 town of Walnut Hill, 1900 Farm,** and **Henry A. Wallace Crop Center.**

MADISON COUNTY (30 miles SW via I-80 and US 169. Chamber of Commerce, 73 Jefferson St., Winterset. 515-462-1185 or 800-298-6119) Much ballyhooed since their movie debut, the six remaining **covered bridges** (originally 19) are listed on the National Register of Historic Places.

Dubuque ·······································

(Iowa Welcome Center, 3rd St. at Ice Harbor. 319-556-4372 or 800-798-8844) French-Canadian Julien Dubuque arrived in the 1780s to trade with the Meskwaki Indians and by 1788 was running their lead mines along the Mississippi. When he died in 1810, the Meskwaki buried him on a river bluff, later marked by the **Julien Dubuque Monument** in **Mines of Spain State Recreation Area.** The Indians reclaimed the mines until 1832, when the land was ceded to the U.S. government. In 1833 the city of Dubuque was settled—making it one of Iowa's earliest communities. By mid-century, the region was supplying most of America's lead, including Civil War lead shot made in the 150-foot-tall **Shot Tower** (E. 4th St. Extension), built in 1856.

During the 1850s, lumbering replaced lead mining as the main industry of this important river port, manufacturing center, and rail hub. The prosperous late 19th century saw a building boom here, reflected in Dubuque's wealth of Victorian mansions. Several **historic districts** preserve an array of structures and styles. One unique landmark, the 1882 **Fenelon Place Elevator** (End of W. 4th St.), still runs cable cars up and down the steep bluff. The rare Egyptian Revival-style **Old Jail,** completed in 1858, holds the **Dubuque Museum of Art** *(E. 8th St. and Central Ave.).*

Effigy Mounds National Monument, Harpers Ferry

Mississippi River Museum *(3rd St. at Ice Harbor. 319-557-9545. Adm. fee)* This complex covers 300 years of history along the great river. The **Woodward Riverboat Museum** focuses on the story of navigation and commerce, with exhibits on Native Americans, fur trading, mining, and logging, while the nearby **National Rivers Hall of Fame** spotlights such notables as Lewis and Clark, Mark Twain, and Robert Fulton. Visitors can board the dockside **William M. Black** *(May-Oct.),* a 1934 steam-powered side-wheeler.

Mathias Ham House *(2241 Lincoln Ave. 319-557-9545. Daily June-Aug.; weekends May and Sept.-Oct.; adm. fee)* The Italianate villa, built in 1856 by an industrialist, offers a glimpse of antebellum life along the upper Mississippi. Also on the grounds are a one-room schoolhouse and a log cabin.

256

Excursion

GALENA, ILLINOIS *(16 miles SE via US 20)* See page 224.

Effigy Mounds National Monument ··········
(3 miles N of Marquette via Iowa 76. 319-873-3491. April-Oct.; adm. fee) As long as 2,500 years ago, prehistoric Indians built numerous earthen mounds here atop the dramatic 300-foot-high limestone bluffs of the upper Mississippi. The peaceful 1,475-acre park preserves 191 *known* mounds, most of which are compound, conical, or linear in shape. Twenty-nine, though, take the form of bear or bird effigies—one of the largest collections of effigy mounds remaining in the Midwest. (While prehistoric mounds are found in much of the country, effigy mounds are concentrated in southern Wisconsin and adjacent regions of Iowa, Minnesota, and Illinois.) The mounds vary in size as well as shape, with the monumental Great Bear Mound measuring 137 feet long and 3.5 feet high. The park is divided into north and south units, with 11 miles of interpretive hiking trails. Be sure to stop first at the Visitor Center for an introduction to the site.

Excursion

VILLA LOUIS, PRAIRIE DU CHIEN, WISCONSIN *(7 miles SE via Iowa 76 and US 18)* See page 236.

Iowa City ·······································
(Convention & Visitors Bureau, 408 1st Ave., Coralville. 319-337-6592 or 800-283-6592) In 1839 Congress legislated that the capital of the new Iowa Territory would be located in Johnson County. A site was chosen on the Iowa River's east bank. The city grew rapidly, attracting a large immigrant population, and remained the seat of government after statehood in 1846. The

state's development toward the west, however, forced lawmakers to shift the capital to more centrally located Des Moines in 1857. In what came to be compensation for Iowa City's loss, they established the **University of Iowa** here. Chartered in 1847, it turned out to be the city's cultural and economic mainstay. A good "walking town," Iowa City has preserved much of its architectural heritage, with several designated historic districts. Focal point of the **downtown historic district** is the gold-domed capitol building.

Old Capitol *(Clinton St. and Iowa Ave. 319-335-0548)* The Greek Revival landmark served as a government seat from 1842 until 1857, when it was deeded to the university. The interior features a rare reverse spiral stairway and chambers restored to represent the capitol's historical periods.

Plum Grove *(1030 Carroll St. 319-337-6846. Mem. Day–Oct. Wed.-Sun.)* In 1844 Robert Lucas, Iowa's first territorial governor, and his wife, Friendly, built their seven-room brick retirement home, now restored and containing period furnishings.

Excursions

HERBERT HOOVER NATIONAL HISTORIC SITE *(10 miles E via I-80, in West Branch. Parkside Dr. and Main St. 319-643-2541. Adm. fee)* In 1874 the 31st President was born to a Quaker family here in the two-room, board-and-batten cottage built by his father, a blacksmith, in 1871. The 186-acre memorial site also contains a reconstructed 19th-century blacksmith shop and schoolhouse, the Friends Meetinghouse, hillside graves of Hoover and his wife, and a newly expanded, interactive library-museum.

257

AMANA COLONIES *(20 miles NW via I-80 and US 151. Welcome Centers off I-80 and in Amana. 319-622-7622 or 800-245-5465)* In the mid-1800s, a group of Germans seeking religious freedom immigrated to Buffalo, New York. Seeking more land, they moved west, resettling in the fertile Iowa River Valley in 1855. They established a self-supporting colony of seven villages based on a religious communal system, and on 26,000 acres they built factories, mills, and shops to supply all their needs. In 1932 the community abandoned this system, incorporated their holdings, and formed the profit-sharing Amana Society, separate from the church. The site—a living museum encompassing the seven rustic villages, more than 400 original structures, and working farms and shops—preserves the look and German heritage of the Amanas.

Plan on spending at least a day here to explore historic sites, shops, restaurants, and byways accessible via the marked **Amana Colonies Trail** *(Iowa 151 and 220)*. Highlights include the **Amana Community Church** *(Homestead)*; the **Barn Museum** and **Communal Agriculture Exhibit** *(South Amana)*; the **Communal Kitchen** and **Cooper Shop Museum** *(Middle Amana)*, and the **Museum of Amana History** *(Amana)*.

Traditional clothing, Amana Colonies

KALONA *(20 miles SW via Iowa 1. Chamber of Commerce, 514 B Ave. 319-656-2660)* Born as a rail stop on a bull-breeder's ranch, charming Kalona proudly boasts the largest Amish community west of the Mississippi River, along with a sizable Mennonite community. The old 1879 **railroad depot** is among the cluster of historic structures, including a traditional

Amish "Grandpa house," displayed at the **Kalona Historical Village** (*Iowa 22 E*), where visitors also find a no-frills little museum filled with Mennonite artifacts and history.

Other Sites in Iowa

Abbie Gardner Cabin (*US 71, in Arnolds Park. 712-332-7248. Mem. Day–Labor Day*) Built in 1856, the restored log cabin was home to young Abigail Gardner, among those kidnapped by Wahpekute Dakota Indians during the Spirit Lake Massacre, when 36 settlers were killed. The only cabin to survive the event memorializes the story.

Cedar Rock (*S of US 20 on Rte. W-35, Quasqueton. 319-934-3572. Tues.-Sun. May-Oct.*) The bluff-top home of Lowell Walter was designed by Frank Lloyd Wright. Finished in 1950, the residence contains built-in furniture, a boathouse, and an entrance tile with the architect's signature—making this Iowa's only "signed" Wright house.

Council Bluffs Sprawled on the banks of the Missouri River, the city was named to commemorate the first meeting of Lewis and Clark with the Missouri and Oto Indians, in 1804. The **Historic General Dodge House** (*605 3rd St. 712-332-2406. Closed Mon. and Jan.; adm. fee*) preserves the 1870 mansion of Civil War officer Grenville Mellen Dodge. A venture capitalist and a military and civil engineer, he made much of his fortune building railroads. The house contains original furnishings and memorabilia. Nearby stands the 1885 **Pottawattamie County Squirrel Cage Jail** (*226 Pearl St. 712-323-2509*), featuring a novel rotary cell system that consists of a metal drum and tiers of cells: To reach a prisoner, the jailer turned a crank to line up the cell door with the drum opening.

Fort Atkinson State Preserve (*Off Iowa 24, in Fort Atkinson. 319-425-4161. Weekends Mem. Day–Sept.*) In the 1840s the U.S. government built a military post here to protect displaced Indians. Sections of the mostly obliterated original fort have been reconstructed. A museum offers historical exhibits.

Fort Museum and Frontier Village (*E of jct. of US 20 and 169, in Fort Dodge. 515-573-4231. May–mid-Oct.; adm. fee*) Original and replicated structures re-create the flavor of early Fort Dodge, founded in 1850 as a military outpost to guard the expanding frontier. The museum displays Native American, military, and pioneer artifacts.

Matthew Edel Blacksmith Shop (*Rte. E-63 off Iowa 14, in Haverhill. 515-752-6664. Mem. Day–Labor Day*) The 1883 shop of the German blacksmith and inventor has been preserved as he left it in 1940. His handmade tools and inventions are on display; interpreters explain early blacksmithing.

National Czech and Slovak Museum and Library (*30 16th Ave. S.W., Cedar Rapids. 319-362-8500. Tues.-Sat.; adm. fee*) The late 19th and early 20th centuries brought many Central Europeans to this region. (According to estimates, about one-fourth of Cedar Rapids residents have Czech or Slovak ancestry.) The museum represents these cultures through exhibits of memorabilia and traditional costumes, art, and crafts.

Vesterheim Norwegian-American Museum (*502 W. Water St., Decorah. 319-382-9681. Adm. fee*) Meaning "western home," the Vesterheim, founded in 1877, claims to be one of the country's oldest museums of immigrant folk culture. Exhibits include traditional domestic items, furnishings, textiles, and art. An outdoor area of the museum contains various 18th- and 19th-century buildings with period furnishings.

Kansas

Front Street, Dodge City

Searching for the land of Quivira—whose fabulous wealth was only a fable—the Spaniard Francisco Vásquez de Coronado explored parts of what is now Kansas in 1541, traversing broad prairies (homeland of the Wichita Indians) where unimaginable numbers of bison roamed. Among the Native American tribes that came here later, the Kaw (Kansa) gave a name to the future state. In the 1800s the Santa Fe Trail became a major route across Kansas, leading to the establishment of outposts such as Fort Riley and Fort Larned. In the mid-19th century, settlers split into pro- and antislavery factions; raids and counterraids escalated into violence that branded the territory "Bleeding Kansas" and presaged the national cataclysm soon to follow. After the Civil War, northbound cattle drives met rail lines at towns such as Abilene and Dodge City, where rowdy cowpokes and stern lawmen helped to shape the legend of the Wild West. The last three decades of the century saw a new wave of European immigrants—Germans, Swedes, Russians, and others— who founded farming towns that maintain their ethnic character today. Kansas' status as the leading wheat-producing state would astound the early explorers who called its treeless plains "the Great American Desert."

Abilene

Once the northern terminus of the Chisholm Trail, Abilene was a wild frontier town in the years after the Civil War; Wild Bill Hickok was among those who tried to keep order.

Eisenhower Center *(S. Buckeye and 4th Sts. 913-263-4751. Adm. fee for museum)* Though born in Texas, Dwight David Eisenhower grew up in Abilene, where the Eisenhower Center preserves the family's two-story frame home. The center also includes the Presidential Library; a museum with exhibits on Eisenhower's service as commander of Allied forces in Europe in World War II and as the nation's 34th President; and the Place of Meditation, where Eisenhower and his wife, Mamie, are buried.

Excursions

FORT RILEY *(30 miles E via I-70 and Kans. 18)* Among the attractions on the military base (founded in 1852) are the **U.S. Cavalry Museum** *(913-239-2743)*, housed in a former Army hospital, with exhibits on American mounted forces from the Revolutionary War to 1950; the 1855 limestone **Custer House** *(913-239-2737. Mem. Day–Labor Day)* (similar to a now destroyed home occupied by George A. Custer and his wife), interpreting frontier life during the 1870s and '80s; and the **First Territorial Capitol** *(913-784-5535. Thurs.-Sun.)*, where a pro-slavery legislature met in 1855 before voting to move to friendlier ground at Shawnee Mission, near Kansas City.

COUNCIL GROVE *(65 miles SE via I-70 and Kans. 177)* This historical town took its name from a grove of trees along the Neosho River, where a treaty was signed in 1825 allowing safe passage for travelers through Osage territory. Many attractions are found along Main Street, which follows the route of the Santa Fe Trail. The **Hays House** *(112 W. Main St. 316-767-5911. Closed Mon.)*, built in 1857 by Seth M. Hays, is Kansas' oldest continuously operating restaurant. **Kaw Mission S.H.S.** *(500 N. Mission St. 316-767-5410. Closed Mon.)*, a three-story stone structure built in 1850-51, was a boarding school for Kaw (or Kansa) boys, and later the area's first school for settlers' children.

First Territorial Capitol, Fort Riley

Dodge City ···························

Fort Dodge was established in 1865 to protect travel on the Santa Fe Trail. The nearby settlement known as Dodge City was founded as a buffalo-hunting center in 1872, and soon became infamous for lawlessness. **Boot Hill Museum** *(Front St. 316-227-8188. Adm. fee)* recalls the Wild West days; it's located at the old Boot Hill Cemetery, where many victims of violence were buried. A reconstruction of 1870s **Front Street** includes the Long Branch Saloon, a printing office, a general store, and actors who reenact gunfights and offer stagecoach rides.

Kansas City Area ·····························

Shawnee Indian Mission State Historic Site *(3403 W. 53rd St., Fairway. 913-262-0867. Closed Mon.)* Between 1839 and 1862, as many as 200 boys and girls at a time, mostly Shawnee or Delaware, lived at this Methodist mission on a branch of the Santa Fe Trail, attending school and learning blacksmithing, carpentry, and sewing. Visitors today can see fine period items in restored living quarters and schoolrooms; the 1841 **East Building** (where the territorial "Bogus Legislature" met in 1855 to pass pro-slavery laws) and 1845 **North Building** are open for tours.

Mahaffie Farmstead and Stagecoach Stop Historic Site *(1100 Kansas City Rd., Olathe. 913-782-6972. Closed Jan. and weekends Feb.-April; fee for tours)* The cornerstone reads "1865" on this two-story house built of locally quarried limestone. The farm was the first stop on the Santa Fe Trail out of Westport, Missouri; until 1869, when the railroad came through, stage passengers took meals in the cellar kitchen-dining room, now restored. Outside, the stone icehouse and barn—the latter built with wooden pegs rather than nails—also date from the stage-stop era.

Fort Leavenworth *(US 73. 913-684-5604)* Military leaders from George Armstrong Custer to Douglas MacArthur served at Fort Leavenworth; established in 1827, it's the oldest continually operational post west of the Mississippi. Historic sites at the fort include the **Rookery,** built in 1834 as the first permanent headquarters, and the **Main Parade Ground.** The fort's premier attraction is the **Frontier Army Museum** *(Reynolds Ave. 913-684-3191),* popular for its collection of military horse-drawn vehicles, including a carriage used by Abraham Lincoln during his campaign for the U.S. Presidency in 1859.

Kansas City, Missouri *(1 mile E via I-70)* See page 265.

Independence, Missouri *(10 miles E via I-70)* See pages 265-266.

Jesse James Farm and Museum, Missouri *(27 miles NE via I-35 and Mo. 92, near Kearney)* See page 266.

Topeka ·····························

(Convention & Visitors Bureau, 1275 S.W. Topeka Blvd. 913-234-1030) Topeka was founded by "free-state" (antislavery) emigrants from New England in 1854 at the Oregon Trail crossing of the Kansas River. A century later, in 1954, the U.S. Supreme Court issued its landmark ruling against school desegregation in the *Brown v. Board of Education of Topeka* case; **Monroe Elementary School** *(1515 Monroe St.),* attended by African-American student Linda Brown when she was denied admission to an all-white school, is under development as a national historic site. The **State Capitol** *(10th and Harrison Sts. 913-296-3966),* started in 1866, houses murals by Kansas artist John Steuart Curry.

Historic Ward-Meade Park *(124 N.W. Fillmore St. 913-368-3888. Adm. fee)* Wheelwright Anthony Ward settled at this site near the Kansas River in 1854; a replica of his log cabin stands near the two-story, brick-and-limestone house he built in the 1870s. Occupied by family members until the 1960s, the Victorian home is furnished with period items. Also located in the 6-acre complex are a **Santa Fe railroad depot** from nearby Pauline and a reconstruction of an early 1900s drugstore—with a working soda fountain—from Topeka's Potwin historic district.

Kansas Museum of History *(Off I-70, at 6425 S.W. 6th Ave. 913-272-8681)*

Chisholm Trail

Though its Kansas heyday was brief—from 1867 to 1884—the Chisholm Trail holds a romantic place in American history, evoking images of leathery cowboys driving longhorn herds northward across the plains. The famous cattle trail was named for Jesse Chisholm, a half-Cherokee trader who pioneered a road from Kansas through Indian Territory. Originally only a small part of the whole, "Chisholm's trail" came to designate a journey of more than 900 miles from southern Texas to Abilene, Kansas. After the Civil War, cattle drives were the only way to get livestock to railheads and eastern markets. The practice ended in the 1880s, a victim of railroad expansion and ranching methods that included barbed wire for carving rangeland into pastures.

261

"Voices from the Heartland" is the theme of the museum's main gallery; exhibits range from artifacts of hunters who roamed the region 5,000 years ago to a flashy McDonald's sign from 1961. Especially noteworthy are a replica Cheyenne buffalo-hide tepee and an 1880 locomotive from the Atchison, Topeka & Santa Fe line.

Wichita ···

(Convention & Visitors Bureau, 100 S. Main St. 316-265-2800 or 800-288-9424) Named for the Wichita Indians, whose villages once dotted the nearby prairie, Kansas' largest city was a booming cattle-marketing center in the late 19th century.

Wichita-Sedgwick County Historical Museum (204 S. Main St. 316-265-9314. Closed Mon.; adm. fee) Wichita's 1892 City Hall now recounts local history with Victorian furnishings, a turn-of-the-century drugstore, and displays on Native Americans, agriculture, and commerce.

Indian Center Museum (650 N. Seneca St. 316-262-5221. Closed Mon. Jan.-March; adm. fee) The museum features traditional artifacts from several Native American tribes.

Old Cowtown Museum (1871 Sim Park Dr. 316-264-0671. March-Oct.; adm. fee) More than 30 restored buildings help visitors experience Wichita's "cowtown" era of the 1870s, with living history interpreters, the first jail, a one-room school, a blacksmith shop, and a saloon.

Excursion

KAUFFMAN MUSEUM (25 miles N via I-135. 27th and Main Sts., North Newton. 316-283-1612. Closed Mon.; adm. fee) "Of Land and People" is the focus of this museum, which concentrates on the Mennonites who emigrated from Europe to settle on the plains in the 1870s. Grassland ecology (visitors walk past a restored tallgrass prairie), the Cheyenne Indians, and frontier farm life are other featured subjects at the museum.

Other Sites in Kansas

Amelia Earhart Birthplace (223 N. Terrace St., Atchison. 913-367-4217. May-Sept. or by appt.; donations) The two-story frame house where the aviatrix was born, in 1897, now displays many of her personal items.

Fort Larned N.H.S. (6 miles W of Larned on Kans. 156. 316-285-6911. Adm. fee) Established in 1860, Fort Larned protected goods and travelers on the Santa Fe Trail from Indian attacks. In 1866-68 the original adobe structures were replaced with the wood-and-sandstone buildings that stand today, including barracks and officers quarters.

Fort Scott N.H.S. (Old Fort Blvd., Fort Scott. 316-223-0310. Adm. fee) The restored and reconstructed buildings here—barracks, stables, living quarters, and auxiliary structures—reflect the fort's role as frontier outpost.

Hollenberg Pony Express Station (2 miles NE of Hanover on Kans. 243. 913-337-2635. Wed.-Sun.) This frame 1857 building, restored to its 1860 appearance, is the only original, unaltered station remaining along the nearly 2,000-mile route of the Pony Express.

Pawnee Indian Village S.H.S. (22 miles NW of Belleville via US 36 and Kans. 266. 913-361-2255. Wed.-Sun.) A museum built around the excavated floor of an 1820s earth lodge interprets life on the Great Plains. A walkway passes other lodge sites, storage pits, and fortifications.

Missouri

Gateway Arch, St. Louis's symbolic portal to the West

French merchants and farmers were the first Europeans to settle in what is now Missouri, founding Mississippi River towns such as Ste. Genevieve and St. Louis in the mid-1700s. The fur trade and cheap land sparked early settlement here. After the Louisiana Purchase of 1803, travel on the Missouri River created Missouri's enduring legacy as gateway to the American West; St. Louis, Independence, and St. Joseph all served as major departure points for westbound pioneers. Missouri entered the Union as a slave state in 1821 following the famous Missouri Compromise, in which the United States attempted—ineffectually, as it turned out—to deal with the divisive issue of slavery. In the 19th century, St. Louis developed into a major manufacturing center, and Kansas City became a hub for the livestock trade; these sprawling metropolitan areas occupy opposite borders of a state that otherwise is mostly rural.

Hannibal

Beginning in 1839, the citizenry of Hannibal included a mischievous boy named Sam Clemens, who occasionally took time off from exasperating his elders to run to the Mississippi riverfront and watch steamboats. Later, the author who called himself Mark Twain drew on those days to create *The Adventures of Tom Sawyer* and *Adventures of Huckleberry Finn*.

Mark Twain Boyhood Home and Museum (*208 Hill St. 573-221-9010. Adm. fee*) The Clemens family moved to Hannibal when Sam was four years old, and into this two-story, clapboard house five years later. A 1990-91 restoration returned the building to a more authentic appearance, adding a missing kitchen and bedroom. The museum displays memorabilia, including one of the writer's famous white suits.

Mark Twain Birthplace S.H.S., near Florida

Excursion

MARK TWAIN BIRTHPLACE S.H.S. *(35 miles SW via US 36 and 24 and Mo. 107. 573-565-3449. Adm. fee)* In 1835 Mark Twain was born in a two-room house in what he later remembered as the "almost invisible" village of Florida. The home was relocated and preserved within a museum, which also houses his carriage, writing desk, and proof sheets of *Tom Sawyer.*

Hermann ···

Founded in the 1830s, Hermann was one of the most successful German settlements in Missouri, and still retains a distinctly Old World flavor. The **Historic Hermann Museum** *(4th and Schiller Sts. 573-486-2017. April-Oct.; adm. fee)* recounts local history in an 1871 schoolhouse. Winemaking was a tradition settlers brought to the frontier: The 1852 **Hermannhof Winery** *(Mo. 100E. 573-486-5959)* and **Stone Hill Winery** *(Mo. 100S. 573-486-2129. Adm. fee),* established in 1847, offer tours and tastings.

Deutschheim S.H.S. *(109 W. 2nd St. 573-486-2200. Adm. fee)* Deutschheim— German home—is dedicated to preserving Missouri's German heritage. The 1840 **Pommer-Gentner House** re-creates a comfortable home of the early period of immigration, with Biedermeier furniture and imported porcelain. The 1842-1869 **Strehly House,** with its vivid colors and authentic furnishings, interprets middle-class life of the 1860s to 1880s.

Jefferson City ··································

(Chamber of Commerce, 213 Adams St. 573-634-3616 or 800-769-4183) Jealousy among towns vying to become state capital in 1821 possibly was a factor in the selection of the new "City of Jefferson," on the Missouri River, as the seat of government. St. Charles served as temporary capital until Jefferson City's first capitol building was completed in 1826.

State Capitol Building *(E. Capitol Ave. 573-751-4127)* After the second structure, like the first, was destroyed by fire, construction began in 1913 on this classical-style building of Missouri limestone. In corridors on either side of the rotunda, the **Missouri State Museum** offers exhibits on history and natural resources. For many visitors, the highlight of a State Capitol tour is the Thomas Hart Benton mural. The artist outraged many legislators in 1937 with his "Social History of the State of Missouri," which unflinchingly depicts slavery, religious intolerance, and crime.

Jefferson Landing S.H.S. *(Jefferson St. at the Missouri River. 573-751-3475)* Three buildings near the capitol date from when Jefferson City was a busy steamboat port. The **Lohman Building** (circa 1839) served as a hotel, grocery, and warehouse; it houses a small museum with exhibits on local history. The **Union Hotel** (1855), built during the river boom days, houses the Amtrak station and an exhibit hall. The **Christopher Maus House**

(1854) is not open to the public, but the exterior has been carefully restored.

Excursion

WINSTON CHURCHILL MEMORIAL AND LIBRARY *(25 miles NE via US 54, in Fulton. 573-592-1369. Adm. fee)* Winston Churchill popularized the phrase "Iron Curtain" in a 1946 speech at Westminster College in Fulton. As a memorial to the British statesman, London's Church of St. Mary the Virgin, Aldermanbury—built by Christopher Wren from 1670 to 1677 and gutted by German bombs in 1940—was brought to the campus and beautifully reconstructed in the 1960s. A museum beneath the chapel displays Churchill memorabilia, including four of his original paintings.

Kansas City ···

(Convention & Visitors Bureau, 1100 Main St. 816-221-5242 or 800-767-7700) Kansas City was born in 1821, when François Chouteau established a trading post near the confluence of the Missouri and Kansas Rivers. Travel on the Santa Fe Trail helped the settlement grow, and by 1885 the city was a railroad and livestock-trading hub.

Kansas City Museum *(3218 Gladstone Blvd. 816-483-8300. Closed Mon.; adm. fee)* The Long Mansion, a 50-room structure built in 1909-1910, houses exhibits on the city's history, from the Osage Indians through the days of steamboats and minstrel shows to the growth of commerce. A natural history hall, planetarium, and Weather Park are other attractions. The Long Mansion is one of several grand 19th- and early 20th-century houses in the **Scarritt Neighborhood,** on a bluff overlooking the Missouri River.

265

Arabia Steamboat Museum *(400 Grand Ave. 816-471-4030. Adm. fee)* On September 5, 1856, the steamboat *Arabia* hit a tree stump and sank in the Missouri River. In 1988 salvagers recovered an enormous collection of trade goods and artifacts. The cargo—Bohemian beads, Wedgwood china, whale-oil lamps, and farming supplies, to name only a few items—provides a fascinating look at frontier life.

American Royal Museum and Visitor Center *(1701 American Royal Court. 816-221-9800. Tues.-Sat.; adm. fee)* The American Royal Livestock Show, begun in 1899, is one focus of this entertaining, hands-on museum. Visitors can learn what a sheep fitter does or, in computer simulation, match hog-grading skills with a professional judge.

Thomas Hart Benton Home and Studio State Historic Site *(3616 Belleview. 816-931-5722. Fee for tours)* Missouri-born artist Thomas Hart Benton moved into this stone-and-shingle house in 1939, at age 50; he lived and worked here for the rest of his life. The studio, where Benton died in 1975, maintains the cluttered look of an active workplace.

Black Archives of Mid-America *(2033 Vine St. 816-483-1300. Mon.-Fri. Adm. fee)* Housed in a historic fire station, the archives include exhibits on local and regional African-American history and culture, as well as an authentic Missouri slave cabin and memorabilia of the "buffalo soldiers," members of formerly all-black units of the U.S. Army.

Excursions

KANSAS CITY, KANSAS *(1 mile W via I-70)* See pages 260-261.

INDEPENDENCE *(10 miles E via I-70 or US 24)* A fine collection of materials recounting the life and times of our 33rd President rewards visitors to the **Harry S. Truman Library** *(US 24 and Delaware St. 816-833-1225. Adm. fee).* A reproduction of the Truman-era White House Oval Office, a 1950 Lincoln limousine, and the *Chicago Daily Tribune* edition proclaiming "Dewey Defeats Truman" are highlights, along with the plaque reading "The buck stops here" that once sat on the President's desk. Almost unchanged since Harry and Bess lived here, the summer White House, now the **Harry S. Truman National Historic Site** *(Tickets for tours of house, 291 N. Delaware St., available at Information Center, 223 N. Main St. 816-254-7199. Closed Mon. Labor Day–Mem. Day; adm. fee),* reflects the President's folksy ways. Truman's hat rests on a rack in the hall; two chairs in the library are reminders that reading was the usual evening entertainment.

Independence was once the most important outfitting post for 19th-century traders and wagon trains heading west on the Santa Fe, Oregon, and California Trails. Exhibits at the **National Frontier Trails Center** *(318 W. Pacific St. 816-325-7575. Adm. fee)* tell the story of people who, in the words of a 13-year-old emigrant girl, "bade farewell to kindred and friends" and set out on the long, difficult, and often dangerous journey.

MISSOURI TOWN 1855 *(20 miles E via I-70 and Mo. 7, S of Blue Springs. 816-524-8770. Mid-April–mid-Nov. Wed.-Sun., weekends only rest of year; adm. fee)* More than 30 buildings re-create a 19th-century farming village. Living history interpreters include blacksmiths, quilters, and gardeners; structures range from the Georgian **Squire's House** to a log **"dogtrot" tavern.**

FORT OSAGE *(20 miles E via US 24, N of Sibley. 816-650-5737. Mid-April–mid-Nov. Wed.-Sun., weekends only rest of year; adm. fee)* Lewis and Clark passed this bluff overlooking the Missouri River in 1804; four years later, Clark returned to build Fort Osage, a trading post intended to strengthen ties with the Osage Indians. The fort, reconstructed as it appeared in 1812, includes a tall stockade fence, blockhouses, barracks, and trade house.

BATTLE OF LEXINGTON S.H.S. *(35 miles E via US 24, N of Lexington. 816-259-4654. Fee for tours)* Centerpiece of this Civil War site is **Anderson House,** an 1853 home used as a hospital by Union and Confederate troops; damage caused by bullets and grapeshot during the September 18-20, 1861, clash is still visible. Furnishings include an immense rococo-revival bed.

JESSE JAMES FARM AND MUSEUM *(22 miles NE via I-35 and Mo. 92, E of Kearney. 816-628-6065. Adm. fee)* The notorious outlaw was born in a small cabin here in 1847. Jesse and brother Frank spent their childhood on this farm before joining the Younger brothers and other outlaws in post-Civil War careers as bank and train robbers. The cabin and nearby museum display many James family artifacts.

Missouri Town 1855

WATKINS WOOLEN MILL S.H.S. *(25 miles NE via I-35, Mo. 92, and US 69, N of Excelsior Springs. 816-580-3387. Adm. fee)* Well worth a detour off the main roads, the three-story brick mill is a 19th-century textile factory with original steam-powered machinery used to card, spin, weave, and finish. Built in 1860, the mill operated until nearly the turn of the century, but the availability of ready-made clothing hastened its demise.

St. Joseph ··

(Convention & Visitors Bureau, 109 S. 4th St. 816-233-6688 or 800-785-0360) Founded in 1843, St. Joseph became an important jumping-off point for settlers and adventurers heading west in the mid-19th century. The romantic but short-lived Pony Express was founded here.

Patee House Museum *(12th and Penn Sts. 816-232-8206. Closed Mon.-Fri. Nov.-March; adm. fee)* Stuffed full of antiques and artifacts—from a steam locomotive to musical instruments to murder weapons (including an electric drill)—the expansive Patee House invites browsing. Built as a luxury hotel in 1858, the structure was later a college, a shirt factory, and an epileptic sanitarium. The Pony Express was headquartered in the hotel, and the Union Army had offices here during the Civil War. The house where Jesse James was shot, in 1882, has been moved to the museum grounds.

Pony Express National Memorial, St. Joseph

Pony Express National Memorial *(914 Penn St. 816-279-5059. Adm. fee)* Well-designed displays in the service's original stables tell the story of the Pony Express, which carried mail between St. Joseph and Sacramento, California, from 1860 until 1861, when the transcontinental telegraph began service. The Express depended on daring young riders to cross nearly 2,000 miles in as few as ten days.

Robidoux Row *(3rd and Poulin Sts. 816-232-5861. Closed Mon. all year and also Sun. Nov.-April; adm. fee)* Completed in the 1850s by Joseph Robidoux, St. Joseph's founder, these brick apartments served as an early motel for newcomers and transients. The surviving four (of seven) apartments have been restored and furnished with period items.

St. Joseph Museum *(1100 Charles St. 816-232-8471 or 800-530-8866. Adm. fee)* Native American artifacts highlight this museum in an 1879 mansion built by local merchant William M. Wyeth. Other exhibits focus on St. Joseph history, from the era of the earliest settlers to the 20th century.

St. Louis ··

(Convention & Visitors Commission, 10 S. Broadway. 314-421-1023 or 800-888-3861) In 1764 French fur trader Pierre Laclede and his deputy Auguste Chouteau established a settlement on the Mississippi River's west bank and named it for Louis IX. After the Louisiana Purchase of 1803, St. Louis's location near the confluence of the Mississippi and Missouri Rivers made it a gateway for westward advancement. Lewis and Clark provisioned here before setting out for the Pacific in 1804. St. Louis grew into a bustling river port during the steamboat days of the mid-1800s.

Jefferson National Expansion Memorial *(11 N. 4th St. 314-425-4465. Adm. fee)* The most conspicuous part of this riverside complex is the graceful, 630-foot-tall **Gateway Arch** *(Fare for tram ride to top)*, a symbolic portal to the West. Designed by Eero Saarinen in 1947 and completed in 1965, the stainless-steel structure is an engineering and architectural triumph. Below the arch, visitors are welcomed to the **Museum of Westward**

Expansion by a bronze statue of Thomas Jefferson, who foresaw that the consequences of his Louisiana Purchase would extend far into the future. The museum recalls explorers, Native Americans, soldiers, cowboys, and farm families of the 19th-century frontier. Two blocks west is the green-domed **Old Courthouse.** The Dred Scott Trial, which led to a national debate on slavery, began here in the late 1840s. The 1839-1862 building now houses exhibits on the city's history.

Interior of Campbell House, St. Louis

The dedication of **Eads Bridge** over the Mississippi on July 4, 1874, occasioned the biggest celebration St. Louis had ever seen, including a 14-mile parade. Its designer, self-taught engineer James B. Eads, used tubular chrome alloy steel to build an elegant structure with intricately braced arches. The bridge can be seen from the grounds of the Gateway Arch.

Old Cathedral (*209 Walnut St. 314-231-3250. Adm. fee for museum*) Pierre Laclede set aside land for a church shortly after founding his riverside outpost in 1764; the present Basilica of St. Louis, dating from the 1830s, occupies the original site, now just a short walk from the Gateway Arch. The interior was gracefully restored in 1960. The adjoining museum includes the tomb of the first bishop of St. Louis.

Campbell House Museum (*1508 Locust St. 314-421-0325. March-Dec. Tues.-Sun.; adm. fee*) Robert Campbell, a wealthy fur trader and banker, bought a house in an upper-class St. Louis neighborhood in 1854; he and his wife, Virginia, decorated it with hand-carved furniture, ornate chandeliers, and marble fireplaces. The 1851 house was occupied by the couple's reclusive bachelor sons until the last died in 1938, leaving a virtual time capsule of Victorian furnishings and design.

Scott Joplin House State Historic Site (*2658 Delmar Blvd. 314-533-1003. Adm. fee*) The great composer of "Maple Leaf Rag" and "The Entertainer" lived here just after the turn of the century, probably around 1902-04. The upstairs apartment has been restored to a period appearance; downstairs exhibits focus on Joplin's life and the development of ragtime.

Missouri History Museum (*Forest Park, off Lindell Blvd. 314-746-4599. Closed Mon.*) The history of St. Louis—from Native Americans to the 1904 World's Fair to Budweiser beer—is included in the museum's collections. Memorabilia from Charles Lindbergh's flight across the Atlantic in *The Spirit of St. Louis* includes his flight suit, sunglasses, and wrappers from the gum he chewed to stay awake.

Excursions

CAHOKIA MOUNDS, ILLINOIS (*7 miles E via I-55/70*) See page 221.
JEFFERSON BARRACKS HISTORIC COUNTY PARK (*10 miles S via I-55, I-255, and Mo. 231. 314-544-5714. Closed Mon. and Jan.*) Site of the country's first infantry "school of practice" (analogous to a basic-training camp), the barracks prepared soldiers to serve in the U.S. military from 1826 to 1946 and to escort settlers who were bound for the West. Restored

19th-century buildings exhibit the post's long and varied history.

THORNHILL (*20 miles W via I-64/40 and Olive Blvd., in Faust County Park, Chesterfield. 314-532-7298. Wed.-Sun. Fee for tours*) The residence of Frederick Bates, Missouri's second governor, was completed in 1823. The two-story wood structure is the oldest governor's home in the state. Nearby, the **St. Louis Carousel** (*Fare for rides*), dating from around 1920, has been beautifully restored.

DANIEL BOONE HOME (*40 miles W via US 40/61, Mo. 94, and Rte. F. 314-987-2221. March-Nov.; adm. fee*) The celebrated frontiersman spent his last years in this four-story house; he died in a second-floor bedroom in 1820. Constructed between 1803 and 1810, the home contains many of the Boone family's possessions.

ST. CHARLES (*30 miles NW via I-70*) Missouri's first legislature met in upstairs rooms of a brick federal-style building here, now the **First Missouri State Capitol S.H.S.** (*200 S. Main St. 314-946-9282. Fee for tours*), from 1821 until 1826, when the capitol in Jefferson City was completed. Exhibits of the famed expedition and some Clark family items highlight the **Lewis and Clark Center** (*701 Riverside Dr. 314-947-3199. Adm. fee*) in the city's attractive historic district.

Ste. Genevieve ····················

Fertile bottomland and a salt spring attracted Native Americans and French colonists to the Mississippi River site that became Ste. Genevieve, the first permanent settlement in Missouri. Founded about 1750, the town began moving to higher ground after floods in 1785. German immigrants who came in the 1840s added more masonry houses to Ste. Genevieve's mostly vertical-log structures. The **Great River Road Interpretive Center** (*66 S. Main St. 573-883-7097*) offers exhibits and a film on local history.

Felix Valle House State Historic Site (*Merchant and 2nd Sts. 573-883-7102. Adm. fee*) This limestone building is one of the most notable structures in the **Ste. Genevieve Historic District.** Built in 1818 in the federal style, it has been restored to reflect use as both a residence and a store.

Bolduc House Museum (*125 S. Main St. 573-883-3105. April-Oct.; adm. fee*) Period furnishings enhance one of the region's finest examples of French colonial architecture. A vertical-log building probably dating from around 1785, the house comprises two rooms connected by a hallway, surrounded by a stockade fence.

Other Sites in Missouri

Arrow Rock State Historic Site (*Mo. 41, in Arrow Rock. 816-837-3330. Fee for tours*) Settled early in the 19th century, the Arrow Rock site comprises such historic buildings as the 1834 Old Tavern and the home of noted frontier artist and politician George Caleb Bingham.

Missouri's Germans
Dreams of land and freedom in "New Germany" brought thousands of German immigrants to Missouri in the mid-19th century, when settlers founded Westphalia, New Hamburg, Rhineland, and Wittenberg. In 1855, a visitor said the Missouri River village of Hermann had "more German sociability than perhaps anywhere else in America." The town retains a distinctly Old World flavor—literally, in the case of its long-established wineries. By 1860 more than half of foreign-born Missourians were German. Their antislavery views greatly influenced the course of the Civil War: St. Louis's Home Guard, largely made up of Germans, defended the federal arsenal from secessionist forces, keeping the vital port city in the Union.

Other Sites in Missouri

Cape Girardeau (*Convention & Visitors Bureau, 2121 Broadway. 573-335-1631 or 800-777-0068*) The history of this Mississippi River town, founded in 1793 by a French trader, is on display at the **Cape River Heritage Museum** (*538 Independence. 573-334-0405. March-Dec. Wed. and Fri.-Sat., or by appt.; adm. fee*). The 1883 **Glenn House** (*325 S. Spanish St. 573-334-1177. April-Dec. Wed.-Sat.; adm. fee*) exhibits period furnishings.

Dillard Mill State Historic Site (*Off Mo. 49, in Dillard. 573-244-3120. Fee for tours*) Huzzah and Indian Creeks join at this picturesque gristmill. Dating from 1904-08, the mill operated until the 1950s; now restored, it lets visitors see how wheat becomes flour the old-fashioned way.

Fort Davidson S.H.S. (*Rte. V, in Pilot Knob. 573-546-3454*) Exhibits depict the September 27, 1864, Battle of Pilot Knob, which lasted less than an hour yet claimed 1,200 casualties. You can still see Union earthworks.

Gen. John J. Pershing Boyhood Home S.H.S. (*Mo. 5, in Laclede. 816-963-2525. Fee for tours*) "Black Jack" Pershing, who pursued Pancho Villa in Mexico and led American forces in World War I, is memorialized in the house where he lived from age six until he left for West Point in 1881.

George Washington Carver National Monument (*Off Rte. V, in Diamond. 417-325-4151*) The African-American agronomist was born into slavery here. A trail winds through prairie and forest that inspired Carver's love of "flowers, rocks, animals, plants, and all other aspects of His creation."

Harry S. Truman Birthplace State Historic Site (*Off US 160, in Lamar. 417-682-2279*) The modest frame house where Truman was born on May 8, 1884, offers tours interpreting the family history. Built in the early 1880s, the six-room house is furnished with period items.

Maramec Museum (*Off Mo. 8, SE of St. James. 573-265-7124. April-Oct.*) Maramec Iron Works, begun in 1826, was the first such enterprise west of the Mississippi; the factory made cannonballs and armor for gunboats during the Civil War. Exhibits and mining artifacts tell the ironworks story; remains of an 1857 blast furnace can be seen nearby.

Missouri Mines S.H.S. (*Mo. 32, in Park Hills. 573-431-6226. Fee for tours*) Visitors to a former milling complex learn about mining in Missouri's Old Lead Belt—for 60 years the major lead-producing district in the U.S.

Dillard Mill State Historic Site

New Madrid A series of earthquakes in 1811-12, caused by slippage along the New Madrid Fault, were among the most powerful ever experienced in North America. The **New Madrid Historical Museum** (*1 Main St. 573-748-5944. Adm. fee*) presents exhibits on the quakes and on area Civil War battles. **Hunter-Dawson S.H.S.** (*Dawson Rd. 573-748-5340. Fee for tours*) offers tours of a 15-room mansion built in 1859-1860 for a local merchant, with mostly original furnishings.

Washington State Park (*Mo. 21, 8 miles SW of De Soto. 314-586-2995*) Indians using this area as a ceremonial site left petroglyphs dating from the period before European exploration.

Wilson's Creek Natl. Battlefield (*Rte. ZZ, SW of Springfield. 417-732-2662. Adm. fee*) A 5-mile auto route winds through the site of the first major Civil War battle west of the Mississippi, in August 1861. It allowed Confederates to occupy Springfield.

Oklahoma

Fort Washita Military Park, northwest of Durant

Many places in America have Indian names, but in no other is that heritage so appropriate as in the Sooner State. "Oklahoma" derives from Choctaw words meaning "red people," and the state's history is inextricably intertwined with that of its Native American population. Designated soon after the Louisiana Purchase as a place of "removal," the region known as Indian Territory only rarely provided a peaceful home for displaced peoples. Immigrant tribes were attacked by fierce Plains Indians; the Civil War split the Indian population; railroads and settlers encroached on lands that had been granted by treaty. Beginning in 1889, land rushes took away more Indian holdings, as the population of the territory tripled between 1890 and 1900. (Some settlers jumped the opening gun, claiming choice areas "sooner" than lawful newcomers and inspiring one of Oklahoma's nicknames.) Statehood in 1907 ended Native American dreams of a separate homeland. Oil and gas discoveries early in this century transformed many Oklahoma villages into boomtowns, bringing prosperity undreamed of by the pioneers.

Muskogee

This city on the Arkansas River is named for the Muskogee people (called Creek by European settlers), one of the Five Civilized Tribes "removed" to Indian Territory from the southeast in the 19th century.

Five Civilized Tribes Museum (*Agency Hill on Honor Heights Dr. 918-683-1701. Adm. fee*) Constructed in 1875 as the Union Indian Agency, the museum houses artifacts of Cherokee, Chickasaw, Choctaw, Creek, and

Seminole, telling the story of the Trail of Tears and settlement in Indian Territory. An art gallery displays works by Native Americans.

Excursions

CREEK COUNCIL HOUSE MUSEUM (*45 miles SW via US 62, in Okmulgee. 918-756-2324. Tues.-Sat.*) A two-story brick building erected in 1878 served as the capitol of the Creek nation until tribal sovereignty was abolished in 1906. Upstairs rooms accommodated the House of Kings and House of Warriors, the two houses of the Creek Legislature. Fine exhibits interpret tribal history from pre-removal days to the modern era.

FORT GIBSON MILITARY PARK (*10 miles E via US 62 and Okla. 80, in Fort Gibson. 918-478-2669. Adm. fee*) Established in 1824 to try to quell conflicts between Osage and Cherokee, Fort Gibson later served as an administrative center, distributing supplies to Cherokee, Creek, and Seminole who had reached the end of the Trail of Tears. The present stockade is a WPA-era reconstruction. The stone barracks and commissary on Garrison Hill date from the mid-1840s to about 1870.

CHEROKEE HERITAGE CENTER (*30 miles E via US 62. 918-456-6007. Adm. fee*) One of the most significant Native American sites in the region, the center encompasses four attractions. The **Cherokee National Museum** (*March-Dec.*) introduces visitors to the tribe's history; **Tsa-La-gi Ancient Village** (*May–Labor Day*) depicts life before European contact; **Adams Corner Rural Village** (*March-Dec.*) demonstrates life after removal to Indian Territory; and the **Trail of Tears Drama** (*July–mid-Aug.*) presents the Cherokee story from the era of removal to Oklahoma statehood in 1907.

Oklahoma City ·······································

(*Convention & Visitors Bureau, 189 W. Sheridan Ave. 405-297-8912*) Having burst into life on April 22, 1889—the day of the Great Land Run—Oklahoma City soon became a dominant settlement. It displaced Guthrie as state capital in 1910, in a move that had as much to do with political scheming as with practicality.

45th Infantry Division Museum (*2145 N.E. 36th St. 405-424-5313. Closed Mon.*) Memorabilia of the Oklahoma-based division that fought with distinction in World War II and Korea highlight this museum. One room is devoted to Pulitzer Prize-winning cartoonist Bill Mauldin, who served in the 45th; tanks, airplanes, and artillery pieces are displayed on the grounds.

Harn Homestead and 1889er Museum (*313 N.E. 16th St. 405-235-4058. Tues.-Sat.; adm. fee*) The pioneer Harn family's 1904 Queen Anne-style farmhouse is the centerpiece of a collection of noteworthy buildings including an 1890s schoolhouse, two smaller homes, and a reconstructed barn with an enclosed windmill.

National Cowboy Hall of Fame (*1700 N.E. 63rd St. 405-478-2250. Adm. fee*) While there are cowboys (and -girls) aplenty here, this museum embraces all aspects of the West, from wildlife and Native Americans to rodeo stars and Western movies. An extensive art collection includes works by Albert Bierstadt, Frederic Remington, and Charles M. Russell. Among the many artifacts on display are Bob Wills's fiddle and a buggy used in the 1889 Oklahoma land run.

Oklahoma State Museum of History (*2100 N. Lincoln Blvd. 405-521-2491. Mon.-Sat.*) Artifacts from the Paleo-Indian period begin a visit to this museum, which takes visitors through the territorial years, when towns sprang up on the prairie like mushrooms, and into the statehood era. An 1860s buffalo-hide tepee and a restored stagecoach are among the striking objects in the collection.

Excursions

CHISHOLM TRAIL MUSEUM (*45 miles NW via Okla. 3 and US 81, in Kingfisher. 405-375-5176. Tues.-Sun.*) Though located on a branch of the Chisholm Trail, this fine collection ranges far beyond the subject of the famed cattle-drive route. Indian artifacts (including a game bag used by Sitting Bull), antique farm implements, an extensive barbed wire collection, and a horse-drawn hearse occupy the museum. Outside are the Bank of Kingfisher (dating from land-run days), a 1902 schoolhouse, and a log cabin once owned by the mother of members of the infamous Dalton Gang. The adjoining 1892 **Seay Mansion** was the home of Oklahoma's second territorial governor.

GUTHRIE (*32 miles N via I-35*) Founded in 1889, the city that was Oklahoma's territorial (and first state) capital contains one of the largest and best preserved historic districts, with dozens of late 19th-century buildings inviting leisurely exploration of its downtown area. The **Scottish Rite Masonic Temple** (*900 E. Oklahoma Ave. 405-282-1281. Tues.-Sun.; adm. fee*) is well worth a visit; its 268,000 square feet comprise a staggering conglomeration of stained glass, elaborate decorative designs, and grand columned spaces. The **Oklahoma Territorial Museum** (*406 E. Oklahoma Ave. 405-282-1889. Tues.-Sun.; donations*) features exhibits on the period between the land runs and statehood; the restored 1902 **Carnegie Library** stands next door. The **State Capital Publishing Museum** (*301 W. Harrison. 405-282-4123. Tues.-Sun.*) is a don't-miss site: Printing equipment and a splendid turn-of-the-century sales office create a time capsule of pioneer commerce.

Tulsa ·····························

(*Chamber of Commerce, 616 S. Boston Ave. 918-585-1201*) Born as a trading center and rail depot, Tulsa boomed when oil was discovered just after the turn of the century. A portion of its newfound wealth went into the construction of splendid art deco buildings, which remain.

Celebration of Eighty-niner Day in Guthrie

Gilcrease Museum (*1400 Gilcrease Museum Rd. 918-596-2700. Tues.-Sun.; donations*) One of Oklahoma's most rewarding attractions, the Gilcrease offers works ranging from John James Audubon's original painting of the wild turkey to a copy of the Declaration of Independence signed by John Hancock and Benjamin Franklin to rooms full of paintings by Frederic Remington, Charles M. Russell, George Catlin, and Thomas Moran. Thomas Gilcrease, the oilman who founded the museum, was one-quarter Creek; he encouraged Native American artists, and the resulting work presents a distinctive view of Western life.

Philbrook Museum of Art (*2727 S. Rockford Rd. 918-749-7941. Tues.-Sun.; adm. fee*) Once the home of oilman Waite Phillips, this majestic Italian

Renaissance-style mansion now houses one of the Southwest's leading art collections. American history enthusiasts will head for the museum's lower level to examine the outstanding collection of Native American baskets, ceramics, clothing, and leather- and beadwork.

Excursions

CLAREMORE (*30 miles NE via Okla. 66*) Over the course of nearly 80 years, Claremore hotel owner J.M. Davis amassed some 20,000 firearms, ranging from a 14th-century "hand cannon" to modern military weapons. This extraordinary assemblage, now in the **J.M. Davis Arms and Historical Museum** (*333 N. Lynn Riggs Blvd. 918-341-5707. Donations*), includes guns used by Wild Bill Hickok and Pancho Villa, ornate antique European flintlocks and dueling pistols, and a rather macabre set of items relating to crime and executions.

Will Rogers Memorial (*1720 W. Will Rogers Blvd. 918-341-0719*) Oklahoma's most celebrated native son was one of the world's best known (and most highly paid) entertainers until his death in 1935. This appealing museum displays all manner of memorabilia, from his saddles to items found in the Alaska plane crash that killed him and aviator Wiley Post. Theaters show such Rogers films as *In Old Kentucky* and *State Fair*.

WOOLAROC RANCH, MUSEUM, AND WILDLIFE PRESERVE (*40 miles N via Okla. 11 and 123, near Bartlesville. 918-336-0307. Closed Mon. Sept.-May; adm. fee*) Frank Phillips (brother of the Philbrook Museum's Waite) built a pine-log lodge in the 1920s that he called Woolaroc (from "woods, lakes, and rocks"). Today's museum collection is extensive and eclectic, to say the least: An African elephant head looms over a Sioux war shirt; an anaconda skin hangs above a 1932 Phillips 66 truck. The nearby lodge contains family memorabilia.

Other Sites in Oklahoma

Black Kettle Museum (*US 283 and Okla. 47, Cheyenne. 405-497-3929. Tues.-Sat.*) The museum's collection contains many local history items, including several artifacts related to an 1868 "battle" in which U.S. troops led by Lt. Col. George Armstrong Custer attacked a band of Cheyenne and killed the peace-loving Chief Black Kettle.

Chickasaw Council House Museum (*Courthouse Square, Tishomingo. 405-371-3351. Tues.-Sun.*) Among the exhibits is the 1856 house that served as the Chickasaw nation's first capitol building in Indian Territory.

Fort Washita Military Park (*16 miles NW of Durant, off Okla. 199. 405-924-6502*) The site holds reconstructed barracks of an Army fort built in 1842 to protect Chickasaw and Choctaw from marauding Plains Indians.

Indian City, U.S.A. (*2 miles S of Anadarko, on Okla. 8. 405-247-5661. Adm. fee*) Reconstructions of Indian dwellings include a Navajo hogan, an impressive Wichita council house, and a Pawnee earth lodge.

Will Rogers memorabilia

Sequoyah's Home Site (*11 miles NE of Sallisaw, on Okla. 101. 918-775-2413. Closed Mon.*) Forced to leave Arkansas in 1828, Sequoyah, inventor of the Cherokee alphabet, moved into this log cabin; the museum displays a few original possessions.

Artillery at Pea Ridge National Military Park

Spaniard Hernando de Soto marched through in 1541. Although his exact route isn't known, he probably camped in the Ouachita Mountains at a spot now in Hot Springs National Park. French explorer Henri de Tonti founded the region's first permanent European settlement in 1686: the "Post of Arkansas." The name derives from an Algonquin word for a local Native American tribe. Land that would become Arkansas—part swamp, part rugged mountains—was largely inhospitable to colonists and later gained a reputation as a lawless frontier quarter. Arkansas suffered much in the Civil War; the 1862 Battle of Pea Ridge was one of the largest fights west of the Mississippi River. In time the "Great Swamp" of eastern Arkansas was drained, its bottomland forests were cleared, and agriculture was developed. Western highlands, however, remained thinly populated until recent times. Despite industrial growth, agriculture and forestry still play a part in the economy.

Eureka Springs

"Healing" waters made Eureka Springs a booming resort in the late 19th century; when changing interests (and medical advances) caused an economic decline, the town passed decades virtually untouched. Today its steep, winding streets are lined with historic Victorian structures. Located in an 1889 stone building, the **Eureka Springs Historical Museum**

(95 S. Main St. 501-253-9417. Closed Mon.; adm. fee) provides a good introduction to the town. The **Bank of Eureka Springs** (70 S. Main St. 501-253-
8241) is worth a look for its nicely restored interior. The **Rosalie House**
(282 Spring St. 501-253-7377. Adm. fee), brick with gingerbread trim, was
built by a local businessman in the 1880s.

Excursion

PEA RIDGE NATIONAL MILITARY PARK (25 miles W via US 62. 501-
451-8122. Adm. fee) "The battle that saved Missouri for the Union" took place
here March 7-8, 1862, when Brig. Gen. Samuel R. Curtis's troops turned
back a Confederate force pushing toward St. Louis. A 7-mile auto tour leads
visitors past battle sites; the highlight is a reconstruction of Elkhorn Tavern, a two-story structure near the center of the fighting.

Fayetteville

(Chamber of Commerce, 123 W. Mountain St. 501-521-1710 or 800-766-
4626) In 1871 this Boston Mountain town was selected as home of the
institution that became University of Arkansas; the UA's twin-towered
Old Main (Arkansas Ave.), completed in 1875, is the city's most famous
building. The 1905 Romanesque **Washington County Courthouse** (College and Center Sts.) was designed by noted Arkansas architect Charles L.
Thompson; it and the nearby 1897 **Old County Jail** were built of hand-
cut, locally quarried stone. Fayetteville's oldest home is the **Ridge House**
(230 W. Center St.), built as a log "dogtrot" house in the 1830s.

Headquarters House (118 E. Dickson St. 501-521-2970. Mon.-Fri.; adm.
fee) Constructed in 1853, this house features fine period furnishings. It
served as headquarters for Union and Confederate forces in the Civil War;
a door shows minié ball damage from the Battle of Fayetteville.

Excursions

PRAIRIE GROVE BATTLEFIELD STATE PARK (10 miles W via US 62. 501-
846-2990) The last major Civil War battle in northwestern Arkansas took place
here on December 7, 1862—a bloody clash that ended when Confederate
forces ran low on ammunition and withdrew. The park interprets this important engagement and the war's disastrous effect on the people of the Ozarks;
several historic buildings have been moved to the site.

SHILOH MUSEUM OF OZARK HISTORY (10 miles N via US 71B. 118 W.
Johnson Ave., in Springdale. 501-750-8165. Closed Sun.) Focusing on the history of six northwestern Arkansas counties, the museum's collection
includes exhibits on railroads that opened the region to development.

Fort Smith

Founded as an Army outpost in 1817, Fort Smith grew into a rowdy
border town, gateway to Indian Territory, and magnet for drifters and
outlaws. The **Visitor Center** (2 N. B St. 501-783-8888) is in the 1890s River
Front Hotel—better known as Miss Laura's, for the businesswoman who
bought it in 1903. A former brothel on the National Register of Historic
Places, it has been restored with appropriate decor. **Clayton House** (514 N.
6th St. 501-783-3000. Closed Mon.; adm. fee), built in the 1850s and enlarged
in 1882, is the place to begin a tour of the **Belle Grove Historic District,**
encompassing several 19th-century structures. A driving guide is available.

Fort Smith National Historic Site *(Rogers Ave. and 3rd St. 501-783-3961. Adm. fee)* Only foundation stones remain from the first fort (1817); the second fort's commissary, completed in 1846, stands as one of the city's oldest buildings. The brick 1851 barracks served from 1875 to 1889 as courtroom for famed Judge Isaac C. Parker, who had jurisdiction over Indian Territory to the west. His court is re-created inside; outside is a reproduction of the gallows where 79 criminals were executed.

Old Fort Museum *(320 Rogers Ave. 501-783-7841. Closed Mon.; adm. fee)* This museum recounts local history from frontier days to the modern era. Exhibits include a display on World War II general William O. Darby, who grew up in Fort Smith, and a nicely restored 1920s pharmacy.

Excursion

VAN BUREN *(5 miles N via US 64)* Across the Arkansas River from Fort Smith, Van Buren's historic Main Street comprises several noteworthy structures. A walking guide is available from the Chamber of Commerce in the 1901 **Old Frisco Depot** *(813 Main St. 501-474-2761)*. The turreted 1889 **Crawford County Bank Building** *(633 Main St.)* is now a bed-and-breakfast inn. Performances are still staged at the restored **King Opera House** *(427 Main St.)*. The Italianate **Crawford County Courthouse** *(4th and Main Sts.)*, constructed in 1842, was rebuilt after an 1877 fire.

Little Rock ·······································

(Convention & Visitors Bureau, 100 W. Markham St. 501-376-4781 or 800-844-4781) When Arkansas Territory was established in 1819, the capital was Arkansas Post, a flood-prone town on the lower Arkansas River. Two years later the seat of government moved upstream to a village named for a navigational landmark called the "little rock." In 1957 Little Rock's **Central High School** *(1500 S. Park St. 501-324-2300)* became the center of a confrontation between the governor and federal troops over integration. (See sidebar on page 278).

Arkansas Territorial Restoration *(200 E. 3rd St. 501-324-9351. Fee for tours)* Original hand-hewn logs and cypress floorboards are visible in a room of the 1820s **Hinderliter Grog Shop,** Little Rock's oldest building. Other restored structures include the brick **Brownlee House** and the frame **McVicar House—** 1840s homes with period furniture.

Old State House, Little Rock

Old State House *(300 W. Markham St. 501-324-9685)* One of the most beautiful structures in Arkansas, this Greek Revival building served as State Capitol from 1836 to 1911. The upstairs House Chamber has been called the most historic room in Arkansas: State constitutions were adopted here, and in 1861 the legislature voted to secede from the Union. A downstairs exhibit focuses on Bill Clinton's 1992 presidential campaign.

Excursions

HOT SPRINGS NATIONAL PARK (*55 miles SW via I-30 and US 70. 501-624-3383*) Native Americans supposedly bathed in the thermal springs here; in the heyday of "taking the waters" early in this century, the resort city of Hot Springs attracted celebrities from Babe Ruth to Al Capone. **Bathhouse Row,** on Central Avenue, is the focal point of today's park: The 1912 neoclassical **Buckstaff** is the only one of eight remaining bathhouses still offering baths. The 1915 Renaissance Revival **Fordyce** has been restored and serves as the Visitor Center; its interior includes steam rooms, a gymnasium, and a stained-glass ceiling.

TOLTEC MOUNDS ARCHAEOLOGICAL STATE PARK (*15 miles SE via I-440 and US 165. 501-961-9442. Closed Mon.; adm fee*) In the 1800s, some people thought these earth mounds had been made by Mexico's Toltec. The mounds are now known to have been erected about A.D. 700 to 1025 by the Plum Bayou culture. A three-quarter-mile trail leads past mounds that may have been used for religious ceremonies or burials; two were aligned according to astronomical observations.

Other Sites in Arkansas

Arkansas Post National Memorial (*15 miles N of Dumas, on Ark. 169, off US 165. 501-548-2207*) Though little physical evidence remains, this peaceful spot on the Arkansas River was the site of the first European settlement in what is now Arkansas. The French explorer Henri de Tonti founded a post here in 1686; for a time in the 18th and early 19th centuries it was an important settlement, but when the territorial capital moved to Little Rock in 1821, Arkansas Post went into decline and never recovered.

Helena (*Tourism Comm., Mayor's Office, 226 Perry St. 501-338-9831*) The site of a bloody 1863 Civil War battle, Helena boasts several historic structures. The **Phillips County Museum** includes Civil War memorabilia; the **Delta Cultural Center,** located in a 1912 rail station, interprets the heritage of the land and people of eastern Arkansas.

Old Washington Historic State Park (*Ark. 4, Washington. 501-983-2684. Fee for tours*) Once a thriving settlement, the town of Washington encompasses many structures from the 19th century. The 1874 **Hempstead County Courthouse** is now the Visitor Center; the 1836 **Courthouse** was the Confederate State Capitol when Little Rock was captured by Union troops.

Ozark Folk Center State Park (*1 mile N of Mountain View on Ark. 5. 501-269-3851. Mid-April–Oct.; adm. fee*) The center keeps alive the crafts and music of the Ozarks: Quilters, potters, candlemakers, and weavers demonstrate their skills; musicians perform folk songs in the auditorium.

Central High

Little Rock made world news in 1957, when resistance to school integration forced President Eisenhower to send troops to Central High (now a National Historic Landmark). Images of 101st Airborne Division soldiers protecting black students from mobs made the city a symbol of the strife that beset education in the 1950s. Federal troops patrolled the halls for the rest of the school year; the next year, Central didn't open at all. Integration later proceeded peacefully, but "the long shadow of Little Rock," as local African-American leader Daisy Bates called it, endures in the memories of the people who lived through that unsettling time.

Texas

The Alamo, San Antonio

Spanish explorers scoured Texas in the 1500s for the fabled golden cities. They didn't find them, but Spain claimed the vast expanse and named it for an Indian word meaning "friendly." Little attempt at settlement was made until the early 1700s, when the Spanish established several fortified missions to counter French expeditions into the region. In 1821 Mexico broke away from Spanish rule and offered generous land grants to settle the Texas region. The colonists who came—among them Missourian Stephen F. Austin with 300 families—soon grew restless under Mexican rule. After seven months of rebellion and devastating defeats at the Alamo and the Battle of Coleto, Gen. Sam Houston's troops crushed the overconfident Mexican Army at the Battle of San Jacinto and won Texas independence in 1836. The Republic of Texas reigned until 1845, when it became the 28th state. After the Civil War, cowboys drove cattle along dusty trails to northern railroad centers. The modern era began in 1901 when a gusher blew at Spindletop oil field.

Austin

(Convention & Visitors Bureau, 201 E. 2nd St. 512-478-0098 or 800-926-2282)
With its clean water and beautiful terrain, the frontier settlement of Waterloo was chosen in 1839 as the state capital and renamed for the great Texas colonizer. But isolation and threats by Indians and Mexico discouraged settlers. The city finally got on the right track with the coming of the railroad in 1871 and the founding of the University of Texas in 1883.

Governor's Mansion (*W. 11th and Colorado Sts. 512-463-5516. Closed weekends and at the governor's discretion*) Built in 1854-56, this 20-room Greek Revival mansion exemplifies the antebellum style of early Texas. Stephen F. Austin's writing desk is among furnishings shown on the guided tour.

State Capitol (*11th St. and Congress Ave. 512-463-0063*) Completed in 1888, the imposing statehouse—built of pink granite and limestone—is taller than the U.S. Capitol. Guided tours highlight paintings, murals, and statues that tell much about the state's early years.

O. Henry Museum (*409 E. 5th St. 512-472-1903. Wed.-Sun.; donations*) While publishing his Austin weekly in 1894-95, William Sydney "O. Henry" Porter lived in this Victorian cottage. You can see period furnishings and many of the short-story writer's personal belongings.

French Legation Museum (*802 San Marcos St. 512-472-8180. Closed Mon.; adm. fee*) The first foreign government to recognize the Republic of Texas, France built the luxurious legation in 1840 for its flamboyant chargé d'affaires. Restored to original splendor, the Greek Revival, bayou-style cottage boasts beautiful antiques and various outbuildings.

Lyndon Baines Johnson Library and Museum (*2313 Red River St. 512-916-5137*) Formal and staid, the library and museum seem at odds with the laid-back style of the 36th President, but three floors honor him with exhibits: ceremonial gifts, an Oval Office replica, and documentary films. Other floors house 43 million documents from his Presidency.

Jourdan-Bachman Pioneer Farm (*11418 Sprinkle Cut-off Rd. 512-837-1215. June-Aug. Sun.-Thurs., Sept.-May Sun.-Wed.; adm. fee*) Snuggled in a bend of Walnut Creek, 16 reconstructed pioneer farm buildings are authentically furnished and staffed by costumed interpreters. Programs presented seasonally include cotton picking, syrupmaking, and candlelight tours.

Dallas

(*Convention & Visitors Bureau 800-752-9222*) John Neely Bryan founded Dallas in 1841 with high hopes of making the Trinity River navigable for trade. He couldn't, so the settlement languished until 1872, when its leaders bribed the Houston and Texas Central Railroad to come to town. Vir-

tually overnight Dallas became a market for cotton and manufactured goods, the population quadrupled, and more than a million dollars was spent on building a modern city. The 1930 oil discovery in east Texas made more Dallas millionaires and added sparkle to the skyline.

The Sixth Floor Museum (*411 Elm St. 214-653-6666. Adm. fee*) On November 22, 1963, Lee Harvey Oswald allegedly crouched at the window here and took aim at President John F. Kennedy in Dealey Plaza

Old City Park, in the heart of modern Dallas

far below. Exhibits describe the life, death, and legacy of the 35th President.

Old City Park (*1717 Gano St. 214-421-5141. Closed Mon.; adm. fee*) Juxtaposed with the gleaming, modern skyline of downtown Dallas, this striking museum village of 38 restored and relocated structures depicts 19th- and early 20th-century rural life in north Texas.

Fair Park (*Between Parry Ave., Cullum Blvd., Fitzhugh Ave., and Washington St. 214-890-2911*) Home of the nation's largest state fair and the annual Cotton Bowl, 277-acre Fair Park was the site of the 1936 Texas Centennial Exhibition. Its many structures, now museums, comprise the largest collection of art deco exhibition buildings in the U.S. Of historical interest are the **Hall of State** (*214-421-4500. Closed Mon.*), with enormous murals depicting Texas history; the **Age of Steam Railroad Museum** (*214-428-0101. Thurs.-Sun.; adm. fee*), an outdoor collection of walk-through train cars from 1900-1950; and the new **African-American Museum** (*214-565-9026. Tues.-Sun.; donations*), with changing exhibits.

El Paso

(*Information Center, 1 Civic Center Plaza. 915-534-0653*) America's largest border city traces its name to a 1598 expedition of Spanish colonials who arrived via El Paso del Norte—a mountain pass cut by the Rio Grande. The **Museum of History** (*12901 Gateway W. 915-858-1928*) chronicles the pageant, from conquistadores to cowboys.

Mission Trail (*915-534-0630 or 800-351-6024*) A 9-mile stretch of Socorro Road links **Mission Ysleta** (*915-859-9848*), Texas' oldest (founded 1691); **Mission Socorro** (*915-859-7718*), a premier example of Spanish Mission architecture; and **Chapel San Elizario** (*915-851-2333*), opened in 1789 to bolster Spanish soldiers patrolling the "Royal Road" from Mexico.

Fort Bliss Museum (*Bldg. 5051, Fort Bliss. 915-568-4518*) In a reconstruction of the still active post's 1857 appearance, period rooms, maps, personal effects, and interpreters in vintage uniforms evoke frontier soldiering.

Magoffin Homestead Historic Site (*1120 Magoffin Ave. 915-533-5147. Wed.-Sun.; adm. fee*) Post-Civil War settlers built wide-porch haciendas from stone, adobe, and timber, creating Southwest Territorial architecture. This 19-room, 1875 adobe, with original furnishings, exemplifies the style.

Excursion

HUECO TANKS S.H.P. (*34 miles E via US 62/180 to Rte. 2775. 915-857-1135. Adm. fee*) For 10,000 years, humans have drunk from natural cisterns of eroded rock here. Ancient peoples left more than 3,000 pictographs in caves and cliff dwellings.

Fort Worth

(*Convention & Visitors Bureau, 415 Throckmorton St. 817-336-8791 or 800-433-5747*) The city got its start in 1849 as a military encampment to protect ranchers from Indians. From 1866 to 1884, more than 10 million head of cattle stomped through the area along the Chisholm Trail. But Fort Worth didn't get its cow-town image until 1873, when Texas and Pacific engines chugged to town, giving rise to the stockyards—second only to Chicago's in size. When oil was discovered in north Texas in 1912, Fort Worth became the operational hub.

Fort Worth Stockyards Historic District (*Visitor Information Center, 130 E. Exchange Ave. 817-624-4741*) Gaslit streets, false-front shops, and rodeos evoke images of old Fort Worth. Begin your tour at the Visitor Center, which has maps, brochures, and a film. Livestock were held for shipping at the

281

adjacent Stockyards Station, where old pens now house shops and restaurants. Across the street, the mission-style **Livestock Exchange Building** (817-625-5082), built in 1902, was the center of activity; cattle sales are still held here. In Suite 113 is the **Stockyards Museum** (817-625-5087).

Sundance Square (*Throckmorton St. to Calhoun St., 2nd St. to 5th St.*) Named for the Sundance Kid, an outlaw who once hid out in town, Sundance Square is a 14-block district filled with restored Victorian structures. One of them now houses the **Sid Richardson Collection of Western Art** (*309 Main St. 817-332-6554*)—featuring 56 works by Frederic Remington and Charles M. Russell. The 1907 **Fire Station No. 1** (*2nd and Commerce Sts. 817-732-1631*) displays the exhibit "150 Years of Fort Worth History."

Cattleman's Museum (*1301 W. 7th St. 817-332-7064. Mon.-Fri.*) Interactive exhibits, films, and artifacts present the story of cattle ranching.

Thistle Hill (*1509 Pennsylvania Ave. 817-336-1212. Sun.-Fri.; adm. fee*) This 1903 Georgian Revival mansion, the luxurious former home of a Fort Worth cattle baron, showcases period furnishings.

Log Cabin Village (*2100 Log Cabin Village Lane. 817-926-5881. Closed Mon.; adm. fee*) A self-guided trail meanders past a collection of pioneer-era log cabins that once belonged to area settlers.

Fredericksburg

(*Chamber of Commerce, 106 N. Adams St. 210-997-6523*) In the remote Texas Hill Country, German immigrants settled Fredericksburg in 1846. You can see examples of *Fachwerk* (half-timber) architecture and several 19th-century Sunday houses—tiny structures used by farmers who traveled to town for Sunday church services. Walking tour brochures are available.

Portraying pioneer life, the 11 relocated structures in the **Pioneer Museum Complex** (*309 W. Main St. 210-997-2835. Adm. fee*) include an 1849 general store and a Sunday house. An eight-sided 1847 structure that was a "people's church," school, and meeting hall is now the **Vereins Kirche Museum** (*100 block of W. Main St. 210-997-7832. Adm. fee*). Reconstructed in 1936, the building contains exhibits on local history.

Admiral Nimitz Museum and Historical Center (*340 E. Main St. 210-997-4379. Adm. fee*) Fleet Adm. Chester Nimitz grew up in the Steamboat Hotel, built in the 1850s by his German grandfather. The hotel now houses a museum tracing Nimitz's story from childhood to World War II hero. Two blocks away, the **History Walk of the Pacific War** wanders among artillery and heavy machinery, including a Japanese "Val" dive-bomber, an amphibious landing vehicle, tanks, and guns.

Log house, Johnson Settlement

Excursion

LBJ STATE AND NATIONAL HISTORICAL PARKS A swath of rolling countryside west of Austin, the Texas Hill Country was home to Lyndon Baines Johnson, 36th President of the U.S. Two districts of the National Park Service and a state park combine to tell LBJ's story. At the **Johnson City District** (*30 miles E in Johnson City, 1 block S of US 290. 210-868-7128*), begin at the Visitor Center for orientation. Across the street is Johnson's boyhood home. A footpath leads to the **Johnson Settlement**, which belonged to LBJ's grandparents and traces the evolution of the local ranching business. At the **LBJ Ranch District** (*13 miles E, near Stonewall off US 290. 210-868-7128. Adm. fee*), the state park Visitor Center (*210-644-2478*) operates a living history farm. But the main reason to come here is the bus tour of the ranch. Though you can't enter the house (Lady Bird Johnson lives there part-time), the tour includes LBJ's first schoolhouse, his birthplace, and the family cemetery.

Galveston

(*Convention & Visitors Bureau, 2106 Seawall Blvd. 409-763-4311 or 800-351-4237*) Discovered in 1528 by a shipwrecked Spanish explorer, Galveston Island subsequently came under French, Spanish again, and Mexican rule. In 1817 privateer Jean Lafitte used the island as a base of operations—some

say his treasure is still buried here. Galveston's port brought wealth in cotton exports and made it Texas' richest town in the 19th century. On Sept. 8, 1900, a hurricane left 6,000 people dead and the town in rubble. Stop by the **Galveston County Historical Museum** (*2219 Market St. 409-766-2340. Donations*).

Strand National Historic Landmark District (*19th to 26th Sts. from Harborside Dr. to Church St. Visitor Center, 2016 Strand. 409-765-7834*) The Strand was once known as the "Wall Street of the Southwest." Thirteen blocks of 19th-century iron-front commercial buildings now house shops and restaurants. At the foot of the Strand is the **Galveston Island Railroad Museum** (*123 Rosenberg St. 409-765-5700. Adm. fee*), with its restored 1932 passenger depot.

Galveston Victoriana

The museum exhibits 45 retired railroad cars.

The Elissa (*Pier 21, end of 22nd St. 409-763-1877. Adm. fee*) One of the oldest merchant ships afloat, the 1877 iron-hulled bark features restored after-cabins and 103-foot-tall masts. Adjacent is the **Texas Seaport Museum**.

Bishop's Palace (*1402 Broadway. 409-762-2475. Adm. fee*) With its jeweled glass windows, cathedral ceilings, and dark woods, the turreted mansion was built for the Walter Gresham family in 1886 and is considered one of the nation's outstanding houses. The name refers to the bishop of Galveston, who took up residence here in 1923.

Surrounding the palace is the 40-block **East End Historic District** (*Between 19th and 11th Sts. and Broadway and Market St.*), a good place to see Victorian Galveston. Your stops should include **Ashton Villa** (*24th St. and Broadway. 409-762-3933. Adm. fee*), built before the Civil War for the illustrious Brown family. The Italianate mansion contains many antiques and family possessions. The opulent existence of the Moody family comes to life on a self-guided tour of the 42-room **Moody Mansion and Museum** (*2618 Broadway. 409-762-7668. Adm. fee*), built in 1893 in the Richardson Romanesque style.

Goliad

(*Chamber of Commerce, Market and Franklin Sts. 512-645-3563*) In 1749 the Spanish moved the Presidio la Bahia and Espiritu Santo Mission to their present locations; the town that grew up around them was one of the first in the state. The **Courthouse Square Historical District** features a Second Empire Courthouse and the infamous Hanging Tree.

Goliad State Historical Park *(1 mile S on US 77A/183. 512-645-3405. Adm. fee)* Centerpiece of this 2,208-acre park is Espiritu Santo Mission, the longest running mission in Texas (108 years). Self-guided tours include the church, granary, convent, and workshop, as well as a museum with colonial and Indian artifacts.

Presidio la Bahia *(1 mile S on US 77A/183. 512-645-3752. Adm. fee)* The Spanish fort is the oldest west of the Mississippi River and the only site from the Texas Revolution that appears as it did in 1836. But the presidio is best known as the scene of the Goliad Massacre. After surrendering to the Mexican Army at the 1836 Battle of Coleto, Col. James Walker Fannin and his 350 men were brought here and executed. A museum displays Texas Revolution memorabilia, plus excavated items showing several levels of civilization found at the site.

Houston ···

(Convention & Visitors Bureau, 801 Congress St. 713-227-3100 or 800-231-7799) Augustus and John Allen settled in 1836 along mosquito-infested Buffalo Bayou, named their property for Gen. Sam Houston, and set about advertising housing plots for the "great interior commercial emporium of Texas." Settlers came, and Houston was named the capital of the Republic of Texas. Yellow fever and political rivalry soon moved the capital to Austin, but Houston prospered, thanks to the growth of the ship channel and the cotton industry. In the 20th century, oil discoveries in east Texas transformed Houston into a modern boomtown.

Sam Houston Park *(1100 Bagby St. 713-655-1912. Fee for house tours)* Eight historic houses brought from around the region create this pleasant historic park, seen by guided tour. Artifacts, photographs, and panels at the **Heritage Gallery** provide details on houses and regional history.

Excursions

SAN JACINTO BATTLEGROUND STATE HISTORICAL PARK *(20 miles E via Tex. 225 and 134. 713-479-2431)* A 570-foot masonry obelisk marks the

spot where, on April 21, 1836, Texans under Gen. Sam Houston triumphed over the numerically superior Mexican Army and won independence. In the monument lobby, a slide show tells the story; a museum describes regional history and has trail maps of the battleground. Berthed nearby is the **USS Texas,** the only surviving naval vessel from both World Wars.

GEORGE RANCH HISTORICAL PARK *(30 miles SW near Richmond, via US 59. 713-545-9212. Weekends April–mid-Dec.;*

San Jacinto Battleground State Historical Park

adm. fee) In the midst of a 23,000-acre family ranch dating from 1824, this 470-acre living history park, staffed with costumed interpreters, expertly explains the ranch's long history. An 1890s Victorian mansion is among several historic buildings that visitors can tour.

San Antonio ·······································

(Visitor Information Center, 317 Alamo Plaza. 210-270-8748 or 800-447-3372) Spanish priests established five missions along the San Antonio River in the early 1700s; among them was Mission San Antonio de Valero, later renamed the Alamo. More than a century later, during the Texas Revolution, the Alamo was the scene of a 13-day stand against the Mexican Army by 189 colonists—including Davy Crockett and Jim Bowie. They lost their lives, but paved the way for Texas independence. After the Civil War, the Chisholm Trail brought wealth to the frontier city. Linked to the rest of the nation by railroad in 1877, the Wild West town softened its image and, in the 20th century, became a favorite tourist destination full of vestiges of its less civilized past.

The Alamo *(Alamo Plaza. 210-225-1391. Donations)* Swarmed by visitors and surrounded by souvenir stands, the Cradle of Texas Liberty is not always a quiet, reflective place. But the church, with its cases of weapons and personal items belonging to the Alamo heroes, poignantly recalls the fallen. Also included in the self-guided tour are a number of exhibits, a documentary, and flower-filled gardens that represent only a portion of the original stronghold.

Spanish Governor's Palace *(105 Military Plaza. 210-224-0601. Adm. fee)* Spanish governors resided in this 1749 dwelling. A self-guided tour of the house, built with materials from Spain and decorated with period furnishings, offers a glimpse of 18th-century Spanish traditions.

Casa Navarro State Historic Site *(228 S. Laredo St. 210-226-4801. Adm. fee)* Texas patriot José Antonio Navarro lived in this adobe-and-limestone residence, which includes a house, a kitchen, and an office.

King William Historic District *(King William St. and surrounding area)* After Texas won statehood, affluent settlers from Germany flocked to San Antonio, where they built gracious Victorian houses along tree-shaded King William Street. Pick up a walking tour map at the San Antonio Conservation Society *(107 King William St. 210-224-6163)*. The only house open to the public is the lavish Second Empire **Steves Homestead**

285

(509 King William St. 210-225-5924. Adm. fee), furnished in period style.

Institute of Texan Cultures (801 S. Bowie St. in HemisFair Park. 210-458-2300. Closed Mon.; adm. fee) From Native Americans to Spanish colonists to Dutch dairy farmers, more than 27 ethnic groups have contributed to the diverse culture of Texas. This popular museum tells their stories with exhibits, interpreters, interactive displays, and a multiscreen presentation.

San Antonio Missions National Historical Park (Visitor Information Center, 317 Alamo Plaza. 210-270-8748)

Chapel at Spanish Governor's Palace, San Antonio

Four missions built during the Spanish reign dot the Mission Trail in the south part of town. (The fifth mission—now the Alamo—is not part of the park.) Each compound included a church, residences, and a granary. For the most part only church buildings remain, but the missions still convey a sense of 18th-century life. If time is limited, don't miss **Mission San José** (6701 San José Dr. 210-932-1001), the largest and most beautiful church, surrounded by barracks, a granary, and Indian quarters. Perched at the edge of town, the small **Mission San Francisco de la Espada** (10100 Espada Rd. 210-627-2021), established in 1731, retains the air of a wilderness outpost.

Excursion

NEW BRAUNFELS (25 miles NE via I-35. Chamber of Commerce 210-625-2385 or 800-572-2626) Lured by promises of utopia, German immigrants flocked to Texas in the 1840s. New Braunfels was settled in 1845 and, thanks to abundant water and rich soil, it became by 1850 one of the state's most prosperous towns. The German heritage still thrives in local architecture, cuisine, and festivals. Built on the site that town founder Prince Carl of Braunfels, Germany, chose for his castle (it was never built), the small **Sopienburg Museum** (401 W. Coll St. 210-629-1572. Adm. fee) exhibits local artifacts and replicas of an early bakery, a doctor's office, and a pharmacy. A half-timbered house, log cabins, a music studio, and a cabinet shop are among eight structures moved to **Conservation Plaza** (1300 Church Hill Dr. 210-629-2943. Closed Mon.; adm. fee) from around the region.

New Braunfels became a minor center for furniture and cabinet crafting in the 19th century. Housed in the 1858 Breustedt-Dillon House, the **Museum of Texas Handmade Furniture** (1370 Church Hill Dr. 210-629-6504. Call for schedule. Adm. fee) boasts 75 handmade works from the period.

Waco ···

Established in the 1840s on the site of a Texas Ranger outpost and named for local Indians, Waco boomed after the Civil War as rough-and-tumble "Six-Shooter Junction" on the Chisholm Trail.

Texas Ranger Hall of Fame and Museum *(Fort Fisher Park. 817-750-8631. Adm. fee)* In 1823 Stephen F. Austin selected ten men to become the first Texas Rangers, responsible for keeping the peace on the wild frontier. Full of 19th-century ranger paraphernalia—pistols, badges, boots, and knives—this museum is a dream come true for Wild West fans.

Other Sites in Texas

Alabama-Coushatta Indian Reservation *(13 miles E of Livingston on US 190. 409-563-4391 or 800-444-3507. Adm. fee)* In the 1850s, Gen. Sam Houston helped create this reservation. A visitor program includes a museum with dioramas and the Living Indian Village, where tribal members make traditional crafts.

Fort Concho *(E of S. Oakes St. between C and D Aves., San Angelo. Adm. fee)* Among the best-preserved frontier forts in the state, the post has a wonderful mix of 23 original and reconstructed buildings. Exhibits tell stories of Indian campaigns, military strategies, and city life.

Fort Davis National Historic Site *(N of Fort Davis at jct. of Tex. 17 and 118. 915-426-3224. Adm. fee)* Established in 1854 to protect travelers on the San Antonio-El Paso Road, Fort Davis is the Southwest's best preserved example of a frontier military post. Its 70 restored adobe and stone buildings include a barracks, commissary, and commanding officers quarters. A museum exhibits weaponry, Indian artifacts, and paintings.

287

Nacogdoches One of the state's oldest settlements, this town grew up around an 18th-century mission, then served for more than a hundred years as an eastern gateway to Texas. Some of the state's most historic landmarks are here, including the **Old Stone Fort** *(Stephen F. Austin State University. 409-468-2408. Closed Mon.),* built in the 1780s as a Spanish house and trading post.

Panhandle-Plains Historical Museum *(2401 4th Ave., Canyon. 806-656-2244. Donations)* A reconstructed pioneer town and the restored T-Anchor Ranch House—one of the Panhandle's oldest buildings—are among the extensive collections that honor Texas pioneers.

Permian Basin Petroleum Museum, Library and Hall of Fame *(1500 I-20 W, Midland. 915-683-4403. Adm. fee)* A marine diorama of the ancient Permian Sea, a re-created 1920s boomtown, and oil rigs are exhibits that describe the fossil fuel story and its importance to the Texas economy.

Sam Houston Memorial Museum *(19th St. and Ave. N, Huntsville. 409-294-1832. Closed Mon.; donations)* Located on 15 acres once belonging to patriot Sam Houston, the museum complex includes two houses where he lived, his law office, and an excellent museum on Texas history.

Spindletop/Gladys City Boomtown Museum *(University Dr. at US 69/96/287, Beaumont. 409-835-0823. Tues.-Sun.; adm. fee)* Anthony Lucas ushered in the petroleum age when his gusher blew on Jan. 10, 1901. The world's first oil boomtown—which grew up around the rich oil field—has been reconstructed with shacks and period equipment.

Washington-on-the-Brazos S.H.P. *(near Washington. 409-878-2214. Fee)* Preserving the flavor of an important town during the era of the Texas Republic, this park includes part of the original townsite, the home of the last Republic President, and the Star of the Republic Museum.

OREGON

IDAHO

Winnemucca

Wells

Ronald V. Jensen
Living Historical Farm
Golden Spike N.H.S.

Great
Salt
Lake

Ogden

80

Antelope Island
S.P.

Salt
Lake
City

Donner-Reed Museum

Utah
Lake

Par
City

Pr

Reno

Bowers
Mansion

Virginia City

Grimes Point
Archaeological
Area

Benson Historic
Grist Mill

Camp Floyd/
Stagecoach Inn
State Park

Fort Churchill
S.H.P.

Austin

Eureka

U T A H

Carson City

Genoa

N E V A D A

Belmont

Territorial
Statehouse
State Park

Cove Fort

Fremont
Indian
State Park

Fruit

Tonopah

Parowan Gap
Petroglyphs

15

Anasazi
State Park

288

CALIFORNIA

Iron Mission State Pa

Washington
Cotton Mill

Rhyolite

Jacob Hamblin
Home

St. George

Pipe Spring
Nat. Mon.

Fredonia

Lost City Museum

GRAND
CANYON
N.P.

Colorado

Las Vegas

15

Old Las Vegas
Mormon Fort S.H.P.

South Rim
Visitor Center

Boulder
City

Hoover Dam

WUPATKI
NAT. MON.

Williams

Flagstaff

40

Montezuma Castle
Nat. Mon.

Waln
Cany
Nat. M

Tuzigoot Nat. Mon.

Jerome S.H.P.

Colorado

Sharlot Hall
Museum

Fort Verde
S.H.P.

A R I Z O N A

Wickenburg

17

Theodore Roosevelt Dam

Salt

10

Phoenix

To
Nat. M

Glob

Casa Grande
Ruins Nat. Mon.

Yuma

8

10

U.S.A.
MEXICO

Tucso

San Xavier Del

Tubac Presidi
S.H.

19

Tumacacor
N.H.P

San Xavier del Bac Mission, near Tucson, Arizona

Southwest

Today much of the region's backcountry is still claimed by the descendants of ancient peoples who left it strewn with the ruins of pueblos and cliff dwellings. From 1540, when Francisco Vasquez de Coronado trekked from Mexico seeking the Cities of Gold, until 1821, when Anglo-Americans opened the Santa Fe Trail from Missouri, the Southwest's historical pageant featured Spanish conquistadores, priests, and settlers who came to conquer, Christianize, and colonize the New World. Discovery of rich gold and silver deposits brought more settlers in the mid-19th century. Mormon pilgrims wanting a haven from religious persecution founded their new world beside the Great Salt Lake in 1847, but, like Apache people led by Cochise and Geronimo, saw dreams of independence from the rest of America overwhelmed by the young nation's expansion.

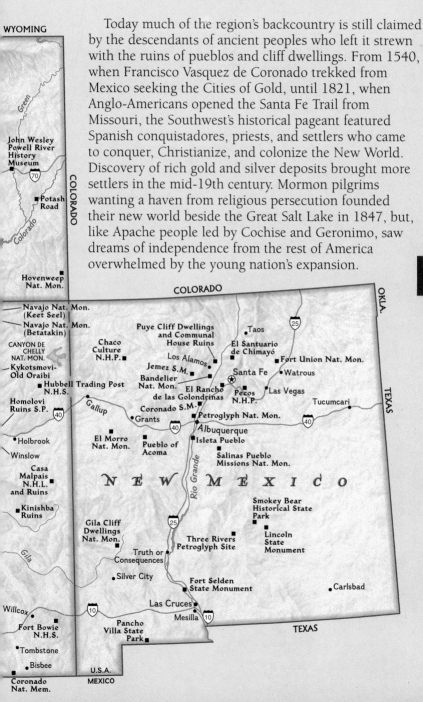

WYOMING

John Wesley Powell River History Museum

70

COLORADO

Green

Potash Road

Colorado

Hovenweep Nat. Mon.

COLORADO

OKLA.

Navajo Nat. Mon. (Keet Seel)
Navajo Nat. Mon. (Betatakin)

CANYON DE CHELLY NAT. MON.

Kykotsmovi-Old Oraibi

Homolovi Ruins S.P.

40

Hubbell Trading Post N.H.S.

Chaco Culture N.H.P.

Puye Cliff Dwellings and Communal House Ruins

Los Alamos

Jemez S.M.

Bandelier Nat. Mon.

El Rancho de las Golondrinas

Coronado S.M.

Gallup

Grants

Taos

25

El Santuario de Chimayó

Santa Fe

Fort Union Nat. Mon.

Watrous

Pecos N.H.P.

Las Vegas

Tucumcari

TEXAS

Petroglyph Nat. Mon.

40

Holbrook

Winslow

El Morro Nat. Mon.

Pueblo of Acoma

Albuquerque

Isleta Pueblo

Salinas Pueblo Missions Nat. Mon.

40

Casa Malpais N.H.L. and Ruins

Kinishba Ruins

NEW MEXICO

Rio Grande

Gila

Gila Cliff Dwellings Nat. Mon.

25

Truth or Consequences

Silver City

Three Rivers Petroglyph Site

Smokey Bear Historical State Park

Lincoln State Monument

Willcox

Fort Bowie N.H.S.

Tombstone

Bisbee

Coronado Nat. Mem.

10

Pancho Villa State Park

U.S.A.

MEXICO

Fort Selden State Monument

Las Cruces

Mesilla

10

Carlsbad

TEXAS

Stone points removed in 1926 from skeletons of extinct bison near Folsom attest to a human presence in New Mexico as early as 10,000 years ago. Pit houses, caves, and cliff dwellings sheltered subsequent farming cultures whose successors rebelled in 1680 against Spanish rule. Europeans returned in 1692, reestablished a provincial capital in Santa Fe, and enforced their will. In 1821 the Santa Fe Trail from Missouri brought commerce and Anglo-American enterprise. The Mexican War, in 1848, brought New Mexico under U.S. dominion; territorial status came in 1850. Union garrisons set up to protect settlers thwarted Confederate attempts to conquer the territory during the Civil War. The short-lived silver, gold, and copper booms brought thousands of immigrants, along with statehood in 1912. Yet New Mexico remained isolated into the 20th century, a key reason it became a center of top-secret government nuclear and military research. The Atomic Age appetite for uranium brought a brief period of mid-century prosperity to a state that remains largely rural and sparsely populated.

Albuquerque

(Visitors Bureau, 20 First Plaza S.W. 505-842-9918) Originally a farming village and military outpost on El Camino Real ("the royal road"), New Mexico's largest city was founded in 1706. Ambitious territorial governor Francisco Valdez supposedly assured superiors that Albuquerque's family count (then 18) exceeded the required 30. The village formed around a plaza, now in **Old Town Albuquerque,** dominated for nearly 300 years by **San Felipe de Neri Church** *(2005 N. Plaza. 505-243-4628. Donations).*

Museum of Art and History *(2000 Mountain Rd. N.W. 505-242-4600. Tues.-Sun.)* The state's cultural mix is celebrated through art and historical displays.

Pueblo Bonito, Chaco Culture National Historical Park

Indian Pueblo Cultural Center *(2401 12th St. N.W. 505-843-7270)* New Mexico's 19 Pueblo tribes operate the center, which presents the history and culture of each tribe. Murals trace traditional Indian rites.

Maxwell Museum of Anthropology *(University Blvd., University of New Mexico campus. 505-277-4404. Donations)* This esteemed museum focuses on Southwest culture. Anasazi exhibits include Chaco Canyon finds.

National Atomic Museum *(SE via Wyoming or Gibson Blvds. to Kirtland A.F.B. 505-284-3243)* Bomb casings and military aircraft are among relics of America's nuclear coming-of-age, starting with World War II's Manhattan Project.

Excursions

PETROGLYPH NATIONAL MONUMENT *(3 miles W on I-40. 505-839-4429. Adm. fee)* Some 15,000 Pueblo images adorn a 17-mile-long escarpment. Most date from A.D. 1300 to 1650; a few may be 3,000 years old.

ISLETA PUEBLO *(13 miles S via I-25. Visitor Center 505-869-3111)* The Tiwa farming town dates from the 1200s. **San Agustin Mission** (1613) is among New Mexico's most striking old churches.

CORONADO STATE MONUMENT *(25 miles N via I-25 and N. Mex. 44. 505-867-5351. Adm. fee)* Ruins of a pueblo where Coronado probably wintered in 1540-41 include a reconstructed kiva and murals recovered from it.

PUEBLO OF ACOMA *(66 miles W via I-40 and N. Mex. 30/32. 800-747-0181. Closed July 10-13 and 1st or 2nd weekend in Oct.; adm. fee)* The Acoma "Sky City" atop a sandstone mesa has been continuously occupied since at least A.D. 1250. **San Esteban del Rey Mission** (1640) may be the largest and most dramatically located Southwest mission.

Chaco Culture National Historical Park......

(Off N. Mex. 44 near Nageezi. 505-786-7014. Adm. fee) One of North America's most important archaeological sites, this 17-mile-long canyon contains 17 multistoried structures known as Great Houses and 400 smaller dwellings. The site dates from A.D. 900 and holds the continent's largest excavated prehistoric building. Five self-guided trails explore major structures, including

Pueblo Bonito, a D-shaped Great House of 800 rooms covering 3 acres. Summer programs include ranger-led tours and campfire programs.

Fort Union National Monument ....

(8 miles NW of Watrous via N. Mex. 161. 505-425-8025. Adm. fee) Chimneys, stone foundations, and adobe walls mark the dimensions of one of the Southwest's largest 19th-century military garrisons, established in 1851 to protect American travelers on this stretch of the Santa Fe Trail. A second fort was built in 1861-62 to repel a Confederate invasion—halted in March 1862 at the Battle of Glorieta Pass. Construction soon began on

an even larger garrison and supply depot that took six years to complete. A self-guided interpretive trail tours the site.

Excursion

LAS VEGAS *(25 miles S via I-25. Chamber of Commerce, 727 N. Grand Ave. 505-425-8631 or 800-832-5947)* More than 900 buildings survive from the town's 19th-century economic boom as New Mexico's chief railhead. Among them is the **Castaneda Hotel,** where Theodore Roosevelt reunited with Spanish-American War comrades in 1900. The **Rough Riders Memorial and City Museum** *(729 N. Grand Ave. 505-425-8726. Mon.-Fri.)* recalls Roosevelt's Cuban adventure.

Fort Union National Monument

Gila Cliff Dwellings National Monument····

(44 miles N of Silver City via N. Mex. 15. Visitor Center 505-536-9461. Adm. fee) Archaeologists believe that 42 rooms in five natural southeast-facing caves were built and occupied by Mogollon families around A.D. 1250. The 10-15 families living here at any one time constructed masonry and adobe structures and produced white pottery decorated with sharply delineated black designs (suggesting a link to Mimbres tribal artistry). A one-mile, self-guided loop trail climbs to the caves.

292

Turquoise Trail

For centuries, Indians gathered the greenish blue mineral from hills along the scenic route between Albuquerque and Santa Fe (now N. Mex. 14). The route first saw outsiders in the 1500s, when Spanish oxcarts creaked along this stretch of El Camino Real, "the royal road" between Mexico City and Santa Fe. In the mid-1850s, the Butterfield Overland Mail stage route, one of the earliest western thoroughfares, also went through here on its way from St. Louis to San Francisco via Los Angeles.

Santa Fe ·······························

(Convention & Visitors Bureau, 201 W. Marcy St. 505-984-6760 or 800-777-2489) Terminus of El Camino Real from Mexico City, the Villa de Santa Fe was declared the capital of Spain's New Mexico province around 1600. The 700-mile Santa Fe Trail from Missouri arrived in 1821, the year Mexico became independent of Spain. The trade routes made Santa Fe the hub of Southwest commerce and the **Santa Fe Plaza** the junction of the Hispanic Southwest and Anglo-American East. Here on August 18, 1846, during the Mexican War, Gen. Stephen Watts Kearny ran up the U.S. flag and annexed the territory (a bloodless feat engineered by James W. Macgoffin, a Santa Fe trader who negotiated behind the scenes with friends in the Mexican government).

Palace of the Governors *(105 Palace Ave. 505-827-6483. Tues.-Sun.; adm. fee to museum)* Built to house the provincial governor and his lieutenants, the adobe complex on the north side of the plaza served as the capital of this part of New Spain for two centuries. It is thus the oldest capitol building in the U.S. An excellent museum displays period rooms and diverse artifacts that reflect Spanish, Mexican, and Anglo-American heritage. Indian artisans selling beneath the palace's arcade continue the plaza's centuries-old trading tradition.

Loretto Chapel (*1 block E of the plaza, 211 Old Santa Fe Trail. 505-982-0092. Adm. fee*) A French architect who was commissioned by Santa Fe's French-born archbishop, Jean-Baptiste Lamy, modeled the church after Paris's Sainte-Chapelle. He commenced work in 1873 but died before he could complete stairs to the choir loft. According to legend, Loretto's Catholic sisters prayed, and an aged, unknown carpenter arrived on a donkey. He built the Miraculous Staircase, which spirals upward without a center pole for support, and rode away, taking no payment.

St. Francis Cathedral (*131 Cathedral Place. 505-982-5619. Donations*) Begun in 1869, this French Romanesque edifice reflects the taste of Jean-Baptiste Lamy, model for the priest in Willa Cather's novel *Death Comes for the Archbishop*. Lamy is buried under the altar, watched over by one of the

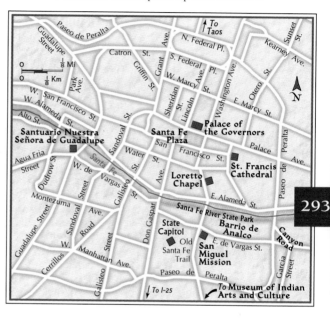

oldest representations of the Madonna in North America.

Santuario Nuestra Señora de Guadalupe (*100 S. Guadalupe St. 505-988-2027. May-Oct. Mon.-Sat., Nov.-April Mon.-Fri.; donations*) The sanctuary (no longer an active church) was completed around 1795, but owes its California mission style to 20th-century repairs. The interior is classic Spanish colonial, with original woodwork. A museum exhibits paintings dating from the 16th century and photographs illustrating the church's survival of fire, revolution, and misguided remodeling.

San Miguel Mission (*401 Old Santa Fe Trail. 505-983-3974. Donations*) This church was built on the site of Indian dwellings dating from the 1300s. Its interior, decorated by 16th-century animal-hide paintings, is an excellent example of New Mexican colonial religious architecture. A circa 1628 document scolding the governor for "impious conduct during the mass" establishes San Miguel as the continent's oldest church structure.

Barrio de Analco One of the oldest residential areas in the U.S. begins on East De Vargas Street, where many houses date from the early 1600s.

Canyon Road Possibly once an Indian trail to Pecos River pueblos, the narrow road is now a chic avenue of galleries, upscale shops, and innovative restaurants, many occupying historic buildings.

Museum of Indian Arts and Culture (*710 Camino Lejo. 505-827-6344.*

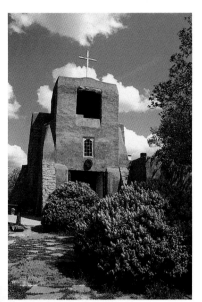

San Miguel Mission, Santa Fe

294

Tues.-Sun.; adm. fee) Art and artifacts from southwestern Indian life celebrate the traditions and contemporary vigor of the culture. The permanent "Pottery of the Southwest" exhibit distinguishes varying tribal traditions.

Excursions

EL RANCHO DE LAS GOLONDRINAS *(15 miles S via I-25 and N. Mex. 599. 334 Los Pinos Rd. 505-471-2261. April-Oct. Wed.-Sun.; adm. fee)* At the last stopping place before Santa Fe on El Camino Real, "villagers" in period dress occupy restored and rebuilt structures. They re-create life in the early 1700s when the 200-acre "Ranch of the Swallows" welcomed colonists en route to Santa Fe.

PECOS NATIONAL HISTORICAL PARK *(25 miles E via I-25, in Pecos. Visitor Center 505-757-6032. Adm. fee)* New Mexico's preeminent pueblo community peaked in the mid-15th century as a cultural crossroads where Plains Indians traded with the Pueblo tribes. Ruins of a 600- to 800-room complex share a knoll with remnants of a Franciscan mission.

EL SANTUARIO DE CHIMAYÓ *(30 miles N via US 84/285 and N. Mex. 76 and 520. 505-351-4889. Donations)* Since 1816, thousands of ailing believers have come on Good Friday to seek the healing power of earth from a pit within this adobe church—a classic of Spanish colonial religious architecture. The village of **Chimayó,** famed for a distinctive family weaving tradition, surrounds Plaza del Cerro, among the few fortified 18th-century squares remaining in New Mexico.

LOS ALAMOS *(30 miles NW via US 84/285, then N. Mex. 502. Visitor Information 505-662-8105 or 800-444-0707)* World War II's Manhattan Project replaced the Los Alamos Ranch School and homesteaders with a secret city of scientists and military personnel. The **Los Alamos Historical Museum** *(1921 Juniper St. 505-662-6272. Donations)* presents the region's geological and human saga. An exhibit recounts the A-bomb project.

PUYE CLIFF DWELLINGS AND COMMUNAL HOUSE RUINS *(35 miles NW via US 84/285 and N. Mex. 30 and 5. 505-753-7326. Adm. fee)* Ruins stretching a mile sheltered ancestors of the Santa Clara Pueblo people from A.D. 1100 to the late 1500s. Some dwellings rose three stories inside cliff-wall caves. Top House, a pueblo

Santa Fe Trail

In August 1821 William Becknell left Missouri with a pack train of goods. He returned from Santa Fe five months later to pay backers $15 for every $1 invested, and the Santa Fe Trail was born. The first wagons were Conestogas pulled by horses or mules, and the 700-mile journey could take 3 months. The Mexican government levied a duty of $500 per wagon, regardless of size, so traders switched to the larger St. Louis-built Murphy, 3 feet wide and 16 feet long. Caravans of 100 wagons crossed Indian country, ready to form squares for defense. When the Santa Fe Railroad reached Lamy in 1800, the trail quickly faded into history.

of 740 rooms, crowns the mesa above. The pueblo is noted for its innovative pottery-making tradition.

BANDELIER NATIONAL MONUMENT *(50 miles NW via US 285 and N. Mex. 502 and 4. 505-672-0343. Adm. fee)* A one-mile loop trail into 600-foot-deep Frijoles Canyon visits cliff ruins, among the hundreds of pueblo remnants in Bandelier's roadless 46-square-mile wilderness.

Salinas Pueblo Missions N.M. ⋯⋯⋯⋯⋯

(Mountainair Visitor Center, US 60 near US 55. 505-847-2585) Anasazi and Mogollon people mixed in the Salinas Valley between A.D. 1100 and 1600, forming an agrarian pueblo society. Sandstone ruins at **Quarai** *(505-847-2290)* were multistoried apartment homes. Completed in the 1630s, Quarai's Franciscan mission, **Nuestra Señora de la Purísma Concepción de Cuarac,** once rose 40 feet on foundations 5 feet wide and 7 feet deep. The **San Gregorio Mission** ruin at **Abó** *(505-847-2400)* combines medieval European church design and pueblo architecture. **Gran Quivira** *(505-847-2770)* was a trade center of 1,500 to 3,000 inhabitants. Remains of two 17th-century Catholic churches, **San Isidro** and **San Buenaventura,** share a limestone knoll. Like Quarai and Abó, Gran Quivira succumbed to drought and disease in the 1670s.

Taos Area ⋯⋯⋯⋯⋯⋯⋯⋯⋯⋯⋯⋯⋯

Taos Pueblo *(505-758-9593. Adm. fees)* Multistoried adobe buildings in the Tiwa-speaking enclave date from A.D. 1000 to 1450. Today, some 200 of the tribe's 2,200 members forsake electricity to live here, hauling river water and baking bread in outdoor earthen ovens. The **Church of San Gerónimo** replaces one destroyed during the 1847 Taos Rebellion.

Taos *(Visitor Information, 1139 Paseo Pueblo Sur. 505-758-3837 or 800-732-TAOS)* Spanish colonials who settled Taos Valley shortly after 1600 were killed during the 1680 Pueblo uprising, but the Spanish returned in 1696 and eventually reestablished Don Fernando de Taos. By 1820 the village was a trading center frequented by beaver-trapping mountain men. In 1847 Taoseños protesting U.S. occupation during the Mexican War killed territorial governor Charles Bent in his home, now the **Governor Bent Museum** *(117A Bent St. 505-758-2376. Adm. fee).* A Civil War takeover by Confederate sympathizers was averted when residents, including Army scout Kit Carson, took up arms. In the early 1900s artists attracted by the region's beauty founded the famed Taos Society of Artists.

Taos Pueblo

Kit Carson Home and Museum *(Kit Carson Rd. 505-758-4741. Adm. fee)* Carson was 33 when he married 14-year-old Josefa Jaramillo and gave her this adobe house as a wedding gift. Period rooms, artifacts, and documents trace his career from mountain man to dime-novel hero.

Blumenschein Home and Museum *(222 Ledoux St. 505-758-0505. Adm. fee)* The queen of Taos "Art Society" adobes was purchased in 1919 and enlarged by society co-founder Ernest Blumenschein and wife, Mary, who decorated it with handmade Taos furniture and their own artwork.

La Hacienda de Don Antonio Severina Martinez *(2 miles S of the plaza on Ranchitos Rd. 505-758-1000. Adm. fee)* The fortresslike adobe, built in the early 19th century, is the state's best preserved late Spanish colonial home.

Church of San Francisco de Asis *(4 miles S via N. Mex. 68. 505-758-2754. Adm. fee)* The massively buttressed apse is a Southwest image made famous by painter Georgia O'Keeffe and photographer Ansel Adams.

Other Sites in New Mexico

El Morro National Monument *(43 Miles SW of Grants via N. Mex. 53. 505-783-4226. Adm. fee)* Since prehistoric times, travelers stopping at the freshwater pool here have etched graffiti into **Inscription Rock.** Anasazi chipped petroglyphs; beginning in 1605, Spanish colonists, mountain men, soldiers, and settlers left initials, dates, and comments. Pueblo ruins cap the mesa.

Fort Selden State Monument *(I-25, 10 miles N of Las Cruces. 505-526-8911)* The post was established in 1865 to protect Mesilla Valley settlers. Photographs along self-guided paths depict the fort's 26 active-duty years, including the time when Gen. Douglas MacArthur's father was commandant. A museum displays old uniforms, weaponry, and equipment.

Jemez State Monument *(13 miles N of Jemez Pueblo via N. Mex. 4. 505-829-3530. Adm. fee)* A member of Coronado's expedition in 1541 found the Jemez dispersed among several pueblos. Around 1600, Franciscan missionaries consolidated them, but famine, war, and tribal resistance to Catholicism left Mission San José de los Jemez abandoned by 1630.

Lincoln State Monument *(US 380, Lincoln. 505-653-4372. Adm. fee)* In 1878-1881 a feud between merchants escalated into deadly battle that ended in a five-day shoot-out. Among the participants was 18-year-old Billy Bonney, alias "The Kid." Five buildings figuring in the conflict are preserved, including the courthouse jail from which Billy escaped by killing two deputies. Living history guides annually reenact key events in the Lincoln County Wars.

Mesilla *(W from Las Cruces via Avenida de Mesilla)* When the 1848 Treaty of Guadalupe Hidalgo ceded land east of the Rio Grande to the U.S., residents of Las Cruces and Doña Ana preferring Mexican domiciles settled the "Little Table" across the river. Mesilla prospered as a trading center and a Butterfield Overland Mail stop until railroaders bypassed it in 1881 in favor of Las Cruces. Historic architecture surrounds the original plaza.

Pancho Villa State Park *(Near Columbus. 505-531-2711. Adm. fee)* Enraged by U.S. support of the Mexican government he was trying to overthrow, rebel Pancho Villa and 500 horsemen attacked Columbus in 1916, killing 18. Gen. John Pershing pursued Villa into Mexico but failed to capture him. The park holds remnants of the 13th Cavalry's Camp Furlong, target of Villa's wrath. The adjoining **Columbus Historical Society Museum** *(505-531-2620. Donations)* occupies a restored railroad depot.

Smokey Bear Historical State Park *(US 380, Capitan. Visitor Center 505-354-2748. Adm. fee)* The Forest Service mascot existed only on fire prevention posters until 1950, when Lincoln National Forest firefighters found a burned bear cub clinging to a tree. The orphan served 26 years as the first real-life Smokey and was buried near the Visitor Center.

Three Rivers Petroglyph Site *(5 miles E of Three Rivers off N. Mex. 54. 505-525-4300)* An old road leads to images chipped into rocks from A.D. 1000 to 1350. A mile-long trail visits reconstructed pueblos and pit houses.

Adobe houses in Barrio Historico, Tucson

A quest for gold brought the Spanish into Arizona in 1540. They found a land of ghost cities left by the Hohokam, Arizona's earliest known people, and the cliff-dwelling ancestral Pueblo. Mission-building Franciscan priests began a campaign to win souls, thwarted by the Pueblo Revolt of 1680. The Spanish returned in the 1700s to crush Indian resistance. The 1848 treaty ending the Mexican War ceded much of Arizona's land to the U.S., but Apache and other Native American resistance continued until 1886, even as mining booms and railroads brought thousands to the territory. Early 20th-century irrigation projects expanded agriculture; rail links brought commerce and, in 1912, statehood—making Arizona the last of the Lower 48 to join the Union. Defense industries that relocated here during World War II began an era of growth that continues unabated.

Bisbee

Discovery of the Copper Queen Lode in the 1870s established Bisbee as the center of one of America's richest copper-producing regions. The city preserves many of its early buildings. Hillside Victorians and old mining cabins overlook the narrow downtown streets of the **Historic District** (*Visitor Center, 7 Main St. 520-432-5421*). The **Bisbee Mining and Historical Museum** (*5 Copper Queen Plaza. 520-432-7071. Adm fee*), in the former headquarters of Bisbee's top mining company, documents the city's first 40 years.

Excursions

CORONADO NATIONAL MEMORIAL (*25 miles W via US 80, Ariz. 92, and Montezuma Canyon Rd. 4101 E. Montezuma Canyon Rd. 520-366-5515. Adm. fee*) Displays of weaponry and armor commemorate the epochal 1540 entry into Arizona by Francisco Vasquez de Coronado, who was beginning his three-year, 4,000-mile expedition of conquest.

TOMBSTONE (*25 miles NW via US 80. Visitor Center, 4th and Allen Sts. 520-457-3929*) An 1877 silver strike made Goose Flats a legend. Exhibits at **Tombstone Courthouse State Historic Park** (*219 E. Toughnut St. 520-457-3311. Adm. fee*) focus on silver mining. The 1881 gunfight that made the **OK Corral** (*520-457-3456. Adm. fee*) famous actually occurred elsewhere. Once bawdy **Bird Cage Theater** (*520-457-3421. Adm. fee*) displays antiques and curios. Many unmarked graves in **Boot Hill Graveyard** (*520-457-9344. Adm. fee*) belong to Chinese who labored in laundries and restaurants to invest in mines and real estate.

Canyon de Chelly National Monument ······

(*3 miles E of Chinle on Ariz. 7. Visitor Center 520-674-5500*) Three deep gorges on Navajo land administered by the National Park Service enclose ruins representing 2,500 years of the Anasazi, a people the Navajo and Hopi revere as ancestors. With one exception, the canyons can be entered only by visitors who are accompanied by rangers or Navajo guides hired at the **Visitor Center,** where exhibits present the canyon's human saga. **North Rim Drive** and **South Rim Drive** feature historic viewpoints. **White House Overlook** on the South Rim begins the only trail into Canyon de Chelly not requiring a guide—a 1.25-mile path to the 60-room **White House** ruin, once home to an entire community.

Canyon de Chelly pictographs

Excursion

HUBBELL TRADING POST NATIONAL HISTORIC SITE (*35 miles SE via US 191 and Ariz. 264. 520-775-3254*) John Lorenzo Hubbell's building opened in 1883, accepting Navajo and Hopi blankets and wool in exchange for brass tokens redeemable for manufactured goods. Hubbell championed Indian causes as a legislator. Free tours of the **Lorenzo Hubbell House** feature a museum-quality collection of rugs, paintings, and baskets.

Flagstaff ·····································

(*Visitor Center, 1 E. US 66. 520-774-9541 or 800-842-7293*) A lumber camp's ponderosa pine flagpole became a landmark for California-bound emigrants, who called it Flagstaff.

Museum of Northern Arizona (*3101 N. Ft. Valley Rd. 520-774-5213. Adm. fee*) This research center probes Colorado Plateau history and science. On permanent view are exhibits exploring the area's cultural development. Changing displays feature works by Native Americans.

Pioneer Museum (*2340 N. Fort Valley Rd. 520-774-6272. Mon.-Sat.; donations*) The 1908 volcanic stone building once was a hospital. Antique toys, signs, and cowboy regalia contrast with medical exhibits.

Riordan Mansion State Historic Park (*1300 Riordan Ranch St. 520-779-4395. Adm. fee*) Two timber baron brothers and their families lived together in the 40-room mansion here, a 1904 masterpiece of the arts and crafts style.

Excursions

HOMOLOVI RUINS STATE PARK (*60 miles E via I-40 and Ariz. 87. 520-289-4106. Adm. fee*) The Hopi consider Homolovi's thousand-year-old pueblo ruins their ancestral home. Forty kiva chambers here presage the elaborately ceremonial nature of Anasazi community life.

WALNUT CANYON NATIONAL MONUMENT (*6 miles E via I-40, Walnut Canyon Rd. 520-526-3367. Adm. fee*) About 850 years ago Sinagua built cliff dwellings into a 400-foot gorge and farmed the land around the rim. A three-quarter-mile footpath leads to 25 of the cliff-dwelling rooms.

WUPATKI NATIONAL MONUMENT (*25 miles N via Ariz. 89, Sunset Loop Rd. 520-679-2365. Adm. fee*) A ball court among 2,600 archaeological sites suggests that ancestral Pueblo living here from A.D. 1100 to 1300 had Mesoamerican ties. Thick-walled Wupatki ("tall house") once rose three stories.

Watchtower at Grand Canyon National Park

TUZIGOOT NATIONAL MONUMENT (*50 miles S via Ariz. 89A, near Clarkdale. Visitor Center 520-634-5564. Adm. fee*) Archaeologists believe that from about A.D. 1000 to 1400 as many as 250 Sinagua at a time occupied this hilltop complex. A museum near the pueblo ruins exhibits tools, weapons, jewelry, textiles, pottery, and beads.

299

MONTEZUMA CASTLE NATIONAL MONUMENT (*50 miles S via I-17, Middle Verde Rd. 520-567-3322. Adm. fee*) The name traces to settlers who thought a pair of 12th-century Sinagua cliff-dwelling ruins here were of Aztec origin. One of them is very well preserved.

JEROME STATE HISTORIC PARK (*55 miles S via Ariz. 89A and State Park Rd. 520-634-5381. Adm. fee*) A museum in a copper-mining mogul's hilltop mansion, constructed in 1916 of adobe brick, commemorates Jerome's one-billion-dollar, 70-year boom, which ended in 1953.

FORT VERDE STATE HISTORIC PARK (*55 miles S via I-17. 520-567-3275. Adm. fee*) Tonto Apache and Yavapai raids brought the U.S. Army in 1871. Restored officers' billets and family housing have authentic furnishings. A museum details the campaign.

Globe ···

A small but stately collection of vintage buildings in the **Globe Historic District** (*Chamber of Commerce, 1360 N. Broad St. 520-425-4495. Mon.-Fri.*) evoke Globe's $134,000,000 silver- and copper-mining bonanza, which lasted from the post-Civil War period to the Depression.

Besh-Ba-Gowah Archaeological Park (*1 mile S via Ariz. 60 and Jesse Hayes Rd. 520-425-0320. Adm. fee*) Hohokam pit houses dating from A.D. 900 underlie a 13th-century Salado pueblo, which you may enjoy exploring on your own.

Excursions

TONTO NATIONAL MONUMENT (*30 miles NW via Ariz. 88. 520-467-2241. Adm. fee*) Well-preserved cliff dwellings built around A.D. 1100 housed Salado farmers who irrigated the valley below for three centuries. A half-mile trail leads to the 19-room **Lower Ruin.** Visitors should make reservations to see the 40-room **Upper Ruin** (*Weekends only Nov.-April*).

THEODORE ROOSEVELT DAM (*35 miles NW via Ariz. 88. Visitor Center 520-467-3200*) In 1911 limestone blocks stacked 280 feet high completed what was then the world's tallest masonry dam and transformed the Salt River Valley into an agricultural cornucopia.

Grand Canyon Region ·····················

Grand Canyon Railway (*233 N. Grand Canyon Blvd., Williams. 520-773-1976 or 800-THE-TRAIN. Mid-March–Oct.; fee*) The spur line used to be the only mode of transportation to the canyon. Revived in 1989, it hauls 1920s-era cars on a 4.5-hour round-trip to a 1908 depot made of logs.

300

Betatakin cliff dwelling, Navajo National Monument

Grand Canyon National Park (*520-638-7888. Adm. fee*) The mile-deep gorge exposes rock 1.7 billion years old. The **South Rim Visitor Center** (*Village Loop Dr. 520-638-7888*) includes historical exhibits. Resembling a European hunting lodge, the 1905 **El Tovar Hotel** (*520-638-2631, ext.6400*) frames canyon-rim views with polished log interiors. Popular **Bright Angel Trail** (*1 mile E of Visitor Center*) to the canyon floor was cut by bighorn sheep, Havasupai Indians, and 19th-century prospectors. Backpackers and mule trains use the 8-mile route, which drops 4,460 feet from the trailhead just west of Bright Angel Lodge.

Tusayan Museum and Ruin (*3 miles W of Visitor Center. 520-638-2305*) Exhibits adjoining an 800-year-old Anasazi village suggest the builders were Hopi forebears. A self-guided trail investigates the ruins.

Navajo National Monument ·················

(*520-672-2366. Adm. fee*) Creek-watered canyons hold two of Arizona's largest cliff dwellings, 150-room **Keet Seel** (*Mem. Day–Labor Day, by advance reservation*) and 135-room **Betatakin** (*May-Sept., by reservation on day of tour*), occupied by Anasazi farmers between A.D. 1250 and 1300. Visitor Center exhibits trace their history and design and display archaeological finds. An overlook permits a distant view of Betatakin, built inside a 452-foot-high alcove of Navajo sandstone. Visiting Betatakin requires a strenuous five-hour, 5-mile round-trip hike, including a steep climb from the valley floor. The 8.5-mile trail to Keet Seel descends a thousand feet and crisscrosses a shallow stream to reach storage areas, ceremonial chambers, and "apartments" beneath a massive overhang. Granaries hold corncobs abandoned 700 years ago.

Phoenix ···

(Convention & Visitors Bureau, 400 E. Van Buren St. 602-254-6500; Mon.-Fri.) A hay camp set up in 1864, Phoenix was named for the mythical bird because it rose from a ruined Hohokam city. A 19th-century Victorian district, **Heritage Square** *(7th and Monroe Sts. 602-262-5071. Tues.-Sun.),* includes **Rosson House** *(6th and Monroe Sts. 602-262-5029. Wed.-Sun. Adm. fee),* an 1895 mansion built for the mayor. The 1900 neoclassical revival **Silva House** *(7th and Adams Sts. 602-236-5451),* a mail-order bungalow, has historical exhibits on turn-of-the-century Phoenix lifestyles.

    Arizona State Capitol Museum *(1700 W. Washington St. 602-542-4675. Mon.-Sat.)* The four-story, copper-domed statehouse opened in 1900 to house the Territorial Legislature. The building, the governor's offices, and the Senate Chamber retain their 1912 appearance.

    Heard Museum *(22 E. Monte Vista Rd. 602-252-8840. Adm. fee)* Native American exhibits include jewelry, pottery, textiles, and kachina dolls.

301

    Pioneer Arizona Living History Museum *(3901 W. Pioneer Rd. 602-993-0212. Oct.-May Wed.-Sun.; adm. fee)* Engaged in activities common to the state's 19th-century pioneers, interpreters in period clothing populate 26 buildings dating from 1861 to 1912.

    Salt River Project History Center Museum *(1521 Project Dr., SRP Admin. Bldg. 602-236-2208. Mon.-Fri.)* Exhibits recount a thousand-year struggle to survive drought, beginning with an explanation of the ingenious irrigation system used by the Hohokam.

Excursion

    CASA GRANDE RUINS N.M. *(50 miles S via I-10 and Ariz. 387 and 287. 520-723-3172. Adm. fee)* Irrigation ditches watered Hohokam cotton and vegetables here between A.D. 950 and 1450, when the desert farmers vanished. The 35-foot-tall structure dominating the ruins was used for ritual or astronomy.

Historic Rosson House, Phoenix

Tucson ··

(Convention & Visitors Bureau, 130 S. Scott Ave. 520-624-1817) Spanish soldiers building a fort in 1775 borrowed the name of a nearby Pima settlement, *Chuk shon* ("spring at the foot of a dark mountain") for El Presidio San Agustin del **Tucson.** Brightly-colored Sonoran adobe architecture decorates the **Barrio Historico** *(Cushing, Simpson, and Kennedy Sts. between Stone and Main Sts.).*

    La Casa Cordova *(175 N. Meyer Ave. 520-624-2333)* Among Tucson's oldest houses (built in the 1850s), La Casa typifies adobe architecture.

Arizona Historical Society Museum and Library *(949 E. 2nd St. 520-628-5774. Donations)* The state's oldest archive documents the influences in Arizona's past—native culture, European exploration, mining, and ranching.

Excursions

SAN XAVIER DEL BAC *(9 miles S via I-19. 1950 San Xavier Rd. 520-294-2624)* In 1797 Franciscans completed their "White Dove of the Desert," the paramount expression of Spanish mission architecture in the U.S.

TUBAC PRESIDIO STATE HISTORIC PARK *(35 miles S via I-19. 1 Presidio Dr. 520-398-2252. Adm. fee)* The site includes remnants of a 1752 presidio in Tubac, regarded as Arizona's first European settlement.

TUMACACORI NATIONAL HISTORICAL PARK *(45 miles S via I-19. 520-398-2341. Adm. fee)* Mission San José de Tumacacori was dedicated in 1691, but Apache hostility and lack of financial support forced its abandonment in 1848. A museum exhibits artifacts from the exquisite church's sad saga.

Other Sites in Arizona

Casa Malpais National Historic Landmark and Ruins *(2 miles NW of Springerville via US 60. Museum, 318 Main St. 520-333-5375. Fee for guided tour of ruins)* Archaeologists excavating the 700-year-old Mogollon pueblo have found a network of burial catacombs.

Fort Bowie National Historic Site *(35 miles E of Willcox via Ariz. 186. Apache Pass Rd. 520-847-2500)* This remote relic of the Army's 1862-1886 campaign against the Apache was built to protect water for troops traveling through the area. Only stone foundations and adobe walls remain.

Hoover Dam *(US 93. Visitor Center 702-293-8321. Adm. fee)* The 726-foot-high concrete dam (the Western Hemisphere's highest) was completed in 1936 to supply water and electricity to the interior Southwest and halt the Colorado River's flooding.

Kinishba Ruins *(7 miles W of Whiteriver via Ariz. 73. 520-338-1230)* The ruins are one of the largest, best preserved Mogollon pueblos in Arizona. Some 2,000 people shared the 400-room complex from A.D. 1100 to 1350.

Kykotsmovi-Old Oraibi *(Ariz. 264. 520-734-2441)* Villages at the center of the Hopi universe, Kykotsmovi nurtures spring-fed peach orchards. Topping Third Mesa 2 miles west since the 1100s, Old Oraibi may be North America's oldest continuously occupied community.

Pipe Spring National Monument *(14 miles W of Fredonia via Ariz. 389. 520-643-7105. Adm. fee)* Site of the only dependable spring in the Arizona Strip, the Mormon cattle ranch was fortified with rock walls in 1871 because residents feared Indian attacks.

Sharlot Hall Museum *(415 W. Gurley St., Prescott. 520-445-3122. Daily April-Oct., Tues.-Sun. rest of year; donations)* Territorial-day Prescott lives on in a dozen buildings, including the original Civil War-era **Governor's Mansion.**

Yuma *(Convention & Visitors Bureau, 377 Main St. 520-783-0071 or 800-293-0071)* A river-crossing point gave the town early importance. The **Fort Yuma Quechan Indian Museum** *(350 Picacho Rd. 619-572-0661. Mon.-Sat.; adm. fee)* exhibits historical photographs, diaries, and artifacts. Granite cellblocks at **Yuma Territorial Prison State Historic Park** *(520-783-4771. Adm. fee)* held prisoners between 1876 and 1909. The **Century House Museum** *(240 Madison Ave. 520-782-1841. Tues.-Sat.; donations)* tells Yuma's story in an 1870s-era adobe residence.

Nevada

Virginia City

Nevada may have been visited by Spanish explorers in 1776, but half a century passed before the arrival of other outsiders. John C. Frémont conducted the first systematic surveys of the area from 1844 to 1845. This helped guide gold-crazed hordes bound for California after 1848, the same year the United States won the region from Mexico. Mormons soon founded Nevada's first permanent settlement, now called Genoa. But Nevada's headline news was yet to break. In 1859 prospectors discovered gold and one of the biggest silver deposits in U.S. history—the Comstock Lode. Nevada cashed in on its new wealth by achieving statehood in 1864, but after the boom began to go bust in the 1880s, the state's population and fortunes dwindled. In the 1930s, Nevada gained notoriety as the home of the "quickie divorce" and legalized gambling. After World War II, the casinos of Las Vegas built the state's biggest industries—gambling and tourism.

Carson City

(Convention & Visitors Bureau, 1900 S. Carson St., Suite 200. 702-687-7410 or 800-NEVADA-1. Mon.-Fri.) In 1858, Abe Curry began promoting this Eagle Valley settlement as Nevada's future capital. It grew into a commercial hub for the Comstock Lode and became the state capital in 1864. You can follow the **Kit Carson Trail** through the historic district.

Nevada State Museum *(600 N. Carson St. 702-687-4810. Adm. fee)* Using Comstock gold and silver, the Carson City mint stamped millions of coins from 1870 to 1893. The museum displays a coin press, examples of coins with the CC mintmark, and a shotgun used to guard bullion shipments.

Orion Clemens House (502 N. Division St. Private) Mark Twain (Samuel Clemens) stayed with his brother in this 1864 house.

Nevada State Capitol (Carson and Musser Sts. 702-687-4810) The 1871 capitol was built of sandstone provided by the state-prison quarry. Displays in the old Senate Chambers include an 1862 map of Nevada Territory and a governor's elkhorn chair.

Nevada State Railroad Museum (2180 S. Carson St. 702-687-6953. Wed.-Sun.; adm. fee) Admire steam locomotives, coaches, and freight cars from the Virginia & Truckee Railroad, a short line that hauled riches from Virginia City. Visitors can ride vintage rail equipment (weekends May-Sept.).

Stewart Indian Cultural Center (5366 Snyder Ave. 702-882-1808. Donations) At a former boarding school (1890-1980), you'll see E. S. Curtis photogravures, regional basketry, and a functioning trading post.

Excursions

GENOA (15 miles SW via US 395 and Genoa Lane) Founded by Mormons in 1851, Genoa is Nevada's oldest settlement. **Mormon Station State Park** (Foothill Rd. and Genoa Ln. 702-782-2590. Mid-May–mid-Oct.; donations) is a replica of the original stockade and trading post; a museum focuses on early settlement. At the **Genoa Courthouse Museum** (702-782-4325. Mid-May–mid-Oct.; donations) you'll see Washo Indian baskets, a schoolroom, a jail, and displays on the original Ferris Wheel (invented by a Genoan) and Snowshoe Thompson, who carried mail to Sacramento.

FORT CHURCHILL STATE HISTORICAL PARK (40 miles E via US 50 and 95A. 702-577-2345. Adm. fee) Nevada's first Army base was built in 1860 to stand guard against Indian raids on the Overland Trail. It also preserved Union allegiance during the Civil War and served as a Pony Express stop before abandonment in 1869. Ruined adobe walls remain near the Carson River, and a Visitor Center brings fort history to life.

VIRGINIA CITY (14 miles NE via US 50 and Nev. 341 and 342. Information 702-847-0311) This 1870s boomtown boasted restaurants serving seafood and champagne, a hundred saloons, the only elevator between Chicago and San Francisco, and a dozen newspapers, one of which gave a start to Mark Twain. Many attractions line C Street: the **Fourth Ward School Museum** (702-847-0975), where visitors learn lessons in Comstock history; the **Nevada Gambling Museum** (702-847-9022. March-Dec.; adm. fee), with its historic gaming tables; the **Mark Twain Museum** (702-847-0525. Adm. fee), featuring original printing presses and Mark Twain's desk; and **The Way It Was Museum** (702-847-0766. Adm. fee), which offers a video program, working models of mines, and Comstock artifacts. Sights on B Street include **Piper's Opera House** (702-847-0433. April-Oct.; adm. fee), where Edwin Booth and Lotta Crabtree performed, and the 1868 **Castle** (702-847-0275. Mem. Day–late Oct.; adm. fee), a residence whose original furnishings include chandeliers and silver doorknobs. The **Virginia & Truckee Railroad** (702-847-0380. May-Oct.; fee) runs steam trains to nearby Gold Hill.

BOWERS MANSION (10 miles N via US 395 and Old 395. 702-849-0201. Mem. Day–Labor Day, weekends May and Sept.-Oct.; adm. fee) "Sandy" Bowers, the first millionaire of the Comstock Lode, built this 1864 granite mansion. To furnish it, he took his wife on a European shopping binge.

RENO (*30 miles N via US 395*) The collection at the **National Automobile Museum** (*10 Lake St. S. 702-333-9300. Adm. fee*) ranges from a 1907 Thomas Flyer (which won the Great Race from New York to Paris) to James Dean's 1949 Mercury from *Rebel Without A Cause*. The **University of Nevada, Reno** (*9th and N. Virginia Sts. 702-784-1110*) dates to the 1880s. On campus is the **Nevada Historical Society** (*1650 N. Virginia St. 702-688-1190. Closed Sun.; adm. fee*), where a self-guided tour looks at people and artifacts—Indians, trappers, miners, and a 1920s whiskey still.

Other Sites in Nevada

Austin After silver was discovered in 1862, Austin grew into Nevada's second largest town. Surviving buildings include the **Gridley Store** and the 1897 **Stokes Castle** (a granite "Roman tower" that was a mining financier's summer home).

Early 20th-century ruin, Rhyolite

Belmont (*45 miles N of Tonopah via Nev. 376. 702-482-3558*) This near-ghost town, founded in 1865, has a fine brick courthouse, dilapidated storefronts, and one saloon still serving drinks.

305

Eureka A highlight of this early mining town, the 1880 **Eureka Opera House** (*10201 Main St. 702-237-6006. Mon.-Fri.*) features a horseshoe balcony and 1924 curtain that advertises local businesses. The **Eureka County Historical Society Sentinel Museum** (*Monroe St. and Ruby Hill Ave. 702-237-5010*) houses the presses and Linotype machines of a frontier newspaper.

Grimes Point Archaeological Area (*10 miles E of Fallon via US 50. 702-885-6000*) A trail leads to petroglyphs pecked into basalt rocks starting from about 7,000 years ago; they depict abstract geometric designs.

Hoover Dam (*10 miles E of Boulder City via US 93. 702-293-8321. Fee for guided tours*) This barrier across the Colorado River rises 726 feet and measures 660 feet thick at the base. Dedicated in 1935, the dam created Lake Mead, providing water for millions of people in the West. Tours descend to generators that can power half a million homes. A Visitor Center has an observation deck and exhibits on Lake Mead and electric power. **Boulder City** was an "instant city" finished in 1932 to house dam workers. The **Boulder City/Hoover Dam Museum** (*444 Hotel Plaza. 702-294-1988. Donations*) displays construction photos, a cable lamp, an old boiler, and other 1930s artifacts.

Lost City Museum (*721 S. Moapa Valley Blvd., Overton. 702-397-2193. Adm. fee*) This small institution is dedicated to the Lost City, or Pueblo Grande de Nevada, a 30-mile stretch of ancestral Pueblo sites. You'll see a rebuilt wattle-and-daub house and displays of pots, jewelry, and tools.

Old Las Vegas Mormon Fort State Historical Park (*908 Las Vegas Blvd. N., Las Vegas. 702-486-3511*) Visitors see remains of Nevada's oldest European-American structure, a Mormon fort built in 1855 to protect travelers.

Rhyolite (*4 miles W of Beatty via Nev. 374. 702-553-2424*) Famous for a house constructed of 53,000 bottles, this early 20th-century mining town once had its own phone company and electrically lighted streets.

Working replicas of *Jupiter* and *No. 119*, Golden Spike National Historic Site

Bands of Paleo-Indians roamed Utah by at least 10,000 years ago. For more than 6,000 years, these Ice Age hunter-gatherers lived in cave dwellings overlooking the Great Salt Lake's freshwater ancestor. About the time of Christ, Utah's northern two-thirds was the domain of the Fremont people. Their contemporaries, the Anasazi, farmed southern Utah's canyon country, but around A.D. 1300 they abandoned their dwellings. Other tribes then arose: the Paiute, Goshute, Shoshone, and Ute, for whom Utah is named. Accounts of the Great Salt Lake Valley's aridity by early 19th-century fur traders offered settlers no encouragement. To Mormons, however, the region's isolation offered a haven from persecution. Their faith and determination to prosper created a culture of astonishing resourcefulness.

Ogden

In 1845 mountain man Miles Goodyear established his claim as Utah's first permanent Anglo-American resident by building a riverside stockade and trading post here. By 1900 Ogden was a major rail hub.

Fort Buenaventura State Park (*2450 A Ave. 801-621-4808. April-Nov.; adm. fee*) A re-creation of Goodyear's outpost was built using methods and tools employed in his day.

Union Station (*2501 Wall Ave. 801-629-8535. Mon.-Sat.; adm. fee to*

museum) First dedicated in 1924, the depot still welcomes travelers to the **Historic District**. Inside, the Ogden Railway Museum displays replicas from the transcontinental railroad completed at Promontory Summit in 1869.

St. George

Mormon colonists on a cotton-raising mission in 1861 founded this city in southwestern Utah. The name honors Church Elder George A. Smith, who discovered that eating raw potatoes cured pioneers of scurvy.

St. George Temple *(490 S. 300 East St. 801-673-5181)* Construction of Utah's first temple (the oldest in use) began in 1871 and lasted nearly six years, employing as a pile driver a cannon bought by Jesse W. Crosby from Commodore Stockton's fleet.

Brigham Young Winter Home *(89 W. 200 North St. 801-673-2517)* The aging Brigham Young moved into this two-story adobe in 1873 and used the residence as a winter home while he stewarded church affairs.

Excursions

WASHINGTON COTTON MILL *(5 miles N via I-15. 375 W. Telegraph Rd., Washington City. 801-634-1880)* The burly, three-story, rock building—a relic of "cotton mission" days—dates from 1865.

JACOB HAMBLIN HOME *(6 miles NW via Utah 18. 3465 Hamblin Rd., Santa Clara. 801-673-2161)* Hamblin had unusual success negotiating peace with tribes resisting the Mormon influx. Sent to Santa Clara to parlay with Paiute, he built the sandstone house in 1863 for his two wives and many of their two dozen offspring.

IRON MISSION STATE PARK *(53 miles N on I-15. 585 N. Main St., Cedar City. 801-586-9290. Adm. fee)* A museum commemorates the Deseret Iron Manufacturing Co., which made an 1850s bid for independence from Eastern suppliers of nails, spikes, stoves, and farm implements. The company's crumbling foundations, the **Old Irontown Ruins,** lie 2.5 miles south of Utah 56, mile marker 41.

Salt Lake City

In 1847 pilgrims led by Brigham Young trekked west from a Mormon colony in Illinois, finding in Utah's fertile Salt Lake Valley a haven from religious persecution.

Temple Square *(S. Temple and Main Sts. 801-240-2534 or 800-447-1818)* Forty years of labor completed the Salt Lake Temple in 1893. **The Mormon Tabernacle** *(801-240-5234)* houses its famed choir and 11,623-pipe organ. Finished in 1867, the hall's 80-foot-high oval dome exhibits astounding acoustics. Music resounds in **Assembly Hall** *(800-537-9703)*, completed in 1880 using granite from the Temple project.

Beehive House *(67 E. South Temple St. 801-240-2671)* The adobe manse was completed in 1854 as an official residence for Young, the first President of the Church of Jesus Christ of Latter-day Saints. The carved beehive on the roof symbolizes industry and thrift.

Utah State Capitol *(300 N. State St. 801-538-3000)* Inheritance taxes on a railroad tycoon's estate funded construction of this Renaissance Revival masterpiece in 1913. Murals in the lofty rotunda depict state history.

Pioneer Memorial Museum *(300 N. Main St. 801-538-1050. Closed Sun. Sept.-May. Donations)* A voluminous collection of artifacts documents the

Salt Lake Temple, Salt Lake City

308

Great Salt Lake Valley pioneer era and the Mormon saga.

Utah State Historical Society Museum (*300 S. Rio Grande. 801-533-3500. Mon.-Sat.*) Exhibits in the heroic 1910 Rio Grande Depot evoke Utah's era of early settlement and industry.

Fort Douglas (*Wasatch Dr. and 500 South St. 801-584-4223*) Mormon dreams of a State of Deseret reaching the Pacific brought the Army to the Wasatch foothills in 1862. Original buildings surround the **Fort Douglas Military Museum** (*Bldg. 32, Potter St. 801-588-5188. Tues.-Sat.*), which celebrates the post's all-black "buffalo soldiers" battalion.

This Is The Place State Park (*2601 Sunnyside Ave. 801-584-8391*) Church lore holds that from this overlook Brigham Young proclaimed the Salt Lake basin his long-sought refuge. Historic buildings moved from around the valley are preserved in **Old Deseret Village.**

Wheeler Historic Farm (*6351 S. 900 East. 801-264-2241. Adm. fee*) Henry and Sariah Wheeler first plowed here in 1887, prospering enough to build a Victorian house in 1898. Docents tend the fields and gardens.

Excursions

ANTELOPE ISLAND STATE PARK (*35 miles N of Salt Lake City off I-15 on Utah 108. Visitor Center, 4528 W. 1700 S. 801-773-2941. Adm. fee*) Explorers Kit Carson and John Frémont named the Great Salt Lake's biggest isle for the pronghorn found here in 1843. A herd of American bison was introduced in 1893.

BENSON HISTORIC GRIST MILL (*15 miles W via Utah 201 and 138. 801-882-7678. May-Nov. Tues.-Sat.*) The mill's stone wheels first turned in 1854, making it one of Utah's oldest buildings—held together without nails by wooden pegs and rawhide strips.

KENNICOT UTAH COPPER MINE (*20 miles SW via I-15, 7800 S. St. 801-322-7300. April-Oct.; adm. fee*) Digging began in 1906 in the world's first and largest open-pit mine. The 2.5-mile-wide, half-mile-deep mine has yielded more wealth than California's gold rush, Nevada's Comstock Lode, and Alaska's Klondike combined.

DONNER-REED MUSEUM (*25 miles W via Utah 201 and 138. Clark and Cooley Sts., Grantsville. 801-884-3348*) Pioneer and Indian artifacts include items jettisoned in 1846 by the ill-fated 87-member Donner-Reed party. Slowed by difficult terrain and Indian raids, the emigrants lost 40 people in a snowbound Sierra Nevada ordeal that led some of them to cannibalism.

PARK CITY (*25 miles SE via I-80 and US 40. Visitor Center, 528 Main St. 801-649-6100 or 800-453-1360*) An 1868 silver strike created a surplus of saloons supplying miscreants to the Territorial Jail, now part of the **Park City Museum** (*528 Main St. 801-649-6104. Donations*). The four-block **Historic Main Street** survived an 1898 fire that nearly consumed the city.

Other Sites in Utah

Anasazi State Park *(Boulder. 801-335-7308. Adm. fee)* From about A.D. 1050 to 1200, Anasazi farming families occupied the 87-room village here.

Camp Floyd/Stagecoach Inn State Park *(Fairfield. 801-768-8932. Mid-April–mid-Oct.; adm. fee)* Fears of a Mormon takeover of Utah brought 3,500 soldiers from Kansas in 1858. Travelers including Mark Twain sojourned at the inn, now the **Stagecoach Inn Museum.**

Cove Fort *(I-70 just E of I-15 jct. 801-438-5547)* The stronghold was built in 1867 as a traveler's way station between Fillmore and Beaver. The 12-room bastion has been restored to its original appearance.

Fremont Indian State Park *(11550 W. Clear Creek Canyon Rd., Sevier. 801-527-4631. Adm. fee to museum)* The largest known settlement of Fremont people was uncovered nearby in 1983 during construction of I-70. A museum adjoins pictographs and petroglyphs and displays artifacts found among 60 pit houses and 40 granaries.

Fruita *(Capitol Reef National Park. 801-425-3791)* About ten Mormon settler families established the village in the 1880s, planting orchards in fields tilled by Fremont Indian farmers between A.D. 600-1200. Restored buildings include a turn-of-the-century farmhouse and log schoolhouse.

Golden Spike National Historic Site *(Utah 83, off I-84. 801-471-2209. Adm. fee)* From May to mid-October, reenactments commemorate the completion of the transcontinental railroad, using reproductions of the locomotives that met here on May 10, 1869.

Hovenweep Natl. Monument *(Off Utah 262. 970-529-4461)* See page 315.

John Wesley Powell River History Museum *(885 E. Main St., Green River. 801-564-3526. Adm. fee)* Antique boats, explorers' journals, and a video recall Utah's early river-running tradition, launched by John Wesley Powell's 1869 expedition down the Green and Colorado Rivers.

Parowan Gap Petroglyphs *(N of Cedar City, 2.5 miles E on Gap Road off Utah 130)* About a thousand years ago, Sevier-Fremont people started chipping designs and depictions of animals and humans into the walls of a wind-gap corridor cut through the Red Hills by an ancient river. The panels rank among America's finest ancient rock art.

Potash Road *(NW of Moab off US 191)* Scenic Utah 279 follows a notch cut by the Colorado River through redrock formations. Viewscopes focus on dinosaur tracks. Petroglyphs 30 feet above the road were etched by ancestral Pueblo people.

Main Street, Park City

Ronald V. Jensen Living Historical Farm *(US 89/91, Wellsville. 801-245-4064. June-Aug. Tues.-Sat.; adm. fee)* Buildings moved from other Cache Valley locations re-create a 127-acre, World War I-era Mormon homestead.

Territorial Statehouse State Park *(Via I-15. 50 W. Capitol Ave., Fillmore. 801-743-5316. Adm. fee)* Naming a new state capital after President Millard Fillmore failed to win Utah's admittance to the Union as the State of Deseret. Funds for a four-winged statehouse petered out, leaving only the south wing completed. The capital was returned to Salt Lake City in 1858.

The Rockies

Few regions retain a landscape that so vividly reflects the past as the Rocky Mountains. Native Americans left their mark, as did the Spanish who pressed into Colorado during the mid-1500s, followed by French, British, and American explorers in the late 18th and early 19th centuries. Fur trappers began hunting here in the early 1800s and later guided emigrants along the Oregon Trail. Gold strikes in the 1860s and '70s poured great wealth into the national economy, but also fueled Indian conflicts. When the tribes were finally contained, settlement began in earnest and the modern West started to take shape.

Pioneer barn in Grand Teton National Park

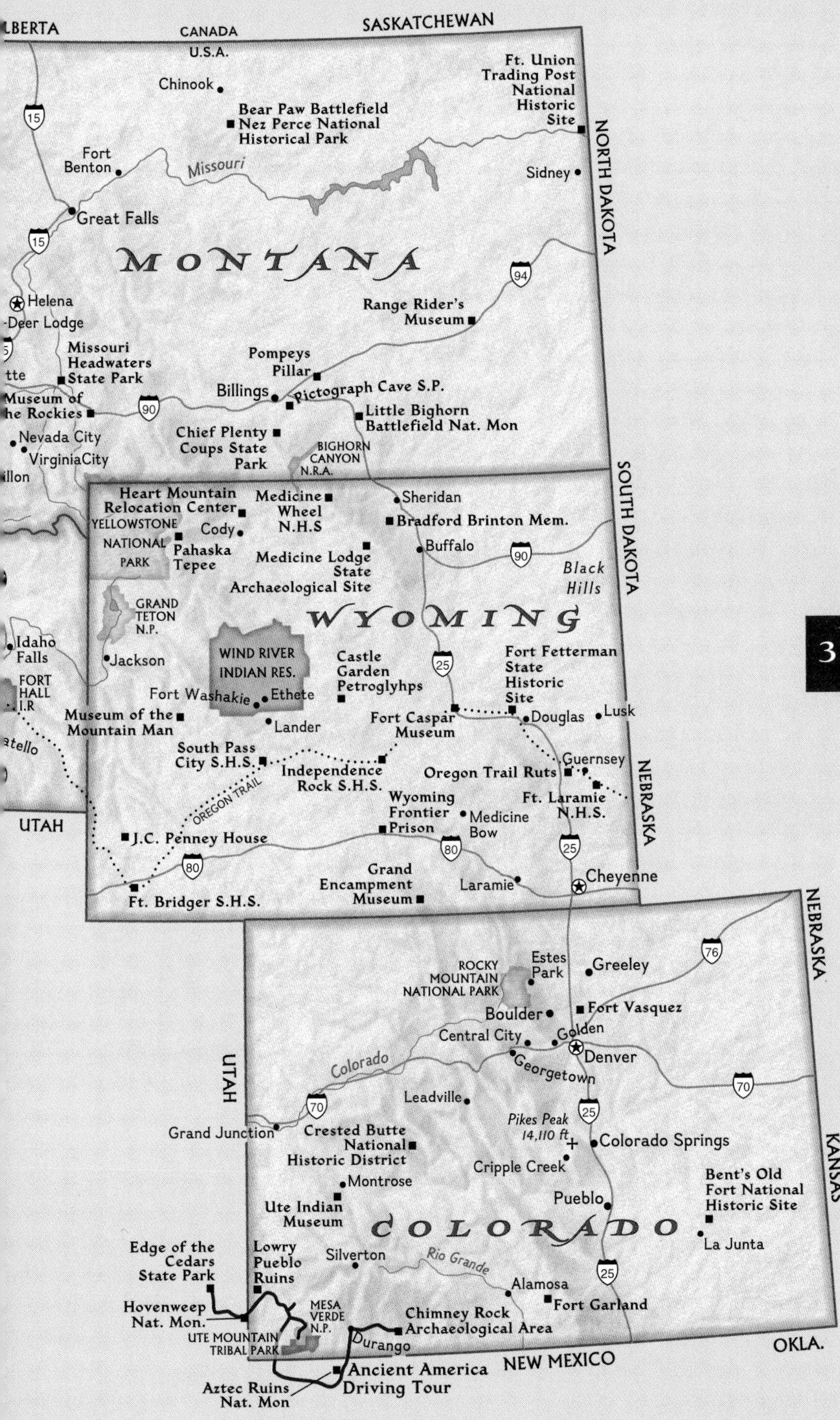

ALBERTA
CANADA
SASKATCHEWAN
U.S.A.
Chinook
Bear Paw Battlefield
Nez Perce National
Historical Park
Ft. Union
Trading Post
National
Historic
Site
Fort
Benton
Missouri
Sidney
NORTH DAKOTA
Great Falls
MONTANA
Helena
Deer Lodge
94
Range Rider's
Museum
Missouri
Headwaters
State Park
Pompeys
Pillar
Museum of
the Rockies
Billings
Pictograph Cave S.P.
Nevada City
Virginia City
Chief Plenty
Coups State
Park
Little Bighorn
Battlefield Nat. Mon
BIGHORN
CANYON
N.R.A.
SOUTH DAKOTA
Heart Mountain
Relocation Center
Medicine
Wheel
N.H.S
Sheridan
Bradford Brinton Mem.
YELLOWSTONE
NATIONAL
PARK
Cody
Pahaska
Tepee
Buffalo
90
Medicine Lodge
State
Archaeological Site
Black
Hills
GRAND
TETON
N.P.
WYOMING
Idaho
Falls
Jackson
WIND RIVER
INDIAN RES.
Castle
Garden
Petroglyphs
Fort Fetterman
State
Historic
Site
FORT
HALL
I.R.
Fort Washakie
Ethete
25
Museum of the
Mountain Man
Lander
Fort Caspar
Museum
Douglas
Lusk
NEBRASKA
South Pass
City S.H.S.
Independence
Rock S.H.S.
OREGON TRAIL
Oregon Trail Ruts
Guernsey
Wyoming
Frontier
Prison
Medicine
Bow
Ft. Laramie
N.H.S.
UTAH
J.C. Penney House
80
25
Cheyenne
Ft. Bridger S.H.S.
Grand
Encampment
Museum
Laramie

ROCKY
MOUNTAIN
NATIONAL PARK
Estes
Park
Greeley
76
NEBRASKA
Boulder
Fort Vasquez
Central City
Golden
Denver
UTAH
Colorado
Georgetown
70
70
Leadville
KANSAS
Grand Junction
70
Crested Butte
Historic District
Pikes Peak
14,110 ft
Colorado Springs
25
Montrose
Cripple Creek
Bent's Old
Fort National
Historic Site
Ute Indian
Museum
Pueblo
COLORADO
La Junta
Edge of the
Cedars
State Park
Lowry
Pueblo
Ruins
Silverton
Rio Grande
Alamosa
Fort Garland
Hovenweep
Nat. Mon.
MESA
VERDE
N.P.
Chimney Rock
Archaeological Area
25
UTE MOUNTAIN
TRIBAL PARK
Durango
Aztec Ruins
Nat. Mon.
Ancient America
Driving Tour
NEW MEXICO
OKLA.

Colorado

Cliff Palace, Mesa Verde National Park

Inhabited by Paleo-Indians thousands of years before Europeans arrived, Colorado was claimed first by Spain and then by France. The United States acquired it in stages beginning with the Louisiana Purchase of 1803. Colorado became a territory in 1861 and the 38th state in 1876. Zebulon Pike explored the area in 1806, and trappers combed its rivers for beaver through the 1840s. Miners and settlers streamed into the mountains during the gold rush years of the 1850s and '60s, and again during the 1870s and '80s, when silver was discovered. Railroads laid track to the rich lodes and smelter towns, and when the U.S. government forced the Plains tribes onto reservations, the railroads opened up Colorado's plains to ranching and farming.

Colorado Springs

(Visitors Bureau, 104 S. Cascade Ave. 719-635-7506) Founded as a resort in 1871, the city sprawls at the foot of Pikes Peak and draws great crowds to its museums, shops, and intensely developed scenic areas.

Western Museum of Mining and Industry *(125 Gleneagle Dr. 719-488-0880. March-Nov., call for off-season hours; adm. fee)* Restored steam engines, drills, hoists, and other exhibits examine mining techniques and history.

Excursions
PIKES PEAK COG RAILWAY *(6 miles W via US 24 in Manitou Springs. 515 Ruxton Ave. 719-685-5401. Late April–late Oct.; fare)* Since 1891 trains have been chugging to the 14,110-foot summit of the peak named for Zebulon Pike, an explorer who saw it in 1806. The trips take 1¼ hours.

CRIPPLE CREEK *(40 miles NW via US 24 and S via Colo. 67. 719-689-2169)* Museums, a mine tour, and redbrick Victorian buildings jammed with operating casinos recall the early days of this gold-mining town. You can also ride a narrow-gauge railroad, pulled by miniature steam locomotives.

Denver ··

(Visitors Bureau 303-892-1112) Colorado's capital city sprang up during the 1860s gold rush and remained closely tethered to the changing fortunes of precious-metal mining through the turn of the century. Architectural reminders of the old days crop up in the city's **Lower Downtown Historic District** and its **Capitol Hill** neighborhood.

Brown Palace Hotel *(321 17th St. 303-297-3111 or 800-321-2599)* This Italian Renaissance-style hotel opened in 1892 and still offers luxurious accommodations for guests, as well as historical exhibits for drop-in visitors.

Museum of Western Art *(1727 Tremont Pl. 303-296-1880. Tues.-Sat.; adm. fee)* Housed in a former brothel, the museum reflects the history of the West through works by Frederic Remington, Charles Russell, and others.

U.S. Mint *(320 W. Colfax Ave. at Cherokee St. 303-844-3582. Mon.-Fri.)* Tours offer glimpses of coin production and tell the history of the mint, which has been stamping out coins here since 1906.

Byers-Evans House Museum *(1310 Bannock St. 303-620-4933. Closed Mon.; adm. fee)* Built during the early 1880s, the restored mansion houses the **Denver History Museum**, which highlights Denver's early days.

Colorado History Museum *(1300 Broadway. 303-866-3682. Adm. fee)* Fine exhibits track history from ancient Pueblo peoples to modern entrepreneurs.

Molly Brown House Museum *(1340 Pennsylvania St. 303-832-4092. Tues.-Sun. in summer; adm. fee)* Guides lead tours through the Victorian home of the "unsinkable" Molly Brown, who survived the 1912 *Titanic* disaster and inspired a 1960s play about her life.

Excursions
GOLDEN *(6 miles W via Colo. 58. Chamber of Commerce 303-279-3113 or 800-590-3113)* The town offers glimpses of the past at the 1867 **Astor House Hotel** *(822 12th St. 303-278-3557 Tues.-Sat.; adm. fee)*, the **Colorado School of Mines Geology Museum** *(16th and Maple. 303-273-3815)*, the **Buffalo Bill Memorial Museum and Grave** *(W on 19th St. to Lookout Mt. Rd. 303-526-0747. Daily in summer; adm. fee)*, and the extensive **Colorado Railroad Museum** *(17155 W. 44th Ave. 303-279-4591. Adm. fee)*.

Pikes Peak Cog Railway

BOULDER *(27 miles NW via US 36. Visitors Bureau 303-442-2911 or 800-444-0447)* This old mining-supply and university town boasts three historic districts. **Chautauqua Park** *(900 Baseline. 303-442-3282)*, in operation since 1897, is the only intact, active Chautauqua site west of the Mississippi River.

FORT VASQUEZ *(25 miles N via US 85. 970-785-2832. Daily in summer)* A reproduction of an 1830s fur-trading post, the fort exhibits artifacts from the original site.

Durango ·····················

(Chamber of Commerce 970-247-0312 or 800-525-8855) Founded in 1880 as a headquarters for the Denver & Rio Grande Railroad, Durango grew into a small city of cheerful Victorian hotels, shops, and houses—many of which survive downtown and along **The Boulevard** *(E. 3rd Ave.)*.

Durango & Silverton Narrow-Gauge Railroad *(479 Main Ave. 970-247-2733.*

Silverton Historic District

May-Oct., call for off-season hours; fare) Ore cars bound for smelters once rumbled along these tracks. Today, coal-fired steam locomotives ply the 45-mile route, pulling 1880s-style passenger cars.

Excursions

SILVERTON HISTORIC DISTRICT *(49 miles N via US 550. 970-387-5654 or 800-752-4494)* An 1870s mining town, Silverton lies in a spectacular alpine setting and retains many of its original buildings, including bars and brothels, grand hotels, storefronts, and the 1902 jail, which now houses the **San Juan County Historical Society Museum** *(1567 Greene St. 970-387-5838. Mem. Day–mid-Oct.; adm. fee)*.

Ancient America Driving Tour ·········
280 miles, 2 days

This drive spans more than a thousand years of Anasazi prehistory, from fifth-century encampments to the pueblo and cliff-dwelling communities abandoned about 1300.

1. Locked in silence and mystery at 7,600 feet, the ruins of a pre-Columbian city crown the 3,160-acre **Chimney Rock Archaeological Area** *(41 miles E of Durango. 970-883-5359. Mid-May–mid-Sept.)*. On Chimney Rock Mesa overlooking the Piedra River, the settlement's multistory masonry design and circular kivas resemble Chaco Canyon's. Anthropologists believe the kivas were used for religious observances between A.D. 950 and 1150.

2. Aztec Ruins N. M. *(W on US 160, S on US 550. 505-334-6174. Adm. fee)* Thinking that the ruins were Aztec in origin, 19th-century settlers misnamed this Anasazi pueblo. Most of the 3-level, 500-room community was built between A.D. 1106 and 1124. The reconstructed Great Kiva, a one-story circular structure, complements the museum's exhibits of pottery and fabrics.

3. Salmon Ruin *(US 550 to Bloomfield, 2 miles W on US 64)* This two-story, C-shaped Chaco Canyon colony was occupied between A.D. 1088 and 1095. Scholars study artifacts recovered here in the adjoining **San Juan County museum** *(6131 US 64. 505-632-2013. Adm. fee)*.

Ancestral Pueblo

The mystery lifts slowly from the ancient people called Anasazi, ancestors of modern Hopi, Zuni, and Pueblo Indians. For over 2,000 years the Anasazi flourished on a Southwest domain the size of New England. Then, just before A.D. 1300, they abruptly retreated southeast to the Rio Grande region, abandoning half of their ancient lands—virtually all of the Colorado Plateau.

4. A 20-mile dirt road leads into **Ute Mountain Tribal Park** *(W on US 64 to Shiprock, N on US 666/160 to Towaoc. 970-565-3751 or 800-847-5485. Reservations required. April-Oct.; adm. fee).* Here hundreds of Anasazi ruins date from the 6th to the 13th century. The park's remoteness and the ruins' fragility make it mandatory to take a guide.

5. Mesa Verde National Park *(N on US 160, 8 miles E of Cortez. 970-529-4465. Park open year-round, visitor facilities open mid-May–mid-Oct.; adm. fee)* An Anasazi cultural center, the site was inhabited between A.D. 550 and 1270. Superbly preserved structures include multistoried dwellings huddled beneath mesa cliffs rising 2,000 feet. Displays in the **Chapin Mesa Museum** *(970-529-4475)* offer insights into the cliff-dweller world. **Spruce Tree House,** Mesa Verde's best preserved structure, stands at the end of a paved quarter-mile trail. North America's largest known cliff dwelling, 217-room **Cliff Palace,** is a short stroll off a 6-mile loop drive.

6. The **Anasazi Heritage Center** *(US 160 W to Colo. 145 at Dolores. 970-882-4811)* A research-oriented museum features interactive exhibits that allow you to practice Anasazi household skills. A half-mile trail zigzags to the **Dominguez and Escalante Ruins,** small rock houses representing two periods of Pueblo architecture.

7. Lowry Pueblo Ruins *(9 miles W of Pleasant View, off US 666. 970-247-4082)* The pueblo is noted for the Great Painted Kiva. Built between A.D. 1090 and 1110, its walls are decorated with painted murals of geometric patterns. Nine other kivas suggest that religious ceremony figured large in the village, whose population may have reached one hundred.

8. Continue SW on a gravel road to **Hovenweep National Monument** *(970-529-4461),* a string of six units occupied from the 5th to the 13th century. The ruins are unique among Great Pueblo period communities by virtue of square, circular, and D-shaped towers that archaeologists think were solar observatories. A 2-mile loop trail visits dwellings and granaries in the Square Tower Group. An 8-mile round-trip trail, open to high-clearance, four-wheel-drive vehicles, follows a dry wash to three other ruins.

9. Edge of the Cedars State Park *(Utah 262 and US 191 in Blanding. 660*

315

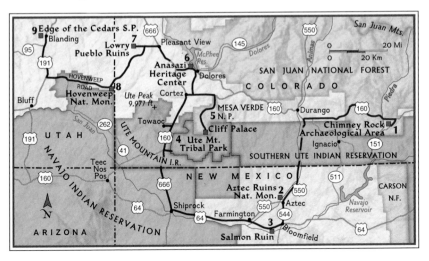

W. 400 North. 801-678-2238) protects a half-dozen complexes dating from A.D. 700 to 1220. The site includes ten kivas and is credited to successive generations of Anasazi, Navajo, and Ute.

Mining Communities

In the 1850s gold and silver drew swarms of miners and led to the construction of narrow-gauge railroad networks and dozens of Victorian towns at high elevations. Some towns survive today as resort communities.

Central City *(Colo. 119. 303-582-5251 or 800-542-2999)* An 1859 gold strike sparked a mining boom that built an elaborate Victorian business district now largely devoted to casino gambling. Spirited tours lead through the 1872 **Teller House** hotel *(120 Eureka St. 303-582-3200)* and the 1873 **Central City Opera House** *(200 Eureka St. 303-292-6700. Adm. fee).*

Georgetown *(Off I-70)* The 1860s mining town preserves 200 original buildings, including residences such as the 1867 **Hamill House** *(305 Argentine St. 303-569-2840. June-Aug.; adm. fee)* and ornate commercial buildings such as the **Hotel de Paris** *(409 6th St. 303-569-2311. Daily June–early Sept., weekends Oct.-May; adm. fee).* From the outskirts of town runs the **Georgetown Loop Railroad** *(1106 Rose St. 303-569-2403. Mem. Day–Sept.; fare),* a narrow-gauge steam train that plies spiraling tracks to historic **Silver Plume.**

Leadville *(US 24)* An 1880's silver boom built Leadville's historic district. Don't miss the **National Mining Hall of Fame and Museum** *(120 W. 9th St. 719-486-1229. Adm. fee);* the 1879 **Tabor Opera House** *(308 Harrison Ave. 719-486 1147. June-Sept.; adm. fee);* and the **Matchless Mine** *(E. 7th St. 719-486-0371. June–Labor Day; adm. fee),* where the legendary Baby Doe Tabor, whose millionaire husband went broke when silver prices fell, died penniless in 1935.

Other Sites

Bent's Old Fort N.H.S. *(8 miles E of La Junta on Colo. 194. 719-384-2596. Adm. fee)* The 1840s fur-trading post has been reconstructed and serves as an outstanding living history museum.

Bent's Old Fort National Historic Site

Crested Butte National Historic District *(Chamber of Commerce 970-349-6438)* Victorian storefronts line the main street of this restored 1880s coal-mining town and ski resort.

Estes Park *(Chamber of Commerce 970-586-4431 or 800-44-ESTES)* Gateway to Rocky Mountain N.P., the town boasts the elegant 1909 **Stanley Hotel** *(333 Wonderview Ave. 970-586-3371 or 800-ROCKIES),* built by the inventor of the Stanley Steamer auto. The **MacGregor Ranch and Museum** *(N on Devil's Gulch Rd. 970-586-3749. Summer)* re-creates an 1870s homestead.

Greeley Begun in 1870 as a utopian agricultural community, the town preserves the **Meeker Home** *(1324 9th Ave. 970-350-9221. Mid-April–mid-Oct. Tues.-Sun.; adm. fee),* which belonged to founder Nathan Meeker.

Ute Indian Museum and Ouray Memorial Park *(3 miles S of Montrose on US 550. 970-249-3098. Mid-May–Sept.; adm. fee)* Exhibits of clothing, weapons, and other items recall the lives of Chief Ouray and other Ute.

Wyoming

Reenactment of a Cheyenne-Deadwood Stage run, Lusk

At times claimed by Spain, France, and England, Wyoming fell within the borders of the U.S. through a handful of treaties beginning with the Louisiana Purchase. It became a territory in 1868 and the 44th state in 1890. During the 1820s and '30s, fur trappers crisscrossed Wyoming, living with and learning from the Apsalooka (Crow), Lakota (Sioux), Shoshone, and other tribes. Emigrants followed, trundling through Wyoming from 1842 to 1868 on the Oregon Trail. In 1867 the nation's first transcontinental railroad began to lay track and establish towns across southern Wyoming. During the 1860s and '70s, Sioux, Cheyenne, and Arapaho fought for control of the Powder River grasslands and the Black Hills. After the defeat of the tribes, settlement and a booming livestock industry helped lay the groundwork for Wyoming's economy, which also relies heavily on coal, oil, and tourism.

Cheyenne

(Visitors Bureau 307-778-3133 or 800-426-5009) Founded in 1867, Cheyenne began as a rowdy construction camp for the Union Pacific. The town prospered as a jumping-off point for the Black Hills gold rush, a shipping point for livestock, and the government seat for the territory and state. In July Cheyenne throws the country's largest outdoor rodeo bash.

Historic Governors' Mansion *(300 E. 21st St. 307-777-7878. Tues.-Sat.)* From 1905 to 1976, Wyoming governors lived in this elegant colonial revival house just a few blocks from the State Capitol.

Cheyenne Frontier Days Old West Museum
(4501 N. Carey Ave. 307-778-7290. Adm. fee)
Rodeo champ videos, autographed hats, and
other memorabilia celebrate the country's largest
outdoor rodeo. Exhibits include cowboy tools
and equipment and Wyoming's finest collection
of restored buggies.

Cody

*(Chamber of Commerce, 836 Sheridan Ave.
307-587-2777)* William "Buffalo Bill" Cody—
Pony Express rider, scout, buffalo hunter, and
showman—lent his name for this 1890s cowboy town. Buffalo Bill's star appeal and the
proximity of Yellowstone National Park made
Cody a popular vacation center.

Buffalo Bill Historical Center

Buffalo Bill Historical Center *(Sheridan
Ave. 307-587-4771. Adm. fee)* This sprawling,
first-class collection of Western art and Americana contains four museums. The **Whitney Gallery of Western Art** exhibits a sensational variety
of original paintings, sculptures, prints, and illustrated letters. The **Cody
Firearms Museum** claims the world's largest collection of American sport
and military guns. The **Plains Indian Museum** displays a wealth of Native
American objects, and the **Buffalo Bill Museum** devotes itself to the life
and times of William Frederick Cody.

Excursion

HEART MOUNTAIN RELOCATION CENTER *(15 miles E via US 14A)*
One of ten camps where the U.S. confined Japanese-Americans during
World War II, Heart Mountain detained 11,000 so-called "evacuees," turn-
ing it into Wyoming's third largest city. A small memorial marks the site.

Grand Teton National Park

(307-739-3600. Adm. fee) Established in 1929, this spectacular mountain park eventually was expanded to encompass much of the floor of the
Jackson Hole Valley. Homesteading began in the 1880s. Dude ranches
and other forms of tourism followed within a generation.

Menor-Noble Historic District *(Ferry runs July-Aug.)* Bill Menor built
a cable ferry across the Snake River in 1892. The old boat and a small
cluster of whitewashed buildings, along with the **Maude Noble Cabin** and
a collection of wagons, recall the settlement era.

Indian Arts Museum *(Colter Bay Visitor Center. May-Sept.)* Extensive
exhibits of traditional clothing, utensils, weapons, children's toys, and
works of art offer intriguing glimpses of Native American life.

Laramie

(Chamber of Commerce, 800 S. 3rd St. 307-745-7339) Founded in 1868 on
the Union Pacific line, Laramie became such a savage, feral, and corrupt
town that it lost its charter and was placed under federal court jurisdiction
until 1874. It soon settled down, though, and prospered as a railroad town,
ranching hub, and site of the state university. Buildings in the **Downtown**

Historic District *(1st and 2nd Sts. between Custer St. and University Ave.)* date from the 1860s and include banks and hotels, a bullet-scored bar, and the site where the first jury with women members convened in 1870.

Laramie Plains Museum *(603 Ivinson Ave. 307-742-4448. Call for schedule; adm. fee)* Housed in the 1892 Ivinson Mansion, a stone-and-shingle Queen Anne, the museum displays toys; furniture; saddles; a piano shipped west in 1868 via riverboat, train, and wagon; and other pioneer memorabilia.

American Heritage Center *(2111 Willett Dr. 307-766-4114. Mon.-Sat.)* A research library and manuscript repository, the center also exhibits an extensive collection of Western art and Americana.

Wyoming Territorial Prison *(975 Snowy Range Rd. 307-745-6161. Mid-May–Sept., call for off-season hours; adm. fee)* Part of Laramie's **Wyoming Territorial Park,** the prison incarcerated outlaws from 1872 through 1901.

Sheridan ···

(Chamber of Commerce 307-672-2485 or 800-453-3650) Sheridan thrived around the turn of the century as a supply and transportation hub for area ranches, farms, and coal mines. Downtown's historic business district is extensive, lively, and largely intact.

Trail End State Historic Site *(400 Clarendon Ave. 307-674-4589. April–mid-Dec., call for off-season hours)* Home of John Kendrick, cattle baron and three-term U.S. senator, this elegant Flemish Revival mansion was built between 1908 and 1913.

Sheridan Inn *(5th St. and Broadway. 307-674-5440)* The sprawling railroad hotel, capped by a huge gambrel roof studded with 69 gables, opened its doors in 1893. The inn schedules tours but books no overnight guests.

Excursions

BRADFORD BRINTON MEMORIAL *(12 miles S on Wyo. 335. 307-672-3173. Mid-May–Labor Day; donations)* The ranch house, once home of a wealthy Illinois manufacturer, and adjacent museum are filled with Western and Native American art.

BUFFALO *(40 miles S via I-90)* The **Jim Gatchell**

Victorian interior, Laramie Plains Museum, Laramie

Memorial Museum of the West *(100 Fort St. 307-684-9331. Daily May-Oct., call for off-season hours; adm. fee)* exhibits pioneer relics and commemorates the violent range wars that swept the state in the 1890s.

Yellowstone National Park ·······················

(307-344-7381. Adm. fee) Explored by Indians, then by trappers and government scientists, Yellowstone became the world's first national park in 1872. At that time, wild lands and wildlife were taken for granted

throughout the West, so the area was set aside primarily because of its many geothermal wonders and the Grand Canyon of the Yellowstone.

The Army administered Yellowstone from 1886 to 1916 and began building **Fort Yellowstone** (*Mammoth*) in 1891. Vestiges remain, including a row of 1909 officers quarters that now house the **Albright Visitor Center.** Exhibits here depict the early days and display photos by W. H. Jackson and watercolor sketches by Thomas Moran. When the Army administered the park, soldiers often lived for months at lonely outposts such as the **Norris Soldier Station** (*Norris Junction*).

During the winter of 1903-04, **Old Faithful Inn,** a masterpiece of stone-and-log construction, was built near the geyser of the same name. The lobby's ceiling slants 84 feet above the floor. Yellowstone's oldest inn, the **Lake Hotel** (*Lake Village*), dates from 1889. It catered initially to wealthy visitors who were escorted through the park on prearranged carriage tours. Teddy Roosevelt camped in the park in 1903, and the **Roosevelt Lodge National Historic District** (*Tower-Roosevelt Rd.*)—a rustic log-cabin lodge, camp, and ranch built in 1920—was named for him.

Excursion

PAHASKA TEPEE (*2 miles outside the East Entrance. 307-527-7701 or 800-628-7791*) William "Buffalo Bill" Cody opened this hunting lodge in 1905.

320

Other Sites in Wyoming

Castle Gardens Petroglyphs (*20 miles S of Moneta*) Ancient depictions of hunters, warriors, and animals decorate a jumble of eroded pinnacles.

Fort Bridger State Historic Site (*Fort Bridger. 307-782-3842. Daily May-Sept., weekends only Oct.-Thanksgiving and March-April; adm. fee*) Originally an 1843 trading post built by fur trapper and mountain man Jim Bridger, the site became an Army base from 1858 to 1890. Many original buildings survive along with a replica of Bridger's old trading post.

Fort Caspar Museum (*4001 Ft. Caspar Rd., Casper. 307-235-8462. Daily mid-May–mid-Sept., Sun.-Fri. rest of year*) Located where the Oregon, Bozeman, and California Trails crossed the North Platte River, the original fort (called the Platte Bridge Station) served to protect travelers bound for the West. The reconstructed 1860s Army fort and adjacent museum include a civilian store, blacksmith, corral, and bridge.

Fort Fetterman State Historic Site (*Near Douglas on Wyo. 93. 307-358-2864. Mem. Day–Labor Day*) Active from 1867 to 1882, the fort functioned as an Army supply outpost. The restored officers quarters and ordnance warehouse date from the 1870s; both house museum pieces.

Fort Laramie N.H.S. (*15 miles E of Guernsey on US 26. 307-837-2221. Adm. fee*) A fur-trading post in 1834, Fort Laramie is considered the first permanent white settlement on the northern plains. Later it became an important stopover along the Oregon Trail, a major Army post, a site of treaty negotiations with the Plains Indians, and a staging area for Army campaigns when those treaties failed. Now a first-rate living history museum, Fort Laramie includes many original buildings, several painstakingly restored.

Oregon Trail Ruts (*S of Guernsey, off Wyo. 26*) Thousands of passing wagons in the 1800s wore these trenchlike ruts into a sandstone ridge. Emigrants also paused at nearby **Register Cliff** to carve their names.

Grand Encampment Museum (*7th and Barnett Sts., Encampment. 307-327-*

5308. *Mem. Day–Labor Day, call for off-season hours; donations)* Ghost-town buildings and mining implements recall the copper boom of the 1890s.

Independence Rock State Historic Site *(45 miles SW of Casper on Wyo. 220. 307-577-5150)* Fur trappers celebrating the Fourth of July named this major landmark on the Oregon Trail. The oblong hump of granite bears thousands of emigrant names carved during the 1840s, '50s, and '60s, and the view from the rock's summit has changed little since then.

Cavalry barracks at Fort Laramie National Historic Site

J. C. Penney House *(701 J. C. Penney Dr., Kemmerer. 307-877-3164. Mem. Day–Labor Day)* The modest home of the department store magnate faces the town square. In 1902 Penney opened his first store, the Golden Rule (no longer standing), in this old coal-mining town.

Lusk *(Jct. of US 18/20 and US 85)* In this eastern Wyoming town, you can tour the Stagecoach Museum *(324 S. Main St. 307-334-3444. Daily in summer; adm. fee)* and see a stagecoach used on the old Cheyenne-Black Hills Stage and Express line.

Medicine Bow *(Jct. of US 287 and Wyo. 487)* The area was the setting for Owen Wister's famous 1902 novel, *The Virginian.* Landmarks include the restored **Virginian Hotel,** a pioneer museum, and a general store where Wister, then a cowpoke from Philadelphia, slept on the counter in 1885.

Medicine Lodge State Archaeological Site *(Near Hyattville)* Ancient petroglyphs and pictographs adorn a broad pink cliff rising from this shady site along Medicine Lodge Creek. Artifacts excavated from streamside campsites cover 10,000 years of occupation.

Medicine Wheel N.H.S. *(W of Burgess Junction, on US 14A. July-Oct.)* An archaeological mystery and sacred Native American site, this ring of stones high in the Bighorn Mountains resembles a large spoked wheel.

Museum of the Mountain Man *(700 E. Hennick, Pinedale. 307-367-4101. May-Sept., by appt. in winter; adm. fee.)* The museum examines the lives, tools, weapons, and trade patterns of fur trappers who combed the Rockies for beaver pelts during the early 19th century.

South Pass City State Historic Site *(S of Lander on Wyo. 28. 307-332-3684. Mid-May–Sept.; adm. fee)* An evocative site, this restored gold-mining town of the mid- to late 19th century includes a variety of furnished shops, houses, cabins, and other original structures.

Wind River Indian Reservation *(N of Lander)* Home to Shoshone and Arapaho tribes, the reservation includes the **grave of Sacagawea** *(Fort Washakie),* the Shoshone woman who guided Lewis and Clark through the Rockies in 1805. At **St. Michael's Mission** *(Ethete)* an Episcopal log church with a great drum for an altar stands within a circle of stone buildings.

Wyoming Frontier Prison *(5th and Walnut Sts., Rawlins. 307-324-4422. Mid-May–Sept., off-season by appt.; adm. fee).* Tours of this old prison, in use from 1901 to 1981, take in cellblocks, a gas chamber, and gallows.

321

Little Bighorn Battlefield National Monument

The United States acquired almost all of Montana in the Louisiana Purchase. The area became a territory in 1864 and the nation's 41st state in 1889. Lewis and Clark traveled through Montana in 1805-06 and were closely followed by trappers, whose trade in beaver pelts dwindled in the 1840s. The 1860s gold rush in the mountains of western Montana brought settlers who established the first towns, but it also helped kick off conflicts, primarily with the Sioux. The battles continued through the 1870s and included Lt. Col. George Armstrong Custer's famous loss at the Little Bighorn in 1876. In time, the tribes were defeated. Ranching boomed and cow towns grew as railroads built across the plains. Mining continued in the west, particularly around Butte, where copper fueled industrial growth during the 1880s and '90s. Today, many Montanans make their livings from agriculture, tourism, timber, mining, and oil production.

Billings

(*Visitor Center, 815 S. 27th St. 406-252-4016 or 800-735-2635*) Founded in 1882 as a railroad town along the Yellowstone River, Billings has grown into a regional center of finance, trade, and transportation.

Moss Mansion (*914 Division St. 406-256-5100. June-Aug., call for off-season hours; adm. fee*) Begun in 1901 for a Billings banker, this red-sandstone mansion contains an eclectic mix of interior design styles.

Peter Yegen, Jr., Yellowstone County Museum (*Billings-Logan Intl. Airport.*

406-256-6811. Sun.-Fri.) A wide-ranging collection of frontier relics and dioramas fills this 1890s log cabin overlooking the city.

Western Heritage Center *(2822 Montana Ave. 406-256-6809. Closed Mon. and Jan.)* Housed in a 1901 Romanesque library, the center depicts Yellowstone Valley's cultural history. Interactive exhibits display artifacts of the Native Americans and immigrant groups who lived here.

Excursions

PICTOGRAPH CAVE STATE PARK *(7 miles S of I-90 via Lockwood exit. 406-252-4654 in season, 406-247-2940 rest of year. Mid-April–mid-Oct.; adm. fee)* Prehistoric hunters lived in sandstone caves here and left intriguing wall paintings.

CHIEF PLENTY COUPS STATE PARK *(35 miles S via Rte. 416. 406-252-1289. May-Sept.; adm. fee)* The park preserves the large log home of Plenty Coups, the last great warrior chief of the Crow. The Visitor Center's museum traces tribal history and describes modern reservation life.

POMPEYS PILLAR *(30 miles E via I-94. 406-875-2233 in season, 406-238-1541 rest of year. Mem. Day–Sept.; adm. fee)* Explorer William Clark carved his name on this sandstone tower in 1806. The rock also bears prehistoric pictographs, petroglyphs, and many other 19th-century signatures.

Butte ··

(Chamber of Commerce 406-494-5595 or 800-735-6814) Founded as a gold camp in the 1860s, Butte became the world's leading copper producer in the 1880s and gained an epithet—"richest hill on earth." Its mines spawned construction of thousands of buildings, and created the smelter city of Anaconda. Perhaps the largest intact historic district in the Rockies, the **Butte National Historic Landmark District** includes some 4,500 Victorian structures. The **Copper King Mansion** *(219 W. Granite St. 406-782-7580. May-Sept.; adm. fee)* dates from the 1880s. Mining tycoon William A. Clark used a half-day's income ($260,000) to build his opulent 34-room home.

Arts Chateau *(321 W. Broadway. 406-723-7600. Adm. fee)* This 1898 turreted mansion, built by William Clark's son, now serves as a gallery and museum.

World Museum of Mining and Hell Roarin' Gulch *(W. Park St. 406-723-7211. Mem. Day–Labor Day, call for off-season hours; adm. fee)* Covering 12 acres, the site includes mining equipment and more than two dozen buildings in a re-created turn-of-the-century Old West town.

Headframe at Butte mine

Excursions

ANACONDA *(25 miles NW via I-90 and Mont. 1)* An 1880s town built to process Butte's copper ore, Anaconda boasts large Queen Annes (for smelter managers) and tightly packed houses where workers lived.

DEER LODGE *(40 miles N via I-90)* Surrounded by a high sandstone wall, the grim 1871 **Old Montana Prison** *(1106 Main St. 406-846-3111. Adm. fee)* housed inmates until 1979. The **Grant-Kohrs Ranch N.H.S.** *(N of town. 406-846-3388. May-Sept.; adm. fee)* was headquarters of Montana's richest ranch. The well-preserved 1,500-acre site has 90 structures, including a house outfitted like a Victorian mansion, plus livestock and old farm machinery.

Glacier National Park ···························

(406-888-5441. Adm. fee) One of America's most spectacular alpine preserves, Glacier was established as a national park in 1910, and became part
of the world's first international peace park in 1932. Human habitation
dates back at least 8,000 years. In recent times, the Blackfeet tribe dominated the eastern slopes of the mountains and fiercely defended the buffalo country from west-side
tribes such as the Kootenai.

Many Glacier Hotel *(602-
207-6000. June–early Sept.)* Built
by the Great Northern Railway,
this striking grand old hotel
opened in 1915. The Swiss-
style lodge stands near an
alpine lake and faces a wall of
glacially carved peaks. Like the
magnificent **Glacier Park Lodge**
in East Glacier, it is made of
native stone and massive logs.

Many Glacier Hotel, Glacier National Park

Going-to-the-Sun Road *(June–Sept.)* Completed in 1932, the 50-mile
route provides one of the finest scenic drives in the Rockies.

Excursions

MUSEUM OF THE PLAINS INDIAN *(13 miles from East Entrance via US 2,
Browning. 406-338-2230. Closed weekends Oct.-May)* Exhibits summarize the
history of the Great Plains tribes; displays include traditional clothing and
beautifully crafted tools, weapons, and ceremonial relics.

CONRAD MANSION *(30 miles from West Entrance via US 2, in Kalispell.
406-755-2166. Mid-May–mid-Oct.; adm. fee)* Built in 1892-95 by Kalispell's
founder, the 26-room mansion blends wealth with taste in a rustic setting.

Great Falls ···

(Information Center 406-771-0885) In 1805 Lewis and Clark spent two
difficult weeks portaging around the thundering cascades that gave the
city its name. Later dammed, the falls provided cheap energy, and Great
Falls flourished as a center of manufacturing, trade, transportation, and
agriculture. Charles M. Russell, "America's cowboy artist," lived and
worked here. The **C. M. Russell Museum Complex** *(400 13th St. N. 406-
727-8787. Closed Mon. Oct.-April; adm. fee)* exhibits the world's largest collection of Russell's oils, bronzes, and illustrated letters. Grounds include
his log-cabin studio and clapboard house.

Excursion

FORT BENTON *(42 miles NE via US 87)* Originally an 1840s fur-
trading outpost, and then a thriving inland steamboat port, the town's historic riverfront district includes a restored 1880s hotel and ruins of the old
fort. The **Museum of the Upper Missouri** *(Old Fort Park. 406-622-5316. Mid-
May–mid-Sept., or by appt.; adm. fee)* celebrates the town's steamboating years,
while the outstanding **Museum of the Northern Great Plains** *(1205 21st St.
406-622-5316. Mid-May–mid-Sept.; adm. fee)* portrays three generations of
farming with antique implements and a restored townsite.

Helena ···

(Chamber of Commerce, 225 Cruse Ave. 406-442-4120) An 1860s gold rush camp, Helena soon expanded as a regional mining center and became the state capital in 1894. Dozens of Gilded Age millionaires built lavish homes here and spent freely in the ornate Victorian commercial district.

State Capitol *(6th and Montana Aves. 406-444-2694. Daily in summer, off-season by appt.)* Tours of the 1902 neoclassical structure depart from the rotunda and take in murals by Charles M. Russell and other Western artists. Nearby, you can walk through the **Original Governors' Mansion** *(304 N. Ewing St. 406-444-2694. Mem. Day–Labor Day Tues.-Sun., call for off-season hours)*, a beautifully preserved brick house built in 1888.

Montana Historical Society Museum *(225 N. Roberts. 406-444-2694)* Artifacts depict Montana's past from prehistory through World War II. The museum also includes photographic and Western art galleries.

Reeder's Alley *(Adj. to S end of Last Chance Gulch)* This restored section of early-day Helena includes modest 1860s houses converted to shops.

Missoula ···

(Chamber of Commerce, 825 E. Front St. 406-543-6623) A natural crossroads of river valleys, the Missoula area has drawn travelers for thousands of years. Lewis and Clark passed through in 1805-06, followed over the next decades by trappers, soldiers, settlers, loggers, academicians, and artists.

Historical Museum at Fort Missoula *(Off South Ave., W of Reserve St. 406-728-3476. Closed Mon.; adm. fee)* Exhibits in a 1911 **Quartermaster's Storehouse** track local history. Several buildings original to Fort Missoula (1877-1947) survive alongside other historic buildings moved to the site.

Excursions

GARNET GHOST TOWN *(35 miles E via Mont. 200 and well-marked forest roads)* This forlorn cluster of warped and creaking houses, cabins, and shops prospered at the turn of the century as a gold-mining town.

FLATHEAD INDIAN RESERVATION. *(15 miles NW via I-90, on US 93)* The grounds of **St. Ignatius Mission National Historic Site** *(St. Ignatius. 406-745-2768)* include an 1854 log cabin built by Jesuit missionaries to the Salish, Kootenai, and Pend d'Oreille Indians. The cabin stands beside an 1891 redbrick church built in high Victorian Gothic style and decorated with 58 beautiful murals by the mission's cook and handyman. Exhibits at the **People's Center** *(Pablo. 406-675-0160. Adm. fee)* and tours of the reservation examine Native American art, history, and culture, and display the region's varied wildlife.

Other Sites in Montana

Bad Pass Trail *(Bighorn Canyon National Recreation Area, S of Hardin on Mont. 313. 406-666-2412. Adm. fee)*

Four Winds Village, Flathead Reservation

This ancient overland route skirts the Bighorn Canyon and has been used for more than 10,000 years—first by Paleo-Indian hunters and traders, then the Apsalooka (Crow) tribe, fur trappers, and others. Signs of habitation include tepee rings, bison kill sites, and hundreds of cairns.

Other Sites in Montana

Bannack State Park (*25 miles SW of Dillon via Mont. 278. 406-834-3413. Adm. fee*) Site of Montana's first major gold strike, in 1862, the ghost town of Bannack once served as the territorial capital.

Daly Mansion (*East Side Hwy., Hamilton. 406-363-6004. Mid-April–mid-Oct.; adm. fee*) Summer home of Butte copper king Marcus Daly, the massive Georgian Revival mansion was built at the turn of the century and boasts 24 bedrooms and 15 baths.

Fort Owen (*E of US 93, near Stevensville. 406-542-5500*) Partially rebuilt, the old trading post offers an 1860s barracks, a furnished homesteader's cabin, exhibits, and a terrific view of the Bitterroot Range.

Fort Union Trading Post N.H.S. (*21 miles N of Sidney on Mont. 200 and N. Dak. 58. 701-572-9083*). Built in 1828, Fort Union thrived for three decades as the preeminent fur-trading post on the upper Missouri. Reconstructed at its original site, the fort is one of the finest living history museums in the region. Visitors can see a fur-trade exhibit at the Bourgeois House.

Little Bighorn Battlefield National Monument (*15 miles SE of Hardin. 406-638-2621. Adm. fee*) Lt. Col. George A. Custer and more than 200 men of the Seventh Cavalry died here on June 25, 1876, during what they had hoped would be a surprise attack on a large camp of Lakota (Sioux) and Cheyenne. Exhibits include weapons and other battle artifacts, as well as Custer's belongings. Films, talks, and tours run throughout the summer.

Missouri Headwaters State Park (*N of Three Forks, off I-90. 406-994-4042. April-Oct.; adm. fee for nonresidents*) Here at the foot of four mountain ranges, the Madison and Jefferson Rivers join to form the Missouri, with the Gallatin flowing in just downstream. Exhibits describe the activities of Lewis and Clark, who paused here in 1805 to plan their westward course.

Museum of the Rockies (*600 W. Kagy Blvd., Bozeman. 406-994-2251. Adm. fee*) Exhibits track geology and natural history from the formation of the planet onward, with special emphasis on the terrain near Bozeman. The museum includes a planetarium, dinosaur displays, and extensive collections of Native American and pioneer artifacts.

Nez Perce National Historical Park (*Montana sites. See page 328 for Idaho sites.*) Evocative and hauntingly serene, the meadow at **Big Hole National Battlefield** (*10 miles W of Wisdom. 406-689-3155. Adm. fee*) was the site of the fourth major battle in the 1877 Nez Perce War. Self-guided trails thread the battlefield, and Visitor Center exhibits trace the conflict's causes and course. The Nez Perce surrendered at **Bear Paw National Battleground** (*16 miles S of Chinook on Mont. 240*) after a six-day siege. A self-guided trail loops through the Nez Perce and Army positions.

Range Rider's Museum (*Miles City. 406-232-6146. April-Oct.; adm. fee*) A gun collection, Indian relics, pioneer artifacts, and replicas of frontier buildings celebrate the cattle boom and homesteading eras of the 1880s and '90s.

St. Mary's Mission (*W end of 4th St., Stevensville. 406-777-5734. Mid-April–mid-Oct.; adm. fee*) The lovingly preserved buildings of this Jesuit mission date from 1866 and include a chapel, residence, log house, and perhaps the nation's first drive-up pharmacy.

Virginia City and Nevada City (*70 miles SW of Bozeman*) These old goldmining towns lie along Alder Gulch, where prospectors found Montana's richest placer deposit in 1863. Original buildings line the main street of Virginia City. The five blocks of the **Nevada City Museum** (*800-648-7588. Late May–mid-Sept.; adm. fee*) hold antique-jammed houses and shops.

Idaho

Silver City ghost town

Explorers Lewis and Clark trekked through Idaho in 1805-06. Fur trappers established a trading post in 1809 and hunted beaver into the 1840s. Idaho became a territory during the 1860s and the nation's 43rd state in 1890. During the 1860s gold rush, settlers poured into northern Idaho. Their presence sparked conflicts with Shoshone-Bannock tribes and, eventually, the Nez Perce. A second gold find, during the 1880s in the Coeur d'Alene River Valley, was soon eclipsed by a silver discovery that spurred a mining boom and spawned violent labor disputes. At the turn of the century, railroads and irrigation projects led to agricultural expansion.

Boise

(Visitors Bureau, 2739 Airport Way. 208-344-7777) Boise grew up around

an 1863 Army outpost built to protect a dangerous stretch of the Oregon Trail. It thrived as a mining supply center during the gold rush, then as an agricultural hub, university town, and seat of state government.

Idaho State Historical Museum (*Julia Davis Park. 208-334-2120. Donations*) Exhibits and a cluster of small historic buildings trace Idaho's history from the frontier era back to Stone Age hunters.

Old Idaho Penitentiary (*2445 Old Penitentiary Rd. 208-368-6080. Adm. fee*) Built in the 1870s and used until the 1970s, the gloomy stone fortress includes exhibits on escape attempts, weapons, and hangings.

Basque Museum and Cultural Center (*611 Grove St. 208-343-2671. Tues.-Sat.; donations*) The center celebrates the area's rich Basque heritage and preserves the **Cyrus Jacobs House,** an 1864 boardinghouse.

Excursions

CELEBRATION PARK (*40 miles S, off Idaho 45*) Trails along the Snake River lead past petroglyphs, and programs examine the area's Native American history. A branch of the Oregon Trail ran along the south bank.

IDAHO CITY (*40 miles NE, on Idaho 21. 208-392-4148*) Placer miners swarmed Idaho City during the early 1860s to work claims that yielded an average of a dollar a pan. The boom failed to last the decade. Many buildings survive as residences, restaurants, saloons, and shops. The **Boise Basin Museum** (*Montgomery and Wall Sts. 208-392-4550. Mem. Day–Labor Day; adm. fee*) publishes an excellent guide to the historic district.

Coeur d'Alene ······················

(*Visitor Center, 1621 N. 3rd. 208-664-3194*) This lovely resort town overlooking a lake of the same name blossomed during the 1880s as a transportation hub for logging and mining. The **Museum of North Idaho** (*115 Northwest Blvd. 208-664-3448. April-Oct. Tues.-Sat.; adm. fee*) celebrates the town's steamboating years, the area's lumberjacks, and the Coeur d'Alene tribe, which once owned the city's land.

Chief Joseph
The famous Nez Perce leader was born in 1840 in Oregon's Wallowa Valley. In 1871 he became chief of a group of Nez Perce who refused to leave land ceded to the U.S. through a fraudulent 1863 treaty. Tall and massively built, Joseph was fair-minded, eloquent, more diplomat than warrior. He strived to retain the Wallowa through negotiation and counseled peace when faced with forceful removal. His group's remarkable 15-week fighting retreat across Idaho and Montana ended in surrender to the Army just short of the Canadian border. "My heart is sick and sad," he said. "From where the sun now stands, I will fight no more."

328

Excursion

OLD MISSION STATE PARK (*18 miles E via I-90. 208-682-3814. Adm. fee*) Idaho's oldest building, a Greek Revival mission church, caps a grassy knoll overlooking the Coeur d'Alene River. Built during the 1850s by Jesuits and Coeur d'Alene Indians, the structure contains chandeliers made from tin cans and an ornate altar carved with a pocketknife.

Nez Perce Natl. Historical Park Driving Tour ········
200 miles, 6 hours

Taking an innovative approach to interpreting Nez Perce history, this park consists of 38 sites in 4 states (see also p. 326). Many sites examine Nez Perce contacts with European Americans, but the park also celebrates traditional culture. The tour visits some of the most important sites in Idaho.

1. Spalding *(Park Hq. 208-843-2261. Adm. fee)* The **Visitor Center** overlooks a bend of the Clearwater River where Henry and Eliza Spalding established a Presbyterian mission to the Nez Perce in 1838. No original buildings remain. The center houses a collection of Nez Perce artifacts—beads, saddles, buckskin clothing, Matthew's Gospel in Nez Perce, and a silk ribbon presented to tribal leaders by Lewis and Clark.

2. Fort Lapwai *(3.5 mi. S on US 95)* served as the N. Idaho Indian Agency. An 1883 officers quarters survives.

3. St. Joseph's Mission *(4 miles S, off US 95. Church open Mem. Day–Labor Day)* Built in 1874, this was the first Catholic mission among the Nez Perce. The grounds held a convent, a school, and an orphanage.

4. Weis Rockshelter *(9 miles S of Cottonwood, off US 95)* Archaeologists estimate that ancestors of the Nez Perce inhabited this cave and the immediate area for at least 7,500 years.

5. White Bird Battlefield *(15 miles S of Grangeville)* On June 17, 1877, some 60 Nez Perce warriors routed 100 cavalrymen here. The fight was the first battle of the Nez Perce War, which involved an epic fighting trek—1,500 miles in four months—toward Canada and freedom. A road winds through the battlefield; an auto-tour brochure describes the action.

6. Heart of the Monster *(E. Kamiah Site, via Idaho 13 and US 12)* An interpretive trail leads to a large hump of basalt, where, according to Nez Perce myth, blood drops from a monster's heart created the tribe. A sign marks the **Lewis and Clark Long Camp** site. Here, the explorers waited for snow to melt in 1806.

7. Lenore *(16 miles W of Orofino)* From 900 B.C. to A.D. 1400, a large village of oval pit houses stood on this site.

Other Sites in Idaho

Fort Hall Indian Reservation *(N of Pocatello)* The **Shoshone-Bannock Tribal Museum** *(I-15. 208-237-9791. Donations)* traces tribal history and illuminates life along the Snake River 7,000 years ago. Fort Hall no longer stands.

St. Joseph's Mission, Nez Perce National Historical Park

Silver City Historic District *(25 miles SW of Murphy, off Idaho 78; rough roads)* The town dates from the 1860s and holds a cluster of old houses and shops, many of which are being restored. Most buildings are closed to the public, but the **Idaho Hotel** still serves meals.

Wallace The **Wallace District Mining Museum** *(509 Bank St. 208-556-1592. Daily in summer, call for off-season hours; adm. fee)* summarizes the town's 1880s mining history. The 1902 **Northern Pacific Depot** *(6th and Pine Sts. 208-752-0111. Spring-fall; adm. fee)* serves as a railroad museum.

329

Far West

Thousands of miles from the nation's birthplace, the Far West was America's final frontier. Furs and gold lured hardy fortune hunters. Fabulous salmon runs and vast forests of towering conifers drew entrepreneurs. Fertile valleys and abundant water attracted farm families. Perhaps most of all, those who came to Washington, Oregon, and California were compelled

CAPE KRUSENSTERN NAT. MON.

CANADA
U.S.A.

Yukon

BERING LAND BRIDGE NATIONAL PRESERVE

Fairbanks

Eagle

YUKON TERRITORY

A L A S K A

Independence Mine S.H.P.

Matanuska Valley Colony

Anchorage

Skagway

Juneau

Southeast Alaska Ferry Tour

B.C.

Sitka

Kodiak

Ketchikan

by an appetite for something new. Such a yearning also drove some people to what might be considered the far, far West: Alaska and Hawaii. The old pioneer cabins, ghost towns, trail routes, and other remnants all attest to the spirit of adventure that defines the history of the West.

Golden Gate Bridge, San Francisco

Wailua River Ancient Sites

Kauai

Niihau

Lihue

Oahu

Honolulu

Kalaupapa N.H.P.

Pearl Harbor

Molokai

Lahaina

Wailuku

Kahului

Lanai

Maui

H A W A I I

Mookini Heiau

Puukohola Heiau N.H.S.

Kailua-Kona

Kona Historical Society Museum

Puuhonua o Honaunau N.H.P.

South Cape

Parker Ranch

Hilo

Hawaii

HAWAII VOLCANOES NATIONAL PARK

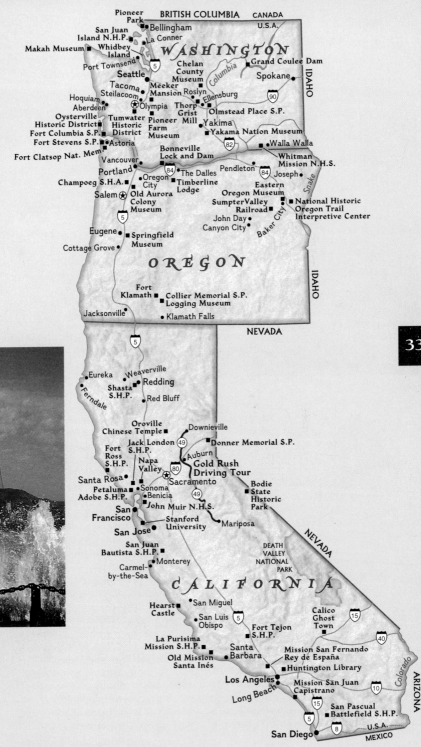

Pioneer
Park
San Juan
Island N.H.P.
Makah Museum
Whidbey
Island
Port Townsend
Seattle
Tacoma
Steilacoom
Hoquiam
Aberdeen
Oysterville
Historic District
Fort Columbia S.P.
Fort Stevens S.P.
Fort Clatsop Nat. Mem.
Astoria
Vancouver
Portland
Champoeg S.H.A.
Salem
Eugene
Cottage Grove

BRITISH COLUMBIA   CANADA
Bellingham   U.S.A.
La Conner

WASHINGTON

Chelan
County
Museum   Grand Coulee Dam
Meeker
Mansion   Roslyn Spokane
Olympia Thorp   Ellensburg
Tumwater Grist   Olmstead Place S.P.
Historic   Mill   Yakima
District Pioneer   Yakama Nation Museum
          Farm
          Museum   Walla Walla

Bonneville
Lock and Dam   Whitman
                      Mission N.H.S.
The Dalles Pendleton
Oregon   Joseph
City   Timberline
       Lodge   Eastern
Old Aurora   Oregon Museum
Colony   SumpterValley
Museum   Railroad   National Historic
                          Oregon Trail
Springfield John Day   Interpretive Center
Museum   Canyon City

OREGON

Fort   Collier Memorial S.P.
Klamath   Logging Museum

Jacksonville   Klamath Falls

IDAHO

NEVADA

Columbia

Snake

Baker City

331

Eureka
Weaverville
Shasta   Redding
S.H.P.
Red Bluff

Ferndale

Oroville
Chinese Temple   Downieville

Fort   Jack London   Donner Memorial S.P.
Ross   S.H.P.
S.H.P.   Napa   Auburn
            Valley Gold Rush
Santa Rosa   Driving Tour
Petaluma   Sacramento
Adobe S.H.P. Sonoma   Bodie
            Benicia   State
San   John Muir N.H.S.   Historic
Francisco   Park
            Stanford
San Jose   University   Mariposa

San Juan   DEATH
Bautista S.H.P. Monterey   VALLEY
Carmel-   NATIONAL
by-the-Sea   PARK

CALIFORNIA

Hearst   San Miguel
Castle
            San Luis   Calico
            Obispo   Ghost
                   Fort Tejon   Town
La Purisima   S.H.P.
Mission S.H.P.
Old Mission   Santa
Santa Inés   Barbara   Mission San Fernando
                        Rey de España
            Los Angeles Huntington Library

            Long Beach   Mission San Juan
                         Capistrano

                    San Pascual
                    Battlefield S.H.P.
San Diego
                         U.S.A.
                         MEXICO

NEVADA

Colorado

ARIZONA

California

Mission Santa Barbara, Santa Barbara

The process by which California's original inhabitants—about 100,000 Native Americans—lost the deed to paradise began in 1542, when Juan Rodríguez Cabrillo sailed into San Diego Bay and claimed the area for the Spanish crown. By 1769 Spain's soldiers and Franciscan padres were forging a chain of missions and forts from San Diego to Sonoma. Mexico later took control, followed by the U.S. in 1848. The same year, glittering flakes discovered at Sutter's Mill put the gold in the Golden State and launched a human stampede. California joined the Union in 1850. Early in the next century, booming agriculture and oil industries prompted more immigration. So did the dream of California as a sunny kingdom of promise, an image fed by Hollywood movies. California is often said to foretell (or even invent) America's future. Its tomorrows may hold social conflict and declining economic power, or a multicultural society that thrives under the sun.

Eureka

(Chamber of Commerce, 2112 Broadway. 707-442-3738 or 800-356-6381) The city of Eureka was founded in 1850 to supply mining camps. Soon Indian hostilities required the building of Fort Humboldt, a lonely post so dispiriting to Ulysses S. Grant that he reportedly repaired to a Eureka saloon. The largely unrestored fort is now the **Fort Humboldt State Historic Park** *(3431 Fort Ave. 707-445-6567)*, with old logging equipment, steam trains, and

Indian artifacts. The city became an important lumber shipping port and a showplace of late 19th-century architecture, especially in **Old Town** *(1st to 3rd Sts., between C and M Sts.)*.

Clarke Memorial Museum *(240 E St. 707-443-1947. Tues.-Sat.)* The collection emphasizes regional Indian artifacts and ceremonial regalia.

Samoa Cookhouse *(W of US 101 over the Samoa Bridge to Samoa Rd. 707-442-1659)* Built in 1892, the West's last surviving cookhouse serves meals amid logging mementos.

Excursion

FERNDALE *(20 miles S via US 101)* This village resembles a pop-up book of Victorian houses, of which the most notable is the 1899 Queen Anne **Gingerbread Mansion** *(400 Berding St. Private)*, with touches of the Eastlake style. Main Street shops offer a historic walking guide to these "butterfly palaces," built by wealth from the 19th-century dairy industry. Old dairy and logging apparatuses and a functioning seismograph are featured at the **Ferndale Museum** *(Shaw and 3rd Sts. 707-786-4466. June-Sept. Tues.-Sun., Wed.-Sun. rest of year, closed Jan.; adm. fee)*.

Los Angeles ························

(Convention & Visitors Bureau, 685 S. Figueroa St. 213-689-8822) Today's multicultural city began in 1781 with the arrival of 11 farm families from Mexico—Spaniards, Mexicans, Indians, and African Americans. By 1848 Los Angeles had become officially American. Oil was discovered in 1892, and the nation's first gas station opened 20 years later, launching L.A.'s love affair with the automobile. In 1913 an aqueduct carried Owens Valley water to the booming population, and Cecil B. DeMille made Hollywood's first feature film. Aircraft manufacturing expanded during World War II.

El Pueblo de Los Angeles Historical Monument *(Bet. Alameda, Arcadia, Spring, and Macy Sts. Visitor Center at Sepulveda House, 622 N. Main St. 213-628-1274. Mon.-Sat.)* Los Angeles began here in 1781. Historic buildings on the 44-acre site include the city's oldest house, the **Avila Adobe** (1818), built by a ranchero who traded cowhides for furnishings; and the oldest place of worship, the simple **Old Plaza Catholic Church** (1822). Brick-paved **Olvera Street** has become a colorful (if synthetic) Mexican marketplace with craft stalls and eateries. The Eastlake Victorian architecture of **Sepulveda House** (1887) illustrates how the Mexican city absorbed Anglo style.

Union Station *(Cesar Chavez and Alameda Sts.)* Its architecture a mix of Spanish colonial revival and streamline moderne, this 1939 depot has marble-and-tile floors and beamed ceilings.

Southwest Museum *(234 Museum Dr. 213-221-2164. Closed Mon.; adm. fee)* Housed in a 1914 mission revival building, the city's oldest museum

Hollywood Be Thy Name
It's hard to believe that Hollywood began with a Prohibitionist. In 1887 teetotaler Harvey Wilcox subdivided 120 acres of land, and his wife christened it "Hollywood." In 1898 Thomas Edison shot a documentary in L.A., and in 1911 the first Hollywood movie studio opened. California's sunshine allowed year-round filming, while its beaches and chaparral country made fine locations. Movie moguls came into being: Cecil B. DeMille directed Hollywood's first feature film in 1913; Carl Laemmle founded Universal Studios; and stars like Mary Pickford built fantasy palaces as unreal as movie sets. That's Hollywood!

showcases renowned Native American collections, including baskets, Plains Indian clothing, and Navajo weavings.

Hollyhock House (*4808 Hollywood Blvd. 213-662-7272. Closed Mon.; adm. fee*) Frank Lloyd Wright's first commission in Los Angeles (1921) features stylized hollyhocks adorning a monumentally scaled stucco house.

Mann's Chinese Theater (*6925 Hollywood Blvd. 213-461-9624*) Resembling a movie set, this green-roofed pagoda of a theater was built in 1927 by showman Sid Grauman. The cement forecourt enshrines the hand- and footprints of some 190 movie stars.

Hollywood Studio Museum (*2100 N. Highland Ave. 213-874-2276. Sat.-Sun.; adm. fee*) In this

Olvera Street, Los Angeles

horse barn, Cecil B. DeMille shot Hollywood's first feature film, *The Squaw Man*, in 1913. On view are silent-movie cameras and props.

Mission San Fernando Rey de España (*15151 San Fernando Mission Blvd. 818-361-0186. Adm. fee*) The original quarters of padres and visitors make up California's largest surviving mission building.

Will Rogers State Historic Park (*1501 Will Rogers State Park Rd., Pacific Palisades. 310-454-8212. Parking fee*) The rustic ranch house of the trick-roping, cowboy-philosophizing humorist of the 1930s is filled with Indian and Western memorabilia, including his lariats.

Excursions

HUNTINGTON LIBRARY, ART COLLECTIONS, AND BOTANICAL GARDENS (*12 miles NE via Calif. 110/Arroyo Pkwy. in San Marino. 1151 Oxford Rd. 818-405-2141. Closed Mon.; adm. fee*) Founded at the turn of the century by rail transportation magnate Henry Huntington, this world-class collection includes rare books and manuscripts (among them a Gutenberg Bible), European and American paintings and decorative art, and 150 acres of gardens.

LONG BEACH (*30 miles S via I-710*) Incorporated in 1888, this beach community is the permanent berth of the **Queen Mary** (*S end of I-710. 310-435-3511. Adm. fee*), the world's largest luxury liner. The 1934 art deco marvel, which steamed across the Atlantic more than a thousand times, offers self-guided tours of decks, the engine room, and the bridge. The city's early days can be visited at **Rancho Los Cerritos** (*4600 Virginia Rd. 310-570-1755. Wed.-Sun.*), an adobe country house built in 1844 in Monterey colonial style; and **Rancho Los Alamitos Historic Ranch and Gardens** (*6400 Bixby Hill Rd. 310-431-3541. Wed.-Sun.*), an 1806 ranch house with dairy barns, farm animals, and a garden designed by the sons of Frederick Law Olmsted.

Monterey ···

(Visitor Center, 401 Camino El Estero. 408-649-1770) Capital of California during both the Spanish and Mexican periods, Monterey played host to the 1849 constitutional convention that led to U.S. statehood. The city became a tourist resort when the elegant Del Monte Hotel opened in 1880, and after the turn of the century it prospered as the "Sardine Capital of the World."

Visitors can tread the Path of History around the waterfront and old downtown, seeing adobe houses and museums. The hub is the 7-acre **Monterey State Historic Park** *(Custom House Plaza. 408-649-7118. Ask about combination tickets)*, which has a number of different sites. Begin your tour at **Stanton Center,** which offers visitor information, a walking tour brochure, and a short history film. It also houses the **Maritime Museum of Monterey** *(408-373-2469. Adm. fee)*, with ship models, whaling artifacts, and a thousand-prism lighthouse lens. California's oldest public building, the adobe **Custom House** was the financial hub of Alta California (Mexico's northern province) from 1822 until 1846; it collected shipping duties and traded in "California bank notes," or cowhides. The building contains 1830s-type cargo. The 1839 **Larkin House** *(510 Calle Principal. Closed Tues. and Thurs.; adm. fee)* shows how New England architecture blended with Mexican, creating a style popular after the 1920s known as Monterey colonial. Furnishings include the desk of merchant, secret agent, and U.S. consul Thomas Larkin. A sea captain built the **Cooper-Molera Complex** *(525 Polk St. Closed Mon.; adm. fee),* which depicts life in the mid-1800s through an adobe house, carriage house, barn, and plantings authentic to the period. At the **Robert Louis Stevenson House** *(530 Houston St. Closed Mon.; adm. fee)* the Scottish author was a roomer in 1879 while courting Fanny Osbourne; personal memorabilia include Stevenson's dining room furniture and books.

335

Other sites along the Path of History include **Colton Hall** *(522 Pacific St. 408-646-5640),* where delegates gathered in 1849 to draft California's first constitution; visitors see the table where the document was signed. Out back is the granite **Old Monterey County Jail** (1854-1956). Finally, all that remains of Spain's original military enclave is the stone-and-adobe **Royal Presidio Chapel** *(Church and Figueroa Sts.).* Built in 1795, it is the oldest structure in Monterey and the state's last original presidio chapel.

Excursion

CARMEL-BY-THE-SEA *(5 miles S via Calif. 1)* Once a stop along El Camino Real, Carmel became an artists colony-beach resort around the turn of the century, which it remains today. Padre Junipero Serra, the Franciscan whose energy forged California's chain of missions, headquartered at **Mission San Carlos Borromeo del Rio Carmelo** *(3080 Rio Rd. 408-624-3600. Adm. fee).* Crude frontier materials and a sublime vision created the sandstone church with a Moorish tower and graceful star window. Another historic structure, poet Robinson Jeffers' **Tor House** *(26304 Ocean View Ave. 408-*

Padre Serra Library,
Mission San Carlos, Carmel-by-the-Sea

624-1813. Fri.-Sat. by reservation; adm. fee), a granite cottage begun in 1916, stands near the coast that inspired his work. His desk, books, and bed beside the window remain as they were in his day.

Redding Vicinity

Shasta State Historic Park (10 miles W via Calif. 299. 916-243-8194. Wed.-Sun.; adm. fee) Amid the ruins of gold rush boomtown Shasta City, a law court, jail, and gallows have been restored as the **Courthouse Museum,** displaying Indian baskets, pioneer six-shooters, and California oil paintings of 1862-1939; the **Litsch Store** re-creates an 1880s general store, with merchandise ranging from a pickle barrel to derby hats.

Weaverville (50 miles NW via Calif. 299. Chamber of Commerce, 317 Main St. 916-623-6101 or 800-487-4648. Historic walking tour map available) In the small town's atmospheric Main Street area, iron-shuttered brick buildings date from the mid-1800s. The 1854 **Weaverville Drug Store** (219 Main St.) is California's oldest pharmacy. Exhibits at the nearby **J.J. (Jake) Jackson Memorial Museum/Trinity County Historical Park** (508 Main St. 916-623-5211. Daily April-Nov., Dec.-March Tues. and Sat. only; donations) include firearms, Chinese artifacts, druggists' remedies, and turn-of-the-century costumes. Also worth a stop, the **Weaverville Joss House State Historic Park** (Oregon and Main Sts. 916-623-5284. Daily mid-May–mid-Sept., call for off-season hours; adm. fee) is a Taoist temple in continuous service since 1874. Used by early Chinese gold miners, it contains carved and gilded screens and pictures of Chinese deities.

Red Bluff (26 miles S via I-5. Chamber of Commerce, 100 Main St. 916-527-6220) Once the head of navigation on the Sacramento River, Red Bluff served as a commercial port for San Francisco steamers until after the turn of the century. The 1880s Victorian home of a sheepman, the **Kelly-Griggs House Museum** (311 Washington St. 916-527-1129. Thurs.-Sun.; donations) displays antique furnishings. Just north of town lies the **William B. Ide Adobe State Historic Park** (21659 Adobe Rd. 916-529-8599. Parking fee). This 1850s adobe honors the first and only president of the Bear Flag Republic of California, which existed for less than a month in 1846. The park includes the house, smokehouse, and carriage shed.

Sacramento

(Convention & Visitors Bureau, 1421 K St. 916-264-7777) The arrival of energetic John Sutter in 1839 at the convergence of the American and Sacramento Rivers sparked the beginning of Sacramento. Soon Sutter's Fort, a famous frontier outpost, was providing pioneers with shelter and supplies. After the California Gold Rush transformed Sacramento into a booming supply town for fortune hunters, the city became the young state's capital in 1854.

California State Capitol Museum (10th St. between L and N Sts., in the capitol building. 916-324-0333) California's opulently domed, Renaissance Revival capitol, built in 1860-1874, contains restored offices of the period 1900-1910, furnished with old desks and leather chairs.

Governor's Mansion State Historic Park (1526 H St. 916-323-3047. Guided tours only; adm. fee) This Second Empire Italianate mansion, built in 1877 for a hardware merchant, housed 13 governors ending with Ronald Reagan. Items left by first families range from inaugural gowns to the dollhouse of Earl Warren's daughter.

Old Sacramento Historic District *(Bet. I-5 and the Sacramento River, from I to L Sts. Walking tour brochure available at Visitor Center, 2nd and K Sts. 916-442-7644)* Sacramento's former business hub along the riverfront, this 28-acre site showcases fine gold rush-era buildings along wooden sidewalks. The 1852 **B.F. Hastings Building** *(2nd and J Sts.)* served as the terminus of the Pony Express, as well as the original home of the California Supreme Court. It now houses a Pony Express exhibit; restored California Supreme Court chambers; and the **Wells Fargo Museum** *(916-440-4263)*, filled with gold displays, a working telegraph, and a restored Concord stagecoach. Nearby, the **California State Railroad Museum** *(2nd and I Sts. 916-448-4466. Adm. fee)*—the nation's largest interpretive railway museum—commemorates Sacramento's role as a terminus of the transcontinental railroad. The collection includes beautifully restored locomotives and cars from the 1860s through the 1960s. Admission includes the nearby 1876 **Central Pacific Railroad Passenger Station** and its train shed.

Also in the district you'll find the **California Military Museum** *(1119 2nd St. 916-442-2883. Adm. fee)*; the wood-and-canvas 1849 **Old Eagle Theatre** *(Front and J Sts. 916-323-6343. Guided tours by appt.)*, California's first building constructed as a theater; and the one-room **Old Sacramento Schoolhouse** *(Front and L Sts. 916-483-8818)*, its desks furnished with slates, chalk, and *McGuffey's Readers.* Docked nearby on the Sacramento

California State Railroad Museum, Sacramento

River, the historic **Delta King** *(916-444-5464)*, which once churned between Sacramento and San Francisco, is now an elegant floating hotel and restaurant.

Sutter's Fort State Historic Park *(2701 L St. 916-445-4422. Adm. fee)* Sacramento's earliest settlement, founded in 1839 by Swiss immigrant John Sutter, conveys the feeling of pioneer life. Reconstructed walls surround the adobe fort's original central building; visitors can tour a bakery, cooper and blacksmith shops, dining room, and living quarters. Nearby stands the **California State Indian Museum** *(2618 K St. 916-324-0971. Adm. fee)*, where baskets and exquisite ceremonial dance costumes highlight Native American artifacts.

Gold Rush Country Driving Tour ······ 200 miles, 2 days

In 1848 a gold strike on the western slope of the Sierra Nevada kicked off a human stampede. Oak-studded hills exploded with gold seekers who ravaged streams for flakes and nuggets, built more than 500 towns, and created the wildest West imaginable. Some boomtowns live on, linked by the fittingly named Highway 49.

1. Sprawled along the Downie and Yuba Rivers, **Downieville**'s picturesque

337

Main Street is lined with gold rush-era buildings. A wood-frame gallows behind the courthouse was used in 1885 to punish a murderer.

2. In **Nevada City,** historic buildings on Broad Street include the 1856 **National Hotel** and the **Nevada Theatre,** where Mark Twain lectured. Firehouse No. 1 is topped with a Victorian bell tower and houses the **Nevada County Historical Society Museum** *(214 Main St. 916-265-5468. Closed Wed. Nov.-April),* with a complete Chinese joss house, Maidu Indian baskets and arrows, and artifacts from the Donner Party.

A 25-mile detour will bring you to **Malakoff Diggins State Historic Park** *(Via Calif. 49, Tyler-Foote Crossing, and Cruzon Grade, then follow signs. 916-265-2740. Adm. fee).* The world's largest hydraulic mining enterprise of the time used huge "monitor" water nozzles to blast the earth and reach deeper gold deposits. Visitors see the eroded pit. Also here is the partially reconstructed townsite of North Bloomfield.

3. **Grass Valley**'s hard-rock mining boom is said to have begun when a farmer, searching for a lost cow, stumbled over a chunk of rock quartz laden with gold. Strollers along Mill and Main Streets see vintage store-fronts and the 1851 **Holbrooke Hotel** *(W. Main St.).* Exhibits at the **North Star Mining Museum** *(Allison Ranch and McCourtney Rds. 916-273-4255. May–mid-Oct.; donations)* focus on hard-rock mining, and include the world's largest Pelton wheel (which generated power for mines). For more mining history, stop by the **Empire Mine State Historic Park** *(10791 E. Empire St. 916-273-8522. Adm. fee).* California's oldest and richest gold mine, it yielded 5.8 million ounces of gold. Visitors can peer down the shaft or examine the mine owner's 1897 cottage, modeled after a Cornish hunting lodge.

4. Old Town **Auburn** preserves a red-and-white firehouse (1891) and other buildings, overlooked by the domed **Placer County Courthouse** of 1898. The **Gold Country Museum** *(Gold Country Fairgrounds, 1273 High St. 916-889-6500. Closed Mon.; adm. fee)* is dedicated to Placer County gold mining. Visitors can pan for gold in a running stream. At the **Bernhard Museum** *(291 Auburn-Folsom Rd. 916-889-6500. Closed Mon.; adm. fee),* an 1851 family home and winery, costumed docents explain daily life back then.

5. Standing on the American River at the **Marshall Gold Discovery**

Gold and scale

State Historic Park *(Calif. 49, in Coloma. 916-622-3470. Adm. fee)* is a working replica of Sutter's Mill, where in 1848 James Marshall spied tiny glinting nuggets in the tailrace; he couldn't keep his mouth shut and thus launched the California Gold Rush. The Visitor Center offers a historical video, Maidu Indian artifacts, mining gear, and James Marshall's own rifle, pocketwatch, and tools. The park includes an 1852 gunsmith shop; a derelict jail; Marshall's cabin; and the Wah Hop Store, where local Chinese bought everything from groceries to opium.

6. In **Placerville**, admire a Concord stagecoach, Pony Express mailbag, Studebaker wagon, and country store at the **El Dorado County Historical Museum** *(El Dorado County Fairgrounds, 104 Placerville Dr. 916-621-5865. Wed.-Sun.; donations)*. A mile north of town at **Hangtown's Gold Bug Park** *(Bedford Ave. 916-642-5232. Mine open May-Oct., weekends only rest of year; adm. fee for mine)*, you can tour the Gold Bug Mine and see a stamp mill. The **Hattie Museum** has mining artifacts.

7. Worth seeing in the uncommercialized village of **Fiddletown** is the rammed-earth **Chew Kee Store Museum** *(14357 Littletown Rd. April-Oct. Sat.)*, a Chinese herbal doctor's shop in business from 1850 to 1913. It contains Chinese remedies, a shrine, and gambling devices.

Farther along Calif. 49, an interesting side trip east via Calif. 88 and Pine Grove-Volcano Road will bring you to **Indian Grinding Rock State Historic Park** *(209-296-7488. Adm. fee)*. For food, Miwok Indians ground acorns on this huge slab of marbleized limestone, leaving 1,185 mortar holes in the surface, as well as faint petroglyphs. The **Chaw Se Regional Indian Museum** displays a replica bark house, dance regalia, animal traps, and other artifacts.

8. Housed in the old Hall of Records, the **Calaveras County Museum** *(30 N. Main St., 2nd fl. 209-754-6579 or 209-754-1058. Adm. fee)* in **San Andreas** displays Native American and pioneer artifacts, including an invitation to a public hanging. Gentleman stagecoach robber Black Bart was tried in the adjacent courtroom and jailed in a cell out back.

9. Among gold rush buildings along **Angels Camp**'s Main Street is the former **Angels Hotel** *(1287 S. Main St.)*, where in 1865 Mark Twain reportedly heard the tale he would write up as "The Celebrated Jumping Frog of Calaveras County." It's

Sutter's Mill replica, Marshall Gold Discovery S.H.P. in Coloma

an apartment building now, but the exterior is unchanged. At the **Angels Camp Museum** *(753 S. Main St. 209-736-2963. Call for hours; adm. fee)* see restored carriages and a mineral display.

10. Preserved as **Columbia State Historic Park** *(2 miles N of Calif. 49 via Parrott's Ferry Rd. 209-532-4301. Activities fees)*, Columbia is a time

339

capsule filling 12 square blocks. Old brick buildings range from a grammar school to a saloon to a Wells Fargo office. Visitors can clatter through the streets aboard a stagecoach, pan for gold, and tour an operating gold mine. The museum has a slide show and exhibits on historical restoration.

11. At the **Railtown 1897 Historic Sierra Railroad Shops** (*Off Main St. on 5th Ave., Jamestown. 209-984-3953*), tour the Sierra Railway's vintage steam roundhouse and see restored locomotives and cars. Steam-train excursions (*May-Nov., call for schedule; fare*) run on the original tracks.

12. The valley hamlet of **Coulterville** boasts a number of mid-1800s buildings, including the Hotel Jeffery, an adobe Chinese store, and a house of ill repute. The **Northern Mariposa County History Center** (*Calif. 49 at Calif. 132. 209-878-3015. April-Dec. Tues.-Sun., weekends only Feb.-March, closed Jan.*) displays gold scales, a rolltop desk, and guns. Outside by the Hanging Tree (once used by vigilantes) is a small mining locomotive.

13. Among historic buildings in **Mariposa** is the **Mariposa County Courthouse** (*Bullion St. between 9th and 10th Sts.*), an 1854 white-frame building said to be California's oldest courthouse in continuous service. At the **Mariposa Museum and History Center** (*Jessie and 12th Sts. 209-966-2924. Daily March-Oct., weekends only Nov.-Feb., closed Jan.; donations*), you'll find a replica Indian village and rooms depicting a gold rush newspaper office, drugstore, saloon, and sheriff's office, as well as mining equipment and a working stamp mill.

San Diego ···

(*Visitor Center, Horton Plaza at 1st Ave. and F St. 619-236-1212*) Some 227 years after explorer Juan Rodríguez Cabrillo landed here in 1542, the Portolá expedition built a presidio and Padre Serra founded California's first mission. On the site of that first settlement in **Presidio Park** stands the **Junipero Serra Museum** (*2727 Presidio Dr. 619-297-3258. Closed Mon.; adm. fee*), which focuses on the period before the American conquest. The city remained isolated until the transcontinental railroad arrived in 1885, then grew during World War I as a Navy home port. The 1915 Panama-California Exposition took place at **Balboa Park** (*Laurel St. between Park and 6th Aves. 619-239-0512*), where fine Spanish revival buildings remain.

Old Point Loma Lighthouse, San Diego

Mission Basilica San Diego de Alcalá (*10818 San Diego Mission Rd. 619-281-8449. Adm. fee*) Dating from 1774, this plain white mission features a wall of bells and Padre Serra's original quarters.

Old Town San Diego State Historic Park (*Off I-5 at Old Town Ave. Visitor Center at Robinson-Rose House. 619-220-5422*) Surrounded by adobe-and-wood buildings, this plaza is an outdoor museum of mid-19th-century San Diego. Highlights include the 1867 **Seeley Stable**, with its collection of stagecoaches and Western gear, and the furnished 1827 **adobe hacienda** of a presidio *comandante*.

Cabrillo National Monument (*1800 Cabrillo Memorial Dr. 619-557-5450. Adm. fee*) Located on the lofty point where Cabrillo first made landfall are a Visitor Center focused on Spanish exploration and the 1855 **Old Point**

Loma Lighthouse, which has been refurbished.

Gaslamp Quarter *(Bounded by 4th and 6th Aves., Broadway, and Harbor Dr.)* This early business district showcases Victorian commercial buildings. Saturday walking tours leave the **William Heath Davis House Museum** *(410 Island Ave. 619-233-4692. Adm. fee),* a New England saltbox house shipped around Cape Horn in 1850.

San Diego Maritime Museum *(1306 N. Harbor Dr. 619-234-9153. Adm. fee)* Moored here are the 1863 bark *Star of India* (the oldest iron-hulled vessel afloat), a steam yacht, and an 1898 ferryboat serving as a nautical museum.

Hotel del Coronado *(1500 Orange Ave., Coronado. 619-435-6611)* This elegant Victorian seaside resort (1888) boasts an early Otis elevator. The cupola roof line inspired guest L. Frank Baum in describing Oz.

Excursion
SAN PASCUAL BATTLEFIELD S.H.P. *(40 miles NE via I-15 and Calif. 78. 619-220-5430. Fri.-Sun.)* In the roughest encounter of the Mexican-American War, U.S. troops were routed by *Californios* in 1846. A Visitor Center at the 50-acre site explains the battle.

San Francisco

(Visitor Information Center, Hallidie Plaza at Powell and Market Sts. 415-391-2000) Spanish colonialism and rowdy American romanticism blend like watercolors in the splashy history of San Francisco. After Spaniards founded a mission and presidio in 1776, a village called Yerba Buena took shape nearby. Americans came in a human tidal wave during the California Gold Rush of 1849. The city became a hub of commerce, built a cable car system, and put up fine Victorian houses. Then in 1906 a great earthquake and fire erased 500 city blocks. The **Jackson Square Historic District** *(Jackson St. bet. Montgomery and Sansome Sts.)* preserves brick buildings that survived the disaster. A rebuilt San Francisco showed itself during the 1915 Panama-Pacific International Exhibition. In the 1930s the Golden Gate and Bay Bridges spanned the bay.

Mission San Francisco de Asís (Mission Dolores) *(16th and Dolores Sts. 415-621-8203. Adm. fee)* Original bells still hang from rawhide thongs at this 1791 church, San Francisco's oldest building. Inside are a baroque altar screen and wooden columns painted to simulate Italian marble.

San Francisco skyline from Alamo Square

Palace Hotel *(2 New Montgomery St. 415-392-8600)* Originally built in 1875 and rebuilt in 1909, the landmark boasts a leaded-glass atrium in the Garden Court and a Maxfield Parrish mural.

Chinatown *(Grant Ave. area between Bush and Washington Sts.)* Chinese immigrants came to California for the gold rush, staying to labor on the Central Pacific Railroad in the 1860s. Chinatown, rebuilt after the 1906 earthquake, boasts colorful Chinese architecture. Don't miss the painted balconies along **Waverly Place** and the peaked roofs and vivid hues of

San Francisco

Marin
Peninsula

Alcatraz

Golden Gate
Bridge

SAN FRANCISCO BAY

San Francisco
Maritime N.H.P.

Coit
Memorial
Tower

GOLDEN GATE

Fort Point N.H.S.

Palace of
Fine Arts

Battery
East
Road

Beach St.

Bay St.

Marina Blvd.

N

Presidio
Museum

San Francisco
Cable Car
Museum

Jackson Sq.
Historic
District

Presidio of
San Francisco

Broadway

0   1 Mi
0   1 Km

Jackson St.

Haas-
Lilienthal
House

Chinatown

Washington

Palace
Hotel

Lincoln
Park

Bush   St.

Geary Blvd.

Pt. Lobos Ave.
Cliff House

Golden   Gate   Park

Mission
San Francisco
de Asís

16th St.

342

the **Chinese Consolidated Benevolent Building** (843 Stockton St.), home of
the Six Companies that brought Chinese laborers to California in the mid-
1800s. Historical exhibits interpreting the experience of Chinese Americans can be found at the **Chinese Historical Society of America** (650
Commercial St. 415-391-1188. Call for hours).

San Francisco Cable Car Museum (Washington and Mason Sts. 415-474-
1887) The city's second cable car (1873) is on view, as is today's working powerhouse of motors and pulleys that drives the cable car network.

Coit Memorial Tower (Top of Telegraph Hill. 415-362-0808. Fee for elevator) This concrete landmark (1933) was a civic benefaction of Lillie
Hitchcock Coit, who as a girl tagged along with an engine company. Some
say her memorial to volunteer firemen resembles a firehose. Depression-
era murals adorn the lobby. Great bay views await at the top.

Haas-Lilienthal House (2007 Franklin St. 415-441-3004. Wed. and Sun.; adm.
fee) A tower, gables, art glass, fancy woodwork, and decorative wallpapers
make this 1886 merchant's home a showplace of Queen Anne Victorian style.

San Francisco Maritime National Historical Park (Beach and Polk Sts.
415-556-3002. Adm. fee to ships) At the Maritime Museum, which resembles an art deco passenger liner, displays include figureheads, harpoons,
and sailor-made ships-in-bottles. At nearby Hyde Street Pier are the 1886
square-rigger **Balclutha,** with its authentically furnished cabins; and an
1890 side-wheel steam ferryboat, the **Eureka.**

Alcatraz (San Francisco Bay. 415-546-2700. Tours leave from Pier 41; reservations recommended; adm. fee) Join the shades of Scarface Al Capone and
the Birdman of Alcatraz at this former federal penitentiary (1934-1963).
Audiocassette tours visit cell blocks, mess hall, and prison library, while
ranger programs allow the public to meet former Alcatraz inmates.

Palace of Fine Arts (Baker and Beach Sts.) Last trace of the 1915 Panama-

Palace of Fine Arts, San Francisco

Pacific International Exhibition, this restored classical revival rotunda and colonnade were designed by Bernard Maybeck to evoke a Roman ruin.

Presidio of San Francisco (*NW area of city. Visitor Center, Main Post Bldg. 102 on Montgomery St. 415-561-4323*) Founded by Spanish soldiers in 1776, the presidio was an active military post until 1994. Two reasons to visit: the scenic location on 1,500 acres of woods and hills by San Francisco Bay, and the **Presidio Museum** (*Funston Ave. at Lincoln Blvd. Wed.-Sun.*). A diorama of 1906 San Francisco shows how the Army set up tent cities for earthquake-displaced residents.

Fort Point N.H.S. (*Off Lincoln Ave. at the presidio. 415-556-1693. Wed.-Sun.*) Founded during the Civil War, this fort has never fired a shot in anger. Visitors explore a brick honeycomb of gunports, see Civil War weapons, and view cannon drill demonstrations. The fort offers a spectacular view from beneath the Golden Gate Bridge.

Golden Gate Bridge (*Viewing area off Lincoln Ave. or off US 101 northbound*) Opened in 1937, this San Francisco landmark is supported by 3-foot-diameter cables slung from twin towers, and its overall length is 8,981 feet. Erected by engineer Joseph Strauss and tinted International Orange, the bridge has been continuously painted since opening day.

Cliff House (*1090 Point Lobos Ave. 415-556-8642*) Located on a bluff overlooking the Pacific Ocean, today's Cliff House (1909) is the latest in a series of structures that since 1858 have included an 8-story French château. A museum exhibits penny arcade and musicmaking machines; there's also a popular bar and restaurant. Nearby you can see the remains of the famous Sutro Baths, which closed in 1952.

Excursions

JOHN MUIR NATIONAL HISTORIC SITE (*35 miles NE via I-80, Calif. 24, and I-680 in Martinez. 4202 Alhambra Ave. 510-228-8860. Wed.-Sun.; adm. fee*) Naturalist and writer John Muir (1838-1914), whose influence helped create Yosemite National Park, lived in this 17-room Italianate house. Built in 1882, it has a redwood-paneled library and a bedroom where the Sierra Club founder refused to hang curtains, since he liked being awakened by the sun.

BENICIA (*40 miles NE via I-80, Calif. 24, I-680, and I-780*) Harking back

343

The Big Four
Four San Francisco merchants who sold wares to the forty-niners got particularly rich: Charles Crocker, Mark Hopkins, Collis P. Huntington, and Leland Stanford. The "Big Four" teamed up to build a railroad monopoly that brought them vast financial and political power. Their Central Pacific line was part of the transcontinental railroad that linked the nation in 1869. Some called them robber barons; Huntington was exposed as a briber of public officials. But some good was done: Leland Stanford endowed Stanford University.

to Benicia's 13 months as California's capital in 1853-54, **Benicia Capitol State Historic Park** *(115 West G St. 707-745-3385. Adm. fee)* contains the state's oldest existing statehouse. Nearby, the **Fischer-Hanlon House** *(135 West G St. 707-745-3385. Sat.-Sun.; adm. fee)* is a gold rush hotel that became a private home; it shows how a middle-class Benicia family lived in the late 19th century.

Memorial Church on Stanford University campus, Palo Alto

San Jose ···

(Convention & Visitors Bureau, 150 W. San Carlos St. 408-977-0900) California's first civilian community was founded in 1777 to grow food for the Spanish military presidios of Monterey and San Francisco. Utterly transformed during the past 30 years, San Jose produces not crops but computer chips, for Silicon Valley. Two reminders of early days are the 1797 **Peralta Adobe** *(175 W. St. John St. 408-993-8182. Closed Mon.)*, last remnant of the city's Spanish colonial settlement; and the adjacent **Fallon House** *(408-993-8182. Closed Mon.)*, a Victorian mansion with furnishings of the pre-Civil War period.

San Jose Historical Museum *(Kelley Park, 1600 Senter Rd. 408-287-2290. Adm. fee)* This 25-acre complex evokes early San Jose through original and reconstructed buildings, including Victorian-furnished houses, an 1888 Chinese temple, and the Bank of Italy (forerunner of the Bank of America). The **Pacific Hotel** has exhibits on local history and communications.

Excursion

STANFORD UNIVERSITY *(20 miles N via US 101, in Palo Alto. Guided tours. 415-723-2560)* Highlights of the 8,200-acre campus, laid out by Frederick Law Olmsted (the designer of Central Park) and opened in 1891, are the Richardson Romanesque sandstone buildings around the Quad and the 1903 Memorial Church, with its Byzantine-style mosaics of biblical scenes.

San Luis Obispo ·····································

(Chamber of Commerce, 1039 Chorro St. 805-781-2777) This sunny city grew up around its 1772 mission, and later prospered as an agricultural center and home of California Polytechnic State University. The chamber's "Heritage Walks" brochure guides you to early adobes, Victorian houses, the 1884 Chinese **Ah Louis Store** *(800 Palm St. 805-543-4332. Call for schedule)*, and other downtown sites. The **Motel Inn** *(Monterey St. exit from US 101)* was the first motel in the world.

Mission San Luis Obispo de Tolosa *(Chorro and Monterey Sts. 805-543-6850. Adm. fee)* One of the first missions to use red-clay tiles for roofing, it has a unique combination belfry and vestibule.

San Luis Obispo County Historical Museum *(696 Monterey St. 805-543-0638. Wed.-Sun.)* Displays at this former Carnegie library include a Victorian parlor, a lighthouse lens, and "flower wreaths" made entirely of human hair. The museum operates the 1853 **Dallidet Adobe and Gardens** *(1185 Pacific St. Mem. Day–Labor Day Sun. p.m.),* built by a French vintner.

Excursions

SAN MIGUEL *(40 miles N via US 101)* Unique among missions, the original decorations of **Mission San Miguel Arcángel** *(775 Mission St. 805-467-3256. Donations)* survive untouched. Painted roses decorate the walls and the Eye of God watches over the sanctuary, all unchanged since the 1820s. Dating from 1846, the **Rios Caledonia Adobe** *(700 S. Mission St. 805-467-3357. Wed.-Sun.; donations)* became a stage stop, tavern, and inn. You'll see bedrooms and a saloon bar of boards laid across two whiskey barrels.

HEARST CASTLE *(45 miles N via Calif. 1. 805-927-2020 or 800-444-4445. Reservations required; adm. fee)* Resembling a slice of Europe on the California coast, the 165-room Spanish-Moorish estate (1919-1947) of publishing mogul William Randolph Hearst boasts a main house and three guesthouses, with Renaissance furniture and tapestries, carved ceilings, a library with 5,200 volumes, and a swimming pool laid out beside a Greco-Roman temple facade.

Santa Barbara 345

(Visitor Information Center, 1 Santa Barbara St. 805-965-3021) Spain claimed this seaside region in 1542, but 240 years passed before Spanish colonists came to Santa Barbara. The city became a tourist mecca in the late 1800s, when wealthy Easterners basked in the Mediterranean climate. After a 1925 earthquake, the city rebuilt in its trademark Spanish colonial revival style.

Casa de la Guerra *(11 E. de la Guerra St. 805-966-6961. Closed Mon.)* During the 1820s presidio *comandante* José de la Guerra completed this fine adobe house, which became the hub of Santa Barbara social life.

Santa Barbara Historical Museum *(136 E. de la Guerra St. 805-966-1601. Closed Mon.)* Artifacts of the city's Chumash, Spanish, Mexican, Yankee, and Chinese cultures range from silver saddles to a gilded Chinese shrine. Two adjacent adobes date from 1817 and 1836.

Santa Barbara County Courthouse *(1100 Anacapa St. 805-962-6464. Tours Mon.-Sat.)* Resembling a Spanish-Moorish castle, this 1929 building delights the eye with red-tile roofs, turrets, Tunisian tiles, open-air stairways, wrought-iron chandeliers, sunken gardens, and historical murals.

El Presidio de Santa Barbara State Historic Park *(123 E. Canon Perdido St. 805-966-9719)* This continuing reconstruction of the Spanish military post includes a chapel and soldiers' quarters. The original 1788 guardhouse is Santa Barbara's oldest building.

Neptune Pool, Hearst Castle

Mission Santa Barbara *(2201 Laguna St. 805-682-4149. Adm. fee)* Called "queen of the missions" for its lovely foothill setting, two pink-domed towers, and sandstone facade of Roman style, the mission was founded in 1786. Original living quarters display vestments, sheepskin psalmbooks for Indian choristers, and crafts.

Excursions

OLD MISSION SANTA INÉS (*45 miles NW via US 101 and Calif. 246 in Solvang. 1760 Mission Dr. 805-688-4815. Adm. fee*) Parts of the church were painted by Indian artists using vegetable colors. Fine old vestments and Latin missals are on display.

LA PURISIMA MISSION S.H.P. (*55 miles NW via US 101 and Calif. 246 near Lompoc. 2295 Purisima Rd. 805-733-3713. Adm. fee*) This restored mission is set among hills and furnished in the manner of 1820. Visitors see the church, workshops, residences, tallow vats, livestock, and an authentically reproduced mission garden of food, fiber, and medicinal plants. Inquire about living history days.

Santa Rosa ··········

(*Chamber of Commerce, 637 1st St. 707-575-1191*) Founded in 1858, the sunny city has some ornate Victorian houses along McDonald Street. But Santa Rosa is perhaps most famous for being the home of Luther Burbank. For four decades beginning in 1885, the self-taught horticulturalist experimented in his gardens, now preserved as the **Luther Burbank Home and Gardens** (*Santa Rosa and Sonoma Aves. 707-524-5445. Gardens open daily, house and museum April-Oct. Wed.-Sun.; adm. fee for tours*). Here he developed more than 800 new plant varieties, including the Shasta daisy. The carriage house museum looks at Burbank's life and work, while the greenhouse contains a replica of his office. His Greek Revival house showcases original furnishings.

Mural Room, Santa Barbara County Courthouse

346

Excursions

PETALUMA ADOBE STATE HISTORIC PARK (*17 miles S via US 101 in Petaluma. 3325 Adobe Rd. 707-762-4871. Adm. fee*) The former ranch headquarters of Mexican general Mariano Vallejo, this 1836 adobe has 3-foot-thick walls and a surrounding veranda. Workrooms, storerooms for the hide and tallow trade, and Vallejo's quarters (containing his own furniture) convey the feeling of a rancho during the era when California was really the northern extension of Mexico.

SONOMA (*24 miles SE via Calif. 12*) Sonoma Plaza was the scene of the 1846 Bear Flag Revolt, in which an informal cadre of Americans imprisoned Vallejo and proclaimed California a republic. Within a month the U.S. government asserted control. Historic sites relating to those days are preserved on the plaza as **Sonoma S.H.P.** (*Spain St. between 2nd St. E. and 3rd St. W. 707-938-1519. Adm. fee*). Here, restored **Mission San Francisco Solano** (1823), the last in California's chain of missions, has an original bell. Vallejo housed his troops at the nearby 1841 **Sonoma Barracks,** a two-story adobe that now displays military bunks and shows a film about the Mexican general. Next door the wood-frame **Toscano Hotel** evokes the 1890s. On tree-shaded grounds a half mile west of the plaza stands the 1851 **Lachryma Montis** *(Spain St. W. and 3rd St. W.),* Vallejo's carpenter Gothic residence, furnished with his belongings. Its New England architecture reflects his acceptance of American life.

Two miles northeast of town, the winery that in 1857 launched California's premium wine industry is now the **Buena Vista Carneros Historic Tasting Room** *(18000 Old Winery Rd. 707-938-1266).* The stone press house and cellars are said to be the state's oldest.

JACK LONDON STATE HISTORIC PARK *(15 miles SE via Calif. 12 near Glen Ellen. 2400 London Ranch Rd. 707-938-5216. Adm. fee)* The 835 acres of rustic Beauty Ranch were the retreat of popular author Jack London after he grew "tired of cities and people." His 1913 mansion, Wolf House, burned before he could move in; the ruined walls and fireplaces are visible. The later **House of Happy Walls** is now a museum displaying a few of London's manuscripts, a model of his sailboat *Snark,* his desk and typewriter, publishers' rejection slips, and South Pacific travel keepsakes.

NAPA VALLEY *(E of Santa Rosa, along Calif. 29. Conference & Visitors Bureau 707-226-7459)* This renowned cornucopia of wine grapes was settled during gold rush days. In the town of **St. Helena,** you'll find two historic wineries. Founded in 1861, **Charles Krug Winery** *(2800 Main St. 707-967-2201)* ranks as Napa Valley's oldest wine operation; visitors see Charles Krug's original winemaking facility with its redwood tanks. The Rhine House mansion at the 1876 **Beringer Vineyards** *(2000 Main St. 707-963-7115)* evokes a German castle. Nonwine history can be found at the **Silverado Museum** *(1490 Library Ln. 707-963-3757. Closed Mon.),* where the life of writer Robert Louis Stevenson, who honeymooned in the valley in 1880, is portrayed through 8,000 items, including childhood lead soldiers and first editions of *Treasure Island* and other works.

In the town of **Calistoga,** the **Sharpsteen Museum** *(1311 Washington St. 707-942-5911. Donations)* showcases a diorama of the town's 1859 hot springs resort, built by Sam Brannan, California's first millionaire. Visitors also see an original resort cottage decorated with tintype photos.

347

Other Sites in California

Bodie State Historic Park *(20 miles SE of Bridgeport, off US 395. 619-647-6445. Adm. fee)* The West's largest true ghost town, Bodie rose in 1859 on wings of gold. By 1880 it had 10,000 people, 30 mining companies, 65 saloons, and plenty of wickedness, badmen, and gunfights. About 170 buildings remain, and the town gives the haunting impression that residents just drifted away, leaving poker chips on casino tables and caskets in the morgue. A museum with mining equipment, hearses, and everyday belongings occupies the Miners' Union Hall. The 3-mile, unpaved access road is difficult in wet weather and may be closed in winter.

Calico Ghost Town *(10 miles NE of Barstow, off I-15. 619-254-2122 or 800-862-2542. Adm. fee)* Once the hub of some 500 silver and borax mines, Calico thrived from 1881 to 1907. Commercialized now with shops and gunfight stunt shows, the town has six original buildings, plus re-creations. Town historian "Lefty" leads walking tours. Five miles farther north on I-15, the **Calico Early Man Archaeological Site** (*619-255-8760. Wed.-Sun.*) encompasses a Pleistocene-Holocene quarry and stone tool workshop. Some artifacts may be 200,000 years old; if that date is ever confirmed, this would be the oldest human site in America. The dig was directed by famous paleontologist Dr. Louis B. Leakey. Excavation workshops are open to the public by reservation.

Death Valley National Park (*619-786-2331. Adm. fee*) In this sunblasted realm of sand and stone, named by struggling pioneers in 1849, you'll visit historic sites relating to borax mining of the 1880s. At Furnace Creek Ranch, the **Borax Museum** displays minerals, wagons, and a steam train used at the mines. Just north, the **Harmony Borax Works** is the ghostly site of a processing plant, adobe buildings, and one of the famous 20-mule-team wagons used to haul refined borax out of the valley. In contrast to its elemental surroundings, **Scotty's Castle** (*Guided tours. Adm. fee*) resembles a Spanish-Moorish palace. It was built in the 1920s with the cash of a Chicago businessman and the fancies of a former showman in Buffalo Bill's Wild West, known as Death Valley Scotty.

Donner Memorial State Park (*Off I-80, 0.5 mile W of Truckee exit. 916-582-7892. Fees for parking and museum*) The **Emigrant Trail Museum** looks at overland travel in the 1840s and the ill-fated Donner Party, which was snowbound nearby during an early winter in 1846. Only 49 of 91 people lived through the six-month ordeal of freezing and starvation.

Fort Ross State Historic Park (*15 miles NW of Jenner on Calif. 1. 707-847-3286. Adm. fee*) In 1812 Russian fur hunters built Fort Ross (short for "Rossiia") to gather sea otter pelts and raise food for Russian colonists in Alaska. Visitors see the original commander's residence, along with reconstructions of a Russian Orthodox chapel and blockhouses with cannon.

Fort Tejon S.H.P. (*Off I-5 in Lebec. 805-248-6692. Adm. fee*) This Army post, built in the 1850s to guard Grapevine Pass and control Indian raiders, briefly experimented with camels as transport in the arid West. Two original adobe buildings survive, including furnished barracks and officers' quarters, with displays of military uniforms and weapons.

Mission San Juan Capistrano (*Camino Capistrano at Ortega Hwy., San Juan Capistrano. 714-248-2048. Adm. fee*) Founded in 1776 and famous for its returning swallows (annual festival on March 19), the mission has lovely gardens and a stone church. The only remaining chapel where Padre Serra said Mass (1777) has a gilded altar and is California's oldest building still in use.

Oroville Chinese Temple (*1500 Broderick St., Oroville. 916-538-2496. Adm. fee*) Built in 1863 for a local community of 10,000 Chinese, the complex consists of the three chapels devoted to Confucianism, Taoism, and Buddhism. There is also a display of embroidered tapestries, parade parasols, bronzes, wood lacquerware, puppets, and more. Chinese plantings fill the gardens.

San Juan Bautista S.H.P. (*Visitor Center at 2nd and Washington Sts., San Juan Bautista. 408-623-4881. Adm. fee*) The park revolves around the original Spanish plaza. Headquarters are in the adobe **Plaza Hotel** (1858), with furnished hotel rooms. Among several buildings open to the public, the residential ground floor of **Plaza Hall** is outfitted with furniture of the late 1800s; and the **Plaza Stable** (1872) displays wheeled vehicles, including two made by the Studebaker brothers of later automobile fame. Adjacent to the park is the 1797 **Mission San Juan Bautista** (*408-623-2127*), the largest mission church; the altar was painted by a ship-jumping American sailor.

348

Oregon

Columbia River at Crown Point, near the end of the trail for Lewis and Clark and the Oregon pioneers

Fur sparked the European era in Oregon. In an effort to cash in on the world's appetite for sea otter and beaver pelts, explorers and traders from several nations came to the Northwest in the late 1700s and early 1800s. The Lewis and Clark expedition, lasting from 1804 to 1806, did much to open this far-off Pacific land to Americans. Soon the U.S. and Great Britain emerged as the main forces in the area, and in 1818 they agreed to share the bounty of Oregon Country, which at this time included the entire Northwest.

During the 1830s, missionaries trickled into Oregon's Willamette Valley. Reports of rich farm land spurred large-scale migration over the Oregon Trail in the 1840s and '50s. The rapidly growing pioneer presence gave weight to U.S. claims to the region, and in 1846 Great Britain and the U.S. signed the treaty that gave British Columbia to the British and Oregon Country to the United States. Though the arrival of railroads and the land grants helped bring thousands of settlers into Oregon during the 1880s, the state remained agricultural until the timber industry took off near the turn of the century; by 1950 Oregon was the nation's leading lumber producer.

Astoria

(Chamber of Commerce, 111 W. Marine Dr. 503-325-6311 or 800-875-6807)
In 1811 the lure of furs prompted John Jacob Astor to send a trade expedition to the mouth of the mighty Columbia River. Setting up shop near

the area where Lewis and Clark had holed up for the winter of 1805-06, the traders established an outpost, inevitably named Astoria. The town later thrived as a port and salmon canning center.

Heritage Museum (*1618 Exchange St. 503-325-2203. Adm. fee*) One unexpected display reveals that in the 1920s nearly 900 Astorians belonged to the Ku Klux Klan. Such surprises—most far more positive—await amid the exhibits on logging, fur trading, and pioneer life.

Columbia River Maritime Museum (*1792 Marine Dr. 503-325-2323. Adm. fee*) Spend a few hours in this expansive museum and you'll grasp an essential truth about Astoria: The sea and the river are its lifeblood. Exhibits range from the flotilla of boats in the vaulting Great Hall to the transplanted bridge of a World War II destroyer in the labyrinth of galleries. Outside, visitors can board the lightship **Columbia,** which used to be stationed at the mouth of the river to help seafarers navigate the notoriously treacherous waters that have claimed hundreds of ships.

Fort Clatsop National Memorial

350

Flavel House (*441 8th St. 503-325-2563. Adm. fee*) One can imagine leading a pampered existence in this grand Victorian residence: evenings of music and witty conversation in the three parlors filled with lovely period furniture. But the life evoked by this 1885 Queen Anne house had its drawbacks, as evidenced by the display of amazingly tiny ladies' shoes.

Excursions

FORT CLATSOP NATIONAL MEMORIAL (*5 miles S via US 101 and Ft. Clatsop Rd. 503-861-2471. Visitor Center open daily in summer, weekends in spring*) The rough, dark, cramped stockade in which the members of the Lewis and Clark expedition passed the cold, rainy winter of 1805-06 is accurately replicated at this memorial. Visitor Center displays tell of elk hunts, beaver trapping, and trading with the savvy local Native Americans.

FORT STEVENS S.P. (*10 miles W via US 101 and Ft. Stevens Hwy. 503-861-2000*) Though its guns were never fired in anger, Fort Stevens guarded the mouth of the Columbia from the Civil War until shortly after World War II. The guns and most of the buildings are gone, but the museum and the massive concrete emplacements echo nearly a century of preparedness.

FORT COLUMBIA S.P., WASH. (*10 miles N via US 101*) See page 365.

Baker City ···

(*Convention & Visitors Bureau, 490 Campbell St. 541-523-3356 or 800-523-1235*) A gold rush in the 1860s gave birth to Baker City. A second min-

House National Historic Site *(713 Center St. 503-656-5146. Closed Mon. and Jan.; adm. fee)*, an 1846 Georgian home built by McLoughlin after he retired from the Hudson's Bay Company.

CHAMPOEG STATE HERITAGE AREA *(30 miles S via I-5 to Donald-Aurora exit. 503-633-8170)* The Visitor Center museum, the 1862-vintage Manson Barn, and a reconstructed 1852 house tell of pioneer life in the Willamette Valley. It was here in 1843 that settlers voted to form a provisional government under the United States, an important step in keeping the region out of the British empire.

VANCOUVER, WASH. *(5 miles N via I-5)* See page 363.

Salem ···

(Convention & Visitors Assoc., 1313 Mill St. S.E. 503-581-4325 or 800-874-7012)
In 1834, nearly a decade before the human tide flowed over the Oregon Trail, Jason Lee and his fellow Methodist missionaries arrived in the Salem area. By the time the first wave of settlers came in the early 1840s, Lee and company had built houses and a sawmill, and founded a university.

State Capitol *(900 Court St. N.E. 503-986-1388)* After the first two buildings burned, the current capitol was built in 1938. In addition to the typical stately renderings in marble, bronze, and oak, four massive murals depicting key moments in Oregon history surround the rotunda.

Willamette University *(900 State St. 503-370-6300)* Founded by Jason Lee and his followers in 1842, Willamette University claims to be the first university in the West. Waller Hall, built in 1867, is the oldest of several venerable brick buildings that grace this small liberal arts college.

Mission Mill Village *(1313 Mill St. S.E. 503-585-7012. Tues.-Sat.; adm. fee)* At the heart of this 5-acre historical complex lies the cavernous **Thomas Kay Woolen Mill,** built in 1889 and productive for some 70 years. Guides take visitors through the intact factory and show them the process from fleece to finished product; cover your ears when they turn on the gigantic 1940s power loom. Jason Lee's 1841 house and several other historic structures also are located on the grounds.

Bush House *(600 Mission St. S.E. 503-363-4714. Closed Mon.; adm. fee)* The 1878 Victorian mansion and most of its furnishings are original and in excellent condition. People come from far and wide just to see the wallpaper.

Deepwood Estate *(1116 Mission St. S.E. 503-363-1825. Sun.-Fri.; adm. fee)* From its renowned stained-glass windows to its golden oak woodwork to its multiple gables, this ornate 1894 Queen Anne attracts admiration, as does the elaborate formal garden.

The Dalles ···

(Chamber of Commerce, 404 W. 2nd St. 541-296-2231 or 800-255-3385)
Just west of The Dalles, the sheer basalt cliffs of the Columbia River Gorge rise right out of the river. This narrowing of the gorge made the townsite a natural stopover for Native Americans, Lewis and Clark, and fur trappers. The site grew even more important in the early 1840s, when Oregon Trail pioneers began pouring in; it was here they had to switch from wagons to rafts and float down the treacherous river waters.

Original Wasco County Courthouse *(W. 2nd Place near Mill Creek. 541-296-2231 or 800-255-3385. Call for hours)* This modest 1859 courthouse once served the largest county ever to exist in the United States: Between

1854 and 1859, Wasco County covered 130,000 square miles, extending east to the Continental Divide in the Rockies.

Fort Dalles Museum (*500 W. 15th St. 541-296-4547. Call for hours; adm. fee*) Stagecoaches and flintlock rifles recall frontier life.

Old St. Peter's Landmark (*W. 3rd and Lincoln Sts. 541-296-5686. Closed Mon.*) The tip of the steeple atop the gracefully louvered belfry reaches 170 feet, making this 1898 Gothic Revival church the visual focal point of The Dalles' historic downtown.

Other Sites in Oregon

Bonneville Lock and Dam (*3 miles W of Cascade Locks via I-84. 541-374-8820*) The first of the massive federal projects that have tamed the Columbia and Snake Rivers to supply water for power and irrigation, Bonneville was completed in 1938. Tours take in the powerhouses and the lock.

Canyon City and John Day A gold strike on Canyon Creek in 1862 spawned the adjacent towns of Canyon City and John Day. The **Kam Wah Chung & Co. Museum** (*Canton St., City Park, John Day. 541-575-0028. May-Oct. Sat.-Thurs.; adm. fee*) tells of the vital role Chinese immigrants played in eastern Oregon, especially in the gold mines; in 1880 there were 960 Chinese miners in Grant County alone. The **Grant County Historical Museum** (*Oreg. 395 in Canyon City. 541-575-0362. June-Sept. or by appt.; adm. fee*) contains gold rush relics, Native American artifacts, and ranching exhibits. On its grounds are the Greenhorn Jail and the cabin of Joaquin Miller, who wrote the turn-of-the-century book *Life Among the Modocs*.

Joseph Chief Joseph and the Nez Perce once roamed this scenic area, which they called Wallowa, or "Valley of the Winding Waters." Fine Indian artifacts can be found at artist David Manuel's handsome **Manuel Museum** (*400 N. Main St. 541-432-7235. Closed Jan.-Feb.; adm. fee*). Just up the street in the old bank building, visitors can browse pioneer exhibits at the **Wallowa County Museum** (*2nd and Main Sts. 541-432-1015. Mem. Day–Sept.*).

Wallowa Valley, 19th-century home of Chief Joseph and the Nez Perce

Old Aurora Colony Museum (*15008 2nd St., Aurora. 503-678-5754. Tues.-Sun.; adm. fee*) In 1856 William Keil, a charismatic German minister, and a group of followers braved the Oregon Trail and established Aurora in the Willamette Valley. The colony split up shortly after Keil's death in 1877, but restored buildings and a museum evoke the dream that drew the faithful west.

Timberline Lodge (*Mount Hood National Forest. 503-272-3311*) One of the Works Progress Administration's flagship projects, this monumental structure sits at tree line on Mount Hood like some Olympian hunting lodge. Titan-sized doors and the towering hexagonal fireplace dwarf visitors. Don't overlook the details wrought by those meticulous 1930s craftspeople, such as the newels carved into such native beasts as ravens and owls.

1848 lighthouse at Fort Canby, near Ilwaco

In the early 1800s, Washington was a part of Oregon Country, the name some gave to the whole Northwest. By 1848, when Oregon Country became Oregon Territory, the thousands of pioneers who had come west on the Oregon Trail lived south of the Columbia River, but only about 300 lived north of it. Residents in the north lobbied Congress to make their side of the Columbia a separate territory. Congress did so in 1853 and Washington Territory was born. The population boomed after the railroads came through in the 1880s, leading to statehood in 1889. The growth of the timber industry and the lucrative outfitting of the Klondike gold rushers in the late 1890s launched the state into the 20th century. The seeds of modern Washington were sown during the 1930s and 1940s with the development of huge hydroelectric dams in the Columbia Basin and the meteoric rise of Boeing and the aircraft industry in the Puget Sound region.

Bellingham

(Convention & Visitors Bureau, 904 Potter St. 360-671-3990 or 800-487-2032) Timber, coal deposits, and an accommodating bay from which to ship them led to the settlement of the Bellingham area in the early 1850s. Booms and busts followed, but the economy stabilized by 1903, when four small hamlets merged to become Bellingham. One of these settlements is now preserved as the **Fairhaven Historic District** *(Harris Ave.*

between 4th and 12th Sts. 360-738-1574), which can trace its ancestry to Dirty Dan, whom some call an entrepreneur and others call a smuggler. First settled in 1852, Fairhaven's streets are lined with dozens of well-preserved historic houses and commercial buildings.

Whatcom Museum of History and Art (121 Prospect St. 360-676-6981. Closed Mon.; adm. fee) Rooms inside the 1892 old city hall feature artifacts from Northwest Coast people, 19th-century toys, and Victorian clothing.

Excursions

PIONEER PARK (10 miles NW via I-5, in Ferndale. 1st and Cherry Sts. 360-384-4006. Park open year-round; tours mid-May–mid-Sept. Tues.-Sun.; adm. fee for tours) Visitors can con-

Whatcom Museum of History and Art, Bellingham

template the rigors of pioneer life represented by this collection of original log structures from around the state, including a post office and school.

HOVANDER HOMESTEAD PARK (15 miles NW via I-5, near Ferndale. 360-384-3444) A self-guided tour of the house, barn (complete with live farm animals), gardens, and orchards at this well-preserved turn-of-the-century homestead provides a graphic picture of early farm life.

Ellensburg ···

(Chamber of Commerce, 436 N. Sprague. 509-925-3137) On July 4, 1889, citizens got an unexpectedly spectacular pyrotechnics display when a fire burned most of the town to the ground. That's why so many of the dozens of late Victorian buildings in the historic district date from 1889—and why they're built of brick. Tucked into one of these buildings is the **Kittitas County Museum** (114 E. 3rd St. 509-925-3778. Call for hours) and its hodgepodge of local artifacts. Kids love the Native American war shirt.

Excursions

OLMSTEAD PLACE STATE PARK (4 miles E via I-90. 509-925-1943. Park open year-round, call for schedule of building tours) Little has changed on this 217-acre spread since Samuel and Sarah Olmstead began farming it in 1875. Visitors see the 1875 cabin, the 1908 farmhouse, the barn, and the granary.

THORP GRIST MILL (6 miles NW via I-90 in Thorp. 509-964-9640. Mem. Day–Labor Day) The mills that could grind grain into flour often lay at the heart of the agricultural communities that dotted the valleys of the Northwest. In Thorp, children even wore clothes made from the mill's discarded flour sacks. The Thorp mill provides a thorough look at the mill and its role.

ROSLYN (*25 miles NW via I-90 or Wash. 10. Chamber of Commerce 509-674-5958*) Made famous as the set for the television series *Northern Exposure*, Roslyn still remains at heart a backwater whose roots reach back to a brief coal boom in the late 1800s. Belly up to **The Brick** (*1 Pennsylvania Ave.*), the old tavern that still has a running-water spittoon.

Hoquiam and Aberdeen

These small twin cities lie on the eastern tip of Grays Harbor, named after Boston trader Robert Gray, the Northwest coast explorer who first entered it in 1792. Settlement of Hoquiam and Aberdeen began in earnest during the last half of the 19th century, when timbering boomed.

Arnold Polson Museum (*1611 Riverside Ave, in Hoquiam. 360-533-5862. Wed.-Sun. in summer, weekends rest of year; adm. fee*) Lumber magnate Arnold Polson gave his son this 26-room mansion as a wedding gift in the 1920s. Now the house contains a wide range of displays on regional history.

Hoquiam's Castle (*515 Chenault Ave., in Hoquiam. 360-533-2005. Daily in summer, weekends rest of year, closed Dec.; adm. fee*) Lumber tycoon Robert Lytle had this elaborate mansion built in 1897. Visitors expect the Tiffany lamps and the 600-piece, cut-crystal Viennese chandelier, but the tacky saloon on the third floor comes as a surprise.

Aberdeen Museum of History (*111 E. 3rd St, in Aberdeen. 360-533-1976. June–mid-Sept. Wed.-Sun., mid-Sept.–May Sat.-Sun.; donations*) The exhibits that cram this cavernous former armory include a huge mosaic fashioned from union buttons, the wheelhouse of a tugboat, and logging paraphernalia.

359

Olympia

(*Visitor Information Center, 14th Ave. and Capitol Way. 360-586-3460*) Settlers claimed this townsite early (1846) because it provided access to Puget Sound, as well as good farming and logging. By 1853, when Washington became a U.S. territory, Olympia boasted 996 residents and the territory's only newspaper, which helped lead to its selection as the capital.

Washington State Capital Museum (*211 W. 21st Ave. 360-753-2580. Tues.-Sun.; adm. fee*) In one early vote on choosing the state capital, Olympia beat out Vancouver (Wash.) 1,239 to 839—voters were pretty sparse back then. Such details regarding the route Olympia took to become the capital form the heart of this museum, housed in a Spanish-style mansion.

Bigelow House (*918 Glass Ave. N.E. 360-753-1215. Sat.-Sun.; adm. fee*) Memories of Daniel and Elizabeth Bigelow, pioneers and civic leaders, abound in this circa 1860 house. It's filled with original pieces because no other family has ever lived here.

Excursion

TUMWATER HISTORIC DISTRICT (*5 miles S via I-5 in Tumwater Call City Hall for tour info 360-754-4160. Donations for tours*) In the shadow of the interstate lie several old houses dating from the first permanent American settlement on Puget Sound, including the 1905 **Henderson House** and the nearby **Crosby House,** built in 1858 by entertainer Bing Crosby's grandfather.

Port Townsend

(*Visitor Information Center, 2347 E. Sims Way. 360-385-2722*) Though named by Capt. George Vancouver in 1792, Port Townsend wasn't settled until 1851. With its fine harbor, the town soon mushroomed into a thriving—and notoriously seamy—seaport. Many well-preserved 19th-century brick buildings line the downtown area along the waterfront, and dozens of fine Victorian houses perch on the bluff above.

Jefferson County Historical Society Museum *(210 Madison St. 360-385-1003. Closed weekdays in Jan.; donations)* Four floors sag with thousands of artifacts in the historic city hall. Don't overlook the basement jail, where you can read about Howard Garner's escape through the 12-by-7-inch food slot.

Fort Worden State Park *(200 Battery Way. 360-385-4730)* Even the forts are Victorian in this town. The decommissioned fort was built around the turn of the century to protect Puget Sound from invasion by sea; gun emplacements and the **Artillery Museum** tell the story.

Seattle ....

(Convention & Visitors Bureau, 8th and Pike Sts. 206-461-5840) Like terrestrial life, Seattle rose from the mud; in 1851 the first hardy pioneers settled on the mudflats of Elliott Bay—the area known today as Pioneer Square. Seattle's forests attracted entrepreneurs such as Henry Yesler, who built a steam-powered mill on a pier above the tidal flats. An unattended glue pot ignited a blaze in 1889 that burned most of Seattle to the ground; out of the ashes rose **Pioneer Square** *(Bounded by Alaskan Way S., S. King St., 4th St. S., and Yesler Way),* a beautifully cohesive district of historic brick buildings.

Klondike Gold Rush N.H.P. *(117 S. Main St. 206-553-7220)* In 1897, 68 prospectors steamed into Seattle and unloaded more than two tons of gold they'd dug out of the Klondike. Within hours North America's last great gold rush began. Historians estimate that Seattle merchants made some $25 million from outfitting gold seekers, while prospectors extracted only about $10 million in gold from the Klondike. The exhibits in this park-museum start visitors in Seattle and take them through the stages of preparation and travel to the Klondike.

Underground Tour *(610 1st Ave. 206-682-4646. Adm. fee)* After the 1889 fire, Seattle raised its streets 8 to 32 feet above the sidewalks and building entrances in an effort to rise above the mud and sewage. For up to five years people had to climb ladders to navigate this waffle-like cityscape. Finally, the city moved up to the new street level, leaving an underground maze that visitors can now explore by tour.

Wing Luke Asian Museum *(407 7th Ave. S. 206-623-*

Pioneer Square, Seattle

5124. Closed Mon.; adm. fee) Visitors to this Pan-Asian museum will see a great breadth of exhibits, including handmade Chinese kites and documents and photos recalling the internment of Seattle's Japanese citizens during World War II.

Pike Place Market *(Main entrance, 1st Ave. and Pike St. 206-682-7453)* The fish, flowers, and food are fresh, but the market itself dates from 1907. Now a cherished institution frequented by all sorts of Seattlites, the market was an important source of cheap food for poor citizens during the Depression.

Northwest Seaport *(1002 Valley St. 206-447-9800. Mon.-Fri., call for weekend hours)* The displays on Northwest maritime history are interesting, and watching craftspeople restoring old ships is great, but at the heart of the seaport lie its ships: the **Wawona,** an 1897 schooner; and the **Arthur Foss,** an 1889 tug.

Mortuary pole, Burke Museum

Located at the south end of Lake Union, the seaport anchors the **Maritime Heritage Center,** a complex that also includes the Center for Wooden Boats and the Puget Sound Maritime Museum.

Museum of History and Industry *(2700 24th Ave. E. 206-324-1126. Adm. fee)* MOHAI is chockablock with fine displays on Seattle and Northwest history, but one exhibit stands out: the sequential photos and artifacts from the great 1889 fire, including the glue pot that started it.

361

Burke Museum *(17th Ave., N.E. entrance, on Univ. of Washington campus. 206-543-5590. Adm. fee)* At this museum of natural and cultural history, the collection of artifacts includes totem poles of Northwest Coast Indians and boats from different cultures around the world.

Nordic Heritage Museum *(3014 N.W. 67th St. 206-789-5707. Closed Mon.; adm. fee)* Fittingly located in the palpably Scandinavian Seattle neighborhood of Ballard, this museum tells the story of the Nordic migration to America. Around the turn of the century, the flow from Scandanavia was sizable: It's estimated that in 1900 one in six Swedes lived in the U.S.

Excursion

MUSEUM OF FLIGHT *(10 miles S via I-5, Boeing Field. 206-764-5720. Adm. fee)* From the nuts and bolts to the ethereal, this vast, appropriately airy museum presents the many facets of aviation history. Visitors can gawk at dozens of aircraft, such as the squat 1950 "Aerocar" and the first presidential jet, decommissioned in 1996.

Spokane ·

(Visitor Information Center, 201 W. Main St. 509-747-3230 or 800-248-3230) In 1810 David Thompson built a trading post near present-day Spokane, but no permanent settlers arrived until 1871. In 1880 Spokane, population 350, was a mere pinprick on the landscape. Then the railroad came to town, and by 1910 the population had skyrocketed to more than 100,000. In the 35 years following a devastating fire in 1889 (the last of three Washington towns to burn down that year), buildings of many styles rose from the ashes. Dozens have been restored and remain in use, notably the **Davenport Hotel** *(807 W. Sprague Ave.)* and the **Old National Bank Building** *(422 W. Riverside Ave.).*

Browne's Addition (*Coeur d'Alene to Oak, between Riverside and 3rd*) Many Spokane residents who grew rich from mining, timber, and railroading between the 1880s and 1905 built opulent homes in this neighborhood. Most prominent is the 26-room, nine-fireplace mansion (*W. 2208 2nd Ave. 509-838-8300*) commissioned by Patrick "Patsy" Clark in 1895. Now a posh restaurant, it has many exquisite original furnishings.

Cheney Cowles Museum & Historic Campbell House (*W. 2316 1st Ave. 509-456-3931. Closed Mon.; adm. fee*) The historical side of this superb museum focuses on the Inland Northwest and Native American cultures. Everyday life in the past is brought out via artifacts, quotes, and even old home movies.

Excursion

COEUR D'ALENE, IDAHO (*35 miles E via I-90*) See page 328.

Tacoma ···

(*Convention & Visitors Bureau, 906 Broadway St. 206-627-2836 or 800-272-2662*) Tacoma's early history followed a classic Northwest pattern. First, fur traders built a post in the area in 1833. Then someone noticed all the surrounding timber and built a sawmill on Commencement Bay in 1852. Finally, the city boomed a few decades later when the railroad came to town.

The motley crews pictured in the historic photos in the **Spar Tavern** (*2121 N. 30th St.*) reveal the nautical origins of this bayside area called **Old Tacoma,** from which Tacoma sprouted. The tavern heads the list of 19th-century buildings that remain in this venerable neighborhood.

With its signature clock tower, the 1893 **Old City Hall** (*S. 7th St. and Pacific Ave.*) anchors the **Old City Hall Historic District.** Just across the street overlooking the bay is **Fireman's Park,** which features several detailed historical displays and an old and very tall totem pole.

Using plans originally meant for a grand hotel, construction began in 1891 on today's **Stadium High School** (*111 N. E St.*), located in the **Stadium-Seminary Historic District.** Other fine old buildings that border this district include the **First Presbyterian Church** (*Division St. and Tacoma Ave. S.*) and the **W. W. Seymour Botanical Conservatory** (*316 S. G St. 206-591-5330*), a 1908 Victorian beauty fashioned from about 5,000 pieces of glass.

Union Station (*Pacific Ave. and 19th St. 206-572-9310. Rotunda closed weekends*) Built in 1911 as the crowning symbol of the importance of the railroad to Tacoma, this beaux-arts-style, copper-domed structure was elaborately restored in recent years. Next door, a notable collection of Northwest Native American and pioneer artifacts can be found at the **Washington State History Museum** (*1911 Pacific Ave. 206-272-3500 or 888-BE-THERE. Closed Mon. Labor Day–Mem. Day; adm. fee*).

Fort Nisqually (*Point Defiance Park. 206-591-5339. Closed Mon.-Tues. Sept.-May; adm. fee*) This reconstructed Hudson's Bay Company post was built in the early 19th century to create a presence in the fur-trading business on Puget Sound. Visitors can wander through the original gentlemen's house and replicas of other structures.

Camp 6 Logging Museum (*Point Defiance Park. 206-752-0047. Mid-Jan.-Oct. Wed.-Sun.*) During the era of steam logging, from the 1880s to the 1940s, entire logging camps—cookhouse, bunkhouses, and more—were mounted on flatcars and moved from site to site. Visitors can see one such railcar camp plus other logging equipment.

Excursions

Fort Nisqually, Tacoma

MEEKER MANSION *(10 miles SE via River Rd. in Puyallup. 312 Spring St. 206-848-1770. April–mid-Dec. Wed.-Sun.; adm. fee)* The wealth Ezra Meeker amassed by growing hops is evident in his 17-room Victorian mansion, completed in 1890.

PIONEER FARM MUSEUM *(35 miles SE via Wash. 7, near Eatonville. 360-832-6300. Call for hours; adm. fee)* Visitors to this replica of an 1880s farm get a hands-on taste of pioneer life, including a chance to milk a cow.

STEILACOOM *(10 miles S via Steilacoom Blvd.)* Among the venerable sites in Washington's first incorporated city (1854) are the **Steilacoom Historical Museum** *(112 Main St. 206-584-4133. Closed Mon. March-Oct., call for winter hours)*; the **Steilacoom Tribal Cultural Center** *(1515 Lafayette St. 206-584-6308. Tues.-Sun.; adm. fee)*; and the town's hub, **Bair Drug & Hardware Store** *(1617 Lafayette St. 206-588-9668)*, dating from 1895.

FORT LEWIS MILITARY MUSEUM *(15 miles SW via I-5, on Fort Lewis Military Base. 206-967-7206. Wed.-Sun.)* Three galleries tell the history of Fort Lewis and of the Army in the Northwest.

363

Vancouver ·······························

(Chamber of Commerce, 404 E. 15th St., Suite 11. 360-694-2588 or 800-377-7084) Two Fort Vancouvers dominate the early history of this area. Hudson's Bay Company, the British concern, built Fort Vancouver in the 1820s as a trading fort. But in 1846, America and Great Britain negotiated the current U.S.-Canada border, stranding this British outpost in U.S. territory. To fortify America's new claim, the U.S. Army built in 1849 a second Fort Vancouver, a military outpost now called Vancouver Barracks and still in use.

Fort Vancouver N.H.S. *(1501 E. Evergreen Blvd. 360-696-7655. Adm. fee May-Sept.)* Some interpreters refer to Fort Vancouver as "K-mart on the Columbia," the place where Native Americans and settlers could buy almost anything they needed. By 1845, the era depicted in this sprawling, meticulous re-creation, Fort Vancouver was the hub for present-day Washington, Oregon, Idaho, and British Columbia.

Officers' Row *(Just N of Fort Vancouver N.H.S. 360-693-3103)* Originally part of Vancouver Barracks, the 21 stately officers' residences, built between 1850 and 1906, offer an architectural smorgasbord of many different styles. Businesses rent most of these buildings now, but visitors can tour the **George C. Marshall House** *(1301 Officers' Row. 360-693-3103)*, the beautiful Queen Anne Victorian where the author of the Marshall Plan once lived; and the 1848 **Grant House** *(1101 Officers' Row. 360-694-5252. Tues.-Sat.)*—the row's oldest house—named for the Civil War hero who visited here several times as a young officer.

Downtown Vancouver Historic high points include **Covington House** *(4208 Main St. 360-695-6750. June-Aug. Tues. and Thurs.)*, an 1848 log structure that served as a boarding school; and monumental **St. James Catholic**

Vancouver

Church (*Washington and 12th Sts.*), an imposing Gothic Revival-style brick church built in 1885. Don't miss the **Clark County Historical Museum** (*1511 Main St. 360-695-4681. Tues.-Sat.*), which offers a wealth of detail regarding everyday life in Clark County's past; and the **Pearson Air Museum** (*1105 E. 5th St. 360-694-7026. Wed.-Sun.; adm. fee*), where planes, photos, and artifacts tell the stories of pioneer aviators.

Excursion
PORTLAND, OREGON (*5 miles S via I-5*) See page 353.

Walla Walla ···
(*Chamber of Commerce, 29 E. Sumach St. 509-525-0850*) Walla Walla is best remembered for an uprising in 1847, in which Cayuse warriors captured and killed many white settlers. The ground beneath the venerable brick buildings on Main Street hosted a U.S. Army encampment in the 1850s and, before that, is thought to have been part of the Nez Perce Trail. Other restored buildings stand nearby, notably the **Kirkman House** (*214 N. Colville St. 509-529-4373. Thurs.-Sun.*), an 1880 Italianate edifice open for tours.
　Fort Walla Walla Museum Complex (*755 Myra Rd. 509-525-7703. April-Oct. Tues.-Sun.; adm. fee*) The area's pioneer heritage gets full treatment in 5 large exhibit buildings and a compound of 16 original and replica structures.

364

Excursions
WHITMAN MISSION N.H.S. (*10 miles W via US 12. 509-522-6360. Adm. fee*) A fine museum and interpretive trails tell about Dr. Marcus Whitman, his wife, Narcissa, and the other missionaries who trekked west to this site in 1836. It was here, in 1847, that profound tensions caused the Cayuse to rise up against the settlers, leaving many dead, including the Whitmans.
　PENDLETON, OREG. (*42 miles SW via Wash. 125 and Oreg. 11*) See p. 353.

Whidbey Island ·································
Early Spanish explorers thought Whidbey was part of the mainland, but members of George Vancouver's 1792 expedition discovered that it was a deceptively long island. Vancouver also noted that it was bountiful; that natural bounty drew traders in the 1830s and settlers a couple of decades later.
　Civilian Conservation Corps Interpretive Center (*Deception Pass State Park 360-675-2417*) "We had an old timer faller . . . and his biggest job was to try to keep us from killing ourselves." This quote from one of the Civilian Conservation Corps men, referring to his logging training, is typical of the information that complements the artifacts housed in the 1930s stone-and-wood structure, built as a CCC project.

Yakima ···
In the 1880s the railroad came, but property disputes pushed the station 4 miles north of town. Determined not to be bypassed, townspeople put the courthouse, banks, saloons, hotels, and dozens of other buildings on rollers and hauled Yakima 4 miles to its present location.
　Yakima Valley Museum (*2105 Tieton Dr. 509-248-0747. Adm. fee*) This large, dynamic museum features an exploration space for kids, much pioneer paraphernalia, and an enormous collection of horse-drawn vehicles.

Excursions

INDIAN PAINTED ROCKS *(5 miles NW on US 12)* No one knows the origins of these ancient petroglyphs, but the 60-odd reddish stick figures and sunburst faces carved in the basalt are thought to be hundreds, perhaps thousands of years old.

YAKAMA NATION MUSEUM *(20 miles S on US 97, in Toppenish. 509-865-2800. Adm. fee)* The museum presents the story of the Yakama people and the Yakima Valley from the perspective of the tribe.

Other Sites in Washington

Chelan County Museum *(600 Cottage Ave., Cashmere. 509-782-3230. Closed Mon. and Nov.-Feb.; adm. fee)* The main building has an extensive collection of pioneer and Native American artifacts, but the old days are evoked best out back amid the 19 original pioneer structures.

Fort Columbia State Park *(2 miles E of Chinook on US 101. 360-642-3078. April-Sept.)* Two museums and several original buildings capture turn-of-the-century life at this 1896 fort.

Grand Coulee Dam *(Wash. 155, near Coulee Dam. 509-633-9265* Built during the Depression, the dam epitomizes the grand public works of that era. A platform at the top yields awesome views of the spillway.

La Conner A number of buildings in this tiny town date back to its earlier beginnings as a fishing village. The past of the area further emerges in the collections at the **Skagit County Historical Museum** *(501 4th St. 360-466-3365. Wed.-Sun.; adm. fee)*.

Fishing boats along historic waterfront, La Conner

Makah Museum *(Makah Reservation, Neah Bay. 360-645-2711. Closed Mon.-Tues. mid-Sept.–May; adm. fee)* Visitors who peruse the superb exhibits here learn that not all Native Americans hunted bison—some harpooned whales from canoes. Thousands of the artifacts came perfectly preserved from a 500-year-old coastal village that had been partially buried in a mud slide.

Oysterville Historic District *(Convention & Visitors Bureau, US 101 and Wash. 103 in Seaview. 360-642-2400 or 800-451-2542)* More than a dozen historic houses line the two-street town of Oysterville.

San Juan Island N.H.P. *(Two sites on San Juan Island. 360-378-2240)* During the tense summer of 1859, American and British forces faced off after the shooting of a British pig by an American farmer ignited the long-simmering dispute over which country got San Juan Island. Restored buildings and displays at the sites of the opposing armies' camps tell the weird tale of the Pig War.

Alaska

Abandoned mine buildings at Independence Mine State Historical Park, Hatcher Pass

The first human to step onto North American soil set foot in Alaska more than 10,000 years ago, when hunter-gatherers from Siberia crossed the Bering land bridge. Modern history started with Vitus Bering's 1741 voyage to Alaska's shores. His crew returned to Russia with sea otter pelts, stimulating a demand that brought many traders to Alaska in the late 1700s. Russia's interest in Alaska dwindled in the mid-19th century as the fur trade declined, leading to the sale of Alaska to the United States in 1867. Some Americans thought Russia had suckered William Seward, who engineered the deal, and the purchase was dubbed "Seward's folly." Alaska was virtually ignored until gold was discovered near Juneau in 1880. The big 1897 Klondike rush and the even bigger 1898 Nome rush really put Alaska on the map. The glamour of gold overshadowed the rapid growth of salmon fishing and canning in the late 1800s, a stable industry that carried Alaska into the 20th century. Still, the state remained sparsely settled. It took World War II and the Japanese invasion of the Aleutians to bring enough people (more than 140,000 military personnel) to Alaska to justify statehood in 1959.

Anchorage

(Convention & Visitors Bureau, 524 W. 4th Ave. 907-276-4118) The metropolis that holds nearly half of Alaska's residents began in 1915 as a tent

city for workers building the Alaska Railroad. But Anchorage didn't boom into the state's major city until World War II, when military personnel came to town.

Anchorage Museum of History and Art (*121 W. 7th Ave. 907-343-4326. Daily mid-May–mid-Sept., closed Mon. rest of year; adm. fee*) The museum's Alaska Gallery lays out the whole parade of Alaskan history. Visitors start at exhibits on the arrival of humans in North America via the Bering land bridge and proceed through the Russian and pioneer eras to modern times.

Oscar Anderson House Museum (*420 M St. 907-274-2336. Daily mid-May–mid-Sept., Tues.-Sat. rest of year; adm. fee*) Amid the mud and tents of 1915 Anchorage arose this pleasant home, one of the city's first wood-frame houses. Completely restored, it contains many original furnishings.

Alaska Aviation Heritage Museum (*4721 Aircraft Dr. 907-248-5325. Daily May-Sept., Tues.-Sat. rest of year; adm. fee*) Vintage aircraft, a slew of photographs, and much more celebrate the daring of both Alaska's bush pilots and the World War II pilots who fought the Japanese in the Aleutian Islands.

Excursions

MATANUSKA VALLEY COLONY (*45 miles NE via Alas. 1, in Palmer. Palmer Visitor Center, 723 S. Valley Way. 907-745-2880. May–mid-Sept.*) In 1935, a New Deal program brought 200 families from the Midwest and settled them in the Matanuska Valley to build a "colony." The **Colony Museum** at the Visitor Center tells their story and provides information on seeing colony houses and farms in the vicinity.

INDEPENDENCE MINE STATE HISTORICAL PARK (*70 miles NE via Alas. 1 and Palmer Fishhook Rd. 907-745-2827. Buildings open June–mid-Sept.; adm. fee*) Between the museum displays and the many remaining buildings, visitors come away with a good feel for the life of a 1930s hard-rock gold miner in Alaska. At its peak this mine employed more than 200 people and covered more than 1,350 acres.

Southeast Alaska Ferry Tour ···················

Each summer thousands of visitors flock to Alaska's Inside Passage to admire its spectacular scenery and wildlife. The towns along this narrow waterway, which runs from just north of Seattle to Skagway, also provide a look back at the early settlement of America's last frontier. While luxury cruise ships ply these waters, the state-run Alaska Marine Highway System (*907-465-3941 or 800-642-0062. Reserve staterooms and vehicles well in advance*) provides a flexible, economical way to see and learn about the region's history. Six vessels serve south-

eastern Alaska communities. With advance planning, passengers can arrive on one ferry and leave on another to extend their stays.

1. Often called the "gateway to Alaska," **Ketchikan** is known for its fishing and logging industries. The **Totem Bight State Historical Park** *(10 miles N of downtown on the N. Tongass Hwy. Daily mid-May–mid-Sept., Mon.-Fri. rest of year; donations)* offers an introduction to southeast Alaska's native people, the Tlingits. Best known for their totem poles, the tribe hunted and fished along the region's coastal waters long before the arrival of European settlers. Originally a Tlingit fishing camp, Totem Bight is now home to 14 renovated and re-created totem poles and a model of a Tlingit clan house. Interpretive signs and a brochure explain the symbolism of each totem.

Totem poles, Sitka N.H.P.

2. The next ferry stop is **Wrangell**, a small logging and fishing community that is the only U.S. town to have been governed by the Russians, British, and Americans. A boardwalk leads to **Petroglyph Beach** *(0.5 mile N of ferry terminal on Evergreen Ave.),* where rocks are carved with faces and other spiral designs. Some archaeologists believe the carvings date back as far as 8,000 years. Connected to downtown Wrangell by a wooden footbridge, **Shakes Island Historic Site** *(Shakes St. 907-874-2023. Open for tour ships and by appointment; adm. fee)* is dotted with totem poles carved during the Depression by native artisans funded by the Civilian Conservation Corps. There is also a re-created Tlingit tribal house.

3. Once the capital of Russian Alaska, **Sitka** is now a thriving tourist destination where well-maintained historic sites chronicle the settlement of southeast Alaska by Russian fur traders. The site of the first Russian settlement in the region is preserved at the **Old Sitka State Historic Site** *(7 miles N of town, just past ferry terminal. Halibut Point Rd. 907-747-6249).* The fur-trading outpost was destroyed and all of its inhabitants killed by the Tlingits in 1802. A short trail and 24-hour interpretive center detail the early history of Russian activity in Alaska.

The Tlingit inhabitants of the area once used the elevation now known as **Castle Hill State Historic Site** *(Lincoln St., next to City Hall. 907-747-6249),* with its sweeping view of Sitka Sound, as a watchtower. The hill was later the site of the Russian-American Company headquarters. Here, too, the transfer of Alaska from Russia to the U.S. in 1867 took place, and the first U.S. flag with 49 stars was raised in 1959, the year of Alaska statehood. The nearby **St. Michael's Cathedral** *(240 Lincoln St. 907-747-8120. Daily mid-May–Sept., Mon.-Sat. rest of year; donations)* is a reconstruction of the first Russian Orthodox cathedral in the Western Hemisphere. Built in the 1840s, the original cathedral was destroyed by fire in 1966. Virtually all the icons were rescued and are on display inside.

Not far away, the **Sitka National Historical Park** *(106 Metlakatla St. 907-747-6281)* commemorates the 1804 Battle of Sitka, which ended in a Russian victory over the Tlingit. Dotted with interpretive signs, a path through temperate rain forest passes the site of the Tlingit fort, as well as the battleground and a number of totem poles. The park's Visitor Center houses a cultural center where visitors can watch native artists at work. The park also includes the **Russian Bishop's House** *(Lincoln St. 907-747-6281),* one of the few remaining examples of Russian colonial architecture in North America.

4. Begun as a gold-mining town, **Juneau** perches on the banks of the Gastineau Channel, surrounded by spectacular mountains and glaciers. In addition to numerous government buildings, the state capital is home to many historic buildings, including hotels, saloons, and shops. The small, onion-domed **St. Nicholas Russian Orthodox Church** *(326 5th St. 907-586-1023. Mid-May–mid-Sept. Mon.-Sat., and by appointment; donations)* is the oldest original Russian Orthodox church (1894) in southeast Alaska. It was established by Tlingit converts long after the Russians had left Alaska. Numerous 19th-century Russian icons and liturgical items are on display. Across the channel on neighboring **Douglas Island,** a hiking trail leads to the abandoned **Treadwell Mine,** one of the area's largest mining operations. Nearly 70 million dollars worth of gold was mined between 1881 and 1917, when the mine was flooded.

5. Alaska's first permanent Army post, **Fort William H. Seward** was built in **Haines** in 1903, partially in response to a border dispute with Canada. Private residences, which served as officers' quarters, ring a parade ground where Alaskan recruits were trained until 1945. The fort hospital is now the **Alaska Indian Arts Skill Center,** where native artists carve totems and masks. The **Sheldon Museum and Cultural Center** *(11 Main St. 907-766-2366. Adm. fee)* has a collection of photographs of the fort as well as a replica of a Tlingit tribal house and other native artifacts.

6. Skagway, the northernmost port of the Alaska Marine Highway System, was a lively staging area in 1898 for the Klondike gold rush. **Klondike Gold Rush National Historical Park** *(2nd Ave. and Broadway 907-983-2921.*

Daily mid-May–Sept., weekdays only rest of year) includes a collection of restored buildings scattered around downtown as well as a museum dedicated to the frantic dash for gold. The White Pass and Yukon Route Railroad Depot serves as the park's Visitor Center, where exhibits and a video tell of the rigors of the 33-mile climb up the Chilkoot Trail. Among the more than 50 historic buildings in the

Fort William H. Seward, Haines

Skagway Historic District is the Arctic Brotherhood Hall, which now houses the **Trail of '98 Museum** *(Broadway and 2nd St. 907-983-3525. Daily mid-May–Sept., by appt. rest of year).* Inside you'll find a collection of gold rush, Native American, and early Skagway memorabilia.

Other Sites in Alaska

Bering Land Bridge National Preserve *(70 miles N of Nome. For access information contact the Superintendent's Office 907-443-2522)* This 2.7 million-acre site sprawls across remote tundra a few miles south of the Arctic Circle. The prehistory it evokes is equally remote: the first appearance of humans in North America between 10,000 and 50,000 years ago, when they walked across the land bridge from Asia. Unless you excavate, you won't see evidence of these first residents, but later peoples left mysterious rock cairns that merit contemplation.

Cape Krusenstern N.M. (*10 miles N of Kotzebue. Superintendent's Office in Kotzebue 907-442-3890. For access information call the Kotzebue Public Lands Information Center 907-442-3760.*) Over the last 4,000 years or so, the shoreline of the Chukchi Sea (part of the Arctic Ocean) has shifted more than a hundred times. Each shift has left a beach ridge containing artifacts of different occupants, from the Denbigh Flint people of 2300 B.C. to the Eskimos who currently follow traditional ways on this isolated coast.

Eagle (*Alaska Division of Tourism 907-465-2010*) Built on the banks of the mighty Yukon, Eagle was the hub of interior Alaska at the turn of the century. Visitors can tour the courthouse, customhouse, and other historic sites. Visitors also can check out **Fort Egbert,** an Army post built in 1899 to keep order among the region's gold miners and maintain the local telegraph line.

Fairbanks (*Convention & Visitors Bureau, 550 First Ave. 907-456-5774 or 800-327-5774*) Dogsledding is an Alaskan passion, and in downtown Fairbanks visitors can share this passion at the **Dog Mushing Museum** (*535 2nd Ave. 907-456-6874. Late May–Aug. Mon.-Sat., Mon.-Fri. rest of year*). The videos of sled dog races are especially compelling. Alaska's past also emerges at **Alaskaland** (*2300 Airport Way. 907-459-1087. Mid-May–mid-Sept.; activities fees*), a pioneer theme park. Amid the souvenir shops and ice-cream parlors are some restored historic buildings, museums, and the

SS **Nenana,** a 1933-vintage stern-wheeler that once plied the Yukon River. The history of the Great Land's native peoples is told via the outstanding artifacts at the **University of Alaska Museum** (*907 Yukon Dr. 907-474-7505. Adm. fee*). Other exhibits cover the Russian presence in Alaska, natural history, and the state's love affair with gold.

Bering Land Bridge National Preserve

Kodiak (*Kodiak Island Convention & Visitors Bureau, 100 Marine Way. 907-486-4782*) Russians in pursuit of sea otter pelts came to Kodiak in the late 1700s, establishing the oldest permanent European settlement in Alaska. Their era is recounted at the **Baranov Museum** (*101 Marine Way. 907-486-5920. Daily Mem. Day–Labor Day, closed Thurs. and Sun. in winter, closed Feb.; adm. fee*), where visitors can see Russian and native artifacts in a former fur storehouse, built by Russians in 1808. **Fort Abercrombie State Historical Park** (*5 miles N on Fort Abercrombie Rd. 907-486-6339. Daily mid-May–mid-Sept., Mon.-Fri. rest of year*) reveals the more recent past; its bunkers, gun carriages, and observation posts date from World War II.

Hawaii

Puuhonua o Honaunau N.H.P., Island of Hawaii

371

Hawaii's first settlers, who voyaged from the Marquesas more than 1,500 years ago, guided their double-hull canoes to the Pacific's farthest outpost solely by their knowledge of stars, winds, and the flight of birds. Capt. James Cook was the first European to arrive, in 1778. The conqueror Kamehameha the Great united most of the islands into a kingdom by 1795.

Currents of change hit Hawaiian shores with the coming of Yankee missionaries in 1820. Then American whalers turned Honolulu and Lahaina into blubber boomtowns. By mid-century sugarcane was king, and workers from China, Japan, Portugal, and the Philippines helped create the multi-ethnic mix of modern Hawaii. Americans owned much of the land, and in 1893 these foreign businessmen (aided by U.S. Marines) managed to overthrow the Kingdom of Hawaii, which soon was annexed by the United States. The U.S. entered World War II when Japan bombed Pearl Harbor near Honolulu in 1941. After Hawaii became the 50th state in 1959, package tourists discovered paradise.

Island of Hawaii

Hawaii—the Big Island—was probably the first Hawaiian island settled by Polynesian voyagers from the Marquesas, between A.D. 300 and 600. Kamehameha I was born here in 1758. And in 1820 came the first New England missionaries, with the first coffee plants—the genesis of a major industry. Sugarcane and cattle followed.

HILO (*Convention & Visitors Bureau, 250 Keawe St. 808-961-5797*) Ever since

Hawaiians came to the mouth of the Wailuku River to barter, Hilo has been a trading center. Step into the missionary era at the **Lyman House Memorial Museum** (*276 Haili St. 808-935-5021. Adm. fee*), a New England-style house (1839) with koa wood floors and original furnishings. The museum focuses on early settlements and immigrant cultures.

KAILUA-KONA (*Convention & Visitors Bureau, 75-5719 Alii Dr. 808-329-7787*) Seven years before his death in 1819, Kamehameha the Great moved to Kailua-Kona. The grounds of his temple, **Ahuena Heiau** (*King Kamehameha Kona Beach Hotel, 75-5660 Palani Rd. 808-329-2911*), include large carved images and a reconstructed prayer tower.

Hulihee Palace (*75-5718 Alii Dr. 808-329-1877. Adm. fee*) Built by a Hawaiian governor in 1838, this two-story house of coral and lava rock became a vacation spa for island royalty. Furnishings include the wardrobe box that Queen Kapiolani took to England to visit Queen Victoria.

Mokuaikaua Church (*Across from Hulihee Palace. 808-329-1589*) New England architecture meets island materials (lava rocks and coral-based mortar) in this 1830s church, which is topped with a landmark steeple. Inside are koa wood pews and a model of the brig *Thaddeus,* which in 1820 carried the first missionaries 18,000 nautical miles from Boston to Hawaii.

Other Sites on the Island of Hawaii

Hawaii Volcanoes National Park (*808-967-7311; eruption update 808-967-7977. Adm. fee*) The surreal home of Pele, the goddess of fire, embraces one of the world's most active volcanoes, Kilauea. On its lower flank are the **Puu Loa Petroglyphs** (*Via trail from Chain of Craters Rd. at mile 17*), at least 15,000 images etched into a lava flow by ancient Hawaiians. The **Wahaula Heiau** (*currently not accessible due to active lava flows*) is a 13th-century temple where human sacrifice was first practiced in Hawaii. The rock platform remains.

South Cape (*20 miles SW of Naalehu via Hawaii 11 and S. Point Rd.*) Here at the southernmost spot in the U.S. are the ruins of a *heiau* (temple) and a fishing shrine. Holes in the cliffside rocks were made by early Hawaiians, who moored their canoes securely with ropes while fishing in the currents.

Puuhonua o Honaunau N.H.P. (*25 miles S of Kailua-Kona via Hawaii 11 and 160. 808-328-2288. Adm. fee*) Established in the 1500s, this sacred refuge

gave sanctuary to violators of *kapu* (religious taboos), as well as to non-combatants, defeated warriors, women, children, and the sick in time of battle. Because breaking a *kapu*—for instance, letting your shadow fall on a chief's palace— might anger the gods and call down a volcanic eruption or other disaster, an offender was pursued and put to death. If he managed to reach a place of refuge, however, a *kahuna* (priest) would perform an absolution ceremony. Visitors see palace

Hawaiian dancers

grounds, a royal fishpond, and a reconstructed temple.

Kona Historical Society Museum (*10 miles S of Kailua-Kona via Hawaii 11, near Kealakekua. 808-323-3222. Mon.-Fri.; donations*) The mid-1800s

Greenwell Store houses family items including ranching artifacts, an old organ, and a spyglass Mr. Greenwell used to look down at Kealakekua Bay. The society offers walking tours *(808-323-2005. Call for times; fee)* of old Kailua and of a 1920s Japanese coffee farm.

Kaloko-Honokohau N.H.P. *(5 miles N of Kailua-Kona on Hawaii 19, phone for directions. 808-329-6881)* Among the remains of several historic villages are temples, house sites, and fishponds used to raise food for chiefs. Petroglyphs depict people and masted sailing ships (reflecting European contact).

Puukohola Heiau National Historic Site *(1 mile S of Kawaihae via Hawaii 270. 808-882-7218)* A prophet told Kamehameha the Great that to conquer the Hawaiian islands, he must build a temple to his war god. In 1790 the warrior erected this huge terraced platform of lava rocks set without mortar.

Lapakahi State Historical Park *(15 miles N of Kawaihae via Hawaii 270. 808-889-5566)* This fishing village, which offered a safe, sheltered canoe landing, was established around 1300. You'll see the foundations of a canoe house, residences, and an area where salt was produced by evaporating sea water.

Mookini Heiau/Kamehameha Birthplace *(Off Hawaii 270 at mile 20 turnoff to Upolu Airport; 2 miles, then left 2 miles on dirt road)* Still in religious use under hereditary *kahuna*, the Mookini temple lies on a hill above a wild, remote coastline. Legend says the 250-foot-long temple was assembled in a single night. Farther along the road is the 1758 birthplace of Kamehameha the Great.

Parker Ranch Visitors Center and Historic Homes *(Visitor Center on Hawaii 19, in Kamuela. 808-885-7655. Adm. fee)* With 55,000 head of cattle, Parker Ranch is one of the largest privately owned ranches in the United States. It began in 1847, when Massachusetts sailor John Palmer Parker was deeded two acres. Exhibits range from poi pounders to old Bibles and a saddle room. You'll see a study in contrasts at two historic houses *(Hawaii 190, 0.75 mile S of Hawaii 19 and 1 mile on side road. Adm. fee)*. One is the lavish **Puuopelu**, begun in 1862; the other, **Mana Hale**, is a modest New England saltbox built in the 1840s.

> **Captain Cook**
> In 1778 the great Pacific explorer Capt. James Cook reached Hawaii during his search for a passage to the Atlantic. The Briton's ships gathered provisions at Kauai and sailed on. The next year they anchored at the island of Hawaii, whose residents acclaimed Cook as an agent of Lono, god of fertility. Storm damage forced the ships to return later—but this time to misunderstandings that ended with Cook being clubbed and stabbed to death. The mariner's remarkable voyages yielded knowledge of the Pacific islands, but also left Hawaiians with new weapons and diseases.

373

Kauai ··

(Convention & Visitors Bureau, 3016 Umi St., Lihue. 808-245-3971) First of the Hawaiian islands to be discovered by Captain Cook in 1778, Kauai was the last to yield to Kamehameha the Great and join the Hawaiian kingdom in 1810. By mid-century, foreigners had established Christian missions and Hawaii's first successful sugar plantation.

LIHUE Grove Farm Homestead Museum *(Nawiliwili Rd. 808-245-3202. Mon., Wed., Thurs., by reserved tours. Adm. fee)* See the old family residence, workers' camp houses, and lush grounds of an 1864 sugar plantation.

Kauai Museum *(4428 Rice St. 808-245-6931. Mon.-Sat.; adm. fee)* A 1920s public library now displays calabashes and other early Hawaiian artifacts.

Alekoko (Menehune) Fish Pond *(Hulemalu Rd. near Nawiliwili Harbor)*

The stone wall that creates this pond is said to have been built in one night by the *menehunes*—the "little people" who settled Hawaii.

Other Sites on Kauai

Wailua River ancient sites From Lihue, Hawaii 56 winds north into an idyllic landscape dotted with places sacred to ancient Hawaiians. At **Lydgate State Park**, you'll find the sketchy site of a *heiau* (temple); flat-backed royal birthing stones, where high-ranking women bore noble children; and a sacred rock where mothers placed the newborns' umbilical cords. Here, too, is a **place of refuge**—a sanctuary where taboo breakers received pardon. If chased down before reaching the place of refuge, they were sacrificed to the gods at **Holoholoku Heiau** *(Inland on Hawaii 580, Wailua River S.P.)*, located near Opaekaa Falls.

Maui ···

(Convention & Visitors Bureau, 1727 Wili Pa Loop, Wailuku. 808-244-3530 or 800-525-MAUI) In 1787 the first foreigner, Jean-François de La Pérouse, came to Maui. Against orders, he declined to claim the isle for the King of France. Three years later Maui was conquered by Kamehameha the Great. In the 19th century New England missionaries and whalers introduced foreign ways. Sugarcane grew to be the island's main harvest, followed in this century by pineapples and tourists.

LAHAINA A wicked whaling boomtown of the mid-19th century, Lahaina preserves many old buildings despite commercialization. A walking tour brochure of the **Lahaina Historical District** is available from the Lahaina Restoration Foundation, housed in the **Master's Reading Room** *(Front and Dickerson Sts. 808-661-3262. Mon.-Fri.)*, where visiting seamen came to beat the heat and read. Next door, the **Baldwin Home** *(808-661-3262. Adm. fee)* was erected of coral blocks and fieldstone by a missionary-physician in 1834; its rooms contain

Iao Valley State Park, Maui

period items. At the wharf is a replica two-masted freighter, the **Brig Carthaginian** *(808-661-3262. Adm. fee)*, now a floating museum with exhibits on whales and whaling. The 1859 **Lahaina Courthouse** *(Wharf St. 808-661-3262)* was built of coral blocks from a royal palace. The **Old Prison** *(Wainee and Prison Sts. 808-661-3262)* used wall shackles, thus its name Hale Paahao, the "stuck-in-irons-house." Finally, the **Wo Hing Museum** *(Front St. 808-661-5553)* is a 1912 Chinese fraternal hall with a temple upstairs; in the cookhouse, see Thomas Edison's own home movies of Hawaii.

Above town, the **Lahainaluna High School** *(Top of Lahainaluna Rd.)* was the first educational institution west of the Rockies (1831). On the grounds is **Hale Pai,** the "house of printing," which in 1834 published Hawaii's first newspaper; inside is a replica press.

WAILUKU-KAHULUI AREA   Bailey House Museum *(2375-A Main St., Wailuku. 808-244-3326. Mon.-Sat.; adm. fee)* Hawaii's first boarding school for girls (1833) became the residence of its principal, Edward Bailey. Thick-walled rooms contain pre-European Hawaiian artifacts, including shark-tooth spears and bark-cloth blankets.

Iao Valley S.P. *(5 miles W of Wailuku via Iao Valley Rd.)* In 1790 the invading Kamehameha the Great crushed Maui's warriors, whose corpses choked the waters of the valley stream. In earlier days the green vale was a sacred place.

Iolani Palace, Honolulu

Alexander and Baldwin Sugar Museum *(Just SE of Kahului in Puunene. Hansen Rd. and Puunene Ave. 808-871-8058. Mon.-Sat.; adm. fee)* Exhibits look at the history of the Hawaiian sugar industry and the cultures of immigrant field laborers, including Japanese and Filipino. There is a working scale model of a cane sugar factory.

375

Oahu······

In 1795 Kamehameha the Great drove the island's defenders over the cliffs at today's Nuuanu Pali lookout and conquered Oahu. The island became the hub of the Hawaiian kingdom, with Honolulu growing into an important Pacific port and trade center. Waikiki Beach was the retreat of Hawaiian royalty (who liked surfing), and by the late 1800s travelers like Robert Louis Stevenson were enjoying early tourist days. Today Oahu ("gathering place") is the most populous Hawaiian island.

HONOLULU *(Convention & Visitors Bureau, 2270 Kalakaua Ave. 808-923-1811)* **Iolani Palace** *(King and Richards Sts. 808-522-0832. Guided tours Wed.-Sat; adm. fee)* The only state residence of royalty in the U.S. is a palace that King Kalakaua built in 1882 in Italian Renaissance style. It reveals his love of European trappings (gilded throne room, formal portraits) and embrace of modernity (electric lights). After his sister-successor, Liliuokalani, was dethroned in 1893, the palace became the capitol; it's now a museum.

Aliiolani Hale *(King and Miliani Sts. 808-539-4999)* Built in the English-inspired ideal of Italian Renaissance style, the 1874 house of the state judiciary looks like the palace it was originally designed to be. In front stands a statue of Kamehameha the Great, which is adorned with leis on June 11.

Kawaiahao Church *(King and Punchbowl Sts. 808-522-1333)* Sunday services are held in English and Hawaiian at this airy house of worship, erected by Congregationalist missionaries in 1842. For building materials, Hawaiians dove to ocean reefs and chiseled slabs of coral.

Mission Houses Museum *(553 S. King St. 808-531-0481. Tues.-Sat.; adm. fee)* Headquarters of the first Christian missionaries to Hawaii, this complex includes the islands' oldest frame house still in existence (1821). The Congregationalist newcomers devised a Hawaiian alphabet and printed a native bible and other religious tracts; a replica of their press is in the **Printing House.** The coral-block **Chamberlain House** (1831) interprets the mission period.

Hawaii Maritime Center (*Honolulu Harbor, Pier 7. 808-536-6373. Adm. fee*) This hands-on museum has ship models, whaling artifacts, a re-created Matson liner stateroom, a chronology of surfboards, and even an exhibit on tattoos. Docked nearby, the 1878 *Falls of Clyde* is the world's last full-rigged, four-masted sailing ship. *Hokulea,* a replica Polynesian double-hulled voyaging canoe, has ventured all over the Pacific to relive ancient journeys, its crew navigating without instruments. At Pier 10 stands the tourist landmark **Aloha Tower** (1926), where steamship passengers were greeted with leis and musical fanfare; the top offers a panoramic view.

St. Andrew's Cathedral (*Beretania and Queen Emma Sts. 808-524-2822*) Kamehameha IV and Queen Emma established this Episcopal church in 1867; its French Gothic architecture is executed in stone from England.

National Memorial Cemetery of the Pacific (*2177 Puowaina Dr. 808-566-1430*) Filling the bowl of an extinct volcano, this military burial ground has 34,000 gravesites, including those of Pearl Harbor victims and World War II correspondent Ernie Pyle. In earlier times, secret burials of Hawaiian royalty took place here, as did human sacrifices.

Royal Mausoleum State Monument (*2261 Nuuanu Ave. 808-587-0300. Mon.-Fri.*) Members of the Hawaiian royal family are interred on the serene grounds, whose centerpiece is an 1865 Gothic Revival chapel of coral blocks.

Queen Emma Summer Palace (*2913 Pali Hwy. 808-595-6291. Adm. fee*) This Greek Revival house was a retreat from Honolulu's heat for Queen Emma, Kamehameha IV, and their son. Cool, shuttered rooms hold furnishings such as bird-feather standards and a canoe-shaped cradle.

Bishop Museum (*1525 Bernice St. 808-847-3511. Adm. fee*) Over a million cultural artifacts and 22 million natural history specimens—from tiny shells to a 55-foot sperm whale—make this the definitive collection of things Hawaiian. You'll marvel at Kamehameha the Great's personal war god, a model temple, wooden clubs used on taboo breakers, and more.

U.S. Army Museum of Hawaii (*Battery Randolph at Fort DeRussy, Kalia and Saratoga Rds. 808-438-2821. Closed Mon.*) The concrete corridors of this coastal defense fortification housed guns capable of hitting enemy ships up to 14 miles away. The museum has a modest display of weaponry, from rocks that early Hawaiians threw in slings to a Cobra helicopter used in Vietnam.

Other Sites on Oahu

Pearl Harbor A profound silence settles over those who come to the **USS *Arizona* Memorial and Visitor Center** (*Off I-H1 at USS* Arizona *Memorial exit. 808-422-0561. Arrive before noon to be sure of getting tickets.*). The Visitor Center documents the Japanese surprise attack on Pearl Harbor, which killed 2,388 persons, sank 8 ships, and damaged nearly 350 airplanes. You'll see newspaper headlines of December 7, 1941; learn about Harvard-educated Admiral Yamamoto, who planned the attack; and view a film about this largest single-day loss in U.S. Navy history. During the attack the USS *Arizona* sank in less than nine minutes, killing 1,177 crew members. Its submerged hull is their tomb and now their memorial. Visitors are ferried out to a gleaming white structure that spans the underwater wreckage.

Next to the Visitor Center stands the **USS *Bowfin* Submarine Museum and Park** *(808-423-1341. Adm. fee)*. Called the "Pearl Harbor Avenger," the *Bowfin* sank 44 enemy ships and even destroyed a dock and a bus. Exhibits include a periscope and a Japanese one-man suicide torpedo.

Keaiwa Heiau *(NE of Pearl Harbor via Aiea Heights Rd.)* Offerings of ti leaves are still left at this stone *heiau* (temple), built around 1600. Here ancient Hawaiian healers worked with medicinal herbs.

Puu O Mahuka Heiau State Monument *(5 miles inland from Waimea via Pupukea Rd.)* Overlooking the dramatic North Shore, low walls of volcanic rock define the island's largest open-air temple, dating from the late 1700s.

Other Sites in Hawaii

Kalaupapa N.H.P. *(Molokai, 1 mile N of Kalae via Hawaii 470, then steep 3-mile descent by foot trail. 808-567-6802. Guided tours only. For muleback descent and tour offered by Molokai Mule Ride call 800-567-7550; fee. For hikers or those arriving by small plane call Damien Tours 808-567-6171; fee)* Isolated from the world by rough waves and the world's tallest sea cliffs, this was a place of exile for sufferers disfigured by leprosy. In 1873 Father Damien arrived from Belgium and showed his saintly devotion by befriending and nursing the sick, burying the dead, and nourishing souls by building St. Philomena's Church (at the earlier settlement of Kalawao nearby). Patients still live at Kalaupapa, their disease controlled and contagion eliminated by modern drugs. Visitors see the village, church, and spectacular setting.

377

Kaunolu Village Site *(Lanai, 15 miles SW of Lanai City via Manele Rd., unpaved pineapple road called Kaupili Rd., and rough dirt track)* Kamehameha the ·Great came here on vacation to fish and hold sporting contests. Overgrown house sites mark the early village on the eastern side of the bay, along with the remains of an old temple.

Molokai Museum and Cultural Center *(Molokai, 2 miles N of Kualapuu via Hawaii 470. 808-567-6436 or 800-998-3474. Closed Sun.)* The museum's main artifact is the R.W. Meyer Sugar Mill *(tours available; fee)*, built in 1878 by a German who married a Hawaiian chiefess. The restored machinery is still powered by a vintage steam engine and the crusher by mules.

Kalaupapa National Historical Park

Illustrations Credits

Cover Ed Cooper Photo; 1 Nathan's Famous, Inc.; 2-3 George H.H. Huey; 4 Sam Abell, National Geographic Photographer; 5 Sepp Seitz/Woodfin Camp & Associates; 7 Bob Krist; 8 (upper) Jake Rajs; 8 (lower) Balthazar Korab; 9 Dianne Dietrich Leis; 11 Steve Dunwell; 12 Jake Rajs; 14-17 (both) Brian Vanden Brink; 19-20 (both) William H. Johnson; 23 Kindra Clineff/The Picture Cube; 25 Fred Hirschmann; 27-28 (both) Walter Bibikow/The Image Bank; 30 Steve Dunwell/The Image Bank; 31 Eric A. Wessman/Stock Boston; 32 James Lemass/The Picture Cube; 34 Dianne Dietrich Leis; 36 Jake Rajs; 37 Dianne Dietrich Leis; 39 Kindra Clineff/The Picture Cube; 41-42 (both) Steve Dunwell; 44-45 (both) Paul Rocheleau; 46 William H. Johnson; 48 James L. Stanfield, Courtesy Mark Twain House, Hartford, CT; 50 Steve Dunwell; 52 John Lewis Stage/The Image Bank; 54 Dr. E.R. Degginger/Folio, Inc.; 56 Lee Snider/The Image Works; 59 Scott Barrow; 61 (upper) Harald Sund/The Image Bank; 61 (lower) Darren P.McGee/New York State Economic Development; 62-64 (both) Carr Clifton; 67 "Lockport on the Erie Canal" painting by Mary Keys, 1832, Munson-Williams-Proctor Institute, Utica, NY; 68 Scott Barrow; 69 Louie Psihoyos, Photographed at Harriet Tubman House, Auburn, NY; 70 Peter Guttman; 72 Corbis-Bettmann; 75 Dianne Dietrich Leis; 76 Sisse Brimberg/Woodfin Camp & Associates; 77 Chuck Place; 78 Jim Schafer; 79 Peter Guttman; 81 George Fistrovich; 82-85 (both) Gene Ahrens; 86 Peter Guttman; 88 Jake Rajs; 90-94 (all) Greg Pease; 96 David Muench; 98 Chad Ehlers/Tony Stone Images; 99-101 (both) Jonathan Wallen; 102 Lelia Hendren/Folio, Inc.; 103 Gail Mooney; 105 Balthazar Korab; 106 Robert Llewellyn; 107 Sisse Brimberg, National Geographic Photographer; 109-110 (both) Paul Rocheleau; 111 Sam Abell/NGS Image Collection; 112 Catherine Karnow/Folio, Inc.; 113 Sam Abell/NGS Image Collection; 115 Jim Richardson; 116-117 Library of Congress, Ref. #LC-B811-1214; 119 Everett C. Johnson/Folio, Inc.; 120 Douglas Peebles; 121 David M. Doody/Uniphoto, Inc.; 123 Library of Congress, Ref. #LCUSZ62-6166A; 124 Victor R. Boswell, Jr. & Larry D. Kinney; 125 David M. Doody/Uniphoto, Inc.; 127 Andre Jenny/Southern Stock; 129 Murray & Associates/Picturesque

Stock Photos; 130 Peter Guttman; 132 Ron A. Rocz; 135 Bob Krist; 137 Ron Colbroth; 139 Thomas Nebbia; 140 Eddie Hironaka/The Image Bank; 141 Jack Gardner/ Stock South/Atlanta; 142 James Blank/Southern Stock; 144 (upper) "Sequoyah and Syllabary," #4016.312, From the Collection of Gilcrease Museum, Tulsa, OK [photographed by Mark Haynes]; 144 (lower) Edward Bower/The Image Bank; 146 Jim Schwabel/ Southern Stock; 148 Jake Rajs; 150 David Muench; 151 (upper) Timothy O'Keefe/Southern Stock; 151 (lower) Edward Slater/ Southern Stock; 153 Robert Frerck/Woodfin Camp & Associates; 154 Bob Libby/Stock Options; 156 David Muench; 158 Paul Rocheleau/Rebus; 159 Ed Malles; 160 Jonathan Wallen; 161 Ed Malles; 163 Culver Pictures, Inc.; 165 Balthazar Korab; 166 Engraving by Jean-Baptiste Michel le Buteaux, 1720, courtesy Edward E. Ayer Collection, Newberry Library, Chicago; 167 Paul Rocheleau/Rebus; 169 Dianne Dietrich Leis; 171 Matt Bradley; 172 Sam Abell, National Geographic Photographer; 174 Peter Guttman; 176 Zandria Beraldo; 179 Fred Hirschmann; 180 Philip Gould; 183 Jonathan Wallen; 184 Fred J. Maroon/Folio, Inc.; 187 Jonathan Wallen; 188 Andre Jenny/Southern Stock; 189 Fred J. Maroon/Folio, Inc.; 190 Sam Abell/NGS Image Collection; 192 Jonathan Wallen; 193 James Archambeault; 195 Fred Hirschmann; 196-197 (both) James Archambeault; 198 Chip Clark; 200 David Fattaleh/West Virginia Division of Tourism; 201 (upper) Courtesy The Historical Society of Pennsylvania; 201 (lower) Fred Hirschmann; 203 Steve Shaluta, Jr./West Virginia Division of Tourism; 204 Ed Cooper Photo; 206 David Muench; 208 Balthazar Korab; 211 Doris De Witt/Tony Stone Images; 212 James P. Rowan/Tony Stone Images; 214 Dan Demspter/Dembinsky Photo Associates; 216 Duomo; 217 Louie Psihoyos; 218 Jon Riley/Folio, Inc.; 220 Terry Donnelly/Dembinsky Photo Associates; 223 (upper) Kevin O. Mooney/ Odyssey/Chicago; 223 (lower) Robert Frerck/Odyssey/Chicago; 224 Gene Ahrens; 225 David Muench/Tony Stone Images; 227 Robert Frerck/Woodfin Camp & Associates; 228-231 (both) Balthazar Korab; 233 Greg Ryan-Sally Beyer; 234 Balthazar Korab; 235 Ken Dequaine/Third Coast Stock Source; 237 G. Alan Nelson/Dembinsky Photo

Associates; 239 Balthazar Korab; 240 Greg Ryan-Sally Beyer; 242 David Muench; 244-246 (both) Jeff Gnass; 247 Ed Cooper Photo; 249 Gene Ahrens; 250 G. Alan Nelson/Dembinsky Photo Associates; 253 Greg Ryan-Sally Beyer; 254 Tom Bean; 256 Terry Donnelly/Dembinsky Photo Associates; 257 Fred J. Maroon/Folio, Inc.; 259-260 (both) Jonathan Wallen; 263 Marvin E. Newman/The Image Bank; 264-266 (both) Jonathan Wallen; 267 Phil Schermeister/Tony Stone Images; 268-270 (both) Frank Oberle/Photo Resources; 271-274 (all) Jim Argo/ Oklahoma Images; 275 Greg Ryan-Sally Beyer; 277 Matt Bradley; 279 Cheryl Brown/Stock Options; 280 Jack Hollingsworth/Stock Options; 282 Harald Sund/The Image Bank; 283 Reagan Bradshaw; 284 Ron Litt/Stock Options; 286 Tom Dietrich/Tony Stone Images; 288 Tom Bean; 290-291 George H.H. Huey; 292 Renee Lynn/Tony Stone Images; 294-295 (both) D.B. Friedrichs; 297 Tom Bean; 298 George H.H. Huey; 299 Greg Probst/Tony Stone Images; 300 George H.H. Huey; 301 Tom Bean; 303 Phil Schermeister/Tony Stone Images; 305 Chuck Place; 306 George H.H. Huey; 308-309 (both) Chuck Place; 310 Jeff Gnass; 312 George H.H. Huey; 313 Tom Bean/ Tony Stone Images; 314 David Barnes/Tony Stone Images; 316 George H.H. Huey; 317 Wells Fargo Bank; 318 Randy Wells/Tony Stone Images; 319 Ted Edeen; 321 Greg Ryan-Sally Beyer; 322 Jeff Gnass; 323-325 (all) John Reddy; 327 Ed Cooper Photo; 329 Jeff Gnass; 330-331 David Epperson/Tony Stone Images; 332 Larry Ulrich/Tony Stone Images; 334 Duane Djck/West Light; 335 Chuck Place; 337 Dan Dry; 339 (upper) Chuck Place; 339 (lower) Ed Cooper Photo; 340 Chuck Place; 341 Jake Rajs; 343 Tom Benoit/Tony Stone Images; 344 Ed Cooper Photo; 345-346 (both) Chuck Place; 349 Fred Hirschmann; 350 Ed Cooper Photo; 352 Chuck Place; 354-356 (both) Bruce Forster/Tony Stone Images; 357 Gary L. Benson/Tony Stone Images; 358 Chuck Place; 360 Ed Cooper Photo; 361-363 (both) Chuck Place; 365 Nick Gunderson/Tony Stone Images; 366 Fred Hirschmann; 368 Tom Bean; 369 Fred Hirschmann; 370 Fred Hirschmann/Tony Stone Images; 371 Wayne Levin/Photo Resource Hawaii; 372 Richard A. Cooke, III; 374 Jim Cazel/Photo Resource Hawaii; 375 Fred Hirschmann; 377 Douglas Peebles.

Index

Index

381

382

Index

384

Compostion for this book by the National Geographic Society Book Division. Printed and bound by R. R. Donnelley & Sons, Willard, Ohio. Color separations by Phototype Color Graphics, Pennsauken, N.J. Paper by Consolidated / Alling & Cory, Willow Grove, Pa.

Library of Congress Cataloging-in-Publication Data

National Geographic Guide to America's historic places / prepared by the Book Division, National Geographic Society.
    p. cm.
    Includes index.
    ISBN 0-7922-3414-6. — ISBN 0-7922-3415-4
    1. Historic sites—United States—Guidebooks. 2. United States -Tours. I. National Geographic Society (U.S.). Book Division. II. Title
    E159.S4 1996
    973—dc20   96-38536

Visit the Society's Web site at http://www.nationalgeographic.com or GO NATIONAL GEOGRAPHIC on CompuServe.